700 - 595 BURRARD STREET
P.O. BOX 49290
VANCOUVER, B.C. V7X 1S8
(604) 687-6789

WORLD WAR LAW AND LAWYER

ISSUES, CASES, AND CHARACTERS

THOMAS J. SHAW

WORLD WAR I
LAW AND LAWYERS

ISSUES, CASES, AND CHARACTERS

Defending Liberty
Pursuing Justice

Cover design by Andrew Alcala/ABA Publishing. Cover images: Brand Whitlock, Félix Gouin, Walter Schücking, David Lloyd George, Woodrow Wilson, Alfred de Bathe Brandon, Henry Morgenthau Sr., Annette Abbott Adams.

The materials contained herein represent the opinions of the author and/or the editors, and should not be construed to be the views or opinions of the law firms or companies with whom such persons are in partnership with, associated with, or employed by, nor of the American Bar Association or the Senior Lawyers Division, unless adopted pursuant to the bylaws of the Association.

Nothing contained in this book is to be considered as the rendering of legal advice for specific cases, and readers are responsible for obtaining such advice from their own legal counsel. This book is intended for educational and informational purposes only.

© 2014 Thomas J. Shaw. All rights reserved.

No part of this publication may be reproduced, stored in a retrieval system, or transmitted in any form or by any means, electronic, mechanical, photocopying, recording, or otherwise, without the prior written permission of the publisher. For permission contact the ABA Copyrights & Contracts Department, copyright@americanbar.org, or complete the online form at http://www.americanbar.org/utility/reprint.html.

Printed in the United States of America.

18 17 16 15 14   5 4 3 2 1

Cataloging-in-Publication Data is on file with the Library of Congress

Shaw, Thomas J. (Attorney) author.
  World war I law and lawyers : issues, cases, and characters / Thomas J. Shaw.
      p. cm.
  Includes bibliographical references and index.
  ISBN 978-1-62722-431-4 (alk. paper)
  1. Lawyers—History. 2. Practice of law—History. 3. World War, 1914–1918—Law and legislation. I. Title.
  K124.W36S53 2014
  341.609'041—dc23
                                2014003412

Discounts are available for books ordered in bulk. Special consideration is given to state bars, CLE programs, and other bar-related organizations. Inquire at Book Publishing, ABA Publishing, American Bar Association, 321 N. Clark Street, Chicago, Illinois 60654-7598.

www.ShopABA.org

DEDICATION

I was inspired in the writing of this book by the wartime experiences of my late grandfather, Albert James Shaw. His experiences as a solider fighting in Europe for Canada in World War I, as part of the British Empire, and losing his older brother there, were passed on to me only after his own death. As they came to me, they also came to my daughter Katie, through his photos, his children, and his wartime personal journal. May she get to know about her great-grandfather's youthful life and times during those war years through this writing and in turn memorialize it for a later telling to her own children and grandchildren.

Albert James Shaw
Courtesy of Alan J. Shaw and Carol M. White

CONTENTS

Foreword ix

About the Author xix

CHAPTER 1

Before the War 1
1.1 Europe: Interlocking Treaties 5
1.2 United States: From Inward To Outward Looking 39

CHAPTER 2

Europe: International and Military Issues 67
2.1 Startng War 71
2.2 Conscription 85
2.3 Execution of Soldiers 94
2.4 Blockade 107
2.5 Unrestricted Submarine Warfare 119
2.6 New Technologies / Uses of Air Power 139

CHAPTER 3

Europe: Domestic Issues 149
3.1 Emergency Powers / Royal Prerogative 152
3.2 Official Secrets / Censorship 164
3.3 Civilian And Military Supply 175
3.4 Proximate Neturality 187
3.5 Treason 200

CHAPTER 4
United States: International and Military Issues — 223
4.1 Distance Neutrality — 226
4.2 Germany In America — 244
4.3 Enemy Assset And Export Controls — 259
4.4 Selective Service — 272
4.5 Articles Of War — 278

CHAPTER 5
United States: Domestic Issues — 295
5.1 Espionage / Freedom Of Expression — 298
5.2 Sedition / Anarchists / Enemy Aliens — 316
5.3 Supplying The War Effort — 323
5.4 Funding The War — 341
5.5 Women And The War — 350

CHAPTER 6
Europe & Elsewhere: War Crimes, Uprisings & Horses — 369
6.1 War Crimes — 372
6.2 Uprisings — 398
6.3 Parity In The Empire — 421
6.4 Animals In War — 429

CHAPTER 7
After the War — 443
7.1 Armistice And Peace Treaties — 446
7.2 Other Impacts Of The War — 475

Afterword — 491

Appendix: List of Lawyers and Judges Profiled — 495

Index — 505

FOREWORD

The sound of coins jingling around inside a pants pocket. That is how we grandkids could usually tell that my grandfather was in the area. Not a verbose man, he did not speak too much to us little ones, beyond his ongoing joke about working at the underwear factory. He certainly did not speak about what he had been involved with more than a half a century before. It was not until much, much later that I became familiar with his early history, including the part that had him fighting in Europe during World War I (WWI). It turned out that he was one of three brothers who had volunteered for military service in this war, only two of whom were to return. Originating from the same small town in Ontario, Canada, as the Canadian minister of militia, he served as part of the British Empire's forces fighting the Central Powers in Europe.

Unlike the glory and good press that World War II (WWII) gathered during my upbringing, WWI was more elusive. Further distant in time, with fewer survivors around to tell the tales, and with the late entry by the United States into the conflict, it was not a subject that one learned much about in school or on television. The only images I recall seeing were those of soldiers who had been victims of poison gas attacks. There were movies like *All Quiet on the Western Front*, *Paths of Glory*, *Lawrence of Arabia*, and, later, *Gallipoli*. But I don't remember any television shows on this conflict or even much in my school history books or homework assignments on it.

It was only much later, after visiting the grave of the Marquis de Lafayette in Paris ("Lafayette, we are here"[1]) and acquiring my own history books, did I begin to understand that there were significant connections between WWI and WWII. When I gained some glimpses into my grandfather's war service, WWI started to appear on my personal radar. Even then it remained a curios-

---

1. Charles Stanton, *"Nous voila, Lafayette"* spoken during a ceremony at Lafayette's grave (July 4, 1917).

ity, until I received a set of older family photos from my father's brother a few years ago. This included a daily journal kept by my grandfather during WWI, which really piqued my interest. Follow-on e-mails with my uncle and aunt about their father and his service to the Canadian army in Europe brought me to the realization that this war also had many stories that could use a modern (re-)telling, from a legal perspective.

As I described in the foreword of *World War II Law and Lawyers: Issues, Cases, and Characters,* when I had already authored several books and was given the chance to propose a legal-history book to the ABA, I first chose WWII. This was the conflict that my own father was involved in and that I had grown up hearing about. But I always had in my mind that there was going to be a companion book about WWI, to thereby complete the familial connection from my daughter back through to my grandfather (her great-grandfather).

Among my passions in life are raising and educating my daughter Katie, writing, the law, the welfare of all sentient life, and history. Writing this book, as authoring the WWII book did, gave me the chance to bring together all of those passions into a single project. So I worked seven days a week for more than four months to complete this book, with my daughter's occasional inputs (she loved to retell the stories about the animals) and with the added knowledge that if I worked hard, fast, and smart enough, it would be published in 2014, exactly 100 years since the start of the conflict. Perfect.

Just like the WWII companion book, what hopefully makes this book unique is its focus on the three main areas suggested by the subtitle: legal issues, cases, and characters. First, it brings together in a single volume the major legal issues surrounding this conflict. Second, it takes a global view, looking at the laws and cases in as many countries as necessary to describe these major issues. And third, it introduces many lawyers and judges from around the world involved with these issues—some famous, some of whom may be little known or long forgotten today.

SCOPE

This book is neither a general history of WWI nor a legal treatise but a legal history lying somewhere in between. Because I am not a professional historian, I defer in the broader themes of this global conflict to those who are professionals. I present significant wartime events to briefly set the stage for the legal issues that arose from them, although with the lapse now of a century, I needed to spend more time setting the stage than I did in the WWII book. I strongly encourage readers who want more background to turn to the many available sources for deeper understandings of this conflict, its origins and resolutions, and the detailed events and time lines. Likewise, many of the cases, lawyers, and judges featured in this work have been the focus of entire books. As a survey of WWI, I merely introduce the topics, from which further reading and research into a deep pool of facts and events can be done.

This war was primarily fought from 1914 to 1918, but the legal issues may extend both further back and into the period after the war. Because the companion WWII volume already covers the post-WWI era up to WWII, much of that era will be referenced accordingly to chapters in that book. Some of the cases do extend to several years or more after WWI, even after WWII. Geographically, WWI centered on Europe, with additional battle action in the Middle East and Asia Minor and acts of sabotage that occurred in countries everywhere, but it is the location of the various belligerents and their legal issues and responses that determined the geographies covered.

As with all of my books, I have tried to present a global viewpoint. As a long-term expatriate living outside the United States, I have had to analyze life through the eyes of other cultures. But this also comes with an acknowledgment of the differences in culture and language and the inherent failure to be able to appreciate or locate certain relevant information or players. I have used and quoted foreign-language (non-English) sources as I was able to identify them, but clearly some researcher bias may be present, unfortunately and unintentionally.

PRESENTATION

This book is organized around legal issues that arose from significant events in the major geographical areas mentioned earlier. Each chapter opens with a brief introduction and a "Prominent Lawyers and Judges in This Chapter" section, which previews the names and roles of the lawyers and judges discussed in the various sections of that chapter. The individual chapter sections typically identify one or more of the major legal issues, and the related statutes, executive orders, decrees, regulations, relevant cases, subsequent events, and modern applicability (where appropriate) are discussed. Sections generally conclude with biographies of the lawyers and judges featured in that section, except when the events are not part of the WWI era.

Because the book centers on legal issues, it follows each issue from beginning to end and, as such, is not in strict chronological order from the first chapter to the last. However, because legal issues typically take many years to play out, from statute to violation to trial to appellate review, it is not possible to follow a precise time line. Each legal issue is presented on the date that it was identified in a statute, executive order, or decree and is then followed to its end, often taking the reader many years into the future, even after the conclusion of the war. I believe that this works better than trying to weave together many story lines on an exact calendar presentation or working backward from when the court cases were decided. The enactment of laws closely follows the sentiment that was present at the time and so clearly presents the historical atmosphere that brought on particular issues.

LEGAL ISSUES

I have highlighted eighty major legal issues from WWI, spread across the chapters of this book. The following is a consolidated list of those issues, mostly in the order in which they are described. Those with an asterisk are linked to a discussion of modern applicability. I have tried to select different issues than those I discussed in the WWII book, and where it is the same issue (e.g., sedition), tried to present it with respect to a different country, under differing circumstances, and/or under a different interpretation. The issues are also shown in greater granularity than those from the WWII book, to truly present that breadth of legal involvement in this conflict.

Making & Changing Alliances	Cultural Superiority
Reasons for Starting War★	Conscription/Conscientious Objectors
Execution of Soldiers/ Shot for Example	Desertion and Disobeying Orders
Mutiny★	Rehabilitation of the Condemned★
Blockade★	Intentional Starvation of Civilians★
Unrestricted Submarine Warfare	Compensation for Illegal War Acts★
Civilians Taking Up Arms	New Technologies★
Uses of Air Power★	Executive Domestic Powers
Royal Prerogative	Compensation for Legal War Acts
Postponing Elections	Official Secrets★
Censorship/Cryptography	Civilian Supply/Rationing
Military Supply	Powers of Organized Labor
Proximate Neutrality	Angary
Smuggling	Interning Soldiers and Sailors
Civilian Refugees	Feeding Starving Populations
Treason	Defeatist/Peace Propaganda
Distance Neutrality	War Risk Insurance
Neighbor Instability	Military Expedition
Sabotage	Seizing Enemy Assets★
Enemy Intellectual Property	Export/Import Controls★
Selective Service	Articles of War
Arbitrary Military Justice★	Racial Segregation of Units
Espionage★	Freedom of Expression
Controlling Public Information	Sedition
Deporting Anarchists	Enemy Aliens

Seizure of Transportation Systems	Raw Material Pricing and Priorities
Control of Food and Fuel	Labor Disputes
Special War Taxes	War Debt Funding
Closing Financial Markets	Women's Employment and Rights
Furthering Social Movements	Surplus Women
War Crimes against Civilians★	War Crimes against POWs
War Crimes at Sea	Use of Poisonous Gases★
Deportations of Civilians	Massacres/Genocide★
Uprisings for Independence★	Country Mandates★
Dividing Regions of Influence	Political Revolutions★
Parity within Empires	Animals during and after War★
Bacterial Warfare★	Armistices/Peace Treaties★
Reparations/Restitution	Limitations on Armaments & Forces
National Self-Determination★	Pandemics★
Care for Veterans★	Cancellation of War Contracts

I have written about each issue as it occurred in only a single country. As Europe is presented first and in greater detail, this hopefully balances out any bias in a book written by an American attorney. Clearly, many of the same issues repeat themselves in many countries; for example, controlling prices was important to all of the warring nations. While I could have discussed, say, how the United Kingdom dealt with war finances, and perhaps contrasted and compared it to how the United States, France, and Germany did so, I felt that the incremental value of that was less than the value of covering more issues.

CASES

Some cases were chosen for their historical significance; others were chosen because they seemed historically more interesting. I have selected both well-known and obscure cases in order to present the themes of each issue as well as the additional situations to which the themes naturally extend. In order to keep the length of the book reasonable, however, I have not featured every relevant case. My intent is to help readers understand the broad strokes of legal history, not the minutiae, so I have not gone into the details of smaller issues raised in the cases. There are articles available elsewhere that do so. The cases are usually, but not always, trials in courtrooms. In some situations, trials were not possible or practical, so other means of attempting to resolve the matter were used.

The outcomes of several of these cases were then (and some remain) controversial. Former enemies are now allies and close friends. Some of those convicted later presented a case of possible innocence, several instances of which I have discussed. I have tried to take a neutral approach, focusing on these issues as seen through the eyes of those adjudicating them in their own time period. This is not a book designed to reinterpret old issues but to relate them as understood when they happened. While I am aware that a few of the people convicted were later exonerated, the records seem to demonstrate that most judges and attorneys involved attempted to mete out justice and balance interests as best they could against the backdrop of a dangerous global conflict in an unstable world.

CHARACTERS

The characters are the lawyers, judges, and legal training graduates involved with negotiating, drafting or influencing policies, treaties, statutes, and executive orders, and then handling the subsequent implementations and resulting litigation and trials. While I could not discuss every lawyer involved in each issue, I have tried to identify a representative group across nationality, race, gender, fame, and geography, with the understanding that during this time in history, not all groups were allowed to fully participate in the legal world.

Although some characters are as well known as prime ministers, presidents, law lords, and Supreme Court justices, others are not as well known. I have tried to find as many people who may not be known to the reader as people who will be instantly recognizable (although perhaps in a role early in their careers or whose prominence was not gained as a practicing lawyer). I hope to bring them all, famous and obscure, to the attention of a new generation of readers.

There are two international points about the characters. One is that the term "lawyer" covers all manner of titles involved in the legal profession, including barrister, solicitor, advocate, *rechtsanwalt*, *advocaat*, *avocat*, *avukat*, counselor, etc. Likewise, "judge" covers justices on the highest courts, appellate courts, trial courts, international courts, arbitration panels, *richter*, *rechter*, *juge*, *yargiç*, magistrate, recorder, and justice of the peace. Also, in the civil-law countries, it is common for those who study the law to go into the civil service of their countries, and as such these people may not be practicing as lawyers in the sense of a common-law lawyer. The important connection is the legal training and mindset that is common to all of the people profiled.

At the end of most sections in each chapter, a "Legal Profiles" section displays a brief biography of one or more characters in that section. The brief bios of the approximately three hundred featured lawyers, judges, and legal training graduates are just that—brief. They are not meant to be in-depth analyses, nor do they contain the legal philosophies particular to these different people. These are merely introductions to the profiled individuals, intended only as a starting point, and I highly encourage the reader to move on to full biographies of this infinitely interesting cast of characters (to further this end, I have tried to provide at least one external citation for each character). (See the appendix for a composite list of the legal personalities discussed in this book.)

SUBSEQUENT EVENTS/MODERN APPLICABILITY

I have also tried to link the legal issues that arose during this war to subsequent events and, where it makes sense, to modern applications. Some of these matters were essentially settled legally long ago, while others still resonate as unsettled even today. The subsequent events typically occurred within a few years of the end of the war, while modern applicability covers events that happened long after the war or may be happening now. Because the modern applicability sections feature characters outside the era of this war, I decided not to provide profiles of lawyers and judges for these sections.

Many of these issues, probably a solid majority, continued into or rose again in WWII. It is remarkable how little the world learned from WWI and how inconsistently it acted upon what it did learn between WWI and WWII. So many of these issues mutated and came back in a more virulent form in WWII. As such, I often point the reader to chapters in the WWII book, to gain a deeper understanding of how an issue arose then. So I also do not address in detail here the subsequent events on some issues that I described more fully in the WWII book.

While I always find the weft and warp in the fabric of history by itself sufficiently fascinating, in telling these stories a starting point is created in the search for answers to current problems. Perhaps surprisingly, some of the legal matters arising from this war from the last century are still with us today and could easily arise in the conflicts of this century. My goal here is not only to inform, educate, and entertain those new to these issues, cases, and characters from one hundred years ago, but also to provide a brief historical foundation for those who must deal with the modern face of these complex issues. I again hope that I have accomplished all of this.

Thomas J. Shaw, Esq.
January 2014

ABOUT THE AUTHOR

Thomas J. Shaw, Esq., Attorney at Law, CPA, CRISC, CIP, CIPP, CISM, ERMP, CISA, CGEIT, CCSK

Thomas J. Shaw, Esq., is an internationally located attorney and frequent author and speaker on legal topics from a global perspective. He is also the author of the 2013 book *World War II Law and Lawyers—Issues, Cases and Characters,* author of the 2013 book *Cloud Computing for Lawyers and Executives—A Global Approach, Second edition,* author of the 2012 book *Children and the Internet—A Global Guide for Lawyers and Parents,* author of the 2011 book *Cloud Computing for Lawyers and Executives—A Global Approach,* and lead author/editor of the 2011 book *Information Security and Privacy—A Practical Guide for Global Executives, Lawyers and Technologists.* He is also the author of the forthcoming book *Pre-Global War Law and Lawyers—Issues, Cases and Characters.*

Mr. Shaw writes extensively on the law and has published dozens of legal articles in many periodicals. He is also the editor/founder of two American Bar Association periodicals: the *Information Security & Privacy News* and the *EDDE (E-Discovery and Digital Evidence) Journal.* In addition to legal authoring and publishing and raising his daughter, Mr. Shaw works with organizations on Internet, information, and international law; compliance; privacy; information security and governance; audit; contracts; new technologies; cloud computing; and risk. He runs CloudRisk Europe and CloudRisk Asia, which risk assess private- and public-sector organizations and cloud service providers (www.cloudriskeurope.com). He also spends significant time helping to make children safe on the Internet. He can be reached at thomas@tshawlaw.com.

CHAPTER 1

BEFORE THE WAR

The "War to End All Wars" was not in fact the end of war, but the start of a revolution in the law of wartime. New to this conflict was the widely held belief that war and its related activities should be prosecuted according to international and national rules. In the Allied and Associated Powers, in the Central Powers, in neutral nations, and in colonies and dominions belonging to empires, new principles of law were created to deal with the effects of modern warfare. Lawyers and judges, in varying roles, had a significant impact on how the new legal rules for twentieth-century conflict were analyzed, drafted, applied, and interpreted. Occurring between smaller late-nineteenth-century conflicts and the larger coming conflict of WWII, the international conventions, treaties, national statutes, articles of war, and decisions of civilian and military courts and international tribunals looked both backward and forward. Backward to the legal foundations and rulings from prior wars and forward to new technologies and geopolitics that restructured the battlegrounds, borders, and life back home, in diplomatic, political, economic, social, and military terms. WWI was to be the mother lode for mining new nuggets from the law of wartime.

Unlike in WWII,[1] where many of the prewar governments were overthrown during the run up to or during the course of the war, in WWI the governments of the belligerents tended to be more stable, and so the rule of

---

1. *See* THOMAS J. SHAW, WWII LAW AND LAWYERS: ISSUES, CASES, AND CHARACTERS (2013).

law held up throughout the conflict, at least until the very final stages. While governmental institutions were more stable, modern economies and new armament technologies running full speed into nineteenth-century military tactics and static battlefield conditions resulted in massive human and resource devastation. The slaughter during WWI was on an unprecedented scale, with more than thirty-five million dead, injured, and missing.[2] New approaches were needed to deal with the legal issues arising from a new kind of warfare, where a total war utilizing the entire suite of national capabilities was brought to bear.

The new legal rules were promulgated differently in each country. This diversity had much to do not only with the countries' various common- or civil-law legal traditions but also with their respective recent experiences with war. France and Germany had fought each other some forty years previous, while the United Kingdom had been involved only in colonial wars in recent times, and the United States had only recently become involved in conflicts beyond its immediate region.[3] The empires of Austria-Hungary, Russia, and the Ottomans had dealt with war as a necessary ingredient of maintaining or revitalizing an empire. All of these countries had experienced varying kinds of conflicts while adding new states or colonies to their declared or undeclared empires.

After the end of the Napoleonic Wars and American colonial wars in the first two decades of the nineteenth century, Europe and the United States entered into decades of relative peace from major conflicts. But starting again around the second half of the century, conflicts began to break out. This included significant belligerency such as the Mexican-American War of the 1840s, the Crimean War (primarily involving Russia, France, and the United Kingdom) of the 1850s, the American Civil War of the 1860s, and the Franco-Prussian War of the 1870s. There were also wars of independence (e.g., in Italy), myriad wars of colonizers against the colonial subjects (e.g., in India, South Africa, Afghanistan, and New Zealand), and wars of expansion (e.g., in Formosa in the 1890s and the American-Indian wars in the United States).

The century ended with the Spanish-American War and two conflicts that spilled into the next century: the Second Boer War in South Africa and

---

2. U.S. DEPT. OF JUSTICE, WWI CASUALTY AND DEATH TABLES.
3. *See* THOMAS J. SHAW, PRE–WORLD WAR LAW AND LAWYERS: ISSUES, CASES, AND CHARACTERS (forthcoming 2015).

the Boxer Rebellion in China. A number of additional conflicts arose in the early twentieth century, leading up to WWI. These included the Russo-Japan War in 1904–5 and the Turko-Italian War over Libya of 1911–12. Even more closely related were the Balkan Wars of 1912–13, which involved the Ottoman Empire and several Balkan states. These came after Bosnia-Herzegovina was annexed by Austria-Hungary in 1908 and during crises involving Morocco and Albania. The Balkans had become the area of Great Power[4] focus, the most likely spot to ignite a larger conflict.

Each of the major European powers had significant influence and control over other countries. This took many forms, from membership in common dominions headed by the more powerful country to outright annexation and subversion of local control. The way these colonies were acquired and ruled had a significant impact not only among the powers in Europe but also in other countries who were not major players in this world war, such as Japan or countries who sought to annex their neighbors, such as Serbia and Bulgaria. The desire for colonies and the riches and influence such colonies entailed led to many prewar conflicts and was a significant factor in the start of WWI.

This chapter focuses on each of the main WWI combatants in the prewar era and their related legal issues. The first section covers Europe, starting with nation and alliance building and the resultant interlocking agreements between countries leading to conflicts, colonies, and conventions that were to impact the war. The second section addresses the United States, a new player on the larger international scene, but one that was not yet committed to being a full-time participant in the wars of others. The chapter covers the legal issues of making and changing alliances and cultural superiority.

PROMINENT LAWYERS AND JUDGES IN THIS CHAPTER

Europe—Interlocking Treaties:
- William Ewart Gladstone (British chancellor of the exchequer)
- Adolphe Thiers (French president)

---

4. The term "Great Power" changed over time, by region, and based on which country created the definition. For purposes of this section, it can be defined to include the leading national powers in Europe at the time, including the United Kingdom, France, Germany/Prussia, Austria-Hungary, Russia, and the Ottoman Empire.

- Otto von Bismarck (Prussian foreign minister)
- Jules Favre (French minister of foreign affairs)
- Giuseppe Mazzini (Italian nationalist)
- Safvet Pasha (Ottoman grand vizier)
- Benjamin Disraeli (British prime minister)
- Ferenc Deák (Hungarian diplomat)
- Sylvain Van de Weyer (Belgian diplomat)
- Paul Cambon (French ambassador)
- Jules Cambon (French diplomat)
- Heinrich VII (German ambassador)
- Edgar Demange (defense attorney)
- Fernand Labori (defense attorney)
- Louis Renault (French jurist)
- Frederick de Martens (Russian diplomat)
- James Francis Thomas (defense attorney)
- Samuel R. Gummere (U.S. ambassador)
- John M. Hay (U.S. secretary of state)
- Titu Maiorescu (Romanian prime minister)

United States—From Inward- to Outward-Looking:
- William McKinley (president)
- William R. Day (secretary of state)
- Eugenio Montero Ríos (Spanish representative)
- Felipe Agoncillo (Philippine representative)
- Joseph Pulitzer (publisher)
- John Sherman (secretary of state)
- Jutarō Komura (Japanese signatory)
- Alfons Mumm von Schwarzenstein (German signatory)
- Henry A. Cooper (congressman)
- Cayetano Arellano (Philippine Supreme Court chief justice)
- Joseph McKenna (Supreme Court justice)
- Edward Douglass White (Supreme Court justice)
- William Nelson Cromwell (lobbyist)
- Charles Merrill Hough (district court judge)
- Heinrich Lammasch (Austrian arbitrator)
- Mineichirō Adachi (Japanese delegate)
- Elihu Root (secretary of state)

- William Howard Taft (president)
- Philander C. Knox (secretary of state)

1.1 EUROPE: INTERLOCKING TREATIES

A. Agreements and Nation-Building: 1814–1879

The dynamics underlying the territorial and political changes in Europe during the nineteenth and early twentieth centuries were significant factors leading to WWI. Among the seven major powers, the United Kingdom changed the least, maintaining its home country borders and the same form of government in the century leading up to this war. France, after the final defeat of Napoleon I in 1815, lost significant imperial territories and, through the next century, switched back and forth from republic to imperial government several times. Germany and Italy, on the other hand, had only in recent times emerged as distinct national political entities. All four of these countries were "empires" with overseas colonies. Three older empires from central and eastern Europe and Asia—the Ottoman, Russian, and Austro-Hungarian—ruled over more closely situated client states. These three empires were in varying states of decay, yet were trying to revitalize.

1. United Kingdom

The post-Napoleonic century was to be the Pax Britannica era, a time of relative peace from large-scale conflicts, with the Royal Navy patrolling the world's oceans. The United Kingdom was the "United Kingdom of Great Britain and Ireland," with Great Britain consisting of England, Scotland, and Wales, and Ireland still some ways away from independence. The rest of the nation's full name was "and of the British Dominions beyond the Seas," and it was in overseas possessions that the kingdom experienced significant changes during this time period. With waning of power by early colonizers such as the Spanish, Portuguese, Dutch, Arabs, and Ottomans, the British and French were in a global contest for influence, riches, and power in Africa, Asia, and the Americas. The use of colonies was to play a vital role in WWI.

Politically, the United Kingdom at home was very stable, having been a constitutional monarchy since the rule of William II, starting in 1688. Democracy was long established, although the franchise was not widespread. In the post-Napoleonic era, Britain was interested in avoiding European affairs, with its most significant role during this era as part of an alliance with the French, Sardinians, and Ottomans against the Russians in the Crimean War, starting in 1853. This war was a complex conflict with origins in Russian desire for Ottoman territory, French and Russian desires for leadership of Christian sites and people in the Ottoman Empire, and concerns about Russian direct access to the Mediterranean Sea. It concluded in 1856 with the Treaty of Paris, principally resulting in the cessation of Russian expansionism, the neutrality of the Black Sea, the quasi-independence of Romania and Serbia, and the continued (albeit temporary) integrity of the territory of the Ottoman Empire.[5]

LEGAL PROFILES

William Ewart Gladstone was the British chancellor of the exchequer during the Crimean War. He was born in England in 1809 and obtained his legal training there, entering Lincoln's Inn[6] in 1833. But he preferred politics, having been elected to the House of Commons in 1832, and he did not complete this barrister training. At various points in a very long political career spanning fifty years and two parties (Liberal and Conservative), he served as a cabinet minister, chancellor of the exchequer again, leader in opposition, and four times as the prime minister. The list of his accomplishments in government is long, but he was known for his deft work with the government finances, deleting the tax on paper (and thereby reducing the distribution costs of free expression), expanding the franchise, supporting Irish home rule (devolution), and his strong religious beliefs and their progeny. When he died in 1898, six years after leaving parliament, such was his reputation that two future kings of England were among his pallbearers.[7]

---

5. General Treaty of Peace between United Kingdom, Austria, France, Prussia, Russia, Sardinia, and Turkey, Mar. 30, 1856.
6. Under the traditional English system of barrister training, one is called to the bar through belonging to one of four professional associations termed Inns of the Court: Gray's Inn, Lincoln's Inn, Inner Temple, and Middle Temple.
7. See *William Ewart Gladstone*, OXFORD DICTIONARY OF NATIONAL BIOGRAPHY 101010787.

2. France

Unlike most of its continental neighbors, France had long been a unified country, going back at least to Charlemagne in the ninth century. While its territory waxed and waned through the centuries with military victories and defeats, metropolitan France had remained more or less stabilized territorially. It was increasingly ruled centrally by absolutist kings under the Ancient Regime until the French Revolution in 1789 brought the First Republic. With the subsequent Napoleonic Wars and the change to an imperial form of government, the size of the French Empire greatly increased and France took on many overseas client states that affected the lead-up to WWI. The Treaty of Paris in 1815 required France to relinquish its conquered territory to the Netherlands, Austria, Prussia, Switzerland, and Sardinia, returning France back to its territorial boundaries of 1790.[8]

After Napoleon I finally left the scene for good via exile in 1815, the Bourbon kings were restored until 1830, when a constitutional monarchy ruled until 1848. In that year, revolutions rippled across Europe[9] and led to the overthrow of the monarchy in France and to the short-lived Second Republic. The first president of the republic, Louis-Napoleon, a descendant of Napoleon I, returned France in 1852 to a Second Empire as Napoleon III, until his eventual overthrow in 1870 after losing in battle to the Prussians. This brought a return to republican rule with the Third Republic, which would last until the Vichy government in WWII.[10] France gained Savoy and Nice during the Second Empire but was to soon lose other territory to Germany.

LEGAL PROFILES

Adolphe Thiers was the French president who led the Third Republic from 1871. He was born in France in 1797 and obtained his legal training there. But he preferred literature and wrote *Histoire de la Revolution Française* in several volumes in the 1820s. In 1830 he was elected a dep-

---

8. Definitive Treaties between Great Britain, Austria, Prussia, Russia, and France, Nov. 20, 1815.
9. Various movements occurring in 1848 included France, Austria, Hungary, Germany, Poland, Denmark, and Italy.
10. *See* THOMAS J. SHAW, WWII LAW AND LAWYERS: ISSUES, CASES, AND CHARACTERS, ch. 5 (2013).

uty in the national assembly, where he served in various roles in the succeeding two decades, including as prime minister and minister of foreign affairs. He was admitted to l'Académie française in 1833. At the start of the Second Empire, he was arrested and banished from France, although he was later allowed to return. He continued to write, authoring the well-regarded *Le Consulat et l'Empire* in 1863. After the fall of the Second Empire in 1870, he was elected as the president of the Third Republic, where he served for several years before resigning in 1873. During this time he was involved with subduing the Paris Commune movement in 1871. He remained in the national assembly for his remaining years before dying in 1877.[11]

3. Germany
a. Treaty of London

What had long been a series of separate entities had been formed into a unified country in 1871. A vast conglomeration of hundreds of political units, some big and some small, the Holy Roman Empire finally fractured, after more than 800 years, with the Napoleonic Wars. The Congress of Vienna in 1815 was called to redraw the map of Europe after more than two decades of war. It created, inter alia, the German Confederation,[12] consisting of more than thirty German states, four free (unaffiliated) cities, and Prussia and Austria. This "perpetual"[13] union had as its objective "the maintenance of the external and internal safety of Germany, and of the independence and inviolability of the confederated States."[14]

The perpetual union lasted only until the ongoing power struggle between leading members Austria and Prussia erupted into war in 1866. The Austro-Prussian War, won by the Prussians in less than two months, resulted in the Treaty of London in 1867.[15] This agreement stated that the confederation was

---

11. *See Adolfe Thiers*, ASSEMBLEE NATIONALE BIOGRAPHIES DES DÉPUTÉS FRANÇAIS DEPUIS 1789.
12. Final Act of the Congress of Vienna, Act IX, June 9, 1815.
13. *Id.* art. I.
14. *Id.* art. II.
15. Treaty between Great Britain, Austria, Belgium, France, Italy, the Netherlands, Prussia, and Russia, May 11, 1867.

terminated.[16] It also took away certain members. Luxembourg would leave this union (it was owned by the royal house of the Netherlands). The treaty created the North German Confederation, which included Prussia and the Protestant Germanic states but left out such southern Catholic German states as Bavaria, Württemberg, and Baden, and, most importantly for the inter-Germanic rivalry, Catholic Austria.

b. Treaty of Frankfurt

The machinations of Prussian Chancellor Otto von Bismarck and Emperor Napoleon III of France would lead to the further enlargement of Germany through addition of the southern states. Through a series of ill-considered responses by the French (and more calculated ones by Prussia, plus selective editing and leaking of secret correspondence) to the proposal for a relative of the Prussian King Wilhelm I to ascend the vacant throne of Spain, France ended up declaring war on the North German Confederation. This soon brought the southern German states to join the North German Confederation, which was shortly thereafter reformed and renamed the German Empire. The Franco-Prussian conflict lasted less than ten months, in large part due to superior German technology and manpower resources. It resulted in the Treaty of Frankfurt in 1871, which was to have lasting impacts.[17]

The Treaty of Frankfurt set borders that required France to give the Alsace-Lorraine region to Germany.[18] This moved the German border with France away from the southern German states and also provided additional natural and human resources to Germany. France's desire to reclaim this area (so-called *revanchism*) was eventually significant in driving France into WWI. Under the Treaty of Frankfurt, the citizens of Alsace-Lorraine could choose to repatriate to France or stay and become German citizens.[19] The French were to pay five billion francs within three years (which they did).[20] And the parties agreed never to go to war with each other again and to maintain a respectful and hon-

---

16. *Id.* art. VI.
17. Treaty of Frankfurt, Fr.-Prus., May 10, 1871.
18. *Id.* art. 1.
19. *Id.* art. 2.
20. *Id.* art. 7.

orable peace.[21] The treaty also recognized the new political entities involved: the German Empire and the Third French Republic.

LEGAL PROFILES

Otto von Bismarck was the Prussian foreign minister who negotiated the Treaty of Frankfurt. Born in Prussia in 1815, and trained in law, he undertook his practical legal training and was admitted to the bar in 1835. He entered the civil service, spent time addressing his military service requirements, and then, from 1839, spent years primarily managing his family's estates. He reportedly was involved in a number of duels, in an age when that was still a method to resolve disputes of honor. He became a member of the parliament in Prussia in 1849. In 1851, he was appointed as the envoy to the Diet of the German Confederation, a role he served in for eight years. He then served as Prussian ambassador to Russia for four years. In 1862, he was appointed minister-president and foreign minister of Prussia. From this position, along with the added roles of chancellor of the North German Confederation (from 1867) and chancellor of the German Empire (from 1871), he was able to engineer the successful Prussian wars with Austria in 1866 and with France in 1871, and the unification of Germany. Among his many accomplishments domestically was initiating some of the world's first social insurance programs for workers. He continued in his role as chancellor until being removed by the new German emperor in 1890. He died in 1898.[22]

Jules Favre was a lawyer and the French minister of foreign affairs who negotiated the Treaty of Frankfurt. He was born in France in 1809 and started his legal practice there. He became a leading advocate for defending political prisoners, including those espousing the republican cause. He was first elected to national office in 1848 but left after the coup d'état that returned republican France to an imperial form of gov-

---

21. *Id.* art. 13.
22. *See Otto von Bismarck*, BIOGRAPHIE DES DEUTSCHEN HISTORISCHEN MUSEUMS.

ernment. He was elected to the Chamber of Deputies in 1858, where he again championed the republican cause, as he was well known as a leading orator, including for freedom of speech and assembly. After his involvement with the Treaty of Frankfurt, where he was widely believed to have been outnegotiated by Bismarck, and his subsequent resignation of his ministry, he was elected to the Senate in 1876. He was admitted to l'Académie française in 1867. He died in 1880.[23]

4. Italy
a. Wars of Independence

Italy was similarly created out of a series of independent kingdoms. Since the fall of the Roman Empire in 476, various entities had ruled parts of the Italian peninsula, including the Frankish Empire of Charlemagne, the Austrian and Spanish Hapsburg empires, the French empire of Napoleon I, the Papal States, and various trade-enriched Italian city-states such as Venice, Genoa, Milan, and Naples. Through a series of three wars of independence between 1848 and 1866, Italy was able to drive out the Austrian Empire. The Treaty of Vienna returned the Venetia region to the new Kingdom of Italy.[24] The remaining foreign troops in Rome departed during the Franco-Prussian War in 1870, and the Papal States, including Rome, were added to the Kingdom of Italy (declared in 1861), finally unifying the peninsula into one country.

LEGAL PROFILES

Giuseppe Mazzini was a lawyer and one of the leading drivers of Italian unification and independence. He was born in Genoa in 1805 and started his legal practice there. Then he turned to writing and support of these political causes, including becoming a member of the Carbonari secret society, for which he was arrested and imprisoned. He then expa-

---

23. *See* Jules Favre, ASSEMBLEE NATIONALE BIOGRAPHIES DES DÉPUTÉS FRANÇAIS DEPUIS 1789.
24. Treaty of Vienna, It-Aust., Oct. 12, 1866.

triated to Switzerland, where he encouraged insurrections in the Italian peninsula. This led to his arrest and deportation from Switzerland and later from France. He went to England in 1837, where he continued to write and foment uprisings in Italy. He led insurrections and was tangentially involved in the First and Second Wars of Italian Independence; he was also part of the triumvirate that briefly ruled Rome as a republic in 1850. He linked up with Italian nationalist leader Giuseppe Garibaldi frequently but was eclipsed by others, as his opposition to nonrepublican forms of government interfered with the actual political entities driving unification. He lived to see the successful reunification of the peninsula and died in 1872.[25]

b. Orsini Trial

The trial of Felice Orsini for the attempted murder of French emperor Napoleon III took place during this time period. On January 14, 1858, Orsini and three other Italians, Giuseppe Pieri, Antonio Gomez, and Carlo di Rudio, tried to kill Napoleon in Paris by throwing several bombs at the royal carriage. The bombs were made to Orsini's design by an English bomb maker and tested by Orsini while in England. Although several people were killed, Napoleon III survived and went on to the opera that night as scheduled. Orsini had believed that Napoleon was the ultimate cause of Italy being unable to unify as a single political entity.

At the trial, it was revealed that when he was young, Orsini had joined the Giovane Italia organization founded by Giuseppe Mazzini. He had also worked for Mazzini during the brief republican government in Rome around 1850. He was sent on a mission to Hungary, where he was captured, then escaped, and finally made his way to England. It was this English connection that provided a source for his bombs. For their roles in the plot, Orsini and Pieri were executed, and Gomez and di Rudio received life sentences. (In an interesting postscript, di Rudio escaped from prison, came to America, joined the U.S. military, became an officer, and fought in the 1876 Battle of the Little Bighorn with George Armstrong Custer. And, unlike Custer, he survived it.)

---

25. *See Mazzini*, N.Y. TIMES (Mar. 12, 1872).

This trial also had political ramifications in several countries. In the Second War of Italian Independence in 1859, France supported the king of Sardinia, the eventual ruler of Italy. Eventually, Lombardy and Tuscany, among other territories, came under the rule of this now-declared king of Italy. In the United Kingdom, home to not only the expatriate Italians involved in the trial but English and French radicals who had supported them, the government of Lord Palmerston soon fell as a result of the inability to pass legislation criminalizing a conspiracy like Orsini's.

The principal British supporters of the Orsini plot fled the country, thereby avoiding prosecution. Conspiracy charges were then brought against French expatriate Simon Bernard for introducing the conspirators to each other. Thanks to a rigorous defense argument and contrary to the instructions of the court, the jury found Bernard not guilty. There were other related prosecutions for libel for various publishers who supported the cause of Bernard or Orsini, but these came to nothing. Besides political ramifications, Orsini's biggest impact may have been on other people who were frustrated about lack of political change. Future assassins cited Orsini as an inspiration, including those who tried to kill Wilhelm I and Bismarck in Prussia in the 1860s.

5. Ottoman

The Ottoman Empire was founded in the thirteenth century and comprised lands in the Asian, European, and African continents. It stood at the geographic and cultural crossroads between Eastern and Western civilizations. One of the largest empires in history, by the nineteenth century, it was showing significant signs of weakness compared to its zenith, during the times of Suleiman the Magnificent in the sixteenth century. Its success in allowing significant freedoms to its client states began to fray as many started to move toward or agitate for varying forms of independence. The empire also continued to lag behind the technological developments of Western Europe. Battles with Russia over the Balkans led to the Russo-Turkish War of 1877–78 and the subsequent Treaty of San Stefano, which called for the independence of Romania,[26] Serbia,[27] and Montenegro;[28] the establishment of an independent Bulgaria;[29]

---

26. Treaty of San Stefano, Rus.-Tur., Mar. 3, 1878, art. 5.
27. *Id.* art. 3.
28. *Id.* art. 2.
29. *Id.* art. 6.

and the opening of the Bosporus and Dardanelles straits in times of peace and war.[30] This treaty, plus others shortly thereafter, took away several client states and so further weakened the Ottoman Empire.

LEGAL PROFILES

Safvet Pasha was the grand vizier of the Ottoman Empire during the negotiation of the Treaty of San Stefano. This role included being the absolute attorney (*vekil-i mutlak*) for the empire. He was born in Turkey in 1805 and entered the service of the sultan (termed the *Sublime Porte* after the gate that led to the imperial offices). He represented the empire at a number of international conferences in the 1850s through the 1870s. He held many positions during his career, including minister of foreign affairs, minister of commerce and public works, minister of justice, and minister of public instruction. He was behind the founding of a number of schools for both genders, and he led the Council for Reform. He was appointed grand vizier in 1878, during the negotiations of the Treaty of San Stefano. He died in 1883.[31]

6. Russia

The Russian Empire was very large in terms of the land it controlled, but was an empire only for those countries contiguous to it. Declared by Peter the Great in 1721 and expanded by Catherine the Great, by the nineteenth century, the Russian Empire was still economically behind the more capitalist Western Europe as it struggled to break fully free of its ties to serfdom. It was frequently involved in disputes with the Ottoman Empire over the Balkans, viewing itself as the protector of Christian Slavs in that region from their Muslim overlords. The Treaty of San Stefano, following the defeat of the Ottomans

---

30. *Id.* art. 24.
31. *See Obituary: Safvet Pasha*, N.Y. TIMES (Nov. 19, 1883).

by the Russians in 1878, was intended to increase the Russian influence in the Balkans.

The Austrians were not happy about this increased influence, and Austria induced Bismarck to host the Congress of Berlin later the same year to address this situation and redraw the map of Europe in a way that was more favorable to Germany. The majority of the articles of the Treaty of San Stefano were revised at this session, under its final act, the Treaty of Berlin.[32] One of the principal revisions was that Macedonia[33] and Eastern Rumelia,[34] which had been part of an autonomous Bulgaria, were to be removed from Bulgaria and returned to Ottoman control. In addition, the provinces of Bosnia and Herzegovina were to be governed and occupied by Austria-Hungary, as was land between Serbia and Montenegro.[35] Austria-Hungary was also to control certain aspects of Montenegro, such as its naval defenses.[36] Although it received some land in return, Russia was the key loser in the new agreement, having both lost the significant influence that the larger Bulgaria would have provided and suffered the impact of the occupying presence of Austria-Hungary in the Balkans.

LEGAL PROFILES

Benjamin Disraeli was British Prime Minister, a solicitor, and one of the participants at the Berlin conference. He was born in England in 1804 and started his legal practice there. But he soon turned to writing, first in newspapers and then in novels (such as *Vivian Grey*), burlesques, and political pamphlets during the 1830s and 1840s. After several defeats, he first won election to the House of Commons in 1837, to which he was repeatedly reelected, although from different districts, until 1876. In 1852 he became chancellor of the exchequer for the first time, a posi-

---

32. Treaty of Berlin, between Great Britain, Austria-Hungary, France, Germany, Italy, Russia, and Ottoman Empire, July 13, 1878.
33. *Id.* art. 2.
34. *Id.* art. 13.
35. *Id.* art. 25.
36. *Id.* art. 29.

tion he would hold several more times. In 1868, he served briefly as prime minister and then again from 1874 to 1880. He was to frequently exchange both of these roles with his great adversary, William Gladstone. In 1876 he moved to the House of Lords as the Earl of Beaconsfield, where he was during the Berlin Conference. The Liberals and Gladstone were back in power in 1880, and Disraeli was leading the opposition Tories when he died in 1881.[37]

---

7. Austria-Hungary

Austria had long existed as a Hapsburg-ruled country that was part of the Holy Roman Empire. It became the stand-alone Austrian Empire in 1804 during the Napoleonic Wars in preparation for the breakup of the Holy Roman Empire in 1806. The Kingdom of Hungary had existed at least since its founding by Saint Stephen in 1000, but it had been under Hapsburg rule since the early sixteenth century, after its defeat to the Ottomans at the Battle of Mohács in 1526. After the losses of territory described previously through the Treaty of Vienna in 1866 and the Treaty of London in 1867, the Austrian Empire was lagging behind the United Kingdom, France, and Germany. To maintain its "Great Power" status,[38] it agreed to create the Austro-Hungarian Empire in 1867.[39] Under this agreement, the Austro-Hungarian Compromise, Hungary was no longer subordinated to Austrian rule: each nation would have its own parliament, prime minister, and laws. The two countries had in common a single ruler as the emperor of Austria and king of Hungary, a common army and navy, a common foreign policy, a common finance department to fund these empire-level entities, and a customs union for currency and external trade. The terms were renegotiable every ten years.

The number of different cultures and countries included in this empire was vast, including not only Austria and Hungary, but all or parts of the modern-

---

37. *See Benjamin Disraeli*, OXFORD DICTIONARY OF NATIONAL BIOGRAPHY 101007689.
38. The term "Great Power" was first used in connection with the Congress of Vienna in 1814, designating which of the victorious countries were able to vote on all issues. The ability to project military, economic, cultural, and political power on a large scale are some of the criteria used to differentiate great from small powers.
39. Austro-Hungarian Compromise (Ausgleich–Ger., Kiegyezěs–Hung.), Feb. 8, 1867.

day countries of the Czech Republic, Slovakia, Croatia, Slovenia, Romania, Serbia, Italy, Poland, Ukraine, Bosnia and Herzegovina, and Montenegro. The number of languages and cultures created innumerable conflicts that pushed the empire into some of the first laws on multiculturalism, including the laws promulgated in Austria after the Compromise that provided, "All races of the empire have equal rights and every race has an inviolable right to the preservation and use of its own nationality and language."[40] The multicultural character of the empire was then recognized as an asset, a far cry from what would occur in Austria some seventy years later.[41]

After the Treaty of Berlin, Austria-Hungary gained a larger presence in the Balkans. Possibly in recognition for the role that Bismarck had played in hosting the Congress of Berlin, making this influence possible, Austria-Hungary signed the Dual Alliance agreement with Germany for their mutual defense.[42] It provided for either mutual armed assistance in case of an attack on either country by Russia[43] or at least "benevolent" neutrality if either was attacked by another European great power (unless the attacker was supported by Russia, in which case the former provision applied).[44] The agreement was to be secret[45] and to initially run for five years but was renewable.[46]

LEGAL PROFILES

Ferenc Deák was a lawyer and the leading figure on the Hungarian side for the Compromise of 1867. He was born in Hungary in 1803 and started his legal practice there. He created a criminal code that gained a measure of international renown. In 1833, he moved into politics in the Hungarian Diet. He was involved in a number of efforts to reform Hungarian laws and to negotiate the relationship of Hungary to Austria. One

---

40. Basic Law on the General Rights of Citizens, Das Staatsgrundgesetz über die aligemeinen Rechte der Staatsbürger, Dec. 21, 1867, art. 19.
41. *See* Thomas J. Shaw, WWII Law and Lawyers: Issues, Cases, and Characters, ch. 5 (2013).
42. Zweibund, Ger.-Aut.-Hun., Oct. 7, 1879.
43. *Id.* art. 1.
44. *Id.* art. 2.
45. *Id.* art. 4.
46. *Id.* art. 3.

of his major causes was the elimination of serfdom from Hungary, and to prove his sincerity, he freed his own serfs. He also supported equality of taxation (the nobility were exempt from tax) and again demonstrated his position by voluntarily paying tax. During the 1848 Hungarian Revolution, he was named as the minister of justice, in which position he attempted a reform of the judiciary. He was a leader in the Diet when negotiating the Compromise and served in subsequent Hungarian governments. He died in 1876.[47]

8. Neutrality of Belgium and Luxembourg

Two other agreements were signed during this time that were to have a significant impact on WWI, involving the neutrality of Belgium and Luxembourg. In the Treaty of London of 1839, the signatories (United Kingdom, France, Austria, Prussia, Russia, and the Netherlands) all agreed that Belgium was to be a neutral state.[48] In the Treaty of London of 1867, the signatories (Great Britain, Austria, France, Prussia, and Russia) guaranteed the neutrality of Luxembourg.[49]

LEGAL PROFILES

Sylvain Van de Weyer was ambassador from Belgium to the United Kingdom and a signatory on the London Treaty of 1867. He was born in 1802 in a part of France that is now in Belgium, and started his legal practice there. He also became a professor of philosophy. In his legal career, he defended journalists and newspapers, including those involved in supporting the Belgian cause for independence. He was involved in the Belgian Revolution of 1830, which led to the independence of Bel-

---

47. *See Obituary: Francis Deak*, N.Y. TIMES (Jan. 29, 1876).
48. Treaty between Great Britain, Austria, France, Prussia, and Russia, and the Netherlands, Apr. 19, 1839, art. 7.
49. Treaty between Great Britain, Austria, Belgium, France, Italy, the Netherlands, Prussia, and Russia, May 11, 1867, art. 2.

gium from the Netherlands, and he became the new country's foreign minister, enlisting British support. He later served as the ambassador to the United Kingdom, which position he held during the negotiations for the Treaty of London. He died in 1874 in London.[50]

B. Alliance-Building Agreements: 1880–1907

Once the nations of Europe had been unified, alliance agreements became the focus. These were precautionary in nature, trying to achieve a balance of power among potential adversaries, to avoid war outright, or to be ready with allies if war came. The countries tried to line up with others that had complementary goals, but often the alliances were as much based on fear of what the other nations, especially Great Powers, might do. The result was a grouping of two principal blocs leading up to WWI: the Triple Entente for the Allied Powers and the Triple Alliance for the Central Powers. There were other alliances, but these two were the key ones. In addition, countries needed to address new international warfare conventions that were agreed upon during this time period, while also being involved in the race for colonies in Africa and Asia.

1. Triple Entente

Actually a series of agreements for disparate purposes, the Triple Entente was made up of separate agreements among France and Russia (the Franco-Russian Alliance of 1894), France and the United Kingdom (the Entente Cordiale in 1904 and Naval Agreement of 1912), and the United Kingdom and Russia (the Anglo-Russian Entente in 1907). The Franco-Russian agreement was based on their potential need to wage a "defensive war, provoked by an attack of the forces of the Triple Alliance against either of them."[51] This was to take effect if France was attacked by Germany or by Italy supported by Germany, or if Russia was attacked by Germany or by Austria supported by Germany.[52] The intent was that Germany would have to "fight simultaneously on the East and on the West."[53]

---

50. *See The Late M. Van De Weyer*, N.Y. TIMES (June 12, 1874).
51. Franco-Russian Alliance Military Convention, Aug. 18, 1892.
52. *Id.* art. 1.
53. *Id.* art. 3.

The Entente Cordiale was the public part of an agreement between the United Kingdom and France regarding spheres of influence in North Africa (the secret part of the agreement is discussed in the following section).[54] It bound France not to interfere with the United Kingdom in Egypt[55] and the United Kingdom not to interfere with France in Morocco.[56] It also guaranteed free passage of the Suez Canal[57] and the Strait of Gibraltar[58] for all countries and stipulated that France would sign a related agreement with Spain[59] (described in the next section). France and the United Kingdom also reached other accords on fishing rights, territory, and rights in Siam. They later entered a naval agreement whereby the French took on Mediterranean naval duties to free up British ships which would then have the primary naval role in the Atlantic, including defending the northwest coast of France.[60]

The Anglo-Russian Entente was based on an agreement addressing issues with Persia.[61] Persia was split into zones of control between the two parties, and additional provisions were also defined for British spheres of influence for Afghanistan and Tibet.

LEGAL PROFILES

Paul Cambon helped to negotiate and signed the Entente Cordiale for France. He was born in France in 1843, received his legal training there, and was called to the bar in Paris. He chose the civil service and spent time in Tunisia as the resident-general. In 1886, he became the French ambassador to Spain, then in 1890 to the Ottoman Empire. In 1898, he became ambassador to the United Kingdom, where he was when he helped to negotiate the Entente. He would serve in this post for twenty-two years. He helped France keep British support during the

---

54. Declaration Respecting Egypt and Morocco, U.K.–Fr., Apr. 8, 1904.
55. *Id.* art. 1.
56. *Id.* art. 2.
57. *Id.* art. 6.
58. *Id.* art. 7.
59. *Id.* art. 8.
60. Anglo-French Naval Convention, July 23, 1912.
61. Agreement Concerning Persia, U.K.–Rus., Aug. 31, 1907.

First Moroccan Crisis, and he was also the French representative to the London Conference after the Balkan Wars in 1912–13 (both described below). With his brother Jules—the ambassador to the United States, Spain, and then Germany—he was able to help France build allies when war finally came. He died in 1924.[62]

Jules Cambon signed the Entente Cordiale for France. He was born in France in 1845 and started his legal practice there. He served in the military during the Franco-Prussian War and then returned to civilian life in the civil service in 1871. He spent time in Algeria over the next twenty years and was appointed governor-general of Algeria in 1891. In 1897, he was appointed French ambassador to the United States. In this position he was able to help represent the Spanish and negotiate a treaty for the Spanish-American War. He was subsequently ambassador to Spain in 1902 and Germany in 1907, before being recalled during WWI to serve in the foreign ministry. He was involved in the Versailles conferences after the war. He died in 1935.[63]

2. Triple Alliance

Germany, Austria-Hungary, and Italy entered into the Triple Alliance in 1882, and the Ottoman Empire and Bulgaria joined later, after the start of WWI.[64] The details of the alliance included support by the original signatories if Italy was attacked by France or if Germany was attacked by France "without direct provocation."[65] It also required mutual support if one of the contracting parties was attacked by two or more Great Powers.[66] In the event that one of the contracting parties was threatened and thus forced to make war, the other two were required to observe "benevolent neutrality."[67] The parties were not to conclude armistices or treaties except with consensus among them.[68] An

---

62. *See Paul Cambon Dies; French Diplomat*, N.Y. TIMES (May 30, 1924).
63. *See Jules Cambon Dies; French Diplomat*, N.Y. TIMES (Sept. 20, 1935).
64. First Treaty of Alliance between Austria-Hungary, Germany, and Italy, May 20, 1882.
65. *Id.* art. II.
66. *Id.* art. III.
67. *Id.* art. IV.
68. *Id.* art. V.

additional declaration stated that the alliance could not be regarded as being directed against England.

The Triple Alliance was much more clearly laid out as an alliance of military support than the Triple Entente. But Italy subsequently undermined its participation by signing secret agreements with France in 1902, Russia in 1909, and the United Kingdom in 1915 that offset its role in the Triple Alliance. Its participation in WWI, therefore, would not be definitively under the Triple Alliance. In actuality, Italy ended up in the war on the side of the Allied Powers.

LEGAL PROFILES

Heinrich VII was the signer of the Triple Alliance for Germany and the earlier Dual Alliance. He was born in the German Confederation in 1825 and obtained his legal education there before joining the military. In 1853 he joined the diplomatic service. He was posted to Paris from 1854 to 1863 and then served as ambassador to Kassel in Hesse and then Munich in Bavaria. In 1868 he became an envoy from the North German Confederation to Russia. In 1871, he was appointed ambassador of the new German Empire to Russia, from which post he resigned in 1876. In 1877 he was ambassador to the Ottoman Empire during the Russo-Turkish War; he then became the German ambassador to Austria-Hungary in 1878, where he was when the Dual Alliance was signed. He retained this post until 1894. He died in 1906.[69]

3. Dreyfus Trial

During this time period came a trial, or set of trials, that divided France regarding its relationship with Germany. In October 1894, artillery Captain Alfred Dreyfus was arrested for allegedly communicating French military secrets on

---

69. *See Heinrich VII, Prinz Reuss-Köstritz*, Neue Deutsche Biographie.

artillery to the Germans through their embassy in Paris. Dreyfus was from Alsace, the former French province now controlled by Germany. He was also Jewish in a still anti-Semitic world. In January 1895, he was convicted by a court-martial of treason, mostly based on evidence that his handwriting appeared on a note, found in a German-embassy wastebasket, by a supposed French agent offering to sell military information to the Germans. Not all evidence considered by the court was made available to the defense. Dreyfus was sentenced to life imprisonment on Devil's Island off French Guiana.

The incoming chief of military intelligence, Lt. Col. Georges Picquart, found in 1896 that another officer, Ferdinand Esterhazy, was likely the guilty party, based on a letter from a known German agent to him and documents in Esterhazy's handwriting that matched that in the Dreyfus note. Before Picquart could follow up his investigation, however, he was transferred to a more remote posting. The suspicions about Esterhazy become public, and he was eventually brought before a court-martial in January 1898 but was acquitted. Picquart was arrested for revealing military secrets to civilians. In the same month, famed novelist Émile Zola wrote to the newspaper a letter titled *J'accuse* ("I Accuse") that went over the evidence in the case. This led to a libel conviction against Zola the next month (which caused him to leave the country for nearly a year), but also brought to light previously undisclosed evidence from Dreyfus's 1894 trial.

Under review by the French Supreme Court of Appeals, the original verdict against Dreyfus was overturned in June 1899 and a new trial was ordered. In September, a court-martial found Dreyfus guilty again, but he was then pardoned by the French president. He chose to pursue full exoneration, and in July 1906, he received it from the Supreme Court of Appeals. The following year, he took an honorable discharge from the military. In 1908, at Zola's funeral, Dreyfus survived an assassination attempt. During WWI, he volunteered for active service and served throughout the war. Despite being in his fifties, he saw out the conflict before finally dying in 1935.

Esterhazy fled to England to live out his life in anonymity. Picquart was exonerated along with Dreyfus and promoted in the French military. He served as minister of war from 1906 to 1909, before being killed in 1914, just before WWI began.

LEGAL PROFILES

Edgar Demange was the defense attorney for Dreyfus in both of his court-martial trials and the related appeals. He was born in France in 1841 and started his legal practice there. In his early career, he gained fame for achieving an acquittal for Prince Pierre Bonaparte in the shooting of journalist Victor Noir in 1870. He worked as a lawyer for more than sixty years, being involved in many of the famous cases of the time. He continued to represent the Dreyfus family. He died in 1925.[70]

Fernand Labori was another defense attorney for Dreyfus from the second court-martial trial and also for Zola and Picquart. He was born in France in 1860 and started his legal practice there. During the second court-martial of Dreyfus, he was the victim of an assassination attempt. Through the Esterhazy trial (representing the Dreyfus family) and the Zola trial, he was able to uncover evidence to help Dreyfus get a new trial. After several failed attempts, in 1906, he was elected to the national assembly, where he served until 1910, when he returned to legal practice. In 1914, he successfully defended Henriette Caillaux, a politician's wife who had shot and killed a newspaper editor who was attacking her husband. Labori died in 1917.[71]

4. International Conventions

Several important conventions related to war were promulgated during this time period. The Hague Conventions on warfare of 1899 and 1907 and the Geneva Convention on sick and wounded soldiers of 1906 were both significant milestones that set the rules for conduct during war. The Hague Peace Conference of 1899, initiated by Russian Czar Nicholas II, produced four conventions and three declarations in July 1899. The conventions agreed to and ratified by the principal nations in WWI were as follows:

---

70. *See Edgard Demange, Noted Lawyer, Dies*, N.Y. TIMES (Feb. 12, 1925).
71. *See Fernand Labori,* ARCHIVES DE L'ASSEMBLEE NATIONALE.

- Hague I: Pacific Settlement of International Disputes
- Hague II: Laws and Customs of War on Land
- Hague III: Adaptation to Maritime Warfare of Principles of Geneva Convention of 1864[72]

The declarations:

- Hague IV, I: on the Launching of Projectiles and Explosives from Balloons
- Hague IV, II: on the Use of Projectiles the Object of Which Is the Diffusion of Asphyxiating or Deleterious Gases
- Hague IV, III: on the Use of Bullets Which Expand or Flatten Easily in the Human Body

U.S. President Theodore Roosevelt then initiated a second peace conference, which, due to the Russo-Japanese War, was not held until 1907. The conference produced thirteen conventions, one draft convention, and one declaration. The following conventions were agreed to and ratified by most of the principal nations in WWI, except those who had ratified the 1899 conventions but not the 1907 conventions (Bulgaria, Greece, Italy, Montenegro, Serbia, and Turkey):

- Hague I: Pacific Settlement of International Disputes
- Hague II: Limitation of Employment of Force for Recovery of Contract Debts
- Hague III: Opening of Hostilities
- Hague IV: Laws and Customs of War on Land
- Hague V: Rights and Duties of Neutral Powers and Persons in Case of War on Land
- Hague VI: Status of Enemy Merchant Ships at the Outbreak of Hostilities
- Hague VII: Conversion of Merchant Ships into War-Ships
- Hague VIII: Laying of Automatic Submarine Contact Mines
- Hague IX: Bombardment by Naval Forces in Time of War
- Hague X: Adaptation to Maritime War of the Principles of the Geneva Convention

---

72. Convention for the Amelioration of the Condition of the Wounded in Armies in the Field, Aug. 22, 1864.

- Hague XI: Certain Restrictions with Regard to the Exercise of the Right of Capture in Naval War
- Hague XII: Creation of an International Prize Court
- Hague XIII: Rights and Duties of Neutral Powers in Naval War
- Draft Convention: Relative to the Creation of a Judicial Arbitration Court

The declaration:

- Hague XIV: extending Declaration I from the 1899 Conference

The conventions entered into force in January 1910, except for XII, which was never ratified.

Following the desire expressed in the final act of the 1899 Hague Peace Conference to "lessen the inherent evils of warfare," and in the wake of the Russo-Japanese War of 1904–5 and its predecessor convention of 1864, the Second Geneva Convention for the sick and wounded was promulgated in 1906.[73] Among its provisions were the requirements for all belligerents to care for sick and injured combatants and to search for them after battles; to protect hospitals and their personnel, including those collecting and transporting the injured; to protect and recognize the neutrality of aid societies; to return information on the dead, sick, and wounded; and to return the sick and wounded to their own country or to a neutral country. The convention was ratified by every principal nation in WWI, except the United Kingdom.

LEGAL PROFILES

Frederick de Martens was a leading Russian diplomat at the Hague Conferences. He was born in Russia in 1845 and got his legal training there. In 1868 he began working with the foreign ministry. In 1871 he joined the international law faculty of St. Petersburg University. In

---

73. Convention for the Amelioration of the Condition of the Wounded and Sick in Armies in the Field, July 6, 1906.

1869 he published the first of many books, *The Right of Private Property in War*. Other well-known volumes include *International Law of Civilised Nations* and more than a dozen volumes on Russian treaties. He served as an international arbiter on many cases, including the first case under the Permanent Court of Arbitration in the Hague (established under the 1899 Hague Convention I). He was also involved in the Treaty of Portsmouth after the Russo-Japanese War. He was involved in numerous international conferences, including the 1906 Geneva Conference. He died in 1909.[74]

Louis Renault was a leading French legal scholar at the Hague Conferences. He was born in France in 1843 and received his legal training there. He became a professor of law in 1868, working first at the University of Dijon and then at the University of Paris. He also worked with the Ministry of Foreign Affairs, consulting on the international law; additionally, he worked as an arbitrator on many of the first cases at the Hague after 1899. He produced volumes on international and commercial law, such as *Traité de droit commercial* in nine volumes and the wartime *First Violations of International Law by Germany*. He was involved in many international conferences across a wide variety of subjects, including intellectual property, aviation, naval affairs, slavery, and the Geneva Convention. He was involved in the negotiations at the Algeciras Conference. In 1907, he was awarded the Nobel Peace Prize, primarily for his work at the 1907 Hague Conference. He died in 1918.[75]

---

5. Colonies
a. Rush for Territory
While the tussle for territory in Europe continued to go on, there was a significant push from European powers in the latter half of the nineteenth century to grab up colonies across the world. With the Americas already spoken for and the Monroe Doctrine in place, Asia and Africa were left as the primary targets

---

74. *See Frederick De Martens Dead*, N.Y. TIMES (June 21, 1909).
75. *See Louis Renault Dead*, N.Y. TIMES (Feb. 10, 1918).

for expansion. The techniques used by the Europeans ranged from outright seizure to playing one local government faction off another in order to reach an agreement with that favored group and to giving more equitable arrangements for those colonies run by colonists expatriated from the home country. The competition in the "scramble for Africa" was such that conferences were held to set spheres of influence and "uniform rules with reference to future occupations . . . of the African Continent."[76] The goals for the colonizer included new markets for the colonizer's goods, new sources of natural and human resource, military advantages, and, of course, regional influence. These would all come into play in WWI.

Britain and France were the leading global colonizers, with Italy and Germany attempting to catch up. Spain, Portugal, and the Netherlands had been the early conquerors of new territory in previous centuries but had been ousted by either the English or the French or local rebellions, and they now controlled relatively few colonies. The far-flung British Empire consisted of all manner of colonies and dominions, which at its zenith encompassed one-quarter of the world's land mass and population. Colonies were directly ruled by the government in London, while dominions were self-ruling except for international relations. For example, the law that established Canada as a nation specified that the commander-in-chief of the naval and military forces was "declared to continue and be vested in the Queen."[77] By the start of WWI, Canada, Newfoundland (which did not join Canada until 1949), Australia, New Zealand, South Africa, and the Irish Free State were dominions in the British Empire, while for India, Egypt, Kenya, Singapore, Hong Kong, Nigeria, Burma, and many Caribbean and Pacific islands, independence was further in the future. The role of these colonies and dominions in supporting the mother countries would be significant in manpower and sometimes geographic terms during WWI.

Generally, the pre-WWI empires of the major powers fell into two broad categories: those that had their colonies principally overseas and those that had their colonies contiguous to the home country. In the former category were the empires of the United Kingdom, France, Germany, and Italy, while in the latter

---

76. General Act of the Berlin Conference, Feb. 26, 1885.
77. British North America Act (Constitution Act), 1867, 30 & 31 Vict., c. 3, art. 15 (U.K.).

category were the Austro-Hungarian, Ottoman, and Russian empires. While trade was a key aspect of all colonization, the global empires tended to be focused more heavily on the economic aspects of colonization rather than pure conquest. This provided a sense of renewal and vigor that was missing in the contiguous empires, all of whom would collapse through the course of WWI.

b. Morant Court-Martial

In a foreshadowing of WWI, the European powers found conflicts arose in trying to lead soldiers from their colonies while handling foreign relations with other countries. One well-known example was the court-martial of Harry Harbord Morant and two of his Australian compatriots while they served the British in their efforts to subdue the Boers in the South African colony in the Second Boer War (1899-1902). Morant, who was born in England and immigrated to Australia, was known as "Breaker" for his skill with horses. As a published poet, he used this nickname as his pen name. He volunteered for service in South Africa and eventually was assigned to a unit called the Bushveldt Carbineers. The British were fighting the Boers there, descendants of the eighteenth-century Dutch settlers of the Cape Colony. The Boers had set up their own republics in South Africa and resented the interference from the British Empire. They had taken up guerilla tactics to resist the British. Among the duties of the Bushveldt Carbineers was to find and bring in Boer people, have them sign loyalty oaths to the British, herd their women and children into concentration camps, and take away their crops and animals, depriving them of means to support a guerilla war. It was a scorched-earth policy to force Boer capitulation.

Morant had become engaged to the sister of friend and fellow officer Percy Hunt's fiancée. When Hunt was later killed after purportedly being tortured by the Boers, Morant became furious. Along with fellow Australians Peter Handcock and George Witton, he was arrested and accused of killing Boer prisoners. At the trial starting on January 16, 1902—the day after they received the formal charges against them—the men claimed that they had been acting under verbal orders not to take prisoners from British intelligence officer Alfred Taylor, who in turn received his orders directly from the British commander Lord Kitchener. To further complicate the situation, the men were accused of also killing a German missionary who had tended to the Boers and had been aware of the extrajudicial killings.

Their trial went through several phases, with the men admitting to killing the prisoners based on orders from above (but not killing the missionary). This was a clear violation of the Hague Convention of 1899[78] and thus constituted a war crime. Kitchener denied through his second-in-command that he had given such orders (although recent research has uncovered a contemporary legal opinion of the deputy judge advocate general that Taylor did issue such orders and should have been tried for murder instead of negligence to report murder).[79] The court determined that there was sufficient evidence to convict Morant and Handcock for the murders of the Boer prisoners, and they were sentenced to be executed. The younger Witton received the same sentence, but his sentence was commuted to life at hard labor (he was later released and wrote a book about his experience, *Scapegoats of the Empire*). Despite recommendations for mercy, on February 27, 1902, the executions, on orders signed by Kitchener, were carried out.

As neither Taylor nor any of the British soldiers involved in similar atrocities were so convicted, the unequal treatment given the "colonials" has long been a source of tension. There was no appeal allowed, one of the points of procedural unfairness claimed by the defendants' supporters. The trial transcripts have disappeared, leading to further doubts about the fairness of the trial. Given the implications of the murder of the German missionary (Kaiser Wilhelm II supposedly complained about it to his British royal relatives), the alleged ordering of war crimes by Kitchener, and the desire to end this war, there were many factors in play far beyond the trial itself that likely affected the outcome. The peace treaty ending that war was signed shortly thereafter.[80] The story became the basis for the award-winning 1980 film *Breaker Morant*.

---

78. Hague Convention (II) with Respect to the Laws and Customs of War on Land and Its Annex: Regulations Respecting the Laws and Customs of War on Land, July 29, 1899, art. 4.
79. *Australian call for justice long denied Breaker Morant*, Daily Telegraph (Oct. 21, 2011).
80. Treaty of Vereeniging, between the United Kingdom and the South African Republic and Republic of the Orange Free State, May 31, 1902.

LEGAL PROFILES

James Francis Thomas, a major in the army, was the defense counsel in this trial. He was born in Australia in 1861 and started his legal practice as a solicitor in rural Australia. He owned and edited a newspaper in New South Wales and was a strong proponent of Australian federalism, which would eventually be realized. He brought a species of flower, the gerbera, to Australia from South Africa. He was also a poet. He was serving in a reserve light cavalry unit when the call came that the British Empire needed men for the Boer War in 1899. After being decorated for heroism during a year in South Africa with his unit, he returned to Australia. Lack of opportunity for many of his men led him to return to South Africa, where he was drafted into his role for this trial. Upon his return to Australia after the trial, he tried to get the government to open an inquiry into the case, published letters in the newspapers on the case, helped Witton with his book, and provided for the children of Handcock. But the outcome of the trial had a devastating effect on Thomas, as his law practice declined, he sold his interest in the newspaper, and he was eventually declared bankrupt, imprisoned, and disbarred. He died in 1942.[81]

C. Prewar Conflicts: 1905–1913

Against the backdrop of these alliances were a series of crises and local wars in the decade before WWI that were significant in the lead-up to the initiation of the larger war. Each of these conflicts in itself could have led to a war at the time, but for various reasons, cooler heads prevailed and agreements were eventually reached:

- Moroccan Crises in 1905–6 and 1911–12
- Bosnian Crisis in 1908–9
- Turko-Italian War in 1911–12

---

81. *See Obituary*, Tenterfield Star (Nov. 12, 1942).

- Albanian Crises in 1913
- Balkan Wars in 1912–13

1. Moroccan Crises
a. First Crisis

The first crisis in Morocco (the Tangier Crisis) involved the German challenge to French influence in Morocco. As part of the European powers' colonization of the African continent, France had attempted to set up a protectorate in still-independent Morocco, including control of the army, police, and customs revenues. France reached secret agreements in 1904 with Spain to partition Morocco[82] and with the United Kingdom over the countries' respective spheres of influence in Morocco and Egypt.[83] Germany wanted to interfere with the French plans, so Kaiser Wilhelm II made a visit to Morocco in March 1905 to consult with the Moroccan leaders. He offered support for the country in case of war or independence from French control. With both France and Germany mobilizing their militaries, the Algeciras Conference, attended by many countries from outside the crisis, was held from January to April 1906 to attempt to settle this issue.

Contrary to its intentions, Germany was not able to line up sufficient support from other conference attendees, and the result did not produce a French separation from control of Morocco, although it did forestall an official French protectorate there for the time being. The final act of the conference[84] produced only certain restrictions on the ability of the French to dominate the local police force, which was to be run by the Moroccans with training by the French and Spanish,[85] and on arms smuggling.[86] France succeeded in including several provisions dealing with revenues; financial dependency of Morocco would help France insist on the need for a protectorate.[87]

---

82. Declaration on Inclusion of Spain in Anglo-French Agreement of 1904, Fr.-Esp., Oct. 3, 1904; Convention on Morocco, Fr.-Esp., Oct. 3, 1904.
83. Declaration Respecting Egypt and Morocco, Secret Articles, U.K.-Fr., Apr. 8, 1904.
84. General Act of the Algeciras Conference Relating to the Affairs of Morocco, between Great Britain, Austria-Hungary, Belgium, France, Germany, Italy, Morocco, Netherlands, Portugal, Russia, Spain, Sweden, and the United States, Apr. 7, 1906.
85. *Id.* ch. 1.
86. *Id.* ch. 2.
87. *Id.* ch. 3–5.

There were several consequences of this conference, beyond the final act itself. One was to strengthen the Entente Cordiale between the United Kingdom and France, which Germany had sought to weaken. This was part of what caused Russia to join the alliance the following year. From Germany's perspective, its bitterness toward France and the United Kingdom increased. The following year, it passed the Third Naval Law, further committing to the expansion and modernization of its navy in order to be capable of taking on the Royal Navy.[88] Root causes were left unresolved and so continued to water the seeds of a future crisis, which came again in 1911.

The United States, a participant in this conference, had the treaty approved by the U.S. Senate, but only after making a statement opposing U.S. involvement in European affairs.[89]

> [I]n giving its advice and consent to the ratification . . . the Senate understands the participation of the United States in the Algeciras Conference . . . was for the sole purpose of preserving and increasing its commerce in Morocco, the protection as to life, liberty, and property of its citizens residing or traveling therein and aiding by its friendly offices and efforts in removing friction and controversy which seemed to menace the peace between the powers . . . all of whom are on terms of amity with this government; and without the purpose to depart from the traditional American foreign policy which forbids participation by the United States in the settlement of political questions which are entirely European in their scope.[90]

b. Second Crisis

In 1909, Germany and France further agreed that France had special interests in Morocco while Germany had economic interests there.[91] Neither this nor the 1906 agreement really addressed the roots of the dispute, leading in 1911 to a second Moroccan crisis (the Agadir Crisis). A rebellion against the leadership

---

88. Novelle zum Gesetze, betreffend die Deutsche Flotte, vom 14, Juni 1900 vom 5, Juni 1906 (RGBI. S. 729).
89. General Act of the International Conference of Algeciras, Apr. 7, 1906, 34 Stat. 2905.
90. *Id.* at 2946.
91. Agreement on Morocco, Fr.–Ger., Feb. 9, 1909.

in Morocco caused the French to move 20,000 troops to the country to suppress the rebellion. In response, Germany sent a gunboat to the port of Agadir. The settlement of this crisis was the Treaty of Berlin in 1911[92] between France and Germany, exchanging Germany's interest in Morocco for French-controlled land in the Congo, and then the Treaty of Fez in 1912, which allowed France to make Morocco a protectorate and Tangier an international city, and also secured Spanish rights over northern Morocco.[93]

LEGAL PROFILES

Samuel R. Gummere was the U.S. ambassador and a representative at the Algeciras Conference and was also involved in the Perdicaris Incident (see below). He was born in 1849 in New Jersey and started his legal practice there. In 1898, he was appointed counsel general in Morocco, where he was during the Perdicaris Incident. In 1905, due to his work in resolving that matter, he was appointed U.S. ambassador to that country, where he was during the Algeciras Conference. He retained that position through 1909, when he retired from public office. His brother William was chief justice of the New Jersey Supreme Court for more than thirty years. Samuel died in 1920 in England.[94]

c. Perdicaris Incident

The Perdicaris Incident occurred just before the first Moroccan crisis in 1904 but was not directly related to it. The incident involved several key actors, including U.S. President Theodore Roosevelt; his secretary of state, John Hay; U.S. Moroccan Consul-General Samuel Gummere; wealthy Greek American Ion Perdicaris; Berber chief and known kidnapper Mulai Ahmed er Raisuli; and

---

92. Conventions on Morocco and Congo, Fr.–Ger., Nov. 4, 1911.
93. Treaty between Morocco, Germany, Spain, and France, Mar. 30, 1912.
94. *See Ex-Envoy Gummere Dies*, N.Y. TIMES (May 29, 1920).

the young sultan of Morocco, Mulai Abd al-Aziz. Perdicaris, initially unknown to the Americans, had renounced his U.S. citizenship many years before, over a possible loss of assets held in the U.S. Confederacy during the Civil War. He had also expatriated, ending up the owner of a significant estate in Morocco.

The incident started when Perdicaris and his stepson were kidnapped by some Berber tribesmen and taken to Raisuli. In this case, the ransom demand included not only money in gold, but also appointment of Raisuli to a government position. Roosevelt dispatched U.S. warships. Hay and Gummere tried to enlist the assistance of the European powers to pressure the sultan to agree to the terms. The message from Roosevelt to the sultan (through Hay and Gummere) that the U.S. government wanted "Perdicaris alive or Raisuli dead!" became a rallying point for Roosevelt's 1904 reelection campaign. The sultan agreed to Raisuli's demands, and Perdicaris was freed.

The event, although not directly impacting events on the ground in Morocco, did positively impact Roosevelt's reelection bid. As described above, Roosevelt was instrumental in calling the 1907 Hague Conference and the U.S. representation in the 1906 Algeciras Conference and its reaffirmation of neutrality in European affairs. This affair inspired the principal story line in the movie *The Wind and the Lion*, the title of which was a quote from a letter that Raisuli had sent to Roosevelt, comparing Roosevelt to the former and himself to the latter. Perdicaris soon left Morocco for England, while Gummere was promoted. Raisuli became pasha of Tangier.

LEGAL PROFILES

John M. Hay was the U.S. secretary of state during the Perdicaris Incident. He was born in 1838 in Indiana and received his legal training at the office of his uncle, who happened to have a law office next door to an Illinois lawyer named Abraham Lincoln. When Lincoln was elected president in 1860, Hay, along with former classmate John Nicolay, became a private secretary to the president. He fought for several months in the Civil War. After Lincoln's death, the two secretaries penned the ten-volume *Abraham Lincoln: A History*. From 1865 to 1870, Hay worked for the U.S. government in several European capitals (Paris, Madrid, and Vienna). Then, for the next eight years, he worked in journalism. In 1878, he was appointed as the undersecretary of state. In 1898, he was named secretary of state, a position he held for the next seven years. His achievements included negotiating an end to the Spanish-American War, promoting the Open Door policy in China, and crafting the treaties to start the work on the Panama Canal. He died in 1905.[95]

---

2. Bosnia Crisis

As described in the previous section, Austria-Hungary had long had designs on expansion in the Balkans. The Treaty of Berlin gave it the freedom to "administer and occupy" Bosnia-Herzegovina, but there was no ability to annex without the approval of the other signatories. Return to constitutional monarchy in the Ottoman Empire in 1908 implied a possible strengthening of the empire, which was the nominal ruler of Bosnia. The foreign ministers of Austria-Hungary (Alois von Aehrenthal) and Russia (Alexander Izvolsky) met in September 1908 and reached agreements for Russia not to oppose the annexation of Bosnia if Austria would not oppose Russian use of the Dardanelles and Bosporus straits for passage of Russian warships from the Black Sea.

Austria-Hungary proceeded with its annexation of Bosnia in early October 1908, while the other powers strongly opposed Russian warships traversing the Dardanelles and Bosporus straits. Serbia, Russia's Slavic ally, wanted Bosnia for itself and mobilized its military in November. But Russia was not prepared to take on Austria's ally Germany at that time and so had to urge Serbia to back down and accept the annexation. The Ottoman Empire, for its loss of territory, was paid by Austria a sum of around £2 million to accept the annexation. This crisis may have given Austria-Hungary an exaggerated sense of its power in the Balkans and Germany a suspicion of Russia's lack of desire to back its ally, which would come up again in a few short years in the Balkans. Russia, double losers in this crisis, and already smarting from its loss in the Russo-Japanese War of 1905, would not want to have to back down next time.

---

95. *See John Hay*, N.Y. TIMES (July 2, 1905).

3. Turko-Italian War

The Italians, seeing the colonialism of their European counterparts, decided to join the fray by invading Libya (which was not yet a unified country but a collection of territories under the Ottoman Empire). In September 1911, the Italians landed more than 100,000 troops in Libya. They had some initial success, but even with superior naval resources, they were not able to get far from the Mediterranean coast of the territory. The Ottomans were not able to easily move troops there because they had to go through occupied territory by land and they had a vastly outgunned navy. Consequently, they had to rely on local troops. After a year and significant expense, Italy moved to settle the conflict, signing the Treaty of Ouchy in October 1912.[96] The treaty required the Ottomans to remove military units from Libya and to give some Mediterranean islands to Turkey (although these transfers were never realized). The ultimate result of this conflict may have been to further weaken the Ottoman Empire and encourage those states that wanted to break away from it.

4. Albanian Crises

Albania had risen in revolt against the rule of the Ottoman Empire, in a series of uprisings from 1909 through 1911, to the final major uprising in 1912 that had the Albanians controlling significant territory in the country, including Kosovo. The Albanians presented the Ottomans with a list of demands relating to their autonomy within the empire, which the empire agreed to in early September 1912. Subsequently, Albania declared independence in November 1912, after the start of the Balkan Wars.

5. Balkan Wars

The various Christian Balkan countries chafed under the Ottoman Empire and looked for independence. The Turko-Italian conflict provided hope against their common enemy. The countries of Bulgaria and Serbia made an agreement to ally against the Austrians but also the Ottomans.[97] The alliance provided guarantees if any of the Great Powers tried to annex or occupy Ottoman territory in the Balkans.[98] A secret appendix allowed for military options based

---

96. Treaty of Ouchy, It.-Tur., Oct. 18, 1912.
97. Treaty of Friendship and Alliance, Bulg.-Serb., Feb. 29, 1912.
98. *Id.* art. 2.

on the weakness in the Ottoman Empire and specified the division of the territory of Macedonia between the two states. Then Bulgaria and Greece made an alliance in May 1912 and Serbia and Montenegro made an alliance in September 1912. With these Balkan League alliances in place, a war for independence against the Ottoman Empire was now possible.

In October 1912, starting with Montenegro, the four members of the Balkan League declared war on the Ottoman Empire, and fighting commenced in the First Balkan War. The Balkan League captured the Ottoman territory in Europe, leading to an armistice in December and a conference in London. Then a coup d'état in Turkey brought a more aggressive leadership to the Ottoman side, which resumed fighting and was able to regain some territory. This war finally ended with the Treaty of London in May 1913.[99] The Ottoman territories in Europe were ceded to the Balkan League, except for Albania.[100] The questions concerning Albania, including its borders, were to be determined by the Great Powers.[101]

Subsequently, Bulgaria and Serbia could not agree on the division of the territory acquired. Serbian troops had driven further than the previously agreed-upon borders and Greece had also. Suspecting Bulgarian intentions, Serbia and Greece had signed a secret alliance in April 1913.[102] Having failed to receive the territory it expected, Bulgaria launched the Second Balkan War against its former allies of Serbia and Greece. Romania and the Ottoman Empire joined in to reclaim disputed land, and Bulgaria lost most of what it had just acquired in the First Balkan War. This led to the Treaty of Bucharest,[103] which delineated Bulgaria's borders with Romania, Serbia, and Greece.[104] Bulgaria and the Ottoman Empire settled in the Treaty of Constantinople in September 1913. While all of the participants in the Balkan Wars gained territory at the expense of the Ottoman Empire, Serbia, as a winner in these conflicts, gained a new feeling of power as well as a grudge at not having acquired Albania. This was a final thread in the tapestry of intrigue and territory seeking that would soon light the fuse that started WWI.

---

99. Treaty of Peace between Bulgaria, Serbia, Montenegro, Greece, and the Ottoman Empire, May 30, 1913.
100. *Id.* art. I.
101. *Id.* art. II.
102. Secret Protocol between Greece and Serbia, Apr. 13, 1912.
103. Peace Treaty between Romania, Greece, Montenegro, Serbia, and Bulgaria, July 28, 1913.
104. *Id.* art. II, III, V.

LEGAL PROFILES

Titu Maiorescu was the Romanian prime minister at the peace conference in Bucharest. He was born in Romania in 1840. He received a PhD in philosophy in Germany and then his legal training in France. From 1862, he started work as a lawyer and taught at Iasi University, which he did until 1874. He later taught at the University of Bucharest. He was also an author and literary critic and a founder of the literary society Junimea ("Youth") in 1863. After the union of Romania in 1859 (from the provinces of Moldavia and Wallachia), he helped to shape Romanian culture in the second half of the nineteenth century. He was a member of the Romanian Academy and served in government as foreign minister from 1910 to 1913, before becoming prime minister. He died in 1917.[105]

1.2 UNITED STATES: FROM INWARD TO OUTWARD LOOKING

America had been mostly inwardly focused since its last major international encounter, with Britain in the War of 1812. The nineteenth century had seen the United States expanding enormously, primarily through purchases from European countries. The Louisiana Purchase, the Gadsden Purchase, the purchase of Alaska, the annexation of Texas, and the purchase of Florida all had the impact of casting the American expansionary urges focused on new territory within expanding borders of the country, with settlers following the growth of railroads and the Homestead Act of 1862. Even its most significant post-1812 foreign war, against Mexico starting in 1846, had the impact of materially increasing U.S. territory. With all of this new land close at hand, there was no real need for the United States to seek land overseas. Its major wars through the balance of the century, the Civil War and the Indian Wars, were fought inside its borders.

---

105. *See Titu Maiorescu*, Universitatea Titu Maiorescu.

This began to change in the 1890s. By that time, the continental United States was territorially defined. In 1889, Washington, North and South Dakota, and Montana became states, and Idaho and Wyoming the next year, thereby fully defining the control of the northern and western borders of the country. From this point on, expansion of territory would have to come from locations outside the continent. The year 1890 brought the start of a new era in the United States, with the passing of the Sherman Antitrust Act and a more active role by the federal government. The Massacre at Wounded Knee also occurred in 1890, symbolically if not actually signaling the end of the Indian wars. America was ready to cast its view abroad.

A. McKinley: 1897–1901

The transitional figure and administration who guided the United States away from its internal view to a more international perspective was William McKinley. The last of the Civil War veterans to be elected president, McKinley was an appropriate bridge between that most bloody of internal conflicts and the disputes that would arise outside U.S. borders. He started to take a more global view, partly based on the desires for new markets and resources for the emerging industrial giants of America. This view was to manifest itself significantly in the Spanish-American War, where the United States was to challenge Spain over its control of Cuba, located right in America's neighborhood.

LEGAL PROFILES

William McKinley was the president of the United States from 1897 to 1901. Born in Ohio in 1843, he started his legal practice there. He fought in the Civil War during its entirety from 1861 to 1865, where he participated in significant battles such as Antietam and befriended future U.S. president Rutherford B. Hayes. After the war, he got his legal license and practiced law, including a term as a prosecuting country attorney from 1869 to 1871. He was elected to the U.S. House of Representatives in 1877, where he remained until he was defeated in 1890. He was elected the governor of Ohio the next year and was reelected in 1893. In 1896 he secured the Republican nomination for president and won election to the U.S. presidency over famed lawyer Williams Jennings Bryan, running a "front-porch" campaign against the famed orator. In 1900 he defeated Bryan for the presidency again. McKinley was the victim of an assassination attempt on September 6, 1901, and died on September 14.[106]

---

1. Spanish-American War

U.S. sympathy for Cuban attempts at independence went back at least thirty years to 1868. When Spain ruthlessly suppressed a renewed independence movement in Cuba in 1895, the United States, under the Monroe Doctrine, tried to intervene, but subsequent negotiations with Spain were not successful. Several actors in the United States, including the "yellow journalism" newspapers of William Randolph Hearst and Joseph Pulitzer, as well as a young assistant secretary of the navy, Theodore Roosevelt, pushed for war, citing often one-sided or exaggerated accounts of actual repressive measures and atrocities. To protect American commercial interests and calm the situation, McKinley dispatched the warship USS *Maine* to Havana, Cuba, arriving on January 25, 1898.

To avoid inflaming events, the ship's personnel were required to remain onboard. Then an explosion occurred on the ship on February 15, 1898, killing more than 260 naval personnel. The navy's inquiry report in March led to a message from McKinley to Congress on April 11 calling for an end to hostilities in Cuba. Congress responded with a joint resolution calling on Spain to exit Cuba and a promise not to annex Cuba in April. Spain refused to accept those terms and instead broke off diplomatic relations on April 21. On the same day, the United States began a blockade of Cuba. On April 23, Spain declared war, and Congress reciprocated on April 25.

The war lasted from April 21 to August 13, 1898. There were confrontations in the Pacific Ocean in Manila Bay and in the Caribbean Sea at Santiago de Cuba Bay, and on land in Guam and Puerto Rico. The Puerto Rican front included the famous charge up San Juan Hill by the Rough Riders, led by future president Theodore Roosevelt, who had resigned his cabinet post to join the war. U.S. naval and military forces were generally victorious in these disparate global engagements, often with the assistance of the local resistance

---

106. *See McKinley, William, Jr.*, BIOGRAPHICAL DIRECTORY OF THE UNITED STATES CONGRESS.

movements. In the end, Spain, lacking an adequate navy presence, requested an armistice and signed the Treaty of Paris in December.[107]

The terms of the treaty provided for the transfer of the Philippines (in exchange for $20 million), Puerto Rico, and Guam to the United States and the independence of Cuba.[108] When Spain left Cuba, the United States began to exert various forms of control that have lasted to this day (e.g., assuming territorial control over Guantanamo Bay). The subsequent Platt Amendment in 1901 provided for an ongoing U.S. presence on the island with the right to "intervene for the preservation of Cuban independence" and the lease of "lands necessary for coaling or naval stations."[109] In addition to the 1898 U.S. annexation of the Republic of Hawaii,[110] suddenly America had a global footprint, a mini-empire with which to project power and influence.

LEGAL PROFILES

William R. Day was the secretary of state who resigned to lead the U.S. peace commission during the negotiation of the Treaty of Paris. He was born in Ohio in 1849 and started his legal practice there in 1872. He practiced law for more than two decades and became friends with future president McKinley. Upon his election, McKinley appointed Day as assistant secretary of state in 1897. Day became secretary when the previous secretary was asked to resign. He was in this job for only five months before joining the peace commission. After the conclusion of the commission, McKinley appointed him to an open seat on the Sixth Circuit Court of Appeals in 1899. President Theodore Roosevelt appointed him to the U.S. Supreme Court in 1903, where he remained

---

107. Treaty of Peace, U.S.-Esp., Dec. 10, 1898.
108. *Id.* art. I–III.
109. Treaty between the United States and the Republic of Cuba Embodying the Provisions Defining Their Future Relations as Contained in the Act of Congress Approved Mar. 2, 1901 (May 22, 1903).
110. Joint Resolution to Provide for Annexing the Hawaiian Islands to the United States, July 7, 1898.

until retiring in 1922. He then worked on the war claims commission. He died in 1923.[111]

Eugenio Montero Ríos was the leader of the Spanish peace commission during the negotiation of the Treaty of Paris. He was born in Spain in 1832 and started his education at a seminary but abandoned that career for the law. He became a professor of canon law and later began a political career by election to the Cortes in 1869, where he was to remain for more than forty-five years. During that time, he held a number of roles in government, including minister of justice several times, president of the Supreme Court in 1888, and then prime minister in 1904. He was a strong advocate of the separation of church and state and renowned as an orator. He died in 1914.[112]

Felipe Agoncillo was the Philippine representative during the negotiation of the Treaty of Paris. He was born in the Philippines in 1859 and started his legal practice there as well as working as a judge. His patriotism resulted in subversion charges against him by the Spanish and eventually led to his joining other members of the Filipino rebellion in Hong Kong. He was appointed by the rebels to the role of negotiating with foreign governments. He traveled to the United States and then France, trying to get Filipino input for the treaty, and, when he was unsuccessful, to block its ratification by the U.S. Senate. He failed there too, and when the wars ended, he returned to the Philippines and took up his legal practice. He also had a political career in the Philippine Assembly beginning in 1907 and was appointed secretary of the interior in 1923. He died in 1941.[113]

---

111. *See Day, William Rufus*, FED. JUDICIAL CTR., BIOGRAPHICAL DIRECTORY OF FEDERAL JUDGES.
112. *See Spanish Statesman Dead*, N.Y. TIMES (May 13, 1914).
113. *See 69th Death Anniversary of Don Felipe E. Agoncillo*, MANILA BULLETIN (Sept. 28, 2010).

2. Board of Inquiry: USS Maine

The loss of the USS *Maine* was a precipitating event leading America onto the global stage. President McKinley ordered an inquiry by the U.S. Navy into the sinking of the ship right after the incident.[114] The Spanish performed an investigation of their own. The U.S. naval board of inquiry, led by Capt. William Sampson, made a number of findings. It found that all ammunition had been handled according to standard procedure and that the keys to the ammunition storage closets had been properly secured and accounted for. All detonators and other combustibles had been stored elsewhere. The coal bunkers had been inspected daily, and had been well ventilated, and the fire alarms had been in working order. The board noted that the coal had been inspected before being allowed on board and that there had never been a case of spontaneous combustion of coal on board the *Maine* (it had happened on other ships, due to a new type of coal being used).

There were two explosions reported by eyewitnesses; the second, larger one was the explosion of forward gun magazines. It was the first explosion that was in question, which the board noted had caused an inverted "V" shape in the hull and keel. Based on the evidence obtained from divers, the court was of the opinion that this damage "could have been produced only by the explosion of a mine situated under the bottom of the ship." But the court did not assign blame to anyone, noting that it was "unable to obtain evidence fixing the responsibility for the destruction of the *Maine* upon any person or persons." This general conclusion was supported by the 1910–11 Vreeland board of inquiry, which was able to drain the water around the boat and examine it in more detail.

The Spanish inquiry, led by naval officers, came to a different conclusion. It found it most likely that the coal had combusted, as the munitions stores were located next to the coal bunkers. It also noted several points not mentioned in the American report. For example, there were no reports of dead fish in the area of the blast, as would have been typical if a mine had exploded. It also noted that there were no cables found, which would have been used to power a mine to reach and explode in contact with the ship. No column of water typical of a mine explosion was reported. And it was not likely that the Spanish in

---

114. Official Report of the Naval Court of Inquiry into the Loss of the Battleship *Maine*, Mar. 21, 1898.

Cuba would have had time to prepare the mine, since they had been notified of the *Maine*'s itinerary only a short time before the ship arrived in Havana.

The Spanish report was basically ignored at the time. There have been other investigations done many decades after the incident, and none have been able to conclusively prove the case one way or the other. No definitive documents have been produced from the Spanish side showing their plans to bomb the USS *Maine*. As with many events in history, it is less the facts than the perception of the facts that mattered most. As this was a significant link in a chain leading to a war that changed America's role in the world, the acts that were fed by perception were the more important.

LEGAL PROFILES

Joseph Pulitzer and his newspapers led the cry for war. Pulitzer was born in Hungary in 1847 and immigrated to America in 1864. He immediately was recruited to join in the U.S. Civil War. After the war, he moved to St. Louis, Missouri, where, while doing odd jobs, he passed the bar exam. He then took a job in journalism, and he soon became an editor and part owner of a newspaper, giving a voice to the common man. He sold his share and then bought and merged two other St. Louis newspapers to create the *St. Louis Post-Dispatch*. In 1883, he bought the *New York World* newspaper, where he would engage in his famous competition with William Randolph Hearst amid cries of "yellow journalism," all the while building the largest newspaper circulation in the country. He also became a member of the U.S. House of Representatives in 1885 (having long before become a U.S. citizen) but served only a year. The Pulitzer Prizes and the Columbia University School of Journalism were founded from bequests funded by Pulitzer. He died in 1911.[115]

John Sherman was the secretary of state at the beginning of the war with Spain. He was born in Ohio in 1823 and started his legal practice there. In 1854, was elected to the House of Representatives. In 1861 he

---

115. *See Joseph Pulitzer Dies Suddenly*, N.Y. TIMES (Oct. 30, 1911).

was elected to the Senate, where, with one interruption, he would serve until 1897. From 1877 to 1881, he served as secretary of the treasury in the Rutherford administration, before returning to the Senate. He also unsuccessfully sought his party's nomination for the presidency on several occasions. In 1890, he authored the Sherman Antitrust Act. In 1897, he was asked to become secretary of state, but he served in this role for only a year. Sherman was the younger brother of William Tecumseh Sherman, the famed Union general in the Civil War. He died in 1900.[116]

3. Problems of Empires

America was soon to learn that controlling empires entailed significant responsibility. This would be seen most quickly in the Philippine-American War that quickly followed the Spanish-American War, and in the Boxer Rebellion in China. America did not have the experience with invading the territory of other nations, but it was to quickly learn from those that did.

a. Boxer Rebellion

The United States had long had a desire to be involved in the Chinese market but had run into many other countries with the same or more aggressive intentions, many with longer histories in China. To attempt to get equal access, U.S. Secretary of State John Hay had sent requests to the major European powers involved in China (the United Kingdom, France, Germany, and Italy) and Japan and Russia to allow such access and not to violate the territorial and administrative integrity of China. Starting in September 1899, Hay sent out notes that pointed out how agreements between the powers could carve out exclusive zones, to the detriment of other powers, and how openness to all was to the benefit of all the interested nations. These notes intended to "remove any cause of irritation and to insure at the same time to the commerce of all nations in China the undoubted benefits."[117] Hay was able to secure agreement from the other nations, but events would soon test this resolve.

---

116. *See Sherman, John*, BIOGRAPHICAL DIRECTORY OF THE UNITED STATES CONGRESS.
117. Letter from U.S. Secretary of State John Hay to U.S. Ambassador to Germany Andrew D. White, Sept. 6, 1899.

The Righteous Harmony Society (labeled the "Boxers" due to their martial-arts regime) was a group that wanted to throw out the imperialist foreign presence that had grown in China during the latter stages of the Qing Dynasty. A centuries-old dynasty (since 1644), the Qing encountered various foreign influences in its affairs as it tried to hold onto power. The European nations, Japan, and Russia were all involved commercially in China and deployed military power as needed to protect those commercial interests. These countries, with the exception of Japan, were primarily Christian, so they brought not only imperialist tendencies, but also missionaries who came to convert the Chinese.

The Boxers wanted to rid China of the foreign commercial and religious influences. To that end, in early 1900 they began to murder both foreigners and Chinese who had converted to Christianity. With the encouragement of the Chinese military and the Empress Dowager Cixi, the Boxers were able to swarm the countryside around Beijing, moving in on the capital. Foreign legations sent out a call for assistance, and hundreds of foreign troops arrived, but this did not prevent a two-month siege. Finally, in August, tens of thousands of troops from the Eight-Nation Alliance (Austria-Hungary, France, Germany, Italy, Japan, Russia, the United Kingdom, and the United States) converged on the capital to relieve the legations.

The Empress Dowager and the Eight-Nation Alliance then agreed on the Boxer Protocol.[118] The principal provision was for China to pay 450 million Haikwan taels (more than 300 million U.S. dollars at the time) as an indemnity to the eight nations.[119] The sum was to be paid over thirty-nine years, with interest. In addition, the protocol stipulated punishments for certain leaders of the rebellion,[120] a short-term prohibition on arms importation into China,[121] the right of the foreign powers to occupy certain areas to keep communication open between the capital and the sea,[122] and permanent prohibition, on punishment of death, for membership in an anti-foreign society.[123] The United States used its part of the reparations to fund a university (Tsinghua) in Beijing and scholarships to educate Chinese students at American universities.

---

118. Peace Agreement between the Eight-Nation Alliance and China, Sept 7, 1901.
119. *Id.* art. VI.
120. *Id.* art. II.
121. *Id.* art. V.
122. *Id.* art. IX.
123. *Id.* art. X.

The United States had committed 5,000 troops to the alliance, which marked a turning point not only in foreign engagements but also in U.S. presidential powers. As there was no declaration of war and no approval from Congress for the U.S. involvement in this conflict, a president had used his powers to commit troops against a sovereign nation for essentially the first time (similar powers had long been used to suppress uprisings). This would become a recurring theme in the twentieth century, starting with the next president.

LEGAL PROFILES

Jutarō Komura was the Japanese signer of the Boxer Protocol. He was born in Japan in 1855. He was selected to study abroad and completed his studies at Harvard Law School in 1878. After returning to Japan, he served in the ministry of justice and as a judge before moving to the ministry of foreign affairs. He served in positions in China, including Manchuria, and in Korea. He helped to draft the Treaty of Shimonoseki, ending the first Sino-Japanese War in 1895. In 1898 he became ambassador to the United States and then in 1901 became foreign minister, the position he held during the signing of the Boxer Protocol. He was also the signer on the 1905 Treaty of Portsmouth. In 1906 he became ambassador to the United Kingdom. He returned to become foreign minister again and signed the 1908 Root-Takahira Agreement with the United States and the 1910 Japan-Korea Annexation Treaty. He died in 1911.[124]

Alfons Mumm von Schwarzenstein was the German signer of the Boxer Protocol. He was born in Germany in 1859 and studied law there. He then entered the diplomatic service and was posted overseas to America, the United Kingdom, Italy, Romania, Luxembourg, Russia, Japan, and China. It was in this latter post that he represented Germany in signing the Boxer Protocol. He retired after the war and died in 1924.[125]

---

124. See *Marquis Komura Dead*, N.Y. TIMES (Nov. 24, 1911).
125. See *Baron Mumm von Schwarzenstein*, N.Y. TIMES (July 12, 1924).

b. Philippine-American War

The Americans had won the battle of the Philippines on the ground due in large part to the work of the Filipinos under President Emile Aguinaldo. But they were not allowed to enter Manila when the Spanish capitulated and were not able to immediately proclaim their long-sought independence. Their partnership with the Americans against the Spanish overlords turned sour when the Americans would not allow the Filipinos to rule their own country. The United States proposed a U.S.-appointed governor-general to oversee a transition to Filipino rule. This led the resistance fighters to turn on the Americans, and from 1899 to 1902, the war raged. The capture of Aguinaldo brought a proclamation of surrender from him, but other resistance forces continued the fight for another year. By April 1902, however, the war was over. During this time, the Philippines was under the oversight of a U.S. military government, by executive order.[126]

The First Philippine Commission was appointed by executive order in January 1899 to "study attentively the existing social and political state of the various populations, particularly as regards the forms of local government, the administration of justice, the collection of customs and other taxes, the means of transportation, and the needs of public improvements."[127] On March 16, 1900, President McKinley appointed the Second Philippine Commission under the leadership of future president and Supreme Court justice William Howard Taft. On April 7, McKinley gave the commission instructions to set up laws and courts in the Philippines. The subsequent transfer of authority from the American military to civilian control was completed by another executive order from President McKinley, effective July 4, 1901.[128] The start of the Philippine control was the Organic Act of 1902, which provided for a bicameral legislature made up of a locally elected lower house and the Philippine Commission as the upper house (changed to locally elected in 1916) and a bill of rights as in the U.S. Constitution.[129] Supervision was to be under the Bureau of Insular Affairs.

---

126. McKinley Exec. Order to the Secretary of War (Dec. 21, 1898).
127. McKinley Exec. Order to the Secretary of State (Jan. 20, 1899).
128. McKinley Exec. Order to the Secretary of War (June 21, 1901).
129. 32 Stat. 691.

LEGAL PROFILES

Henry A. Cooper authored the Philippine Organic Act. He was born in Wisconsin in 1850 and started his legal practice there after a brief time in Illinois. He was elected a district attorney several times, starting in 1880. In 1887 he was elected to the state senate and in 1893 to the U.S. House of Representatives. He served in Congress until 1931, except for a single election after WWI where he was voted out of office, perhaps due to his opposition to the war. He returned to Congress in the next election and died while in office in 1931.[130]

Cayetano Arellano was the first chief justice of the Supreme Court of the Philippines. He was born in the Philippines in 1847 and started his legal practice there. He worked on a commission that determined that the Philippines was not ready for self-rule immediately after the handover from Spain. His interest was in the Philippines becoming a U.S. state. From 1901 to 1920, he served as the chief justice of the Philippine Supreme Court. Before that, he was a magistrate under Spanish rule, and he served as the provisional chief justice for several years. He also received an honorary law degree from Yale University in 1904, at the recommendation of William Howard Taft. He died in 1920.[131]

4. The Insular Cases

One of the major issues in the Senate approval of the Treaty of Paris was whether the U.S. Constitution allowed the United States to acquire an empire. More specifically, could the United States, which had acquired territory through purchase as described in the previous section, also acquire it via treaty? And in the newly acquired territory, which U.S. statutes and which constitutional protections applied? A number of cases that confronted these questions soon made their way to the Supreme Court. Starting in 1901 and depending on the definition, these Insular Cases continued into the 1930s and

---

130. *See Cooper, Henry Allen*, BIOGRAPHICAL DIRECTORY OF THE UNITED STATES CONGRESS.
131. *See Ex-Chief Justice Arellano*, N.Y. TIMES (Mar. 21, 1921).

contained from seven to more than twenty cases. Three of the more prominent are reviewed here, while others are referenced.

At the start of the *De Lima* case,[132] the U.S. solicitor general summarized the significant time differences among the original Insular Cases. The plaintiffs in these cases were seeking the return of duties on goods imported into Puerto Rico from the United States or duties on goods imported into the United States from Puerto Rico. For the goods imported into Puerto Rico, there were three relevant time periods when the duties were collected:

- "during the military occupation of the island, after the signing of the protocol and before the ratification of the treaty of Paris"[133] (*Armstrong* case[134])
- "during the military occupation, but after the cession of Porto Rico by the ratification of the treaty and before the passage of the Porto Rican act"[135] (*Armstrong* case and first *Dooley* case[136])
- "after the taking effect of the Porto Rican act"[137] (second *Dooley* case[138])

For goods imported into the United States from Puerto Rico, there were two relevant time periods:

- "after the ratification of the treaty of Paris and before the taking effect of the Porto Rican act"[139] (*De Lima* case)
- "after the Porto Rican act took effect"[140] (*Downes* case)

a. De Lima v. Bidwell[141]

This case involved the De Lima sugar importing company trying to recoup custom duties from the customs inspector of New York, George Bidwell. The Court framed this case as involving a single question: whether the sugars, com-

---

132. De Lima v. Bidwell, 182 U.S. 1 (1901).
133. *Id.* at 126.
134. Armstrong v. United States, 182 U.S. 243 (1901).
135. *De Lima*, 182 U.S. at 126.
136. Dooley v. United States, 182 U.S. 222 (1901).
137. *De Lima*, 182 U.S. at 127.
138. Dooley v. United States, 183 U.S. 151 (1901).
139. *De Lima*, 182 U.S. at 126–27.
140. *Id.* at 127.
141. De Lima v. Bidwell, 182 U.S. 1 (1901).

ing "from a port alleged to be domestic,"[142] were imported from a foreign country as defined by the tariff laws. The Court's opinion looked at the definition of a foreign country as "defined by Mr. Chief Justice Marshall and Mr. Justice Story to be one exclusively within the sovereignty of a foreign nation, and without the sovereignty of the United States."[143] Quoting a prior case, *Fleming v. Page*,[144] it stated that

> there was no act of Congress establishing a custom house at Tampico [Mexico], nor authorizing the appointment of a collector; and consequently there was no officer of the United States authorized by law to grant the clearance and authenticate the coasting manifest of the cargo in the manner directed by law, where the voyage is from one port of the United States to another; that the only collector was one appointed by the military commander.[145]

The Court also quoted another ground from the *Fleming* case: "The United States, it is true, may extend its boundaries by conquest or treaty, and may demand the cession of territory as the condition of peace, in order to indemnify its citizens for the injuries they have suffered, or to reimburse the government for the expenses of the war. But this can be done only by the treaty-making power or the legislative authority, and is not a part of the power conferred upon the President by the declaration of war."[146]

Contrary to what it termed the "dicta" in *Fleming*, the Court looked back at territory that the United States had acquired by treaty in Louisiana, Florida, Texas, California, and Alaska. It found that the concurrent trend had been for "a district ceded to and in the possession of the United States" to be no longer considered a foreign country.[147] The Court held that because the United States had both possession and control of a ceded Puerto Rico after the Treaty of Paris was ratified, it was no longer a foreign country, and as such, the duties on

---

142. *Id.* at 176.
143. *Id.* at 180.
144. Fleming v. Page, 50 U.S. 603 (1850).
145. *De Lima*, 182 U.S. at 182–83.
146. *Id.* at 182.
147. *Id.* at 194.

goods imported from Puerto Rico to the United States had been improperly collected in the United States.

A dissenting opinion reemphasized *Fleming*'s statement that "The department, in no instance that we are aware of, since the establishment of the government, has ever recognized a place in a newly acquired country as a domestic port, from which the coasting trade might be carried on, unless it had been previously made so by act of Congress."[148] The dissenters also looked at the accessions of both Louisiana and California to find that the laws of the United States did not apply immediately after cession and possession. The difficulty with the majority opinion was that it "assume[d] that the territory referred to was incorporated by the treaty into the United States, an ever-recurring and misleading fallacy, in our judgment."[149]

b. Downes v. Bidwell[150]

The Court framed the question in this case, a claim by Samuel Downes for a refund of import duties collected in New York, in terms of the *De Lima* case. That case had held that "upon the ratification of the treaty of peace with Spain, Porto Rico ceased to be a foreign country, and became a territory of the United States, and that duties were no longer collectible upon merchandise brought from that island."[151] In the current case, the Court was asked to hold that Puerto Rico had "became a part of the United States within that provision of the Constitution [art. 1 sec. 8] which declares that 'all duties, imposts and excises shall be uniform throughout the United States.'"[152]

The opinion of the Court, looking to the case of the acquisition of Florida from Spain, was that "the government and laws of the United States do not extend to such territory by the mere act of cession."[153] It ruled that "where the Constitution has been once formally extended by Congress to territories, neither Congress nor the territorial legislature can enact laws inconsistent therewith."[154] But it noted that in adopting the Thirteenth Amendment, Congress had recognized a "distinction between the United States" and "any place

---

148. *Id*. at 205.
149. *Id*. at 217.
150. Downes v. Bidwell, 182 U.S. 244 (1901).
151. *Id*. at 248–49.
152. *Id*. at 249.
153. *Id*. at 264.
154. *Id*. at 271.

subject to their jurisdiction,"¹⁵⁵ which meant that "there may be territories subject to the jurisdiction of the United States, which are not *of* the United States."¹⁵⁶ The Court suggested that "there may be a distinction between certain natural rights, enforced in the Constitution by prohibitions against interference with them, and what may be termed artificial or remedial rights, which are peculiar to our own system of jurisprudence."¹⁵⁷ Noting but not following Chief Justice Marshall in *Loughborough*¹⁵⁸ on direct federal taxation of the District of Columbia and Chief Justice Taney in *Dred Scott*¹⁵⁹ on the applicability of federal statutes to territories, the Court held that Puerto Rico was a territory "belonging to . . . but not part of the United States."¹⁶⁰

In a lengthy concurring decision, Justice White instead framed the argument thus: "On the one hand, it is affirmed that, although Porto Rico had been ceded by the treaty with Spain to the United States, the cession was accompanied by such conditions as prevented that island from becoming an integral part of the United States, at least, temporarily, and until Congress had so determined. On the other hand, it is insisted that by the fact of cession to the United States alone, irrespective of any conditions found in the treaty, Porto Rico became a part of the United States, and was incorporated into it."¹⁶¹ Fully acknowledging that "the government of the United States . . . has the full right to acquire territory enjoyed by every other sovereign nation,"¹⁶² he continued, "The general principle of the law of nations . . . is that acquired territory, in the absence of agreement to the contrary, will bear such relation to the acquiring government as may be by it determined."¹⁶³ He could not conceive that the Constitution's "treaty-making power by a mere cession can incorporate an alien people into the United States without the express or implied approval of Congress." This position was eventually adopted as the majority position of the Court and remains so.

---

155. *Id.* at 277
156. *Id.* at 278.
157. *Id.* at 282.
158. Loughborough v. Blake, 18 U.S. 317 (1820).
159. Dred Scott v. Sandford, 60 U.S. 393 (1857).
160. *Id.* at 287.
161. *Id.* at 299.
162. *Id.* at 302–3.
163. *Id.* at 306.

LEGAL PROFILES

Joseph McKenna wrote the dissenting opinion in *De Lima*. He was born in Pennsylvania in 1843 and started his legal practice in California. He served as a district attorney in the state from 1866 to 1868 and then was elected in 1875 to the state assembly. He was elected to the U.S. House of Representatives in 1885, where he served until being nominated to the bench on the Ninth Circuit Court of Appeals in 1892. In 1897, President McKinley selected him to be the attorney general of the United States and then the following year nominated him to serve on the U.S. Supreme Court as an associate justice. He remained on the bench until 1925, when he resigned for health reasons. He died in 1926.[164]

Edward Douglass White wrote the concurring opinion in *Downes*. He was born in Louisiana in 1845 and started his legal practice there. Before he started work as a lawyer, the Civil War interrupted his studies, and he fought with the Confederate Army. After the war, he was in private practice. He then spent time in the Louisiana state senate from 1874 to 1879 and on the state Supreme Court for a year. He was appointed to the U.S. Senate in 1891, but his three-year tenure there was cut short by subsequent appointment to the U.S. Supreme Court as an associate justice by President Cleveland in 1894. He held this position until 1910, when he was elevated to the chief justice position. He held this position until his death in 1921.[165]

B. Roosevelt: 1901–1909

The assassination of President McKinley in September 1901 saw his vice president, Theodore Roosevelt, ascend to the presidency and bring an even more

---

164. *See McKenna, Joseph*, Biographical Directory of the United States Congress; *McKenna, Joseph*, Fed. Judicial Ctr., Biographical Directory of Federal Judges.
165. *See White, Edward Douglass*, Biographical Directory of the United States Congress; *White, Edward Douglass*, Fed. Judicial Ctr., Biographical Directory of Federal Judges.

muscular and engaged foreign policy to American global dealings. Under the purportedly borrowed mantra of "Speak softly and carry a big stick," Roosevelt redefined America's relationship with the world, setting the country on a path that would eventually lead to its involvement in WWI. The previous section described his involvement in initiating the 1907 Hague Peace Conference. Some other examples of this newfound role can be found in four major foreign policy activities Roosevelt was involved with as president from 1901 to 1909:

- Panama Canal
- Roosevelt Corollary
- Mediating Global Disputes
- Great White Fleet

1. Panama Canal
a. Acquiring the Rights

Just as the Suez Canal was built to shorten the travel between Europe and Asia, the idea of a canal across Central America had long been on the agenda of the European powers, eager to cut time off of the trip from the east coast of America and the Caribbean to the west coast of America and Asia. The first concrete result was a railway across the isthmus of Panama in 1855. Then the French, who had built the Suez Canal, tried for many years to build a sea-level canal in Panama (then a province of Colombia), but they eventually gave up due to extensive loss of both money and lives.

The United States expressed an interest in building the canal. It first negotiated with the British on the right to build such a canal by itself, resulting in the Hay-Pauncefote Treaty in November 1901.[166] This treaty was needed because a previous agreement, the Clayton-Bulwer Treaty of 1850, prohibited either country from acquiring sole control of such a canal. To provide shipping access to all countries, the United States agreed to follow the model of 1888's Convention of Constantinople, which allowed free navigation of the Suez Canal.[167] The U.S. Congress then passed the Panama Canal Purchase Act (the

---

166. Hay-Pauncefote Treaty, U.K.-U.S., Nov. 18, 1901.
167. *Id.* art. III.

Spooner Act) in 1902, which allowed the United States to purchase the assets of the defunct French construction effort for $40 million if the government of Colombia would agree to allow construction and operation of the canal across its territory.[168]

The administration then negotiated an agreement with the Colombian government to be able to build the canal. In January 1903, the Hay-Herran Treaty[169] was signed and subsequently ratified by the U.S. Senate. The terms of this agreement called for a lump-sum payment and annual payments from the tenth year for a lease of the Canal Zone in perpetuity. The Colombian legislature thought these payments were too low and would not ratify the treaty. The United States, unwilling to offer more, instead gave their support to Panamanian rebels, who declared independence from Colombia as the new country of Panama. President Theodore Roosevelt sent U.S. Navy ships to block the Colombian military's access to the rebels. The United States then negotiated the Hay–Bunau-Varilla Treaty,[170] on essentially the same terms as the Hay-Herran Treaty, in November 1903, with the new Panamanian administration. Roosevelt later visited the canal during its decade-long construction, becoming the first sitting president ever to leave the United States while in office.

LEGAL PROFILES

William Nelson Cromwell was one of the main players behind getting the Panama Canal Purchase Act passed. He was born in New York in 1848 and started his legal practice there. He first worked as a railroad accountant and then became a partner in a well-known law firm in 1879. As a corporate and international lawyer, he was involved in reorganizations of many large firms, including the National Tube Company, U.S. Steel, Wells Fargo, Northern Pacific Railroad, and the Illinois Central Railroad, all of which made him quite wealthy. For the Panama Canal, he was part of the group that may have emphasized the impor-

---

168. Panama Canal Purchase Act, Pub. L. No. 57-183 (1902).
169. Hay-Herran Convention, U.S.-Col., Jan. 22, 1903.
170. Convention for the Construction of a Ship Canal, U.S.-Pan., Nov. 18, 1903.

tance of volcanoes in Nicaragua to help influence the votes of senators in favor of building the canal in Panama (see section C below). He was also involved in the treaties necessary for its construction. He was a prodigious supporter of philanthropic causes, especially those for the blind. He died in 1948.[171]

b. Legal Action against the Press

In an interesting aftermath to acquiring the rights to build the Panama Canal, Roosevelt was attacked in an editorial by Joseph Pulitzer's *New York World* newspaper for having allowed individuals close to him, including his brother-in-law, to make significant profits from the purchase of the French Panama Canal Company. Roosevelt convinced a local prosecutor to convene a grand jury to indict Pulitzer and his paper for criminal libel. When this matter came before Judge Charles Merrill Hough, a Roosevelt appointee, in January 1910, he quashed the indictment as contrary to established law. But it was appealed up to the U.S. Supreme Court, where a unanimous court in January 1911 agreed with Hough and affirmed the decision not to prosecute Pulitzer for the attack on Roosevelt.[172]

LEGAL PROFILES

Charles Merrill Hough was the federal judge who quashed the indictment of Pulitzer and his company. He was born in New York in 1858 and started his legal practice there in 1884. He continued in private practice until 1906, when he was appointed to the district court position he held during this case. In 1917, he was elevated to the Second Circuit Court of Appeals. He remained in this position until his death in 1927.[173]

---

171. *See W.N. Cromwell, 94, Attorney, Is Dead*, N.Y. TIMES (July 20, 1948).
172. United States v. Press Publ'g Co., 219 U.S. 1 (1911).
173. *See Hough, Charles Merrill*, FED. JUDICIAL CTR., BIOGRAPHICAL DIRECTORY OF FEDERAL JUDGES.

2. Roosevelt Corollary

The Monroe Doctrine was the philosophical basis of American protection of other American countries from European interference. First elucidated by President James Monroe in his seventh annual message to Congress on December 2, 1823, it stated that "as a principle in which the rights and interests of the United States are involved, that the American continents, by the free and independent condition which they have assumed and maintain, are henceforth not to be considered as subjects for future colonization by any European powers." Regarding existing versus new colonies, it said, "With the existing colonies or dependencies of any European power we have not interfered and shall not interfere. But with the Governments who have declared their independence and maintain it, and whose independence we have, on great consideration and on just principles, acknowledged, we could not view any interposition for the purpose of oppressing them, or controlling in any other manner their destiny, by any European power in any other light than as the manifestation of an unfriendly disposition toward the United States."

The Monroe Doctrine was long used by U.S. presidents to keep the Americas, only recently rid of colonizers, free from overt European recolonization. Roosevelt, when advocating U.S. action against Spain over Cuba before the Spanish-American War, had relied upon the Monroe Doctrine. Then, in late 1902, when Venezuela refused to pay its debts to several European countries, including Germany, Italy, and the United Kingdom, these countries began a naval blockade of Venezuela. The blockade lasted two months and was settled when Venezuela and the blockading countries partially agreed on certain terms and then agreed to arbitration for the remaining terms (and with the implied threat of U.S. naval intervention). The use of force to compel agreements over financial matters in the Western Hemisphere led to the Roosevelt Corollary.

a. The Corollary

The principle of the Roosevelt Corollary was that the United States now had the right to intervene if other countries in the Americas were in financial difficulties with European creditors. The United States' interest was to avoid the possibility of a European country intervening and perhaps colonizing the debtor country to seek return on the investment. In his fourth annual statement to Congress on December 6, 1904, Roosevelt laid out this policy as follows:

> It is not true that the United States feels any land hunger or entertains any projects as regards the other nations of the Western Hemisphere save such as are for their welfare. All that this country desires is to see the neighboring countries stable, orderly, and prosperous. Any country whose people conduct themselves well can count upon our hearty friendship. If a nation shows that it knows how to act with reasonable efficiency and decency in social and political matters, if it keeps order and pays its obligations, it need fear no interference from the United States. Chronic wrongdoing, or an impotence which results in a general loosening of the ties of civilized society, may in America, as elsewhere, ultimately require intervention by some civilized nation, and in the Western Hemisphere the adherence of the United States to the Monroe Doctrine may force the United States, however reluctantly, in flagrant cases of such wrongdoing or impotence, to the exercise of an international police power.

b. Permanent Court of International Arbitration

As agreed, the parties to the Venezuela dispute had agreed to arbitration on the unresolved matters in the Hague under the relatively new Permanent Court of Arbitration.[174] Specifically, they had agreed, "The question as to whether or not Germany, Great Britain and Italy are entitled to preferential or separate treatment in the payment of their claims against Venezuela, and its decision shall be final. Venezuela having agreed to set aside 30 per cent of the customs revenues of La Guayra and Puerto Cabello for the payment of the claims of all nations against Venezuela, the Tribunal at The Hague shall decide how the said revenues shall be divided between the Blockading Powers on the one hand and the other Creditor Powers on the other hand, and its decision shall be final."

In this case,[175] the court looked to the fact that the three blockading powers (especially Germany and Great Britain) had long insisted on preferential dis-

---

174. Protocols of Washington of May 7, 1903.
175. Germany, Great Britain, and Italy v. Venezuela, Preferential Treatment of Claims of Blockading Powers against Venezuela, Award of the Tribunal, Permanent Court of Arbitration (Feb. 22, 1904).

tributions, that the Venezuelan government had not specifically disagreed with this preferential treatment and had several times agreed to those preferential distributions for the blockading countries, and that the seven other creditor nations involved had not objected. It also noted that there was no negative impact on the other creditor nations. So the court ruled that the three blockading countries had "a right to preferential treatment for the payment of their claims against Venezuela."

LEGAL PROFILES

Heinrich Lammasch was one of the arbitrators on the Permanent Court of Arbitration for the Venezuela case. He was born in Austria in 1853. He started teaching at the University of Vienna in 1878 and became an international law expert. He was a delegate of Austria-Hungary to both the 1899 and the 1907 Hague Peach Conferences. He served at the Permanent Court of Arbitration from 1904 to 1910, hearing four cases, including this one. At the end of the war, he was part of the peace movement and served as the final minister-president of imperial Austria. He was involved with the postwar peace treaty between Austria and the Allied Powers. He died in 1920.[176]

3. Mediating Global Disputes
a. Russo-Japanese War

In a demonstration of the U.S. desire for peaceful arbitration of disputes and an implicit acknowledgment of its new global standing, President Roosevelt was involved in helping bring two international disputes to resolution. The first was the Russo-Japanese War. Roosevelt had extended the offer to act as a mediator between the two parties, both potential rivals of the United States in the Pacific. Russia and Japan eventually accepted his proposal and met in Portsmouth, New Hampshire. The result was the Portsmouth Treaty.[177]

---

176. See *Austrian Ex-Premier Lammasch Dead*, N.Y. TIMES (Jan. 9, 1920).
177. Treaty of Peace, Jap.-Rus., Sept. 5, 1905.

This agreement ended the war and brought decades of peace between the parties by, for example, the parties agreeing to vacate Manchuria (including their militaries)[178] and to keep their railways there only for commercial and industrial purposes.[179] But it also sowed the seed of future disputes by having Russia agree to transfer its lease of the Liaotung Peninsula,[180] recognize Japan's "paramount rights" to Korea,[181] and transfer the southern half of Sakhalin Island to Japan.[182] For his efforts in bringing the sides together, Roosevelt was awarded the Nobel Peace Prize in 1906, becoming the first U.S. president ever to receive the award.

b. First Moroccan Crisis

As described in the previous section, the United States had been involved in Morocco with the Perdicaris Incident in 1904. To facilitate the settlement of the First Moroccan Crisis, also described in the previous section, President Roosevelt had, at the urging of the German emperor and others, called the many parties together for what became the Algeciras Conference. His ability to deal effectively with disparate national leaders was part of the ultimate success of the conference. When the conference was at a point of failure, for example, he was able to remind the Germans of previous commitments made to him. As explained above, the resulting peace treaty avoided a potential war and helped to raise America's global profile.

LEGAL PROFILES

Mineichirō Adachi was one of the Japanese delegates to the Portsmouth Conference. He was born in Japan in 1870 and received his legal education there. He joined the foreign ministry and was posted to Rome from 1893 to 1896 and then in Paris from 1899 to 1902. Upon returning to Japan, he taught law and served as a judge. He was part of the Portsmouth Peace Conference in 1905. In 1907, he returned to Paris

---

178. *Id.* art. III.
179. *Id.* art. VII.
180. *Id.* art. V.
181. *Id.* art. II.
182. *Id.* art. IX.

and then in 1912 moved to Mexico City for three years. He served in Belgium from 1917, where he took part in the 1919 Paris Peace Conference. He served as Japanese ambassador to Belgium from 1920 to 1927 and to France from 1927 to 1930. He was president of the Permanent Court of International Justice from 1931 until his death in 1934.[183]

4. Great White Fleet

In an effort that again raised the international profile of America, in his final years in office, President Roosevelt sent the U.S. Navy on a global tour. As a former assistant secretary of the navy, Roosevelt understood the importance of a strong navy to a country's global power. He had been pushing Congress to pass funding to build up the number of ships in the navy and increase its personnel, and so between 1904 and 1907 eleven new battleships were commissioned. By December 1907, a fleet of sixteen battleships was ready to depart Virginia for a fourteen-month circumnavigation of the globe. With white hulls signifying peace, the voyage was a combination of goodwill tour; display of global projection of power; subtle enforcement of peace treaties; warning to potential adversaries; shakedown exercise for the ships, men, design, facilities, and tactics; political diversion from recent financial problems; and coming-out party for the new world power. It was an appropriately bold and multifaceted finale for the international efforts of the Roosevelt presidency.

LEGAL PROFILES

Elihu Root was the secretary of state of the United States from 1905. He was born in New York in 1845 and started his legal practice there. He was involved with many corporate clients and well-known private clients but also was involved in defending William "Boss" Tweed. He was later named a U.S. attorney in 1883. He served as secretary of war for the U.S. from 1899 to 1904, where, among other reforms, he initiated the General Staff and the U.S. Army War College. In 1905, he became

---

183. *See Judge Adachi, 65, Dies in Amsterdam*, N.Y. TIMES (Dec. 29, 1934).

secretary of state, a position he held until 1909, where he negotiated the Root-Takahira agreement and dozens of bilateral agreements, and was involved in stabilizing the situations in both Cuba and the Philippines. In 1909, he was elected a U.S. senator, where he became involved in the dispute about the United States' nonpayment of tolls in the Panama Canal. After one term, he did not seek reelection. In 1912, he was awarded the Nobel Peace Prize for all of his international work. In 1913, he was president of the Hague Tribunal of Arbitration that mediated among several countries regarding church property. In 1922, he was part of the Washington Naval Conference. From 1910 to 1925, he led the Carnegie Endowment for International Peace. He was instrumental in founding the Permanent Court of International Justice. He died in 1937.[184]

C. Taft: 1909–1913

The new U.S. president was William Howard Taft, who would take a more economy-centric approach to foreign policy. Taft had significant experience overseas, having served on the commission responsible for the Philippines and then as governor-general there. It was expected that he would be able to continue and expand the policies of Roosevelt. He based his efforts on expanding foreign economic investment and trade by America, the so-called dollar diplomacy. As Taft articulated in his fourth message to Congress, the intent was to increase stability and "to respond to modern ideas of commercial intercourse." He continued, "This policy has been characterized as substituting dollars for bullets. . . . It is an effort frankly directed to the increase of American trade upon the axiomatic principle that the Government of the United States shall extend all proper support to every legitimate and beneficial American enterprise abroad."[185] With a more visible U.S. presence and investment in foreign countries, both the United States and the recipient countries were supposed to benefit. Two examples of this were in Nicaragua and China; however, in neither case was this policy of Taft's a success. Instead, it led to the anti-imperialist direction of his successor in the lead-up to WWI.

---

184. *See Root, Elihu*, BIOGRAPHICAL DIRECTORY OF THE UNITED STATES CONGRESS.
185. President Taft, Fourth Annual Message to Congress, Dec. 3, 1912.

1. Nicaragua

When the idea of a canal across Central America was being considered, there were actually two competing routes, one through Panama and the other through Nicaragua. The commission responsible for the study actually recommended Nicaragua, but the effective lobbying campaign by William Nelson Cromwell and others tilted the decision toward Panama. This did not mean that other European powers could not follow through with their own competing canal through Nicaragua. For this reason, and under the dollar diplomacy policy, Taft was supportive of American investment in Nicaragua. In 1911, in order to protect American interests Taft sent troops to support a rebellion against an anti-American ruler. When the rebels took over, the United States would not recognize them until they signed a treaty swapping out their European national debt for American private loans.

The Knox-Castrillo Convention was signed in June 1911, and while it was being debated in the U.S. Senate, private businessmen went ahead and initiated the refunding of the Nicaraguan national debt with private loans from United States parties, using the national railroad as collateral, implementing financial reorganization, and gaining control of local customs revenues. In May 1912, the Senate rejected the treaty, but to further protect American interests there, when another rebellion arose in July 1912, more than two thousand U.S. marines were sent. Some of the marines were required to stay for more than a decade and became a cause of local and regional resentment, as did similar intervention efforts during these years in Haiti, Mexico, Honduras, and the Dominican Republic.

LEGAL PROFILES

William Howard Taft was the U.S. president and a lawyer. Born in Ohio in 1857, he started his legal practice there. In 1881, he was an assistant county prosecuting attorney, before going into private practice. In 1887, he was a judge in Ohio, but in 1890, he was selected to be the U.S. solicitor general at the age of only 32 years. In 1891, he was appointed to the Sixth Circuit Court of Appeals. In 1900, he was appointed to lead the U.S.-Philippine Commission and in 1901 to the new role of governor-general of the Philippines. In 1904, he became secretary of war for four years. This led to his being elected president of the United States in 1908. He was defeated in his reelection bid due to a third-party challenge from his former mentor Theodore Roosevelt. He then taught law for many years. In 1921, he was appointed the chief justice of the United States. He remained in this role until his death in 1930.[186]

2. China

In an effort not to be left out of the rush to the riches that were to be had in China, Taft encouraged further U.S. investment and loans in Manchuria. There were attempts to invest in the regional railroads, but all the other nations involved (Germany, France, United Kingdom, Russia, and Japan) were already vying for the same territory and economic advantages there. U.S. plans to become part of the consortium to finance and build railroads were successful, but these fell victim to the revolution in China in 1911. Other plans to buy the existing railroads in Manchuria controlled by the Russians and Japanese and return them to the Chinese were rejected by the countries involved. The Open Door policy had not proven as easy to implement as it had been to negotiate.

LEGAL PROFILES

Philander C. Knox was a lawyer and the secretary of state of the United States from 1909. Born in Pennsylvania in 1853, he started his legal practice there. He built up a legal practice that included the foundation of the United States Steel Corporation. In 1901, he was named as the U.S. attorney general. In 1904, he was appointed and then elected to a seat in the U.S. Senate. In 1909, he was appointed as U.S. secretary of state by incoming president Taft, a position he served in throughout that administration. In 1916 he was reelected to the Senate, where he remained until his death in 1921.[187]

---

186. *See Taft, William Howard*, Fed. Judicial Ctr., Biographical Directory of Federal Judges.
187. *See Knox, Philander Chase*, Biographical Directory of the United States Congress.

CHAPTER 2

EUROPE: INTERNATIONAL AND MILITARY ISSUES

The year 1914 dawned with contrary expectations, grudges, desires, and realities among the various nations tied together by the myriad agreements described in Chapter 1. In addition to the agreements and the geopolitics were the military concerns. Russia and Germany had both started significant military upgrade programs. An upgraded Russian military, in alliance with France and Great Britain, could prove to have more military might than Germany and its alliance partners could handle. The United Kingdom continued to build ships to stay ahead of Germany on the seas. The following metrics provide insight into the relative positions of the two major alliances before the start of the war:[1]

	Central Powers	Allied Powers
Population (millions)	128	256
GDP (billions of dollars)	$421	$624
Major ships/submarines	154	443

These metrics (population, GDP, and ships/submarines), which change more slowly than do troop or armament levels and so better indicate fundamental

---

1. Population and GDP figures are for the year 1913 for the six political entities (less the Arab countries under the Ottoman Empire) from *Aggregate and Per Capita GDP in Europe, 1870–2000: Continental, Regional and National Data with Changing Boundaries*, Broadberry and Klein (Oct. 2011); warship counts, steel production, and troop levels from 2 PURNELL'S HISTORY OF THE TWENTIETH CENTURY (A. J. P. Taylor, ed.-in-chief 1971).

military strength, seemed to indicate a mismatch. But there were other metrics that evened out the balance, such as Germany's very high troop-to-population ratio and Russia's and Great Britain's very low ratios[2] (Great Britain's military was still all volunteer at this point; see Section 2.2). In addition, Germany had developed its steel production capabilities to have greater output levels than the three Allied Powers combined.[3] One more factor in this equation was the economic and manpower resources of the British and French dominions and colonies, which would seem to swing the balance back over to the Allied Powers. To address this, and the favorable geographic positions of Allied Powers surrounding their opponents, the Central Powers needed a special military strategy, which they believed they had in the Schlieffen Plan.

This plan, originally envisioned by German Army Chief of Staff Alfred von Schlieffen in 1905 after the start of the Triple Entente, called for rapid action and victory against France before Russia could mobilize its large military. Sweeping through the Low Countries, which would not interfere, and around French defensive forts built to stop just such an advance, and using the vast majority of the German army, this quick strike would encircle Paris and force the French army to surrender. These troops could then be moved east to take on the Russian army, where Germany's superior economics could win a longer war against Russia alone. The United Kingdom, after the loss of France, would be too discouraged to fight a European land war.

For their part, France had Plan XVII. This was based on several assumptions, including that France needed to go on the offensive because it had a disadvantage in its number of troops relative to Germany. It also assumed that Germany would attack through Alsace-Lorraine or perhaps Belgium, so it provided the flexibility to move into either of those areas based on the circumstances. The plan was based partly on military strategy and partly on revanchism, calling for the return of the country's lost provinces. Russia, as well, had Plan XIX, which called for an advance into East Prussia. Austria-Hungary had plans for sending out armies against both Serbia and Russia. The United Kingdom, while it did not have a military plan as such, had been working secretly for some time with France for a British Expeditionary Force (BEF) to come to the aid of France in case of a land war with Germany. It also had naval support protecting the English Channel and France's Atlantic coast.

---

2. *Id.*
3. *Id.*

With these factors in play, the penultimate event leading to the start of the war was the assassination of the successor to the throne of Austria-Hungary, archduke Franz Ferdinand, on June 28, 1914. That murder triggered a wave of demands, mobilizations, and declarations of war. It also led to the trial of the accused assassins. As the nations of Europe fell into their respective camps based on preexisting commitments, war started with shelling of Belgrade, Serbia, by Austria-Hungary on July 29 and the incursions by Germany into Luxembourg, France, and Belgium at the beginning of August. Over the next four plus years, tens of millions would become casualties in a conflict that militarily accomplished almost nothing. But it would change Europe politically, in both philosophical and geographic terms—seemingly forever.

As the war progressed from declarations to engaging in hostilities, legal issues began to arise. Many troops were needed to fight the battles as ever-increasing casualties took unprecedented tolls on the armies of all nations involved. Acquiring replacements became an urgent requirement. While having a volunteer-only force might normally be sufficient for the United Kingdom, with the scale of losses, it did not suffice, and military service conscription laws became necessary. These caused problems for men of certain religious beliefs, and those who were already in the military objected to becoming victims in the carnage all around them. Mutinies and desertions began to occur in units of all belligerents across the Western Front.

Strangling an opponent's supply chain was a common tactic to force them from the field. Given the global nature of this conflict, the supply chains of the military stretched far afield. To choke off German supply by utilizing its superior naval capabilities, the United Kingdom deployed a blockade upon Germany. But Germany was not without its own abilities to deal with the supply chains of its opponents, and used its new U-boat fleet to attack the supplies flowing from North America to the Allied Powers. Germany eventually began to target nonbelligerents, which would lead to the entry of the United States into the war (see Chapter 4).

Submarines were just one of a host of new technologies fully deployed during this war. But one stood out as offering a whole new literal dimension to warfare: the use of the airplane in battle. War had previously been affairs of land and sea but now destruction could rain down from high above, while airborne surveillance was also carried out. Disguising troop movements, at least when the war was mobile, became more important now that they could be spotted from the air. The use of air power brought a whole new legal aspect to warfare.

This chapter focuses on the international and military legal aspects of the war in Europe, beginning with the acts and declarations that started the war. The legal issues that are covered are conscription and conscientious objectors; mutiny, desertion, and disobeying orders leading to execution of soldiers, with some shot for example but rehabilitated postwar; blockades and intentional starvation of civilians; unrestricted submarine warfare; compensation for illegal wartime acts; citizens taking up arms; new technologies in warfare; and the use of air power.

PROMINENT LAWYERS AND JUDGES IN THIS CHAPTER

Starting War:

- Leopold Berchtold (Austro-Hungarian foreign minister)
- István Tisza (Hungarian prime minister)
- Theobald von Bethmann-Hollweg (German chancellor)
- René Viviani (French prime minister)
- Henry Herbert (H. H.) Asquith (British prime minister)
- Alois Curinaldi (presiding judge)
- Antonio Salandra (Italian prime minister)

Conscription:

- David Lloyd George (British secretary of state for war)
- Louis Barthou (French prime minister)
- George Cave (British solicitor general)
- Philip Morrell (member of British parliament)
- Timothy Michael Healy (Irish Anti-Conscription Committee)

Execution of Soldiers:

- Raoul Péret (French minister of justice)
- Louis Nail (French minister of justice)
- Henri Guernut (appeal counsel)
- Alexandre Millerand (French minister of war)
- René Coty (lawyer-soldier)
- Félix Gouin (lawyer-soldier)
- Robert George Raper (lawyer-soldier)

Blockade:

- Robert Cecil (minister of blockade)
- Samuel Thomas Evans (president of British prize court)
- Robert John Parker (Privy Council member)
- Joseph Chappell Hutcheson Jr. (arbitrator)
- Edward Carson (British first lord of the Admiralty)

Unrestricted Submarine Warfare:

- William Jennings Bryan (U.S. secretary of state)
- James W. Gerard (U.S. ambassador to Germany)
- John Bigham (British wreck commissioner)
- F. E. (Frederick Edwin) Smith (British solicitor general)
- Julius M. Mayer (trial judge)
- Lucius H. Beers (petitioner's counsel)
- Wilhelm Kiesselbach (mixed claims German commissioner)
- Thomas Bloomfield (passenger on the *Lusitania*)
- Walther Schücking (head of postwar court of inquiry)
- Edwin B. Parker (mixed claims U.S. commissioner/umpire)

New Technologies/Use of Airpower:

- Richard Haldane (secretary of war)
- Alfred de Bathe Brandon (New Zealand fighter pilot)
- Tobias Asser (leader/influencer of Hague Conferences)
- John Bassett Moore (president of the Commission of Jurists)
- Frank D. Slee (Australian fighter pilot)

2.1 STARTING WAR

A. Statutes
1. July Crisis
The assassinations in late June 1914 led to the "July Crisis," where Austria-Hungary had to determine how to respond. This included lining up support from Germany in case, as expected, Russia intervened to protect its Slavic cousins in Serbia. The Austro-Hungarian leadership, with the exception of the

Hungarian prime minister, believed that immediate war was the only way to keep Serbia from further pushing for its goal of uniting the Slavic populations of the Balkans.[4] As such, and with German "blank-check" backing for whatever strategy it pursued against Serbia,[5] Austria-Hungary planned to issue demands that Serbia would not agree to. With this approach approved by the Emperor Franz Joseph, it issued the following demands to the Serbian government, requiring a response within forty-eight hours:[6]

- Publish on the front page of its official journal a renunciation of the policies and acts of certain organizations that were trying to separate parts of the Austro-Hungarian Empire, and prosecute such activities in the future.
- Suppress publications inciting hatred of Austria-Hungary and remove such from instruction in schools, while accepting collaboration of Austro-Hungarian agents within Serbia in suppressing the propaganda.
- Dissolve the Narodna Odbrana (National Defense) organization implicated in the assassination.
- Remove from the military and government those people issuing propaganda against Austria-Hungary, and explain such statements made since the assassination.
- Arrest certain individuals involved in the assassination, including those who were involved in its planning and those who helped them cross the border into Bosnia, and accept Austro-Hungarian support in the judicial investigation.

The Serbian government of Prime Minister Nikola Pašić, with the counsel of both Russia and Great Britain, determined that it was best to accept these demands where it could, despite not being directly responsible for the murderous events. Serbia accepted in essence all the demands except for Austria-Hungary running its own criminal investigation in Serbia, which Serbia held was contrary to its constitution. It also said it could not locate one of the named

---

4. Minutes of Ministerial Council on Affairs of State (July 7, 1914).
5. German Response to Letter from Emperor Franz Joseph, Communication from German chancellor Bethmann-Hollweg to German ambassador to Austria-Hungary von Tschirschky (July 6, 1914).
6. Austria-Hungary Ultimatum to Serbia (July 23, 1914).

individuals. Serbia stated that if Austria-Hungary had any concern about this response, Serbia would accept the decisions on the matter made either by the World Court in the Hague or by the Great Powers. Austria-Hungary was likely surprised at the amount of acceptance of its demands, but according to its original intent to reject any response offered, it deemed the response to be insufficient and declared war on Serbia.

LEGAL PROFILES

Leopold Berchtold was the Austro-Hungarian foreign minister during the July Crisis. He was born in Austria in 1863 and obtained his legal training there. He joined the foreign service of the Dual Monarchy in 1893. He served at embassies across Europe, including in Paris, the United Kingdom, and Russia. In late 1906, he was named ambassador to Russia, where he was involved with deals that eased the Austro-Hungarian annexation of Bosnia-Herzegovina in 1908 (see Chapter 1). In early 1912 he was appointed by the emperor as the imperial foreign minister, the position he held during this crisis. He was later forced to resign over an inability to get Italy into the war on the side of the Central Powers. He died in 1942.[7]

István Tisza was the Hungarian prime minister in the Dual Monarchy system during the July Crisis. He was born in Hungary in 1861 and obtained his legal training there and in Germany. In 1887, he was first elected to parliament. In 1903, he was elected prime minister, like his father, who had been prime minister for fifteen years. He held this post for two years, until his party lost their electoral majority. He was speaker of the legislature in 1912, when he was the target of an assassination attempt. In 1913, he again became the prime minister, the position he held during this crisis and through most of the war, until May 1917. His policies were not popular with his peers, and he frequently was chal-

---

7. *See Count Berchtold of Austria is Dead*, N.Y. TIMES (Nov. 22, 1942).

lenged to duels. His initial stand against the war was not well known, and as such, he was identified with the war and targeted for assassination several more times. An assassin finally succeeded in October 1918.[8]

---

2. Declarations of War

Both before and after this initial declaration of war, governments across the region, especially the Allied Powers, were working to contain the crisis. Russia was in the middle of a modernization of its forces that would not be complete for several years; France was aware of its own military strength vis-à-vis Germany; and the United Kingdom had no desire to be involved in a European war any more than it had the Franco-Prussian War forty years before. But Russia was mindful that it had to back down in previous Balkan crises, an action it would not repeat. Among the Central Powers, Austria-Hungary had long desired to rid itself of Serbian interference in the Balkans, and Germany had assured its support against France and Russia. There seemed to be no path leading back to a situation where all parties could win.

The declaration of war by Austria-Hungary was followed not only by mobilizations of troops but also by a cascade of declarations of war based upon the prewar alliances, older treaties, and current circumstances. In 1914 alone, the following declarations of war were made by the six powers in the two major alliances, presented in person and by telegraph:

- July 28: Austria-Hungary declared war on Serbia.
- Aug. 1: Germany declared war on Russia.
- Aug. 3: Germany declared war on France.
- Aug. 4: Germany declared war on Belgium.
- Aug. 4: The United Kingdom declared war on Germany.
- Aug. 6: Austria-Hungary declared war on Russia.
- Aug. 12: France declared war on Austria-Hungary.
- Aug. 12: The United Kingdom declared war on Austria-Hungary.
- Aug. 28: Austria-Hungary declared war on Belgium.
- Nov. 2: Russia declared war on the Ottoman Empire.

---

8. See *Ex-Premier Tisza Slain by Soldier*, N.Y. TIMES (Nov. 2, 1918).

- Nov. 5: France declared war on the Ottoman Empire.
- Nov. 5: The United Kingdom declared war on the Ottoman Empire.

There are a number of points to note. First, military conflicts were not always preceded or followed by formal declarations of war. As can be seen from this list, Russia never formally declared war on Germany or Austria-Hungary. Instead, Russia's general mobilization of its troops in reaction to Austria-Hungary's declaration of war on Serbia and its refusal to demobilize led to Germany and then Austria-Hungary declaring war on Russia. Also, Germany had already invaded French and Belgian territories before it officially declared war on them.

Second, declarations of war were not necessarily based on attacks or threats of attack. After Germany failed to receive assurances from France that France would not side with Russia, with whom Germany was now at war with, Germany declared war on France. To get there while avoiding significant French defenses, German troops, utilizing the Schlieffen Plan, had first entered neutral Luxembourg in violation of the 1867 Treaty of London (see Chapter 1). It then asked for free passage through Belgium to deal with France. When Belgium refused to grant that, saying it would defend its own neutrality,[9] Germany invaded anyway, violating the 1839 Treaty of London, and declared war on Belgium. Germany admitted early on that these incursions in the territory of neutrals were violations of international law.[10]

Third, the two major alliances did not necessarily produce responsive declarations of war by alliance partners. The United Kingdom officially declared war on Germany not because of the invasion of France or the declaration of war on Russia, but because of the invasion of Belgium, which violated the neutrality treaty from 1839, of which the United Kingdom was a guarantor. But later declarations of war by France and the United Kingdom were based on declarations of war/attacks by Austria-Hungary and the Ottoman Empire on Russia. Italy did not declare war on the Allied Powers because it viewed its Central Power alliances as defensive, and since Germany and Austria-Hungary had invaded other countries, Italian military response was not required. Italy

---

9. Belgian Response to German Ultimatum, Communication from Belgian foreign affairs minister Davignon to German ambassador to Belgium von Below Saleske (Aug. 3, 1914).
10. German chancellor von Bethmann Hollweg Address to Reichstag (Aug. 4, 1914).

would later sign an agreement with[11] the Allied Powers and declare war in support of them.

Fourth, with the lack of Italian support, the Central Powers added a third participant to their alliance. The Ottoman Empire and Germany signed a secret agreement on August 2, even though it was not fully supported inside the empire (the sultan did not sign it).[12] This new treaty required the Ottoman Empire to remain neutral in the conflict between Austria-Hungary and Serbia, unless the Central Powers went to war with Russia, in which case the Ottoman Empire would intervene on the side of Germany and Austria-Hungary. The latter situation is what occurred on October 29, when the Ottomans attacked the Russian-held (Ukrainian) port of Odessa on the Black Sea. Shortly thereafter, the Allied Powers all declared war on the Ottoman Empire.

Fifth, the declarations of war were often made on quite dubious grounds, especially in the west. The declaration of war by Germany on France stated that French airplanes had encroached on German and Belgian airspace and Germany would not tolerate such aggressive incursions.[13] The declaration of war on Belgium stated that France was planning on deploying troops into Belgium, in violation of her neutrality, for an attack upon Germany, and so Germany had to enter Belgium to reach France and forestall this threat to Belgian neutrality.[14] France and Belgium's governments vigorously denied that any French aviator had flown into Belgium or committed hostile acts in Germany.[15]

Sixth, the declarations of war were not necessarily approved by representative government institutions. The German ambassador communicated to Russia Germany's declaration of war without first seeking the approval of the Bundesrat (the federal council made up of the empire's member states). The Bundesrat, which controlled the supreme legal authority of the empire,[16] under the 1871 constitution (see Chapter 1) was to consent to any war declared

---

11. Treaty of London, It.-U.K.-Fr.-Rus., Apr. 26, 1915.
12. Treaty of Alliance, Ger.-Tur., Aug. 2, 1914.
13. German Declaration of War on France, Letter from German Ambassador to France von Schoen to French President Poincaré (Aug. 3, 1914).
14. German Ultimatum to Belgium, Communication from German Ambassador to Belgium von Below Saleske to Belgian Foreign Affairs Minister Davignon (Aug. 2, 1914).
15. French Prime Minister Viviani's Statement for the National Assembly (Aug. 4, 1914).
16. Verfassung des Deutschen Reiches, art. 7 (Ger.).

by the German emperor that was nondefensive in nature.[17] The Bundesrat approved the declaration after the fact. The declaration of war in the United Kingdom against Germany was done legally but was not voted on by Parliament or authorized by the Cabinet. It was legally approved solely by King George V (albeit with Cabinet urging), under the ancient Royal Prerogative (a set of powers reserved to the monarch; see Chapter 3). And there was no vote in the parliaments of its dominions (except Canada[18]), just the assents provided by the respective governors-general.

Seventh, the declaration of war by Germany on Russia was preceded by several days of communications back and forth between the related monarchs of Germany, Russia, and the United Kingdom. George V of the United Kingdom and Kaiser Wilhelm II of Germany were both grandsons of England's Queen Victoria (through their father and mother, respectively), and George V and Czar Nicholas II of Russia were both grandsons of Denmark's Christian IX (through their mothers). Nicholas and Wilhelm, in a more than halfhearted, but perhaps not fully committed set of telegraph conversations over several days, with both dealing with militaristic advisers who wanted war, looked for ways to keep their countries out of a larger European conflict using their own influences and offices. But they ultimately succumbed to, inter alia, the geopolitical pressures, the military complexities of mobilizing troops over large areas, the differing interpretations of the intent of military mobilizations, the varying national leanings toward war, the unfounded belief that a war with so many potential participants could be contained, and perhaps their own imperial egos and lack of developed negotiating skills. Both men would be out of a job before the end of the war.

LEGAL PROFILES

Theobald von Bethmann-Hollweg was the German chancellor when war was declared. He was born in Prussia in 1856 and obtained his legal training there. The grandson of a noted legal scholar, he entered the Prus-

---

17. *Id.* art. 11.
18. War Measures Act, 1914, 5 Geo. 5, c. 2 (Can.).

sian government service in 1882, eventually rising to the presidency of Brandenburg in 1899. In 1905, he became Prussian interior minister and in 1907 the imperial interior minister. In 1909 he was appointed chancellor of the German Empire, the position he held when war was declared. After attempting to resign over his role in initiating the conflict but being persuaded by the emperor to remain, he held on to this office until July 1917. During the war years, he was frequently overshadowed by the military leadership, derided internationally for his "scrap of paper" comment questioning why Britain was determined to respect its treaty (the scrap of paper) in defending the neutrality of Belgium, and compared unfavorably to the previous war chancellor, Bismarck. He died in 1921.[19]

René Viviani was the French prime minister when war was declared. He was born in Algeria in 1863 and obtained his legal training in France. He practiced law in Algeria and in France, especially defending Socialists and trade unionists, and became involved with the Socialist Party. He was first elected to the national assembly in 1893, where he remained until 1902, was reelected in 1906 and served until 1922. He helped found a newspaper and was able to get a law passed that allowed women to become lawyers in France. He served in the cabinet in several governments in positions such as minister of labor, and he was appointed prime minister shortly before the July Crisis and declarations of war. He held this office until October 1915 and was succeeded by Aristide Briand.[20] He then served in the government until 1917 as minister of justice. Afterward, he traveled to America to enlist its aid in the war; he returned there after the war for the Washington Naval Conference.[21] He was elected to the French Senate in 1922 and died in 1925.[22]

Henry Herbert (H. H.) Asquith was the British prime minister when war was declared. He was born in England in 1852 and obtained his legal training there. He began his practice in 1876 and then worked at

---

19. *See Theoblad von Bethmann-Hollweg*, BIOGRAPHIE DES DEUTSCHEN HISTORISCHEN MUSEUMS.
20. *See* THOMAS J. SHAW, WWII LAW AND LAWYERS: ISSUES, CASES, AND CHARACTERS, ch. 1 (2013).
21. *Id.*
22. *See René Viviani*, ASSEMBLEE NATIONALE BIOGRAPHIES DES DÉPUTÉS FRANÇAIS DEPUIS 1789.

the chancery bar. He was appointed queen's counsel in 1890. He was first elected to parliament in 1886 and joined the cabinet as home secretary in 1892, where he served until the Liberals lost power in 1895. When the party regained power, he returned to the cabinet in 1905 as the chancellor of the exchequer. In 1908, he became the prime minister. Before the war, he was instrumental in getting the Parliament Bill of 1911 passed that took away the ability of the House of Lords to veto legislation passed by the House of Commons and tried to deal with Irish home rule (see Chapter 6). During the war, he formed a grand coalition cabinet, but eventually resigned as prime minister at the end of 1916 and was succeeded by David Lloyd-George.[23] Asquith lost his seat in Commons in the 1918 election, won it back in 1920, and lost it again in 1924. He was subsequently elevated to the House of Lords and died in 1928.[24]

B. Cases

The assassinations of the archduke and his wife were planned by and carried out by Serbian secret police and nationalists, to foment discontent that could lead to further Serbian gains in the Balkans and possibly a Greater Serbia. This plan was the brainchild of Col. Dragutin Dimitrijević (code name "Apis"), the Serbian chief of military intelligence and leading member of the secret Black Hand (Crna Ruka) Society, who was focused on recovering Bosnia and Herzegovina after its 1908 annexation by Austria-Hungary. This plot came after other similar plots, some of which succeeded, such as the 1902 assassination of the king and queen of Serbia, and some of which did not, including several plots to kill the king of Montenegro and the 1911 plot to kill Emperor Franz Joseph.

The assassinations of Franz Ferdinand and his wife happened in Sarajevo, Bosnia, and were committed by Bosnians. There were three main groups involved: those who trained and planned the assassination from Serbia; those who helped get some of the assassins back into Bosnia from Serbia, recruited local Bosnians, or otherwise assisted the plot; and those who actually were assigned to carry out the killings. Of the latter group, six men were identified:

---

23. *See* WWII Law and Lawyers, ch. 1.
24. *See Herbert Asquith*, Oxford Dictionary of National Biography 101030483.

Gavrilo Princip, Nedeljko Čabrinović, Trifko Grabež, Vaso Čubrilović, Cetres Popović, and Muhamed Mehmedbašić, the last of whom escaped into Serbia and was not part of the ensuing trial.

The Black Hand Society's Major Vojislav Tankosić had trained Princip, Grabež, and Čabrinović in Belgrade and provided bombs/grenades, pistols, maps, and money, as well as cyanide for suicide. The other three assassins had been recruited locally in Bosnia by Danilo Ilić. On the day of the assassination, both Čubrilović and Mehmedbašić failed to carry out their assigned functions as the archduke's motorcade passed. Čabrinović threw a bomb, which hurt other spectators but not the archduke. The motorcade then sped away, leaving the other three without a chance to perform their designed functions. But Princip would not be denied, and as the archduke was on his way to the hospital to visit those who had been wounded by the bombing, Princip ran to the car and shot both Franz Ferdinand and his wife to death.

The trial opened in Sarajevo on October 12, 1914, with a three-judge tribunal (no jury). The twenty-five defendants, including the five actual and intended assassins, were charged with high treason, murder, and accessory to high treason and murder. This included the people who had helped the assassins get into Bosnia, helped them while in the country, or coordinated their activities, but not those in Serbia who had initiated these acts with irredentist objectives (i.e., to annex territory belonging to another state but containing people of one's own ethnicity).

During the eleven days of trial, the defendants—especially the younger ones—tried to deflect attention from the Serbian connection. Princip, for example, said, "Only I thought of the assassination." They also spun tales about Freemason involvement. On the other hand, there was detailed disclosure by the defendants of the many people in Bosnia who had helped them.

One of the legal issues in the trial was whether Princip had been born on June 26 1894, as the prosecution contended, or on July 26, 1894, as he contended. The issue was significant because if the earlier date was correct, he would be subject to execution if convicted. His mother and parish priest were both called, and even then, the issue was not settled, as there were two conflicting birth records. Ultimately, the court ruled in the light most favorable to the defendant, for the later date.

Of further legal interest was the issue raised by defense counsel Dr. Rudolf Zistler that the defendants could not actually be tried for treason, since Bosnia was not legally part of Austria-Hungary. This was because the annexation of the country had never been legally approved by the parliaments of Austria and Hungary, although bills to do so had been submitted in both. As such, Bosnia and Herzegovina were not part of the empire; therefore the Bosnian citizens on trial could be tried only for murder, not treason. The court did not accept this reasoning.

Of the twenty-five people rounded up and brought to trial, fifteen were convicted as the sentences were handed down on October 28. The five actual and intended assassins, including Princip and Čabrinović, were under the age of twenty, which meant they could not face the death penalty. Instead, all of the five were convicted of treason and murder and given sentences of up to twenty years. Death sentences and eventual executions were handed down to those who had assisted them in Bosnia, including Ilić and four others, two of whom had their sentences commuted on appeal. Princip, Čabrinović, and Grabež would later die in prison of tuberculosis.

In 1917, perhaps as part of a deal to return Serbia's exiled government to power by silencing destabilizing influences, or perhaps solely to rein in agents that had been involved in acts of terror over the years, the government of Serbian Prime Minister Nikola Pašić moved against the Black Hand. Court-martial proceedings under charges of treason for conspiring to overthrow the government and attempted murder of the crown prince were initiated against Dimitrijević and others (Tankosić had died in battle in 1915) in March 1917, leading to his conviction and subsequent execution. Mehmedbašić was also convicted but was released after the war.

LEGAL PROFILES

Alois Curinaldi was the presiding judge in the 1917 Black Hand trial. He was born in Croatia in 1865 and obtained his legal training in Austria. He was a district court public prosecutor in Mostar, Bosnia and Herzegovina. In 1913 he joined the supreme court. In the first two years of WWI, he was part of the state government of Bosnia and Herzegovina, rejoining the supreme court after that. He was a professor of canon law in Sarajevo, where he spent the later years of his life at a Jesuit facility and died in 1940.[25]

C. Subsequent Events
1. Reasons for Starting War

There were to be many more declarations of war in 1915 and beyond, especially after Italy declared war and as the United States entered the war in 1917 and brought a number of regional allies with it. In the end, more than twenty major belligerents were involved, and about that many other nations were minor belligerents. The individual reasons for declaring involvement in this war varied, with many of the later declarations based on alliances. As will be seen, the United States' involvement was based primarily upon acts committed against it while it attempted to stay neutral, a policy it announced almost from the beginning of the war.

Although a topic of unending complexity, perhaps at its base, the decisions of the original belligerents to go to war—beyond the obvious immediacy of responding to the threat or reality of attack—seem to be based on three primary factors. The first is the desire to protect the status quo of empire, which would apply to France, Germany, and the United Kingdom. The second is the desire to enhance the status quo or reputation/influence, which would include Russia, Austria-Hungary, and the Ottomans. The third is the desire for the recovery or integration of related territory, which applies most obviously to the revanchist motives of France and the irredentist drive of Serbia.

In yet another reminder that the seeds of future wars are planted by acts in the current one, it was the use of similar irredentist reasoning by Adolf Hitler regarding the need to unite the Germanic peoples in the Czechoslovak Sudetenland and Austria with Germany that led to the early aggression in WWII. Germany, between the wars and through WWII, also evidenced the revanchist desire for the return of Alsace and Lorraine and parts of what were Prussia and became parts of a reconstituted Poland, all of which were retaken in early attacks in 1939 and 1940.

---

25. *See Curinaldi, Alois (1865–1940), Jurist,* Österreichisches Biographisches Lexikon 1815–1950.

2. Italy Changes Alliances

Italy did not enter the war as expected in 1914 with Germany and Austria-Hungary. Looking at the Triple Alliance agreement, Italy found that the requirements for her participation arose when Germany or Austria-Hungary were attacked. Given that those countries had attacked Serbia, Russia, France, and Belgium, Italy had no obligation to enter the war. Instead, it signed the secret Treaty of London with France and the United Kingdom.[26] Under this agreement, it would gain significant territory on the Adriatic Sea from the Austro-Hungarian Empire and possibly territory from the Ottoman Empire at the end of the war.[27]

The intent of the agreement was for Italy to strike at the Central Powers from the bottom and "to use her entire resources for the purpose of waging war jointly with France, Great Britain, and Russia."[28] Those countries, in turn, were to support Italy's military on land (Russia)[29] and on sea (France and Britain).[30] Italy revoked its participation in the Triple Alliance on May 3, 1915, and declared war on Austria-Hungary three weeks later. In actuality, Italy did not make any significant military impact, spending years trying to make territorial gains into Austria-Hungary. This would have an effect on the country's ultimate acquisitions at Versailles.

LEGAL PROFILES

Antonio Salandra was the Italian prime minister at the start of war. He was born in Italy in 1853 and obtained his legal training there. He taught administrative law at the University of Rome before entering the national parliament in 1886. He was appointed as minister of agriculture in 1899, minister of finance in 1906, and minister of treasury in 1910. He became prime minister in March 1914, serving in that role until June 1916, after further military setbacks in the battles against the Austro-

---

26. Treaty of London, U.K.-It.-Fr.-Rus., Apr. 26, 1915.
27. *Id.* art. 4–9.
28. *Id.* art. 2.
29. *Id.* art. 1.
30. *Id.* art. 3.

Hungarians. He attended the Paris Peace Conference and was the Italian representative to the League of Nations. In 1928, he became a member of Italy's Senate. He then published a book on Italy's decision to abandon neutrality and its negotiations with both alliances to achieve maximum benefit for Italy.[31] He died in 1931.[32]

D. Modern Applicability

The desire for a Greater Serbia never really disappeared. Upon the disintegration of Yugoslavia in the early 1990s, Serbia again went to war to claim territory it felt belonged to it. The many parts of Yugoslavia that have been pieced together since WWI, including Slovenia, Croatia, Bosnia and Herzegovina, Macedonia, Montenegro, and Kosovo, all broke off from Serbia, even though ethnic Serbians resided in several of these new republics. But not without first having to go to war against first the armed forces of Yugoslavia, then Serbia. That latter conflict brought in NATO air strikes, which were followed on with significant trials for war crimes. The International Criminal Tribunal for the former Yugoslavia prosecuted participants on all sides, but significantly the civilian and military leaders of Serbia. Through April 2013, the tribunal has indicted 161 persons for serious violations of international humanitarian law committed in the territory of the former Yugoslavia during these new wars to create a Greater Serbia.[33]

Perhaps the most egregious modern example of finding any reason for starting a war was the U.S. invasion of Iraq in 2003. It was based on a set of justifications that began with that country supposedly having nuclear weapons and eventually became just that Saddam Hussein was a "bad guy." The former ally of the United States against its longer-term adversary in Iran became the new enemy, after its invasion of Kuwait had been rolled back in the early 1990s. But it is ambiguity in peace treaties that may prove to be the reason for a possible future war unrelated to national defense, as the growing national powers in North Asia provoke and then make amends back and forth over treaties

---

31. *See Italy's War Deals Told by Ex-Premier*, N.Y. TIMES (Feb. 8, 1931).
32. *See A. Salandra Dead; Italian Ex-Premier*, N.Y. TIMES (Dec. 9, 1931).
33. UN ICTY, *Key Figures of ICTY Cases* (Apr. 15, 2013).

stretching back to WWII[34] and sometimes centuries beforehand, over islands located between them.[35]

2.2 CONSCRIPTION

A. Statutes

The initial enthusiasm for war proved short lived, after all the declarations of war and faltering initial attacks. Germany executed the modified Schlieffen Plan, advancing through Luxembourg and Belgium before entering France, but its progress was eventually stopped by the combined forces of the British Expeditionary Force and the re-deployed French army. The availability of the French troops came in part due to the failure of Plan XIX to recapture Alsace and Lorraine. Being now on French and Belgian soil, the Germans literally dug in, with a massive trench system. The British and French reciprocated. The Western Front then became, for the next several years, a massive abattoir of men, as each side tried to dislodge the other using antiquated tactics of massive frontal assaults, only to be met with deadly new technologies such as machine guns, tanks, and poison gas.

The costs of stopping the German advance were unprecedented in the history of warfare. The appalling losses clearly dictated the need for a change in tactics, which was not forthcoming, and an increase in manpower, which was. At the First Battle of the Marne in September 1914, the total casualties (killed, missing, and wounded) among all the participants were around half a million, while the First Battle of Ypres in October–November 1914 had total casualties of more than a quarter million. By the end of 1915, British casualties amounted to upward of half a million men, including those incurred at Gallipoli.[36] Such attrition was not sustainable under the current British system of recruiting soldiers only voluntarily.

Most of the major powers in this conflict had conscription laws, which gave them sizable standing armies, both active and reserve. For example, the

---

34. *See* WWII LAW AND LAWYERS, ch. 8.
35. *See Japan's Leader Gives No Ground in Islands Dispute*, N.Y. TIMES (Sept. 27, 2013).
36. GREAT BRITAIN WAR OFFICE, STATISTICS OF THE MILITARY EFFORT OF THE BRITISH EMPIRE DURING THE GREAT WAR, 1914–1920 (1922).

French had just extended the period of national conscription the previous year.[37] But the United Kingdom, as an island nation with a significant overseas empire, had long relied on its navy to project power globally and maintained a smaller, all-volunteer army. When the battle requirements for more men arose, both from the increasing size of the conflict and from the appalling number of casualities taken, the response was not sufficient. The large battle death tolls were regularly published in the newspapers, denting the early patriotic fervor that produced significant enlistments.

This shortage of troops was despite the massive numbers of volunteers who had responded to the call from Secretary of State for War Lord Kitchener. More than two million men had volunteered through the end of 1915. In the second half of 1915, Lord Derby attempted to raise volunteers through encouraging the "pal" system of having friends volunteer together. While again producing significant results, it was not sufficient. Estimates ranged from 600,000 to 1 million single men[38] who had not responded to the "Derby Scheme," which sought voluntary assent to being called to active duty only if needed. Social pressure was also prevalent, with women giving white feathers to men who had not volunteered and red "not at home" badges being placed in windows. Even the outrage at the execution of British nurse Edith Cavell (see Chapter 3) did not bring enough volunteers, so the government had to turn to a national conscription law.

First passed in January 1916, the Military Service Act provided that each single (unmarried or widower without children) British male in Great Britain between the ages of eighteen and forty-one was to be considered enlisted for the duration of the war.[39] "Enlisted" meant being subject to call-up to active military service by class and placement in the reserves before then. This did not include British subjects who ordinarily resided in the dominions or were in Britain only for education. The list of those who were excepted from the act included those who had been already discharged or rejected from the service, those who were disabled or ill, and the clergy.

Additionally, men could be exempted upon application and decision by local military service tribunals. Exemptions could be claimed for those serving

---

37. Loi des tres ans de 1913 (Fr.).
38. Hansard HC Deb 05 Jan. 1916 vol. 77 cc949-1074.
39. Military Service Act of 1916, 5 & 6 Geo. 5 c. 104 (U.K.).

in or training for an important national function (e.g., producing or transporting munitions, coal mining, agriculture), those to whom it would pose a severe hardship (e.g., financial or domestic), those who were ill, and those who conscientiously objected to combatant service and could be assigned to noncombatant service. Certificates of exemption from these tribunals could be absolute, conditional, or temporary. Training or financial hardship could only be temporary. Those on conditional exemption had to notify the authorities if their circumstances changed, subject to a fine for not doing so. Those who misrepresented their situations could receive jail time.

Applications for exemption were made by the men or their employers to local military service tribunals in districts defined by the National Registration Act,[40] a law passed in 1915 to gain an understanding of the number of men available for military service. Appeals of exemption decisions could be made to the military service appeal tribunal or (on approval from the appeal tribunal) to the central military service tribunal in London. There were also exemptions that could be made by government departments for occupations of national importance. These exemptions began with the Munitions of War Act, which prevented people working in the munitions industry from leaving their jobs without permission.[41]

To provide some perspective on the scale of exemptions, a British government report after the war[42] detailed the number of exemptions as of April 1917, a little more than a year after the Military Service Act became effective. It lists three categories of exemption: those approved by the military service tribunals, those in protected trades and occupations, and miscellaneous. Those exempted by military service tribunals totaled 779,936 men, broken down into 40,146 receiving absolute exemption, 372,979 receiving a conditional exemption based on a reserved occupation (munitions, railways, transport, agriculture, coal miners, shipbuilding), 206,191 receiving a conditional exemption based on domestic and related grounds, and 160,620 receiving temporary exemptions.

Men in protected occupations (government-controlled firms, coal mining, railways, government departments, and organizations such as the Red Cross) totaled 1,796,728. Men in the "miscellaneous" category, including those who

---

40. National Registration Act of 1915, 5 & 6 Geo. 5 c. 60 (U.K.).
41. Munitions of War Act of 1915, 5 & 6 Geo. 5 c. 54 (U.K.).
42. GREAT BRITAIN WAR OFFICE, STATISTICS OF THE MILITARY EFFORT OF THE BRITISH EMPIRE DURING THE GREAT WAR, 1914–1920 (1922).

had had appeals dismissed and were awaiting assignment, as well as those still in tribunal adjudication, totaled 165,324. The grand total of men under some form of exemption or adjudication in April 1917 was 2,741,988. In comparison, at that time the monthly deficit of troops recruited compared to the number needed was around 240,000 men. The number of British military deployed overseas in expeditionary forces at the end of the war totaled only 2,075,275 men.

Almost as soon as it was enacted, discussion arose in Parliament about the specifics of the exemptions. For example, did Irish laborers on English farms qualify for exemption? Did sons of widows qualify for exemption?[43] To clarify some of this and to widen the pool of potential recruits, the Military Service Act was further refined in May 1916.[44] The changes included adding married men and removing the exceptions for those men who had been discharged or rejected. The massive casualty rates led to the act being further revised three times in 1917 and 1918—changing the age bands to seventeen and fifty-one, reducing the number of jobs exempted from services, allowing those previously wounded to be reconsidered for service, and expanding the enlistment area to include Ireland (then part of the United Kingdom), the Isle of Man, and the Channel Islands.

LEGAL PROFILES

David Lloyd George was the British secretary of state for war in 1916 and soon to be the prime minister. He was born in England in 1863 but raised in Wales and obtained his legal training there. He started his practice in Wales and entered politics there in 1889 on a county council. He was elected to the British House of Commons in 1890, remaining there for fifty-five years. He opened a solicitor's office in London and, after gaining a national reputation, joined the cabinet of the government in 1906. In 1908 he became chancellor of the exchequer until the war

---

43. *See, e.g.*, Hansard HC Deb 21 Feb. 1916 vol. 80 cc414-5; HC Deb 23 Feb. 1916 vol. 80 c704W; HC Deb 24 Feb. 1916 vol. 80 cc788-9; HC Deb 29 Feb. 1916 vol. 80 cc859-60; HC Deb 29 Feb. 1915 vol. 80 c865; HC Deb 01 Mar. 01 1916 vol. 80 cc1043-4.
44. Military Service Act of 1916 (Session 2), 6 & 7 Geo. 5 c. 15 (U.K.).

dictated new roles. In May 1915, he took on the new role of minister of munitions after the Shell Crisis (see Chapter 3). After the death of Lord Kitchener in June 1916, he became secretary of state for war, and in December, he succeeded Asquith to become prime minister, a position he held until 1922. After the war, he joined the peace talks and presided over several acts of social reform. After 1922, he remained in Parliament until his death in 1945.[45]

Louis Barthou was the French prime minister in 1913, when the conscription period in France was extended to three years. He was born in France in 1862 and obtained his legal training there. In 1889, he was elected to the National Assembly, where he remained until being elected a senator in 1922. He served in the cabinets of many governments, including as minister of the interior, of public works, and of justicer before becoming prime minister in 1913. His son died in the war in 1914, and Barthou only returned to active politics as minister of foreign affairs in 1917. After the war, he served as minister of war, of justice, and of foreign affairs. He was also an author of some renown and was elected a member of l'Académie française.[46] In 1934, he was assassinated along with the King of Yugoslavia on the latter's visit to France.

B. Cases

Of the large numbers of men applying or qualifying for exemptions from active military service, a small percentage responded to their enlistment notice by claiming conscientious objector status. Prime Minister Asquith, in introducing the Military Service Act to Parliament, had likened the history of the conscientious objector to exemptions from militia duty given to the Quakers during the Napoleonic Wars.[47] He also referenced similar wordings used by South Africa and Australia when they had adopted conscription laws for military training and service.

---

45. *See David Lloyd George*, OXFORD DICTIONARY OF NATIONAL BIOGRAPHY 101034570.
46. *See Louis Barthou*, ASSEMBLÉE NATIONALE HISTOIRE.
47. Hansard HC Deb 05 Jan. 1916 vol. 77 cc949-1074.

To qualify for exemption as a conscientious objector, those who demonstrated that they had a firmly held belief were given a choice of taking on some form of noncombatant military service in the Non-Combatant Corps (NCC), or nonmilitary civilian service, such as in the government's Home Office Scheme. But there were some thousands of enlistees who refused to have anything to do with the war in any role, the so-called absolutists. For these objectors, besides the immense social distain they were subject to in both military and civilian life, prison was often the result, along with other penalties, such as the loss of the franchise (i.e., voting) for several years after release, and the complete inability to obtain employment.

In actuality, many of the applications for conscientious objector status were denied and the men sent to combatant units. Those who continued to refuse to do any type of service were "handed over to military authorities, shut up in cells, some damp and dark; put in irons, badly fed, bullied, roughly handled, threatened with death, bayonet placed against the heart, sentenced to solitary confinement for seventy, or one hundred, or one hundred and sixty two days, or to two years' hard labour."[48]

Opposition to the Military Service Act from conscientious objectors came in two forms. One was from those who were not enlisted and so carried on a campaign of civil disobedience to the war and to the requirement to fight. The other was from those who were enlisted. The Non-Conscription Fellowship (NCF) was headed up by figures such as Clifford Allen (the future Lord Allen) and Archibald Fenner Brockway (future MP and Baron Brockway), who were both later imprisoned for not accepting conscription. The fellowship had support and involvement from the likes of Bertrand Russell. For signing their names to pamphlets protesting conscription, these men were fined and, if they did not pay (Russell's fine was paid for from sales of his books), imprisoned under the Defence of the Realm Act (see Chapter 3). They also set about to assist conscientious objectors wherever they could, including intervening politically.

There was soon a need for such assistance. When absolutists refused to obey any orders, they were court-martialed and turned over to the military, where they became objects of ridicule, abuse, and constant verbal intimidation. This reached a high point when the army determined that it must make a point of

---

48. Hansard HC Deb 15 May 1916 vol. 82 cc1194-230.

those conscientious objectors who refused to serve in any manner. It shipped seventeen of them over to France, forcing their conscription into the NCC. When they would not perform any services whatsoever, they were given various forms of military field punishments, including being handcuffed to a fixed object (the replacement for flogging as a punishment), often similar to "crucifixion." When word of these punishments reached England, a Liberal member of Parliament asked the British solicitor general if the military could execute these men as conscientious objectors. The answer was no, but as they were now in the military, the solicitor general replied, "Is it fair to ask a commander in the field . . . to inquire into the motive why a soldier disobeys?... When men are drafted into the Army they must be subjected to military rule in the ordinary way."[49]

Soon, another group of absolutist conscientious objectors, called the "Richmond 16" for their incarceration in the prison at Richmond Castle, was sent overseas. After arriving at a military camp in northern France, these men refused to do any work, such as unloading supplies. This was a violation of the Army Act, and for this disobedience while on active service, the men were convicted at field general courts-martial. The sentences were pronounced on June 24, 1916. Each man was led up and his offense and sentence announced as being execution by firing squad. After a significant pause each time a sentence was announced that day, it was subsequently announced that the sentences had been commuted to ten years penal servitude at hard labor. Luckily for these men, Lord Kitchener, who had wanted to make an example of these men for those who disobeyed orders, had been killed by a German mine on June 5. At that point, the British government decided to stop transferring absolutist conscientious objectors to the military and to begin confining them, as appropriate, to civilian prisons and domestically-situated labor camps.

This story has an interesting tangent, in that one of the Richmond 16 had a brother who was serving at the same time in the active military in the trenches of Europe. Philip Brocklesby was a second lieutenant while his older brother Bert was a conscientious objector and one of the Richmond 16. Soon, Philip would be involved in the very bloody Battle of the Somme (more than one million total casualties). By chance, they happened to meet each other briefly while in France. Philip was in training and Bert was being brought to where he

---

49. *Id.*

was to be sentenced. Despite the disparate roles in and reactions to service in the war, the brothers respected each other's beliefs, as did their father, a justice of the peace. After the war, Bert was unable to find employment in his hometown, due to the very strong feeling against absolutist conscientious objectors, and so spent many years overseas doing missionary work.[50]

LEGAL PROFILES

George Cave was the British solicitor general in 1916. He was born in England in 1856 and obtained his legal training there. Starting in 1880, he practiced as a barrister in chancery and became a king's counsel in 1904. He was elected to the House of Commons in 1906. He served as counsel to both the University of Oxford and the Prince of Wales. He advised the Foreign Office on blockade issues (see Section 2.4) at the start of the war and was named solicitor general in 1915. The following year, he was appointed home secretary, a position he held for three years. In 1919, after his ennobling, he was appointed as a lord of appeal. In 1922 he became the lord chancellor (responsible for the courts and the judiciary), a position he held until 1925. In that year he was elected chancellor of the University of Oxford. He died in 1928.[51]

Philip Morrell was the Liberal MP who inquired about the status of the first conscientious objectors who were sent to France in 1916. He was born in England in 1870 and obtained his legal training there. He started out in practice in his father's law firm. He was first elected to Parliament in 1908, where he remained for the next ten years. During the war, he was a leading figure in the antiwar movement's Union of Democratic Control, which wanted to avoid future wars through prohibiting secret agreements and avoiding punitive peace terms. He also used his home (his family were wealthy brewers) to shelter conscientious

---

50. *See Brothers at War: The WW1 Soldier and the Pacifist ... but Who Was the Hero?*, DAILY MAIL (Feb. 14, 2008).
51. *See George Cave*, OXFORD DICTIONARY OF NATIONAL BIOGRAPHY 101032329.

objectors and provide them with alternative work. He and his better-known wife, Ottoline, supported aspiring authors and socialized with the Bloomsbury Set, including D. H. Lawrence, Aldous Huxley, Virginia Woolf, W. B. Yeats, T. S. Eliot, E. M. Forster, and Bertrand Russell. He died in 1943.[52]

C. Subsequent Events

The final revision to the Military Service Act in 1918 expanded conscription to Ireland. Although around 200,000 Irish nationals had volunteered for service in the military,[53] the conscription law caused significant resistance in Ireland, as home rule had still not been implemented. The movement was led by the Irish Anti-Conscription Committee, who, along with church and union leaders, held rallies, communicated resistance through church parishes, and called general strikes. The resistance, somewhat analogous to the linguistic, religious, and political dynamics that took place in Canada after its conscription law was passed in 1917 between the francophone and English-speaking segments of society, came as the tide of the war was turning in favor of the Allied Powers. The war would end later that year, and no Irish conscripts were ever called up. But the resistance movement helped to set the stage for the coming battle over Ireland's status in the United Kingdom (see Chapter 6).

The issues of conscription and conscientious objectors were both to return in the early stages of WWII. The start of war in 1939 meant that again men between the ages of eighteen and forty-one could be drafted, with exceptions for the clergy, the unfit, and those in reserved occupations. Conscientious objectors had to state their case before a tribunal, and if their beliefs were judged to be firmly held, they could be assigned to the NCC, conditionally exempted upon performing certain kinds of civilian work, or unconditionally exempted. As the war intensified, the upper age for conscription was again raised, to fifty-one years of age, and this time, women between twenty and thirty years old could be called up as well. So the conscientious objectors in WWII also included women.

---

52. *See Ottoline Morrell*, OXFORD DICTIONARY OF NATIONAL BIOGRAPHY 101035111.
53. Dept. of the Taoiseach/Roinn an Taoisigh, *Irish Soldiers in the First World War.*

LEGAL PROFILES

Timothy Michael Healy was an Irish politician and a member of the Irish Anti-Conscription Committee. He was born in Ireland in 1855 and obtained his legal training there and in England. He was elected to the British Parliament from an Irish district in 1880. He was aligned with Charles Stewart Parnell and the Irish Home Rule movement. He was called to the Irish bar in 1884 and the English bar in 1910. He maintained various political affiliations, all with the goal of Irish Home Rule, but often with the major participants at odds with each other. His legal career continued to prosper, including involvement in the investigation into the 1907 theft of the Irish Crown Jewels. He was appointed the first governor-general of the new Irish Free State in 1922, after the Anglo-Irish Treaty of 1921. He held this position until early 1928. He died in 1931.[54]

2.3 EXECUTION OF SOLDIERS

A. Statutes

The carnage from battles was only to worsen. The casualties from the battles of the Somme, Verdun, and others would each total more than a million men. The death toll rose in inverse proportion to the display of original military thinking by the leadership of the combatants. The utter insanity of the collective military tactics being deployed did not in any way correlate to a lessening of the resolve of the military commanders to keep sending men to the slaughter and to punish those who would no longer participate. Unlike the conscientious objectors described in the previous section, who were only threatened with execution, the reality of the battlefront meant that hundreds of men met their deaths not from the enemy but in front of firing squads made up of their

---

54. *See Timothy Michael Healy*, OXFORD DICTIONARY OF NATIONAL BIOGRAPHY 101033788.

compatriots. The punishments for mutiny, desertion, and cowardice were swift and severe.

All of the military powers had these problems. The will to fight, the early patriotic fervor, had long subsided. This was visible in troops of the belligerents, including those that had significant numbers of soldiers who belonged to other nations, such as the Austro-Hungarian Empire and the Ottoman Empire. The czar of Russia, facing an exhausted and unwilling army, was forced to abdicate in March 1917 (see Chapter 6). But it was on the Western Front, so stagnant but full of death and seemingly devoid of progress of what was intended to be a war that was "over by Christmas," where the resistance of those fighting the battles was most clearly on display. Germany and the United Kingdom had their own troubles with desertions (more than three hundred men from the United Kingdom were executed for desertion in the war), but it was the French who seemed to have the bigger problem with mutinies.

The French infantry troops suffered greatly during the war. After they saved their nation from being overrun by German forces, the horrors of the following two and a half years of trench warfare and stalemate destroyed the morale of the average soldier. The new deadly technologies of machine guns and poison gases had made both defensive and offensive actions lethal. The soldier could not move; he could not stay still. He was locked into a very long subterranean world, stretching from Switzerland to the North Sea, that was often flooded by rainwater. And he was not only hounded by constant thoughts of mortality but also was pounded relentlessly by the elements, disease, snipers, and artillery barrages. Add to this the futility of going "over the top" into barbed wire and withering machine gun fire for little gain, and it is a wonder not that there were mutinies but that there were so few.

The life of soldiers in the trenches was one of both variability and constancy. The variability came from the sudden appearance of death and disease. Death could strike as quickly when peeking over the trench wall and being met by sniper fire. Diseases brought on by the weather, the poor hygiene, the atrocious living and sleeping conditions, the proximity to dead bodies and latrines, and the various and omnipresent vermin were a significant source of casualties. The constancy came from being stuck in several cycles. These included the shelling cycles, the daily routine cycle, and the trench rotation cycle. Soldiers were posted in the front-line trenches, then in front-line supporting trenches, then in reserve, and then had rest times. The daily cycle of watching for attacks, performing menial tasks, doing weapons checks and inspections, taking care of personal needs, and the sheer boredom was relieved only by those times when the soldiers had to journey close to or into the no-man's-land between the trenches or to repel enemy attacks.

Trench warfare was famously described in the books *All Quiet on the Western Front*[55] (*Im Westen nichts Neues*) and *Goodbye to All That*.[56] The former gave voice to the thoughts of soldiers in the trenches, highlighted in the following brief excerpts:

I am young, I am twenty years old; yet I know nothing of life but despair, death, fear

Our knowledge of life is limited to death

We are little flames poorly sheltered by frail walls against the storm of dissolution and madness, in which we flicker and sometimes almost go out

Bombardment, barrage, curtain-fire, mines, gas, tanks, machine-guns, hand-grenades—words, words, but they hold the horror of the world

[H]ow senseless is everything that can ever be written, done, or thought, when such things are possible. It must be all lies and of no account

[D]eath is not an adventure to those who stand face to face with it. It will try simply to tell of a generation of men who, even though they may have escaped shells, were destroyed by the war.

Under the revised 1857 French military code that was in effect during WWI,[57] *les tribunaux militaires* (more specifically *le conseil de guerre*, councils of war) could sentence those under its jurisdiction who committed a crime to punishments ranging from death to deportation to banishment to military

---

55. ERICH MARIA REMARQUE, IM WESTEN NICHTS NEUES, (Little Brown and Co. 1929) (translation A.W. Wheen).
56. ROBERT GRAVES, GOODBYE TO ALL THAT, Anchor (1929).
57. Code de justice militaire pour l'armee de terre, June 9, 1857 (Fr.).

degradation (loss of rank, pension, ability to serve, etc.).[58] The available military-specific crimes included insubordination and desertion,[59] revolt (mutiny) and rebellion,[60] crimes and offenses against military duty,[61] and treason and espionage.[62] The leaders of a mutiny could be punished by execution.[63] The military ranks of the members making up a tribunal were based on the rank of the accused. Executions were to be carried out by twelve men standing 6 meters in front of the condemned, who was tied to a post.[64] The ammunition was to be loaded before the arrival of the condemned, and the officer and military doctor were to be ready in case a coup de grâce was necessary after the initial shots were fired. Just as the war was starting, the military established *les conseils de guerre spéciaux* (or *cours martiales*) that provided simplified procedures for expedited trials, with only three judges comprising the tribunal, no appeals, and executions within twenty-four hours.[65]

LEGAL PROFILES

Raoul Péret was the French minister of justice for a few months in 1917, following René Viviani and Aristide Briand. He was born in France in 1870 and obtained his legal training and started his legal practice there. He entered national politics by election to the National Assembly in 1902, where he would remain as a deputy until 1926. He was three times the president of this Chamber of Deputies. During this time, he held a number of cabinet positions, including minister of commerce in 1914, minister of finance in 1926, and minister of justice again in 1930. In 1927, he was elected to the Senate, where he served until 1932. In 1931, he was embroiled in a conflict of interest regarding assistance he had

---

58. *Id.* art. 185.
59. *Id.* art. 230 et seq.
60. *Id.* art. 217 et seq.
61. *Id.* art. 209 et seq.
62. *Id.* art. 204 et seq.
63. *Id.* art. 217.
64. Décret du 25 octobre 1874 sur les executions militaires (Fr.).
65. Décret du 2 août 1914 sur les conseils de guerre spéciaux; Décret du 6 septembre 1914 sur les conseils de guerre spéciaux (Fr.).

supposedly given to a client while in office that had led to the failure of a bank, but the Senate acquitted him. He died in 1942.[66]

Louis Nail was the French minister of justice from late 1917 to 1920, following Péret. He was born in France in 1864 and obtained his legal training there. After obtaining his license, he started his practice in Lorient and joined the general council for the department of Morbihan in 1898. He was the mayor of Lorient from 1904 to 1912 and president of the general council there from 1913. He was a member of the National Assembly from 1910 to 1920, where he served in an undersecretary role in the cabinet in 1915, before taking the justice position. He died in 1920, when he was struck by an automobile.[67]

B. Cases

With the potential loss of their country in the balance, the leadership of the French army utilized strict measures to deal with those whom it determined were acting contrary to the defense of the homeland or influencing others to do so. This included a variety of offenses, from dereliction of duty to disobedience in the presence of the enemy to desertion to outright mutiny. The following are four examples, which stretched from the buoyant but desperate early phases of the war until its exhausted but still desperate later stages, of how France dealt with its own soldiers for noncompliance with orders on the Western Front.

1. Shot for Example—Dereliction of Duty

On November 27, 1914, in the small village of Vingré, the front-line trenches holding French soldiers in a reserve infantry regiment (298th) were heavily bombed for hours. The trenches, not very strongly built at this early stage of the war, began to collapse and were then overrun by German soldiers in a late-day charge. The French soldiers, on a command from their leader Lt.

---

66. *See Raoul Péret*, Assemblee Nationale Biographies des Les Présidents de l'Assemblée Nationale.
67. *See Louis Nail*, Assemblee Nationale Biographies des Députés Français depuis 1789.

Paulaud, fell back to their support trenches, regrouped and rallied, and ended up retaking the ground that had been surrendered. The battalion, believing that they should not have retreated at all, ordered twenty-four of the men to spend the next week in the front-line trenches. But this was not sufficient for the commanding general, Étienne de Villaret. Determined to set an example, he instead had these infantry men arrested and charged with abandoning their posts under article 211 of the military code.[68]

On December 3, a special council of war was called. The defense counsel, second lieutenant Bodé, was given only hours to interview the men and prepare a defense, after himself returning from the front-line trenches. Before the tribunal, Lt. Paulaud denied that he had given an order to retreat. Even though Lt. Bodé presented the facts that the men had retired as directed in good order and had regained the temporarily lost area, the tribunal (Lt. Col. Pinoteau, Lt. Diot, adjutant Pothonnier) decided that all twenty-four men were guilty. Six of the men who had purportedly been on the right side of the trench, where the attack started, were selected to be made an example of and sentenced to death. Jean Blanchard, Francisque Durantet, Paul-Henri Floch, Pierre Gay, Claude Pettelet, and Jean Quinault were executed the next morning. Being in the reserves, most of these men were in their thirties. Both Floch and Gay had actually been captured that day and managed to escape, only to be executed by their own army. The other soldiers in the regiment were marched by to view the corpses.

In addition to losing their husbands and fathers, the families of the executed men were socially castigated. After the war, the case was taken up again, and in January 1921, in part based on Lt. Paulaud's own repeated statements of the innocence of these men, the appellate Court of Cassation determined that their convictions should be annulled (*casse et annule*).[69] The men were determined to have died for France (*morts pour la France*), and the trial testimony of Lt. Paulaud was discredited. Lt. Paulaud himself was brought before a military tribunal in October 1921 and charged with perjury, but given the long period of time since the actual incident, it was difficult to establish his guilt, and he was not convicted. None of the senior officers was ever tried, even though Floch's brother brought a complaint in 1929. More than 600 soldiers were

---

68. Code de justice militaire pour l'armee de terre (Fr.).
69. La Cour de Cassation, Jan. 29, 1921, JOURNAL OFFICIEL, Feb. 18, 1921.

known to have been shot as examples (*soldat fusillé pour l'exemple*) during WWI by France.[70]

In excerpts from the final letter from Floch, who was a clerk of the court in his hometown (*greffier de la justice de paix*), to his wife, he stated his innocence:[71]

> My dearest Lucie,
>
> When this letter reaches you, I will be shot dead. Here's why: On November 27, around five p.m., after a violent bombardment of two hours on a front-line trench, the Germans came into the trench and took me prisoner with two other friends. I escaped from the Germans following my friends, and then I was accused of dereliction of duty in the presence of the enemy.
>
> Twenty-four of us were tried last night by the War Council. Six were sentenced to death, including me. I am no guiltier than the others, but it is being used as an example. . . . I ask your humble forgiveness for all the trouble I caused you and the embarrassment. . . . My little Lucie, again, sorry. I die innocent of the crime of dereliction of duty. If instead of escaping from the Germans, I had remained a prisoner, I would still have survived. It is fate . . .
>
> Henry Floch

2. Shot for Example—Disobedience in the Face of the Enemy

In 1915, the case of the four corporals of Souain was another typical instance of the French military punishing a few to set an example for all. On March 10, 1915, after many days of death but no advancement at Souain in northern France, men were sent to cut some of the barbed wire in front of their trenches. Twenty-four men—six corporals and eighteen soldiers—of the 336th infantry regiment were among those ordered into the maelstrom of machine gun fire from the German side and the barely-in-front of them artillery fire

---

70. Assemblée Nationale, Quest. 19915, JOURNAL OFFICIEL, Mar. 5, 2013.
71. Letter from Henri Paul Floch to Lucie Floch (Dec. 3, 1914).

from the French side. To encourage his men to advance, their general, Geraud Réheilhac, commanded that the artillery be temporarily directed into the trenches on his own men. The artillery commander Bérubé refused without a written order.

Stuck in shell holes, surrounded by the bodies of their fallen comrades, aware of the futility of the advance, with the barbed wire fully 150 meters ahead in the killing zone, the men could not advance without dying. In the trial of these twenty-four men on March 16, 1915, they were charged with disobedience in the presence of the enemy. The special council of war did not sentence the infantry men, as they had been randomly chosen, two from each squad or two of the corporals (who, they determined, could not hear the command to advance). But the other four corporals (Louis Girard, Lucien Lechat, Louis Lefoulon, Théophile Maupas) were held responsible and took the blame for the entire group's actions. Over the protest of their immediate commander, the four corporals were convicted and then executed the following day.

After the war, Blanche Maupas, the wife of Théophile Maupas, brought a case before the criminal chamber of the Court of Cassation twice, in 1922 and 1926. She even wrote a book about the case,[72] but she failed to achieve a result like that of the case from Vingré. This case would become part of the inspiration for the 1935 book and the 1957 movie *Paths of Glory*. Kirk Douglas stars as Col. Dax, a criminal defense lawyer in civilian life who defends soldiers at trial but finds that their fate, as in certain special councils of war, may have been preordained before the tribunal began. In the film, as in the Souain case, men are chosen to die as representatives of their unit.

Finally, a forum was created by law to deal with these remaining cases from the special councils of war: the Court of Special Military Justice (*Cour spéciale de justice militaire*).[73] These courts were composed of both legal personnel (counselors from the Paris court of appeal) and current and former soldiers. On March 3, 1934, noting their long time in the trenches, their physical and mental exhaustion, the poorly aimed artillery strikes, the dead bodies of fallen comrades, the distance to the barbed wire, the esteem of their men, and their impeccable records in civilian life, the court decided to rehabilitate the four

---

72. B. Maupas, LE COMBAT D'UNE ÉPOUSE POUR LA RÉHABILITATION DE SON MARI, LE CAPORAL MAUPAS (THÉO), L'UN DES QUATRE FUSILLÉS DE SOUAIN EXÉCUTÉS LE 17 MARS 1915 (1934).
73. Loi du 9 mars 1932 (Fr.).

corporals. The court annulled the previous judgment, acquitted the men, and ordered "*décharge leur mémoire des condamnations prononcées*" (discharge of the memory of their convictions). The widows of Maupas and Girard received one franc apiece in damages.

3. Mutiny

What finally pushed French troops over the line into mutiny was the failure in the spring of 1917 of the battles of the Aisne. After the losses in 1916 and then a bitterly cold winter, the troops needed success in some measure. Despite fighting on their own soil, the French military doctrine of constant offensives did not translate into successes in the well-fortified positions of the trenches. The futility of the assaults led to soldiers taking into their own hands what was obvious from their perspectives, the decision to no longer engage in meaningless and deadly en masse frontal assaults.

In May and early June of 1917, French troops began to disobey orders to return to the front-line trenches when their turn in the rotation came, or they moved on their own to the rear from the front-line trenches. This disobedience involved large numbers of troops, perhaps one-third to one-half or more of the French divisions on the Western Front. In some cases significant numbers of troops in a division were involved; in other cases smaller groups of soldiers in the different divisions decided to mutiny or disobey orders. These were usually soldiers in the infantry divisions, since those were the ones involved in the en masse charges.

The French military command responded in several ways. The commander who ordered the attacks on the Aisne, Robert Nivelle, was relieved, and Philippe Pétain was given command. He undertook a two-part approach. First, large numbers of rebellious troops were arrested and brought in front of a court-martial. Of the tens of thousands who were arrested, around 3,500 (approximately 10 percent of the mutineers) were convicted of a serious offense under the military code, including more than 600 sentenced to be executed. Of those, only forty-three are actually known to have been executed.[74] Second, Pétain stopped the en masse offensive assaults for the most part. He was waiting for more technology, such as newer tanks. He was also waiting for the arrival of the American troops, not just for the new bodies, but also for

---

74. *See, e.g.*, G. PEDRONCINI, LES MUTINERIES DE 1917 (1st ed. 1967, 2nd ed. 1983).

the impact on the morale of the French soldiers. And for the French troops, he provided more frequent and longer periods of rest during their rotations through the trench cycle.

4. Desertion and Capitulation

Jean Jacques Chapelant was a young French lieutenant leading a small artillery squad supporting the 98th infantry regiment. On October 7, 1914, he surrendered near Roye after his area was overrun, his guns went out of service, and he was shot in the leg. He managed to escape from his captors, bad leg and all, but his commander, Lt. Col. Didier, charged him with several offenses under military code:[75] capitulating in the open field to the enemy,[76] desertion,[77] and encouraging the desertion of others[78] and so convened a special council of war. Chapelant became the ranking leader after the infantry captain had been killed, which magnified the severity of his actions and made him responsible not only for leading the counterattack but also for the actions of the soldiers at hand. He was convicted by the three-man tribunal (Cmdr. Gaube, Capt. Raoux, Lt. Bourseau), and the next day, lying in a stretcher due to his wounds that was tied to an apple tree, he was shot. Before this, Lt. Col. Didier had allegedly tried to give him a pistol to take his own life, which Chapelant refused to do. Despite the efforts of his parents, Chapelant was not rehabilitated by the Court of Special Justice in the 1930s.

LEGAL PROFILES

Henri Guernut was the counsel assisting many of the families in clearing the names of the executed French soldiers. He was born in France in 1876 and obtained his legal training there. In 1912 he became the secretary general of the *Ligue des droits de l'homme* (League of Human Rights), a position he held for twenty years, championing the rights of, among others, Algerians, lawyers, and women. From 1928 to 1936, he

---

75. Code de justice militaire pour l'armee de terre (Fr.).
76. *Id.* art. 210.
77. *Id.* art. 238.
78. *Id.* art. 242.

served in the National Assembly. In 1936, he also served as the minister of education. After WWII started, he took up the cause of French refugees in England. He died in 1943.[79]

Alexandre Millerand was the minister of war when many of these cases took place. He was born in France in 1859 and obtained his legal training there. He was involved in some high-profile trials after becoming a lawyer in 1882, including defending Paul Lafargue, the son of Karl Marx. He entered the Chamber of Deputies in 1885, where he would remain until 1920. He joined the cabinet several times, including as the minister of commerce and public works. He was administrator for the recovered provinces of Alsace and Lorraine after the war. In 1920, he became the French president, a position he held until 1924. He was elected to the Senate in 1925, where he served until 1940. He died in 1943.[80]

C. Subsequent Events

Ultimately the mutinies died down, thanks to both the steps taken by Pétain and the successes that came after the arrival of the American troops and new equipment. Pétain was, however, to become quite the leading figure in his country once again, but this time for the wrong reasons. He led Vichy France during WWII and would die disgraced.[81] The special councils were stopped later in the war and were removed from future consideration when the military code was revised in 1928.[82] This revision also gave the civil courts, at least in peacetime, oversight of certain acts by the military that occurred on French soil. As previously mentioned, in the 1930s the Court of Special Justice was able to rehabilitate dozens of the soldiers executed during the war.

---

79. *See Henri-Alfred Guernut*, ASSEMBLEE NATIONALE BIOGRAPHIES DES DÉPUTÉS FRANÇAIS DEPUIS 1789.
80. *See Alexandre Millerand*, ASSEMBLEE NATIONALE BIOGRAPHIES DES DÉPUTÉS FRANÇAIS DEPUIS 1789.
81. *See* WWII LAW AND LAWYERS, ch. 5.
82. Loi du 9 mars 1928 Portant revision du Code de justice militaire pour l'armee de terre (Fr.).

The British, who operated under the rather strict code of the centuries-old Mutiny Act of 1689, had more problems with desertions and other crimes that led to over 300 soldiers, including those from the Commonwealth, being executed. The 1964 British movie *King and Country* depicts a WWI deserter. But mutinies did continue to erupt, including the biggest British mutiny of the war, at the training area of Étaples in France in September 1917.

Mutinies were not restricted only to the land; several occurred on the seas, both shortly before and after this war, such as the mutiny by the German High Seas fleet in November 1918 and the mutiny in the Black Sea Fleet of France in 1919. The Communist revolution occurring in Russia had a hand in some of these uprisings. Mutinies continued in WWII, in the forces of all countries, including the United States.[83] They occurred in the armies of the modern powers even up to the Vietnam War, albeit in much smaller and more easily resolved disputes.

LEGAL PROFILES

René Coty was a lawyer serving in the trenches during the war. He was born in France in 1882 and obtained his legal training there, beginning his practice in 1902 in Le Havre. He was elected to the city council there in 1908. When war broke out, he volunteered and was sent to the front in November 1914, where he remained until January 1919. He was elected general counsel for Le Havre in 1919. He was elected to the National Assembly in 1923, and he served alternately there and in the Senate until 1953. He served from 1954 to 1959 as the president of the Fourth Republic. In 1959, he was a member of the Constitutional Council that led to the Fifth Republic and the takeover of power by Charles de Gaulle. He died in 1962.[84]

Félix Gouin was another lawyer serving in the trenches during the war. He was born in France in 1884 and obtained his legal training

---

83. *See* WWII LAW AND LAWYERS, ch. 2.
84. *See René Coty*, ASSEMBLEE NATIONALE BIOGRAPHIES DES DÉPUTÉS FRANÇAIS DEPUIS 1789.

there, receiving his license in 1907. He became the general counsel for the department of Bouches-du-Rhône in 1911. When the war started, he volunteered and spent the entire war in the front lines. In 1924, he was elected to the National Assembly, where he remained, in its various forms, until 1958. He was one of only eighty deputies in the National Assembly to vote against ceding power to Pétain in Vichy in 1940.[85] He was part of the provisional government in WWII in Algiers and then Paris and headed the provisional government in 1946 after de Gaulle's resignation. He continued in the new government, but in 1958, he objected to the new constitution and left politics. He died in 1977.[86]

Robert George Raper was another lawyer serving in the trenches during the war, but one who did not survive the conflict. He was born in England in 1877 and obtained his legal training there. He was working as a solicitor in Sussex when the war started. He transferred from the territorial reserves to the South Staffordshire Regiment, an active service unit, and was made a major. In leading his men through the French village of Fricourt in the Battle of the Somme, he was killed on July 2, 1916. He was buried there, and a local street is named after him.[87]

D. Modern Applicability

Mutinies still occur in modern times and are put down with varying degrees of severity. For example, in 2009, there was a mutiny in the army of Bangladesh. The soldiers of the Bangladesh Rifles unit mutinied over inadequate pay and harsh treatment they had received while serving in the military. Scores of people, mostly senior military officers, were attacked and killed by the mutineers. In a trial in a civilian court lasting several years, more than 800 of these soldiers were put on trial together. The court eventually handed down death

---

85. *See* WWII Law and Lawyers, ch. 5.
86. *See Félix Gouin*, Assemblee Nationale Biographies des Les Présidents de l'Assemblée Nationale.
87. *See Killed in Action*, The Times (July 8, 1916).

sentences to more than 150 of the defendant soldiers, on charges including murder, rape, and arson.[88]

One of the questions that arises after every war is what to do with the legacies of those who may have been wrongly convicted in the haste and hurry of battlefield conditions. With the calm and certainty of a postwar peace, the decisions of long ago can be revisited and, where grossly wrong, modified as appropriate. This was the case with the martyrs of Vingré and the corporals of Souain, in the decades following the war. But efforts are still taking place in modern times. In 1998, Prime Minister Lionel Jospin memorialized those executed in the mutinies of 1917, at a speech at Craonne near the Chemin des Dames starting point of the mutiny. And most recently, the Ministry of Veteran Affairs decided to classify Lt. Chapelant as having died for France (*morts pour la France*).[89]

It is impossible, short of new, authenticated records that clearly depict the conditions and actions under which these men were convicted, to know the whole truth. The British passed a law in 2006 pardoning all of those executed in the commonwealth during WWI, including for the offenses of casting away arms, cowardice, leaving a post without orders, mutiny, sedition, disobeying or striking an officer, and desertion.[90] Defence Minister Desmond Browne said, "I do not want to second-guess the decisions made by commanders in the field. . . . I believe it is better to acknowledge that injustices were clearly done in some cases, even if we cannot say which—and to acknowledge that all these men were victims of war."[91] Perhaps French Prime Minister Lionel Jospin's 1998 words said it best: that these men had fully returned to "our collective memory" ("*réintégrer aujourd'hui, pleinement, notre mémoire collective nationale*").

2.4 BLOCKADE

A. Statutes

Defeating an enemy is not just defeating its soldiers on the ground or sailors on the sea. It also includes destroying its ability to make war. One way to do

---

88. *See 152 Soldiers Sentenced to Die for Mutiny in Bangladesh*, CNN (Nov. 5, 2013).
89. Ministry of Veteran Affairs, Opinion No. 353-2012 (Nov. 8, 2012) (Fr.).
90. Armed Forces Act of 2006, c. 52, § 359 (U.K.).
91. *Pardoned, the 306 Soldiers Shot at Dawn for 'Cowardice,'* The Telegraph (Aug. 16, 2006).

this is to cut off the supply lines providing food and the raw materials used to produce food and armaments. Being a naval power, the United Kingdom began a blockade at sea to cut off the supplies coming into Germany, a practice it had used on its enemies for hundreds of years. Because of the new technologies of submarines, mines, and airplanes, it no longer deployed a "close" (to the enemy's ports) blockade as in previous wars, but a "distance" blockade (interdicting ships heading to an enemy's ports). The story of this blockade is tied closely with the response to the blockade, the submarine warfare as practiced by Germany (covered in the next section), rationing in Germany (covered in the next chapter), and embargo and export controls by the United States (covered in Chapter 4).

The international law applicable to blockades starts with the laws on interdicting ships of neutral countries. Under the applicable Hague Convention of 1907,[92] ships could not be captured or searched in the territorial waters of a neutral country,[93] and neutral countries could not supply warships or war materials to the belligerents[94] but neutrals were not required to prevent the export or transit of such materials to the belligerents.[95] To further define a code of rules for prizes captured and awarded in the prize court foreseen in Convention XII of the 1907 Hague Convention, further discussions took place at the London Naval Conference in 1908–9, which produced the London Declaration.[96]

This declaration required that for a blockade to be binding, it had to be effective (a question of fact),[97] it had to be declared (with a start date and geographic limits) and notified,[98] it must be applied impartially,[99] and it was to operate close to the ports and coast of the enemy.[100] Further, neutral vessels could not be captured for breaching the blockade without knowledge of it,[101]

---

92. Convention on the Rights and Duties of Neutral Powers in Naval War (Hague XIII) (Oct. 18, 1907).
93. *Id.* art. 2.
94. *Id.* art. 6.
95. *Id.* art. 7.
96. Declaration Concerning the Laws of Naval War, 208 Consol. T.S. 338 (1909).
97. *Id.* art. 2–3.
98. *Id.* art. 8–9.
99. *Id.* art. 5.
100. *Id.* art. 1.
101. *Id.* art. 14.

but a breaching vessel that had (or was presumed to have) such knowledge would be subject to confiscation of its cargo.[102] Neutral vessels could only be captured in the area of a blockade for breaching it; blockades could not be implemented over neutral ports or coasts; and ships could not be captured if they were heading for a nonblockaded port, even if their ultimate destination was a blockaded port.[103]

Under the London Declaration, goods were broken into the three categories: absolute contraband[104] (always seizable as directly war-related materials); conditional contraband (seizable if "susceptible" to war use), which included items such as foodstuffs, clothing, animal food, money, vehicles, vessels, fuel, horseshoes, and harnesses);[105] and noncontraband (never seizable), which included cotton, wool, rubber, paper, soap, agricultural equipment, items exclusively for the sick and wounded, and feathers. This declaration was not ratified by a majority of the belligerents in the war, but was a point of reference for neutrals such as the United States in asking that naval belligerents like the United Kingdom and Germany adhere to it.

There were several parts to the British strategy of blockading Germany and its allies. First, the Royal Navy would patrol the North Sea (as the French would do in the Mediterranean and Adriatic Seas to blockade Austria-Hungary), stopping any ships suspected of carrying prohibited materials. Second, there were contraband lists, which contained those items that would not be allowed into Germany and so could be seized. Third, there were minefields laid by the Royal Navy, to deter both enemy ships and also those of neutral countries sending contraband to Germany. Ships of neutral nations could get inspected in a British or neutral port for contraband, and, when approved, they would be safely guided through the minefields. Fourth, the North Sea was declared a British military area by the Admiralty (under First Lord Winston Churchill), subjecting both German and neutral ships to blockade rules.[106]

The blockade was not a plan that was complete from the start, but was repeatedly modified, based on what the British discovered and on the responses

---

102. *Id.* art. 21.
103. *Id.* art. 17–19.
104. *Id.* art. 22.
105. *Id.* art. 24.
106. British Admiralty, Declaration of North Sea War Zone, Nov. 3, 1914 (U.K.).

of the Germans and of neutral countries. The British adopted the London Declaration but revised it several times with regard to what was contraband and how ships could be seized.[107] These revisions included making "conditional contraband" into "absolute contraband," seizing ships heading not directly to blockaded ports ("continuous voyage"), and requiring inspected ships to travel to a port for inspection. Items that were added to contraband included those that were controlled by the German government when rationing was implemented, so rationed foodstuffs became contraband. After Germany declared the seas around the British Isles a military region,[108] the British blockade practice was changed: they began to seize all German goods regardless of the port of origin and to capture any merchant ships coming from or going to German ports, and they expanded the list of contraband.[109] Ultimately, it was the interdiction of neutral ships with goods potentially going to Germany that was the key to the blockade's success, so the United Kingdom had to maintain good relations while enforcing an effective blockade, which was not easily done.

To convince neutral countries not to ship contraband goods to Germany, the British Foreign Ministry tried to negotiate agreements with the principal countries involved: Sweden, Denmark, Norway, and the Netherlands. It was perhaps most focused on the goods flowing through the port of Rotterdam, but the government of the Netherlands would not agree to British terms, for fear of showing partiality and so violating its neutrality. Considering what had happened with the invasion of neutral neighbor Belgium, this was a real concern. So instead, the United Kingdom was able to conclude a nongovernmental agreement with the Netherlands Overseas Trust (NOT; *Nederlandsche Overzee Trustmaatschappij),* which accepted pledges from private shipping companies regarding use of contraband goods only in the Netherlands. The NOT board provided these to the British government.

Besides negotiating with the other northern European neutral countries to limit exports to Germany and the need to continually revise its contraband lists, Britain participated in a number of other blockade-related activities, includ-

---

107. Order in Council, Declaration of London, Aug. 20, 1914, Order in Council, Declaration of London No. 2, Oct. 29, 1914; Proclamation Regarding Contraband, Aug. 4, 1914, Additions to List of Contraband, Sept. 21, 1914, Revision of List of Contraband, Oct. 29, 1914 and Dec. 23, 1914 (U.K.).
108. Chief of Marine Staff Von Pohl, Declaration of Blockade around the United Kingdom, Feb. 4, 1915 (Ger.).
109. Order in Council, Mar. 15, 1915 (U.K.).

ing granting export licenses. To oversee much of this activity, the Ministry of Blockade was created in February 1916. This ministry was responsible for coordinating all the activities in the Foreign Ministry and elsewhere, including ensuring that European neutrals did not import more than their prewar levels (a sure sign that they were acting as a transshipment point to belligerents); that British financial firms did not provide credits to neutrals engaged in restricted trade; that other British entities did not export to the enemy; and that American exports to the European neutrals during U.S. neutrality were delivered according to a preapproved process.

The United Kingdom and France later moved away from the London Declaration completely and extended the blockade of neutrals. They seized contraband from neutral vessels bound for neutral ports if the goods were eventually destined for a Central Power.[110] Later, they reversed the burden of proof in such cases so that all ships came under suspicion unless they could prove their destination port was neutral[111] (previously, the burden of proof had been on the interceptor, with destination provable merely by paperwork). After the Russian withdrawal and American entry into the war,[112] they extended these practices even further, seizing all exports from neutral European countries. The Russian withdrawal meant that Britain no longer needed the goodwill of Scandinavian countries for transshipment of supplies to Russia. (See Chapter 3 for a discussion of European neutrality during the war.)

LEGAL PROFILES

Robert Cecil was the British minister of blockade. He was born in England in 1864, the son of a prime minister, and obtained his legal training there. He was engaged in practice from 1887 to 1906, including becoming queen's counsel in 1899. In 1906 he was first elected to the House of Commons, where he would remain, with a brief exception, until 1923. After serving with the Red Cross at the start of the war, he

---

110. Order in Council, Mar. 30, 1916 (U.K.).
111. Order in Council, Maritime Rights, July 7, 1916 (U.K.).
112. Order in Council, Oct. 18, 1917 (U.K.).

joined the Foreign Ministry, where he remained during the rest of the war. He became minister of blockade in 1916 and performed this role through mid-1918. After the war, in 1923, he was the Lord Privy Seal and became a peer. From 1919 on, he was heavily involved in negotiating for and supporting, in various roles, the League of Nations during its entire lifetime. He received the Nobel Peace Prize for these actions in 1937. He died in 1958.[113]

B. Cases

When a vessel is captured by a blockade, it may then be confiscated, declared a "prize," and the vessel and its cargo become subject to the rulings of a prize court. The first case discusses one such case that went through the British prize court and was appealed up to the Privy Council. The second case concerns an American ship that was seized by the British as part of its blockade efforts to keep contraband out of Germany and the decades-long effort to receive compensation for the seizure.

1. SS Zamora

In the SS *Zamora* case, the Privy Council reviewed the British prize court decision regarding a Swedish ship seized in 1915.[114] The ship was captured by the British on April 8, 1915, as it sailed from New York to Stockholm and was taken to a British port and seized as a prize. A writ was issued for confiscation of both cargo and vessel. The cargo was copper, considered contraband belonging to the enemy and allegedly heading to an enemy port, although there was no proof of this. The War Department requisitioned the copper, under an order in council for rules of the prize courts,[115] which in turn was based on statute.[116] Owned by the Swedish Trading Company, the cargo had not been condemned as contraband before being requisitioned (and paid for). The appellants argued that requisition was available only for "naval stores"

---

113. *See Robert Gascoyne Cecil*, Oxford Dictionary of National Biography 101032335.
114. *In re* Part Cargo *ex* SS Zamora, Judicial Committee of the Privy Council (Apr. 7, 1916).
115. Order in Council, Prize Court Rules, Mar. 23, 1915 (U.K.).
116. Prize Court Act of 1894, 57 & 58 Vict., c. 39 (U.K.).

(absolute contraband), which did not include copper, even though copper was used heavily by the navy.

The Crown had argued before the prize court that it had the right to requisition the goods, stating that under common law it had "in times of public danger the prerogative right of entering upon and seizing for military or naval purposes all lands or chattels within the jurisdiction." But this claim was rejected as inapplicable to the prize courts, which operated under international, not municipal, law. The Crown also advocated that the prize court could order vessels or cargo to be requisitioned at the behest of the Crown, including before condemnation or after an appraisal. So in the analysis of the Privy Court, a discussion point was whether this rule was required to be followed, and if not, under what circumstances the War Office could requisition seized cargo.

The Privy Council looked back to the prize court rule-enabling statute and found that it granted the court power to create only procedural rules that would take effect after a judge had determined that the requisition of a vessel or its goods was based on a power originating from a different source. The Crown had said that this source was the Royal Prerogative (see Chapter 3), but the Privy Council rejected this idea, saying, inter alia, the law of prize courts was international law, which could not be defined by the Royal Prerogative. Orders in council were to be given appropriate weight but "short of treating it as an authoritative and binding declaration of law." So the rule that the Crown could requisition goods was not a requirement for prize courts.

Instead, based on international law, the Privy Council held that the right to requisition the goods and vessels of neutrals was "not an absolute right, but a right exercisable in certain circumstances and for certain purposes only." Under its reasoning, the right of requisition should generally be exercised after a captured vessel has been brought to a prize court for adjudication. There needs to be an urgent requirement for the vessel or the goods in defense of the realm or prosecution of the war, as determined by the prize court. Because in the case described, the prize court did not have sufficient evidence that the right was exercisable (i.e., that there was an urgent national need for the goods), the ruling of the prize court ordering the requisition of the copper was reversed by the Privy Council.

LEGAL PROFILES

Samuel Thomas Evans was the president of the British prize court during the war. He was born in Wales in 1859 and obtained his legal training there. He was in private practice in Wales and became a queen's counsel in 1903 (the final one appointed during the reign of Queen Victoria). He was elected to the House of Commons in 1890, where he would serve until 1910. In 1908, he was appointed as the solicitor general of the United Kingdom. In 1910, he left Parliament to become president of the High Court of Justice, Probate, Divorce and Admiralty Division (in Prize), the position he held during the decision described in this section. He died in 1918.[117]

Robert John Parker presented the Privy Council's opinion in *Zamora*. He was born in England in 1857 and obtained his legal training there. He started to practice in 1883. He later worked as a junior equity counsel to the Treasury from 1900 to 1906. He was then appointed to the High Court, where he served until 1913. In 1913, he was made a Lord of Appeal, the position he held when the *Zamora* opinion was rendered. In 1916, he became president of the Judiciary Committee of the Privy Council. He served in this appeals role until his death in 1918.[118]

2. SS Lisman

The case of the SS *Lisman* involves another neutral vessel, this time American, that was carrying contraband cargo.[119] Leased from another company along with three other ships by Interocean Transportation Company of America, it sailed from New York on May 22, 1915, after being inspected by the British consul general. Its cargo was to be partly offloaded in London and then partly offloaded in Rotterdam. Its cargo to Rotterdam was consigned to several individuals as well as to the Netherlands Overseas Trust (NOT), but without

---

117. *See Samuel Thomas Evans*, OXFORD DICTIONARY OF NATIONAL BIOGRAPHY 101033043.
118. *See Robert John Parker*, OXFORD DICTIONARY OF NATIONAL BIOGRAPHY 101035388.
119. SS Lisman, U.K.-U.S., Disposal of Pecuniary Claims Arising out of the Recent War (1914–1918) (Oct. 5, 1937).

NOT's knowledge or consent to this consignment. The bill of lading included the provision that in case of war, the goods could be offloaded at any port if the voyage became unsafe.

When it arrived in London on June 9, the Contraband Committee examined its cargo list and required that the *Lisman*'s phosphate of soda be offloaded and placed with the prize court and that the contraband goods being shipped to individuals in the Netherlands be reconsigned to NOT or offloaded in London. NOT refused to accept the reconsignment without a significant financial guarantee. Interocean's attempts to get the ship released were unsuccessful, and the ship finally discharged all of its contraband, which was then seized for the prize court. The ship was allowed to depart on July 9. Its sister ship had a similar experience, and as a result, the lightly funded company was forced into bankruptcy on September 27, 1915.

Originally the solicitors, and later the bankruptcy trustee for Interocean, had filed a claim for the seized goods in the British prize court. The grounds for the claim included that the *Lisman* was a neutral ship going from and to neutral ports; that it had named consignees in Rotterdam; that it had been inspected by the British consul general with affidavits of no re-export from the consignees; and that it had been unduly detained (thirty-two days instead of the nine days offloading should have taken), leading to loss of business, reputation, and credit and ultimately to bankruptcy. The prize court ultimately ruled in November 1919 and rejected the claims, as it found no unlawful seizure or detention, as it was admitted that all the contraband or enemy property or goods being shipped to Germany were liable for seizure.

Instead of appealing, the trustee chose to utilize diplomatic channels, but the U.S. State Department did not forward the message to the British. Under a 1927 agreement to settle war claims, the United States was allowed to stand in the stead of the United Kingdom for valid claims by American nationals that had not been satisfied in British claims courts. This meant that those with claims who had exhausted their remedies in the British prize courts, because the prize courts had disregarded principles of international law or that the possible remedies offered were illusory, now had a forum for their claim. The trustee's claim was examined, but the United States also rejected the claims, after the trustee took a wholly inconsistent position from the original claim (that the seizure and detention were lawful) and did not appeal the prize court's ruling. After this rejection, the State Department and the trustee agreed to arbitration. The arbitrator found only a single question for consideration—

whether there had been a denial of justice—but felt the prior decisions were appropriate and that there was no merit in the claim and so rejected it.

LEGAL PROFILES

Joseph Chappell Hutcheson Jr. was the arbitrator in the *Lisman* case. He was born in Texas in 1879 and obtained his legal training there. He was in private practice from 1900 until 1918. He also served as counsel to the city of Houston from 1913 to 1917 and as mayor of that city from 1917 to 1918. In 1918, he was appointed to the federal district court in the Southern District of Texas. In 1930, he was appointed to the bench of the Fifth Circuit of Appeals, the position he held when acting as an arbitrator for this case. He was chief judge of the circuit court from 1948 to 1953, assuming senior status in 1964. He died in 1973.[120]

C. Subsequent Events

After the war ended, unlike in WWII, Germany was not occupied. There was nothing preventing Germany from restarting hostilities, despite the armistice being in place. To ensure German follow-through on its commitment to end the war, the blockade of Germany was kept in place until the signing of the Versailles Treaty (see Chapter 7). The success of the blockade employed by the British was spelled out in a memorandum to the cabinet: "All the evidence tends to show that, with some minor exceptions, practically no goods coming from overseas are getting through to Germany."[121] The varied tactics included rationing neutral states based on prewar import levels and the Navicert preapproval system used by Americana shippers. Where these devices failed, the memorandum stated, "Our only plan is to detain the goods as long as possible, and, if necessary, put them in the Prize Court."[122] This memo also described tactics used to stop exports of select products to Germany from neighboring

---

120. *See Joseph C. Hutcheson* Jr., FED. JUDICIAL CTR., BIOGRAPHICAL DIRECTORY OF FEDERAL JUDGES.
121. Memorandum to U.K. War Cabinet in Regard to the Present Position of the Blockade, First Lord of the Admiralty Edward Carson (Jan. 1, 1917).
122. *Id.*

neutral countries. These strategies included not exporting butter to Sweden and then prohibiting exports of Swedish butter to Germany; buying up Norway's fishing catch (normally headed to Germany); and controlling the copper market sufficiently to force Norway into an agreement to swap copper imports for German-bound pyrite exports.

The effect of the blockade on Germany was devastating. Imports fell by more than half. Intercepted goods included not only war materials but also imported foodstuffs and the fertilizers used to grow food. And many of the farm laborers went off to war as well. This led to a drastic decline in caloric intake from many staples of the prewar German diet. Upward of one million people in Germany died from malnutrition during and after the war. Germans ended up eating the plentiful radishes as a substitute for other vegetables and created a new kind of bread, the *kriegsbrot* ("war bread," made of rye, wheat, and potato meal).

It is uncertain how decisive a role the blockade played in the ultimate surrender of Germany, but in any analysis, its impact on both the military and civilian populations of the Central Powers was very significant. In addition, due to the lack of nutrition and the privations of war, Germans may have been more susceptible to the "Spanish flu" pandemic that hit Europe starting in 1918 (see Chapter 7). This led to perhaps half a million more deaths in Germany compared to the normal mortality levels, with Europe as a whole suffering up to three million additional deaths during the height of the pandemic. The global impact of this disease was an estimated forty million or more deaths—the most lethal pandemic known in human history.[123]

LEGAL PROFILES

Edward Carson signed the blockade memorandum to the cabinet and also presented the Crown's case to the prize court in *Zamora*. He was born in Ireland in 1854 and obtained his legal training there. He started his legal career in 1877 and became a queen's counsel in 1889. He was involved in a number of famous cases, including the libel suit by Oscar

---

123. *See* Ansart et al., *Mortality Burden of the 1918–1919 Influenza Pandemic in Europe*, 3 INFLUENZA AND OTHER RESPIRATORY VIRUSES 99 (2009).

Wilde. In 1892, he was elected to the British House of Commons and in 1900 became solicitor general, a role he held through 1905. In 1914 he was appointed as the attorney general, the position from which he presented the *Zamora* case. In 1917 he became first lord of the Admiralty, the role he held during the blockade memorandum. In 1921 he was appointed as a lord of appeal. He was also heavily involved in the Unionist (Ulster) cause and was a vociferous opponent of Irish home rule (see Chapter 6). He died in 1935.[124]

D. Modern Applicability

The use of blockade has continued in modern wars. Despite the increased use of airplanes to deliver supplies, the majority of items that do not get sent overland by rail or road are still delivered via ships on the seas. From the Cuban missile crisis to the Vietnam War to the Falklands War to NATO's war on Serbia regarding Kosovo to the 2003 Iraq War to the blockade of Hezbollah in Lebanon in 2006, blockades or embargoes have been used in modern times to prevent supplies from reaching belligerents. These have typically been less of a total blockade than those used during WWI. Blockades are still being used, for example, by the Israelis to blockade Hamas in Gaza.

The law regulating blockades has changed, moving in part from its traditional place as customary international law to being supported by mention in the UN Charter, as an action that the UN Security Council may undertake in its role to maintain or restore peace and security.[125] But as Security Council actions place the whole UN membership against a single offending nation, leaving no neutral parties, the situation is quite different than a war with just a few belligerents and many neutral nations. Another modern effort to bring shape to the law of blockades was the San Remo Manual.[126] This treatise, although not legally binding, states that, inter alia, attempts to starve populations or secondary impacts that produce starvation are no longer permissible under modern customary international law of blockades.

---

124. *See Edward Carson*, Oxford Dictionary of National Biography 101032310.
125. UN Charter, art. 42.
126. International Institute of Humanitarian Law, San Remo Manual on International Law Applicable to Armed Conflicts at Sea (1994).

The intentional starvation of civilian populations is a tool of warfare still practiced in the modern world. In 2012, the leaders of the country of Sudan were charged with not only bombing but with intentionally starving the civilian populations of their country living in those regions straddling the border with the breakaway nation of South Sudan.[127] These acts included the expelling of aid workers, the interception of food for the starving people in the region, and bombings done without regards to non-combatants being targeted. The 2005 peace accord that had brought an end to the decades-long civil war in Sudan left several contested areas along the border, some which continued to be used as bases by forces loyal to the non-occupying nation.

2.5 UNRESTRICTED SUBMARINE WARFARE

A. Statutes

In response to Britain's blockade (and partly out of realization that it could not compete with the United Kingdom's surface fleet, especially after the Battle of the Falklands), Germany issued its own declaration on February 4, 1915, making the area around the United Kingdom a war region. It announced it would sink British, French, and Russian ships in this area without notice.[128] Neutral ships were also at risk there, due to the dangers of both being in a war region and also the British government's alleged direction to misuse neutral country flags for its shipping. The declaration was issued by the German chief of marine (naval) staff and supported by the chancellor and the kaiser as well as the Foreign Ministry but opposed by the naval minister, Alfred von Tirpitz. It was to begin on February 18, 1915. When the neutral countries, especially the United States, strongly protested this policy, the German Foreign Ministry withdrew the declaration.

So began a two-year set of back-and-forth diplomatic exchanges between Germany and the United States, the former trying to keep America out of the war and the latter trying to stay out. The initial response from Washington to Berlin was termed the "Strict Accountability" warning. The administration of

---

127. *See Starving Its Own Children*, N.Y. Times (June 2, 2012).
128. Chief of Marine Staff Von Pohl, Declaration of Blockade around the United Kingdom, Feb. 4, 1915 (Ger.).

U.S. President Woodrow Wilson, six days later, sent the following message to the German foreign minister:

> [The U.S. Government] requests the Imperial German Government to consider, before action is taken, the critical situation in respect of the relation between this country and Germany—which might arise were the German naval force, in carrying out the policy foreshadowed in the Admiralty's proclamation, to destroy any merchant vessel of the United States or cause the death of American citizens. It is, of course, not necessary to remind the German Government that the sole right of a belligerent in dealing with neutral vessels on the high seas is limited to visit and search, unless a blockade is proclaimed and effectively maintained, which this Government does not understand to be proposed in this case. To declare or exercise a right to attack and destroy any vessel entering a prescribed area of the high seas without first certainly determining its belligerent nationality and the contraband character of its cargo would be an act so unprecedented in naval warfare that this government is reluctant to believe that the Imperial Government of Germany in this case contemplates it as possible. . . .
>
> If the commanders of German vessels of war should act upon the presumption that the flag of the United States was not being used in good faith and should destroy on the high seas an American vessel or the lives of American citizens, . . . the Government of the United States would be constrained to hold the Imperial Government of Germany to a strict accountability for such acts of their naval authorities, and to take any steps it might be necessary to take to safeguard American lives and property and to secure to American citizens the full enjoyment of their acknowledged rights on the high seas.[129]

This did not mean that there would be no U-boat activity or American fatalities. On March 28, 1915, a U-boat sank the British passenger ship SS *Falaba* without warning off the coast of Africa, killing an American citizen.

---

129. Note from U.S. Secretary of State Bryan to Germany Foreign Minister von Jagow (Feb. 10, 1915).

President Wilson, however, did not respond. On May 1, the U.S. tanker SS *Gulflight* was torpedoed, with three American deaths. Then, on May 7, the RMS *Lusitania* was sunk by a German U-boat. With more than a thousand deaths, and more than a hundred of them American, President Wilson had to respond. He did so over the course of several messages of protest to the German government. In the first, sent through the U.S. secretary of state and the ambassador to Germany, he recalled these and other attacks on shipping that had caused American deaths. He also pointed out the impossibility of using submarines for the role of searching merchant ships suspected of hiding their true nationality or carrying contraband cargo. He then tried to shift the blame to allow the German government room to disavow the sinking: "Long acquainted as this government has been with the character of the Imperial German government and with the high principles of equity by which they have in the past been actuated and guided, the government of the United States cannot believe that the commanders of the vessels which committed these acts of lawlessness did so except under a misapprehension of the orders issued by the Imperial German naval authorities."[130]

The German foreign minister Gottlieb von Jagow replied[131] by defending each of the mentioned incidents but then focused on the *Lusitania*. He made several points supporting his contention that this ship was not an unarmed merchant ship. First, he noted the role of the ship as an auxiliary cruiser and its placement on the navy list and initial funding by the British government. He then noted that such ships had masked guns and alluded to a British policy of using neutral flags, of ramming submarines, and getting rewarded for doing so. As such, Germany could no longer consider such ships in the declared war zone as subject to the standard practice of "stop and search." He also noted that the ship had been carrying Canadian troops and a significant amount of ammunition, proven by the explosions that had led to its quick sinking (and the resultant high loss of life). As such, Germany felt justified in having sunk such a ship in self-defense.

Wilson then followed up with another message, in which he informed the German government that it had been misinformed about the military capabil-

---

130. Note from U.S. Secretary of State Bryan to German Foreign Minister von Jagow through U.S. Ambassador to Germany Gerard (May 13, 1915).
131. Note from German Foreign Minister Gottlieb von Jagow to U.S. Ambassador Gerard (May 28, 1915).

ity of the *Lusitania*, otherwise the United States would have been negligent in clearing such a vessel from a U.S. port as a neutral merchant vessel. He also said the ship was not a troop transport and was not carrying any cargo in violation of U.S. laws: "Only her actual resistance to capture or refusal to stop when ordered to do so for the purpose of visit could have afforded the commander of the submarine any justification for so much as putting the lives of those on board the ship in jeopardy."[132] More than a month later, Wilson sent another message to Germany, this time with stronger language: "Repetition by the commanders of German naval vessels of acts in contravention of those rights must be regarded by the Government of the United States, when they affect American citizens, as deliberately unfriendly."[133]

When a U-boat sank another British ship, SS *Arabic*, on August 19, 1915, and two Americans were among the forty-four deaths, Wilson insisted that unless Germany wanted to break off diplomatic relations with the United States, it had to cease the sinking of passenger ships without warning. Finally, on September 1, the Germans agreed not to target passenger ships that did not try to resist. But this left open the possibility for U-boats to attack merchant ships in addition to warships. One such attack occurred on the English Channel ferry SS *Sussex* in April 1916, again without warning and with Americans among the eighty fatalities.

This attack led Wilson to protest to Germany that "the Government of the United States has been very patient. At every stage of this distressing experience of tragedy after tragedy. . . . It has accepted the successive explanations and assurances of the Imperial Government. . . . It has made every allowance for unprecedented conditions. . . . If it is still the purpose of the Imperial Government to prosecute relentless and indiscriminate warfare against vessels of commerce by the use of submarines . . . the Government of the United States is at last forced to the conclusion that there is but one course it can pursue. . . . Unless the Imperial Government should now immediately declare and effect an abandonment of its present methods of submarine warfare against passenger and freight-carrying vessels, the Government of the United States

---

132. Note from U.S. Secretary of State Lansing to German Foreign Minister von Jagow (June 9, 1915).
133. Note from U.S. Secretary of State Lansing to German Foreign Minister von Jagow (July 21, 1915).

can have no choice but to sever diplomatic relations with the German Empire altogether."[134]

Von Jagow replied by pointing out that the British had continually flouted international law. He compared the millions of Germans whom the Allied Powers had intended to starve with the hundreds lost in U-boat attacks. He did relay, however, that U-boats would then be told that merchant vessels, wherever located, "shall not be sunk without warning and without saving human lives unless the ship attempts to escape or offer resistance."[135] But the use of unrestricted submarine warfare was to arise again in early 1917. By then, the situation for Germany was becoming militarily and economically desperate. The U-boat attacks may have offered their only path out of the strangling blockade being deployed by the British. There was a bit of a gamble to be taken: that by redeclaring unlimited submarine warfare—knowing that it would cause the Americans to break off diplomatic relations and declare war—the British could be defeated before the Americans could fully deploy in Europe, and perhaps the war could be thus brought to a successful conclusion.

So on January 31, 1917, Germany, through its ambassador to the U.S. Johann von Bernstorff, announced that it was resuming unrestricted submarine warfare the next day. This entailed a blockade of Great Britain, France, Italy, and the eastern Mediterranean Sea and applied to both belligerent and neutral shipping within these blockade zones. All such ships would be sunk. Germany cited the lack of progress in peace negotiations (see Chapter 7), and the poor wheat harvest necessitating the urgent need for food imports. Increased submarine production supporting unrestricted submarine attacks would disrupt shipments of coal, timber, and iron ore to the Allied Powers and could bring them to conclude a viable peace. As he had threatened in his message of the year before, President Wilson then gave instructions to break off diplomatic relations between the United States and Germany. Declarations of war would follow within two months (see Chapter 4).

---

134. Note from U.S. Secretary of State Lansing to German Foreign Minister von Jagow (Apr. 18, 1916).
135. Note from German Foreign Minister von Jagow to U.S. Secretary of State Lansing (May 4, 1916).

LEGAL PROFILES

William Jennings Bryan was the U.S. secretary of state who responded to the U-boat attacks in 1915. He was born in Illinois in 1860 but started his legal practice in Nebraska. His wife also became a lawyer (and their daughter was later elected to Congress). In 1890, he was first elected to the U.S. House of Representatives, where he served two terms. In 1896, he ran, as the youngest major-party candidate ever, for the office of U.S. president. Backing free silver and opposing the gold standard, he was defeated by William McKinley. Running again in 1900, he lost a second time to McKinley. Again in 1908, he tried to be elected president, only to lose to William Howard Taft. When Woodrow Wilson was elected president in 1912, he chose Bryan as secretary of state. Bryan remained in that position until resigning over the responses sent in the *Lusitania* sinking. A populist known as the "Great Commoner," one of the great public speakers of the era, and a supporter of Prohibition, he campaigned for the Eighteenth Amendment, which passed in 1918. He also was passionately opposed to Darwinism, including evolution and social Darwinism, and gave many speeches on it in the 1920s, culminating in the famous *Scopes* "monkey" trial in 1925 and his tête-à-tête with defense attorney Clarence Darrow. He died in 1925, just a few days after the end of the *Scopes* trial.[136]

James W. Gerard was the U.S. ambassador to Germany during the *Lusitania* sinking. He was born in New York in 1867 and obtained his legal training there. During the Spanish-American War, he served in Cuba. He was elected to the New York Supreme Court in 1909. In 1913, he was appointed as the U.S. ambassador to Germany. He served in this role until the severing of diplomatic relations with Germany in 1917, including spending time visiting and comforting those in prisoner-of-war camps and representing the Allied Power governments to the German government during America's neutrality. In 1914, he had defeated Franklin D. Roosevelt in the Democratic primary for a U.S. Senate seat

---

136. *See* Bryan, William Jennings, BIOGRAPHICAL DIRECTORY OF THE UNITED STATES CONGRESS.

(but had lost in the general election). After WWI, he returned to his legal practice. He was also active in war relief efforts globally during both WWI and WWII, and in other philanthropic activities. He died in 1951.[137]

B. Cases

The sinking of the *Lusitania* gave rise to a number of different legal adjudications in varied forums, including inquests by the Board of Trade in the United Kingdom, court trials in the United States, and international committees sitting in arbitration of unresolved claims, some of which occurred during the conflict and some after the war. Additionally, there was the case of the British merchant captain who followed the Admiralty's directions to resist U-boats and his subsequent capture and court-martial by Germany.

1. The Lusitania: British Court of Inquiry

The Mersey Court of Inquiry, named after wreck commissioner Lord Mersey, examined the various positions of responsibility for the sinking and reported these to Parliament.[138] Its overall conclusion was clear: that "the loss of the said ship and lives was due to damage caused to the said ship by torpedoes fired by a submarine of German nationality whereby the ship sank. In the opinion of the Court the act was done not merely with the intention of sinking the ship, but also with the intention of destroying the lives of the people on board." The court's investigation looked into several major aspects of the planned trip from New York to Liverpool, including the ship itself, the voyage, the navigation of the ship, and the torpedoing of the ship.

The British Board of Trade had ordered this inquiry and had put a number of questions to the court. The court issued findings in answer to each of these questions. The important questions and answers that focused on whether the sinking had a legal basis are excerpted below:

---

137. *See James W. Gerard, 84, Dies; Envoy to Germany 1913–17*, N.Y. TIMES (Sept. 7, 1951).
138. Loss of the Steamship *Lusitania*, Report of a Formal Investigation into the circumstances attending the foundering on 7th May, 1915, of the British Steamship *Lusitania*, of Liverpool, after being torpedoed off the Old Head of Kinsale, Ireland, Wreck Commissioner's Court of Inquiry (July 17, 1915).

1. When the *Lusitania* left New York on 1st May, 1915 . . . (b) Were there any troops on board? *No.*

2. Did the *Lusitania* before leaving New York comply with the requirements of the Merchant Shipping Acts, 1894 and 1906,[139] and the Rules and regulations made thereunder? *Yes.*

9. Before and at the time the *Lusitania* was attacked . . . (e) What flag was the *Lusitania* flying? *None.*

10. Before the submarine made the attack (a) Was any, and if so, what warning given to the *Lusitania* by the submarine of her presence or intention to attack, or was any, and if so, what signal was given or communication made by the submarine to the *Lusitania*? *No.* (b) Was any, and if so, what request made by the submarine to the *Lusitania* to stop? *No.* (c) Was any, and if so, what opportunity given to any persons on board the *Lusitania* to leave her? *No.*

11. Was any, and if so, what action taken by those on board the *Lusitania* before she was attacked (1) To escape from the submarine? (2) To resist visit or search? (3) To avoid capture? *No such action was taken.*

12. Was the *Lusitania* armed? If so, how was she armed? *No.*

14. Did any cargo or other thing on board the *Lusitania* explode or ignite or increase the damage caused by the torpedo? *No cargo or other thing exploded or ignited.*

19. What was the cause of the loss of the *Lusitania*? What caused the loss of life? *The loss of the* Lusitania *and the loss of life was caused by the sinking of the ship by torpedoes from a submarine.*

---

139. Merchant Shipping Act of 1906, 6 Edw. 7, c. 48 (U.K.).

LEGAL PROFILES

John Bigham, Lord Mersey, was the British wreck commissioner heading the inquiry into the *Lusitania* sinking. He was born in England in 1840 and obtained his legal training there. He developed a commercial law practice around his native Liverpool, becoming a queen's counsel in 1883. After several unsuccessful attempts, he was elected to Parliament in 1895. He left politics in 1897 when he was named a judge on the Queen's Bench. In 1909 he was named to head the Probate, Divorce, and Admiralty division of the court but resigned after a year. In 1912 he was appointed to head the commission of inquiry investigating the sinking of RMS *Titanic*. In 1914 he had the same role investigating the sinking of RMS *Empress of Ireland* and in 1915 heading the *Lusitania* commission. He continued to judge periodically and died in 1929.[140]

F. E. (Frederick Edwin) Smith was the British solicitor general representing the Board of Trade during the inquiry into the *Lusitania* sinking. He was born in England in 1872 and obtained his legal training there. He became a king's counsel in 1908, two years after he was finally elected to Parliament after several unsuccessful attempts. He remained in the Commons until 1919, when he was elevated to the House of Lords. In 1915 he was appointed as the solicitor general, the position he held during the *Lusitania* inquest. Later, in 1915, he was appointed attorney general. After the war, he became lord chancellor in 1919, a position he held until late 1922. In 1924 he became the secretary of state for India and served until 1928. He died in 1930.[141]

---

140. *See John Charles Bigham*, OXFORD DICTIONARY OF NATIONAL BIOGRAPHY 101031884.
141. *See Frederick Edwin Smith*, OXFORD DICTIONARY OF NATIONAL BIOGRAPHY 101036137.

2. The Lusitania: U.S. Trial

The sinking of the *Lusitania* brought many lawsuits, so the owner of the ship, the Cunard Steamship Company, sought to have its liability limited by petitioning in U.S. federal court.[142] More specifically, it sought to ascertain that the company (petitioner) was "not liable for any loss or damage arising out of the attack on, or the sinking of, the *Lusitania*, but that if the court shall adjudge the petitioner is liable, then that the court limit the petitioner's liability to its interest in the *Lusitania* and her pending freight."[143]

One way of limiting this liability was via the contract printed on each ticket between the passengers and the steamship company, which stated, "The Company will use all reasonable means to insure the ship being sent to sea in a seaworthy state and well found, but is not otherwise liable for loss of, or injury to, the passenger or his luggage, or delay in the voyage, whether arising from act of God, King's enemies, perils of the sea, rivers or navigation, barratry or negligence of the Company's servants (whether on board the steamer or ashore) defect in the steamer, her machinery, gear or fittings or from any other cause of whatsoever nature."[144]

Cunard asserted that this contract limited its liability because the sinking of the ship had clearly been caused by the German U-boat's torpedo. The company could not be held liable for negligent acts based on an intervening illegal act by a third party. The claimants alleged several acts of negligence that had exposed the ship to attack. The petitioner responded that even if there had been acts of negligence, which it denied, it was the torpedoing of the ship that was the proximate cause of the sinking. These included many of the same issues covered by the British Wreck Commissioners Court involving where negligence could be found, such as the preparing and then lowering of the boats before and after the torpedoing. One alleged act of negligence was the captain ignoring the instructions of the Admiralty regarding zig-zagging (turning in short arcs or at right angles), but as the practice was understood in 1915, it was "better adapted to an armed naval vessel whose destination is not known than to an unarmed passenger vessel whose destination was well known."[145]

---

142. *In re* Cunard SS Co. Ltd. as Owners of SS Lusitania for Limitation of Liability, 251 F. 715 (S.D.N.Y. 1918).
143. *Id.*, Brief on the Facts for the Petitioner, at 1.
144. *Id.* at 2.
145. *Id.* at 67.

In its opinion, the court found that the ship was not armed and did not contain explosives. The minimal amount of ammunition could not have caused an explosion, leading to its rapid sinking but instead found that two torpedoes struck the ship. It found no fault with any of the procedures utilized on the voyage, for example, in regards to the deployment of the life boats. All important port holes and watertight doors had been closed. The launching of the lifeboats went as well as could be expected, given the significant listing of the ship to the starboard side after the torpedo struck. The crew had had adequate training. In all of these areas of possible negligence, the court found none.

Then the court focused on what it termed "the only debatable question of fact in the case, *i.e.*, whether Captain Turner was negligent in not literally following the Admiralty advices and, also, in not taking a course different from that which he adopted." The court stated that captains must be allowed to use their judgment while trying to follow the Admiralty advice as closely as possible, which had been "(1) to give the headlands a wide berth; (2) to steer a mid-channel course; (3) to maintain as high a speed as practicable; (4) to zig-zag and (5) to make ports, if possible, at dawn, thus running the last part of the voyage at night." The court focused on the likelihood that an unarmed merchant vessel would, even if it followed all these procedures exactly, have been rather an easy target for a group of submarines lying in wait and so ruled "as a fact, that the captain and, hence, the petitioner, were not negligent."[146]

Even if there had been negligence, the court said there was no liability if the negligence was not the proximate cause of the loss. And it could not be the proximate cause if there had been an intervening illegal act by a third party. The question was, then, was the torpedoing of the *Lusitania* an illegal act? The court declared that international law was clearly part of U.S. law, then looked at how the U.S. government analyzed the legalities. In particular, it looked to the German Foreign Ministry communication of May 4, 1916: "In accordance with the general principles of visit and search and destruction of merchant vessels recognized by international law, such vessels, both within and without the area declared as naval war zone, shall not be sunk without warning and without saving human lives, unless these ships attempt to escape or offer resistance."[147] Looking to American, British, Russian, Japanese, and German

---

146. *Id.*, Opinion of Court.
147. *Id.*

prize codes, the court found them all congruent to the principles. As such, "the cause of the sinking of the *Lusitania* was the illegal act of the Imperial German Government,"[148] and so the court granted the petition and dismissed the claims.

LEGAL PROFILES

Julius M. Mayer was the judge in the *Lusitania* trial in the United States. He was born in New York in 1865 and started his legal career there. He practiced from 1886 to 1912, taking on the role of attorney general for the state of New York in 1903, a role he held for four years. In 1912, he was named to the federal bench in the southern district of New York, where he served during this trial. He remained in this position until he was elevated to the court of appeals for the Second Circuit in 1921. He served in this role for three years until resigning in late 1924. He died in 1925.[149]

Lucius H. Beers was the counsel for the petitioner in the *Lusitania* trial. He was born in New York in 1860 and started his legal practice there. Besides Cunard and other maritime clients that he defended, he also practiced probate law and was involved in a number of high-profile estate cases. During the war, he was part of the navy's antisubmarine board. After the war, besides continuing his practice, he authored legal articles[150] and brought cases before the Supreme Court.[151] He died in 1948.[152]

---

148. *Id.*
149. *See Julius Marshuetz Mayer*, FED. JUDICIAL CTR., BIOGRAPHICAL DIRECTORY OF FEDERAL JUDGES.
150. *See, e.g., Poison Gas or a League of Nations?*, THE OUTLOOK (Feb. 12, 1919).
151. *See, e.g.,* Betts v. United States, 273 U.S. 762 (1926).
152. *See Lucius Beers Dead; Lawyer 65 Years*, N.Y. TIMES (Oct. 3, 1948).

3. The Lusitania: Mixed Claims Commission

After the war, Germany and the United States agreed to create the Mixed Claims Commission to deal with open claims by U.S. nationals against Germany and German nationals arising from the war.[153] Some of those claims were related to the sinking of the *Lusitania*. The commission was set up to deal with the type of claims defined in the Treaty of Berlin[154] (incorporating provisions of the Versailles Treaty) at the end of war (see Chapter 7). Specifically, it was intended to address the claims of American citizens that had arisen since the start of the war for property seized or damaged in Germany, debts owed to Americans by German nationals or the German government, or other claims for loss or damage as a consequence of the war.

The court, in its opinion controlling how individual claims would be addressed,[155] discussed how damages for death (of the *Lusitania*'s passengers) were typically calculated. It noted that at common law, there was no compensation for the death of a human being, but statutes in British law and, later, U.S. state law and the German civil code provided for such compensation, although with widely varying approaches. The common guideline was that awards were granted for the loss to the claimants (i.e., heirs), not to the deceased or to insurance companies.[156]

From these models, the court derived its method for paying the death benefit. Importantly, it did not deduct for any life insurance proceeds received (contrary to the opinion of the German commissioner because life insurance contracts are absolute payment contracts based on premiums paid, not indemnity payments) and it did not allow for punitive damages (contrary to the opinion of the American commissioner because, inter alia, the Treaty of Berlin did not contemplate punitive damages). It calculated the amount due to the

---

153. Agreement between the United States and Germany Providing for the Determination of the Amount of the Claims Against Germany, Aug. 10, 1922, U.S.T.S. 665 (Ger.-U.S.); Agreement Affected by Exchange of Notes between the United States and Germany, Extension of the Jurisdiction of the Mixed Claims Commission–United States and Germany, Dec. 31, 1928, U.S.T.S. 766 (Ger.-U.S.).
154. Treaty of Aug. 25, 1921, U.S.T.S. 658 (Ger.-U.S.).
155. Mixed Claims Commission, United States and Germany, Opinion in the *Lusitania Cases* (Nov. 1, 1923).
156. Provident Mutual Life Insurance Co. and Others v. Germany (Sept. 18, 1924).

individual claimants based on a discounted present value of the sum of the following amounts:[157]

- Which the decedent, had he not been killed, would probably have contributed to the claimant
- The pecuniary value to such claimant of the deceased's personal services in claimant's care, education, or supervision
- Reasonable compensation for such mental suffering or shock, if any, caused by the violent severing of family ties, as claimant may actually have sustained by reason of such death" (contrary to the opinion of the German commissioner, who would accept these type of claims only "if real and actual")

Many claims were awarded, and others were denied. Among those awarded was a claim for loss of life to the survivors of John Page, who at the time of his death had been forty-five years old, in good health, and vice president at the Mark Cross Company, with an annual salary of $2,500, and "His future business prospects were bright."[158] His wife had been fully dependent on him, and they had no dependent children, so she was awarded $80,000 by the commission. Albert Hopkins also perished aboard the *Lusitania*, leaving behind a wife and a young child. He had been the president of a shipbuilding company, with an annual salary of $25,000, and at forty-four years old was described as "healthy, active, and industrious."[159] The commission awarded his wife $50,000 and his daughter $80,000.

There were also awards to survivors. James T. Houghton was a doctor who was going to Belgium to work for the Red Cross treating injured soldiers during the war. He was the son of Warren Houghton, a judge on the New York Supreme Court. He was carrying medical supplies with him to use in his medical practice. He was injured and spent about five hours in the water after the sinking, but he survived. Afterward, he "was unable to practice his profession for more than a year and remained in a nervous state for about two

---

157. Mixed Claims Commission, United States and Germany, Opinion in the *Lusitania Cases*.
158. U.S. *ex rel*. Page v. Germany (Feb. 21, 1924).
159. U.S. *ex rel*. Gilmer v. Germany (Feb. 14, 1924).

years."[160] For his injuries and their impact on his profession, he was paid $9,000, plus an additional award for his lost medical supplies.

The court ruled that the deaths of British nationals who were spouses or parents of American nationals could be compensated under the Treaty of Berlin. Americans with British national spouses or dependents, however, had to seek compensation through the Versailles Treaty. The key was the nationality of the survivor, not the decedent.[161] But there were often more diverse facts. For example, the claim of a surviving spouse who got remarried to a French citizen in 1917 and lost her American citizenship was denied, as claimants needed to be American citizens as of November 11, 1921 (the date of the Treaty of Berlin).[162] This was despite her August 1915 claim to the U.S. secretary of state, before her remarriage. Another American woman lost her U.S. citizenship when she married a British citizen, who later perished on the ship. But she regained her U.S. citizenship on his death, since she resided in the United States (and subsequently married an Ohio lawyer)[163] and so could receive damages.

Even the wealthiest tried to partake of claims for loss and damage. The estate of Alfred G. Vanderbilt, who had perished heroically (offering his life vest to a young mother with an infant even though he himself could not swim) on the *Lusitania* (he had just avoided sailing on the last voyage of the *Titanic* three years earlier), was valued at more than $15 million, but the court could find "no evidence offered of producing power of decedent" (i.e., he had lived off his assets and related income), so no damages were awarded.[164] And the famous theater owner Charles Frohman (Dustin Hoffman's role in the movie *Finding Neverland* about playwright J. M. Barrie and the creation of *Peter Pan*), although a fabulous moneymaker in North America (but not in Europe), had no children or survivors except his older, nondependent siblings, so the siblings' claims were denied.[165]

---

160. U.S. *ex rel*. Houghton v. Germany (Feb. 21, 1924).
161. Administrative Decision No. VI (Jan. 30, 1925).
162. U.S. *ex rel*. De Gennes v. Germany (Mar. 11, 1925).
163. U.S. *ex rel*. Williams v. Germany (Mar. 11, 1925).
164. U.S. *ex rel*. Baker and Vanderbilt v. Germany (Mar. 11, 1925).
165. U.S. *ex rel*. Frohman v. Germany (Sept. 24, 1924).

LEGAL PROFILES

Wilhelm Kiesselbach was the initial German mixed claims commissioner. He was born in Germany in 1867 and obtained his legal training there and in England and America. He practiced in Hamburg, running unsuccessfully for political office. He was named to the Mixed Claims Commission in 1922, serving until 1932. In 1929, he was selected judge of the regional court, but due to differences with the Nazi regime, he was removed in 1933 in the Nazi purge of judges.[166] After WWII, until 1950, he was involved with reorganizing the judiciary around Hamburg, as part of the postwar Allied denazification programs.[167] He died in 1960.[168]

Thomas Bloomfield was a lawyer and a passenger who perished on the *Lusitania*. He was born in England in 1865 but obtained his legal training in the United States and was naturalized in 1892. He was licensed to practice in several states (Illinois, Massachusetts, Minnesota, and New York) and dedicated his practice to insurance-related matters, such as casualty and reinsurance. It was for this business that he was traveling on the *Lusitania*. Although his body was never found, it is assumed that he died on May 7, 1915.[169] His surviving American spouse filed a claim with the Mixed Claims Commission and, based on the facts that they had no children and that he had been fifty years old and had made $6,000 a year, she was awarded $45,000 for the loss of her husband.[170]

4. The Brussels

There was another well-known case dealing with submarine warfare involving the court-martial of Captain Charles Fryatt. An English merchant ship captain, Fryatt was following the orders of the British Admiralty to act aggressively

---

166. *See* WWII LAW AND LAWYERS, ch. 6.
167. *Id.*
168. *See Wilhelm Kiesselbach*, NEUE DEUTSCHE BIOGRAPHIE.
169. *See Fifty New Yorkers Lost in First Cabin*, N.Y. TIMES (May 9, 1915).
170. U.S. *ex rel.* Bloomfield v. Germany (Feb. 21, 1924).

toward submarines if attacked, as he had previously had fended off attacks by U-boats while on his United Kingdom–Netherlands English Channel commercial route. The British Admiralty, after the February 4, 1915, German declaration of the war zone around the British Isles, had on February 10 issued orders that merchant vessels should avoid or, in certain situations, engage hostile submarines: "No British merchant vessel should ever tamely surrender to a submarine, but should do her utmost to escape . . . If the submarine is seen at a distance . . . alter course to bring the boat astern and proceed at full speed. . . . If a submarine comes up suddenly close ahead of you with obvious hostile intention, steer straight for her at your utmost speed. . . . She will probably then dive."[171]

On March 28, 1915, Fryatt was captaining the SS *Brussels* in the English Channel, close to the Maas Lightship on the way to Rotterdam, when it was signaled to stop by German submarine U-33. Fearing that he was about to be torpedoed (correctly, as the log of the U-33's captain states that he had cleared one torpedo tube and intended to fire it), he instead followed one part of the Admiralty's direction and headed toward the submarine, trying to cause it to dive, which it did. For his refusal to surrender his vessel, Fryatt was acclaimed in Parliament, along with other merchant captains.[172] Over the next several months, the *Brussels*, helmed by other captains, was to be attacked by U-boats four more times.

More than one year later, German naval ships surrounded and captured Fryatt, his crew, and his ship SS *Brussels*. Taken to occupied Belgium, he was held, often in isolation, and interrogated. In late July, Fryatt was brought before a court-martial of the German Marine Corps for the attempted sinking of the U-33 (i.e., a civilian taking up arms against the German forces and attempting to cause injury to them). The court, led by Dr. Zäpfel, had appointed Fryatt's counsel, a civilian attorney now Major Neumann, only just before the start of the trial. Using the testimony and affidavits of the officers and sailors on the U-33 and its log book, but not the log book of the *Brussels*, and considering the commendation in Parliament and Fryatt's interrogation answers, but not allowing cross-examination of the U-33's captain, the court convicted Fryatt.

---

171. U.K. Admiralty, Instructions for Owner and Masters of British Merchant Ships Issued with Reference to the Operations of German Submarines against British Shipping (Feb. 10, 1915).
172. Hansard HC Deb 28 Apr. 1915 vol. 71 c698.

He was convicted of being a civilian taking up arms against the military (*franc-tireur*), who had tried to ram the U-33, even though Fryatt would only admit to trying to get the submarine to dive. The *franc-tireur* rules applied to civilians taking up arms against the opponent's military on the land (see Chapter 6) but had not been applied to merchant captains resisting capture on the sea. Fryatt could perhaps have escaped the charge of being a *franc-tireur* by asserting that he had been following the commands of a military authority (the Admiralty) in what he did, as opposed to making his own decisions to resist the U-boat.

It was generally accepted under the prize court rules of the major shipping nations that merchant vessels could resist a "visit" by a warship trying to take them as a prize or sink them. The German prize court rules had a variation, in that armed merchantmen could resist, while unarmed merchant vessels were supposed to submit without resistance. Fryatt was sentenced to be executed. Without any appeal, the sentence was carried out the same day, July 27, 1916. Notice of the death was published on posters in several languages in Bruges by the German military officials.

After the armistice was signed, in 1919 a court of inquiry in the new German government reviewed the Fryatt decision and found it to be correct in its conclusion, by looking at Captain Fryatt's decision to turn toward the submarine. This action was in defiance of the Admiralty orders that had dictated fleeing if there was sufficient time to do so. The court had contended that there had been sufficient time when first sightings had been made with the submarine. Therefore, Fryatt had clearly been trying to ram the submarine and so bring harm to it. The court did note that Captain Fryatt should not have been executed on the same day as his sentencing and that he had had a right of appeal, which he had declined to exercise. There is no mention of a right to appeal in the trial records.

LEGAL PROFILES

Walther Schücking was the head of the postwar court of inquiry that reviewed the Fryatt court-martial. He was born in Germany in 1875 and obtained his legal training there. He became a professor of law, first at the University of Breslau in 1900 and then at the University of Marburg in

1902. He taught constitutional and international law there until 1920. After the war, he was elected to the Reichstag, where he served until 1928. A committed pacifist, he was appointed as one of the German delegates to the Paris Peace Conference. In 1918, he was appointed to head this commission, looking into violation of international law in regard to prisoners of war, including the Fryatt case. In 1930, he was named to the Permanent International Court of Justice in the Hague. When the Nazis came to power, they attempted unsuccessfully to remove him from this position. He died in 1935.[173]

C. Subsequent Events

The unrestricted submarine warfare by Germany during the war eventually led to the use of the convoy system of Allied Power warships protecting merchant shipping. The Treaty from the London Naval Conference of 1930 stipulated that submarines had to "conform to the rules of international law" and, unless there was active resistance to visit or search or persistent refusal to stop, that a merchant vessel's passengers and crew had to be placed in a "place of safety" before it was sunk.[174] But unrestricted submarine warfare was to arise again in several geographic areas during WWII, especially in the Battle of the Atlantic. This again would lead to the use of convoys to protect shipping coming from North America to the United Kingdom and the Lend-Lease program.[175] After WWII, the creation of the United Nations would provide the forum for refined definitions of the waters under the jurisdiction of coastal nations[176] and so shrink the amount of "high seas" where warfare on neutral shipping would be possible.

During its lifetime, which ran from 1922 to 1930, the Mixed Claims Commission, United States and Germany, disposed of more than 20,000 claims, about one-third of which resulted in money being awarded. The amounts paid out, under the Settlement of War Claims Act of 1928,[177] not including interest, were more than $180 million ($2.5 billion in 2014 dollars). As for the

---

173. *See Walther Schücking*, NEUE DEUTSCHE BIOGRAPHIE.
174. Treaty for the Limitation and Reduction of Naval Armaments, art. 22, Apr. 30, 1930.
175. *See* WWII LAW AND LAWYERS, ch. 2.
176. *See, e.g.,* UN Convention on the Law of the Sea, 1833 U.N.T.S. 3 (Dec. 10, 1982).
177. Pub. L. No. 70-122 (1928).

cause of the large loss of life on the *Lusitania*, although the British court of inquiry and the U.S. trial court seemed to agree on there having been a second torpedo that struck the ship, the U-boat's log showed that only a single torpedo had been fired. Many theories have been advanced since that time to account for the very rapid sinking time, including espionage (see Chapter 4), coal dust explosions, aluminum dust explosions, ammunition explosions, and boiler explosions. Due to the positioning of the ship on the sea bed and the Irish government's reluctance to disturb this underwater gravesite, the answer may never be known.

LEGAL PROFILES

Edwin B. Parker was the initial American mixed claims commissioner and, shortly thereafter (with the death of William R. Day; see Chapter 1), the umpire of the Mixed Claims Commission. He was born in Missouri in 1868 and started his legal practice there. He then moved to Texas in 1897, where he had obtained his legal training, to continue his practice. When WWI started, he went to Washington, DC, as a volunteer, serving, for example, on the War Industries Board. He also served after the war on the United States Liquidation Commission; as a commissioner in the Mixed Claims Commission, United States and Mexico; and as commissioner of the Tripartite Claims Commission between the U.S., Austria, and Hungary from 1926. He served on the U.S.-Germany Mixed Claims Commission from 1922 until his death in 1929.[178]

D. Modern Applicability

The definition of what is a legal and illegal act of war is sometime blurred by the differing perspectives of the belligerents involved. There have been numerous incidents in modern times where compensation was paid for acts of war but the legality or illegality of the act was not always agreed upon. In 1988, the USS *Vincennes* mistakenly shot down an Iranian civilian airliner it had

---

178. *See In Memoriam: Judge Edwin B. Parker*, 24 AM. J. INT'L L. 139 (Jan. 1930).

identified as a military aircraft during the latter stages of the Iran-Iraq War, for which the United States paid compensation while expressing "deep regret over the loss of lives."[179] In the Falklands War between Great Britain and Argentina, the sinking of the Argentine warship *General Belgrano* in 1982 outside the British-declared exclusion zone around the Falkland Islands and the loss of more than 300 Argentine sailors did not lead to the payment of compensation between the nations, as the British viewed it to be a legitimate act of war while Argentine leaders have variously held it to be war crime.[180] In the air war that occurred as part of the conflict over Kosovo in 1999, U.S. warplanes under NATO forces admitted to accidentally bombing the Chinese embassy in Belgrade instead of the Yugoslav Federal Directorate for Supply and Procurement and paid compensation for doing so.[181]

2.6 NEW TECHNOLOGIES / USES OF AIR POWER

A. Statutes

One of the constants of warfare is that new technology provides an advantage, albeit a temporary one, to the side that first successfully deploys it. The modern corollary to that is that the law addressing the new technology will lag its battlefield deployment by at least one major conflict. WWI saw the deployment of new or improved technologies that included submarines, machine guns, artillery, tanks, poison gas, and air power. To some extent, as discussed in the previous section, submarines were controlled by existing naval rules for surface ships. The use of machine guns, artillery, and tanks could be addressed under existing rules for land warfare. Some initial rules for poison gas had been implemented in the Hague Conventions (see Chapter 1). But it was the new use of air power that truly outpaced the legal regimes then in place.

The rules that could be applied to air power included the following. The Hague Convention of 1899 prohibited "the discharge of projectiles and explo-

---

179. *See* Settlement Agreement on the Case Concerning the Aerial Incident of 3 July 1988 before the International Court of Justice.
180. *Cristina: Lo del Belgrano fue un crimen de Guerra*, El Tribuno (May 3, 2012).
181. *See* Final Report to the Prosecutor by the Committee Established to Review the NATO Bombing Campaign Against the Federal Republic of Yugoslavia, Intl. Crim. Tribunal for the former Yugo.

sives from balloons or by other new methods of a similar nature."[182] The latter part of this phrase could encompass airplanes. The 1907 Hague Convention expanded the time period to which this prohibition attached.[183] The ratifiers of the 1899 convention included Austria-Hungary, France, Germany, and the United States, but not Turkey. The 1907 convention, by the time of which the 1899 convention's five-year life had expired, was ratified only by Great Britain and the United States. This meant that Germany, Austria-Hungary, and France were no longer bound by it, and, given the statement "It shall cease to be binding from the time when, in a war between the contracting Powers, one of the belligerents is joined by a noncontracting Power," in essence, neither were the United States and the United Kingdom.

In addition, the Hague 1907 rules for warfare on land were modified to include the phrase "by whatever means" to the following revised clause: "The attack or bombardment, *by whatever means*, of towns, villages, dwellings, or buildings which are undefended is prohibited"[184] (emphasis added). This could be expanded to include attacks by airplane. The 1899 and 1907 conventions already included the following in regard to bombardments from land: "[A]n attacking force must, before commencing a bombardment . . . warn the authorities. In sieges and bombardments all necessary steps must be taken to spare, as far as possible, buildings dedicated to religion, art, science, or charitable purposes, historic monuments, hospitals, and places where the sick and wounded are collected, provided they are not being used at the time for military purposes."[185] There were also similar rules for bombardments from sea.[186]

Heavier-than-air flight had been possible only since the decade before, so at the beginning of the war, air warfare was not a strategic component of the belligerents. That began to change, both as the varied uses of air power met with success and as technology continued to improve the capabilities of airplanes and dirigibles. What went up into the air in this war were reconnaissance planes to spy on enemy movements; various types of bombers, including planes and dirigibles, to cause damage to enemy forces and capabilities; and fighter airplanes, to protect or shoot down other airborne objects.

---

182. Hague IV, Declaration I on the Launching of Projectiles and Explosives from Balloons (July 29, 1899).
183. Hague XIV, Declaration on the Launching of Projectiles and Explosives from Balloons (Oct. 18, 1907).
184. Hague IV, Laws and Customs of War on Land, Annex, art. 25 (Oct. 18, 1907).
185. Hague IV, Laws and Customs of War on Land, Annex, art. 26–27 (Oct. 18, 1907).
186. Hague IX, Concerning Bombardment by Naval Forces in Time of War (Oct. 18, 1907).

LEGAL PROFILES

Richard Haldane was the British secretary of war who initiated the Advisory Committee for Aeronautics in 1909, which centralized the research and solutions on the issues with flight. He was born in Scotland in 1856 and obtained his legal training there and in England, being called to the bar in 1879. In 1890 he became a queen's counsel. In 1885 he was elected to Parliament. He was appointed secretary of state for war in 1905 (a position he held until 1912) and reformed the British military, including creating an imperial general staff and organizing the British Expeditionary Force, which was to be essential in WWI. In 1911 he was raised to the House of Lords, and in 1912 he was appointed as lord chancellor, a role he served until 1915. He was appointed to this position again in 1924. He also served on the judicial committee of the privy council, the court of appeal for cases within the British Empire. He died in 1928.[187]

The use of the air for reconnaissance was demonstrated early in the war, such as at the First Battle of Marne, where planes helped spot gaps in the enemy's lines and contributed to artillery positioning. Airplanes were used as fighters to escort Allied planes or pursue enemy planes and for ground attack on enemy troops and capabilities. Flying aces such as Germany's Manfred von Richthofen, France's René Fonck, Canada's Billy Bishop (whose father was a lawyer), and England's Mick Mannock became famous for their chivalry and derring-do, in stark contrast to the soldiers of the land war who were stuck in the trenches.

But it was the use of air power to drop bombs that was a (small) part of the war's strategic direction and where legal issues were to arise. Bombs were dropped from two types of new technology: the bomber planes of varying configurations and also the slow-moving but majestic dirigibles. More effective bomber planes did not really appear until late in the war and did not have the significant impact they would have in WWII. The dirigibles, on the other hand, were available from the start of the war and actually had several

---

187. *See Richard Haldane*, OXFORD DICTIONARY OF NATIONAL BIOGRAPHY 101033643.

advantages for bombing: their long range, their ability to fly higher than fighter planes, and their bomb-carrying capacity.

An example of the use of dirigibles was the raid over England (including London) on September 23, 1916, and the story of the zeppelin airship L-33. This was a bombing mission of eleven super-zeppelins that left occupied Belgium around noon. After crossing the English Channel at night and making its way to London, starting close to midnight, L-33 began to drop its complement of bombs as it moved across London and surrounding area, killing almost a dozen people. But the long time spent over the city and its powerful searchlights brought antiaircraft fire and then a British fighter, which fired explosive, incendiary bullets into the ship full of flammable hydrogen. The net effect of these defensive measures started to bring the airship down, and despite the crew throwing over all ballast and removable objects that they could, the zeppelin finally crashed to the ground about ninety minutes after it had started dropping bombs. The crew of more than twenty men was eventually captured, and the design of the dirigible became available for British engineers to study. The ability of the British to bring down the dirigibles eventually led to Germany significantly reducing the use of zeppelins for strategic bombing.

LEGAL PROFILES

Alfred de Bathe Brandon was the Allied fighter pilot who shot down the L-33 zeppelin and was a lawyer in civilian life. He was born in New Zealand in 1883 but obtained his legal training in England. After being called to the bar in England in 1906, he returned to New Zealand to practice in his father's law firm. When the war started, he returned to England to take flight training at his own expense. Six months before his engagement with the L-33, he had been involved in the downing of another zeppelin, the L-15. After the war, he returned to New Zealand and his law practice. He died in 1974.[188]

---

188. *See Brandon, Alfred de Bathe*, DICTIONARY OF NEW ZEALAND BIOGRAPHY.

B. Cases

While there were not many cases regarding air power from the war, bombings did cause damage. As such, civilians tried to seek compensation for that damage. Two cases were brought before the Greco-German Mixed Arbitral Tribunal in Paris, presided over by M. Asser, for damages that had been caused to Greek nationals by German air attacks. This tribunal was similar to the Mixed Claims Commission, United States and Germany, discussed above, set up under the Versailles Treaty article 304, which provided for mixed arbitral tribunals. The Greco-German tribunal ended up dealing with more than 700 claims by Greek nationals and entities against Germany.

While it looked at the circumstances of damages sought by the individual claimants, the tribunal also had reason to analyze the rules of war under which some of these damages had been sustained. In particular, it looked at how the Hague IV Convention rules for land warfare bombardments could be applied to air warfare bombardments. There were several cases involving damages from German air bombings of neutral Greek property, during the period before Greece entered the war on the side of the Allied Powers.

In one case,[189] damages were sought for damage to the plaintiffs' coffee crop that had been destroyed by a zeppelin bombardment onto the island of Salonica (now Thessaloniki) in 1916. The tribunal agreed that because the neutral territory had been occupied by the Allied Powers, Germany had been justified in attacking it. But this "did not absolve her from the duty of observing the established rules of international law in the matter of bombardment. It was one of the generally recognized principles of internal law that the belligerent ought to respect, so far as possible, the life and the property of the civilian population." The tribunal then applied to air warfare Hague IV Annex article 26's requirement for a warning before a bombardment, as "there was no reason why the rules as to land bombardment should not apply to bombardment from the air." Noting that the bombing had been done at night and the city's lights had been turned off, the tribunal said that it would have been "impossible to aim the bombs with the accuracy required to spare private dwelling-houses and commercial establishments." It found that the aerial bombing without warning, despite the military advantage it conveyed, was "generally inadmissible" and "contrary to international law."

---

189. Coenca Bros. v. Germany, Greco-German Mixed Arbitral Tribunal Case No. 389, 4 Ann. Dig. 570 (1927).

A second case took place several years later[190] for another aerial bombing in 1916, this time by airplanes onto the city of Bucharest, leading to the death of a civilian. The tribunal noted that Hague IV Annex article 25's prohibition on attacking and bombing undefended towns had been modified in 1907 by adding the phrase "by whatever means" to include attacks delivered via air war. The tribunal again supported the requirement for advance notice on an undefended city, under both Hague IV Annex article 26 and Hague IX article 6. Regardless of whether an air force was trying to occupy or just to destroy a town, air forces needed to give advance notification. With airplanes flying at altitude and often at night (not to mention the general inaccuracy of bombing technology in those early days), aerial bombing was "not in a position to direct with precision the fall of bombs so as to ensure that they hit only the fortifications and war munitions, without harm being done to the person and the property of non-combatants."

LEGAL PROFILES

Tobias Asser was the Dutch lawyer who was instrumental in the Hague Peace Conferences of 1899 and 1907 and the International Court of Arbitration. He was born in the Netherlands in 1838 and obtained his legal training there. He started a legal practice in 1860, but in 1862 he was appointed as an international, civil, and commercial law professor at the University of Amsterdam. He was able to convince the Dutch government to host several conferences on international private law starting in the 1890s, which he led. As the Dutch delegate to the 1899 (as well as the 1907) Hague Peace Conference, he was able to add the convention[191] to a Permanent Court of Arbitration, for which he would win the Nobel Peace Prize in 1911. He also sat on that court's first arbitration case in 1902 (*US-Mexico Pious Fund*). He was involved as a foreign affairs adviser to the Dutch government, providing counsel on all major treaties, and became a member of the Council of State in 1893. He founded several

---

190. Kiriadolou v. Germany, Greco-German Mixed Arbitral Tribunal Case No. 301, 5 Ann. Dig. 516 (1930).
191. Hague I, Convention for the Pacific Settlement of International Disputes (1899).

international private law institutes and an international law review. He died in 1913.[192]

C. Subsequent Events

The lack of rules for the new technologies used in air warfare was something that clearly needed to be addressed. After the war, a new proposal was put forward in a set of Hague Convention rules in early 1923.[193] The rules, applying to those both heavier (i.e., planes) and lighter (i.e., dirigibles) than air craft, prohibited aerial bombardment that was for the purpose of "terrorizing the civilian population, of destroying or damaging private property not of a military character, or of injuring non-combatants."[194] Places of worship, historic monuments, hospitals, etc., were to be spared.[195]

Aerial bombardment was to be considered legitimate only if it was directed exclusively at a military objective (one whose destruction would convey a military advantage), which included "military forces; military works; military establishments or depots; factories constituting important and well-known centres engaged in the manufacture of arms, ammunition, or distinctively military supplies; lines of communication or transportation used for military purposes."[196] Towns could not be bombarded if it would cause the "indiscriminate bombardment of the civilian population," unless they were in the "immediate neighborhood" of the operations of land forces and there existed "a reasonable presumption that the military concentration is sufficiently important to justify such bombardment, having regard to the danger thus caused to the civilian population." Belligerent states in violation were liable for damage or injury caused. This convention was never ratified.

In 1938, the League of Nations, after the atrocities of the Spanish civil war, unanimously passed a resolution on protecting civilian populations from bombing.[197] It stated three principles:

---

192. *See Tobias Asser*, Norwegian Nobel Academy, Prize Biography.
193. Draft Hague Convention, Rules of Air Warfare (1923).
194. *Id.* art. 22.
195. *Id.* art. 25.
196. *Id.* art. 24.
197. League of Nations Resolution, Protection of Civilian Populations Against Bombing From the Air in Case of War (Sept. 30, 1938).

- Intentional bombing of civilian populations was illegal.
- Only identifiable, legitimate military objectives should be bombed.
- Such bombardments should avoid bombing neighboring civilian populations.

The League of Nations resolution called for a meeting of the Bureau of the Conference for the Reduction and Limitation of Armaments to draft regulations on air warfare, which resulted in a draft convention protecting civilian populations.[198] Stating that civilians were not to be "objects of an act of war,"[199] this convention prohibited attacks on undefended towns. A town was considered undefended when it did not contain "combatant troops . . . military, naval or air establishment, or barracks, arsenal, munition stores or factories, aerodromes or aeroplane workshops or ships of war, naval dockyards, forts, or fortifications for defensive or offensive purposes, or entrenchments."[200] A defended town could not be bombed if it would terrorize the local population or lead to indiscriminate bombardment of civilians. This proposal also was never ratified, as the hostilities of WWII had just started.

LEGAL PROFILES

John Bassett Moore was the president of the Commission of Jurists at the 1922–23 Washington Conference on the Limitation of Armaments appointed to look at the rules of aerial warfare (and radio in time of war). He was born in Delaware in 1860 and obtained his legal license there. He started to work at the State Department in 1883, rising to assistant secretary. In 1891, he was appointed to a new international-law professorship at Columbia University, where he remained until 1924. He was involved with the State Department during the Spanish-American War and at the peace conference afterward. He was involved in several international arbitrations and conferences before the war. He served on

---

198. Draft Convention for the Protection of Civilian Populations Against New Engines of War (1938).
199. *Id*. art. 1.
200. *Id*. art. 2.

the Hague Tribunal from 1912 to 1938 and as a judge on the World Court (Permanent Court of International Justice) from 1920 to 1928. He died in 1947.[201]

Frank D. Slee was a WWI Australian fighter pilot and a lawyer who almost changed the air-war history of WWII. He was born in Australia[202] in 1894 and obtained his legal training there. He left his law clerk position and volunteered in 1915 to join the war in Europe. He was in the trenches in France when he was injured and sent to England. He then volunteered for flight training. He found himself flying his first (and last) mission over Belgium in June 1917. He had a chance to shoot down a German plane but was soon surrounded by his target and two other German planes, who teamed up to shoot him down. He was captured, and the three German pilots came to visit him. The leader, who had been in the plane Slee had been shooting at, was Lt. Hermann Goering, who would become the head of the Luftwaffe in WWII and would later be tried at Nuremberg for war crimes.[203] After spending time as a prisoner of war,[204] Slee returned to civilian life in Australia to work at his law firm and become a barrister and solicitor. He died in 1967.[205]

D. Modern Applicability

WWII introduced the terror of nuclear weapons dropped from airplanes, which is discussed in detail in the companion book.[206] In 1949, Geneva Convention IV was promulgated (the first three Geneva Conventions in 1949 dealt, respectively, with sick and wounded armed forces in the field, sick and wounded armed forces at sea, and prisoners of war). Dealing with civilian

---

201. *See John Bassett Moore*, N.Y. TIMES (Nov. 14, 1947).
202. *See Bunbury's Sportsmen, No. 1 Frank D. Slee*, THE MIRROR (Oct. 25, 1924).
203. *See* WWII LAW AND LAWYERS, ch. 6.
204. *See* British Red Cross Society, Notification from the Central Prisoners War Committee (July 27, 1917).
205. *See The Aussie WWI Flying Ace Who Had Hermann Goering in His Gunsights*, THE AUSTRALIAN (Apr. 25, 2011).
206. *See* WWII LAW AND LAWYERS, ch. 7.

populations, it was revised based on the events of WWII.[207] More significantly, in 1977 the First Additional Protocol to the 1949 convention reiterated much of what was stated in the 1923 and 1938 draft agreements regarding the protection of civilian populations.[208]

In the attempts by NATO in the late 1990s to protect Kosovo from being overrun by Serbia in the long-running dissolution of Yugoslavia, accusations of bombing of civilian populations were submitted to the prosecutor's office for the International Criminal Tribunal for the former Yugoslavia. The accusations included deliberately or recklessly attacking civilian populations, by attacking from heights to avoid air defenses (which also precluded differentiating between military and civilian targets). Accusations were made for more than twenty incidents, ten of which had resulted in the deaths of ten or more civilians. Unlawful attacks were those that were directed against civilian populations or against military objectives causing disproportionate civilian casualties.

The prosecutor decided not to issue indictments, explaining why in a report to the UN Security Council. The committee appointed by the prosecutor's office was not able to easily state which attacks had been disproportionate, in looking at several of the specified incidents. It recommended no further investigations, saying, "In all cases, either the law is not sufficiently clear or investigations are unlikely to result in the acquisition of sufficient evidence to substantiate charges against high level accused or against lower accused for particularly heinous offences."[209]

The Additional Protocol also introduced the obligation that when countries introduce a new warfare technology, they must ascertain its legality. The article in full states, "In the study, development, acquisition or adoption of a new weapon, means or method of warfare, a High Contracting Party is under an obligation to determine whether its employment would, in some or all circumstances, be prohibited by this Protocol or by any other rule of international law applicable to the High Contracting Party."[210]

---

207. Geneva Convention (IV) Relative to the Protection of Civilian Persons in Time of War (1949).
208. Protocol Additional to the Geneva Conventions of 12 August 1949, and relating to the Protection of Victims of International Armed Conflicts (Protocol I), art. 51 (June 8, 1977).
209. Final Report to the Prosecutor by the Committee Established to Review the NATO Bombing Campaign against the Federal Republic of Yugoslavia (2000).
210. Protocol Additional to the Geneva Conventions of 12 Aug. 1949, art. 36.

CHAPTER 3

EUROPE: DOMESTIC ISSUES

In addition to dealing with other countries, both politically and militarily, governments during the war had to continue to govern their own populations. This included not only providing the usual health and welfare functions but doing so while persevering through a time of extreme stress. There were stressors on the labor force, on the raw materials feeding into the economic cycle, and on the flow of information. So governments in Europe began to pass new laws and give themselves new powers to deal with these extraordinary circumstances. Starting slowly at first and then ratcheting up as individual crises began to be more pronounced, these powers became autocratic compared to their prewar authority.

Every belligerent country's government began to take steps to give itself more power.[1] This was pronounced in long-standing democracies such as the United Kingdom, which had deep traditions opposed to such grabs of power since wrestling it away from the king many centuries before. The Crown still retained certain but not clearly defined powers, which would be used along with statutory powers to control a large swath of domestic activity during the war. But this use, though legal, sometimes brought the need to compensate those affected by it. Related to the need for more centralized government power was the need to direct the flow of information and communications on

---

1. *See, e.g.,* Enabling Act of 1914, *Gesetz über die Ermächtigung des Bundesrats zu wirtschaftlichen Maßnahmen und über die Verlängerung der Fristen des Wechsel- und Scheckrechts im Falle kriegerischer Ereignisse*, RGBl. 1914, S. 327 (Ger.).

the home front. Morale of the population was as important as the protection of military secrets, and governments needed to both limit and shape what was to be disclosed.

Every country had supply problems, deriving both from the need to divert raw materials from civilian to military uses and from the significantly decreased imports due to the cut-off of supply and trade routes. Initially these supply problems were manageable, but as the war began to drag on, they became more acute. The countries involved all depended to varying degrees on imports for both their military needs and their food supplies, and now those were being put at risk, so systems needed to be created to continue to supply the war while keeping the civilian populations alive.

For those countries that tried to remain neutral but were proximate to the front lines, the war caused special issues in neutrality. Stuck between "the devil and the deep blue sea," a veritable Charybdis and Scylla, the countries closest to the front tried to stay neutral but were constantly threatened by imminent invasion. They had to have a flexible neutrality policy in both directions to survive. The war also found many civilians accused of betraying their own countries or their enemies' countries, through acts of espionage; by communications, collaboration, or commerce with the enemy; or through acts of patriotism to their native countries.

This chapter focuses on domestic legal aspects of the war in Europe, beginning with the powers that governments gathered to themselves to fight the war, including those originating in the executive branch or monarchy; the compensation they had to pay for using those powers; and the deferral of elections in a democracy. The legal issues covered also include the ability to protect confidential information; the ability to control the supply of food to civilians and munitions to the military; the war's impact on workers' power; the issues of neutrality for countries located next to the battle zone, including internment of humans and materials, refugees, starvation, smuggling, and confiscated vessels; and the varying sources and reasons for committing treason.

EUROPE: DOMESTIC ISSUES | 151

PROMINENT LAWYERS AND JUDGES IN THIS CHAPTER

Emergency Powers/Royal Prerogative:

- Reginald McKenna (British home secretary)
- Gordon Hewart (solicitor general)
- Leslie Frederic Scott (petitioner's counsel)
- Charles Swinfen Eady (appeals court judge)
- John Simon (petitioner's counsel)
- Ernest Pollock (solicitor general)
- Andrew Murray (law lord)
- John Fletcher Moulton (law lord)
- John Hamilton (law lord)

Official Secrets/Press Censorship:

- John Buchan (war correspondent)
- James Atkin (court of appeals justice)
- Archibald Bodkin (prosecutor)
- Edward Tindal Atkinson (defense counsel)
- Rufus Isaacs (lord chief justice)
- Travers Humphreys (defense counsel)
- Max Aitken (Ministry of Information)

Civilian and Military Supply:

- Adolf von Batocki (head of war food program)
- Georg Michaelis (state nutrition office)
- Wilhelm von Waldow (head of war food program)
- Henry Holman Gregory (defense counsel)
- Charles Darling (appeals justice)
- William Gloag (munitions tribunal chairman)
- Thomas A. Fyfe (munitions tribunal chairman)
- Edward Rosslyn Mitchell (defense counsel)
- Robert Munro (secretary for Scotland)

Proximate Neutrality:

- Theo Heemskerk (Dutch prime minister)
- Pieter Cort van der Linden (Dutch prime minister)

- John Loudon (Dutch minister of foreign affairs)
- A. A. H. Struycken (arbitration counsel)
- Seerp Gratama (*Hoge Raad* justice)
- Charles Ruijs de Beerenbrouck (refugee commissioner and prime minister)
- Fridtjof Nansen (high commissioner for refugees)

Treason:

- Raymond Poincaré (French president)
- Edouard Clunet (defense counsel)
- Pierre Bouchardon (investigating magistrate)
- Gaston de Leval (American legation counsel)
- Sadi Kirschen (defense counsel)
- Brand Whitlock (U.S. minister to Belgium)
- Daniel Mérillon (prosecutor)
- Joseph Caillaux (defendant)
- Léon Bourgeois (president of the Senate)
- Anatole de Monzie (defense counsel)
- Vincent de Moro-Giafferri (defense counsel)
- Merton E. Lewis (state attorney general)
- Albert Salle (defense counsel)
- André Mornet (prosecutor)
- Stanley Buckmaster (British solicitor general)
- Aristide Briand (French prime minister)
- Henri Robert (president of Paris bar)
- Felix Cassel (British judge advocate general)

3.1 EMERGENCY POWERS / ROYAL PREROGATIVE

A. Statutes

At the start of the war, the United Kingdom's government acquired additional powers for itself by passing the Defence of the Realm Act (DORA).[2] This law covered a wide variety of activities and grew over time; it was amended several

---

2. Defence of the Realm Act of 1914, 4 & 5 Geo. 5, c. 29 (U.K.).

times as the war progressed.[3] The act as consolidated stated that "His Majesty in Council" (in essence, the British cabinet) had the ability to create regulations focused on stopping espionage and communications with the enemy, to prevent false reports or those that would affect loyalties to the country or within the armed forces or relations with foreign powers; to suspend regulations on the acquisition or use of land; to take possession of munitions factories; and to protect communications, troops, ships, and transportation facilities.

Violators could be subject to courts-martial as if they were members of the British military, and people who intended to assist the enemy were eligible for the death penalty. Later revisions also allowed trial by jury in civil courts for British citizens and provided specific rules for acquisitions of land by the government to prosecute the war. They also provided a way for parties to cancel a contract, stating that breach of contract was defensible if the act that violated the contract was carried out in order to comply with DORA.

In addition to the statutes, there were regulations that were issued as orders in council under the statutes and department orders under the regulations. By the war's end, more than two hundred regulations had been issued, but by the end of 1914, when the DORA Consolidation Act was passed, only sixty-three such regulations had been issued. These covered the following areas and powers:

- Controlling (and occupying) land and buildings, food supplies, securities, war materials, coal, petroleum, and the means of production, and interfering with private property rights for public safety or the defense of the realm
- Clearing areas, removing suspects, interning aliens, requiring people to remain indoors, preventing meetings, and stopping leisure travel
- Controlling canals, coal mines, pub hours, lights, and sounds
- Prohibiting the gathering and disseminating of military-related information (including troop or ship movements, defenses, munitions, and the

---

3. Defence of the Realm Act (No. 2) of 1914, 4 & 5 Geo. 5, c. 63 (U.K.); Defence of the Realm Consolidation Act of 1914, 5 Geo. 5, c. 8 (U.K.); Defence of the Realm (Amendment) Act of 1915, 5 Geo. 5, c. 34 (U.K.); Defence of the Realm (Amendment) (No. 2) Act of 1915, 5 Geo. 5, c. 37 (U.K.); Defence of the Realm (Amendment) (No. 3) Act of 1915, 5 & 6 Geo. 5, c. 42 (U.K.); Defence of the Realm (Acquisition of Land) Act of 1916, 6 & 7 Geo. 5, c. 63 (U.K.).

conducting of operations), photographing certain places, and communicating with the enemy
- Prohibiting tampering with telegraphic equipment or possessing wire telegraphic equipment or carrier pigeons (or liberating them), possessing cipher keys, using secret or nonpostal means of communication
- Prohibiting the publication of false or prejudicial reports that undermined the armed forces, the public confidence, or military recruiting, or the publication of secret meetings, such as those of the cabinet, or anonymous and unapproved propaganda
- Prohibiting access to military areas, shipbuilding yards, and munitions factories and causing harm to railways, dealing in or sabotaging war materials, forging or altering military documents, and inciting mutinies or violating regulations
- Prohibiting assisting prisoners of war or internees to escape

Some of the regulations seemed misplaced, unnecessary, or even humorous or trivial. Subject to being banned were the following activities: holding dog shows or fairs; whistling for cabs; allowing deer or bunnies to injure crops or trees; increasing the agricultural acreage used for growing hops (for beer); treating others to a round of drinks at the pub; supplying cocaine, opium, or cannabis to members of the military (e.g., doctors) who were not authorized to give out these drugs on nonrepeatable prescriptions; and operating a brothel in an area that housed members of the armed forces.

LEGAL PROFILES

Reginald McKenna was the British home secretary when DORA was introduced. He was born in England in 1863 and obtained his legal training there. He became a barrister before being first elected to Parliament in 1895. He served in the House of Commons through the end of WWI, holding a number of different positions in government. He was head of the board of education in 1907 and first lord of the Admiralty from 1908 to 1911. In 1911, he became the home secretary, the role he held when this law was passed. He held this position until 1915, when he was appointed as the chancellor of the exchequer, where he served for a year. After defeat in the 1918 parliamentary election, he moved on from politics to become chairman of Midland Bank. He died in 1943.[4]

B. Cases
1. DORA Violations

The number of violators actually incarcerated under DORA was not that great, as most people taken into custody were enemy aliens.[5] What was more common were fines for first-time minor offenses. A well-known case of a first-time offender is that of Prof. Bertrand Russell, who was fined £100 and costs, as an alternative to two months in prison (and subsequently lost his post at Cambridge), for making comments that appeared in an anticonscription pamphlet of the Non-Conscription Fellowship (see Chapter 2). His second conviction in 1918, for advocating against U.S. participation in the war, led to a six-month prison sentence.

The antiwar positions of Communists and Socialists made them a target of the government. Convicted under DORA was Glasgow school teacher and Marxist John Maclean, who was sentenced in 1915 for uttering comments against recruiting and was fined £5 or the alternative of five days in prison (he then lost his teaching job). In early 1916, he was convicted again for making speeches against conscription and was sentenced to three years in prison. He was subsequently released after a little more than a year in jail. In the spring of 1918, he was convicted of seditious activities and sentenced to five years in jail. After the war, he was pardoned. A number of others in the militant trade-unionist movement were imprisoned during the war for resisting both conscription and the employment restrictions on munitions work.

Other parts of the wide-ranging regulations under DORA led to convictions, such as those for drug use, which had not previously been illegal. These new restrictions led to the well-publicized 1916 trial of an ex-solider, Horace Dennis Kingsley, and his associate, Rose Edwards, for selling cocaine on multi-

---

4. *See Reginald McKenna*, Oxford Dictionary of National Biography 101034744.
5. *See* Hansard HC Deb 06 June 1918 vol. 106 cc1731-2.

ple occasions to the Canadian troops in the United Kingdom, after the troops' commander had noticed that dozens under his command had developed a drug habit. Kingsley and Edwards were sentenced to six months in prison. But it was not only those working in the underworlds who were convicted. The department store Harrods (and its pharmacists who packaged drug products for sale) was also convicted under DORA regulation 40B of selling illicit drugs in 1916 and was fined £5.

2. De Keyser's Royal Hotel

The most far-reaching case decided under DORA regarded the requisition of a hotel by the military and the subsequent nonpayment for its occupation and use. This case involved not only DORA but also the definition of the scope of the Royal Prerogative. The issue of the Prerogative had been raised in the previous case on the SS *Zamora* (see Chapter 2) but was fully explored here for different reasons. The Royal Prerogative is best understood as the remnants of the absolute powers of the monarchy from predemocratic times in the United Kingdom. As the power of Parliament had grown and statutes replaced arbitrary royal rule, the powers available under the Royal Prerogative diminished. But the exact scope of what it had diminished to was not defined anywhere, so when the Prerogative was part of the assertion of the powers under which this requisition occurred, the courts needed to study history.

In the previous year, the court of appeals had reviewed a case on the ability of the Crown to requisition for national defense purposes.[6] The *Shoreham Aerodrome* case involved the government requisitioning land for an air combat unit on the coast in Sussex, invoking both DORA and the Royal Prerogative. The property owners complained about the offered compensation and wanted a declaration that they were legally entitled to proper compensation instead of just *ex gratia* (voluntary without legal obligation) compensation. The court of appeals, upholding the trial court, said that there was no legal right under the Prerogative to compensation for property temporarily seized. The case was then settled before the judgment on the subsequent appeal to the House of Lords was final, as the law lords were not supportive of the Crown's argument. So the appeals court's decision remained the state of the law.

---

6. *In re* A Petition of Right, "Shoreham Aerodrome Case" 3 K.B. 649 (1915).

In the present case, the Royal Flying Corps had requisitioned real property (a hotel) for its headquarters in London, not property for a fighting unit. It was unable to settle on an amount with the owner and referred the matter to a commission charged with assessing actual monetary losses under DORA (the Defence of the Realm Losses Commission). Instead, the hotel filed a petition asking to be paid a higher rent for the use and occupation of the hotel based on the government's statutory obligation under the Defence Acts, including the principal current version, the Defence Act of 1842.[7] The government replied that it had requisitioned the property using its powers under DORA and the Royal Prerogative and was not required to pay compensation. The trial court[8] felt compelled to follow *Shoreham*, ruling for the Crown that the requisitioning was necessary for the public safety and defense of the realm and no compensation was due.

LEGAL PROFILES

Gordon Hewart was the British solicitor general appearing for the Crown during this case. He was born in England in 1870 and obtained his legal training there. He spent time working as a journalist but was called to the bar in 1902. In 1912 he became a king's counsel. He was first elected to Parliament just before the start of the war in 1913 and joined in Privy Council in 1918. In 1919, after briefly serving as solicitor general, he become attorney general, where he remained for three years before being appointed as the lord chief justice for England and Wales in 1922. He held this position until resigning in 1940. He died in 1943.[9]

Leslie Frederic Scott was one of the attorneys for the petitioner in this case. He was born in England in 1869 and obtained his legal training there. He was called to the bar in 1894. In 1910, he was first elected to Parliament, where he remained until 1929. He served as the solicitor

---

7. Defence Act of 1842, 5 & 6 Vict., c. 94 (U.K.).
8. De Keyser's Royal Hotel, Ltd. v. R., 34 T.L.R. 329 (1918).
9. *See Gordon Hewart*, OXFORD DICTIONARY OF NATIONAL BIOGRAPHY 101033846.

general in 1922 for six months. In 1935, he was appointed to the court of appeals, where in 1940 he became the senior lord justice. He retained this role through his retirement from the bench in 1948. He died in 1950.[10]

The court of appeals took a different approach.[11] Partly this was based on a months-long search of the historical legal records, going back centuries, for situations where the Crown had requisitioned property without paying for it. The court was not able to find such examples. While the petitioners had claimed the Defence Acts required compensation for temporary use and occupancy of land, the Crown had insisted that in time of war, the Royal Prerogative allowed for such seizure without compensation, as the prerogative was independent of and not restricted by statutes. The court, in a 2–1 decision, found that under the Defence Act of 1842, the hotel was owed rent for its use by the military, under an implied contract.

LEGAL PROFILES

Charles Swinfen Eady was one of the two judges (Thomas Warrington was the other) in the majority opinion on this case and was the Master of the Rolls. He was born in England in 1851 and obtained his legal training there. He became a solicitor in 1874, a barrister in 1879, and a queen's counsel in 1893. In 1901 he was appointed a judge in the chancery court, where he served until 1913. In that year, he joined the Privy Council and was appointed a lord justice of appeal, where he served until 1918, when he became Master of the Rolls (inter alia, head of the court of appeals). He died in 1919.[12]

---

10. *See Leslie Scott*, OXFORD DICTIONARY OF NATIONAL BIOGRAPHY 101035992.
11. De Keyser's Royal Hotel, Ltd. v. R., 35 T.L.R. 418 (C.A. 1919).
12. *See Charles Eady*, OXFORD DICTIONARY OF NATIONAL BIOGRAPHY 101032952.

John Simon was the lead counsel for the petitioners in this case. He was born in England in 1873 and obtained his legal training there. He was called to the bar in 1899 and first elected to Parliament in 1906. In 1910 he was appointed as solicitor general, where he served until 1913, when he was appointed as attorney general. He left this position to become home secretary in 1915 for six months. This was a role he reprised from 1935 to 1937, after spending the years 1931 to 1935 as foreign minister, where he was noted for appeasing the Japanese invasion of Manchuria.[13] In 1937, he became chancellor of the exchequer, and in 1940 the lord high chancellor. He served in this role through the end of WWII and died in 1954.[14]

Ernest Pollock was the new solicitor general appearing for this appeal. He was born in England in 1861 and obtained his legal training there. He was first elected to Parliament in 1910 and was appointed as solicitor general in 1919, remaining there until 1922. He briefly served as attorney general before being named as Master of the Rolls in 1923, when he also left his seat in Parliament. He remained in this position until resigning in 1935. He died in 1936.[15]

The House of Lords opinion affirmed the court of appeals, but for different and differing reasons.[16] Lord Dunedin's opinion first found that there had been no mutual assent to the seizure of property, so there was no implied contract between the parties, as the court of appeals had ruled. As there had been a legal repossessing of the property, the only question to be considered was whether compensation must be paid. Looking at the Royal Prerogative, Dunedin said, "If the whole ground of something which could be done by the Prerogative is covered by the statute, it is the statute that rules." Quoting the role of restrictions on the Prerogative by statute in the court of appeals decision, he said,

---

13. *See* THOMAS J. SHAW, WWII LAW AND LAWYERS: ISSUES, CASES, AND CHARACTERS, ch. 7 (2013).
14. *See John Simon*, OXFORD DICTIONARY OF NATIONAL BIOGRAPHY 101036098.
15. *See Ernest Pollock*, OXFORD DICTIONARY OF NATIONAL BIOGRAPHY 101035562.
16. Att.-Gen. v. De Keyser's Royal Hotel, Ltd., A.C. 508 (H.L. 1920).

"What use would there be in imposing limitations if the Crown could, at its pleasure, disregard them and fall back on Prerogative?"

The Dunedin opinion looked back at the historical activities for several centuries and found that statutes had been passed allowing compensation for property taken and that agreements had been reached with property owners for such seizures. However, it could find no case where the Prerogative had been used and compensation not paid. The statutes passed included those during the Napoleonic Wars and before, which eventually led to the Defence Act of 1842 (more research on the historical statutes had been done since the court of appeals decision). With this plethora of statutes, this opinion stated that it was not possible to assert an "unrestricted Prerogative right as existing alongside with the statutory powers authorizing the Crown to acquire on certain terms. The conclusion is that the Crown could not take the Petitioners' premises by the powers of the Prerogative alone."

The Dunedin opinion then looked at DORA and the ability under the regulations to take property needed for the public safety and defense of the realm. Granting that the government had the authority to take the property, Dunedin wondered whether the DORA provision that "regulations may provide for the suspension of any restrictions on the acquisition or use of land—under the Defence Acts, 1842 to 1875" applied to compensation. He ultimately ruled that it did not, that the obligation to make payment was not a restriction that could be "swept away."

The other lord justices wrote their own opinions, with differing logic, but reaching a unanimous decision to dismiss the appeal and affirm the court of appeals decision. Lord Atkinson stated that "when such a statute expressing the will and intention of the King and of the three Estates of the Realm is passed, it abridges the Royal Prerogative while it is in force to this extent, that the Crown can only do the particular thing under and in accordance with the statutory provisions, and its Prerogative power to do it is in abeyance" and found in those statutes the requirement to pay for use of the property. Lord Moulton found that the requisition had clearly been made utilizing DORA, not the Royal Prerogative, so statutory compensation was required. Lord Sumner stated that the Defence Acts' powers for "requisitioning buildings in time of war were in no way inconsistent with an intention to abate the Prerogative in this respect, if not absolutely" and said, "There is no prerogative right to elect not to pay."

Lord Parmoor's opinion stated, "The growth of constitutional liberties has largely consisted in the reduction of the discretionary power of the Executive, and in the extension of Parliamentary protection in favour of the subject under a series of statutory enactments. The result is that whereas at one time the Royal Prerogative gave legal sanction to a large majority of the executive functions of the Government, it is now restricted within comparatively narrow limits. The Royal Prerogative has, of necessity, been gradually curtailed, as a settled rule of law has taken the place of an uncertain and arbitrary administrative discretion." It went on, "Since Magna Carta the estate of a subject in lands or buildings has been protected against the Prerogative." He concluded that statutory regulations requiring such compensation needed to be obeyed, and "as far as such regulation is inconsistent with the claim of a Royal Prerogative right, such right can be no longer enforced."

LEGAL PROFILES

Andrew Murray, Lord Dunedin, gave the first opinion in this case. He was born in Scotland in 1849 and obtained his legal training in Britain. A son and grandson of Scottish lawyers, he was called to the bar in 1874, became a queen's counsel in 1891, and was elected to Parliament that same year. He held a variety of Scots-related posts in the United Kingdom, including solicitor general of Scotland, and in 1896, lord advocate (the top legal adviser on Scots law), a position he held until becoming secretary for Scotland in 1903. In 1905, he left Parliament upon being appointed lord justice general and lord president of the court in session (the top judicial position in Scotland). In 1913 he became a British law lord. He served in this role until resigning in 1932. He died in 1942.[17]

John Fletcher Moulton gave another of the opinions in this case. He was born in England in 1844 and obtained his legal training there. In addition to being a barrister, he was a scientist, a mathematician, and a fellow at the Royal Society. These occupations assisted his patent law

---

17. *See Andrew Murray*, OXFORD DICTIONARY OF NATIONAL BIOGRAPHY 101035154.

practice, in which he was involved with Guglielmo Marconi's first British wireless patent in 1897. He was first elected to Parliament in 1885, the year he also became a queen's counsel. In 1906 he was appointed to the court of appeals, and in 1912, he became a law lord. During the war, from 1914, he was involved with munitions and headed up the government's explosives department in the Ministry of Munitions. He died in 1921.[18]

C. Subsequent Events

Since the legal cases were not favorable to the British government in the immediate postwar era,[19] the government sought protection against litigation. The Indemnity Act of 1920[20] was an attempt by the government to minimize its liability for wartime acts. This law provided that there should be no liability for government agents (ministers, civil servants, members of the military) who committed illegal or unauthorized acts as long as the acts had been performed in good faith and in defense of the realm, for public safety, in regard to military discipline, or generally in the public interest. The government itself could not be sued, except in specific circumstances, such as for breach of contract.

The Royal Prerogative would be the focus of a much later case arising out of government actions during WWII.[21] The British government had ordered the destruction of oil wells, pipelines, refineries, and other related British facilities in Burma, before that country was overrun by the Japanese in February 1942 in the early days of the conflict in the Pacific. The question before the law lords was whether the demolition of these facilities, done under the power of the Royal Prerogative, was compensable to the facilities' British owners. The court ruled the answer was yes, that it was not battle damage (which would not likely be compensable), and that the "weight of opinion was against there being any general rule that no compensation can be due for loss caused by an exercise of this prerogative."[22] (The obligation for payment here was in fact voided by subsequent passing of the War Damages Act of 1965,[23] whose

---

18. See John Moulton, OXFORD DICTIONARY OF NATIONAL BIOGRAPHY 101035132.
19. See, e.g., Newcastle Breweries Ltd. v. R., 1 K.B. 854 (1920).
20. 10 & 11 Geo. 5, c. 48 (U.K.).
21. Burmah Oil v. Lord Advocate, UKHL 6 (1964).
22. Id.
23. C. 16, 1965 (U.K.).

purpose was to "abolish rights at common law to compensation in respect of damage to, or destruction of, property effected by, or on the authority of, the Crown during, or in contemplation of the outbreak of, war.") Limitations on the Prerogative's various powers are still being debated today.[24]

DORA Regulation 40B in 1916, which banned the selling of cocaine and opium, was the first serious drug law in the United Kingdom. It would be followed by the Dangerous Drugs Act of 1920,[25] reflecting the 1912 Hague Opium Convention and the Versailles Treaty's commitment to bring that convention into force, banning the global opium trade.[26] Instead of treating drug use as a medical problem, this law began to penalize the use of and addiction to drugs like heroin, cocaine, and morphine by banning their import and export without a license. The regulations that followed in 1921 limited the production, prescription, and possession of drugs to medical professionals or others with licenses and required extensive record keeping on dangerous drugs by both doctors and pharmacists.

LEGAL PROFILES

John Hamilton, Lord Sumner, was one of the law lords in the *De Keyser* case and was also a participant in the Versailles conference. He was born in England in 1859 and obtained his legal training there. His practice focused on commercial matters. He became a king's counsel in 1901 and then a High Court judge in 1909. He was appointed to the court of appeals in 1912 and then as a law lord in 1913. He took part in the Paris Peace Conference in 1919, as part of the reparations committee. He resigned as a law lord in 1930 to lead the Indian Empire Society that advocated continued rule of India by Britain. He died in 1934.[27]

---

24. MP's Armed Forces (Parliamentary Approval for Participation in Armed Conflict) Bill 16 of British HC Session 2005-6.
25. 10 & 11 Geo. 5, c. 46 (U.K.).
26. Treaty of Peace between the Allied and Associated Powers and Germany, art. 295, June 28, 1919.
27. *See John Hamilton*, Oxford Dictionary of National Biography 101033670.

In addition to giving itself more power during the war years, one other thing the government did was to keep itself in power longer. When the grand coalition government came together as a unified national political leadership in 1915, it became clear that stability of the government meant not only a unified but also a consistent voice. As such, this government passed a number of laws to defer the time for holding elections. This was justifiable based not only on the need to avoid the distraction from the war effort that electioneering would occasion and the trouble that a turnover in leadership would bring, but also the practical problem that many of the electorate were on the battlefields or otherwise engaged in the war effort, as were members of Parliament. It would also be a poor use of paper to use it for ballots during wartime.

The laws postponing elections started with the first act in 1915[28] and continued with five more acts[29] passed during the war. All were deferrals of short durations, considering the sensitivity of suspending the franchise in a long-standing democracy. The main features of these laws were to suspend local and national elections and allow for the selection of people into municipal positions for the lifetime of the acts, which were never more than a few months long. This same suspension occurred in other countries during the war and was to reoccur during WWII.

3.2 OFFICIAL SECRETS / CENSORSHIP

A. Statutes

In the years leading up to the war, the British passed the Official Secrets Act (OSA).[30] While officially a revision of the 1889 Official Secrets Act, it set out useful provisions to protect appropriate information during a war. For example, it criminalized spying, in the forms of approaching or entering prohibited places or making, obtaining, or communicating sketches (including photographs), information, or documents that might be "directly or indirectly useful

---

28. Elections and Registration Act of 1915, 5 & 6 Geo. 5, c.76 (U.K.).
29. Parliament and Local Elections Act of 1916, Parliament and Local Elections Act of 1917 (U.K.); Parliament and Local Elections (No. 2) Act of 1917 (U.K.); Parliament and Local Elections Act of 1918 (U.K.).
30. An Act to Re-enact the Official Secrets Act, 1889, with Amendments, 1 & 2 Geo. 5, c. 28 (U.K.).

to an enemy."[31] It also penalized civil servants who received, communicated, or retained any such unauthorized sketch or document containing such prohibited information[32] and those who harbored spies.[33]

This list of what was considered a "prohibited place" was quite extensive:

(a) any work of defence, arsenal, factory, dockyard, camp, ship, telegraph or signal station, or office belonging to His Majesty, and any other place belonging to His Majesty used for the purpose of building, repairing, making, or storing any ship, arms, or other materials or instruments of use in time of war, or any plans or documents relating thereto; and

(b) any place not belonging to His Majesty where any ship, arms, or other materials or instruments of use in time of war, or any plans or documents relating thereto, are being made, repaired, or stored under contract with, or with any person on behalf of, His Majesty, or otherwise on behalf of His Majesty; and

(c) any place belonging to His Majesty which is for the time being declared by a Secretary of State to be a prohibited place for the purposes of this section on the ground that information with respect thereto, or damage thereto, would be useful to an enemy; and

(d) any railway, road, way, or channel, or other means of communication by land or water (including any works or structures being part thereof or connected therewith), or any place used for gas, water, or electricity works or other works for purposes of a public character, or any place where any ship, arms, or other materials or instruments of use in time of war, or any plans or documents relating thereto, are being made, repaired, or stored otherwise than on behalf of His Majesty, which is for the time being declared by a Secretary of State to be a prohibited place for the purposes of this section, on the ground that information with respect

---

31. *Id.* § 1.
32. *Id.* § 2.
33. *Id.* § 7.

thereto, or the destruction or obstruction thereof, or interference therewith, would be useful to an enemy.[34]

In addition to prohibiting disclosure of official secrets, the British government was involved in watching for disclosures through postal censorship and initiated press censorship over war reporting. Under both the OSA and DORA, the military banned the newspapers' war reporters from the front lines and instead set up the War Office Press Bureau in 1914 to issue censored reports of war activity. This bureau first utilized a single war reporter, Lt. Col. Ernest Swinton, as the lone official reporter from the battlefront (who, after witnessing the killing fields caused by machine gun technology, was instrumental in proposing what became the battle tank). This sole-source reporting lasted only until early 1915, when pressure from the press finally caused the military to allow a pool system of five reporters from the major publications to report heavily censored details from the battlefront.

But this led to a very controlled and often very misleading depiction of what was actually happening at the front. For example, the first day of the Battle of the Somme resulted in more than 50,000 casualties for the British army, the worst single day in the nation's history. This is how the battle was reported after the first two days in a leading British newspaper: starting on page 10, behind such important stories on earlier pages as "Farmers and the Wool Clip," "Vegetable Growing," and "More Summer Sales," was the headline "The Day Goes Well."[35] The report filed on the first day of the battle (July 1) contained the phrase "as far as can be ascertained, our casualties have not been heavy," and early on the second day (July 2) it said, "Troops are in excellent spirits." More reports from July 1: "Sir Douglas Haig telegraphed last night that the general situation was favourable";[36] and from the end of July 2: "The general situation may be regarded as favourable." A story on the same page from "Our Military Correspondent" subtitled "Saving the Infantry"[37] included this: "[A]t the exact hour when the Allied offensive on the Somme began and [I] had the pleasure of communicating the first news of the Anglo-French success . . . everything has gone well. Our troops have successfully carried out their missions. . . .

---

34. *Id.* § 3.
35. *'The Day Goes Well,' Details of the Fighting,* THE TIMES (July 3, 1916) at 10.
36. *Forward in the West, Start of a Great Attack,* THE TIMES (July 3, 1916) at 8.
37. *New Tactics, General Joffre's Strategy, Saving the Infantry,* THE TIMES (July 3, 1916) at 8.

Thanks to the very complete and effective artillery preparation, thanks also to the dash of our infantry, our losses have been very slight." The page in between these articles had a patriot report seemingly out of some romantic ballad, of the hours before the battle of the Somme, where "Our Special Correspondent" described "Our Men Marching Up"[38] and how "detachments of our troops could be seen swinging across country . . . [a]nd always as they passed they whistled softly in unison. Some whistled 'Tipperary,' some 'Come back, my Bonny, to me,' and some, best of all in the place and surroundings, 'La Marseillaise' . . . always the steady tramp-tramp, tramp-tramp as they shouldered by; and always they were whistling. Now and then a laugh broke out at some unheard joke, a completely careless laugh, as of a holiday-maker."

LEGAL PROFILES

John Buchan was a lawyer and one of the first of the war correspondents allowed to go to the war front. He was born in Scotland in 1875 and obtained his legal training there. He bracketed being called to the bar in 1901 with time serving in South Africa in the diplomatic service and running for a seat in Parliament. All the while, he was authoring a number of books, many set in Scotland or South Africa. When the war broke out, he worked first for the War Propaganda Bureau, where he wrote a serialized, heavily propagandized "history" of the war. Then he worked for the *Times* newspaper as one of the war correspondents. He later enlisted in the military, serving in military intelligence, writing for the General Headquarters. He was then drafted into running the Department of Information (see below). After the war he returned to writing (in his lifetime he authored more than thirty novels and several biographies), was elected to Parliament in 1927 and served until 1935, and was appointed in 1935 to be the governor-general of Canada. He was serving in this position when he died in 1940.[39]

---

38. *The Great Battle, Special Account, 'The Biggest British Offensive'*, THE TIMES (July 3, 1916) at 9.
39. *See John Buchan*, OXFORD DICTIONARY OF NATIONAL BIOGRAPHY 101032145.

B. Cases

There were a number of prosecutions during the war under the OSA, of which the following cases are illustrative. The first case concerned a foreign national working as a civil servant in the censorship of mails. The second case was an example of an initially unsuccessful prosecution of a former civil servant who passed information that may not have been useful to the enemy. The third case involved a former German citizen who passed armaments information on new weapons to a German armaments company. The fourth case had a foreign national from a neutral country conspiring to obtain and pass information about a prohibited place on the coast of England to the enemy. The fifth case involved a Ministry of Munitions engineer who provided armaments information to help his own commercial prospects. A separate prosecution under DORA in 1918 for war reporting that might have assisted the enemy illustrates the extent of the control the British government had over press reporting.

1. Postal Censors

This early 1915 case[40] involved the criminal trial of a Belgian professor, Emile Jules Dupuis, for violations of the OSA. He had been working examining letters for the postal censor for neutral-country correspondence. He was accused of informing a person whose mail was being monitored of the fact of the monitoring. It turned out that the woman he had informed was not seriously involved in any political issues, but the judge was concerned that it could have turned out to be a serious matter in wartime if she had been a different type of person. Dupuis was warned not to repeat information that had passed through his review in court to the jury, as this would be a further transgression of the OSA. He was sentenced to twelve months' imprisonment. His appeal was turned down, with the court of appeals justices noting his prior six convictions in South Africa, including for fraud.

2. War Office Employee

Not all cases recommended for OSA prosecution were initially successful. In one case brought in January 1919, one Albert Hennington Crisp, who used to work as a clerk in the War Office, allegedly passed information and documents to Arthur J. Homewood, the secretary of a firm of tailors. The information

---
40. R. v. Dupuis, Central Crim. Ct. (1915).

regarded contracts for officers' uniforms. The supposed plan was not only to acquire the future contracts for Homewood's firm but also to help him use the tailoring work as an excuse to avoid military service. The judge did not find that this information was something that might be used to assist the enemy and so dismissed the case against Crisp and Homewood under the OSA. But the prosecution refiled the case, and in February 1919, the two defendants pleaded guilty.[41] The court had ruled that although the information might not have been official secrets, it could be considered useful to the person to whom it was given. The defendants were fined but not imprisoned.

3. Lord Mayor

This case[42] involved the former lord mayor of Sheffield, a former German citizen, for violations of the OSA. Sir Joseph Jonas was indicted in 1918 for having conspired to obtain and communicate to the enemy information on a prohibited area. He had come to Britain as a young man and gotten involved in the steel industry, creating a firm that eventually became a significant supplier of weapons to the British government. He had become a British citizen more than forty years before and had gotten involved in the city council in Sheffield. In 1913, he had numerous discussions with Charles Alfred Vernon, another naturalized British citizen (formerly German) and member of the Ministry of Munitions, regarding a new rifle and the plant where it was being manufactured. This information also involved another German national leading an armaments firm in Germany, who was a friend and customer of Jonas and a former employee of an armaments maker in the United Kingdom. Jonas claimed that by getting information and passing documents about the design on new weapons in 1913 he was merely following up on the competitive information requested by his friend in Germany and had not intended to harm the interests of the state (i.e., of the United Kingdom). The jury found that he did not intend to injure the interests of the state and so was not liable for a felony, but he was convicted of a misdemeanor for obtaining and communicating information about a prohibited place (the British armaments factory). He subsequently lost his knighthood.

---

41. R. v. Crisp and Homewood, Central Crim. Ct. (1919).
42. R. v. Jonas and Vernon, Central Crim. Ct. (1918).

4. Neutral Country Citizen

This case involved a Swede who tried to obtain military information for some German friends.[43] In early 1915, Ernst Gustav Waldemar Olsson had asked another Swedish national long residing in England about naval and military forces and defenses along the northeast coast of England. He requested this information over three conversations for some German friends who were serving as masters on ships in Rotterdam. This questioning led to Olsson's conviction under OSA. He was sentenced to four years in prison. He appealed the judgment, based, inter alia, on a card he was carrying when arrested that contained signaling information. This card was not allowed to be introduced into evidence, due to its sensitive nature, but it was discussed at the trial. Because the defense could not cross-examine prosecution witnesses about the card, which the defense said was commonly available and had been in the possession of the accused for several years, the defense asserted that it was prejudiced by inadmissibility. Because the contents of the card were not disclosed in court and the judge had issued instructions to the jury that they should not assume anything about the card, the appeals court found no prejudice to the defendant and the appeal was dismissed.

5. Ministry of Munitions

This case[44] involved an electrical engineer in the Ministry of Munitions machine tool department, who in 1916 had obtained a ministry report about machine tools in Switzerland. The defendant, Alfred Horswill Gibbings, sent the report with a letter to a Hans Schmidt in Switzerland, who was involved with machine tool production there and suggested that he might become the local agent of Swiss machine tool makers. Gibbings had visited that country previously to investigate machine tools for the British ministry. His stated intention in his letter was to resign and find more lucrative work representing the Swiss tool firms in London. The report, which a senior technical officer had created about Swiss machine tool capabilities, was intercepted by the postal censors and led to the indictment. The court found Gibbings guilty of violating the OSA for attempting to communicate information he had obtained

---

43. R. v. Olsson, Court of Appeals (1915).
44. R. v. Gibbings, Central Crim. Ct. (1916).

from his position with the government. He was sentenced to four months' imprisonment.

6. Publication Assisting the Enemy

This case[45] involved the well-known war reporter Charles à Court Repington, who had reported on many conflicts, such as the Russo-Japanese War, and after a long military career had special contacts within the army. He was the impetus for the "Shell Crisis" (see Section 3.3) through his reporting (which came with the tacit approval of the head of the British Expeditionary Force). In this 1918 case, he was accused, along with editor Howell Arthur Gwynne of the Morning Post, of disclosing information that could be used to assist the enemy. What was published was a decision of the Versailles Council to retain and name the commander of general reserves, but the defense contended that this information had been known in Germany (and Italy) for some time before the *Morning Post* printed it. In addition, what was published was a criticism of that decision, based on Repington's own military knowledge. The court ruled that despite the information's prior publication elsewhere, the disclosure remained a violation of DORA, and it fined each of the two defendants £100.

LEGAL PROFILES

James Atkin was the judge in the first case. He was born in Australia in 1867 and obtained his legal training in England. He was called to the bar in 1891 and became a king's counsel in 1906, focusing on commercial law. In 1913, he was appointed as a judge on the High Court. In 1919, he was appointed as a justice on the court of appeals. In 1928, he became a law lord, where he was involved in the well-known case of *Liversidge v. Anderson*.[46] He lost his oldest son in WWI, and his daughter Rosaline was called to the bar in 1937. He died in 1944.[47]

---

45. R. v. Repington and Gwynne, Central Crim. Ct. (1918).
46. *See* WWII LAW AND LAWYERS, ch. 5.
47. *See James Atkin*, OXFORD DICTIONARY OF NATIONAL BIOGRAPHY 101030492.

Archibald Bodkin was the prosecutor in the second case. He was born in England in 1862 and obtained his legal training there, being called to the bar in 1885. He spent many years working primarily for prosecutors, including prosecuting George Chapman (thought by some police to be Jack the Ripper) for (different) murders. During the war, he was involved in many OSA and spying cases. In 1920 he was named the director of public prosecutions, a role he fulfilled thoroughly until 1930. He then returned to a prior role as a recorder, which he retained until 1947. He died in 1957.[48]

Edward Tindal Atkinson was the defense counsel in the third and final case. He was born in England in 1878 to a father who was a county judge, and he obtained his legal training there, being called to the bar in 1902. During the war he served with the Royal Air Force. After the war, he served as a legal adviser to the peace conference. Returning to his practice, in 1930, he was named as the director of public prosecutions, a position he held until 1944. He died in 1957.[49]

Rufus Isaacs was the lord chief justice presiding over the appeal in the fourth case. He was born in England in 1860 and obtained his legal training there, being called to the bar in 1887. He was elected to Parliament in 1904, remaining there until 1913. In 1910, he briefly served as solicitor general and then was appointed attorney general, a role he held until 1913. From this position, he participated in the investigation into the sinking of the RMS *Titanic*. In 1913, he was appointed the lord chief justice (head of the court of appeals). During this period, he served as the ambassador to the United States at the end of the war. From 1921 to 1926, he was the viceroy of India, where he imprisoned another famous lawyer, Mohandas K. Gandhi (see Chapter 6). Isaacs died in 1935.[50]

Travers Humphreys was the defense counsel in the fifth case. He was born in England in 1867, the son of a solicitor, and obtained his legal

---

48. *See Archibald Bodkin*, OXFORD DICTIONARY OF NATIONAL BIOGRAPHY 101031942.
49. *See Edward Atkinson*, OXFORD DICTIONARY OF NATIONAL BIOGRAPHY 101030494.
50. *See Rufus Isaacs*, OXFORD DICTIONARY OF NATIONAL BIOGRAPHY 101034119.

training there, being called to the bar in 1889. He was involved in a number of well-known cases, including those of Oscar Wilde and many murder cases. He became a High Court judge in 1928 but also heard many criminal appeals, including those of William Joyce for treason after WWII.[51] He retired from the bench in 1951 and died in 1956.[52]

C. Subsequent Events

The OSA was revised after the war in 1920,[53] based on the experience gained during the conflict. Revisions to the statute included prohibitions on forgery, impersonations, the unauthorized use of uniforms to gain access to prohibited places, the unauthorized use or possession of government stamps, communicating secret codes or passwords, interfering with those guarding prohibited places, and inciting or aiding and abetting a violation of the act. An addition to the statute was a requirement for anyone with information on violations of the act to provide it to police as requested, under specific procedures. Communicating with a foreign agent led to the presumption of having obtained or attempted to obtain information that was directly or indirectly useful to the enemy.

The government did not only work with the major newspapers on both censorship and propaganda but also created a Ministry of Information in 1918 that was headed up by one of the major newspapermen in the United Kingdom, Lord Beaverbrook. This ministry subsumed the Department of Information, which had taken over from the War Propaganda Bureau. The means of providing propaganda was not only through the press but also through newsreels, a very popular way, in the days before radio and television, to experience the war for those on the home front. To help propel propaganda, the government had recruited many famous British authors to write for it, including Arthur Conan Doyle, H. G. Wells, J. M. Barrie, Rudyard Kipling, and Thomas Hardy. The functions of this new ministry were split into those for domestic propaganda, those for foreign propaganda, and those involving the military. Given the proximity

---

51. *See* WWII LAW AND LAWYERS, ch. 5.
52. *See Travers Humphreys*, OXFORD DICTIONARY OF NATIONAL BIOGRAPHY 101034053.
53. Official Secrets Act of 1920, 10 & 11 Geo. 5, c 75 (U.K.).

of the end of the war, however, the ministry had only a short time to make an impact before its functions were scaled down and transferred back to the Foreign Office after the war. The various propaganda activities, aimed at persuading neutrals (especially America), and at keeping up domestic morale, by both hiding the scale of Allied battle losses and playing up bad acts by the Central Powers (see Chapter 6), seem to have succeeded in both aspects.

Efforts were made by all sides not only to prosecute the unauthorized obtaining of secrets but also to protect against the disclosure of secrets, through various types of encoding techniques. There were diplomatic codes between home country and ambassadors, codes for communications between allies, and cryptography used to protect military communications, with trench codes used along the front lines. The French had experts like Étienne Bazeries and Georges Painvin; the Germans had Arthur Scherbius (developer of the Enigma machine); the British had the occupants of Room 40 (of the Old Admiralty Building), the people who eventually decoded the Zimmermann telegram that was part of the impetus that pushed America to join the war (see Chapter 4); and the Americans had Col. Parker Hitt and Herbert Yardley.

Perhaps the biggest weapon in cryptography that the Americans brought with them to Europe was Native American soldiers. In seeing that many of the communications on the front seemed to be intercepted by the Germans, the Americans decided to use Native Americans, especially those of the Choctaw tribe, to speak on the telephone in their own language. With many Native American languages being entirely oral (never committed to writing), this was an extremely secure method for encoding phone messages (and much faster and safer than runners). Like the more well-known Navajo code talkers in WWII, the Choctaw code talkers of WWI contributed to the success of American forces late in the war.

LEGAL PROFILES

Max Aitken, Lord Beaverbrook, was the first head of British Ministry of Information. He was born in Canada in 1879 and obtained his legal training there but never practiced. Instead, he got involved in a number of businesses, including power generation in Canada. He then sold his business interests and moved to England in 1910. There he also got involved in businesses, including Rolls-Royce and then newspapers. He was also elected to Parliament. In 1918 he took on the role of minister of information; then, after the war, he returned to his newspaper empire, including the leading paper the *Daily Express*. During WWII, he was appointed minister of aircraft production. He died in 1964.[54]

D. Modern Applicability

The OSA was also used significantly during WWII and later during times of relative peace.[55] The OSA has become a common tool for pursuing civil servants who disclose confidential information in government custody. The number of prosecutions under OSA during the decades since the war is large and has included politician Edgar Lansbury (father of actress Angela Lansbury); foreign embassy code clerk Tyler Kent; Soviet double agents George Blake, cryptographer Geoffrey Prime, Michael Bettany, and Michael Smith; magazines such as *Leveller* and *Isis*; Foreign Office clerk Sara Tisdall; journalists Crispin Aubrey and Duncan Campbell; civil servants David Keogh and Richard Jackson; members of Parliament William Owen and Jonathan Aitken; and Ministry of Defense civil servant Clive Pointing. The latter three were prosecuted but acquitted by a jury.

3.3 CIVILIAN AND MILITARY SUPPLY

A. Statutes

The shortages of goods during the war to both civilians and the military had several causes. One was the fact that the military was taking up a disproportionate amount of the available supplies, meaning that all things being equal, civilians had to do with less. But all things were not equal, as the supply sources had been severely restricted by blockades, submarine attacks, and other economic warfare tactics. This second factor severely impacted all of the participants, but

---

54. *See William Aitken*, Oxford Dictionary of National Biography 101030356.
55. *See* WWII Law and Lawyers, ch. 5.

especially Germany, as explained in Chapter 2. A third factor was that even with economic civilian restrictions, including supply controls (rationing) and price controls, the military could not get certain items needed to fight the war successfully, which led to crises in both Germany and the United Kingdom.

1. Civilian Supply

The rationing systems introduced for consumer goods were based on both a moral authority founded in patriotism and a legal authority from statutes and regulations. These systems were found in all of the major countries involved in the war but were introduced at different times. Germany, subject to the blockade and cut off from supply sources on both fronts, began forms of rationing early, in 1915. Austria-Hungary also found itself cut off from traditional suppliers, but within the kingdom, the problem was exacerbated by grain producer Hungary having more wheat available for its citizens than Austria did. Britain and France, each having their own production still available and able to receive supplies from neutrals like America and from within the empire from countries like Canada, did not implement compulsory rationing until later in the war, in 1918.

The German economic situation was such that civilians were asked to sacrifice for the good of the nation, so that production could be shifted to military needs. While this affected all aspects of consumer goods, clearly it is food that was hit the hardest. As Germany was not self-sufficient in food production, being cut off from prewar sources of food made it very difficult to supply the military and civilian needs, necessitating the early attempts at rationing. What made the food supply situation even worse was that one of the items targeted in the blockades was the fertilizers used heavily in agriculture. In addition, the military manpower needs had taken large numbers of farm workers from agricultural regions to the front. And then difficult winters and poor harvests exacerbated the food shortage.

Nationally, there was initially no coordinated effort to address rationing, as the cities and states took on most of this responsibility. Many of the initial activities were reactionary, such as the 1915 slaughter of the millions of pigs (*Schweinemord*), which both saved the crops that would have been fed to them and made the pigs themselves into food, or the price controls on bread, which led to more potato consumption as a replacement. Starvation and deprivation in the larger cities began to occur, and then food riots and work strikes. To provide a coordinated response, a national War Food Office (*Kriegsernährungsamt*)[56] was created in May 1916 to determine how to keep the population from starvation and deal with food transportation. It implemented rationing of items including bread, sugar, meat, cheese, milk, butter, potatoes, rice, coffee, cocoa, and tea. But a lack of political prowess and comprehensive strategy by the office led the states to make their own efforts, such as those in Prussia, which appointed a state commissioner for public nutrition in February 1917.

In the United Kingdom, the unrestricted submarine warfare finally was having an impact. Previously, the cabinet had set maximum prices on essential foods, but by 1917, shortages were causing long lines for different types of food. So the government determined that it should implement mandatory national rationing under a food controller, starting in 1918. Items that were eventually rationed (the timing of each was different) included sugar, butter, margarine, meat, jam, and cheese. Registration with a butcher and a grocer and possession of a ration card was required to purchase these items. Unlike in Germany, the British scheme, when started, would within the first year cover every type of food of which there was scarcity.

But rationing, minimum price controls (to encourage supply), and maximum price controls (to discourage inflation) were not the only options for civilian supply. Another was to increase the supply, for example, by increasing the amount of arable land under production. The British Corn Production Act of 1917 was an example of a way to increase the domestic food supply by guaranteeing a minimum price for cereal crops and minimum wages for farm laborers.[57] This and other efforts led to a significant increase in agricultural acreage by war's end. And unlike in Germany, women were pressed into service, with the Women's Land Army taking many responsibilities in agriculture to free up male farm workers for military service.

DORA was used as a way to control food, with the role of "food controller" given extensive responsibilities under regulations to maintain the food

---

56. Auf Grund des Artikels 4 der Verordnung des Bundesrats über Kriegsmassnahmen zure Sicherung der Volksernährung vom 22 Mai 1916 (RGBl. S. 401) (Ger.).
57. 7 & 8 Geo. 5, c. 46 (U.K.).

supply. The food controller was responsible for "orders regulating, or giving directions with respect to the production, manufacture, treatment, use, consumption, transport, storage, distribution, supply, sale or purchase of, or other dealing in, or measures to be taken in relation to any article (including orders providing for the fixing of maximum and minimum prices where it appears to him necessary or expedient to make any such order for the purpose of encouraging or maintaining the food supply of the country, and making such provisions as to entry, inspection, or otherwise as appear to him necessary or expedient for the purpose of his duties)."[58] The position of minister of food was later created to take over the role of the food controller.[59]

2. Military Supply

The "Shell Crisis" arose in the United Kingdom after military leadership blamed the lack of munitions for the failure of the March 1915 offensive at Neuve Chapelle. When this news was leaked to the press, the ensuing furor led to two laws being passed in June and July: the Ministry of Munitions Act and the Munitions of War Act of 1915. The former law[60] and a related order in council[61] detailed the oversight role, first filled by David Lloyd George (see Chapter 2), and functions related to the supply of munitions, including responsibility for munitions supply and munitions factory labor. These responsibilities included to handle munitions contracts and inspections[62] and to "institute such inquiries on behalf of His Majesty and do all such other things as he may consider necessary or expedient for the effective performance of his duties."[63]

The latter act[64] was addressed to the "efficient manufacture, transport, and supply" of munitions for this war. It did not allow for strikes or lock-outs at munitions plants[65] and referred disputes to arbitration tribunals.[66] It gave the ministry the ability to declare nongovernment munitions factories as "controlled establishments," which brought them under the control of the ministry.

---

58. DORA Regulation 2F, Jan. 10, 1917 (U.K.).
59. New Ministries and Secretaries Act of 1916, 6 & 7 Geo. 5, c. 68 (U.K.).
60. Ministry of Munitions Act of 1915, 5 & 6 Geo. 5, c. 51 (U.K.).
61. Order in Council, Ministry of Munitions, June 16, 1915 (U.K.).
62. *Id.* § 2.
63. *Id.* § 4.
64. Munitions of War Act of 1915, 5 & 6 Geo. 5, c. 54 (U.K.).
65. *Id.* § 2.
66. *Id.* § 1.

This meant that there were restrictions on the profits that could be earned, and wage increases had to be approved by the minister of munitions.[67] DORA was also amended to regulate workers in munitions plants.[68] The Munitions of War Act also had provisions making it extremely difficult for munitions workers to leave employment there to find work elsewhere, requiring a certificate from the former munitions employer.[69]

The munitions work eventually came under such demands that the minister of munitions in early 1917 was forced to prioritize munitions work into A, B, and C classes, with class A encompassing contracts from the Admiralty or the War Office, for merchant shipping, or from allied governments, and class B including exports, maintenance and repairs, or contracts certified as necessary for the efficient conduct of the war. Class C included all other contracts. Further acts allowed the ministry to control the wages of the employees there, many of whom were women ("munitionettes") stepping in for men sent to the front lines.[70] In addition, overseas munitions production in British Empire countries such as Canada was overseen by the Imperial Munitions Board to produce munitions for the European war.

To deal with the gap in the supply of domestically produced armaments, Germany introduced the Hindenburg Program. With the early expectations that the war would be "over by Christmas," the stalemate had Germany at a severe disadvantage in what had become a war of attrition. Originating from the Raw Materials Office set up in August 1914 by Walter Rathenau of conglomerate AEG and the War Ministry's direction, the plan in August 1916 was to draw all remaining available resources and devote them to the war effort, with production targets of doubling munitions and tripling artillery and machine guns by May 1917. These goals necessitated increased construction of munitions factories. It also required drafting all available human resources into working on the war effort, moving to a centrally controlled, total-war economy.

As the new (in 1916) army chief of staff Paul von Hindenburg stated, "The quality of troops, whose value can never be rated high enough, is no longer decisive; instead, superiority in artillery, munitions, and machine guns is

---

67. *Id.* § 4.
68. *Id.* § 9.
69. *Id.* § 7.
70. Munitions of War (Amendment) Act of 1916, 5 & 6 Geo. 5, c. 99; Munitions of War Act of 1917, 7 & 8 Geo. 5, c. 45 (U.K.).

increasingly decisive . . . we can only win the war if we supply the army with enough military equipment that it confronts the enemy armies from a position of equal strength. . . . maximum performance can, however, be achieved only if the German people in its entirety puts itself at the service of the Fatherland. All other considerations have to take a back seat. . . . Every man must be put into service according to his skills, be it at the lathe, in the office, or in any other occupation where he best serves the state."[71] So the Reichstag passed a law[72] that obligated every German male between the ages of eighteen and sixty who was not in the armed forces to participate in national auxiliary service. Those in government, agriculture, forestry, health care, or the war industry were considered to be rendering national service, and those in agriculture or forestry, necessary to feed and supply the nation, were not to be removed from those important occupations.[73]

LEGAL PROFILES

Adolf von Batocki was the first head of the German War Food Office. He was born in Germany in 1868 and obtained his legal training there. After schooling he entered the Prussian civil service, working as a court clerk and then an assessor. From 1900 to 1907, he was a district administrator in Königsberg. From 1907 to 1914, he was involved with the chamber of agriculture in East Prussia. After outbreak of the war, he was appointed president of the province of East Prussia and was involved with reconstruction of that province after Russian attacks. Then, in 1916, he became the head of the new War Food Office. He later served in the war on the Italian front and became a governor there. After the war he defended against a Communist uprising in East Prussia and worked on reconstruction there. He was also active in agricultural policy and taught economics at university. He died in 1944.[74]

---

71. Von Hindenburg letter to Bethmann Hollweg (Sept. 13, 1916).
72. Auxiliary Service Law of 1916, Hilfsdienstgesetz (Ger.).
73. *Id.* § 2.
74. *See Adolf von Batocki-Friebe*, Neue Deutsche Biographie.

Georg Michaelis was in charge of the state of Prussia's food program. He was born in Germany in 1857 and obtained his legal training there. After getting his doctor of law, he moved to Tokyo, Japan, to teach German law from 1885 to 1889. Upon returning to Germany, he was involved as a prosecutor in the Prussian administration, including various regional roles and as the undersecretary of the Prussian Ministry of Finance from 1909. From 1915, he headed the Prussian food program (*Reichsgetreidestelle*) for production of cereals and also advised the other Central Powers on nutrition. He then succeeded Bethmann-Hollweg as the chancellor of Germany in July 1917 (the first non-aristocrat), but only until the end of October. He served as the president of Prussia and then in 1918 as the president of the Prussian province of Upper Pomerania. He died in 1936.[75]

Wilhelm von Waldow was the second leader of the War Food Office. He was born in Germany in 1856 and obtained his legal training there. He then joined the Prussian administration, where he served in a number of administrative and leadership posts, including in Königsberg and in Posen. In 1911 he was elected the president of Upper Pomerania. In 1917 he took over the War Food Office. He also served in the Prussian state parliament from 1894 to 1898 and as Lord Mayor of Cologne. He died in 1937.[76]

B. Cases

Violations of the statutes addressing supply to civilians and the military came to trial in several ways. For civilians, there were trials related to the hoarding of food, which was contrary to the goal of rationing to make food available equally to all. For the military, the supply of munitions brought cases relating to violations of the Munitions of War acts, which were tried under the acts' munitions tribunals. These cases were closely tied to the labor union movement for establishing the rights of workers. In addition, labor activities arising

---

75. *See Georg Michaelis*, NEUE DEUTSCHE BIOGRAPHIE.
76. *See Wilhelm von Waldow*, NEUE DEUTSCHE BIOGRAPHIE.

from the act's apparent undermining of labor's gains by dilution of the union rights came to a head in these trials, which also led to extrajudicial punishments by the government. When the actions of the labor movement extended into directly inciting violations of DORA against the war effort, it led to prosecutions.

1. Food Hoarding

The following case was illustrative of government attempts to control the food supply. In April 1917, food hoarding was banned. In *Ex parte Murdoch*,[77] the defendant's house was raided by the local Food Control Committee, which found excess tea, sugar, meat, flour, milk, and other items. "Excess" was defined as that which exceeded the quantity that would be ordinarily required for the residents' use and consumption. The prosecution was able to show significant deliveries of both sugar and flour in the time between the effective date of the Food Hoarding Order and the raid on the house in November 1917. In addition, the defendant's grocer said the defendant had purchased his ration amount of these items from the store. As such, the defendant was fined and ordered to forfeit all of the excess sugar and flour that had been confiscated by the police in the raid (which had been seized under DORA regulatory authority).

In the appeal, the defendant argued that he should have been charged with separate offenses for each item (hoarding of sugar and flour) and for each of the four occasions when he took excess delivery, but the penalty had been for only one count (food hoarding over the seven-month period). The court of appeal held that the regulation was not for having more food than ordinarily required but possession of excess quantities of individual items. As such, the defendant had been convicted of two separate offenses but had only a single penalty imposed (duplicity), so the conviction was quashed.

---

77. R. v. Hammick and Another, JJ. (*ex parte* Murdoch), K.B. Court of Appeal (1918).

LEGAL PROFILES

Henry Holman Gregory appeared for the defendant in the food hoarding case. He was born in England in 1864, the son of a solicitor, and obtained his legal training there, being called to the bar in 1897. He became a king's counsel in 1910. He held several judicial positions, including as recorder of Bath in 1916 and of London in 1934. He also served on the central criminal court in 1929. In 1918 he was elected to Parliament, where he served until 1922. He was also involved with a number of commissions and arbitrations dealing with labor issues and unemployment insurance. He died in 1947.[78]

Charles Darling was the judge who announced the decision for the court in the food hoarding case. He was born in England in 1849 and obtained his legal training there, being called to the bar in 1874. In 1885, he became a queen's counsel. He was elected to Parliament in 1888, where he served until 1897. In that year, he was appointed a High Court judge on the Queen's Bench. The position also served in an appellate role, where he was when this case was decided. He served in this role until retiring in 1923 and then entering the House of Lords in 1924. He died in 1936.[79]

2. Munitions Tribunals

The Munitions of War acts had made provision for munitions tribunals to settle any differences between labor and management at munitions plants. These issues ranged from strikes of varying degrees, to refusal to work overtime, to the inability of workers to get leaving certificates to go to other positions. Two related trials occurred at one firm in the Glasgow, Scotland, area in 1915. Glasgow was the biggest center of labor unrest due to large numbers of workers involved in munitions and shipbuilding. The first trial involved a shortage of coppersmiths, which led management at the Fairfield company to want to introduce plumbers into these roles. The union agreed to having plumb-

---

78. *See Sir Holman Gregory, K.C.*, THE TIMES (May 10, 1947).
79. *See Charles Darling*, OXFORD DICTIONARY OF NATIONAL BIOGRAPHY 101032714.

ers on the ships but not in the copper shops themselves. Since the firm was a controlled establishment under the Munitions Act, management's direction to start dilution (the use of semi-skilled and unskilled workers in skilled positions) seemed to weaken the role of the coppersmiths' trade union. So the coppersmiths walked out en masse. In early August 1915, twenty-eight of these strikers were put on trial before the munitions tribunal. At the trial, despite many protests about the legitimacy of the actions of management, the strikers agreed to return to work and had to pay a de minimis fine.

A short while later, two shipwrights at the same company were dismissed for loitering on the job. When the company refused to reinstate them, other shipwrights struck, and in September, twenty-six of the leaders were brought to trial before the munitions tribunal. The tribunal focused on the illegality of the strike rather than the fairness of the dismissals of the two workers. The strike's illegality was not in dispute, so the strikers were fined £10 each and given three weeks to pay or risk imprisonment.

The following year, the dilution movement under the Munitions Act came to a head in Glasgow with the shop stewards deportation case. In the first months of 1916, the government had been trying to implement dilution in the munitions plants. The engineers went on strike over this. The government responded by ordering the arrest and deportation of ten implicated shop stewards from Glasgow. Thirty strikers were brought before the munitions tribunal in March 1916 and were convicted and fined £5 each.

This was the peak of significant munitions labor trials during the war, although later there were prosecutions under DORA. The Clyde Workers Committee was an unofficial workers' organization involved in protesting the Munitions Act and its prohibition on workers' mobility (the leaving certificates) and dilution (including the use of women in factories). An article was published in the committee's journal, *The Worker*, titled "Should the Workers Arm?" The article led to a prosecution in which the leader of the committee, Willie Gallacher, and the journal's publisher, John William Muir, were convicted under DORA of inciting violations of the act and so against the war effort and received sentences of six and twelve months, respectively.

LEGAL PROFILES

William Gloag was the chairman of the munitions tribunal in the first case. He was born in Scotland in 1865, the son of a judge, and obtained his legal training there, starting his legal career in 1889. He first became a law instructor at the University of Edinburgh in 1902 and then a professor of law at the University of Glasgow in 1905. He became a king's counsel in 1909. He authored several well-known legal books, including *Introduction to the Law of Scotland*. He died in 1934.[80]

Thomas A. Fyfe was the chairman of the munitions tribunal in the second case. He was born in Scotland in 1852 and obtained his legal training there. He practiced commercial law, with an emphasis on shipping firms. He was appointed sheriff (trial judges in civil and criminal courts) in Fyfe in 1895 and in Glasgow in 1900. He authored several publications on law, including on the Munitions of War acts and on sheriff courts, and he was involved in the Sheriff Court Act of 1908. He lost both of his sons in WWI. He died in 1928.[81]

Edward Rosslyn Mitchell was the defense counsel in the deportations case. He was born in Scotland in 1879 and obtained his legal training there, starting as a solicitor in 1904. He first got involved with the Glasgow Town Council by being elected in 1909, where he would remain active for decades. After an unsuccessful attempt in 1922 against soon-to-be prime minister Bonar Law, he was elected to Parliament in 1924 by defeating former prime minister H. H. Asquith. He served there until 1929. He died in 1965.[82]

---

80. See *William Gloag*, OXFORD DICTIONARY OF NATIONAL BIOGRAPHY 101037461.
81. See *Sheriff-Substitute Fyfe*, THE TIMES (Mar. 16, 1928).
82. See *Mr. E.R. Mitchell*, THE TIMES (Nov. 3, 1965).

C. Subsequent Events

After the war, the need for an extraordinary supply of munitions was no longer a major issue, and many munitions factories were dismantled. Civilian rationing did not immediately cease, however, because supply and demand had to resume its equilibrium. As mentioned in Chapter 2, significant numbers of Germans starved, and the survivors were in such a weakened state that the Spanish flu pandemic hit the country hard. Rationing was to return in even a bigger way in the United Kingdom in WWII, starting right from the early stages of the war. In Germany, the WWII rationing system also started early, but warily, as Nazi officials did not want any impact on the people's prosperity. So in the first few years of that war, rationing did not impact Germans' lives significantly, but as the war wore on and the adverse results became more significant, the effects of rationing on the German people became more severe.

After WWI, labor unrest returned, but for different reasons. The decrease in the massive government needs from the war years led to a decrease in economic demand that could not be offset by the increase in consumer consumption. To add to this, the return of soldiers meant a new source of competition on the labor front for the union movement. Faced with raising unemployment, the unions determined that they should try to bargain for a shorter, forty-hour workweek. This would mean available work for more workers. A general strike was called for in the Glasgow area in late January 1919. During negotiations with the Lord Provost of Glasgow, violence broke out in what was called the Battle of George Square. The British government intervened by sending in nonlocal troops to restore order. Many of the labor leaders, including Willie Gallacher, were jailed, and the forty-hour workweek was not achieved at that time.

During WWI, all of the additional government spending on munitions and ships not only rebalanced the economy away from domestic to military consumption (domestic British consumption fell from 77.2 percent of GDP in 1913 to 60.7 percent in 1918, while government expenditures increased from 8.7 percent of GDP in 1913 to 37.7 percent in 1918),[83] it also greatly strained the government finances, which meant new sources of revenue were needed to fund the war. As always, these included raising new taxes, borrowing, and print-

---

83. *The United Kingdom During World War I: Business as Usual?*, Broadberry and Howlett, tbl. 5 (2003) (quoting Feinstein (1972), *National Income, Expenditure and Output of the United Kingdom, 1855-1965*).

ing money. The new taxes included increasing rates for income and ad valorem taxes and a new excess-profits duty of up to 80 percent on businesses.[84] There were also significant increases in domestic and overseas debt issuance and the use of inflationary techniques to increase short-term revenues and make the interest payments and principal repayments of government debt cheaper. The total budget deficit of the United Kingdom from the beginning to the end of the war grew from £706 million in 1913–14 (26.2 percent of GDP) to £7,482 million in 1918–19 (127.5 percent of GDP),[85] a whopping increase of almost 1,000 percent!

LEGAL PROFILES

Robert Munro was the secretary for Scotland during these riots. He was born in Scotland in 1868 and obtained his legal training there, starting as an advocate in 1893. He became a king's counsel in 1910, the same year that he was elected to a seat in Parliament, where he served until 1922. In 1913, he became the lord advocate, a position he held until late 1916, when he became secretary for Scotland. In 1922, he was appointed to the bench as the lord justice clerk, where he remained until 1933. He died in 1955.[86]

3.4 PROXIMATE NEUTRALITY

A. Statutes

Neutrality was a position in foreign relations that several countries in Europe attempted to maintain. These included Denmark, Luxembourg, the Nether-

---

84. Finance (No. 2) Act of 1915, 5 & 6 Geo. 5, c. 89 (U.K.).
85. *The United Kingdom During World War I: Business as Usual?*, Table 9 (quoting Wormell (2000), The *Management of the National Debt of the United Kingdom, 1900-32* and Feinstein (1972)).
86. *See Robert Munro*, OXFORD DICTIONARY OF NATIONAL BIOGRAPHY 101040352.

lands, Norway, Spain, Sweden, and Switzerland.[87] Of these, it was the Netherlands that was both geographically closest to the battle and most consistently being tested on its position of neutrality by the demands of the Allied and Central Powers. Geographically contiguous to Germany and close across the English Channel to Great Britain, the Netherlands had to try to maintain neutrality while being located in the middle of these two leading powers. This position included dealing with trade, as the Netherlands had significant prewar relationships with both countries, which reached not only into goods but also into its ships, ports like Rotterdam, and financial credits for trade. It also involved dealing with its own territorial integrity, with possible incursions by the belligerents and influxes of victims of the war, such as the refugees from neighboring Belgium.

The requirements of neutral countries during wartime were spelled out in the Hague Conventions V[88] and XIII.[89] Hague V did not allow belligerents to move troops or munitions across the territory of a neutral[90] or for a neutral to allow such movement.[91] Regarding trade, "A neutral Power is not called upon to prevent the export or transport, on behalf of one or other of the belligerents, of arms, munitions of war, or, in general, of anything which can be of use to an army or a fleet,"[92] but any restrictions that are put in place were required to be applied impartially.[93] Further, it was not a violation of neutrality for a person of a neutral country to furnish supplies or makes loans to one of the belligerents.[94] But as discussed in the section on blockades (see Chapter 2), neutral states could not provide belligerents "war-ships, ammunition, or war material."[95]

When the declarations of war specified in Chapter 2 began in August 1914, the Dutch responded to each with a declaration of strict neutrality. Among the provisions it passed was prohibition of use of its territorial waters by belligerent

---

87. For information on Switzerland's neutrality during WWII, see WWII LAW AND LAWYERS, ch. 5.
88. Convention on the Rights and Duties of Neutral Powers and Persons in Case of War on Land (Hague V) (Oct. 18, 1907).
89. Convention on the Rights and Duties of Neutral Powers in Naval War (Hague XIII) (Oct. 18, 1907).
90. Hague V, art. 2.
91. *Id.* art. 5.
92. *Id.* art. 7.
93. *Id.* art. 9.
94. *Id.* art. 18(a).
95. Hague XIII, art. 6.

warships[96] (more stringent than Hague XIII, which allowed passage by warships through neutral waters).[97] It also prohibited use of its airspace,[98] a rather novel concept in the days before significant use of airplanes in war. To enforce its neutrality, the Dutch used its small army and limited navy to guard its coast and land borders. These forces had to act both to protect the neutrality provisions and to provide a defense against possible invasion, as neutral neighbor Belgium had suffered. While all the major powers had accepted the Netherlands' declarations of neutrality, as the war wore on, the initial advantages of Dutch neutrality to the powers (an economic transit conduit for Germany; the lack of another front and blocking of German access to English Channel ports for the United Kingdom and France) began to mean less.

To help prepare for the war, the Dutch had passed several laws increasing the human resources capabilities of the military, including the field army,[99] the primary reserves,[100] and the secondary reserves.[101] Eligibility for call-up in case of a war was extended to practically all males under forty to support the field army (*landstorm*) and the primary reserves (*landweer*). The soldiers, especially the primary reserve forces, had additional duties in dealing with a variety of different foreigners who came into the Netherlands after the start of the war. Civilian refugees in large numbers (up to one million) came from Belgium after the initial German invasion there (although many later returned home or went on to Great Britain). Military personnel came, including those of the belligerents who had intentionally or unintentionally entered the country, and also escaped prisoners of war (POWs) and POWs who had been exchanged between Belgium, Germany, and England and then interned in the Netherlands. After the Germans marched on Antwerp, tens of thousands of defeated Belgian soldiers also made their way to the Netherlands, initially overwhelming the Dutch capabilities to intern them.

Under Hague V, the Netherlands was required to intern belligerent soldiers away from the front lines and ensure that they did not rejoin the war.[102]

---

96. Declaration of the Neutrality of the Netherlands in the European War, art. 4, Aug. 5, 1914 (Neth.).
97. Hague XIII, art. 10.
98. Staatsblad no. 354, 1914 (Neth.).
99. Militiewet, Staatsblad no. 21, 1912 (Neth.).
100. Landweerwet, Staatsblad no. 148, 1913 (Neth.).
101. Landstormwet, Staatsblad no. 149, 1913 (Neth.).
102. Hague V, art. 11.

This was also a provision in the Dutch declaration of neutrality, to disarm these troops and intern them until war's end.[103] For POWs who had escaped from imprisonment by one of the belligerents, they were not required to be interned but could remain at liberty, if they were to stay in the neutral country at all.[104] In addition, sick and wounded soldiers who came into the Netherlands were to be guarded to ensure they did not return to the conflict, but they were also accorded all rights under the Geneva Conventions.[105]

One of the items that made guarding the southern border somewhat easier on the Dutch was that Germany built an immensely long "Wire of Death" along the border of Belgium and the Netherlands. The 300-kilometer electrified wire, running along the whole of the northern Belgian border and carrying up to 6,000 volts, was deadly for both humans and animals. Its purpose was to diminish the flow of refugees and troops into the Netherlands from Belgium on the south, but it did not address Belgium's eastern border with Germany or its coastal borders on the west and north. Several thousand people died trying to get over, under, or through the wire from its installation date in August 1915. It did demonstrate Germany's intention to let the Netherlands remain neutral.

In addition to guarding its land borders, the Dutch had to guard a very long coastline with a significant number of ports. These included not only its own ports, but also Belgium's, in the case of Antwerp. The opening to the sea for that city was in Dutch territory, lying on the Scheldt River. Because of the potential use of the river as an entry into Antwerp, the Netherlands took steps to maintain its neutrality by rearranging the buoys and lights there. In a note to the Belgian government,[106] the Dutch said that they would allow sailing up the river to Antwerp only during the daytime and only with Dutch pilots, thereby serving "both the Dutch interests in the defense of Netherlands territory and

---

103. Declaration of the Neutrality of the Netherlands in the European War, art. 3, Aug. 5, 1914 (Neth.).
104. Hague V, art. 13.
105. Amelioration of the Condition of the Wounded on the Field of Battle, Aug. 22, 1864; Convention for the Amelioration of the Condition of the Wounded and Sick in Armies in the Field, July 6, 1906.
106. Note addressed to the Belgian Government to announce that the Netherlands may be obliged to institute war buoying on the Scheldt, Aug. 3, 1914 (Neth.).

Belgian interests in the navigation of Antwerp."[107] The Dutch also requested the removal of the lightships in that area.

The Hague Conventions also dealt with the right of "angary," the seizure of the property of neutrals by belligerents for use during the war. This right was only to be used by sovereign states when absolutely necessary and required an indemnity payment for its use. It was something else that the Dutch, with their significant merchant fleet, had to deal with. As an example, when the United States entered the war, it had to transport vast amounts of men and materials to Europe and so needed all the ships it could locate. It tried to enter agreements with the countries that remained neutral for use of their available shipping. It entered one with the Dutch government, but due to German pressure, the Dutch were forced to renege. As such, the American government, in March 1918, utilizing the authority of a statute passed the previous year,[108] began to requisition Dutch merchant ships wherever they were located within U.S. territory and waters.

LEGAL PROFILES

Theo Heemskerk was the Dutch prime minister leading up to the war. He was born in the Netherlands in 1852 and obtained his legal training there. He was elected to the Tweede Kamer (house of representatives) in 1888 and served there until 1908. He also served in the Amsterdam city council, from 1889 to 1895 and from 1900 to 1908. He served as interior minister from 1908 while he was serving as prime minister (i.e., minister president), a position he held until 1913. He then joined the council of state. From 1918 to 1925, he served as justice minister. He returned to the Tweede Kamer in 1925 and became minister of state in 1926. In 1930 he was president of a conference on the codification of

---

107. *Id.*
108. Pub. L. No. 65-24, An Act to Punish Interference with the Foreign Relations, the Neutrality, and the Foreign Commerce of the United States, to Punish Espionage, and Better to Enforce the Criminal Laws of the United States, and for Other Purposes (1917).

international law held at the Hague. He served in the Tweede Kamer until his death in 1932.[109]

Pieter Cort van der Linden was the Dutch prime minister during the war. He was born in the Netherlands in 1846, the son of a lawyer, and obtained his legal training there. He started in private practice in 1869. In 1881, he became a professor, first at the University of Groningen and then at the University of Amsterdam. From 1897 to 1901, he served as the minister of justice. Even though not a member of the legislature, he was the prime minister and the interior minister of the Netherlands from 1913 to 1918. As a result of his backing for universal suffrage, the widened electorate brought in new leadership in 1918. From 1918 to 1934, he was a member of the council of state. He served on the Permanent Court of Arbitration and led the Carnegie Foundation (Netherlands). He died in 1935.[110]

B. Cases

The cases that arose from proximate neutrality showed the balance that the Dutch had to maintain between the Central and Allied Powers. The first case discussed here deals with the interning of submarines that could not leave the Netherlands. The second involves the sinking of neutral ships. The third case concerns the Dutch government's response to smuggling.

1. Interning Submarines

The Dutch needed to protect their neutrality in all of the areas discussed above. They protected their territorial integrity by interning troops that came across the borders, but denied that in the early offensive of the war the Germans invading through Belgium and Luxembourg had used the Dutch roads near Vaals. On the water, they interned ships and submarines as per their declaration of neutrality,[111] including two U-boats that ran aground within a few weeks of

---

109. *See Heemskerk, Theodorus*, BIOGRAFISCH WOORDENBOEK VAN NEDERLAND 3.
110. *See Linden, Pieter Cort van der*, BIOGRAFISCH WOORDENBOEK VAN NEDERLAND 1.
111. Declaration of the Neutrality of the Netherlands in the European War, art. 4, Aug. 5, 1914 (Neth.).

each other: the UB-30 near Walcheren Island in February 1917 and the UB-6 near Voorne Island in March 1917 (UBs were more coastal versions of the oceangoing U-boats called *Unterseeboot*). In a resolution based on international arbitration between the Dutch and the Germans that showed the practical side to remaining neutral under constant pressure from belligerents, the UB-6 was scuttled and its crew interned for the rest of the war. The UB-30 was eventually released back to the Germans in August 1917, where it proceeded to sink many more ships, only to be sunk itself by depth charges from a British armed trawler one year later, on August 13, 1918.

This incident greatly incensed the Germans, as compared to their response to the British armed merchantman *Princess Melita* in the same month. When approaching Rotterdam, the *Princess Melita* was ordered by the Dutch to leave neutral waters under threat of internment. The ship departed, but having thrown its gun overboard, as per instructions, it returned, and after it was verified that the ship was unarmed, it was permitted to proceed on to Rotterdam without internment. This led the Germans to consider, but never follow through on, an occupation of the Netherlands. The Dutch maintained their policy of interning belligerents' warships, whether they were submarines or armed merchantmen, causing ongoing consternation to both the Germans and the British.

2. Sinking of Neutral Ships

As the war progressed and the Netherlands continued to hold tight to its neutrality principles, one action that may have tried its patience as much as any other was the sinking of the Dutch steamer ship SS *Tubantia*. In the investigation subsequent to this March 15, 1916, incident, torpedo fragments belonging to German submarine UB-13 were found in the remnants of the ship and a number of its launches. This matter was not fully addressed until after the war, when it was submitted to international arbitration.[112] The German government claimed that the fragments were from a torpedo that had been fired ten days before the *Tubantia* sunk, at a British destroyer, and that had missed its target and lain in the water for the *Tubantia* to run into. While the court could

---

112. Hague International Commission of Inquiry, Loss of the Dutch Steamer *Tubantia*, Germany v. the Netherlands, Feb. 27, 1922.

not rule that out, they found credible the testimony of the crew members who saw the wake of a torpedo being fired at them.

Dutch meteorology experts claimed that if a torpedo fired ten days previous to the sinking had lain in the water since then, it would have drifted almost 20 nautical miles from where the explosion and sinking took place by the time the *Tubantia* sunk. They also found that the ship had been sufficiently lighted and identifiable as a neutral (Dutch) ship, although there had been fog on that night. The Germans also claimed the submarine had been elsewhere at the time of the sinking, but the original log books had been destroyed and so there was no authenticated copy to prove that. The court ruled the most likely cause of the sinking of the *Tubantia* was the direct firing of a torpedo from UB-13, and more than £800,000 was awarded to the Dutch owners of the ship for their losses.

An interesting follow-up to this case concerned the wreckage of this ship. Two groups of salvagers claimed the right to the wreck. It had long been thought that there was a rich collection of several million British pounds' worth of gold coins on this ship. As such, the competition to get the sunken treasure was intense. One of the parties in the subsequent case was war hero aviator Sydney Sippe (he had bombed zeppelin factories inside Germany early in the war), who claimed that he had found the wreck and started salvage work on it in 1922, while his competitor had not started until 1923. The court found that Sippe had indeed started first, marked the wreck, and initiated dives there.[113] This decision constituted sufficient possession, and so Sippe was able to exclude the other salvaging party while he was doing his salvaging work. He eventually abandoned the effort, due to the cost and the great difficulty in getting to the wreck.

3. Smuggling

Neutrality also played a role in the flow of economic goods. Chapter 2 discussed the British blockade and the role of the Dutch in ensuring the imported goods did not come into the Netherlands for re-export to the Central Powers. But in addition to legal imports and exports, there was the problem of illegal exports being smuggled from the Netherlands into Germany along their long border. With economic pressure from Germany to provide goods such as food

---

113. *The Tubantia*, All ER 615 (1924).

(since if it did not, Germany would not reciprocate with coal and timber), the Dutch government responded in several ways. Numerous cases of border guards taking bribes were brought to light in newspapers,[114] leading the Dutch to pass a law at the end of 1915 to prevent these acts of smuggling through increases in customs enforcement and military assistance.[115]

To further assist the fight against smuggling, the use of the "state of siege" was implemented, providing additional powers to the government. Under the war law of 1899,[116] the government was allowed to declare either a state of war (*staat van oorlog*) or a state of siege (*staat van beleg*), with the latter a form of martial law providing more extensive control to the military leaders by allowing them to dictate to local governments instead of consulting first with them. The Dutch government declared a state of war in certain areas initially in August 1914, but subsequently it declared states of siege across the country, including in those areas along the borders with Germany and Belgium. One of the state-of-siege powers was to restrict the movement of people and goods into or out of the implicated area,[117] so military controls were able to more efficiently combat smuggling of goods into Germany than civilian channels.

Because of the unclear nature of the respective limits of military versus civilian powers under this law, the Dutch supreme court (high council, *Hoge Raad der Nederlanden*) decided a number of cases involving the military's use of its powers under state of siege, clarifying those powers. These included a case in 1918 in which the court ruled that because states of siege were declared around local, not national, areas, military powers in these areas did not extend beyond the respective civilian government powers. This meant that the military did not have the power to issue regulations on trade to stop smuggling, as that was a national government power, so the military was liable for the impacts of its smuggling regulations. This ruling came as the war was drawing to a close and so did not severely impact the use of the Dutch military in the fight against smuggling from the Netherlands into Germany.

---

114. *See, e.g.*, *Smuggling in Holland, A Notorious Abuse*, THE TIMES (Feb. 7, 1916).
115. Staatsblad. no. 533, 1915 (Neth.).
116. *Oorlogswet*, Staatsblad. no. 128, 1899 (Neth.).
117. *Id.* art. 23.

LEGAL PROFILES

John Loudon was the Dutch minister of foreign affairs during the war, negotiating with Germany and the United Kingdom. He was born in the Netherlands in 1866 and obtained his legal training there. He then moved into diplomacy, serving overseas from 1895 to 1913, first in Italy then China, France, the United Kingdom, Japan, and finally the United States for the final five years. In 1913, he became the foreign minister, a role he held until 1918. He defended Dutch neutrality from this post. In 1919 he served as an envoy to the Paris Peace Conference and then became the ambassador to France for twenty years, remaining in France until it was overrun in WWII. He died in 1955.[118]

A. A. H. Struycken was the Dutch counsel in the SS *Tubantia* arbitration. He was born in the Netherlands in 1873 and obtained his legal training there. He was appointed as a constitutional and international law professor at the University of Amsterdam in 1906, a position he held full time until the start of the war and part time thereafter. In 1914 he joined the Dutch council of state. After the war, he was a delegate to the Paris Peace Conference and the Hague Conference on Russian Affairs in 1922. He was also a member of the Permanent Court of Arbitration. He wrote several legal treatises, including on Dutch law and on the war and international law. He died in 1923.[119]

Seerp Gratama was a justice and vice president of the Dutch supreme court, the *Hoge Raad*, who ruled on the smuggling rules during the war. He was born in the Netherlands in 1858, the son of a law professor, and obtained his legal training there. After private practice and work as a state archivist from 1887 to 1896, he was appointed as a judge in the Rotterdam district court in 1896. In 1904, he was appointed a justice on the *Hoge Raad*, becoming vice president of the court in 1918. He headed up a commission that worked on reform of the civil procedure

---

118. *See* Linden, Pieter Cort van der, BIOGRAFISCH WOORDENBOEK VAN NEDERLAND I.
119. *See Struiken, Antonius Alexis Hendrikus,* BIOGRAFISCH WOORDENBOEK VAN NEDERLAND I.

and was involved in legal historical organizations and publications. He died in 1923.[120]

C. Subsequent Events

After the war, the refugees and internees of all types eventually returned to their countries of origin. This had begun already with the changing military situation. But as the war was ending, the Netherlands got perhaps its most problematic refugee when Kaiser Wilhelm abdicated the German imperial throne and left Germany, being treated in the Netherlands as a private-citizen refugee. As such, all privileges applied to him, one of which was the refusal of the Netherlands to return him to Germany. The Allied Powers wanted to bring him to justice and try him for his role in starting the war, as allowed by the Versailles Treaty.[121] On June 28, 1919, the president of the Paris Peace Conference (see Chapter 7) requested that the Dutch government extradite him, as he was still a symbol of the German war party. Further attempts were made on January 16, 1920, and February 14, 1920, but the Netherlands, in one of the final acts of neutrality from this war, refused all such requests, and Kaiser Wilhelm lived out his life there, dying in 1941 as Nazi Germany was occupying the neutral Netherlands.

Interestingly, the kaiser's son Prince William, who had served a military role leading German armies during the war, instead of being treated as a refugee, was treated on his arrival in the Netherlands as a belligerent soldier and interned. He was interned for five years before he was allowed to return to Germany. The problems of neutrality, refugees, military internees and trading with belligerents would arise again in WWII for another of WWI's neutral countries, Switzerland, which, unlike the Netherlands, was completely surrounded for much of WWII by belligerents from one alliance.[122] But there were additional factors involving the financial services sector and banking secrecy, as well as the Holocaust, that made neutrality so different in WWII than it had been in WWI.

---

120. *See Gratama, Seerp*, BIOGRAFISCH WOORDENBOEK VAN NEDERLAND I.
121. Treaty of Peace Between the Allied and Associated Powers and Germany, art. 227, June 28, 1919.
122. *See* WWII LAW AND LAWYERS, ch. 5.

LEGAL PROFILES

Charles Ruijs de Beerenbrouck was a government commissioner for Belgian refugees during the war and the Dutch prime minister at the end of the war. He was born in the Netherlands in 1873 and obtained his legal training there. He started practice in 1896 and was elected in 1899 to the Maastricht city council, where he served until 1918. In 1905, he was elected to the Tweede Kamer, where he served until 1918. From 1914 to 1918 he served as commissioner for Belgian refugees. In September 1918, he became prime minister, dealing with the return of soldiers and the residency of Kaiser Wilhelm. He served in this role until 1925, when he became the president of the Tweede Kamer. He was also interior minister from 1918 to 1923. In 1929, he again became the prime minister, serving until 1933. He then switched back to being the president of the Tweede Kamer, remaining in this post until his death in 1936.[123]

For the Netherlands, the escalating blockade and demands for food from Germany and food parity from Britain led to hunger for the civilian population by 1918. But this was significantly less extreme than the hunger situation in Belgium almost from the start of the war. Belgium was not a significant food producer, and with its food requisitioned by the invading German army, the Belgians' starvation situation rapidly deteriorated. Originating out of the U.S. embassy in London but run and funded by civilian efforts, the Commission for the Relief of Belgium (CRB) was able to purchase, ship, and deliver millions of tons of food to Belgium during the war. Through a combination of agreements reached with the belligerents not to sink its ships as well as rigorous oversight of the distribution process, the CRB helped keep the country and millions of citizens fed. This organization was led by mining consultant and London resident Herbert Hoover. The future U.S. president was also to lead the U.S. Food Administration after the United States entered the war, as well as the postwar American Relief Administration, which helped to feed Europe, including Germany, Poland, and Russia.

---

123. *See Ruijs van Beerenbroek, Charles*, BIOGRAFISCH WOORDENBOEK VAN NEDERLAND I.

The civil war in Russia, the deportation of Armenians (see Chapter 6), and other conflicts contributed to the refugee problem after the war. Unlike the Belgian refugees, who could return to their home country, these new refugees had been expelled from their home countries and were, in essence, stateless. This problem was given to the League of Nations (see Chapter 7), which, through its high commissioner for refugees, Fridtjof Nansen, was able to provide temporary relief from famine while tackling the unique problem of the statelessness of these refugees through the design of the "Nansen passport," which was used as a form of identification for these stateless people to get resettled somewhere.

LEGAL PROFILES

Fridtjof Nansen was the League of Nations high commissioner for refugees after the war and among the most famous explorers in the world. He was born in Norway (then in union with Sweden) in 1861, the son of a lawyer. Although not a trained lawyer himself, Nansen spent the second part of his career deeply involved in legal issues. He was first to traverse Greenland in 1888, and in his specially built Fram (later used by Roald Amundsen to find the route of the long-sought Northwest Passage), he attempted to reach the North Pole. In 1905, he was a strong advocate for the separation of Norway and Sweden, negotiating with both Germany and England to gain support and promoting a Danish prince to become the new king of Norway. In 1906 he became the ambassador to the United Kingdom. When Norway joined the League of Nations, he was one of its delegates. Through his work in assisting the repatriation of POWs, he was asked to help with those displaced by the Russian revolution and civil war. For his work in assisting refugees and POWs, he was awarded the Nobel Peace Prize in 1922. He continued to assist refugees until his death in 1930.[124] After his death, the League of

---

124. *See Fridtjof Nansen*, N.Y. TIMES (May 14, 1930).

Nations created the Nansen International Office for Refugees to continue his work.

3.5 TREASON

A. Statutes

The crime of treason is the most basic betrayal of one's country, be it the country of one's birth, of one's ancestors, or where one has been naturalized. But the treason laws used in this war and their applications were surprisingly different. The differences arose in detailing what acts were considered treasonable; defining espionage versus treason (e.g., acts committed by a citizen might be treason, but the same acts by a noncitizen might be espionage); differences between gathering intelligence, commerce, and communicating with an enemy; differences between "high" treason (trying to bring down the state, or treasonous acts when the state is at war) and treason (other crimes against the state or its leadership or treasonous acts when the state is at peace); the interplay between military and civil/criminal laws for treason; the use of military instead of civil courts to try the cases; and applicability of domestic law to foreign neutrals, enemies, and those in occupied countries.

In England, the treason statute in effect during the war was the centuries-old Treason Act.[125] In 1351, the Treason Act was promulgated, punishing acts directly affecting the king, such as killing or plotting to kill the king, his wife, or his heir; having relations with the women around the king; levying war on the king; adhering to the king's enemies by giving them aid and comfort; or killing the king's high officials, including justices. Later statutes[126] made it treason just to plan to do some of these acts, including to deprive the king of his crown, to levy war on the king, or to incite foreigners to invade the country.

Treason under the French military code[127] was mentioned briefly in Chapter 2 for the mutinies in the trenches. The code's section for treason and espio-

---

125. Treason Act of 1351, 25 Edw. 3, Stat. 5, c. 2 (U.K.).
126. *See, e.g.*, Sedition Act of 1661, 13 Car. 2, Stat. 1, c. 1 (U.K.).
127. Code de justice militaire pour l'armee de terre de 1857 (Fr.).

nage called for death and degradation for those who provided to the enemy secret plans, passwords, supplies, shipments, negotiations, or information about arsenals, ports, and harbors; maintained contact with the enemy to assist its operations; participated in a conspiracy to force the surrender or capitulation of a besieged site; or caused a problem negating a rally in the presence of the enemy.[128] Anyone who entered military establishments to procure documents or information for the enemy, provided such documents or information to the enemy, harbored such spies, or entered military establishments in disguise were also subject to execution,[129] as were those who passed weapons or means or recruited men for a power that was at war with France.[130]

In Germany, the treason statute under the military penal code[131] described high treason (*hochverrath*), treason against the state (*landesverrath*), and treason during war (*kriegsverrath*). Military personnel who committed *hochverrath* or *landesverrath* were subject[132] to the civilian penal code,[133] while those who committed *landesverrath* in the field during wartime were subject to the *kriegsverrath* provisions.[134] Those provisions stated that anyone who aided the enemy or harmed the German military or its allies could be sentenced to death for any of the following acts:[135]

- Committing a *landesverrath* offense under §90 of the German penal code, which included sabotage of war materials or means of communications, recruiting Germans as spies or soldiers, spying, betraying military plans or other secrets, and inciting military desertion or mutiny
- Destroying telegraph stations
- Providing the enemy a signal book or an extract from such
- Betraying secret communications or other secrets
- Making false reports about the enemy or failing to make reports
- Acting as a guide for the enemy against the Germans or as a guide for the Germans and leading the troops astray

---

128. *Id.* § 205.
129. *Id.* § 206–207.
130. *Id.* § 208.
131. Militär Strafgesetzbuch für des Deutsche Reich von 1872 (Ger.).
132. *Id.* § 56.
133. Strafgesetzbuch des Deutsche Reich of 1872 (Ger.).
134. Militär Strafgesetzbuch für des Deutsche Reich, § 57.
135. *Id.* § 58.

- Making signals to confuse or mislead the troops or to escape
- Disobeying or altering a military command
- Communicating with the enemy about the conduct of the war
- Disturbing the army with hostile opinions or other notices
- Ignoring proper care of the troops' food
- Freeing enemy POWs

Penalties in this section of the military code were permitted to be applied, during times of war against Germany, to both German nationals and foreigners.[136]

LEGAL PROFILES

Raymond Poincaré was the French president during the entire war. He was born in France in 1860 and obtained his legal training there. His early legal work included a defense of the author Jules Verne. He was first elected to the National Assembly in 1887 and joined his first cabinet in 1893, where he was often finance minister. He served in the cabinet until 1903, when he was elected to the Senate, where he served until 1913. He became prime minister in 1912 and was then elected president of France in 1913. After his term ended, he was again elected to the Senate, serving until 1934. He again became prime minister in 1922, holding the position until 1924, and later became foreign minister, prime minister again, and finally finance minister. He died in 1934.[137]

B. Cases

There were so many cases of treason prosecuted during the war by the European nations that the following examples are merely representative. These cases

---

136. Militär Strafgesetzbuch für des Deutsche Reich, § 160.
137. See *Raymond Poincaré*, Assemblee Nationale Biographies des Députés Français depuis 1789.

can be broken down into the following groups: spying for the enemy, helping enemies' countrymen and allies, political treason, undermining the morale of a nation, and helping one's former countrymen as a naturalized resident of a new country. In this first category is the trial of Dutch dancer Mata Hari in France. In the second category is the trial of British nurse Edith Cavell by Germany in Belgium. In the third category are the trials of French politicians Louis Malvy and Joseph Caillaux in France. In the fourth category are the trials of Paul Bolo and those associated with *Le Bonnet Rouge* newspaper in France. In the fifth category is the trial of former German consul Nicholaus Ahlers in the United Kingdom. One other well-known treason case from WWI, the trial of Irish politician Sir Roger Casement, is discussed in Chapter 6.

1. Mata Hari

The case of Margaretha Geertruida Zelle, an exotic dancer known by her stage name of Mata Hari (meaning "eye of dawn" in Indonesian), was well known in its time and involved the French, Germans, and British. Mata Hari, born in the Netherlands and left on her own after the death of her mother and the bankruptcy and departure of her father, had an unsuccessful early marriage to a military man twenty years her senior. After the loss of their son, they moved back to the Netherlands after spending five years in the Dutch East Indies (Indonesia). Mata Hari eventually left her husband and took up exotic Asian dancing, becoming quite famous in the capitals of Europe. She was able to travel the continent, giving performances in a variety of venues and milieus for a decade. She also lived the life of a courtesan, liaising with military officers of all nationalities during her travels, including those in Germany. Glamorous and famous, she was often in the news.

When the war started, it was no longer easy for her to move about freely to maintain her lifestyle. She was initially stuck in Germany, without income, as her costumes had been seized. Making her way back to the Netherlands, she was offered money in late 1915 by German consul Karl Kroemer to spy for Germany. She did little to follow through on the deal, feeling she was owed for her financial losses in Germany. Instead, she kept the money while sending the Germans information of little value. In July 1916, she fell in love with a Russian officer fighting with the French, Vladimir de Massloff, eighteen years her junior. After he was wounded in battle by mustard gas, needing funds for their possible future together and a military pass to see him in the military hospital, she accepted an offer from Georges Ladoux of the French counterintelligence unit to spy on the Germans.

On the way from France to the Netherlands via England, the British detained her as a potential spy, and she was not allowed to enter the United Kingdom. Instead she went to Spain, met German Major Arnold von Kalle, and found out certain unimportant information from him, which she passed on to the French. The French did not believe the information, and on Mata Hari's return to France in February 1917, she was arrested as a spy for the Germans. She was brought before the investigative magistrate for espionage crimes. The investigation initially found nothing, neither any disclosures of military importance by any of the several score of military officers who had been her lovers, nor any definitive spying apparatus (e.g., invisible ink) in her personal effects.

Then, Ladoux produced a communication from Kalle in Madrid to Berlin describing a spy working for the Germans code-named Agent H21 (this was Mata Hari). It was not clear why the Germans would wirelessly transmit such information in a code already known to have been broken by the Allied Powers. Ladoux, later arrested as a double agent, may have created or enhanced the cable himself, or the Germans may have deliberately sent the information to get rid of an agent working for the other side. After a long investigation, Mata Hari was put on trial in July 1917 and charged with espionage and treason that had led, in the words of one of the tribunal's seven judges, to the deaths of 50,000 French soldiers (whose transports had been torpedoed and sunk based on the information she had passed to the Germans).

The eight charges included meeting with and giving information to Kroemer, meeting with Kalle, and, most significantly, endangering the security and operations of the French military through the information she passed. The trial lasted only two days (July 24–25), with little in the way of hard evidence except character witnesses against her (and one in support of her) and her own admissions of meeting and receiving money from the Germans. One of the witnesses, who claimed he had told her nothing of importance during his visit(s), was diplomat Jules Cambon (see Chapter 1). Her own attorney, more than seventy years old and an expert in international commercial but not criminal law, was outside his area of practice. She was convicted on all eight counts, although not unanimously. Appeals were filed on her behalf, including by the Dutch government, but none successfully. On October 15, 1917, with the exhaustion of her appeals and with no presidential pardon forthcoming, she was executed by firing squad in France at age forty-one.

In a way, the verdict, based on questionable spying techniques leading to information of perhaps little value, has to be understood as a product of the war situation, as it took place in the same year that the failed spring offensives led to the mutinies discussed in Chapter 2. Without a clear way forward on the morale front, apart from the arrival of the Americans, the French needed a boost for their population, and taking down a German spy certainly was a useful way to do it. Spying for the enemy is a crime, regardless if it leads to more or less valuable information. Also, there was a peace movement at that time within the French government, which would lead to other treason trials (see Subsections 3 and 4 below). The particular circumstances of those months produced a result that might have been significantly less severe if the trial had been held after the conclusion of the war.

LEGAL PROFILES

Edouard Clunet was the defense counsel for Mata Hari. He was born in France in 1845 and obtained his legal training there. He served in the French military in the Prussian-Franco war of 1870–71. He moved to Paris, where he became known for international law cases involving many nations, including Germany, England, Belgium, the Netherlands, Spain, the United States, and France. He served as the legal adviser to the English and Spanish embassies. He served as the president of the Institute of International Law (*Institut de Droit International*), presiding over the 1911 meeting in Madrid. He died in 1922.[138]

Pierre Bouchardon was the investigating magistrate in the Mata Hari trial. He was born in France in 1870, the son of a lawyer, and obtained his legal training there. He started as a magistrate in 1895, rising to the head of criminal affairs in the department of justice in 1908. During the war, he was investigating magistrate for the third council of war in

---

138. *See Edouard Clunet, Noted Lawyer*, N.Y. TIMES (Oct. 13, 1922).

Paris, involved with the cases of Mata Hari, Bolo, *Le Bonnet Rouge*, Louis Malvy, and Joseph Caillaux. He was appointed to the court of appeal in Paris, becoming its president in 1924, then moved to the Court of Cassation, serving from 1929 until 1940. Remaining loyal to France in WWII, despite his son's being sent to a concentration camp, he was involved in the postwar high-court trials of Philippe Pétain and Pierre Laval. He was also the author of dozens of books about criminal cases in France in the nineteenth and twentieth centuries. He died in 1950.[139]

2. Edith Cavell

A case that occurred two years before that of Mata Hari but was more well known at the time was the trial by Germany of British nurse Edith Cavell. Unlike in the Mata Hari case, there was little doubt about the facts. Edith Cavell had come to Belgium in 1907 to teach nursing after training in England. When the war started, she continued her nurse training, heading *L'École Belge d'Infirmières Diplômées*, but as casualties mounted, she treated the wounded of all nationalities. In addition, she sheltered several hundred Allied soldiers and Belgians of military age, helping them to escape from Belgium to the Netherlands. Betrayed by Georges Quien (who was himself tried and convicted after the war for collaboration), she was arrested in August 1915, along with thirty-four others, mostly women, and was put on trial for treason.

After a period in solitary confinement, she admitted that she had helped the men she had sheltered to escape to the Netherlands. At the trial, the evidence against her was her own confession and a postcard from an escaped soldier who had made it all the way to England thanking her for her assistance. This was the ultimate fear of the German military and the essence of the charge against her: that the soldiers she had assisted would return to their units and fight against Germany.[140] Cavell was charged with the crime of war treason for conducting soldiers to the enemy, a charge that applied to foreigners as well as Germans. Additionally, even though the 1906 Geneva Convention would have protected

---

139. *See M. Pierre Bouchardon*, THE TIMES (Nov. 13, 1950).
140. Strafgesetzbuch des Deutsche Reich, § 90 (1) 3.

her as a medical person,[141] acts that were "injurious to the enemy" stripped her of that protection.[142]

She was brought to trial and confirmed her confession on October 7, 1915. She admitted that she had received confirmation that soldiers she had helped into the Netherlands had indeed made it to England, which not only made it easier to convict her but also changed what might have been viewed as an attempt to assist soldiers in reaching their lines into an accomplished fact. She was convicted and sentenced on October 11, late in the day. Many efforts were made on her behalf, including those by the Americans, still neutral, acting for the British. The Americans had been trying to see her and appoint legal counsel since August. But under German military law, pretrial meetings with the attorney were not required, and only lawyers registered to practice before the court could be appointed attorney for the defendant.

These rules meant that Cavell received a different and perhaps separately motivated counsel for this trial, who did a poor job of communicating with the counsel for the U.S. Legation. After her conviction and sentencing, the U.S. minister to Belgium, Brand Whitlock, sent an urgent note to the German military governor, asking for a reprieve or pardon for Cavell based on her nursing work for both sides.[143] The secretary to the American Legation, Hugh Gibson, along with the legation's counsel and the Spanish minister to Belgium, went to see the German Governor-General Baron von der Lancken. But even though he spoke with both the trial court judge and the military governor, he was unsuccessful in prevailing upon them to wait even a day further, despite Cavell's being incarcerated already. Cavell was then executed early on October 12, some nine hours after being convicted and secretly sentenced, after uttering the famous phrase that "Patriotism was not enough."[144]

The ensuing outcry was significant, but the German response was initially diplomatically tone deaf. This changed when Kaiser Wilhelm was quick to reprieve the death sentences of others sentenced along with Cavell. But the damage had been done, and between the atrocities in Belgium (see Chapter

---

141. Convention for the Amelioration of the Condition of the Wounded and Sick I the Armies of the Field (July 6, 1906), art. 6.
142. *Id.* art 7.
143. Letter from Whitlock, U.S. Minister to Belgium to German Governor-General von der Lancken and German Military Governor von Bissing (Oct. 11, 1915).
144. Account by Rev. H. Stirling Gahan, on the Execution of Edith Cavell (Oct. 12, 1915).

6), the sinking of the *Lusitania* (see Chapter 2), and now this execution of a female nurse who had aided soldiers on both sides, Germany was fast losing the war's public-relations battle (one reason why the Nazis were to pay particular attention to controlling their message in the events leading up to WWII). The mindset of those involved was perhaps best displayed by an assistant to Governor-General von der Lancken, who, upon hearing the American pleas for leniency, responded that his "only regret was that [they] did not have three or four [other] old English women to shoot."[145]

LEGAL PROFILES

Gaston de Leval was the counsel for the American Legation in Belgium. He was born in Belgium and obtained his legal training there. After the Cavell case, he published articles and gave speeches in England and the United States[146] on German law as it applied to occupied Belgium and this case, and he was made an honorary member of the American Bar Association. He was threatened by the occupiers and fled Belgium with his family for London during the occupation.

Sadi Kirschen was the actual defense counsel for Cavell. He was born in Belgium in 1877 and obtained his legal training there, becoming a member of the Brussels bar. He and de Leval got into quite a heated debate about Kirschen's role in defending Cavell, such that it led to blows. The Belgian bar council decided in 1921 that while the physical violence by Kirschen against de Leval should be censured, de Leval's role in attacking Kirschen's credibility, was more reprehensible, and de Leval was reprimanded. Kirschen also wrote about this time in a 1919 book.[147] He died in 1934.

---

145. *Germans Gloried in Cavell Murder*, N.Y. TIMES (Sept. 26, 1917).
146. *Cavell Lawyer Comes to America*, N.Y. TIMES (Aug. 14, 1917).
147. Sadi Kirschen, *Devant les conseils de guerre allemands* (1919).

Brand Whitlock was the U.S. minister (later ambassador) to Belgium during the war. He was born in Ohio in 1869 but was admitted to the bar in Illinois in 1894 and Ohio in 1897. After a series of jobs in journalism, he worked in state politics. In 1897, he returned to Ohio, where he practiced law until 1905 and was then elected the mayor of Toledo and reelected three times. For his work on Woodrow Wilson's election campaign, he was appointed minister to Belgium in 1913 and was instrumental in the success of the Committee for Relief in Belgium (see above) and stopping deportation of Belgian citizens to Germany as forced laborers. When the United States entered the war, he was forced to leave Belgium but returned after the war as its U.S. ambassador. He retired in 1922. Throughout his career, he continued to write prolifically, including books and articles. He died in 1934.[148]

---

3. Political Treason

The French rightist parties have long believed that the country was being sold out by the Socialists, especially when peace overtures to Germany started to be made in 1917. With Georges Clemenceau taking over as prime minister in November 1917, vowing to deal with pacifists and betrayers, the cases against the appeasers could be made and several treason trials were held. The first involved former Minister of the Interior Louis Malvy, the second former Minister of the Interior and Prime Minister Joseph Caillaux. Both of these men were from the same radical-socialist political party that was part of the *union sacrée*, which was the political agreement that helped the various parties to work together during the war and to avoid labor disputes.

a. Malvy

Louis-Jean Malvy, a radical Socialist member of the Chamber of Deputies since 1906, held several short-term roles in government from 1911 through 1914 before becoming the minister of the interior in March 1914. He held this post until August 1917 through many changes in the government. After the failure of the Battle of Chemin des Dames, he resigned. Rightist journalist and royalist

---

148. *See Brand Whitlock, Diplomat, is Dead*, N.Y. TIMES (May 25, 1934).

Léon Daudet, in a letter sent to French president Raymond Poincaré, accused Malvy of leading or supporting the defeatist/pacifist movement within France and passing information learned as a member of the council of war to Germany. Malvy had this letter read in front of the National Assembly. The short-term prime minister Paul Painlevé took no action against Malvy but instead had the offices of Daudet raided. When the government fell and Clemenceau became prime minister in November, the situation for Malvy changed, and to clear his name, he as a deputy requested a trial before the French Senate.

Malvy was initially charged with treason, based on the Daudet letter, for providing Germany with information, including the plans for the offensive at Chemin des Dames and provoking or inciting mutiny among the troops. After a dozen hearings, no clear evidence could be found for these charges, so instead he was charged with culpable negligence and criminal disregard for the duties of the minister of the interior for not taking appropriate actions against treasonable enterprises. After a long investigation, he was finally brought to trial before the Senate acting as a high court in July 1918, where his activities as the minister of the interior were reviewed in detail, under a law that allowed the Senate to review the crimes of ministers.[149]

These activities included failing to strongly address labor actions and anti-war subversive elements within France or to deal with the peace propaganda filtering through the military, which had led to the mutinies of 1917 (see Chapter 2). He had been asked to keep troops on leave from being inundated with peace propaganda that would affect them when they returned to the front lines. In addition, he was alleged to have protected a number of others who would be prosecuted for treason, such as his mentor Joseph Caillaux and *Le Bonnet Rouge* newspaper (see below), and to have done nothing to stop the activities of the spy Leopold Lipscher, who had been trying to initiate peace negotiations with the French government. Although defended by the former prime ministers in whose cabinets he had served, Malvy was convicted in early August 1918, and instead of receiving five years in solitary confinement, he was banished from France for five years.

---

149. Loi du 16 juillet 1875 sur les rapports des pouvoirs publics, art. 12 (Fr.).

LEGAL PROFILES

Daniel Mérillon was the prosecutor in this trial. He was born in France in 1852 and obtained his legal training there. He was a member of the Bordeaux city council from 1878, as its deputy mayor and counsel. He was elected to the Chamber of Deputies in 1885, where he served until 1889, when he lost reelection. He was appointed assistant attorney general to the court of appeal in Paris in 1897, rising to be its president. In 1917, he was appointed as the attorney general for the Court of Cassation. He was also very active in the world of sport shooting, being elected as the first president of the International Union of Shooting (L'Union Internationale de Tir) in 1907. He was responsible for getting this sport included in the 1920 Olympic Games in Antwerp. He died in 1925.[150]

b. Caillaux

Joseph Caillaux had been a member of the Chamber of Deputies since 1898 and served in several roles, primarily as minister of finance but also briefly as interior minister, as well as prime minister in 1911, a position from which he was forced to resign for conducting secret negotiations with Germany. He was anathema to the conservative politicians for his opposition to conscription and his support for an income tax. He had also become known for his wife's 1914 murder trial, where she was accused of killing the editor of a newspaper that had politically attacked her husband (and may have been about to publish her letters to Caillaux written when she was his mistress and they were both married to others).

During the war, Caillaux led the efforts to seek a negotiated peace with Germany. After Georges Clemenceau became the French prime minister, Caillaux was considered another of the leading defeatists/pacifists who needed to be removed in order for France to concentrate on total war and victory. The Chamber of Deputies voted overwhelmingly in December 1917 to remove his immunity and bring him to trial. In January 1918, he was arrested and imprisoned. A lengthy investigation was delayed not only by Caillaux's requested

---

150. *See Daniel Mérillon*, Assemblee Nationale Biographies des Députés Français depuis 1789.

time spent responding to the magistrate's inquiries but also by the final year of the war and the follow-up peace conference, the difficulty of getting witnesses from many countries, and perhaps the hope that more Socialists would be voted out of office in the next election. After the investigation, Caillaux was finally brought to trial before the Senate in February 1920.

The charge against him at the start of the trial was treason for having tried to weaken the security of the country by intrigue, machinations, and intelligence with the enemy. Evidence included a safe deposit box in Florence, Italy, where he had kept the contents of a plan to change the French government during the war, as well as cables he had allegedly sent to and received from the Germans. In addition, he was linked to most of the main characters who had been involved in the newspaper treason trials (see below), plus a number of other players involved in trying to subvert the French morale during the war. His trips to Spain, Italy, and South America drew particular notice for what may have occurred there (in Spain in 1911, he allegedly threatened the Spanish king, and after the South America trip in 1915, he started his strong peace push).

His lawyers claimed that the contents of the Italian safe deposit box contained merely the aspirations for a new type of government in France, not an actual plan to overthrow the government. But they could not so easily argue away the communications between Caillaux and German agents or aspirants—some supplied by foreign governments, including the United States—and communications by German ministers claiming that Caillaux was their man in France, one whom they would help to return to power, including through the purchase of French newspapers (see below). Caillaux ultimately was convicted not of the capital charge of treason for maintaining an understanding with the enemies of France and facilitating their entry into the country,[151] but instead of corresponding with a hostile power resulting in the enemy gaining information prejudicial to the military or political situation of France.[152] His punishment was three years of imprisonment, but he was credited for the time

---

151. Code Pénal of 1810, art. 77 (Fr.).
152. *Id.*, art. 78.

he had already served since his arrest. He was also banished from France and lost his civil rights.

LEGAL PROFILES

Joseph Caillaux was the defendant in this trial. He was born in France in 1863 and obtained his legal training there. He entered the civil service in 1888, serving in Algeria. He entered the Chamber of Deputies in 1898, where he would remain until 1919, when he was imprisoned. He was the minister of finance six times, starting in 1899. He was minister of the interior from June 1911 to January 1912, when he also served as prime minister. After being pardoned in 1924, he was elected to the Senate in 1925, where he would remain until his death in 1944.[153]

Léon Bourgeois was the president of the Senate and this court in this trial. He was born in France in 1851 and obtained his legal training there. He entered the civil service and held a number of positions. He was elected to the Chamber of Deputies in 1889, where he soon entered the cabinet and held various ministries. He became prime minister in 1895. In 1899 and 1907 he was delegate to the Hague Peace Conference and joined the Permanent Court of Arbitration in 1903. He was elected president of the Chamber of Deputies in 1902 and was elected to the Senate in 1905. In 1906 he was the minister of foreign affairs during the Algeciras Conference (see Chapter 1). After the war, he became the president of the council of the League of Nations, for which he won the Nobel Peace Prize. He was president of the Senate from 1920 to early 1923. He died in 1925.[154]

---

153. *See Joseph Caillaux*, Assemblee Nationale Biographies des Députés Français depuis 1789.
154. *See Léon Bourgeois*, Assemblee Nationale Biographies des Députés Français depuis 1789.

Anatole de Monzie was one of the many lawyers defending Caillaux in this trial. He was born in France in 1876 and obtained his legal training there. He got started in local politics including serving as a mayor and general counsel. He was elected to the Chamber of Deputies in 1909 and served there until 1919 and then again from 1929 to 1942. In 1913, he joined the cabinet and frequently served in a ministerial role there, including as minister of justice, of finance, and of education. He was elected to the Senate in 1920, where he served until 1929. He was a prolific writer and was responsible as minister of education for the publication of the *Encyclopédie français* in 1932, along with historian Lucien Febvre. He died in 1947.[155]

Vincent de Moro-Giafferri was another of the lawyers defending Caillaux. He was born in France in 1878 and obtained his legal training there. During WWI, he served in the military, being wounded at the Battle of Verdun, and receiving the Croix de Guerre honor. He was first elected to the Chamber of Deputies in 1919, serving there until 1928. He became famous as a top criminal lawyer and orator, defending some of the highest-profile cases. He was active in supporting Jewish lawyers fleeing from the Nazis into France in the 1930s after the loss of their ability to practice.[156] He returned to the National Assembly in 1946, where he remained until his death in 1956.[157]

---

4. Treason by Newspapers

It was through newspapers that public opinion could be swayed, and it was here that Germany sought to change French opinion. Two different cases involved French newspapers connected with activities that would bring them to trial. Paul Bolo, later styled as Bolo Pasha after his dealings with the leader

---

155. *See Anatole de Monzie*, ASSEMBLEE NATIONALE BIOGRAPHIES DES DÉPUTÉS FRANÇAIS DEPUIS 1789.
156. *See* WWII LAW AND LAWYERS, ch. 6.
157. *See Vincent de Moro-Giafferri*, ASSEMBLEE NATIONALE BIOGRAPHIES DES DÉPUTÉS FRANÇAIS DEPUIS 1789.

of Egypt, was arrested and brought to trial for trying to use German money to buy up French newspapers to sway opinion toward German positions. The newspaper *Le Bonnet Rouge* was an evening newspaper being financed by Germany through Switzerland.

a. Bolo Pasha

Paul Bolo was a native of France who became involved in international intrigue. He was the son of a lawyer, and after practicing as a dentist and a barber, starting several failed business ventures, and spending time in Spain and South America and in prison for fraud, he suffered the death of his second wife (he had not yet divorced his first wife). She was older than him and wealthy, and she left him with significant assets, some of which he used philanthropically to fund homes for underprivileged children. He met the ruler of Egypt, Abbas Hilmi, who gave him the title Bolo Pasha. As the financial adviser to the German-leaning Hilmi, the two of them and their agents hatched a plan over many months and meetings to invest in French newspapers to slant the reporting to favor German interests.

The German government agreed to fund these newspaper purchases and in spring 1915 started sending money through intermediaries to Bolo, representing this as the fortune of the now former ruler of Egypt (he had been deposed by the British). These large transactions were noticed by the French government, so it was determined that the neutral United States would be a better place to transact this business. In March and April 1916, Bolo traveled to the United States and was able to enlist the help of the German ambassador there, Johann Heinrich von Bernstorff, in this scheme. It was von Bernstorff who approved the funding of the plan. The vast documentation of the financial aspects of this relationship created in America helped to later convict Bolo. It was U.S. federal and state authorities who identified the information documenting the planned activities and notified the French government.

Bolo was arrested in September 1917 and placed on trial by court-martial for treason in February 1918, before the same court, the third council of war (*conseil de guerre*) of Paris, that had tried Mata Hari. Against Bolo, the charge of treason was that he had conspired with Abbas Hilmi to aid Germany and that he had received money from Germany to fund pacifist propaganda within France. Witnesses included Bolo's first wife and Joseph Caillaux. The evidence produced at this trial included that $1.7 million had been transferred in March and April 1916 from the Deutsche Bank to the Royal Bank of Canada branch in New York, passing through several other financial institutions and transaction types to hide its origin. It was for use by Bolo, his wife, and the owner of *Le Journal* in Paris, Senator Charles Humbert, all through financial credits now available back in France. The transaction also included a letter from Bolo dictating these distributions. Bolo was found guilty and sentenced to death on February 14, 1918. Despite the plea of his well-known prelate brother Monseigneur Bolo, he was executed on April 17, 1918.

LEGAL PROFILES

Merton E. Lewis was the attorney general of New York State. He was born in New York in 1861 and started his legal practice there in 1887. He served as mayor of Rochester from 1895 to 1896. He was elected to the New York State Assembly in 1897, serving through 1901, and then the state senate in 1902, serving through 1906. He then ran unsuccessfully for state comptroller in 1906 but was appointed as deputy state attorney general in 1915. In 1917, he was elected state attorney general upon the resignation of his predecessor. He held this position until the end of 1918, when he ran unsuccessfully for governor of the state and returned to private practice. From 1926 to 1930, he was a special U.S. attorney. He died in 1937.[158]

Albert Salle was the defense counsel in this trial. He was born in France in 1863 and obtained his legal training there, receiving admittance to the Paris bar in 1882. His practice focused more on civil and commercial practice, and he was the counsel for the Bank of France. As the soon-to-

---

158. *See M.E. Lewis is Dead; Ex-State Leader*, N.Y. TIMES (May 3, 1937).

be head (*bâtonnier*) of the Paris bar (in 1921), he was appointed to the role of defending Bolo in such a difficult case. He died in 1937.[159]

---

b. Le Bonnet Rouge

Two months later, in April 1918, another trial was held in the same court, this time involving the newspaper *Le Bonnet Rouge*. This paper was started just before the war and included as its editor anarchist Miguel Almereyda (born Jean-Baptiste Vigo). It became known for defeatist articles and criticism of the French High Command. These articles were censored, but there was a distribution network to get the uncensored versions into the hands of the military. When the manager of the paper, Emile Joseph Duval, was captured at the Swiss-French border with a check for 150,000 francs from German banker Mannheim Marx, it was discovered that Marx was fronting for the German government. A legitimate prewar relationship had become treasonous after the start of the war, and in July 1917 the newspaper was suspended and Duval was arrested.

The Interior Ministry's chief of staff, Jean Leymarie, was involved in this affair, with the ministry funding the newspaper and Leymarie granting permission for Duval to go to Switzerland some twenty times to meet Marx without hindrance. Leymarie had even returned the seized check to Duval, but when Prime Minster Alexandre Ribot heard of this seizure and the ensuing investigation, he had Leymarie dismissed; Louis Malvy then resigned as interior minister. Almereyda, Duval, Leymarie, and five other reporters and editors from the newspaper were arrested. Almereyda died in jail—whether by suicide or murder was never determined—but the remaining seven were brought to trial.

Evidence introduced at the trial included an investment by Joseph Caillaux into this newspaper at the time of his wife's murder trial in 1914. The paper had given very favorable coverage of his wife during the trial, at which she was acquitted of murder. The evidence also showed that the paper was a leader in the defeatist press, having printed articles that tried to demoralize soldiers

---

159. *See* A. Salle, *Defender of Spy, Bolo Pasha*, N.Y. TIMES (Apr. 16, 1937).

by describing what their wives and girlfriends might be doing back home or by saying the Allied soldiers were temporarily marrying French girls and then abandoning them when the war was over. The paper had also advocated against American intervention in the war and had tried to glorify Germany's wrongdoings. The court-martial found all the defendants guilty, with Duval sentenced to death and the other six defendants sentenced to various terms of imprisonment at hard labor.

LEGAL PROFILES

André Mornet was the prosecutor in the Mata Hari, Bolo Pasha, and *Bonnet Rouge* trials. He was born in France in 1870 and obtained his legal training there. He became a magistrate in Reims in 1898. In 1903, he moved to Paris as a deputy magistrate. In 1912 he became attorney general. During the war, he was assigned to various councils of war as a lieutenant, including near the front lines and then, in 1917, in Paris, where he also dealt with the trials of *Le Journal*. In 1922 he became general counsel to the Court of Cassation, a role he held for eight years. He then became an adviser to the civil chamber in 1930. He was once again in the middle of wartime legal trials in WWII, as prosecutor both in the early-war Vichy Riom trials and the postwar trial of Vichy leadership (see below). He died in 1955.[160]

5. Ahlers

Nicholaus Ahlers was a former German consul who was charged with high treason in 1914 for recruiting German nationals in the United Kingdom for the war effort. Ahlers had been a naturalized British citizen since 1905 and claimed innocence because he said he had not known that Germany and the

---

160. *See Andre Mornet, French Prosecutor, Dies; Led Petain, Laval, and Mata Hari Trials*, N.Y. TIMES (July 23, 1955).

United Kingdom had gone to war when he performed his recruiting efforts in Britain. Most of the incidents had occurred on August 5, 1914. In his trial in December 1914, the judge looked at the Treason Act of 1351 and did not find a requirement of knowledge of a war for a judgment of treason, but the judge decided to require it. Ahlers, the German consul at Sunderland, claimed he had known on August 4 that Germany was at war with France, Russia, and Belgium, but not the United Kingdom, even though the German consul general had notified him on August 1 that German ships in British ports should consider leaving in case diplomatic relations were broken, and on August 4 that German males should return home.

The defense claimed that the declaration of war that had occurred at 23:00 on August 4 and had been printed in the newspaper Ahlers read the morning of August 5 was not credible, and that Ahlers had believed it was just another sensationalist headline. The prosecution countered that it was not believable that a consul would not have had the information by August 5 that war had been declared, also pointing to Ahlers's knowledge that a German ship had been seized that day. So the purchase of eight tickets, which Ahlers admitted to having done to send eight men back to Germany, must have been done with the full knowledge that the United Kingdom was at war with Germany, and, having been done by a British citizen, was a treasonous act. The jury found the defendant guilty and, with death the only sentence possible for this crime, the court sentenced him thus.

The court of criminal appeal later that month considered five points of appeal. These were (1) that the defendant had no knowledge of the state of war; (2) he did not know his acts were wrongful, given, for example, that it is common to give aliens a grace period to return home; (3) that he acted in good faith without treasonous intent; (4) that the prosecutor alluded to the fact that the sentence was unlikely to be carried out; and (5) that the notice of the home secretary giving aliens a five-day grace period to return home was misconstrued by the trial judge to mean that it applied only to aliens unable to bear arms. The prosecutor stated that the defendant was guilty of trying to raise an enemy army in the United Kingdom, clearly a treasonous act, which a grace period would not affect at all.

The court of appeal noted that the Alien Restriction Act was passed on August 5, 1914,[161] followed by a related order in council, and, from that, the notice from the home secretary that aliens had until August 11 to depart. This chronology provided support for the appellant's belief that it was typical for aliens to have a grace period in which to depart. The court ruled that the trial court should have put forward two possible views of the defendant's intentions to the jury. The jury should also have been presented with the possibility that the appellant had intended no hostile act to England, and had only been performing his job. As such, the court quashed the conviction. Ahlers was later interned, as was his wife, who died in internment in England in 1917. After the war, in 1919, Ahlers's British naturalization certificate was revoked for disloyalty.

LEGAL PROFILES

Stanley Buckmaster was the prosecutor for this case and British solicitor general. He was born in England in 1861 and obtained his legal training there, being called to the bar in 1884. He became a king's counsel in 1902. He was elected to Parliament in 1906, lost his seat in 1910, and was elected again in 1911. From 1913 to 1915, he served as the solicitor general. He was then appointed the lord chancellor, a role he held through the end of 1916. He served in the House of Lords for the remainder of his life, dying in 1934.[162]

C. Subsequent Events

Mata Hari was not the only spy executed, nor was Edith Cavell the only woman condemned for work in service of her country. Another example was the Belgian Red Cross worker Gabrielle Petit, who assisted British intelligence

---

161. 4 & 5 Geo. 5, c. 12 (U.K.).
162. *See Stanley Buckmaster*, OXFORD DICTIONARY OF NATIONAL BIOGRAPHY 101032159.

in gathering information about German troop movements but was finally discovered, tried, and executed in April 1916 for her efforts. Other spies, such as German Carl Lody, were tried by military courts for war treason, convicted, and executed. Other newspaper trials took place, such as for the people connected with using enemy funds to buy *Le Journal*, including the conviction and execution of Pierre Lenoir. The images of many of the people convicted in these trials continued to live on in various ways, such as Cavell, whose execution was a large propaganda point for the British and led to tens of thousands signing up for military service in the wake of her execution. Malvy and Caillaux both were politically rehabilitated after the war and returned to French politics in the National Assembly. And efforts are still underway to rehabilitate the memory of Mata Hari by presentation of new evidence.[163]

Some of the laws and players described here were to be involved in WWII. In the United Kingdom, the treason law was at first determined to be procedurally difficult to apply, so the Treachery Act[164] was passed in 1940, before the Treason Act itself was revised in 1945.[165] And André Mornet continued to fulfill his role as the prosecutor at the center of French treason trials during WWII, in two very different ways.[166] He was the prosecutor in the Riom trial in the early part of the war, on behalf of the Vichy regime, that tried to prosecute the French leadership for their role in the downfall of France before the Nazi blitzkrieg. Then, after the war, he was the prosecutor in the trial of Pierre Laval, the right-hand man to Philippe Pétain in running the despised Vichy collaborationist regime in France during the war.

LEGAL PROFILES

Aristide Briand was the French prime minister before, during, and after the war, and a future Nobel Peace Prize winner. He was born in France in 1862 and obtained his legal training there. He was elected

---

163. *Mata Hari 'was framed'*, BBC News (Oct. 16, 2001).
164. 3 & 4 Geo. 6, c. 40 (U.K.).
165. 8 & 9 Geo. 6, c. 44 (U.K.).
166. *See* WWII Law and Lawyers, ch. 5.

to the Chamber of Deputies in 1902, where he championed the 1905 law separating church and state in France,[167] and the later reconciliation with the Vatican. He became prime minister for the first of eleven times in 1909, his last in 1929. His role as foreign minister in 1925, which he would hold through 1932, led to the Treaty of Locarno recognizing the permanent borders of Germany, France, and Belgium, for which he won the Nobel Peace Prize.[168] In 1926, he negotiated the Kellogg-Briand Pact, which renounced war as a tool to solve conflicts between nations. He died in 1932.[169]

Henri Robert was the president of the Paris bar association during the war. He was born in France in 1863 and obtained his legal training there, being admitted to the bar in 1885. He became a top criminal law attorney, handling top cases including murder and fraud, before moving to civil litigation after the war. He was the *bâtonnier* (head) of the Paris bar from 1913 to 1919. He was the author of a number of books and a historian and was elected to the French Academy in 1923. He died in 1936.[170]

Felix Cassel was the British judge advocate general during the war, overseeing war treason cases. He was born in Germany in 1869 to a German-English family and so obtained his legal training in England, being called to the bar in 1894. In 1904 he became a queen's counsel. In 1910, he was elected to Parliament, where he served until 1916. When the war started, he first went to France with the army but from 1915, he was made judge advocate general, a position he remained in until 1934. He died in 1953.[171]

---

167. Loi du 9 décembre 1905 concernant la séparation des Églises et de l'État.
168. *See* WWII LAW AND LAWYERS, ch. 1.
169. *See Aristide Briand*, ASSEMBLEE NATIONALE BIOGRAPHIES DES DÉPUTÉS FRANÇAIS DEPUIS 1789.
170. *See Henri Robert*, ACADÉMIE FRANCAISE.
171. *See Felix Cassel*, OXFORD DICTIONARY OF NATIONAL BIOGRAPHY 101075606.

CHAPTER 4

UNITED STATES: INTERNATIONAL AND MILITARY ISSUES

The war that began in August 1914 in Europe was very far away for a country that had not been in a major international war in a century. The United States, as explained in Chapter 1, had increasingly begun to be engaged with other nations. Most of those nations were in the Western Hemisphere, but through commerce with China and Japan, war in the Philippines, and dealing with pirates in Africa, the country had a new foreign exposure. It had long had relationships with European countries, but it had not engaged in war with or against Europeans since its own wars of independence had ended (except for the brief war with Spain in 1899). Its relationships were politically balanced, with enduring friendships with France, Great Britain, and Germany. So America's default reaction was to be neutral in the new European war, but to also allow commerce with all the belligerents, supplying the needs of nations that were blockading each other.

The United States quickly declared its neutrality in the conflict. Although its legal and linguistic inheritance from the United Kingdom and its eighteenth-century military alliance with France tilted the balance of this neutrality toward the Allied Powers, the large German immigrant population in the United States, plus anti-British sentiment in its large Irish immigrant population, initially had America trying to balance its approach to the conflict. It was a series of acts by the Central Powers, including the sinking of the *Lusitania* (see Chapter 2), the execution of Edith Cavell (see Chapter 3), the atrocities in Belgium (see Chapter 6), the actions taken with Mexico (below), and the 1917 resumption of unrestricted submarine warfare (see Chapter 2), that finally pushed the United States out of its biased neutrality to a position of active participation in the war.

Before the United States became a belligerent, it was a target, for varying reasons; then joining the war brought with it new restrictions on its ability to trade with the enemy. It also required that America find a source of manpower to fill the ranks of its troops that were to be deployed to the European theater and to implement a new military code of justice for its massively larger armed forces. This chapter focuses on America's neutrality at the start of the war and its efforts to stay neutral, Germany's interference with that neutrality via sabotage and other plans, and the events that finally brought America into the war. It also covers the legal issues involved with harming the economic capabilities of the enemy and their assets in America, use of the selective service system to raise military manpower, and the implementation of a new military code of justice and problems with that system.

PROMINENT LAWYERS AND JUDGES IN THIS CHAPTER

Distance Neutrality:
- Woodrow Wilson (U.S. president)
- Arthur Zimmermann (German foreign minister)
- Frederick William Lehmann (appellant's counsel)
- John M. Woolsey (petitioner's counsel)
- Louis D. Brandeis (Supreme Court justice)
- James M. Beck (U.S. solicitor general)
- Oliver Wendell Holmes (Supreme Court justice)
- Robert Lansing (U.S. secretary of state)
- Edwin Hubble (soldier and astronomer)

Germany in America:
- William W. Canada (U.S. consul)
- Luis Cabrera (Mexican representative)
- John Hay (congressman)
- Eliseo Arredondo (Carranza government agent)

- John Hessin Clarke (Supreme Court justice)
- William van Fleet (trial judge)
- Julier Clyde Hizar (defendant)
- Louis T. Hengstler (defendant)
- John W. Preston (prosecutor)
- Heinrich Albert (commercial attaché)
- Alexander Bruce Bielaski (Bureau of Investigation chief)

Enemy Asset and Export Controls:

- A. Mitchell Palmer (alien property custodian)
- Louis Marshall (counsel for appellant)
- George Langham Ingraham (counsel for appellee)
- Willis van Devanter (Supreme Court justice)
- James A. Fowler (counsel for appellee)
- George Sutherland (Supreme Court justice)
- Edward Terry Sanford (Supreme Court justice)
- Henry W. Anderson (counsel for appellant)
- Frank L. Polk (State Department counselor)
- Patrick Garvan (president of Chemical Foundation)

Selective Service:

- Enoch Crowder (judge advocate general)
- Walter Nelles (amicus curiae)
- Robert Szold (assistant to solicitor general)
- Hugh S. Johnson (Judge Advocate General's Corps)

Articles of War:

- John J. Pershing (leader of the American Expeditionary Forces)
- Newton D. Baker (secretary of war)
- George E. Chamberlain (senator)
- Samuel T. Ansell (deputy judge advocate general)
- John A. Hull (judge advocate)
- Franklin Delano Roosevelt (assistant secretary of the navy)
- James B. Morris (lawyer-soldier)
- William H. Lewis (assistant U.S. attorney general)

4.1 DISTANCE NEUTRALITY

A. Statutes
1. Declaring Neutrality
With the outbreak of war in Europe in July and August 1914 as described in Chapter 2, the United States, as a large neutral country with political and commercial relations with both alliances, had to state its intentions. The Allied Powers, with their larger GDP and populations and their control of the seas, could win an extended conflict, as long as they could still get supplied by the United States and other neutrals. So they did not need the United States to enter the war in 1914. The Central Powers expected to win the war in 1914, and they did not want a neutral America favoring the Allied Powers. From Kaiser Wilhelm to businessmen, diplomats, and scholars, Germans appealed to America with the righteousness of their cause.

But before the United States government could be concerned with how to respond to foreign governments, it had to be concerned with its own citizens. As soon as war was declared by both alliances, Congress passed a joint resolution that provided monies for relief, protection, and transportation for American citizens caught up in the "existing political disturbance in Europe."[1] The resolution required citizens receiving government relief or transportation to reimburse the government, if they were financially able to do so. It also authorized the president to use military vessels, personnel, and supplies as needed. Congress also later granted the American Red Cross the power to charter ships to transport nurses and supplies in order to carry out its functions.[2]

To help Americans stranded in Europe, President Woodrow Wilson issued an executive order on August 5, 1914.[3] It called for the secretaries of state, war, navy, and treasury to take on roles in getting relief to stranded Americans: the secretary of the navy was to provide transportation for the people and supplies involved in the relief effort, the secretary of war was to provide the onsite personnel for the relief and to charter ships, the secretary of the treasury was

---
1. Pub. Res. No. 42, Joint Resolution for the Relief, Protection, and Transportation of American Citizens in Europe and for Other Purposes (Aug. 5, 1914).
2. Pub. Res. No. 43, Joint Resolution Granting Authority to the American Red Cross to Charter a Ship or Ships of Foreign Register for the Transportation of Nurses and Supplies and for All Uses in Connection with the Work of That Society (Aug. 20, 1914).
3. Exec. Order No. 2012, For the Relief, Protection and Transportation Home of Americans in Europe at the Outbreak of the European War of 1914 (Aug. 5, 1914).

to fund the effort, and the secretary of state was to provide diplomatic support. All were to work in a coordinated fashion as the Board of Relief.[4]

Two weeks after the start of the war, President Wilson then went before Congress and declared that the United States intended to follow the path of neutrality in this conflict. On August 19, 1914, his message to Congress emphasized neutrality as something that emanated as much from the average American citizen as from government:

> The effect of the war upon the United States will depend upon what American citizens say and do. Every man who really loves America will act and speak in the true spirit of neutrality, which is the spirit of impartiality and fairness and friendliness to all concerned. The spirit of the nation in this critical matter will be determined largely by what individuals and society and those gathered in public meetings do and say, upon what newspapers and magazines contain, upon what ministers utter in their pulpits, and men proclaim as their opinions upon the street.
>
> The people of the United States are drawn from many nations, and chiefly from the nations now at war. It is natural and inevitable that there should be the utmost variety of sympathy and desire among them with regard to the issues and circumstances of the conflict. Some will wish one nation, others another, to succeed in the momentous struggle. It will be easy to excite passion and difficult to allay it.
>
> Those responsible for exciting it will assume a heavy responsibility, responsibility for no less a thing than that the people of the United States, whose love of their country and whose loyalty to its government should unite them as Americans all, bound in honor and affection to think first of her and her interests, may be divided in camps of hostile opinion, hot against each other, involved in the war itself in impulse and opinion if not in action.

---

4. Exec. Order No. 2013, Establishing Board of Relief for Benefit of Americans Stranded Abroad during the European War of 1914 (Aug, 6, 1914).

Such divisions amongst us would be fatal to our peace of mind and might seriously stand in the way of the proper performance of our duty as the one great nation at peace, the one people holding itself ready to play a part of impartial mediation and speak the counsels of peace and accommodation, not as a partisan, but as a friend.

I venture, therefore, my fellow countrymen, to speak a solemn word of warning to you against that deepest, most subtle, most essential breach of neutrality which may spring out of partisanship, out of passionately taking sides. The United States must be neutral in fact, as well as in name, during these days that are to try men's souls. We must be impartial in thought, as well as action, must put a curb upon our sentiments, as well as upon every transaction that might be construed as a preference of one party to the struggle before another.[5]

One of the issues that the United States had to address concerned the arming of merchant ships. A statement from the early days of the war[6] allowed merchantmen belonging to belligerent nations entering U.S. ports to carry weapons, but only for defensive purposes. There was a presumption that the use of weapons would be for offensive purposes, and the burden was on a ship to show otherwise, during an investigation that would be launched upon entry into a U.S. port. Factors determinative of weapons' purpose included the caliber and quantity of weapons and ammunition, whether the vessel used the usual trade routes, the types of cargo, whether the crew size was typical, the types of passengers (not of a military character), and whether the supplies and fuel onboard were sufficient only to get to the next port.

In the case of the United States, neutrality had a different twist. The newly opened Panama Canal was protected by the U.S. government, so rules for its neutral use were issued by proclamation from the president in late 1914.[7] All vessels that directly were "prosecuting or aiding hostilities" were to be treated as ships of war, except for hospital ships.[8] Warships could not take on fuel,

---

5. Woodrow Wilson, *Message to Congress,* 63rd Cong., 2d Sess., Senate Doc. No. 566 (Washington, 1914).
6. Dept. of State, Arming of Merchant Vessels (Sept. 19, 1914).
7. Exec. Proclamation No. 1287, Neutrality: Panama Canal Zone (Nov. 13, 1914).
8. *Id.* Rule 2.

supplies from the U.S. government, munitions, or troops and could not linger in Canal Zone waters. No more than three ships belonging to either alliance could be transiting the canal at any one time. When adversaries both had ships in the canal at the same time, the second ship could not depart the Canal Zone waters until twenty-four hours after the first ship had left. Belligerent vessels returning to Canal Zone waters would lose their departure precedent privileges vis-à-vis vessels of the other alliances. Repair facilities of the Canal Zone could not be used to repair warships. The radio capabilities of warships could not be used during transit except for canal business. Belligerent aircraft could not be used in the Canal Zone.

Implementing neutrality at a distance, while not being subject to the concern of proximate neutrals of possible invasion, did have the ongoing difficulty of the pressure from both of the alliances. There were a number of complaints directed at the United States during its period of neutrality from August 1914 to April 1917. The complaints of the Central Powers included favoritism shown in several areas by America to the Allied Powers, such as the lack of objections to seizures on the high seas by Britain, the prohibition on war loans but not armament sales, and the censorship of wireless communications (which were favored by Germany) but not wired communications.

The policy of providing general war loans to belligerents evolved from the time when William Jennings Bryan was secretary of state to when Robert Lansing took over that role. Bryan was opposed to such loans, and helped kill such a request from J. P. Morgan to loan money to the French government in 1914 because it was contrary to the spirit of neutrality and could divide the loaning nation into factions that would each try to influence their neutral government in favor of the country they had loaned to (to ensure repayment). But American financial institutions wanted to loan money to foreign governments to fund the purchases of American goods that were in such demand from Europe during the war. In addition, the financial situation of the European governments started to deteriorate, as their gold reserves were being depleted by the need to import more from America than they could export. A credit squeeze would severely impact both European countries and the American economy. As such, in the second half of 1915, the U.S. government changed its stand on such war loans and decided no longer to oppose them.

Another significant complaint involved the shipping of munitions to the Allied Powers. Austria-Hungary complained to the United States that its reliance on Hague neutrality conventions[9] was in danger due to the large volumes of munitions that it was shipping to the Allied Powers.[10] It called upon America to consider an embargo on munitions shipments to the Allied Powers as a way to maintain that neutrality, to address what to Austria-Hungary and its ally Germany was a legally constructed blockade against their receiving munitions from the United States. It also called on the U.S. government to improve its relationships with the Central Powers and to allow the delivery of arms and munitions on the high seas instead of in a port. It also pointed out that the preamble of Hague XIII allowed neutral nations to make exceptions, based on necessity.

In reply, Secretary Lansing said that far from being partial, the United States was acting impartially and would not change its position to favor one side over the other based on the capability of that power to obtain goods.[11] The British blockade was making it difficult for the Central Powers to receive American goods, which were available to all, but each nation had to take those goods in its own ships from U.S. ports, not in American ships. America would not embargo the goods of one alliance to equalize the receipt of its goods of the other alliance. Lansing also said that the necessity exception in the preamble to the Hague XIII Convention was one that only neutral nations could decide for themselves; belligerents could not do so for the neutral countries. He noted that during the Second Boer War, the countries of the Central Powers had sold arms and munitions equally to the British and the Boers. Lansing also said that the history of the United States was to keep a small supply of munitions and arms domestically and to rely on acquiring further supplies from other nations through trade in case it found itself at war, so it would be inconsistent to deny the same recourse to the nations now engaged, lest the world become an "armed camp."[12]

---

9. Convention Respecting the Right and Duties of Neutral Powers and Persons in Case of War on Land (Hague V), art. 7, Oct. 18, 1907; Convention on the Rights and Duties of Neutral Powers in Naval War (Hague XIII), art. 7, Oct. 18, 1907.
10. Letter from Austro-Hungarian Foreign Minister von Burian to U.S. Secretary of State Lansing (June 29, 1915).
11. Letter from U.S. Secretary of State Lansing to Austro-Hungarian Foreign Minister von Burian (Aug. 13, 1915).
12. *Id.*

LEGAL PROFILES

Woodrow Wilson was U.S. president before and during WWI. He was born in Virginia in 1856 but started his legal practice in Georgia. He then returned to academia, getting a PhD in history and political science in 1886. He taught at several universities before teaching law at Princeton University. He remained there, and was appointed as the president of Princeton in 1902, serving until 1910. He was then elected the governor of New Jersey, a position he held from 1911 to 1913. While in that role, he ran for and was elected president of the United States in 1912. During his two terms in office, the Federal Reserve was created, the income tax was established, trusts and price fixing were further curtailed, the Federal Trade Commission began policing unfair business practices, the Panama Canal opened, and support was provided for farmers and child laborers. While stumping for the League of Nations after the war (see Chapter 7), he suffered a debilitating stroke in October 1919, which marred the remainder of his term until early 1921. He died in 1924.[13]

2. Declaring War

Staying neutral became impossible in 1917, with the restarting of unrestricted submarine warfare by Germany. With Russia soon to drop out of the war, Germany hoped that its planned spring offensive, supplemented by forces redeployed from the Eastern Front, could end the land war in Europe. Germany took the calculated gamble that it would control enough geography and have armistices in place before America could sufficiently deploy its forces. The stalling of its spring offensive and the rapidity of American involvement, initially more in the materials area, would prove the gamble a risk not worth taking, as American capabilities and German exhaustion would end the war late the following year.

---

13. *See Career of Woodrow Wilson as College Executive, Governor and President*, N.Y. TIMES (Feb. 4, 1924).

Although Wilson had won reelection to the presidency in 1916 with the slogan "He kept us out of war," several related events occurred in early 1917 to finally change the American perspective on the war. The first was the sending of a telegram from Berlin to the German embassy in Mexico, the "Zimmermann telegram." The second was the announcement of the resumption of unrestricted submarine warfare by Germany (see Chapter 2). The Zimmermann telegram, from the German Foreign Minister Arthur Zimmermann to German ambassador in America Johann von Bernstorff and then to German minister in Mexico Heinrich von Eckardt, stated that Germany hoped that the resumption of unrestricted submarine warfare would not bring the United States into the war, but if it did, then Germany would align with Mexico to allow it to reconquer the U.S. states of Texas, New Mexico, and Arizona, which the United States had purchased in the Treaty of Guadalupe Hidalgo in 1848.[14] It also suggested Mexico bring Japan into this alliance.

Although sent in code by the Germans and intercepted by the British on January 19, 1917, and then decoded by British cryptoanalysts, the message was not delivered to the U.S. government until late February. On January 31, Germany announced the resumption of its policy of unrestricted submarine warfare (i.e., sinking of all ships, neutrals as well as belligerents) around Great Britain, France, Italy, and the eastern Mediterranean, to be effective from February 1. As President Wilson had clearly explained to Germany in April 1916 (see Chapter 2) and to Congress,[15] unrestricted submarine warfare would lead to the United States severing its diplomatic relationship with Germany. And that is what the U.S. government did on February 3, 1917.

In an address to Congress, where President Wilson first recounted the history of the submarine attacks and the political responses during the war, he said he found it difficult to believe that Germany really intended to sink all neutral ships, but "if American ships and American lives should in fact be sacrificed by their [German] naval commanders in heedless contravention of the just and reasonable understandings of international law and the obvious dictates of humanity, I shall take the liberty of coming again before the Congress, to ask that authority be given me to use any means that may be necessary for the protection of our seamen and our people in the prosecution of their

---

14. Treaty of Peace, Friendship, Limits, and Settlement with the Republic of Mexico, U.S.-Mex., Feb. 2, 1848.
15. Woodrow Wilson, Address to a Joint Session of Congress on German Violations of International Law (Apr. 19, 1916).

peaceful and legitimate errands on the high seas. I can do nothing less. I take it for granted that all neutral governments will take the same course. We do not desire any hostile conflict with the Imperial German Government. We are the sincere friends of the German people and earnestly desire to remain at peace with the Government which speaks for them."[16]

In another speech to Congress several weeks later, President Wilson recounted that while only two American ships had been sunk since the February 1 start of unrestricted submarine warfare, due perhaps to "fortunate circumstances," overall commerce was suffering because ships were avoiding traveling into those areas, given a lack of insurance protection.[17] He then asked Congress for the authority to defensively arm merchantmen (the House passed the Armed Ship Bill, but a Senate filibuster killed it) and also for sufficient war risk insurance credits. A war risk insurance bureau had been created by statute in September 1914[18] to secure coverage when American vessels or shippers could not get adequate war risk insurance, but now Congress amended that act to raise the amount available for paying losses from $5 million to $15 million.[19]

After getting unanimous support from his cabinet members, President Wilson called Congress back early and went to that body on April 2, 1917. Stating that "armed neutrality, it now appears, is impracticable,"[20] he said that Germany had sunk not only neutral merchant ships, but hospital ships and ships carrying relief to Belgium: "There is one choice we cannot make, we are incapable of making: we will not choose the path of submission and suffer the most sacred rights of our Nation and our people to be ignored or violated. The wrongs against which we now array ourselves are no common wrongs; they cut to the very roots of human life. . . . Our object now, as then, is to vindicate the principles of peace and justice in the life of the world as against selfish and autocratic power. . . . The world must be made safe for democracy."[21] And so

---

16. Woodrow Wilson, Address to a Joint Session of Congress on the Severance of Diplomatic Relations with Germany (Feb. 3, 1917).
17. Woodrow Wilson, Address to a Joint Session of Congress on a Request for Authority to Arm Merchant Vessels (Feb. 26, 1917).
18. Pub. L. No. 63-193, An Act to authorize the establishment of a Bureau of War Risk Insurance in the Treasure Department (1914).
19. Pub. L. No. 64-387, An Act to amend an Act entitled "An Act to authorize the establishment of a Bureau of War-Risk Insurance in the Treasury Department," approved September second, nineteen hundred and fourteen. (1917).
20. Woodrow Wilson, Address to a Joint Session of Congress on Reasons for Declaring War on Germany (Apr. 2, 1917).
21. *Id.*

he asked Congress to declare that the United States was in a state of war with Germany and to provide the manpower, materials, and financial credits to address this war.

Congress passed a joint resolution on April 6 declaring that a state of war existed between Germany and the United States.[22] Because Germany had committed "repeated acts of war" against the United States, it resolved that the state of war "which has thus been thrust upon the United States is hereby formally declared." It then gave the president the power "to employ the entire naval and military forces of the United States and the resources of the Government to carry on war against the Imperial German Government; and to bring the conflict to a successful termination all of the resources of the country are hereby pledged by the Congress of the United States."

LEGAL PROFILES

Arthur Zimmermann was German foreign minister. He was born in Germany in 1864 and received his legal training there. He began to practice but then entered the diplomatic service in 1893. He served in China from 1896 to 1900 as vice consul, then consul. In 1902 he joined the foreign office's diplomatic branch. In 1911, after becoming a director, he was appointed as the undersecretary for foreign affairs, where he was involved in supporting the Easter Rising in Ireland in 1916 (see Chapter 6). In November 1916, he became the secretary after the resignation of von Jagow, which was the position he held when he sent his telegram to the German minister in Mexico and the United States declared war with Germany. He remained in this role until August 1917, when he retired from politics. He died in 1940.[23]

---

22. Pub. Res. No. 65-1, Declaring That a State of War Exists between the Imperial German Government and the Government and the People of the United States and Making Provision to Prosecute the Same (1917).
23. *See Dr. Zimmermann Dies in Germany*, N.Y. TIMES (June 8, 1940).

B. Cases

The types of cases that arose from neutrality included cases involving violations of neutrality and how to keep commerce going as a neutral country through war risk insurance. Three U.S. Supreme Court cases looked at these different aspects. The first case addressed whether prize captures could be brought into a neutral country's ports and held there indefinitely. The second case had the Court reviewing the changes in the circumstances of a prewar debt, from one involving two belligerents in a neutral country's court, to one where the court was now in a belligerent country and one party was an enemy alien. The third case involved war risk insurance and the payouts by the government for losses that may have been typical maritime risks instead of war risks. The fourth case was for claims to recover the costs of war risk insurance from Germany.

1. Neutrality and Prizes

In *The Steamship Appam*,[24] the U.S. Supreme Court was asked to look at what started as two separate suits, one to recover a vessel, a prize ship brought into a U.S. port during the war while America was still neutral, and one to recover its cargo. The SS *Appam* was a British merchant ship captured on January 15, 1916, by the German warship *Moewe*. It was taken on a return trip from West Africa to Liverpool, England. The crew offered no resistance and were kept as prisoners, except for some who were used to operate the ship. Bombs were placed on the ship, with German sailors close at hand with revolvers. The crew were told they would be shot if they did not cooperate. Despite the fact that the ship was twice as far from the nearest American port as the nearest German port, the captain ordered the captured ship to sail to the nearest American port (Hampton Roads, Virginia) and to "lay up,"[25] which is where it arrived at the end of January.

The German ambassador then requested that the crew and ship be detained in the U.S. port by American authorities. The American government instead released the crew, and then the owner of the ship sued for its return, claiming its detention had been a violation of neutrality. The German government answered that the ship had been brought into the nearest American port as a

---

24. The Steamship Appam, 243 U.S. 124 (1917).
25. *Id.* at 146.

prize under a century-old treaty[26] between the United States and Prussia that did not allow for putting under legal process prizes brought into the other nation's ports.[27] It also claimed that since a prize court in Germany was handling this matter, the U.S. court had no jurisdiction.

The Supreme Court resolved that there were three questions to answer: (1) Was the use of U.S. ports in this manner a violation of neutrality under international law? (2) Was use of the U.S. port covered by existing treaties between Germany and the United States? (3) Did a U.S. court of admiralty have jurisdiction and condemnation rights over this ship? The Court noted the extreme distance traveled and the fact that the ship did not qualify for the usual exceptions under Hague XIII, "unseaworthiness, stress of weather, or want of fuel or provisions," under which it should have left as soon as possible.[28] The German government's argument was that this article did not apply because the British had not ratified that convention.

The Court noted that, dating back to the Neutrality Act of 1794, the United States had not allowed belligerent ships the use of its ports for fitting out and arming. The United States had taken a reservation to article 23 of Hague XIII, which allowed prize ships into neutral ports to await adjudication by prize courts. Given the country's clear stand against its ports being used to store prizes and with no way to remove the ship except through augmenting the crew, which would have violated neutrality principles, the court ruled that use of the U.S. port for holding prizes was a violation of neutrality. On the second question, the Court interpreted the Prussian–U.S. treaty of 1799 as being only for temporary stays and when a warship accompanied a prize, neither of which was true in this case.

On the third question, citing two of its cases from 1794[29] and 1822,[30] the Court found that federal district courts had the right to adjudicate these types of cases, stating, "The violation of American neutrality is the basis of jurisdiction, and the admiralty courts may order restitution for a violation of such neutrality. In each case the jurisdiction and order rests upon the authority of

---

26. Treaty of Amity and Commerce between the Kingdom of Prussia and the United States of America, July 11, 1799.
27. *Id.* art. XIX.
28. Hague XIII, art. 21.
29. Glass v. The Sloop Betsey, 3 Dall. 6 (1794).
30. Santissima Trinidad, 7 Wheat. 283 (1822).

the courts of the United States to make restitution to private owners for violations of neutrality where offending vessels are within our jurisdiction, thus vindicating our rights and obligations as a neutral people."[31] So it ruled that the lower courts had jurisdiction to rule on this matter and affirmed the rulings in favor of the *Appam* for return of the ship and cargo.

LEGAL PROFILES

Frederick William Lehmann was the lead counsel for the appellants. He was born in Germany in 1853 and immigrated to America at a young age. After leaving home at the age of ten and spending many years working as a farm laborer, he was employed by judge Epenitis Sears, who helped him attend college and then start his legal practice in Iowa. He moved to Nebraska, then Missouri in 1890 and further built his practice. He became the president of the American Bar Association in 1908 and served for two terms. In 1910, President Taft appointed him as the solicitor general, where he remained for the balance of Taft's term before returning to private practice. He died in 1931.[32]

2. Neutrality and Contracts

In *Watts*,[33] the British libellant (plaintiff) had supplied to the Austro-Hungarian defendant corporation bunker coal before the declarations of war but was not paid and so brought suit after obtaining jurisdiction in personam by seizing one of the defendant's ships that had been supplied with the coal. The respondent claimed that under Austro-Hungarian and British law, a neutral country could not require a transfer of funds from one belligerent to another. The libellant claimed that the payment of a debt due was legal in the place of performance, either where the coal had been loaded (Algeria) or where payment

---

31. The Steamship Appam at 156.
32. *See F.W. Lehmann Dies in St. Louis at 78*, N.Y. TIMES (Sept 13, 1931).
33. Watts, Watts & Co. v. Unione Austriaca di Navigazione, 248 U.S. 9 (1918).

was to be made (London), and so Austro-Hungarian law was not involved. Additionally, the jurisdiction of this court would not violate U.S. neutrality. The U.S. district court claimed that it did have jurisdiction but then declined to exercise it, as Great Britain and Austria-Hungary were now at war and it was a matter of their municipal laws.

Between the time that the trial court decision was made and arguments were heard on this case in the U.S. Supreme Court in April 1918, the United States had declared war on Austria-Hungary in December 1917.[34] So the Court determined that it had to take into account both the changes in law and in fact that had occurred since the trial court ruling. With Austria-Hungary now an enemy alien, suit could be brought in U.S. courts against it. Although defended by counsel, the Court felt that to provide an adequate defense, there needed to be intercourse between the defendant's counsel in the United States and company personnel in Austria-Hungary. As this was now prohibited by U.S. law (i.e., the Trading with the Enemy Act; see Section 4.3), the Court remanded the case back to the district court, to be heard when the United States and Austria-Hungary returned to a condition of peaceful relations.

LEGAL PROFILES

John M. Woolsey was the lead counsel for the petitioners in *Watts*. He was born in South Carolina in 1877 but started his legal practice in New York. From 1901 to 1929, he was in private practice there, including a practice in admiralty law. In 1929, he was appointed to the federal bench in the Southern District of New York by President Hoover, where he served actively until 1943. While there he became well known for his decision to allow the importation of the novel *Ulysses* into the United States, when the book had been previously banned by censors for being obscene.[35] The publisher then printed his decision inside the American editions of the book. He died in 1945.[36]

---

34. Pub. Res. No. 65-17, Declaring That a State of War Exists between the Imperial and Royal Austro-Hungarian Government and the Government and the People of the United States and Making Provision to Prosecute the Same (1917).
35. United States v. One Book Called "Ulysses", 5 F. Supp. 182 (S.D.N.Y. 1933).
36. *See Woolsey, John Munro*, FED. JUDICIAL CTR., BIOGRAPHICAL DIRECTORY OF FEDERAL JUDGES.

Louis D. Brandeis delivered the opinion of the Court in *Watts*. He was born in Kentucky in 1856 and started law school at the age of eighteen, graduating as valedictorian. He briefly practiced in Missouri, and then moved to Boston in 1879, where he was a law clerk and later became a partner in a new law firm. It was in 1890 that he and his law partner published the seminal article "A Right to Privacy,"[37] which laid the initial groundwork for a whole new area of law. Brandeis's practice of progressive law supported working people and pitted him against many of the largest economic interests of the day. After the election of President Wilson in 1912, Brandeis acted as an adviser to the administration and helped to get the Federal Reserve System Act[38] and the Federal Trade Commission Act[39] passed. He was appointed by President Wilson in 1916 as an associate justice on the U.S. Supreme Court, becoming the Court's first Jewish member. He served in this role until 1939 and was instrumental in many key decisions, including those involving privacy,[40] free speech,[41] and the Erie doctrine.[42] He died in 1941.[43]

---

3. War Risk Insurance: Control

In *Standard Oil*,[44] claims under the war risk insurance program were being made for the loss of a ship, the SS *Llama*, which had sailed in October 1915 with a cargo of oil from New York to Copenhagen but had been diverted en route by British warships on blockade. On its detour, the ship had struck rocks and sunk, a total loss. The insurer had taken on the following risks: "takings at sea, arrests, restraints and detainments of all kings, princes, and peoples, of what nation, condition or quality soever, and all consequences of hostilities or warlike operations, whether before or after declaration of war."[45] But the defense

---

37. S. Warren and L. Brandeis, *The Right to Privacy*, 4 Harv. L. Rev. 193 (1890).
38. Pub. L. No. 63-43 (1913).
39. Pub. L. No. 63-203 (1914).
40. *See, e.g.*, Olmstead v. United States, 277 U.S. 438 (1928).
41. *See, e.g.*, Whitney v. California, 274 U.S. 357 (1927).
42. *See* Erie Railroad Co. v. Tompkins, 304 U.S. 64 (1938).
43. *See Brandeis, Louis Dembitz*, Fed. Judicial Ctr., Biographical Directory of Federal Judges.
44. Standard Oil Co. of N.J. v. United States, 267 U.S. 76 (1925).
45. *Id.* at 77.

argued that the rocks had been the proximate cause of sinking and that they were a marine peril and not something covered by its insurance.

The Court looked at the issue of who was in "paramount control"[46] of the ship at the time of the accident and found that it was the British officer. It did not matter how often he gave orders, whether the intervening British ship was armed or not, or how much the ship's own master seemed to navigate; what mattered was who had the ultimate control. This was deemed to have been the British officer. As their intervention was determined to have been a taking, all acts consequent to that taking were part of it, including the sinking, and so this risk fell under the insured risks and the libellants prevailed on their claim for the loss of the ship.

LEGAL PROFILES

James M. Beck was the U.S. solicitor general, on the brief for this case. He was born in Pennsylvania in 1861 and started his legal practice there in 1884. From 1888 to 1892, he served as an assistant district attorney, and he became a district attorney in 1896, serving until 1900, when he became an assistant to the U.S. attorney general. He held this role until 1903, when he began to practice in New York. In 1921, he became solicitor general, a position he held until 1925. In 1927, he was elected to Congress, where he served until 1934, when he resigned. During WWI, he made speeches in France and England, supporting the cause of the Allied Powers. He was made a master of the bench at Gray's Inn, the first foreigner so invited in hundreds of years. He also received many honors in Europe and was called to the English bar after the war, in 1922. He died in 1936.[47]

Oliver Wendell Holmes Jr. delivered the opinion of the Court in *Standard Oil*. He was born in Massachusetts in 1841 and started his legal practice there. But first he volunteered for and fought in the American

---

46. *Id.* at 78.
47. *See Beck, James Montgomery*, BIOGRAPHICAL DIRECTORY OF THE UNITED STATES CONGRESS.

Civil War, being wounded at the battles of Antietam and Chancellorsville. In 1866, he began to practice law in Boston. In 1882, he was appointed to the Massachusetts Supreme Judicial Court, eventually becoming the chief justice in 1899. In 1902 he was appointed as an associate justice on the U.S. Supreme Court by President Roosevelt. He was to remain on the Court until 1932, where his best-known opinions and dissents included those covering sedition[48] and free speech.[49] He died in 1935.[50]

4. War Risk Insurance: Premium Claims

In *U.S. Steel Products*,[51] several companies were trying to seek refunds from Germany for war risk insurance premiums that they had paid. The refunds were sought through the postwar mixed claims commission discussed in Chapter 2. The opinion of the commission described the risks for the United States' merchants during its period of neutrality as limited to cases when part or all of the cargo was contraband, when the shipping violated a blockade, when a ship encountered mines, and when a shipment was under a belligerent flag. Because the contraband lists kept changing, blockaded ports and the location of mines were uncertain, and belligerent countries needed to use their ships, the war risk insurance was vital for American commerce. But the commission listed the commercial benefits of this insurance, detailing as an example how the prices of shipped goods stopped falling and began to increase after war risk insurance became available in America.

The commission also described how cotton, even after being declared contraband, was being purchased at contract price if seized by the British and French blockades. It made the point that the decrease in the price of cotton before war risk insurance became available was ultimately borne by the cotton producer, and the increase in the price of cotton after war risk insurance became available was ultimately borne by the cotton consumer. But in neither

---

48. *See, e.g.*, Schenck v. United States, 249 U.S. 47 (1919).
49. *See, e.g.*, Abrams v. United States, 250 U.S. 616 (1919).
50. *See Holmes, Oliver Wendell Jr.*, FED. JUDICIAL CTR., BIOGRAPHICAL DIRECTORY OF FEDERAL JUDGES.
51. Mixed Claims Commission, United States and Germany, U.S. Steel Products Co. (United States) v. Germany; Costa Rica Union Mining Co. (United States) v. Germany; South Porto Rico Sugar Co. (United States) v. Germany (Nov. 1, 1923).

case was it borne by the shippers, who were making the claims here. The commission stated that the losses sustained by American nationals for recovery under the commission had to be caused by Germany or its agents in order to qualify for refunds, but that there were no claims for injury or damage by Germany, only general costs of being at war.

Instead, these were costs of war that had to be borne by each country, like the cotton producer and consumer. The commission stated, "If the terms of the Treaty can be so expanded by forced construction as to embrace such claims, then they will include all increased living costs, increased railroad freights, increased income and profits taxes, in a word *all* costs or consequences of the war, direct or remote, to the extent that such costs were paid or losses suffered by American nationals. The rejection of such a construction must follow its mere statement."[52] As such, war risk insurance premiums claims were not allowed either during the period of U.S. neutrality or during its later period of belligerency, as these costs were related not to direct actions of Germany but to the "very existence of a state of war."[53]

LEGAL PROFILES

Robert Lansing was the American secretary of state during the war. He was born in New York in 1864 and started his legal practice there in 1889. He was involved in many international law cases from then until the war. He joined the State Department in 1914 after representing the United States in maritime-related arbitration with Great Britain. He became secretary in 1915 in follow-up to the sinking of the RMS *Lusitania*, when William Jennings Bryan resigned. He was the lead U.S. representative at the Paris Peace Conference. He continued as secretary of state until resigning in 1920 and returning to his international law private practice. He died in 1928.[54]

---

52. *Id.*
53. *Id.*
54. *See Robert Lansing, Wilson War Aide, Dies in Capital*, N.Y. TIMES (Oct. 31, 1928).

C. Subsequent Events

After war was declared, President Wilson took a number of steps to prepare the country rapidly for war, including the following wide-ranging directives issued as executive orders. Under his war powers (and the Act to Regulate Radio Communication, of 1912), he ordered the seizure of radio stations to be used by the government and the closing and removal of the equipment for others.[55] Federal employees could now be dismissed on security grounds, for their "conduct, sympathies or utterances, or because of other reasons growing out of the war."[56] A committee on public information was created, comprising the secretaries of war, navy, and state, headed by a civilian appointed by the president.[57] The Council for National Defense was allowed to utilize whatever person they thought appropriate, even if not a federal government employee.[58] The eight-hour workday limit was suspended on war-related work.[59] Censorship was imposed on submarine cables and telephone and telegraph lines for communications sent outside the United States.[60] Based on Congressional authorization,[61] German vessels lying in American-controlled waters were to be seized[62] and ships were ordered to be built,[63] and the American registry of foreign ships was made easier.[64]

---

55. Exec. Order No. 2585/2605A, Taking Over Necessary and Closing Unnecessary Radio Stations (Apr. 6/30, 1917).
56. Exec. Order No. 2587A, Federal Employees Removal on Security Grounds (Apr. 7, 1917).
57. Exec. Order No. 2594, Creating Committee on Public Information (Apr. 13, 1917).
58. Exec. Order No. 2600, Employees of Council of National Defense (Apr. 17, 1917).
59. Exec. Order No. 2605, Suspending Eight-Hour Law in Contracts under the War Department (Apr. 28, 1917).
60. Exec. Order No. 2604, Censorship of Submarine Cables, Telegraph and Telephone Lines (Apr. 28, 1917).
61. Pub. Res. No. 2, Authorizing the President to Take Over for the United States the Possession and Title of Any Vessel within Its Jurisdiction, Which at the Time of Coming Therein Was Owned in Whole or in Part by Any Corporation, Citizen, or Subject of Any Nation with Which the United States May Be at War, or Was under Register of Any Such Nation, and for Other Purposes (May 12, 1917).
62. Exec. Orders No. 2619A, German Boats (May 14, 1917), No. 2621 (May 16, 1917), No. 2624 (May 22, 1917), No. 2625 (May 22, 1917), No. 2635 (June 12, 1917), No. 2651 (June 30, 1917), No. 2653 (July 3, 1917), No. 2709 (Sept. 27, 1917), No. 2748 (Nov. 2, 1917).
63. Exec. Order No. 2664, Exercise of Authority under the Emergency Shipping Fund Act (July 11, 1917); Exec. Order No. 2687, Exercise of Authority under the "Naval Emergency Fund Act," and Others (Aug. 21, 1917).
64. Exec. Order No. 2696, Suspending Law Admitting Foreign-Built Ships to American Entry (Sept. 7, 1917).

LEGAL PROFILES

Edwin Hubble was an American soldier in this war and a future renowned astronomer. He was born in Missouri in 1889 and received his legal training at the University of Chicago and the University of Oxford, where he was a Rhodes Scholar. He practiced law briefly in Kentucky in 1913, but his heart was with astronomy, so he changed his study and received his PhD in 1917, just in time to volunteer for the U.S. Army, and eventually served overseas. After the war, he returned to astronomy, not law. Among his many discoveries at the Mt. Wilson observatory in California included many galaxies outside of the Milky Way Galaxy, Hubble's law on the distance of galaxies based on the red-shifting of the light received from them, and Hubble's sequence on the grouping of galaxies. The Hubble Space Telescope was named for him. During WWII he again volunteered for service and led a group working on ballistics of ordinance. He died in 1953.[65]

4.2 GERMANY IN AMERICA

A. Statutes

The request in the Zimmermann telegram was ultimately turned down by the Mexicans, but that was not the first or last time that America's southern neighbor was involved during the war. Nor was this the only time that Germany was involved in schemes or attacks on U.S. soil during the war. Germany had been involved in a series of plans, starting before the war, to foment difficulties for the British that involved tie-ups with similarly motivated anti-British groups located in the United States. When its war began, Germany also got involved in various attempts at sabotaging the U.S. munitions producing capabilities that were supplying the Allied Powers. The latter two interventions are more fully discussed in the "Cases" section below.

---

65. *See Dr. Edwin P. Hubble*, 74 THE OBSERVATORY No. 878, at 32 (1954).

During WWI, the United States would intervene militarily not only with Mexico, but also in the Dominican Republic, Panama, Nicaragua, Cuba, and Haiti, sometimes based on direct involvement of Europeans and sometimes based on the fear of their involvement. As was discussed in Chapter 1, the Taft administration had been involved in swapping out European debt for American debt in Nicaragua in 1907 and then intervened as it deemed necessary. The troubles with Mexico were more multifaceted and started just before the war, with the Tampico Incident in April 1914.

1. Tampico Incident

Mexico was in the middle of a decade-long revolution that started in 1910, and it was not certain who the ruling authorities were, as there were a number of different and shifting centers of power. One of these factions, led by General Victoriano Huerta, had briefly seized U.S. sailors in the Mexican port of Tampico trying to refuel their ship from a German supplier. President Wilson went before Congress, asking for authority to respond to this incident.[66] The Mexicans had offered apologies and an explanation that the area was under martial law and no one was allowed to land at the time.

But the U.S. commander Rear Admiral Henry Mayo focused on the fact that several of the sailors were forced off of a U.S. boat (i.e., American territory) to be arrested, and he asked for further demonstration of remorse from the Mexicans, which they refused. Wilson put this in the context of other incidents that had happened involving the same faction, which he attributed to the U.S. government's refusal to recognize Huerta's faction as the legitimate one in Mexico. Congress followed the president's request with a joint resolution that allowed use of military force to seek out "unequivocal amends for certain affronts and indignities committed against the United States . . . [but] disclaims any hostility to the Mexican people or any purpose to make war upon Mexico."[67]

Then a second Mexican port became the focus later in April 1914. Trying to stop a shipment of small arms from Germany from reaching Huerta, Wilson had ordered the navy to stand off of the port of Veracruz and intercept the

---

66. Woodrow Wilson, Address to a Joint Session of Congress on the Tampico Incident (Apr. 20, 1914).
67. Pub. Res. No. 63-22, Justifying the Employment by the President of the Armed Forces of the United States (Apr. 22, 1914).

German ship SS *Ypiranga* from Hamburg. With the arrival of the ship imminent, based on reports from the U.S. consul there, Wilson ordered U.S. commander Rear Admiral Frank Friday to take over at least the port area of the town. This led to taking over the whole town and imposing martial law. After Huerta was overthrown and the new government of Venustiano Carranza was in place, the United States eventually withdrew from Veracruz, in November 1914. To help those impacted by the "disturbances" in Mexico, Congress provided funding for the repatriation of U.S. citizens.[68]

Congress, concerned about the impact of the Mexican Revolution, had previously instituted a U.S. arms embargo to the Americas in March 1912.[69] This prohibited the export of arms or munitions to any country in the Western Hemisphere where domestic violence existed, if the president determined that U.S. arms would promote such violence. President Taft had drawn on this privilege immediately, cutting off arms shipments to Mexico.[70] Presidents could allow exceptions to the embargoes, which Wilson did for the U.S.-favored Carranza faction in the Mexican Revolution. This meant that other groups had to turn to Europe for their arms. This is why the SS *Ypiranga* was to land at Veracruz, a place controlled by Huerta forces, against whom the U.S. embargo was being enforced. But the U.S. troops there had no legal authority to detain the ship, as the United States and Mexico were not at war and no formal blockade was in place. The ship was allowed to leave and was able to deposit its arms for Huerta at a Mexican port to the south of Veracruz.

LEGAL PROFILES

William W. Canada was the U.S. consul at Veracruz. He was born in Indiana in 1850 and started his legal practice there. He was active in local politics, leading to his being named to the consul position at Veracruz in 1897. While serving in this position, he survived being shot in one of

---

68. Pub. L. No. 63-88, An Act Providing an Appropriation for the Relief and Transportation of American Citizens in Mexico (1914).
69. Pub. Res. No. 62-22, To Amend the Joint Resolution to Prohibit the Export of Coal or Other Material Used in War from Any Seaport of the United States (Mar. 14, 1912).
70. Pub. Proclamation No. 1185, Proclamation by the President of the United States of America Regarding the Export of Arms, Etc., to Mexico (Mar. 14, 1912).

the uprisings during the Mexican Revolution. He resigned as consul in 1916 and died in 1921.[71]

2. Pancho Villa Raid

In March 1916, another major incident occurred in Mexico, with suspected but unproven German support. Francisco "Pancho" Villa entered the United States and killed more than a dozen civilians and soldiers in New Mexico, after previously killing a similar number of American citizens working in Mexico in January. This attack led President Wilson to order General John Pershing into Mexico in pursuit of Villa. Although initial battles were favorable to the Americans, Villa was never captured, as Wilson was trying to avoid provoking a war with Mexico by going too far into the country. In any event, the U.S. entry into WWI would require the recall of Pershing for deployment to Europe. Negotiations between the two governments at Niagara Falls eventually led to the departure of U.S. troops in early 1917. One of the U.S. troops who had been pursuing Villa in this expedition was the future WWII general Lt. George S. Patton, the son of a lawyer.

The Villa raid sparked the passage in Congress of the National Defense Act of 1916,[72] which laid the groundwork for many of the capabilities of the U.S. military during WWI. The active military[73] and National Guard[74] were significantly increased in size; an Officer's Reserve Corps,[75] Enlisted Reserve Corps,[76] and Reserve Officers Training Corps (ROTC)[77] were created; and the president was authorized to call up the National Guard in times of war.[78] Wilson did subsequently deploy significant numbers of National Guard to patrol the U.S.-Mexico border, providing essential training for these men and officers that would prove useful during their subsequent service in Europe in the following years.

---

71. *See William W. Canada Dead*, N.Y. TIMES (May 18, 1921).
72. Pub. L. No. 64–85 (1916).
73. *Id.* § 3.
74. *Id.* § 62.
75. *Id.* § 37.
76. *Id.* § 55.
77. *Id.* § 40.
78. *Id.* § 111.

LEGAL PROFILES

Luis Cabrera was the Mexican representative to the Niagara Falls talks to end the cross-border raids. He was born in Mexico in 1876 and started his legal practice there in 1901. In addition to practicing, he wrote articles speaking out against the long-ruling government. He also taught at law school and became director of Escuela Nacional de Jurisprudencia. In 1912, he was elected to the federal legislature. He supported the Carranza faction and so was appointed finance minister in 1914 and also tried to negotiate an end to the U.S. arms embargo that year. Besides this activity, he was involved with the Plan of Guadalupe for relegitimizing Mexico after the assassination of President Madero in 1913. He also drafted the Agrarian Law (*la Ley Agraria*) in 1915 and was involved with the 1917 constitution. Continuing his writing, sometimes under pen names, he was briefly deported to Guatemala in 1931. He twice turned down the opportunity to run for president of Mexico. He died in 1954.[79]

James Hay was the primary drafter of the National Defense Act of 1916. He was born in Virginia in 1856 and started his legal practice there in 1877. In 1883, he became an attorney for the state, a role he held until 1896. In 1885, he was elected to the state legislature, serving until 1889, and in 1893, to the state senate, serving until 1897. In that year he was elected to the U.S. Congress, where he served until 1916, including as the head of the Committee on Military Affairs, the position he held when he drafted the National Defense Act. In 1916, he retired from Congress and was nominated by President Wilson to the Court of Claims, where he served actively until resigning in 1927. He died in 1931.[80]

---

79. *See Luis Cabrera*, MEMORIA POLITICA DE MEXICO, Oct. 30, 1911.
80. *See Hay, James*, BIOGRAPHICAL DIRECTORY OF THE UNITED STATES CONGRESS; *Hay, James*, FED. JUDICIAL CTR., BIOGRAPHICAL DIRECTORY OF FEDERAL JUDGES.

B. Cases

There were cases that arose from the Mexican Revolution that reached U.S. courts, including one concerning the legitimacy of the current Mexican government and whether actions of that government could be challenged in U.S. courts. Also, there were several cases of German involvement in the Americas, first for trying to undermine the British rule in India and second for destroying production capabilities of U.S. munitions plants during U.S. neutrality. The first case deals with Mexico during its revolution and Pancho Villa, the second case with the German-Indian (sometimes called the German-Hindu) conspiracy trial, and the third case with German sabotage activities within America.

1. Military Assessments and Pancho Villa

In *Oetjen*,[81] the U.S. Supreme Court looked at Pancho Villa's ability to speak for the Mexican government. The plaintiff was trying to get the return, in replevin, of two large consignments of hides that had been acquired directly from a Mexican business. The defendant asserted that it had acquired the hides from a Texas company that had acquired them directly from Pancho Villa. The plaintiff claimed that the hides had been confiscated by Villa in violation of the Hague Convention IV of 1907.

When the Mexican Revolution started and soon led to the resignation of longtime president Porfirio Diaz, reformer Francisco Madero was elected president in 1911. But he was assassinated in 1913, and several power factions sprang up, including those led by Victoriano Huerta and Venustiano Carranza. Villa was associated then with Carranza and responsible for the military action in the northern region of Mexico. In October 1913, Villa captured the city of Torreon and demanded a military assessment. The owner of the hides, Martinez, was a supporter of Huerta and fled, but the hides were taken and sold to a Texas company.

The Court took judicial notice that on October 19, 1915, the U.S. government (along with Latin American countries) recognized the Carranza government as the de facto ruler of Mexico, thanks in part to the agent of the Carranza government in the United States. And on August 31, 1917, the Carranza government was recognized as the de jure representative of Mexico after Carranza was elected president by the Mexican legislature in 1917. The Court

---

81. Oetjen v. Central Leather Co., 246 U.S. 297 (1918).

also noted that the Hague Convention applied to international conflicts, not civil wars, and even if they did, there were articles that allowed armies to levy occupied territories.

The Court then described three "settled principles of law"[82] upon which to apply the facts. The first was that the use of the political power of the executive is not subject to judicial review. Second, who is sovereign of a country is a political, not a judicial, question, which the U.S. government had decided in the case of Mexico. Third, de jure recognition is retroactive to the time when a government began, so the 1913 action of Villa as the representative of Carranza was covered by the 1917 de jure recognition of that government (even though Villa would soon fall out with Carranza). The actions by a Mexican government representative regarding an action with a Mexican citizen (or an American citizen[83]) could be reviewed only in a Mexican court or through the U.S. government's political function, not by a U.S. court. The Court affirmed the award to the defendant of the hides acquired from Pancho Villa through the Texas company.

LEGAL PROFILES

Eliseo Arredondo was the agent for the Carranza government in the United States. He was born in Mexico in 1870 and started his legal practice there in 1900. He also served as a district judge. He was the governor of the state of Coahuila from 1911. He then served in several roles, including interior minister of the new Carranza government (he and Carranza were first cousins) during the revolution. He went to the United States to act as the agent of the Carranza government (ambassador-designate) before being appointed as the ambassador to the United States in late 1917. In 1918, he became the ambassador to Spain. He died in 1923.[84]

---

82. *Id.* at 302.
83. *See* Ricaud v. Am. Metal Co., 246 U.S. 304, 310 (1918).
84. *See Eliseo Arredondo Dead*, N.Y. TIMES, (Oct. 20, 1923).

John Hessin Clarke delivered the opinion for this case. He was born in Ohio in 1857 and started his legal practice there in 1878. Besides his legal practice, he owned a newspaper and was very active in Democratic politics in the state. He failed in an election bid for the U.S. Senate in 1904. In 1914, he was appointed to the federal bench for the Northern District of Ohio by President Wilson. In 1916, he was then appointed to the United States Supreme Court. He served there until 1922, when he resigned. He spent time promoting the League of Nations after his resignation. He died in 1945.[85]

---

2. German-Indian Conspiracy

To remove the British from India, Indian nationalists globally aligned with various other groups, such as Irish nationalists, who had similar goals of freedom from British domination. With the start of the war, one of these groups, the Ghadar Party, found common cause with Germany. The leader of the party in the United States, Har Dyal, had jumped bail and gone to Europe after being indicted for violating U.S. neutrality law. Together this new partnership launched a series of efforts to undermine British rule in India, primarily by inciting Indian soldiers serving with the British military to revolt. Their joint efforts culminated in a series of mutinies in 1915 from Singapore to the Punjab, which were finally suppressed by the British, with the perpetrators brought to trial in various locations, including Lahore, India.

The German consulate in San Francisco served as the focus of the seditionist efforts in America. In this new plot, the Germans acquired small arms in the United States and had them delivered to San Diego. From there they were ostensibly to be shipped to the Carranza faction in the Mexican revolution (see previous case) on the SS *Annie Larsen*. In reality, they were destined for India, after being transferred to a second ship, the SS *Maverick* off of the coast of Mexico. The *Annie Larsen* had a German navy captain in charge of the cargo (the "supercargo"), and the *Maverick* was crewed by German sailors. In fact, the ships did not rendezvous, and both ships were captured, with the person in charge of the supercargo on the *Maverick* confessing to his role and the cargo

---

85. *See Clarke, John Hessin*, Fed. Judicial Ctr., Biographical Directory of Federal Judges.

still on the *Annie Larsen* being sold at auction, despite German government intervention to stop it.

The British trials, the details from this new gun-running scheme, and other intelligence efforts produced evidence of a plot utilizing the still-neutral United States to foment dissent in the British Empire by arming nationalists back in India. This led to arrests of Germans, Americans, and Indian nationalists in the United States and a trial that began in November 1917 based on violation of neutrality laws for conspiring to overthrow British rule. What the defendants were charged with, inter alia, was violating the U.S. criminal code by conspiring[86] to commit the offense of organizing a military expedition against a friendly power.[87] Among those arrested were German consul general Franz Bopp and vice consul Eckhart von Schack, who had previously been convicted of violating U.S. neutrality on similar grounds for conspiring to destroy munitions intended for the Allied Powers by blowing up several tunnels in Canada.[88]

During the trial,[89] one of the defendants, Dr. C. K. Chakravarty, claimed that the German government had provided hundreds of thousands of dollars of funding in America for their cause. The judge compared the Indian defendants to "mere catspaws of the ruthless Prussian military system." The jury handed down the sentences on April 30, 1918. Of the thirty-four people who had been brought to trial, fourteen of the Germans and Americans were convicted and sentenced to imprisonment and fined, and two were only fined, while fifteen of the Indian defendants were convicted and sentenced to imprisonment. Two of the Indians were killed as the trial was ending, with defendant Ram Singh shooting his codefendant Ram Chandra in the courtroom and then being shot himself by a U.S. marshal. The leaders of the German consulate, Bopp, von Schack, and military attaché Baron Wilhelm von Brincken, were given the maximum sentence allowed of two years' imprisonment, running consecutively with their prior convictions for the Canada offenses (concurrently for von Brincken).

---

86. U.S. Criminal Code § 37.
87. *Id.* § 13.
88. United States v. Bopp, Case No. 5885, 230 F. 723 (1916).
89. United States v. Bopp, Case No. 6133, 254 F. 635 (1917).

LEGAL PROFILES

William van Fleet was the judge in this trial. He was born in Ohio in 1852 but moved to California and started his legal practice there in 1873. He became an assistant district attorney in 1878. In 1881, he was elected to the state assembly and, starting in 1883, was the director of the state prison system. From 1884 to 1892, he was a judge on the Superior Court of California. He was appointed to the California Supreme Court in 1894, where he served until 1899. In 1907, he was appointed by President Roosevelt to the federal bench in the Northern District of California. He served there until his death in 1923.[90]

Julier Clyde Hizar was a defendant in this case. He was born in Ohio in 1871 but moved to California and started his legal practice there in 1894. He was the one who leased the *Annie Larsen* and also was responsible for getting the arms loaded on it, posing as a representative of Carranza. He was convicted and sentenced to a year in the county jail and fined five thousand dollars. He died in 1946.[91]

Louis T. Hengstler was also a defendant in this case. He was born in Germany to a family of lawyers and started his legal practice there. He came to California in 1886 and was admitted to the bar in 1887. He was also a mathematician and taught at the University of California in both mathematics and law. He was convicted at this trial and sentenced to jail time, but he made a patriotic plea to the court and ultimately was only fined five thousand dollars and not imprisoned.[92] He was subsequently involved in quite a number of cases that reached the U.S. Supreme Court, especially those involved with admiralty law.

John W. Preston was the prosecutor in this case. He was born in Tennessee in 1877 and started his legal practice there in 1897. He came

---

90. *See Van Fleet, William Cary*, FED. JUDICIAL CTR., BIOGRAPHICAL DIRECTORY OF FEDERAL JUDGES.
91. *See Hizar, Julier Clyde*, State Bar of California.
92. *See San Francisco Consuls Sentenced to Prison*, N.Y. TIMES (May 1, 1918).

to California to try a probate matter and eventually came back to stay, getting his California license in 1903. He served in the California legislature from 1908 to 1910 and then in 1914 took on the role of U.S. attorney for the Northern District of California, the position he held during this trial. He remained there through 1918, when he resigned to work as assistant attorney general for the United States for war work. In late 1926, he was appointed an associate justice on the California Supreme Court, where he served until retiring in 1935 and returning to practice before the Supreme Court. He died in 1958.[93]

3. Munitions Sabotage

Although there were several incidents that occurred during U.S. neutrality that demonstrated German intent to sabotage American munitions capabilities, including information gained from the July 1915 theft of the briefcase of the German commercial attaché by U.S. intelligence agents, it was two major incidents that confirmed German involvement. These were fires and explosions that destroyed a storage depot at the Black Tom Terminal in New York harbor on the nights of July 29–30, 1916, and another explosion that destroyed the Kingsland munitions plant in New Jersey on January 11–12, 1917. In both cases, sabotage by German agents was suspected. With the imminent entry of the United States into the war, there was no opportunity to resolve these cases during the conflict.

As discussed in Chapter 2, after the war, a mixed claims commission was initiated to resolve claims by U.S. nationals against Germany and German nationals that had arisen during the war, including during the time of American neutrality.[94] These two cases were submitted to the commission by the owners of the two properties, and a judgment was rendered in 1930 stating that the

---

93. *See In Memoriam, Honorable John W. Preston*, 2 CAL. REP. 50.
94. Agreement between the United States and Germany Providing for the Determination of the Amount of the Claims against Germany, Aug. 10, 1922, U.S. T.S. 665 (Ger.-U.S.); Agreement Affected by Exchange of Notes between the United States and Germany, Extension of the Jurisdiction of the Mixed Claims Commission–United States and Germany, Dec. 31, 1928, U.S.T.S. 766 (Ger.-U.S.).

Kingsland fire had not been caused by an "authorized German agent" and that for the Black Tom fire, the cause was "not sufficiently proved."[95]

But in 1933, the cases were resubmitted to the commission, based on allegations of material fraud, collusion on the part of German witnesses, and the suppression of evidence. For several years, arguments were made on whether the cases could be reopened and then whether the evidence of fraud should be considered separate from the merits of the cases. Finally, by January 1939, all evidence had been submitted and the commission began to meet to review it all, on both the question of fraud and the merits. There was a disagreement from the German commissioner, who insisted that the misleading of the commission in 1930 was not material if the United States had met its burden of proof. The commission was examining this question when the German commissioner retired from the commission on March 1, 1939. Given that the Nazi Party was now in power in Germany, the commissioner was not replaced.

The remaining two members of the commission, looking to the commission's own rules and to precedent from U.S. Supreme Court decisions,[96] determined that they had the power to proceed with a decision, as an objecting arbitrator cannot defeat the operation of a commission by withdrawing. Since commission decisions required only a two-member majority, the outcome would not likely have changed even if the German commissioner had been in place. On a voluminous amount of information presented, evidence introduced, and arguments made, the commission highlighted some key points. General evidence produced included a message in January 1915 sent from the German army general staff to the military attaché in the United States, Franz von Papen, naming persons capable of committing sabotage in the United States and Canada (information that von Papen claimed he never acted on) and telegrams showing authority to sabotage oil fields in Tampico, Mexico, that were controlled by Standard Oil and supplied oil to the Allied Powers.

Statements were taken and other evidence collected suggesting that German American Frederick Herrmann had organized saboteurs in America and provided them with incendiary devices, as well as statements from German-American Paul Hilken that he was the paymaster for these operations in

---

95. Mixed Claims Commission, United States and Germany, Lehigh Valley Railroad Company, Agency of Canadian Car and Found Company, Limited, and Various Underwriters (United States) v. Germany (Oct. 16, 1930).
96. Republic of Columbia v. Cauca, 190 U.S. 524 (1903).

America, under direction from the German general staff's *Sektion Politik*. Both men had traveled to Europe after the war had started to receive instructions from this group. The most important evidence was a coded message written in lemon juice and pin pricks on a magazine that had been sent by Herrmann in Mexico (most saboteurs had left the United States after the declaration of war, as they would be subject to execution) in April 1917 to Hilken in the United States. It mentioned both the Black Tom and the Kingsland fires, the German government connection, and the need for funds to blow up the Tampico oil fields.

Extensive proof was offered to demonstrate the authenticity of this message. The contents of this short message, as summarized later by the mixed claims umpire, were "conclusive proof to any reasonable man that (a) Herrmann and Hilken knew the Kingsland fire and the Black Tom explosion were the work of German agents and (b) that [interned merchant captain Friedrich] Hinsch, Hilken, and Herrmann, undoubted agents, were privy thereto, and (in the light of the record before the Commission) (c) that [Michael] Kristoff [the suspected Black Tom bomber] and [Theodore] Wozniak were active participants in these events. As the American Agent has well said, I may utterly disregard all the new evidence produced and still, if I deem this message genuine, hold Germany responsible in both of the cases."[97] The German commissioner did not object to this statement in this opinion.

Theodore Wozniak, who worked at the Kingsland munitions plant cleaning ammunition shells with rags dipped in alcohol, admitted that the Kingsland fire had started at his workbench. His testimony in the 1930 commission decision led the commission to believe that the fire had been an accident. Subsequent evidence was produced suggesting that Wozniak had been paid by the Germans for his testimony before the commission in 1930. And he later admitted having been in contact with German spies operating in and around the munitions plant, as well as with Herrmann. Evidence was produced of payments to other plant workers for testifying that the machines they used in cleaning the shells had sparked (the original claim about the source of the fire), but it was later shown that the machines in the plant did not spark.

The commission ruled that "material fraud in evidence presented by Germany seriously misled Commission and affected its decision in favour of Ger-

---

97. Mixed Claims Commission, United States and Germany, Umpire's Opinion (Dec. 3, 1932).

many" and so set aside its 1930 decision.[98] In addition, the commission found "on the record as it now stands, that the liability of Germany in both the Black Tom and Kingsland cases has been established."[99] With WWII now upon them, there was no settlement for this issue until long after the war had finished and the Federal Republic of Germany had come into being, with upward of $50 million in damages and interest eventually paid to settle these claims.

LEGAL PROFILES

Heinrich Albert was the German commercial attaché whose briefcase was stolen. He was born in Germany in 1874 and started his legal practice there. He came to America in 1915 as commercial attaché to collect funds for the Red Cross, but his main role was to finance clandestine German operations, such as spying, labor strikes, and attacks on munitions plants, which was uncovered in the contents of the briefcase. In February 1917, he returned to Germany and became undersecretary of state and finance minister and agreed to become chancellor, although his bid was not successful because he could not form a government. He then returned to legal practice, especially in German-American financial issues.[100] He died in 1960.

C. Subsequent Events

The German involvement with America's neighbors showed up prominently in at least two other places during the war. One was at the Battle of Ambos Nogales in August 1918, where the U.S.-Mexico border literally ran right down the middle of the street. Movement across the border had been curtailed, leading to several deaths, and so tensions were high, when a gun battle erupted

---

98. Mixed Claims Commission, United States and Germany, Lehigh Valley Railroad Company, Agency of Canadian Car and Found Company, Limited, and Various Underwriters (United States) v. Germany (June 15, 1939).
99. Mixed Claims Commission, United States and Germany, Order (June 15, 1939).
100. *See With North German Lloyd*, N.Y. TIMES (May 13, 1932).

over suspected smuggling from the American side in the state of Arizona to the Mexican side in the state of Sonora. The famed Tenth Calvary (one of the units composed of African American Buffalo Soldiers) was stationed nearby and assisted in the action. Many sources, including testimony from participants, cited involvement by German personnel in this battle. The result was a border fence down the middle of the street.

Fear of German involvement led to the U.S. takeover of the Dominican Republic in 1916. As explained in Chapter 1, the United States had previously intervened in this country, due to a fear that its European debts would allow one of its creditors to take over the country and use it for a base to launch attacks against the United States. The situation deteriorated through successive Dominican administrations, so in 1916, the United States took over the country, based on a purported violation of the 1907 treaty involving customs collections, and retained control of it through the remainder of the war and beyond, with the troops finally departing in 1924.

There were also other German espionage efforts during the war. Military attaché Franz von Papen and naval attaché Karl Boy-Ed were both very active in building spy and sabotage networks, for which they were asked to leave the United States in late 1915. Franz von Rintelen, who came to the United States in 1915, organized (among other subversive activities) incendiary devices to be placed onto merchant ships, causing fires in their munitions cargos. He was captured by the British, then held by the Americans until the end of the war.

The "pencil bomb" devices used for this sabotage had been created by Dr. Walter Scheele, who had been carrying on industrial espionage in the United States, and after being caught fleeing the country, avoided prison by changing sides to work for the Americans. Part of this work included creating a process for safely loading explosives into shells before transporting them. Biological warfare capabilities were also prepared in the United States by Anton and Carl Dilger (see Chapter 6).

LEGAL PROFILES

Alexander Bruce Bielaski was the chief of the Justice Department's Bureau of Investigation during the war, responsible for investigating many subversive activities. He was born in Maryland in 1883 and started his legal practice there in 1904. He joined the Justice Department that year, working his way to becoming assistant to the chief. He was then made chief in 1912, a role he remained in until 1919. He then returned to private law practice. He worked as a special assistant to the attorney general in prosecuting smugglers when Prohibition was in effect. He also headed, from 1929 to 1959, the National Board of Fire Underwriters arson investigation team. He died in 1964.[101]

4.3 ENEMY ASSET AND EXPORT CONTROLS

A. Statutes

When the United States entered the war, it went from dealing with the war's belligerents under the rules of neutrality to being a belligerent itself, with defined allies and enemies. This changed the situation from one of being able to supply all materials (at least those not declared contraband) of the belligerents of both alliances to one where exports to the enemy and their assets within the United States had to be controlled. To this effect, Congress passed the Trading with the Enemy Act in October 1917,[102] following from a similarly named act passed in the United Kingdom in 1914.[103] The U.S. act led to a number of executive orders from the president, one of which created the role of "alien property custodian" later that month.[104]

The Trading with the Enemy Act made it unlawful for persons in the United States, unless licensed, to have commercial communication with, extend credit to, execute a contract with, or pay a debt to an enemy, including anyone allied to an enemy or anyone residing in an enemy-occupied country.[105] It was illegal to transport an enemy.[106] It was unlawful to send a letter, telegram, book, map,

---

101. *See Bruce Bielaski, Justice Aide, Dies*, N.Y. TIMES. (Feb. 20, 1964).
102. Pub. L. No. 65-91, Trading with the Enemy Act (1917).
103. Trading with the Enemy Act of 1914, 4 & 5 Geo. 5, c. 87 (U.K.).
104. Exec. Order No. 2744, Fixing Salary of, and Vesting Certain Power and Authority in, the Alien Property Custodian Appointed under Trading with the Enemy Act (Oct. 29, 1917).
105. Trading with the Enemy Act § 3(a).
106. *Id.* § 3(b).

plan, or wireless message to an enemy or an enemy's ally. It was lawful for the president to censor communications to any foreign country.[107] The president could regulate transactions in foreign exchange and the export of gold or silver coin or bullion.[108] The president was authorized to appoint an alien property custodian (APC) to hold and administer all property and money received[109] that belonged to unlicensed enemies.[110] Imports could also be regulated after presidential proclamation.[111] Foreign-language news items could not be published unless a translation was provided.

By executive order, President Wilson assigned responsibilities to many of these functions.[112] He set up a War Trade Board to issue licenses for all exports, except for those of coin, bullion, or currency. Just two months earlier, he had created the Exports Administrative Board[113] under the Espionage Act (see Chapter 5), which was now to be subsumed by the War Trade Board. The treasury secretary was given responsibility for both the trade in foreign exchange and bullion and coin and the prohibitions on communications with enemies. A censorship board was set up to censor communications with other countries. The Federal Trade Commission was given responsibility for enemy intellectual property, including registering and licensing the use thereof. The postmaster general was responsible for the publication of foreign-language news items within the country. The APC was given all the responsibilities specified in the act and was later given additional responsibilities by another executive order.[114]

---

107. *Id.* § 3(c).
108. *Id.* § 5(b).
109. *Id.* § 6.
110. *Id.* § 7(c).
111. *Id.* § 11.
112. Exec. Order 2729A, Vesting Power and Authority in Designated Officers and Making Rules and Regulations under Trading with the Enemy Act and Title VII of the Act Approved June 15, 1917 (Oct. 12, 1917).
113. Exec. Order No. 2687-A, Establishing an Exports Administrative Board and an Exports Council (Aug. 21, 1917).
114. Exec. Order 2744, Fixing Salary of, and Vesting Certain Power and Authority in, the Alien Property Custodian Appointed under Trading with the Enemy Act (Oct. 29, 1917).

LEGAL PROFILES

A. Mitchell Palmer was the first APC during the war. He was born in Pennsylvania in 1872 and started his legal practice there. He was first elected to Congress in 1909, serving for three terms until 1915. In 1917, he was appointed as the first APC, a role he held until early 1919. He then became, in March 1919, the attorney general of the United States, serving until 1921, throughout many of the postwar strikes and "Red Scares." He ran unsuccessfully for the 1920 Democratic Party nomination for president and then returned to legal practice and involvement with Democratic Party politics. He died in 1936.[115]

B. Cases

As would be expected in placing controls on financial assets, there was much litigation filed against the APC regarding alien assets. Many of these cases reached the Supreme Court. This section looks at a number of these cases. The first case involves the beneficial ownership of shares in an American corporation by a German corporation. The second case covers the seizure of a joint account when one of the account holders was not an enemy. The third case discusses when to value a partnership interest in a partnership of Germans and Americans that was dissolved before the start of the war. The fourth case discusses the impact of import regulations on the revenue realized from the regulated sale of wool. The fifth case involves the sales to a special corporation of intellectual property seized under the Trading with the Enemy Act.

1. Enemy Ownership of Shares

In *Stoehr*,[116] shares of a New Jersey corporation that were owned by a German corporation were seized by the APC and were to be sold. The Supreme Court, noting that the Trading with the Enemy Act was rooted in Congress's

---

115. *See Palmer, Alexander Mitchell*, BIOGRAPHICAL DIRECTORY OF THE UNITED STATES CONGRESS.
116. Stoehr v. Wallace, 255 U.S. 239 (1921).

article 1 constitutional power to "make rules concerning captures on land and water," detailed some of the powers of the APC under the revised act. These included that any money or property "owing or belonging to or held for, by, on account of, or on behalf of, or for the benefit of, an enemy or ally of enemy not holding a license granted by the President hereunder, which the President after investigation shall determine is so owing or so belongs or is so held, shall be conveyed, transferred, assigned, delivered, or paid over to the Alien Property Custodian, or the same may be seized by the Alien Property Custodian; and all property thus acquired shall be held, administered and disposed of as elsewhere provided in this Act."[117]

Corporations were also to cancel shares held by enemies and issue the shares instead in the name of the APC. The APC was described as "[having] 'all of the powers of a common-law trustee' in respect of all enemy property coming into his hands and is given authority, subject to the President's supervision, to manage and dispose of the same, by sale or otherwise, as if he were the absolute owner, save as the power of disposal may be suspended by a suit. . . . As respects the ultimate disposition of the property or its proceeds § 12 says: 'After the end of the war any claim of an enemy or of an ally of enemy to any money or other property received and held by the alien property custodian or deposited in the United States Treasury, shall be settled as Congress shall direct.'"[118]

The appellant's claim here was that the shares in the New Jersey corporation, Botany Worsted Mills, were owned by a New York corporation, Stoehr & Sons, Inc., not the German corporation, Kammgarnspinnerei Stoehr & Co., AG, and as such were not subject to seizure except under Fifth Amendment considerations determined through a judicial proceeding. The shares in Botany Worsted Mills had been owned by the German corporation, but when the war broke out, the New York corporation had been created and the Botany shares had been transferred to it from the German corporation by contract. The district court found that the German corporation was the beneficial owner of the New Jersey corporation's shares and not licensed, so it dismissed the suit.

One objection raised was that the seizure was done by the APC without judicial determination. The Court stated, "That Congress in time of war may authorize and provide for the seizure and sequestration through executive

---

117. Pub. L. No. 65-91, Trading with the Enemy Act, § 7(c) (1917).
118. *Stoehr* at 244.

channels of property believed to be enemy-owned, if adequate provision be made for a return in case of mistake, is not debatable.... There is no warrant for saying that the enemy ownership must be determined judicially before the property can be seized; and the practice has been the other way.... [T]he property is to be retained by the Custodian to abide the result and, if the claimant prevails, is to be forthwith returned to him."[119]

The bigger question was whether the contract made the German corporation the beneficial owner of the shares in Botany. The German corporation was family-owned by father Eduard Stoehr and three sons, all German citizens except one who had naturalized American citizenship and a second who was a resident in the United States. The German corporation's shares in Botany had been transferred first to a partnership of the two U.S.-located sons and then to the newly created New York corporation. A contract for the sale of the Botany shares at book (not fair market) value between the German corporation and the New York corporation allowed for the transfer back to the German corporation if the shares were not paid for in five annual installments (no installments had been paid). The German corporation retained the share certificates, and the dividends from the Botany shares were not paid to the New York corporation, as would be expected if it was the effective owner. The Court ruled that the contract "was not intended as a genuine business transaction"[120] and affirmed the district court in the seizure by the APC.

LEGAL PROFILES

Louis Marshall was the counsel for the appellant in this case. He was born in New York in 1856 and started his legal practice there in 1878. He had a focus on both appellate law and arbitration, arguing numerous cases before state and federal appeals courts, including the U.S. Supreme Court. He was active in the legal support of minority groups such as the NAACP; Jewish causes, as the head of the American Jewish Committee

---

119. *Id.* at 245.
120. *Id.* at 251.

and at the Paris Peace Conference; and conservationist efforts and legislation. He died in 1929.[121]

George Langham Ingraham was one of the counsels for the appellee in this case. He was born in New York in 1847, the son of a judge, and started his legal practice there in 1869. He was first elected a judge in 1882 in the Superior Court of New York City. In 1891, he was elected to the New York Supreme Court. He joined the appellate division in 1896, becoming the presiding justice in 1910, serving until 1915, when he resigned. He went into private practice and during the war also served on the appeals draft board. After the war, he worked on the advisory sales committee of the APC. He died in 1931.[122]

Willis van Devanter was the justice who delivered the opinion of the Court in this case. He was born in Indiana in 1859 and started his legal practice there in 1881. After three years, he moved to Wyoming, where he practiced and also served as city attorney and chief judge of the territory and then the state. From 1896 to 1903, he served in the Interior Department as an assistant attorney general and also taught at law school. In that year, he was nominated by President Roosevelt for a seat on the new Eighth Circuit Court of Appeals. In 1910, William Howard Taft nominated him for the U.S. Supreme Court. He would serve on the Court until 1937. He died in 1941.[123]

2. Joint Account with Nonenemy

In *Commercial Trust*,[124] a trust was set up to pay investment returns to the joint account of two individuals, one living in France and the other living in Germany. The APC determined the French resident was a neutral. The trust document allowed either of the beneficiaries to withdraw all of the trust assets. The trustee, therefore, would not surrender the property because a neutral was

---

121. *See Louis Marshall Dies Abroad in 73d Year after a Brave Fight*, N.Y. TIMES (Sept. 12, 1929).
122. *See Notables at Funeral of Ex-Judge Ingraham*, N.Y. TIMES (Jan. 28, 1931).
123. *See Van Devanter, Willis*, FED. JUDICIAL CTR., BIOGRAPHICAL DIRECTORY OF FEDERAL JUDGES.
124. Commercial Trust Co. of N.J. v. Miller, 262 U.S. 51 (1923).

able to withdraw all the assets. The APC was equally adamant that because an enemy alien could also withdraw all of the assets, they were seizable.

Because the APC succeeded in the interests held by the alien enemy, he also succeeded in the ability to withdraw all of the funds. As the actions of the APC were only preemptory, with the right of return if he was mistaken, the Court dismissed other challenges. One other challenge was that because the war had ended, the statute no longer applied and property should revert. The Court noted that Congress had specially exempted this act from its revocation of other wartime acts, and instead "provided that all property subject to that act shall be retained by the United States 'until such time as the Imperial German Government ... shall have ... made suitable provision for the satisfaction of all claims.'"[125]

LEGAL PROFILES

James A. Fowler was the counsel for the appellee in this case. He was born in Tennessee in 1863 and started his legal practice there in 1886. Throughout his years of private practice, he made several unsuccessful political runs, including for governor of Tennessee in 1898 and for U.S. Senate in 1928. He was appointed an assistant U.S. attorney general in 1908, a role he held until 1914. He was appointed again in 1921, serving until 1926. In 1927, returning to Tennessee, he was elected to the Knoxville city council and served as its mayor. He then returned to private practice; he died in 1955.[126]

3. Partnership Valuation

In *Sutherland*,[127] a partnership between a naturalized American and three German nationals was effectively terminated by the war. The APC was able to

---

125. *Id.* at 57.
126. *See* Fowler, James Alexander, WHO'S WHO IN TENNESSEE.
127. Sutherland v. Mayer, 271 U.S. 272 (1926).

seize the enemy partnership assets minus the American's share, so he tried to obtain an accounting to determine the value of the assets and liabilities of the partnership. The district court had ruled that the value of the American's interest should be valued at the exchange rate on the day that war was declared (18 cents on the dollar), while the appellant wanted to value his shares at the postwar rate when the hearings began (0.48 cents on the dollar). The district court used the former date, since the partnership had been dissolved before the declaration of war.

The Supreme Court concurred in this, saying, "Upon the dissolution of a partnership, the general rule is that the liquidating partner or partners must settle up the partnership affairs within a reasonable time and, after payment of the partnership debts and liabilities . . . [t]he rule is not different because the dissolution is the result of war."[128] The loss due to the delay caused by cessation of communication during wartime was differently focused, as "[t]he prohibition against doing anything for the benefit of an enemy contemplates his benefit during the war and not the possible advantage he may gain when peace comes."[129]

Whether the partnership interest was valued at the 1917 exchange rate or the partnership was liquidated and the funds held in marks at that date, the effect was the same to the American partner. The Court held that the proper exchange rate should be the rate on the date when a war trade board regulation had been issued,[130] 7.875 marks to the dollar, restoring the "right of commercial intercourse and of communication between citizens of this country and Germany."[131]

LEGAL PROFILES

George Sutherland was the justice who delivered the opinion of the Court in this case. He was born in England in 1862 but moved to America as an infant. He started his legal practice in Michigan, then moved to

---

128. *Id.* at 289.
129. *Id.*
130. War Trade Board Regulation No. 802, July 14, 1919, and No. 814, July 20, 1919.
131. *Sutherland* at 295.

Utah. He was a state senator there from 1897 to 1901. He was elected to Congress in 1900, serving only a single term before being elected to the U.S. Senate in 1905. He was defeated in 1916 and returned to private practice. In 1922, he was nominated to the U.S. Supreme Court by President Harding. He served on the Court until 1938. He died in 1942.[132]

4. Import Restrictions

In *L. Richardson*,[133] the president by proclamation had required a license for the import of wool and other materials into America. The War Trade Board had required that wool importers first give the U.S. Army the option to purchase whatever wool they were importing. In the plaintiff's case, the government had purchased only part of the wool the plaintiff had imported from South Africa, causing a significant reduction in the realized revenue from the remaining wool sold elsewhere. The Court, in reviewing all of the announcements and regulations, found that the requirement concerned only options to purchase, not a commitment to purchase, and as such, the government was not liable for the reduction in revenue despite its import regulation requiring that it be offered the option to purchase the wool.

LEGAL PROFILES

Edward Terry Sanford was the justice who delivered the opinion of the Court in this case. He was born in Tennessee in 1865 and started his legal practice there in 1890. He also taught at law school starting in 1898. In 1905, he was appointed an assistant attorney general of the United States. In 1908, President Roosevelt appointed him to the federal district bench in the Middle and Eastern districts of Tennessee. In 1923, Presi-

---

132. *See Sutherland, George*, BIOGRAPHICAL DIRECTORY OF THE UNITED STATES CONGRESS; *Sutherland, George*, FED. JUDICIAL CTR., BIOGRAPHICAL DIRECTORY OF FEDERAL JUDGES.
133. L. Richardson & Co. v. United States, 266 U.S. 541 (1925).

dent Harding nominated him for the U.S. Supreme Court. He served on the Court for seven years, until his death in 1930.[134]

5. Sale of Seized Enemy Intellectual Property

In *Chemical Foundation*,[135] the provisions of the Trading with the Enemy Act allowing the sale of enemy intellectual property were challenged. As recited by the Court's opinion, at the start of the war, Germany held an unassailable advantage in certain industries like chemicals for explosives, dyes, and medicines. First due to the British blockade and then the declaration of war, these products became unavailable in the United States. The Trading with the Enemy Act gave the APC the power to seize and sell the intellectual property of the enemy, acting like a common-law trustee,[136] and so the Chemical Foundation was incorporated just after the end of the war to acquire and then license seized enemy patents to the United States and American nationals. The foundation's president and head of the board was the APC.

President Wilson made an executive order giving Frank Polk, a counselor at the State Department, the ability to authorize the APC to make a private, unadvertised sale of the patents to the Foundation, which he subsequently did.[137] Many reasons were provided for this private sale, including that "the Foundation had been incorporated to hold the patents as a trustee for American industries affected by the patents, to eliminate hostile alien interests, and to advance chemical and allied industry in the United States, and that it was obligated to grant nonexclusive licenses upon equal terms to qualified American manufacturers and was empowered to grant free licenses to the United States; that the public interest would be best served by a wide use of the inventions, which most readily could be promoted by licenses which the Foundation was

---

134. *See Sanford, Edward Terry*, Fed. Judicial Ctr., Biographical Directory of Federal Judges.
135. United States v. Chem. Found., Inc., 272 U.S. 1 (1926).
136. Pub. L. No. 65-109, An Act Making Appropriations to Supply Urgent Deficiencies in Appropriations for the Fiscal Year Ending June 30, 1918, and Prior Fiscal Years, on Account of War Expenses, and for Other Purposes (1918); Pub. L. No. 65-233, An Act Making Appropriations to Supply Deficiencies in Appropriations for the Fiscal Year Ending June 30, 1919, and Prior Fiscal Years, on Account of War Expenses, and for Other Purposes (1918).
137. Exec. Order No. 3016, Vesting Certain Powers under the Trading with the Enemy Act in Property Custodian and Frank L. Polk (Dec. 3, 1918).

obligated to grant; [and] that a private sale would prevent the patents from falling into the hands of purchasers unwilling or unable to use the inventions, or who would use them for speculative purposes."[138]

Public and political opinion brought the United States government itself to investigate the sale of the intellectual property to the Chemical Foundation and bring this lawsuit. The Court, though, could find no wrong. It looked at the Trading with the Enemy Act and the authority of the president, in the public interest, not to sell the items seized by the APC at public auction; the broad powers given to the APC to sell assets under his custody, "as though he were the absolute owner";[139] the structure, financial incentives of officers, and organizational roles of the Chemical Foundation; the power of the president to delegate under the act; the details of the individual patent sales to the Chemical Foundation; the orders made by Frank Polk; and the subsequent executive order by the president on February 13, 1920, ratifying the sales. Based on this evidence, the Court affirmed similar findings and rulings by the lower courts.

LEGAL PROFILES

Henry W. Anderson was the counsel for the appellant in this case. He was born in Virginia in 1870 and started his legal practice there in 1898. During WWI, he headed up the American Red Cross in Romania, staying until he was driven out in 1918. He returned after the war to provide further service with the Red Cross in Europe.[140] He mounted several unsuccessful political campaigns but mostly focused on law, including bankruptcy law during the Great Depression. He died in 1954.

Frank L. Polk was the State Department counselor who set the private sales of the enemy intellectual property. He was born in New York in 1871, the grandnephew of U.S. President James K. Polk, started his legal practice there in 1897, and served in the Spanish-American War. Besides

---
138. *Chemical Foundation* at 8.
139. *Id.* at 11.
140. *See Balkans Owe Much to Red Cross Aid*, N.Y. TIMES (Aug. 11, 1919).

legal practice, he served on city commissions, including the Municipal Civil Service Commission. In 1914, he was appointed as the corporate counsel for the city of New York. In 1915 he was appointed as counselor to the State Department, a role he performed until 1919. He then was appointed undersecretary of state, which included being part of the American delegation to the Paris Peace Conference. He then returned to private practice as a partner in a law firm. He died in 1943.[141]

C. Subsequent Events

After the war, the Trading with the Enemy Act was one of the few war-related statutes that did not get repealed by the joint resolution after the war.[142] It was to arise again in WWII, under the First War Powers Act. Even more seizures of enemy assets were made in that war than in WWI, and they took several decades after the war to unwind.[143] Also arising in WWII was the control of exports, but in a much bigger way, given the United States' earlier entry into that conflict.[144] An export control administrator was charged with restricting a whole list of materials and products that may have been of use to the enemies of the United States, directly and indirectly (through neutral countries). This control of exports dealing with any military aspects was tightly controlled, including any dual-use technology and nuclear weapons.[145]

During the war, the APC controlled more than 30,000 unique accounts relating to business enterprises and individuals, holding nearly $1 billion in assets.[146] In 1928, the Settlement of War Claims Act was passed.[147] One of the roles the act created was that of the war claims arbiter, who was to look into claims related to any enemy merchant vessels that were seized, radio stations

---

141. *See Frank L. Polk Dies; Cabinet Ex-Aide*, 71, N.Y. TIMES (Feb. 8, 1943).
142. Pub. Res. No. 66-64, Declaring That Certain Acts of Congress, Joint Resolutions, and Proclamations Shall Be Construed as If the War Had Ended and the Present or Existing Emergency Expired (Mar. 3, 1921).
143. *See* THOMAS J. SHAW, WWII LAW AND LAWYERS: ISSUES, CASES, AND CHARACTERS, ch. 3 (2013).
144. *See* WWII LAW AND LAWYERS, ch. 2.
145. *Id.*
146. Alien Property Custodian Annual Report 1918–1919.
147. Pub. L. No. 70-122, An Act to Provide for the Settlement of Certain Claims of American Nationals against Germany, Austria, and Hungary, and of Nationals of Germany, Austria, and Hungary, against the United States, and for the Ultimate Return of All Property Held by the Alien Property Custodian (1928).

that were seized and sold to the United States, or patents that were seized and sold to the United States.[148] Because the assets sold by the APC to the Chemical Foundation were not sold to the United States, the original German patent holders could not be compensated for their lost patents. The return to Germany of German government assets held by the APC was to be offset by the results of the Mixed Claims Commission.[149] This was further impeded in 1934 by a joint resolution of Congress[150] that, because payments under the Mixed Claims Commission were in arrears, stopped payments related to the return of German property held by the APC until such arrears were resolved.

LEGAL PROFILES

Patrick Garvan was the second APC and second head of the Chemical Foundation. He was born in Ohio in 1875 and started his legal practice there in 1899. He worked as a district attorney in New York from 1900 until being appointed assistant district attorney for New York City. He worked at the local office of the U.S. Bureau of Investigation during the war, before becoming APC in 1919. He was also dean of the law school at Fordham University from 1919 to 1923. In 1919, he was appointed as the president of the Chemical Foundation, becoming a strong advocate for the sciences in the United States, a position he held until his death in 1937.[151]

D. Modern Applicability

Seizing assets, interdicting trade, and blocking access to credit are all methods used modernly to deny declared and undeclared enemies the use of their overseas commercial capabilities to fund wars or terrorist activities. In recent years, the United States and the European Union have worked in conjunction with

---

148. *Id.* § 3.
149. *Id.* § 10(d).
150. Pub. Res. No. 73-53, To Amend the Settlement of War Claims Act of 1918, as amended (1934).
151. *See Francis P. Garvan, Lawyer, Dies Here*, N.Y. TIMES (Nov. 8, 1937).

the international community to restrict the abilities of North Korea, Iran, Iraq, Cuba, the Taliban, Al Qaeda, Hezbollah, and other countries and organizations. Numerous programs based on statutory restrictions are run under the U.S. Treasury Department to oversee these activities.[152] Import/export controls are quite a common feature of the modern world, used to control the access to a wide variety of technologies, especially those dealing with national defense, such as encryption protocols and nuclear weapons.[153]

4.4 SELECTIVE SERVICE

A. Statutes

The likelihood of the United States going to war after it severed diplomatic relations with Germany meant that a significant number of soldiers would be required. The all-volunteer force that the United States had long used would not be sufficient for the needs of the European conflict it was entering, and the National Defense Act, while increasing manpower (see Section 4.1), had not produced the desired number of volunteers. As such, Congress passed a new law in May 1917 that introduced conscription for the first time since the Civil War.[154] The statute called for the men in the National Guard and its reserves to be drafted into military service, and for initially 500,000 new men, plus four divisions of infantry volunteers, to be enlisted.[155] These enlisted men were to be raised from those between the ages of twenty-one and thirty, inclusive, who were citizens or were declaring to be citizens and were not enemy aliens. The newly enlisted men were to serve "for the period of the existing emergency unless sooner discharged."[156]

No one was allowed to pay someone else to substitute for them in their selective service obligation (unlike in previous wars).[157] Conscientious objectors were recognized, and full or partial exemptions were made for those employed in armories, arsenals, and navy yards; those employed in agriculture, the postal system, or customs; pilots and mariners; employees of industries

---

152. *See* WWII LAW AND LAWYERS, ch. 3.
153. *See* WWII Law and Lawyers, ch. 2.
154. Pub. L. No. 65-12, An Act To Authorize the President to Increase Temporarily the Military Establishment of the United States (1917).
155. *Id.* § 1.
156. *Id.* § 2.
157. *Id.* § 3.

supporting the military establishment; those supporting dependents "which render[ed] their exclusion or discharge advisable"; those who were physically or morally deficient; and, of course, members of Congress.[158] Local draft boards were to be created to review exemptions, with the right of appeal up to district boards.[159] Registration was required of all potential draftees, subject to criminal penalties for refusing willfully to do so.[160]

Anyone who made a false or incorrect registration or anyone who "aid[ed] another to evade the requirements" of the act was also subject to criminal prosecution.[161] Those who wanted to enlist could, if they were between the ages of eighteen and forty.[162] The president could prohibit the sale of alcohol "in or near military camps and to offices and enlisted men" or "while [enlisted men were] in uniform," but alcohol could be sold and used "for medicinal purposes."[163] The secretary of war was authorized to "suppress and prevent the keeping or setting up of houses of ill fame, brothels, or bawdy houses" near military camps or the receiving "for immoral purposes any person into any place . . . used for the purpose of lewdness, assignation, or prostitution."[164]

Then the president, as required by the National Defense Act, issued a proclamation that the time and place of registration would be on June 5, 1917.[165] Eligible men were to register at the designated registration place within their home district. Those who could not attend on that date, because of illness or travel, could register by agent, by mail, or in the location where they were on the designated day. President Wilson also used this proclamation to send a message: "[T]he men who remain to till the soil and man the factories are no less a part of the army that is in France. . . . It is not an army that we must shape and train for war—it is a Nation. . . . The Nation needs all men, but it needs each man, not in the field that will most pleasure him, but in the endeavor that will best serve the common good. . . . It is nothing less than the day upon which the manhood of the country shall step forward in one solid rank in defense of the ideals to which this Nation is consecrated."

---

158. *Id.* § 4.
159. *Id.*
160. *Id.* § 5.
161. *Id.* § 6.
162. *Id.* § 7.
163. *Id.* § 12.
164. *Id.* § 13.
165. Pub. Proclamation No. 1370, Conscription (May 18, 1917).

LEGAL PROFILES

Enoch Crowder was the judge advocate general during the war and was responsible for the drafting of the National Defense Act. He was born in Missouri in 1859 and, after graduating from the U.S. Military Academy, was admitted to the bar in 1884. He then taught and got his law degree. He was involved in the Indian Wars and served in several locations as judge advocate, including the Philippines during the Spanish-American War and on the Philippine Supreme Court. In 1901, he became the deputy judge advocate general, then spent two years observing the Russo-Japanese War. In 1911, he became judge advocate general, a position he held through 1923. Here he also oversaw the revision of the Article of War (see next section) and the registration and induction of enlisted men under the draft as provost marshal. From 1923 to 1927, he was American ambassador to Cuba. He then entered private practice. He died in 1932.[166]

B. Cases

The challenge to selective service was quickly raised, both on the street and legally. The legal response reached the Supreme Court in late December 1917 and was decided shortly thereafter. Known as the Selective Draft Law Cases, these cases consolidated six different suits into a single decision. In addition to that landmark decision, there were several decisions relating to those who were tried and convicted for opposing the draft, either by direct opposition or by encouraging others to avoid selective service. Some of these cases were tried under the Espionage Act (see Chapter 5), but the Selective Service Act had provisions criminalizing this conduct.

1. Selective Draft Law Cases

In this opinion,[167] the Supreme Court reviewed a number of challenges to the Selective Service Act. The plaintiffs had all qualified to register for selec-

---

166. See *Gen. Crowder Dead; War Draft Author*, N.Y. TIMES (May 8, 1932).
167. Arver v. United States, No. 663; Grahl v. United States, No. 664; Otto Wangerin v. United

tive service but had not registered and had been tried and convicted for failing to do so. The Court found the power to raise and support armies and to make rules for land and naval forces in Article I of the Constitution, as well as the power to make laws carrying into execution these powers. The appellants' contention—that this right was only the right to raise volunteer armies with the citizens' consent—was swept away by the Court by reference to the current English Service Act, colonial American acts, states' constitutions after independence, and documents dating back to ancient times in England, where "it is certain that before the Norman Conquest the duty of the great militant body of the citizens was recognized and enforcible."[168]

The Court differentiated the states' limited rights under the Constitution regarding militias and those for raising armies, with the states' role in training the militias based on Congress's determination of when the militias would need to be utilized. This distinction minimized the number of times that the army power had to be used by Congress. The Court noted that in the War of 1812, when conscription had been required, the legality of conscription had been based on the power to raise armies, not the militia powers. In the Civil War, the Court noted separate acts of Congress to raise volunteers, to increase the size of the militia, and then to require conscription when the first acts were not sufficient in raising the needed manpower. The only case to challenge the Civil War draft had been decided along similar lines, as had draft challenge cases in the Confederacy. Finally, brushing aside a challenge claiming that the draft was involuntary servitude banned by the Thirteenth Amendment, the Court upheld the constitutionality of the law and the convictions for resisting the draft.

LEGAL PROFILES

Walter Nelles filed an amicus curiae brief with the Court in the Selective Draft Law Cases. He was born in Kansas in 1883 and started his legal practice in New York in 1911. During the war, he joined the National

---

States, No. 665; Walter Wangerin v. United States, No. 666; Kramer v. United States, No. 681; Graubard v. United States, No. 769; 245 U.S. 366 (1918).
168. *Id.* at 378–79.

Civil Liberties Union, the forerunner of the American Civil Liberties Union, as one of its cofounders and its counsel. He wrote a biography of fellow cofounder (along with Roger Baldwin) attorney Albert DeSilver. He tried many cases tied to Socialists, conscientious objectors, pacifists, and aliens, as well as other civil rights cases and those involving the labor movement and injunctions. He also taught at Yale Law School beginning in 1929 and published numerous law review articles. He died in 1937.[169]

2. Encouraging Others to Avoid the Draft

In *Ruthenberg*,[170] Alphones Schue was indicted for failing to register for the draft. Several others, including Charles Emil Ruthenberg, were charged with aiding, abetting, counseling, commanding, and inducing Schue not to register. The Court noted that the primary constitutional challenges to the draft had been settled in the Selective Draft Law Cases. It turned down claims that the Socialists who had been convicted had been denied their constitutional rights because the juries had been composed of property owners; that the jurors were not allowed to be asked about the difference between Socialists and anarchists; and that the indictment did not specify the citizenship requirements of the defendant. The Court affirmed the convictions for aiding and abetting the failure to register for the draft under the National Defense Act.

LEGAL PROFILES

Robert Szold filed "on the brief" for both of these cases. He was born in Illinois in 1889 and started his legal practice in 1912. He served as assistant to the U.S. solicitor general from 1915 to 1918. In 1915, he wrote briefs that led to the first federal child labor law. Besides private practice, he was also heavily involved in the Zionist movement and Palestine. After the war, he became administrator of the town of Jerusalem

---

169. *See Prof. Walter Nelles of Yale Law School*, N.Y. TIMES (Apr. 1, 1937).
170. Ruthenberg v. United States, 245 U.S. 480 (1918).

in Palestine and helped create endowment funds for education. He died in 1977.[171]

C. Subsequent Events

The National Defense Act was amended later to expand the draft-eligible age to a range of eighteen to forty-five years old.[172] The military draft ended with the end of the fighting in this war, but it would be a major factor again in WWII.[173] Selling the public on the draft was part of the job of the ministry of public information (see Chapter 5), which enlisted labor leaders like Samuel Gompers in trying to persuade men to enlist or volunteer. In the end, more than 2.8 million U.S. males were inducted into the military through the selective service system in 1917 and 1918.[174] And unlike in the Civil War, perhaps because of the late entry of the United States into WWI, there were no large-scale draft riots. Resistance was both political, as discussed in Chapter 5, and passive (not registering or not showing up for service). An estimated 24 million men did register, while several hundred thousand who were required to do so failed to register or respond. Few people, however, were imprisoned for failure to comply with the draft.

LEGAL PROFILES

Hugh S. Johnson was a primary drafter of the regulations for the National Defense Act. He was born in Kansas in 1882, the son of a lawyer, and graduated from West Point in 1903. He started his legal practice in the Judge Advocate General's Corps during the war. In 1916, as judge advocate, he joined the expedition to Mexico to find Pancho Villa (see

---

171. *See Robert Szold, Zionist Leader*, N.Y. TIMES (Nov. 10, 1977).
172. Pub. L, No. 65-210, An Act Amending the Act Entitled "An Act to Authorize the President to Increase Temporarily the Military Establishment of the United States," Approved May 18, 1917 (1918).
173. *See* WWII LAW AND LAWYERS, ch. 4.
174. Selective Service System, History and Records, Induction Statistics.

above). He left the military after the war to go into private business with the former head of the War Industries Board, Bernard Baruch (see Chapter 5). In 1932, he joined the Roosevelt administration and led the National Recovery Administration for more than a year, before it was declared unconstitutional by the Supreme Court. He then turned to writing newspaper columns. He died in 1942.[175]

4.5 ARTICLES OF WAR

A. Statutes

After several years of review, in August 1916, new Articles of War passed Congress, to take effect the following March.[176] The previous version had been in existence since 1806 and contained 101 articles. The 121 articles in the revised version constituted a major modification. These articles were organized into major sections, with topics including who was subject to military law, how courts-martial operated, and what was considered a crime under military law. Naval personnel had their own rules (nicknamed "Rocks and Shoals"), so those subject to the new articles included members of the regular army, volunteers, people drafted into service, cadets, marines who served with the army, anyone accompanying the army in the field outside the United States during peacetime or anywhere during wartime, and anyone who became subject to courts-martial.[177]

Courts-martial were of three types: general, special, and summary.[178] The composition of the court depended on the type of court-martial. For general and special courts-martial, a judge advocate and assistants were to be appointed,[179] with the judge advocate responsible for prosecution.[180] General

---

175. *See Hugh S. Johnson*, N.Y. TIMES (Apr. 16, 1942).
176. Pub. L. No. 64-242, An Act Making Appropriations for the Support of the Army for the Fiscal Year Ending June 30, 1917, and for Other Purposes, § 3 (1916).
177. Articles of War, art. 2.
178. *Id.* art. 3.
179. *Id.* art. 11.
180. *Id.* art. 17.

courts-martial could try any person subject to military law for any crime;[181] special courts-martial could try any person except an officer, a person charged with a capital crime, or a person facing confinement in excess of six months;[182] summary courts-martial could try any person except an officer, a noncommissioned officer if he objected, a person charged with a capital crime, or a person facing confinement in excess of three months.[183] Prohibitions on compulsory self-incrimination[184] and double jeopardy[185] were included.

The punishments of flogging, branding, marking, and tattooing on the body were prohibited,[186] but the articles allowed the names of defendants convicted of cowardice or fraud to be published in newspapers and in camps, stating, "it shall be scandalous for an officer to associate with him."[187] A simple majority of the court could convict and sentence a defendant, except for determining a death penalty, which required a two-thirds majority.[188] Confirmation by the U.S. president was required in cases involving officers and death sentences, except in time of war,[189] and the president's powers included the ability to disapprove findings and confirm lesser sentences.[190]

Punishable crimes included desertion[191] (which in times of war was punishable by death), being absent without leave,[192] disobeying or assaulting a superior officer,[193] and mutiny or sedition or failing to suppress such.[194] Under the category of "war offenses" were misbehavior before the enemy (e.g., abandoning one's post),[195] improper use of countersigns or forcing a safeguard,[196] corresponding with or aiding an enemy,[197] and spying, which was punishable by

---

181. *Id.* art. 12.
182. *Id.* art. 13.
183. *Id.* art. 14.
184. *Id.* art. 24.
185. *Id.* art. 40.
186. *Id.* art. 41.
187. *Id.* art. 44.
188. *Id.* art. 43.
189. *Id.* art. 48.
190. *Id.* art. 49.
191. *Id.* art. 58.
192. *Id.* art. 61.
193. *Id.* art. 64.
194. *Id.* art. 66.
195. *Id.* art. 75.
196. *Id.* art. 77–78.
197. *Id.* art. 81.

death in times of war.[198] Other crimes included damage to or loss of military property;[199] drunkenness while on duty;[200] provocative speech or gestures;[201] dueling;[202] murder or rape;[203] manslaughter, mayhem, arson, burglary, robbery, larceny, embezzlement, perjury, or assault;[204] fraud against the government;[205] conduct unbecoming an officer and a gentleman;[206] and disorders or conduct bringing discredit to the military (although this last was not specifically listed).[207]

LEGAL PROFILES

John J. Pershing was the leader of the American Expeditionary Force (AEF) that went to Europe to fight in WWI. He was born in Missouri in 1860 and graduated from West Point in 1886. After years of active military service, he got his legal degree in 1893. He was appointed to teach at West Point in 1897. He served in both the Spanish-American War, beginning in 1899, and the Philippine-American War, beginning in 1901. He did tours in Japan, the Balkans, and the Philippines again. President Roosevelt promoted him to brigadier general in 1905, skipping several ranks. After losing his wife and most of his children in a fire, he was involved in the 1916 raids into Mexico to capture Pancho Villa (see Section 4.2). In 1917 he was named as major general in charge of the AEF, which in a short time grew from fewer than a hundred thousand men to more than two million men. After the war, he was thanked

---

198. *Id.* art. 82.
199. *Id.* art. 83.
200. *Id.* art. 85.
201. *Id.* art. 90.
202. *Id.* art. 91.
203. *Id.* art. 92.
204. *Id.* art. 93.
205. *Id.* art. 94.
206. *Id.* art. 95.
207. *Id.* art. 96.

by Congress[208] and named general of the armies of the United States,[209] the only person to ever hold that rank during his lifetime. In 1921, he became army chief of staff, retiring in 1924. He died in 1948.[210]

Newton D. Baker was the secretary of war during the U.S. time of belligerency in WWI. He was born in West Virginia in 1871 and started his legal practice in 1894. He was the private secretary to the U.S. postmaster general in 1896. He served as the city solicitor for Cleveland, Ohio, winning elections in 1905, 1907, and 1909. In 1912 and again in 1914, he was elected Cleveland's mayor, while turning down cabinet positions. He cofounded a law firm, where he would return after the war. In 1916, he was named secretary of war, a role he served in until 1921. Most famously for someone in this position, he was a pacifist, who declared, "I'm so much of a pacifist that I'm willing to fight for it." In 1928, and again in 1935, he was appointed to the Permanent Court of Arbitration. He died in 1937.[211]

B. Cases

After the war, there came to light numerous cases where the military justice system was alleged to have failed. Based on the public outcry, Secretary of War Baker asked the judge advocate general (JAG) in writing to reply to these charges. This was after members of the JAG Corps had appeared before the Senate Military Affairs Committee to explain the cases.[212] Feeling that the public, and especially the families of the accused, needed to hear what Congress had heard, the secretary asked the JAG to disclose the facts about these cases. The JAG replied,[213] citing three cases highlighted by those in Congress who

---

208. Pub. Res. No. 66-15, Joint Resolution Tendering the Thanks of the American People and the Congress of the United States to General John J. Pershing, and to the Officers and Men of the American Expeditionary Forces (1919).
209. Pub. L. No. 66-45, An Act Relating to the Creation of the Office of General of the Armies of the United States (1919).
210. *See Pershing of A.E.F. is Dead; On Service Rolls 62 Years*, N.Y. TIMES (July 16, 1948).
211. *See Newton D. Baker Dies in Cleveland*, N.Y. TIMES (Dec. 26, 1937).
212. Letter from Secretary of War Baker to Maj. Gen. E. H. Crowder (Mar. 1, 1919).
213. Letter from Maj. Gen. E. H. Crowder to Secretary of War Baker (Mar. 10, 1919).

had complained, in which he hoped to demonstrate that the criticism was not warranted. He also replied to each of the specific criticisms leveled against the military justice system used during the war. But what caused more changes to the operation of the military justice system and its system of review was a trial held in Texas in late 1917 that led to postwar revisions in the Articles of War.

1. Specific Cases Cited by the JAG

The three cases cited by the JAG were termed the military police case, the conscientious objector case, and the death sentences in France case. In the first case,[214] a soldier acting as a member of the military police was caught on the scene of a burglary and was arrested. In his trial, he was found not guilty, but on request of the commanding officer, a reconsideration was performed, and he was then found guilty. This reconsideration was portrayed as an abuse of the commanding officer's authority, but in actuality, the JAG Corps in Washington had recommended that while there had been no legal error and the evidence did sustain the finding, it did not raise to the level of proof of guilt beyond a reasonable doubt. Another reconsideration was done by the local judge advocate, but he confirmed the finding of guilt beyond a reasonable doubt, and so did his officer. The verdict demonstrated the powers of review; in the words of the JAG: "[T]he reconsideration which was actually given by the Judge Advocate, on the point of proof beyond a reasonable doubt, was a measure of protection which the law does not provide in any civil court in the United States for the control of a jury's verdict."[215]

In the second case, a soldier who was a conscientious objector and was not given noncombatant status disobeyed an order to drill and was found in possession of seditious literature.[216] The court sentenced him to death, but the JAG advocated disapproval of the sentence because the order to drill had not been lawful, and therefore disobeying it was not a crime. He also said that the defendant had not demonstrated intention to distribute the seditious literature. The president agreed with the JAG and disapproved the sentence, and the defendant was discharged. The JAG said that the result showed how well the military justice system was working.

---

214. JAG record No. 110595, tried Jan. 24, 1918.
215. Letter from Crowder, *supra* note 212.
216. JAG record No. 116790, tried June 17, 1918.

The third case involved two death sentences handed out to privates Sebastian and Cook for sleeping while on sentinel duty in a front-line trench during a battle in November 1917, after being awake for several days. General John J. Pershing believed that these sentences were vital to the welfare of his army as a whole, as they not only protected American troops occupying a salient, but also adjacent French troops. The JAG, however, had recommended clemency to the secretary of war, even though no extenuating circumstances were found. The JAG Corps staff had fully reviewed the case and could find no reversible error or problem with the facts, but on recommendation from the JAG, the president eventually pardoned the men.

LEGAL PROFILES

George E. Chamberlain was head of the Senate committee holding these hearings. He was born in Mississippi in 1854 and started his legal practice in Oregon in 1879. In 1880 he was elected to the state legislature. From 1884 to 1902, he was both a district attorney and a state attorney general. In 1902, he was elected governor of Oregon; he was reelected in 1906. In 1908, he was elected to the U.S. Senate, serving until 1921. He headed up the Committee on Military Affairs for six years. He then returned to private practice. He died in 1928.[217]

2. Allegations against the Military Justice System

There were fourteen specific accusations that the JAG responded to. These are listed here, with each followed by a brief summary of the response that the JAG presented.

1. That the general treatment of accused soldiers is not according to the rigid limitations of law as embodied in the Criminal Code, but is according to the arbitrary discretion of the commanding officer in each case.

---

217. *See Chamberlain, George Earle,* BIOGRAPHICAL DIRECTORY OF THE UNITED STATES CONGRESS.

First, the JAG demonstrated the multiple steps of review required for decisions within the JAG Corps and the depth of the questions that had to be answered. His reply also said that military and civilian law operate similarly, although they were for different purposes. Quoting General William Tecumseh Sherman, he said, "The object of civil law is to secure to every human being in a community the maximum of liberty, security, and happiness, consistent with the safety of all. The object of military law is to govern armies composed of strong men, so as to be capable of exercising the largest measure of force at the will of the Nation."[218]

Noting favorably the military's review of cases vis-à-vis the civil courts, he mentioned that for cases involving penitentiary sentences, six JAG officers had to review and sign off on the court's opinion before it went to the JAG for final review. With death-sentence cases, seven JAG officers had to concur on the opinion. This was after the local reviewing authority and judge advocate had reviewed the case. This review was automatic; the defendant did not need to insist on an appeal to get a review. The JAG also noted that the sentences were all stated as maximums with no minimum time, meaning a properly motivated convicted soldier could work his way back into the military by his own efforts, despite the length of the maximum sentence handed out.

> *2. That the military Criminal Code itself is not modern and enlightened, but is an archaic code which systematically belongs to medieval times.*

In response to this criticism, the JAG pointed out that the articles of war had only recently been passed by Congress, after four years of deliberation. At the same time, he also noted that the war had brought to light several possible improvements to the code, which he recommended be added.

> *3. That a soldier may be put on trial by a commanding officer's arbitrary discretion, without any preliminary inquiry into the probability of the charge.*

The JAG pointed out the similarities to the civil system on this point, and the fact that the local judge advocate needed first to review any serious charge.

---

218. Letter from Crowder, *supra* note 212.

Article 76 of the new articles required just such an inquiry, the results of which had to be given to the defense before anyone could be put on trial.

4. That commanding officers do thus put on trial a needlessly large number of trivial charges.

The JAG explained that there were about 300,000 men in the army at the start of the war, less than half of whom were in the regular army. By the time of the armistice, there were close to 4.2 million men in the military. This massive number of new recruits meant that there were large numbers of people not familiar with military rules. Despite this, the JAG contended that the officers were actually more lenient than they had been before the war. The statistics before the war for general courts-martial were about one man in 20, special courts-martial about one man in 42, and summary courts-martial about one man in 3, but during the war, general courts-martial were about one man in 200, special courts-martial about one man in 165, and summary courts-martial about one man in 12.

5. That the court-martial is composed of and the defense is conducted by men not acquainted with military law.

The JAG pointed out that the court was primarily a finder of fact, while the judge advocate's job was to supply the points of law. In addition, the automatic appeal and the exhaustive records ensured that the law was correctly applied. He also pointed to the training provided to officers on military law and the ample copies of the military code distributed throughout the services.

6. That the Judge Advocate combines incongruously the functions of prosecutor, judicial adviser of the court, and defender of the accused.

The JAG believed that there was some confusion about the difference between the staff judge advocate and the trial judge advocate. The staff judge advocate reviewed each decision for legal and factual errors and advised each military commander in its role as reviewing authority. The trial judge advocates were not typically part of the JAG office, and they did act as prosecutors, but they were different people in a different organization than the staff judge advocate reviewing the trial record.

7. That second lieutenants "knowing nothing of law and less than nothing of court-martial procedure" are assigned to the defense of "enlisted men charged with capital or other most serious offenses."

The JAG believed that the convening officer tried to find men who had legal experience to act as defense counsel, but this was not always possible. He said, "The main object of the Army is victory, not trials."[219] Again, he noted that the system of automatic review would catch deficiencies in the application of the law.

8. That a plea of guilty is received from an accused on a charge for which the sentence of death may be imposed.

Due to the vast number of cases, it was difficult to respond directly to this charge, but even if a defendant pled guilty, the prosecution still had to present its case. This was essential where the punishments were discretionary. Courts had the option to change the plea to "not guilty" if the evidence did not support a guilty plea.

9. That commanding generals, as reviewing authorities, send back for reconsideration judgments of acquittal.

The JAG discussed the reviewing authorities' ability to disapprove findings, assign a sentence for a lesser offense, or eliminate all or part of a sentence, noting that these powers were as much a part of their role as reconsiderations. But a reconsideration meant only another look at the evidence and was typically used as a way to correct the facts as stated in the trial record. To support this claim, he pointed to a recent review that had showed that of a thousand cases returned to the court-martial for reconsideration, only eighteen had changed

---

219. *Id.*

an acquittal into a guilty verdict. Even with those low numbers, however, the JAG recommended removing this power from the reviewing authority.

10. That the judgment of the court is kept secret until after the action of the reviewing authority is taken, even when the initial judgment is an acquittal.

This secrecy was because of the need for the reviewing authority to perform its consideration, and if it was for a reconsideration of an acquittal, then announcing the judgment could cause problems.

11. That the sentences imposed by courts-martial are as a rule excessively severe.

To answer this charge, the JAG looked at the three most common crimes. Of the 3,000 cases of desertion brought to trial, only twenty-four had resulted in death sentences, and all of those sentences had been commuted or remitted. The average sentence handed out was just over seven years' imprisonment—not a severe punishment compared to the potential death sentence that was mandated by Congress. For convictions of being absent without leave, which in many cases may have really been desertions that could not be proved because the army changed locations so rapidly, the average sentence was only 1.5 years, again not severe compared to a death sentence. For the crime of disobeying an officer—again, in time of war, punishable by death—the average sentence was a little more than four years, with half of the sentences less than two years. Out of 200,000 total sentences handed down for military offenses, all but 7,000 were by special and summary courts-martial, meaning their sentences could not be more than six months. And again, these were maximum sentences and the time actually served was often significantly less, as men were returned to duty.

12. That the sentences imposed by courts-martial are variable for the same offense.

The JAG noted that there were variations in sentences, especially in certain time periods (as the war was escalating) and in certain commands, but sometimes they balanced out (longer sentences for desertion but shorter ones for being absent without leave).

13. That the Judge Advocate General's office either partakes in the attitude of severity or makes no attempt to check it by revisory action.

The JAG had a division that looked exclusively at the remission or mitigation of sentences. A sample of one year showed that more than 12 percent of sentences were recommended for reduction, and many of those reductions were for significantly less punishment time.

14. That the action taken in the Judge Advocate General's office is ineffectual to enforce military law and procedure, because its rulings do not have the force of a Supreme Court mandate, but are only recommendatory, and are either ignored by the division commanders or vetoed by the Chief of Staff.

In only about 2 percent of the cases reviewed were the recommendations of the JAG Corps not followed. To ensure that severe sentences could not be carried out without JAG review, General Order No. 7 (discussed in the following case) required the reviewing authority to suspend sentences pending a JAG review.

LEGAL PROFILES

Samuel T. Ansell was the acting JAG after Enoch Crowder was appointed provost marshal to run selective service. Ansell was born in North Carolina in 1875 and started his legal practice after graduating from West Point in 1899. He served in the Philippines and in Mexico. He and Crowder got into quite a public dispute over whether the JAG Corps reviews should be considered optional recommendations or mandatory advice for the reviewing authority and over the propriety of the whole court-martial system. He resigned from the military after this debate and returned to private practice, although many of his proposals ended up in the revised Articles of War. He died in 1954.[220]

---

220. *See Gen. S. T. Ansell, Lawyer Was 79*, N.Y. TIMES (May 28, 1954).

3. Houston Riot Trials

In August 1917, the arrest and beating in Houston of an African American solider, Pvt. Alonzo Edwards, who had been trying to help a woman arrested for sheltering a minor criminal, led to a major riot and deaths around a military camp in Texas. Afterward, Military Police Cpl. Charles Baltimore was arrested and beaten by police when he inquired about Edwards's arrest. This occurred in an area of the country where "Jim Crow" laws were still prevalent, and racial animosity and outright racism were openly on display daily. These events led the other members of the Twenty-Fourth Infantry Regiment to collect their weapons and march on the jail to seek revenge for the treatment of their fellow black soldier, despite orders from their commander to remain in camp and turn in their weapons. The incident became a battle with local law enforcement and resulted in the deaths of more than a dozen people. More than one hundred soldiers were arrested and brought to trial.

The soldiers were charged with violating four of the Articles of War: Article 64, for willfully disobeying a lawful command of their superior officer; Article 66, for creating or joining a mutiny at a camp; Article 92, for committing murder while under military law; and Article 93, for committing assault with intent to commit a felony. The punishment for these offenses was death, life imprisonment, or such other punishment as a court-martial may direct. The crime was aggravated by occurring during a time of war, although these soldiers had been stationed far from the front lines in Europe.

The men were tried in large groups, with the first sixty-three tried together,[221] but only assigned a single counsel. The defense counsel, Harry S. Grier, taught law and had been in courts-martial, but he does not appear to have been a licensed lawyer. Evidence was produced that Cpl. Baltimore had already returned to camp after the intervention of his commanding officers, that the police officer involved had been suspended, and that all soldiers had been ordered to remain on base that night. Despite extra guards on duty and interventions by their commanding officer, more than a hundred men left camp with rifles, marching in military columns, under Sgt. Vida Henry and Sgt. William Nesbit. After randomly killing or wounding several dozen people in the area, the soldiers returned to camp (except Henry, who committed suicide).

---

221. United States v. William C. Nesbit, Sgt., Company I, 24th Infantry, et al.

On November 28, 1917, of the sixty-three men on trial, fifty-four were convicted on all four counts, with forty-one sentenced to life imprisonment and thirteen sentenced to be executed (five men were acquitted and four convicted of lesser offenses). The thirteen death sentences were carried out on December 11, before the trial records could be reviewed by the JAG Corps in Washington, DC. It was not until late January 1918 that these records were reviewed and approved by the acting JAG, Col. J. J. Mayes. Gen. Ansell was irate when he discovered what had happened, leading to the issuance in mid-January of Army General Order 7, requiring a review by the JAG before any executions could take place. This order led to the creation of the JAG boards of review, finally codified in 1920. Subsequently, two other trials for crimes during these events took place.[222] Of fifty-five additional defendants, fifty-two were found guilty, and six more executions (this time under JAG review) were carried out, but only after President Wilson commuted the death sentences of ten of the men.

The president filed a memorandum with the adjutant general of the army, so that his actions in affirming or commuting these sentences would be a matter of public record. He commuted most of the death sentences, he said, "because I believe the lesson of this lawless riot will have been adequately pointed by the action already taken and that now directed, and also because I desire the clemency here ordered to be a recognition of the splendid loyalty of the race to which these soldiers belong and an inspiration to the people of that race to further zeal and service to the country of which they are citizens and for the liberties of which so many of them are now bravely bearing arms at the very front of great fields of battle."[223]

LEGAL PROFILES

John A. Hull was the judge advocate assigned to oversee the legal aspects of this trial (trial judge advocate Dudley V. Sutphin prosecuted the case). Hull was born in Iowa in 1874 and started his legal practice

---

222. United States v. Washington (1917); United States v. Tillman (1918).
223. Woodrow Wilson, Memorandum to Adjutant General of the army (Aug. 31, 1918).

there in 1895. During the Spanish-American War, he joined the military and the JAG Corps. During WWI, he was judge advocate for the Central Department, and he served as legal adviser to the governor-general of the Philippines between 1913 and 1921. In 1924, he was made the judge advocate general, a position he remained in until 1928. From 1930 to 1932, he again advised the Philippine governor-general. In 1932, he was appointed to the Philippine Supreme Court, departing in 1936, when only Filipinos were allowed to serve in these positions. He died in 1944.[224]

C. Subsequent Events

After the war, there were further minor changes to the Articles of War in 1918 and 1919, but more significant revisions were made in 1920.[225] These changes included the appointment of defense counsel and the requirement that no one who acted as a trial judge advocate could then work on the same case as a staff judge advocate. Sentences of death, life imprisonment, or imprisonment of more than ten years required approval from three-fourths of the members of the court-martial, and all other sentences required the approval of two-thirds of the members of the court-martial. No sentences could be carried out until the trial records had been referred to the staff judge advocate or the JAG. Commanding officers could commute serious sentences before they reached the president. A JAG board of review was created for use on presidential-level decisions (e.g., executions), and no sentence could be carried out without the board's approval and that of the JAG.

The U.S. Navy also had its own court-martial system during the war, but one of its biggest trials came just after the war was over. Concerned over allegations of homosexual behavior within the navy in Newport, Rhode Island, a court of inquiry decided that an investigation was warranted. It was approved by the assistant secretary of the navy. The investigation was unorthodox, tracking the activities of suspects across a wide range of different locations and

---

224. *See Maj. Gen. Hull, 69, Legal Authority*, N.Y. TIMES (Apr 18, 1944).
225. Pub. L. No. 66-242, An Act to Amend an Act Entitled "An Act for Making Further and More Effectual Provision for the National Defense, and for Other Purposes," Approved June 3, 1916, and to Establish Military Justice, c. II (1920).

milieus. As a result, a number of sailors were eventually arrested and put on trial for sodomy, which was considered "scandalous conduct tending to the destruction of good morals" under the Navy Articles of Justice. The courts-martial convicted seventeen sailors and sent them to prison and gave them dishonorable discharges.

LEGAL PROFILES

Franklin Delano Roosevelt was the assistant secretary of the navy during the war. He was born in New York in 1882 and started his legal practice there in 1908. He was first elected to the Senate in New York State in 1910, but he resigned to become assistant secretary of the navy in 1914. He held this role until 1920, when he ran unsuccessfully on the Democratic national ticket as the vice-presidential candidate. He was elected governor of New York in 1928 and in 1932 was elected U.S. president, the first of four such wins for this office, where he would become the central figure for Americans in the Great Depression and the world in WWII. He died in office in 1945.[226]

Under prodding from black organizations like the NAACP, the military set up an officer training school at Fort Des Moines, Iowa, for African American officers in 1917. Its location was remote from the media and had been previously used by the Buffalo Soldier units. The first training started in May 1917. More than one thousand candidates, mostly college graduates from schools like Tuskegee and Howard, but also Yale and Harvard, along with several hundred noncommissioned officers, started the training. More than half of these men completed officer training in October and then were shipped off to basic training. By spring 1918, they had joined other Americans in being sent to the theater of war in Europe, where many of them were wounded in the fierce fighting at the end of the war.

---

226. *See A Leader Dies, With Victory Close*, N.Y. TIMES (Apr. 15, 1945).

LEGAL PROFILES

James B. Morris was a graduate of the Des Moines officer training school and a lawyer. He was born in Georgia in 1890 and started his legal practice in Iowa in 1917. He joined the officer training school and was sent to Europe in May 1918 after he graduated. Working in the intelligence service, he was seriously wounded. He returned to practice law in Iowa after the war and then, in 1922, bought a local newspaper, which he ran for fifty years. In 1925, he became a founder of the National (originally Negro) Bar Association, an organization founded because the American Bar Association (ABA) did not at the time admit black lawyers. Morris died in 1977.[227]

William H. Lewis was the first African American admitted to the ABA and was an assistant U.S. attorney general. He was born in Virginia in 1868, and after attending law school at Harvard, he was hired to coach football there in 1895. He also served in state and local political office in Massachusetts before being appointed as an assistant U.S. attorney in 1903 by President Roosevelt. In 1910, he was appointed the assistant U.S. attorney general by President Taft. His membership in the ABA caused such a stir in 1912, despite his defense by U.S. attorney general George Wickersham, that the ABA did not admit another black member for thirty years. Lewis returned to private practice after his time in Washington. He died in 1949.[228]

D. Modern Applicability

To decrease the potential for arbitrariness in trial verdicts and to streamline and standardize the procedures across the entire armed forces, the Uniform Code of Military Justice was established in 1950.[229] Among other items, the

---

227. *See Morris, J.B.*, Des Moines Register (Feb. 11, 2009).
228. *See W.H. Lewis is Dead; Boston Lawyer, 80*, N.Y. Times (Jan. 2, 1949).
229. Pub. L. No. 64-506, An Act To Unify, Consolidate, Revise, and Codify the Articles of War, the Articles for the Government of the Navy, and the Disciplinary Laws of the Coast Guard, and to Enact and Establish a Uniform Code of Military Justice (1950).

code provides for additional levels of appellate review for decisions resulting in long imprisonments or death sentences. The law member is now a military judge who must be a member of the bar and the officers sit more like a civilian jury. The code, along with the Manual for Courts-Martial[230] (which contains both the Rules for Courts-Martial and Military Rules of Evidence), reflects and sometime precedes similar rules used in the federal civilian courts. One item that is still unique to the military is the ability for the convening authority to "take action" on a sentence (i.e., review and either accept or reject a sentence).[231] Specifically, "the convening authority may for any or no reason disapprove a legal sentence in whole or in part, mitigate the sentence, and change a punishment to one of a different nature."[232] Recent cases have led Congress to consider whether this unique element of military justice that allows the overruling of the decision of a military judge and jury outside the military judicial appeals process is still appropriate.[233]

---

230. Exec. Order No. 13593, 2011 Amendments to the Manual for Courts-Martial, United States (Dec. 13, 2011).
231. Rules for Courts-Martial No. 1107, Manual for Courts-Martial, United States (2012).
232. *Id*. at No. 1107(d)(1).
233. *Hagel Orders Review of Military Judicial Authority*, CNN (Mar. 12, 2013).

CHAPTER 5

UNITED STATES: DOMESTIC ISSUES

As did all countries entering the war, the United States had to ensure that the homeland was secure and its civilian population was supporting the war effort. Beyond the few incursions by Germany and Mexico described in Chapter 4, the territory of the United States did not come under military attack. That did not mean there were no security threats to face at home. The possible spying by agents of foreign governments while the United States was neutral and by agents of enemy governments after the United States joined the war was a constant concern. Another concern was for those resident in the United States, both citizens and enemy aliens, who were using the opportunities of a distracted government in wartime to plot its overthrow. So laws were passed that proscribed both espionage and sedition, but these ran into the constitutional protections of the freedom of expression.

The need to build a war economy ran into many difficulties, including acquiring and transporting sufficient supplies, dealing with labor issues, and ensuring vital industries ran as efficiently as necessary. This required the U.S. government to take extraordinary measures, including taking over vital industries. As with all nations, the vast increase in governmental expenditures meant that new sources of funding were required. Public revenues had to be increased, and borrowing sources had to be found. While all of this was going on, the government could not ignore the needs of over half its population. The labor of women was necessary to support the war effort, as were their social and emotional contributions to maintain the morale of the country. Several causes women had long led and supported came to fruition with this conflict.

This chapter focuses on the domestic legal issues in the United States during the war, starting with how the country controlled public information and responded to espionage, freedom of expression, sedition, anarchists, and enemy aliens. It then covers the economic aspects of ensuring there was an adequate supply of natural and human resources for the production of war materials, including rationing, priority setting, and taking over transportation systems shipping the war materials. Next is the response—including bond sales, taxes, and the closing of financial markets—to the significant public funding shortfalls and capital flows out of the country to fund the Europeans' militaries. The chapter closes by looking at some of the legal issues that particularly involved women both during and after the war, in their employment and their rights, the social issues that they had long championed, and the impact of the war's lethality on women.

PROMINENT LAWYERS AND JUDGES IN THIS CHAPTER

Espionage / Freedom of Expression:
- Edwin Y. Webb (House sponsor)
- Charles Allen Culberson (Senate sponsor)
- Alfred Bettman (appellee brief)
- Thomas Watt Gregory (attorney general)
- James C. McReynolds (Supreme Court justice)
- Seymour Stedman (appellant counsel)
- Isaac Edward Ferguson (appellant brief)
- Kenesaw Mountain Landis (trial judge)
- Benjamin Franklin Bledsoe (trial judge)
- John E. Joyce (assistant U.S. attorney)
- Learned Hand (trial judge)
- Thomas G. Patten (postmaster)
- William H. Lamar (defense counsel)
- Seth Shepard (amicus curiae)
- Josephus Daniels (secretary of the navy)

Sedition / Anarchists / Enemy Aliens:

- Kenneth Douglas McKellar (Senate co-sponsor)
- William Paul Dillingham (Senate co-sponsor)
- J. Edgar Hoover (Bureau of Investigation)
- John William Abercrombie (acting secretary of labor)
- Zechariah Chafee Jr. (law professor)

Supplying the War Effort:

- Walker D. Hines (assistant director general of railroads)
- Robert S. Lovett (War Industries Board priorities commissioner)
- Albert C. Ritchie (War Industries Board general counsel)
- Asbury F. Lever (legislation sponsor)
- Harry Augustus Garfield (fuel administrator)
- Felix Frankfurter (War Labor Policies Board head)
- Frank P. Walsh (National War Labor Board co-chairman)
- John Barton Payne (counsel for Railroad Administration)
- Alfred A. Wheat (counsel for United States)
- William D. Guthrie (amicus curiae brief)
- Joseph Sill Clark Sr. (appellant counsel)
- John Jacob Esch (House co-sponsor)

Funding the War:

- William Gibbs McAdoo (secretary of treasury)
- Mahlon Pitney (associate justice)
- Charles Evans Hughes (chief justice)

Women and the War:

- Belva Ann Lockwood (suffrage movement)
- Belle Case La Follette (suffrage movement)
- Catherine Waugh McCulloch (suffrage movement)
- Inez Milholland (suffrage movement)
- Etta H. Maddox (suffrage movement)
- Morris Sheppard (Prohibition laws' sponsor)
- Wayne Wheeler (legislation drafter)
- Wade H. Ellis (appellees counsel)

- Oscar Leser (plaintiff)
- William L. Frierson (assistant U.S. attorney general)
- Annette Abbott Adams (assistant U.S. attorney general)

5.1 ESPIONAGE / FREEDOM OF EXPRESSION

A. Statutes

After the start of the war, Congress was quick to pass the Espionage Act[1] to deal with spying on military establishments. This law passed included thirteen titles; this section focuses on Title I, Espionage, and Title XII, Use of the Mails. Title I included a wide-ranging set of different prohibitions on activities contrary to the war effort. If a person was involved in one of these activities intending, with regard to national defense information, to hurt the United States or to assist a foreign nation in doing so, they were in violation of the statute.

Title I of the Espionage Act would punish the person who goes to any "vessel, aircraft, work of defense, navy yard, naval station, submarine base, coaling station, fort, battery, torpedo station, dockyard, canal, railroad, arsenal, camp, factory, mine, telegraph, telephone, wireless, or signal station, building, office, or other place connected with the national defense,"[2] or places where naval vessels, aircraft, arms, munitions or war materials were "made, prepared, repaired, or stored"[3] and, at that location, "copies, takes, makes, or obtains, or attempts, or induces or aids another to copy, take, make, or obtain, any sketch, photograph, photographic negative, blue print, plan, map, model, instrument, appliance, document, writing or note of anything connected with the national defense."[4]

Also punished was the person who obtained or helped another obtain a "document, writing, code book, signal book, sketch, photograph, photographic negative, blue print, plan, map, model, instrument, appliance, or note, of anything connected with the national defense"[5] or communicated, transmitted, or attempted to communicate or transmit one of these items to someone

---

1. Pub. L. No. 65–24, An Act to punish acts of interference with foreign relations, the neutrality, and the foreign commerce of the United States, to punish espionage, and better to enforce the criminal laws of the United States, and for other purposes (1917).
2. *Id.* Title I, § 1(a).
3. *Id.*
4. *Id.* § 1(b).
5. *Id.* § 1(c).

not authorized or retained it. It was illegal for a person entrusted with one of the items but with gross negligence allowed it to be "removed from its proper place of custody or delivered to anyone in violation of his trust, or to be list, stolen, abstracted, or destroyed."[6]

Anyone who transmitted to a foreign government any "document, writing, code book, signal book, sketch, photograph, photographic negative, blue print, plan, map, model, note, instrument, appliance, or information relating to the national defense" during a time of war could be punished by death (compared to a twenty-year maximum prison sentence during peacetime).[7] Someone who collected, published, or communicated information on "the movement, numbers, description, condition, or disposition of any of the armed forces, ships, aircraft, or war materials" or the military or naval operations of the United States, or information about fortifications or the public defense that "might be useful to the enemy" could also be sentenced to death.[8]

Someone who during wartime intentionally made false reports or false statements intending to interfere with the U.S. naval or military forces or help the enemy willfully, or caused or attempted to cause "insubordination, disloyalty, mutiny, refusal of duty, in the military or naval forces of the United States" during wartime, or obstructed "the recruiting or enlistment service of the United States,"[9] was subject to imprisonment of up to twenty years. It was a crime to conspire to do these acts[10] or to harbor someone who had done or was conspiring to do these acts[11]—these were also subject to imprisonment.

Under Title XII, any letter, newspaper, pamphlet, book, photograph, or circular that violated the act was considered nonmailable.[12] Any such item that contained any matter that advocated "treason, insurrection, or forcible resistance to any law of the United States" was also considered nonmailable.[13] Use of the postal system for any matter declared to be nonmailable subjected the person to possible incarceration in the place it was mailed, was carried, or was to be delivered.[14]

---

6. *Id.* § 1(e).
7. *Id.* § 2(a).
8. *Id.* § 2(b).
9. *Id.* § 3.
10. *Id.* § 4.
11. *Id.* § 5.
12. *Id.* Title XII, § 1.
13. *Id.* § 2.
14. *Id.* § 3.

LEGAL PROFILES

Edwin Y. Webb was the sponsor of the Espionage Act in the House. He was born in North Carolina in 1872 and started his legal practice there in 1894. He was elected to the state senate in 1900 and then to the U.S. House in 1902, serving in that role through the war. In 1919 he resigned after President Wilson appointed him to the federal bench in the Western District of North Carolina. He served there until he retired in 1948. He died in 1955.[15]

Charles Allen Culberson was the sponsor of the Espionage Act in the Senate. He was born in Alabama in 1855 and started his legal practice in Texas in 1877. In 1890 he became the attorney general of the state of Texas, serving there until 1894. In that year he was elected governor of the state, where he served until 1898. In that year he was elected to the U.S. Senate, serving there until he lost the election in 1922. He died in 1925.[16]

B. Cases

There were several very well-known cases that arose out of the Espionage Act. The first five cases deal with Title I of the act, addressing conduct obstructing the selective service system. The sixth and seventh cases involve Title XII of the act. Opinions in the first three cases were issued within a week of each other and were all drafted by the same Supreme Court justice. The mediums vary across the cases, with the first involving leaflets, the second and seventh a newspaper, the third a speech, the fourth various forms of communication, the fifth a motion picture, and the sixth a periodical.

---

15. *See Webb, Edwin Yates*, BIOGRAPHICAL DIRECTORY OF THE UNITED STATES CONGRESS; *Webb, Edwin Yates*, FED. JUDICIAL CTR., BIOGRAPHICAL DIRECTORY OF FEDERAL JUDGES.
16. *See Culberson, Charles Allen*, BIOGRAPHICAL DIRECTORY OF THE UNITED STATES CONGRESS.

1. Free Speech in Publications (1)

In *Schenck*,[17] the U.S. Supreme Court looked at the implications of the Espionage Act on free speech. Charles Schenck was the general secretary of the Socialist Party of the United States and was responsible for printing and mailing war-related flyers to 15,000 men who had been drafted for military service. His co-defendant in the case, Dr. Elizabeth Baer, was a member of the Executive Committee of the party, recording the minutes during the meeting the party had decided to create the mailing. The violations of the Espionage Act, brought against them in court, were in trying to cause insubordination in the armed forces, in obstructing the military recruiting and enlistment process while the United States was at war, and conspiring to use and unlawfully using the postal system for nonmailable matter.

The mailed leaflets had on one side the contents of the Thirteenth Amendment, which had outlawed slavery and involuntary servitude. It claimed that the Selective Service Act (see Chapter 4) violated this and that "a conscript is little better than a convict."[18] It advocated changing this situation through peaceful means, such as revocation of the law. On the other side, enlistees were told to "assert your opposition to the draft," that "silent consent to the conscription law as helping to support an infamous conspiracy," and that "you must do your share to maintain, support and uphold the rights of the people of this country."[19] The Court asserted that the intended effect was to influence draftees to obstruct the draft, to which the defense did not strongly object.

The main contention made by the defense was that this speech was protected by the First Amendment. The Court responded by saying first that "in many places and in ordinary times the defendants . . . would have been within their constitutional rights. But the character of every act depends upon the circumstances in which it is done."[20] As an example, the Court said, "The most stringent protection of free speech would not protect a man in falsely shouting fire in a theatre and causing a panic" or "protect a man from an injunction against uttering words that may have all the effect of force. . . . The question in every case is whether the words used are used in such circumstances and are of

---

17. Schenck v. United States, 249 U.S. 47 (1919).
18. *Id.* at 50-51.
19. *Id.* at 51.
20. *Id.* at 52.

such a nature as to create a clear and present danger that they will bring about the substantive evils that Congress has a right to prevent."[21]

The Court continued, stating, "It is a question of proximity and degree. When a nation is at war many things that might be said in time of peace are such a hindrance to its effort that their utterance will not be endured so long as men fight and that no Court could regard them as protected by any constitutional right."[22] The Court then noted that as conspiracy to commit the crime was a part of the statute, it was not necessary to prove that some men actually obstructed the draft based on the defendants' publication. As such, the Court unanimously affirmed the decision convicting the defendants. Schenck was sentenced to six months' imprisonment and Baer to three months.

LEGAL PROFILES

Alfred Bettman was on the brief for the prosecution team in this trial. He was born in Ohio in 1873 and started his legal practice there in 1898. He was a country attorney from 1909 to 1911 and city solicitor from 1912. During the war he was brought in to work on Espionage Act cases such as this one. After the war he served on the Wickersham Commission, dealing with criminal activity related to Prohibition, on the committee to draft the standard city planning and zoning enabling acts, and on the plan that became the Tennessee Valley Authority. He is best known for his work on urban planning and zoning, writing the amicus brief in the *Village of Euclid* case, which turned the Court's opinion in favor of upholding zoning regulations.[23] He served as the president of the American Society of Planning Officials from 1934. He died in 1945.[24]

---

21. *Id.*
22. *Id.*
23. Village of Euclid v. Ambler Realty Co., 272 U.S. 365 (1026).
24. *See Alfred Bettman*, N.Y. TIMES (Jan. 23, 1945).

2. Free Speech in Publications (2)

In *Frohwerk*,[25] issued the week after *Schenck*, defendant Jacob Frohwerk was charged with conspiracy to violate the Espionage Act, through the overt acts of twelve articles written and published in the state newspaper *Missouri Staats Zeitung*. His articles were, according to the Court, intended to "cause disloyalty, mutiny and refusal of duty in the military and naval forces."[26] The Court noted its decision on *Schenck*, adding that "the First Amendment while prohibiting legislation against free speech as such cannot have been, and obviously was not, intended to give immunity for every possible use of language . . . We venture to believe that neither Hamilton nor Madison, nor any other competent person then or later, ever supposed that to make criminal the counselling of a murder within the jurisdiction of Congress would be an unconstitutional interference with free speech."[27]

After going through examples of the publications, the Court reiterated, "It may be that all this might be said or written even in time of war in circumstances that would not make it a crime. We do not lose our right to condemn either measures or men because the Country is at war."[28] Noting that in the record there was no evidence that the publication was intended to reach men subject to the draft—or even what the quantity of its publication was—the point was that it could not rule out that "the circulation of the paper was in quarters where a little breath would be enough to kindle a flame."[29] Dismissing the defense argument that there was no intent to obstruct recruiting, the Court said that "conspiracy to obstruct recruiting would be criminal even if no means were agreed upon specifically by which to accomplish the intent. It is enough if the parties agreed to set to work for that common purpose."[30] The Court unanimously affirmed the conviction of ten years' imprisonment.

---

25. Frohwerk v. United States, 249 U.S. 204 (1919).
26. *Id.* at 205.
27. *Id.* at 206.
28. *Id.* at 208.
29. *Id.* at 209.
30. *Id.*

LEGAL PROFILES

Thomas Watt Gregory was the attorney general during the war and was behind the drafting of the act and prosecutions under it. He was born in Mississippi in 1861 and started his legal practice in Texas in 1885. Besides private practice and his own law firm, he served as city attorney of the city of Austin from 1891 to 1894. He turned down appointments for both the state assistant attorney general and district judge positions. His work as special counsel to the state in antitrust cases led to his serving from 1908 to 1913 as a special assistant attorney general for the United States for antitrust cases. In 1914 he was appointed attorney general. He remained in this position until 1919 and attended the Paris Peace Conference that same year. He died in 1933.[31]

James C. McReynolds was one of the justices in this unanimous decision. He was born in Kentucky in 1862 and started his legal practice in Tennessee in 1884. He ran unsuccessfully for Congress in 1896. He taught law from 1900 until 1903, when he was appointed assistant attorney general for the United States. He served in this role until 1907, leaving for private practice in New York and then returning to the government for a year starting in 1910 to work on antitrust cases. In 1913 he was appointed as the U.S. attorney general. In 1914 President Wilson nominated him for a seat on the U.S. Supreme Court, where he served until retiring in 1941. He died in 1946.[32]

3. Free Speech in Public Speaking

In *Debs*,[33] the Court faced another case that fell under the Espionage Act, this one issued the same day as *Frohwerk* but having a much more high profile defendant. Eugene Debs had originally risen to prominence for his role in

---

31. *See T.W. Gregory Dies; in Wilson Cabinet*, N.Y. TIMES (Feb. 26, 1933).
32. *See McReynolds, James Clark*, FED. JUDICIAL CTR., BIOGRAPHICAL DIRECTORY OF FEDERAL JUDGES.
33. Debs v. United States, 249 U.S. 211 (1919).

the 1894 Pullman Strike and was the Socialist candidate for president in 1900, 1904, 1908, and 1912. The two charges against him were based on a speech he made on June 16, 1918, during which he intended to "incite insubordination, disloyalty, mutiny and refusal of duty in the military and naval forces . . . [and] to obstruct the recruiting and enlistment service of the United States."[34] In its opinion, the Court focused on the latter of the two charges, as demonstrated by extracts from his speech.

In the June 16, 1918, speech, Debs had said that he had just returned from visiting those convicted of aiding a draft resister (see *Ruthenberg v. United States* in Chapter 4) and that he was proud of them. He then expressed support for others convicted of obstructing the draft, namely Kate Richards O'Hare and Rose Pastor Stokes. Regarding the latter, he declared that "if she was guilty so was he, and that he would not be cowardly enough to plead his innocence."[35] In continuing with his speech, Debs said that "you need to know that you are fit for something better than slavery and cannon fodder."[36] The Court said that with the overall tone of the speech opposing this war, that "its natural and intended effect would be to obstruct recruiting."[37]

Before his speech, he had also declared his support for an "Anti-War Proclamation and Program" whose first recommendation was "continuous, active, and public opposition to the war, through demonstrations, mass petitions, and all other means within our power."[38] The Court reasoned that if he "accepted this view and this declaration of his duties at the time that he made his speech [doing so] is evidence that if in that speech he used words tending to obstruct the recruiting service he meant that they should have that effect."[39] With the sentences for conviction on the two charges running concurrently, the Court did not review the first charge and affirmed the conviction. Debs would run again for president, from jail, in 1920 and would then be pardoned by that presidential race's victor, Warren G. Harding.

---

34. *Id*. at 212.
35. *Id*. at 214.
36. *Id*.
37. *Id*. at 215.
38. *Id*. at 216.
39. *Id*.

LEGAL PROFILES

Seymour Stedman was the counsel for the defense. He was born in Connecticut in 1871 and started his legal practice in Illinois in 1891. He became involved early in what would become the Socialist Party, supporting Eugene Debs in his various runs for the U.S. presidency. He was the vice president on the 1920 Socialist ticket. During the war he defended others, such as Rose Pastor Stokes, who were also charged under the act. He was later elected to the state legislature and ran for mayor of Chicago. He died in 1948.[40]

Isaac Edward Ferguson was on the brief for the defense. He was born in Canada in 1888 and started his legal practice in Illinois in 1912. After spending several years in Wyoming, he returned to Chicago to become involved in the Socialist and Communist parties and defended their members. In 1920 he and Communist Party executive secretary Charles Ruthenberg were put on trial for criminal anarchism, convicted, and sentenced to five years' imprisonment for the publication of a Communist manifesto advocating overthrow of the government by force. He was released early[41] and resumed his legal practice. He died in 1964.

4. Wobblies

In *Haywood*,[42] the U.S. government had raided the national offices of and then brought to trial over one hundred members of the Industrial Workers of the World (IWW or "Wobblies"), including their leader, William "Big Bill" Haywood. The Wobblies' leaders and agents had conspired to have their members, who were working in munitions factories, "break machinery, spoil materials, strike, and use force to prevent other workmen from taking their places; also to have their members refrain from registering in obedience to the Selective Service Act, to have them desert, if brought into registration offices, and rescue

---

40. *See Seymour Stedman, Chicago Lawyer, 78*, N.Y. TIMES (July 10, 1948).
41. *See Radicals' Release Ordered by Court*, N.Y. TIMES (Apr. 20, 1922).
42. Haywood et al. v. United States, 268 F. 795 (7th Cir. 1920).

them by force, if caught; and also, in defiance of the Espionage Act, to cause all whom they could influence by speeches, pamphlets, and newspapers to keep out of the military service."[43]

They were convicted under four counts by the trial court and sentenced to concurrent terms of imprisonment on each count. Counts one and two were conspiracy to use force to prevent the execution of any law of the United States, while counts three and four were for conspiracy to violate the Selective Service Act and the Espionage Act, respectively. The laws that count one addressed included the declaration of war, national defense appropriations, and those dealing with enemy aliens, selective service, and espionage. The appeals court struck those parts of count one that had to do with the Selective Service and Espionage Acts, then asked if interfering with work in a munitions plant with which the government had a contract was forcible prevention for executing the declaration of war and appropriations acts. As these acts related to interference with private individuals rather than government officials, count one was struck.

Count two involved conspiracies to injure citizens who were exercising their rights and privileges under the Constitution and laws. But the Court said that contracts for selling war munitions to the government were not rights and privileges of citizens, as, for example, foreign governments and companies had sold munitions to the United States. As such, count two was struck. But the appeals court turned down Fourth and Fifth Amendment arguments by the appellants regarding the materials seized in the raids and let stand the convictions and sentences of twenty years for each of the counts of conspiracy to violate the Espionage and Selective Service Acts. Haywood, while out on bail, fled the country and went to Russia, where he died in 1928.

LEGAL PROFILES

Kenesaw Mountain Landis was the trial judge in this case. He was born in Ohio in 1866 and started his legal practice in Illinois in 1891. He served as private secretary to the U.S. secretary of state, former judge Walter Q. Gresham, between 1893 and 1895. He then turned down

---
43. *Id.* at 799.

an offer to become U.S. ambassador to Venezuela, returning instead to private practice. In 1905 he was nominated by President Roosevelt for a seat on the federal bench in the Northern District of Illinois. While on the bench, he was the trial judge for another group of defendants convicted in early 1918 under the Espionage Act, including Victor L. Berger, editor of the Socialist *Milwaukee Leader* newspaper (see case 7 below). This case was overturned by the Supreme Court because he did not recuse himself when allegations of bias were raised.[44] He served on the bench in 1922, when he resigned to take a new full-time position as the first commissioner of major league baseball, which had recently been hit by the "Black Sox" scandal during the 1919 World Series. He served as the baseball commissioner from 1920 until his death in 1948.[45]

---

5. Free Speech in Motion Pictures

In this case,[46] a 1917 silent movie made about the Revolutionary War portrayed U.S. ally Great Britain in a bad light through its actions during that conflict. Depicted were some factual and some fictional acts committed by British soldiers, loyalists, and allies against American patriots and settlers, acts that included the bayonetting of an infant and the assault of a young woman. It was produced by Robert Goldstein, whose family had emigrated from Germany and now ran a costume shop supplying the film industry in California. He was in some part trying to emulate what D.W. Griffiths had done for the Civil War in the 1915 film *Birth of a Nation*, in which he had been involved. After his movie ran afoul of film censors at its opening in Chicago, he cut the offending scenes to get censor approval but reinserted them when it opened in Los Angeles.

For this, he was arrested and prosecuted for trying to cause insubordination in the military and obstruct recruiting through arousing "antagonism, hatred and enmity" between the United States and Great Britain, as well as aiding

---

44. Berger v. United States, 255 U.S. 22 (1921).
45. *See Landis, Kenesaw Mountain*, FED. JUDICIAL CTR., BIOGRAPHICAL DIRECTORY OF FEDERAL JUDGES.
46. United States v. Motion Picture Film "The Spirit of '76," 252 F. 946 (S.D. Cal. 1917).

Germany by use of this film. It could not have helped the defendant that a fictional scene depicted American Benjamin Franklin (the namesake of the trial judge) being punched in the face by British King George III. He was convicted and sentenced to ten years' imprisonment, and the film was seized. This conviction was upheld by the court of appeals, finding that the appellant desired to obstruct "the necessary cooperation between the allied countries against the enemy."[47] The film was allowed to be publicly viewed in 1921, without federal government objections, sponsored by an Irish-affiliated company with possible ties to Sinn Féin, an Irish republican political party.

LEGAL PROFILES

Benjamin Franklin Bledsoe was district judge in this trial. He was born in California in 1874 and started his legal practice there in 1896. From 1900 to 1914 he was a judge on the superior court in the state. In 1914 President Wilson appointed him to the federal bench in the Southern District of California. He served there until resigning in 1925 to run unsuccessfully for mayor of Los Angeles. After this he returned to private practice. He died in 1938.[48]

John E. Joyce was the assistant U.S. attorney who approved the showing of this film after the war. He was born in 1889. He served in the criminal branch of the U.S. attorney's office during the 1920s, eventually leading it. He became a federal bankruptcy referee in 1932 and was involved in many high profile cases. He died in 1963.[49]

---

47. Goldstein v. United States, 258 F. 908 (9th Cir. 1919).
48. *See Bledsoe, Benjamin Franklin*, FED. JUDICIAL CTR., BIOGRAPHICAL DIRECTORY OF FEDERAL JUDGES.
49. *See John E. Joyce*, N.Y. TIMES (Nov. 18, 1963).

6. Postal System—Nonmailable

In *Masses Publishing*,[50] the charges concerned Title XII of the Espionage Act. The New York postmaster, Thomas G. Patten, had determined that the August 1917 issue of *The Masses*, a graphical New York-based Socialist periodical, contained material in violation of the Espionage Act and so was nonmailable. The violation of the act was four pieces of text and four cartoons describing and depicting the heroism of resistance to the war effort, including the futility of conscription and the praising of draft resisters. The government alleged that such depictions would incite a mutinous attitude among the troops. The magazine sought an injunction requiring the postmaster to mail the periodical, as, it argued, the government's action infringed on First Amendment rights of free expression.

Trial judge Learned Hand looked at the three clauses from section 3 of the Espionage Act that were the basis for the charges. The first clause was about the spreading of false reports or statements, where Hand ruled that the materials were in the form of opinion and criticism, not factual statements that could be interpreted as false. As such, they were within the bounds of the "right to criticize either by temperate reasoning, or by immoderate or indecent invective, which is normally the privilege of the individual in countries dependent upon free expression of opinion as the ultimate source of authority."[51]

The second clause was about causing insubordination, disloyalty, mutiny, or refusal to duty in the military. The key word here was "causing" these results, as interpreting it too broadly would lead to the "suppression of all hostile criticism, and of all opinion except what encouraged and supported the existing policies." Hand did not believe that all criticism against the war could be suppressed, with the differentiation between legitimate criticism and the inciting of violent resistance, as one "may not counsel or advise others to violate the law as it stands." The magazine had not actually violated the act if it stopped "short of urging upon others that it is their duty or their interest to resist the law."[52]

The third clause was about obstructing the recruiting or enlistment services. The magazine's text included praise both for those convicted of conspiring to induce others to not register for the draft and for conscientious objectors.

---

50. Masses Publ'g Co. v. Patten, 244 F. 535 (S.D.N.Y. 1917).
51. *Id.* at 539.
52. *Id.* at 539–41.

Without direct advocacy in the text to follow these models of action, Hand did not find that the defendants had violated section 3 of the act. As such, he granted the injunction requiring the postmaster to not deem the magazine as nonmailable. But this ruling was quickly stayed by injunction and overturned by the court of appeals a few months later.[53] The magazine soon ceased publication due to mailing restrictions, and its editors were put on trial, though not convicted, for violating the Espionage Act.

LEGAL PROFILES

Learned Hand was the judge in this trial. He was born the son of a judge in New York in 1872 and started his legal practice there in 1897. He was appointed by President Taft to the federal bench for the Southern District of New York in 1909. He served there until 1924, when he was nominated by Calvin Coolidge for the Court of Appeals for the Second Circuit. He served as chief judge from 1948 to 1951, when he retired. He died in 1961.[54]

Thomas G. Patten was the New York postmaster whose reactions to the magazine started this trial. He was born in New York in 1861 and obtained his law training there. Instead of legal practice, he became involved in operating a fleet of tugboats. He was then elected to Congress in 1910, serving until 1917. After an election loss in 1916, he was appointed as New York postmaster general. He served in this role until 1921, when he moved to Hollywood to work on motion picture distribution. He died in 1939.[55]

---

53. Masses Publ'g Co. v. Patten, 246 F. 24 (2nd Cir. 1917).
54. *See Hand, Learned*, FED. JUDICIAL CTR., BIOGRAPHICAL DIRECTORY OF FEDERAL JUDGES.
55. *See Patten, Thomas Gedney*, BIOGRAPHICAL DIRECTORY OF THE UNITED STATES CONGRESS.

7. Postal System—Privileges

In *Milwaukee*,[56] a local newspaper went to court in September 1917 for articles in violation of the Espionage Act, making the paper nonmailable. On appeal, the postmaster general approved the order to revoke the newspaper's second-class mailing privileges. The publisher then brought suit, claiming the act was unconstitutional in giving the postmaster such powers, including under First and Fifth Amendment grounds. The Court reviewed a law from 1879, which had classified mail into four classes of mailable matter, newspapers falling under the second class. Because the revenue for second-class service was significantly lower than the costs of actually providing it, the privilege of using this second-class mail required a permit demonstrating, inter alia, that the newspaper or periodical was mailable.

The postmaster general stated that since the declaration of war and continuing until the revocation of its privilege, this newspaper frequently published false reports and statements, intending to interfere with the success of the U.S. military, support the success of its enemies, and obstruct recruiting and enlistment. He provided examples of fifty such articles from April to September 1917. Using the same power the postmaster had exercised for forty years, he then revoked the second-class mailing privileges of the newspaper. The Court opined, "Freedom of the press may protect criticism and agitation for moderation or repeal of laws, but it does not extend to protection of him who counsels and encourages the violation of the law as it exists. The Constitution was adopted to preserve our Government, not to serve as a protecting screen for those who while claiming its privileges seek to destroy it."[57] The Court affirmed the postmaster's order.

In dissent were Justices Holmes and Brandeis. Justice Brandeis narrowed this to the consideration of whether Congress gave the postmaster general the power to deny second-class mailing privileges on these grounds. Answering whether the postmaster could close the mails to all future issues of a newspaper, Brandeis said that this would make the postmaster "the universal censor of publications."[58] He said that the postmaster's role is to follow the criteria set by Congress, without discretionary power. To have such power would violate

---

56. United States ex rel. Milwaukee Social Democratic Publ'g Co. v. Burleson, Postmaster Gen. of the U.S., 255 F. 407 (1919).
57. *Id.* at 414.
58. *Id.* at 423.

First, Fifth, Sixth, and Eighth Amendments and Article III of the Constitution. Justice Holmes said that he was "satisfied that the Postmaster cannot determine in advance that a certain newspaper [issue] is going to be nonmailable and on that ground deny to it not the use of the mails but the rate of postage that the statute says shall be charged."

LEGAL PROFILES

William H. Lamar was counsel for the appellant in this trial. He was born in Alabama in 1859 and started his legal practice in Washington, DC, and Maryland in 1885. He had gone on the second relief attempt in 1883 to rescue Lt. Adolphus Greely's ill-fated Arctic expedition. He was elected to the Maryland legislature in 1894. During the Spanish-American War, he served as a Signal Corps captain and was also involved in public relations campaigns for the war. From 1906 to 1913 he worked for the Department of Justice, then became solicitor for the U.S. post office, where he served until 1921. He returned to private practice with his son. He died in 1928.[59]

Seth Shepard co-wrote an amicus curiae brief with the Court that was used posthumously. He was born in Texas in 1847 and started his legal practice there in 1868, after serving in the Civil War. In 1874 he was elected as a state senator. In 1893 he was appointed to the federal bench by President Cleveland in the Court of Appeals for the District of Columbia. He served as chief justice of this court from 1905 until his retirement in 1917. He was a law lecturer at Georgetown University from 1895 to 1910. He died later in 1917.[60]

---

59. *See William H. Lamar; Postoffice Department Solicitor in Wilson Administration Dies*, N.Y. TIMES (Feb. 12, 1928).
60. *See Shepard, Seth*, FED. JUDICIAL CTR., BIOGRAPHICAL DIRECTORY OF FEDERAL JUDGES.

C. Subsequent Events

The Espionage Act was modified by the Sedition Act in 1918 (see next section), leading to more trials. Although ostensibly created to deal with spies, in fact no spies were tried under this statute during the war. It was used primarily to deal with Americans who opposed the war. The issue of freedom of expression would rise up again in the next war. Relying on the decision in the *Milwaukee Leader* case, the postmaster general in WWII again took away second-class mailing privileges from out-of-favor magazines.[61] The Espionage Act survived the peacetime revocation of most wartime acts and was revised in the run-up to WWII to deal with peacetime violations. Again it was not heavily utilized in WWII but did deal with both those targeting the military with publications and disfavored groups who supported the goals of the enemy.[62]

To deal with the negative publicity of the antiwar groups and put a positive spin on the war, President Woodrow Wilson created the Committee for Public Information.[63] This was to be composed of the secretaries of state, war, and the navy and be headed by a civilian, a journalist named George Creel. The committee was composed of a number of different divisions, including films, pictures, and publications "for the purpose of stimulating recruiting and patriotic interest in the war; to the end that the utmost cooperation of all citizens in the successful prosecution of the war be secured."[64] It set up speakers to stump at rallies ("Four-Minute Men"), created posters, and put out a newspaper of its own under its News Division, all delivering positive news and images. It also had overseas operations, such as a foreign picture service "for the purpose of stimulating interest in the war and furnishing entertainment and instruction by means of motion pictures to American Soldiers at home and abroad, also to lend similar aid to the armies and citizens of our allies."[65]

---

61. *See* WWII Law and Lawyers, ch. 4.
62. *See* WWII Law and Lawyers, ch. 2.
63. Exec. Order No. 2594, Creating Committee on Public Information (Apr. 14, 1917).
64. Exec. Order No. 2708, Creating Divisions of Pictures, Films and Publications under the Committee on Public Information (Sept. 25, 1917).
65. Exec. Order No. 2774A, Division Created Under the Public Information Committee (Dec. 17. 1917).

LEGAL PROFILES

Josephus Daniels was the secretary of the navy during the war. He was born in North Carolina in 1862 and was admitted to the bar in 1885. However, he turned from law to politics and publishing and became editor of the *State Chronicle* newspaper from 1885. In 1894 he bought Raleigh's *News & Observer,* merged it with the *State Chronicle,* and used it to provide vigorous support to the Democratic Party. After the election of President Wilson, Daniels was appointed as secretary of the navy in 1913, a position he held until 1921, including serving on the Committee for Public Information. After this, he returned to running his newspaper. He also served as U.S. ambassador to Mexico from 1933 to 1941. He died in 1948.[66]

D. Modern Applicability

This act continues to be modernly relevant, right into current news headlines. In the last few years, those who have disclosed information have become subject to the Espionage Act. Eight individuals have been charged under the act by the U.S. administration of President Barack Obama since 2009, for wide-ranging disclosures of national security information. Bradley Manning was among these, having disclosed national defense information that was published on WikiLeaks and being convicted in 2013 of six counts of violating the Espionage Act (but not on the charge that releasing the information publicly was aiding the enemy). More recently, Edward Snowden disclosed certain surveillance activities of the National Security Agency and was charged with unauthorized communication of national defense information (in violation of 18 U.S.C. 793(d)) and willful communication of classified communications intelligence information to an unauthorized person (in violation of 18 U.S.C. 798(a)(3)).[67]

---

66. *See Josephus Daniels Dies at Age of 85*, N.Y. TIMES (Jan. 16, 1948).
67. United States v. Edward J. Snowden, Criminal Complaint, June 14, 2013.

5.2 SEDITION / ANARCHISTS / ENEMY ALIENS

A. Statutes

The U.S. government was concerned not only about espionage but about other activities that were contrary to the war effort, national security, and public morale. There were three different pieces of legislation passed removing dissent: targeting those wanting to disparage and resist the government, those who believed in violent overthrow of the government or no government at all, and those who were possibly loyal to a different government. Those targeting the war effort and resisting the U.S. government were addressed by the Sedition Act. Anarchist aliens trying to overthrow the U.S. government were addressed by the Immigration Act of 1918. Enemy aliens who might be aiding their native country through word and action were addressed through existing laws and new presidential proclamations and regulations.

1. Sedition Act

This statute,[68] passed in May 1918, was a revision to the Espionage Act of the previous year. It modified section 3 of Title I and section 4 of Title XII. The Title I change included adding a prohibition on obstructing U.S. bond sales while the United States was at war, as well as language against any who might "willfully utter, print, write or publish any disloyal, profane, scurrilous, or abusive language about the form of government of the United States," the Constitution, military or naval forces, flag, or army or navy uniforms or language "intended to bring [these] . . . into contempt, scorn, contumely, or disrepute, or shall willfully utter, print, write, or publish any language intended to incite, provoke, or encourage resistance to the United States or promote the cause of its enemies."[69] This included displaying the enemies' flags, advocating curtailing production of war materials or advocating, teaching, or defending any of these things. The Title XII change had the postmaster add the words "mail to

---

68. Pub. L. No. 65-150 An Act to amend section three, title one, of the Act entitled "An Act to punish acts of interference with the foreign relations, the neutrality, and the foreign commerce of the United States, to punish espionage, and better to enforce the criminal laws of the United States, and for other purposes," approved June fifteenth, nineteen hundred and seventeen, and for other purposes (1918).
69. *Id.* § 1.

this address undeliverable under the Espionage Act" to mailings that were in violation of the act and were thus returned to the sender.[70]

2. Immigration Act

To deal with alien anarchists, the Immigration Act of 1918 was passed in October 1918.[71] It excluded from admission into the United States aliens who were anarchists, believed in or advocated forceful or violent overthrow of the U.S. government, advocated or taught the assassination of public officials, unlawful destruction of property, or all forms of law or opposition to all forms of government or were members in groups holding, teaching, or advocating such beliefs.[72] Any alien who was or thereafter fell into one of these classes was subject to being deported.[73] An attempt to further enter the country after deportation was considered a felony and would lead to arrest and imprisonment.[74]

3. Enemy Aliens

The day that Congress declared war, under existing law,[75] President Wilson proclaimed that as war now existed between the United States and Germany, rules regarding enemy aliens within the United States needed to be established.[76] In his role as commander-in-chief and under statutory authority,[77] he directed that enemy aliens (nonnaturalized German males from the age of fourteen upwards) were liable to be "apprehended, restrained, secured, and removed as alien enemies." He added that "All alien enemies are enjoined to preserve the peace towards the United States and to refrain from crime against the public safety, and from violating the laws of the United States and of the States and Territories thereof, and to refrain from actual hostility or giving information, aid or comfort to the enemies of the United States."[78] This included strictly complying with regulations that the president would promulgate.

---

70. *Id.* § 2.
71. Pub. L. No. 65-221 An Act to exclude and expel from the United States aliens who are members of the anarchistic and similar classes (1918).
72. *Id.* § 1.
73. *Id.* § 2.
74. *Id.* § 3.
75. U.S.C. § 4067.
76. Pub. Proclamation No. 1364, Declaring That a State of War Exists Between the United States and Germany (Apr. 6, 1917).
77. U.S.C. § 4068-70.
78. Pub. Proclamation No. 1364.

He then said that those who obeyed the law could peacefully continue their lives but that those who did not would be liable for restraint or deportation. He then issued the following regulations:

- Enemy aliens were not allowed to possess weapons or explosives.
- Enemy aliens were not allowed to use or operate any aircraft, wireless apparatus, signalling device, cipher code, or documents in cipher or invisible writing.
- Enemy aliens could not approach a fort, camp, arsenal, aircraft station, government or naval vessel, navy yard, or factory producing munitions or army or navy goods.
- Enemy aliens were not to write or publish attacks or threats against any government entity, measures or policies, or against the person or property of persons in the U.S. armed forces or civil service.
- Enemy aliens were not to commit or abet any hostile acts against the United States, or give information, aid, or comfort to its enemies.
- Enemy aliens were not to reside in any prohibited area.
- Enemy aliens were to register, and those who violated these regulations could be interned, deported, or arrested and tried and have offending items seized.

In November of 1917 the president issued another proclamation,[79] listing additional prohibited places, such as canals, wharves, warehouses, elevators, railroad depots or yards, or being on the water within three miles of a shoreline, except on a public ferry. Flying of airplanes, balloons, or flying ships was not permitted, nor was entry into the District of Columbia or the Panama Canal. All enemy aliens needed to register and carry registration cards and neither change their residence or occupation nor travel without complying with these regulations. These regulations were extended in April 1918 to include women,[80] which because they had now become enemies, included both Austro-Hungarian and German native females over fourteen.[81] It was

---

79. Pub. Proclamation, Prescribing Additional Regulations for Enemy Aliens (Nov. 16, 1917).
80. Pub. L. No. 65-131, An Act to amend section four thousand and sixty-seven of the Revised Statutes by extending its scope to include women (1918).
81. Pub. Proclamation, Extending Regulations Prescribing the Conduct of Alien Enemies to Include Women (Apr. 19, 1918).

made a crime to enlist in the military or navy of a foreign state, unless that state was also at war along with the United States, against a common enemy.[82]

LEGAL PROFILES

Kenneth Douglas McKellar was senator co-sponsoring the Sedition Act. He was born in Alabama in 1869 but started his legal practice in Tennessee in 1892. He was first elected to Congress in 1911, serving until 1917. In 1916 he was elected to the Senate, where he served until 1953. After losing the 1952 election, he retired. He died in 1957.[83]

William Paul Dillingham was senator co-sponsoring the Immigration Act of 1918. He was born in Vermont in 1843 and started his legal practice there in 1867. He was a county prosecutor from 1872 to 1876. From that year he held a variety of state roles, including being elected to the state house of representatives in 1876 and 1884, to the state senate in 1878 and 1880, as the state tax commissioner from 1882 to 1888, and as governor in 1888. He was first elected to the U.S. Senate in 1900 and served there until his death in 1923.[84]

B. Cases

The actions of government officials under these acts led to the deportations of anarchists under the Immigration Act. Emma Goldman (previously convicted of obstructing the draft)[85] and 248 of her fellow anarchists were deported back to Russia, and anarchist and bomber Luigi Galleani was deported back to Italy. The Bureau of Investigation's Enemy Alien Registration Section in the Justice Department was responsible for identifying, interviewing, and, as need be, arresting and detaining German nationals under the proclamation of

---

82. Pub. L. No. 65-10 An Act to amend section ten of chapter two of the Criminal Code (1917).
83. *See McKellar, Kenneth Douglas*, BIOGRAPHICAL DIRECTORY OF THE UNITED STATES CONGRESS.
84. *See Dillingham, William Paul*, BIOGRAPHICAL DIRECTORY OF THE UNITED STATES CONGRESS.
85. Goldman v. United States, 245 U.S. 474 (1918).

the president. In total, several thousand Germans were placed into internment camps but were released at the end of the war.

The principal case decided under the Sedition Act was the Supreme Court case of *Abrams*.[86] In this case, five defendants, all Russian nationals living in the United States and self-described anarchists or Socialists, were charged under the Sedition Act with publishing 5,000 illegal circulars. The four counts were to conspire during wartime to write and publish "disloyal, scurrilous and abusive language about the form of Government of the United States," language "intended to bring the form of Government of the United States into contempt, scorn, contumely and disrepute," language "intended to incite, provoke and encourage resistance to the United States in said war," and to "urge, incite and advocate curtailment of production of things and products, to wit, ordnance and ammunition, necessary and essential to the prosecution of the war."

The two circulars, one in English and one in Yiddish, urged workers in munitions plants to stop working and others not to buy government bonds. It called for a labor strike, all intending to assist the revolution in Russia but also to defeat the war effort in the United States. The Court affirmed the convictions, stating that the wording in the circulars showed that, "while the immediate occasion for this particular outbreak of lawlessness, on the part of the defendant alien anarchists, may have been resentment caused by our Government sending troops into Russia as a strategic operation against the Germans on the eastern battle front, yet the plain purpose of their propaganda was to excite, at the supreme crisis of the war, disaffection, sedition, riots, and, as they hoped, revolution, in this country for the purpose of embarrassing and if possible defeating the military plans of the Government in Europe."

Justice Holmes (and Justice Brandeis) dissented. Justice Holmes, as had the Court in its opinion, focused on the third and especially the fourth counts, which he said required intent "to cripple or hinder the United States in the prosecution of the war."[87] He did not feel this had been proved, as the act could only be done with the intent to produce the result if "the aim to produce it is the proximate motive of the specific act, although there may be some deeper motive behind."[88]

---

86. Abrams v. United States, 250 U.S. 616 (1919).
87. *Id.* at 626.
88. *Id.* at 627.

But his real objection was related to the First Amendment, which he said could only be restricted, even in wartime, with "the present danger of immediate evil or an intent to bring it about." Stating that "nobody can suppose that the surreptitious publishing of a silly leaflet by an unknown man, without more, would present any immediate danger that its opinions would hinder the success of the government arms or have any appreciable tendency to do so,"[89] he could foresee assistance being had to Russia without affecting the war effort of the United States. Then "the ultimate good desired is better reached by free trade in ideas—that the best test of truth is the power of the thought to get itself accepted in the competition of the market, and that truth is the only ground upon which their wishes safely can be carried out. . . . I think that we should be eternally vigilant against attempts to check the expression of opinions that we loathe."[90]

LEGAL PROFILES

J. Edgar Hoover was the Bureau of Investigation official responsible for monitoring enemy aliens during the war and getting anarchists like Emma Goldman deported. He was born in Washington, DC, in 1895 and after getting his law degree in 1917 he joined the Justice Department's Bureau of Investigation, where he oversaw enemy aliens during war. After the war, he headed the General Intelligence Division, then in 1921 was the deputy director of the bureau and in 1924 was named the director. In 1935 the organization became the Federal Bureau of Investigation (FBI), where Hoover was named first director. With its expanded powers and his leadership there, his outsized influence on American political life and domestic security continued until his death in 1972.[91]

John William Abercrombie was acting secretary of labor who signed Emma Goldman's deportation order. He was born in Alabama in 1866

---

89. *Id.* at 628.
90. *Id.* at 630.
91. *See John Edgar Hoover*, FEDERAL BUREAU OF INVESTIGATION HISTORY.

and started his legal practice there in 1888. From 1896 to 1898 he served in the state senate and then until 1902 as Alabama's state superintendent of education. From 1902 until 1911 he was president of the University of Alabama. In 1912 he was elected to Congress, where he served for two terms. From 1918 to 1920 he was the solicitor and acting secretary of labor. From 1920 to 1927 he served as the superintendent of education in Alabama. He died in 1940.[92]

C. Subsequent Events

The Sedition Act was repealed after the war, enemy aliens were disinterred and repatriated, and the immigration law was revised a number of times. One of the outgrowths of these cases under the Espionage and Sedition Acts was summarized the following year by a Harvard University professor who had corresponded about their respective opinions with Holmes, Hand, and Brandeis. Zechariah Chafee's seminal 1920 treatise *Freedom of Speech* laid the groundwork for many of the subsequent decisions on First Amendment expression rights, leading up to the Supreme Court's 1969 *Brandenburg* decision.[93] Before that decision, new sedition and immigration laws were to play a large role in WWII, as the government once again put on trial Socialists, Communists, and anarchists for their anti-government expressions.[94]

LEGAL PROFILES

Zechariah Chafee Jr. was a law professor who wrote the seminal paper on freedom of speech in 1920. He was born in Rhode Island in 1885 and started his legal practice in Massachusetts in 1913. In 1916 he started teaching law at Harvard University, where he remained until 1956. He worked on the Wickersham Commission from 1929, drafted the federal

---

92. *See Abercrombie, John William*, Biographical Directory of the United States Congress
93. Brandenburg v. Ohio, 395 U.S. 444 (1969).
94. *See* WWII Law and Lawyers, ch. 2.

interpleader statute in 1936, and worked on apportioning seats in Congress based on the ten-year census results from 1930, 1940, and 1950. He was involved as amicus curiae with the leading free expression case[95] during WWII.[96] He died in 1957.[97]

5.3 SUPPLYING THE WAR EFFORT

A. Statutes

As critical as any other activity in the war was maintaining the U.S. economy effectively and efficiently. This was no easy feat, as the vast demands of the military created shortages in all the inputs to production: raw materials, labor, capital, fuel, and transportation. This put upward pressure on prices and a downward trend on the availability of products for the civilian consumers. The shortage of labor in turn provided opportunities for the nascent labor movement. It also gave those who ran nationally vital industries, like the railroads or the fuel suppliers, a chance to utilize their monopolistic powers. To address all of these competing interests while ensuring success for military production and consumer availability and pricing, a blizzard of different statutes, executive orders, and regulations were issued and government oversight bodies created.

1. Railroads

The defense appropriations act of August 1916[98] had a clause included that stated, "The President, in time of war, is empowered, though the Secretary of War, to take possession and assume control of any system or systems of transportation, or any part thereof, and to utilize the same, to the exclusion as far as may be necessary of all other traffic thereon, for the transfer or transportation of troops, war material and equipment, or for such other purposes connected

---

95. W. Va, State Bd. of Educ. v. Barnette, 319 U.S. 624 (1943).
96. *See* WWII LAW AND LAWYERS, ch. 4.
97. *See Zechariah Chafee Jr., 71, Dead; Lawyer, Civil Liberties Champion,* N.Y. TIMES (Feb. 9, 1957).
98. Pub. L. No. 64-242, An Act making appropriations for the support of the Army for the fiscal year ending June thirtieth, nineteen hundred and seventeen, and for other purposes (1916).

with the emergency as may be needful or desirable.[99] Despite voluntary efforts of many of the railroads to organize themselves cooperatively for the war, more was needed to support the war effort. Using this statutory authority, President Wilson, after conferring with the Interstate Commerce Commission (ICC), issued a proclamation in late December 1917 taking control of the railroads within the continental United States.[100]

This proclamation specified that it was necessary to take possession and control of the railroads (and their water-related systems but not street electric passenger railways and subways) on December 28, 1917, perhaps excluding nonwar traffic to the preference of transporting troops, war material and equipment, and anything else necessary for the war efforts. This was to include "terminals, terminal companies and terminal associations, sleeping and parlor cars, private cars and private car lines, elevators, warehouses, telegraph and telephone lines and all other equipment and appurtenances commonly used upon or operated as a part of such rail or combined rail and water systems of transportation."

The president appointed the first director general of the railroads, William McAdoo, who was to operate the railroads, at least at the start, through the employees of the railroads already working there. The director general was to enter agreements with the railroads for "just and reasonable compensation" for their use and control that was equivalent to the operating income for the railroads over the last three years, without impacting stock or bondholders or creditors as to payments of dividends and interest. Attachments of the common carriers' property could not be levied, but lawsuits could still be maintained.

President Wilson explained his decision to Congress (the takeover had occurred during a Congressional absence), saying it was "necessary to do to secure the complete mobilization of the whole resources of America by as rapid and effective means as can be found. Transportation supplies all the arteries of, mobilization. Unless it be under a single and unified direction, the whole process of the nation's action is embarrassed . . . only under government administration can the entire equipment of the several systems of transportation be fully and unreservedly thrown into a common service without

---

99. *Id.* § 1.
100. Pub. Proclamation No. 1419, Government Assumption of Control of Transportation Systems (Dec. 26, 1917).

injurious discrimination against particular properties. Only under government administration can an absolutely unrestricted and unembarrassed common use be made of all tracks, terminals, terminal facilities and equipment of every kind. Only under that authority can new terminals be constructed and developed without regard to the requirements or limitations of particular roads."[101]

In March 1918, Congress passed the Railroad Control Act to give further support to the actions of the president.[102] The statute specified that the president was authorized to agree with the railroads on just compensation, not to exceed the past three-year average operating income of the railroad, and excess returns were to be retained by the government, while making allowances for reserves to keep the railroads' property in good repair.[103] Competing connecting railroads not under government controls were also entitled to the benefits of the act. Only 90 percent of the three-year operating income was to be paid to railroads with whom no agreement could be reached.[104] Disputes on just compensation were to go to a board appointed by the ICC and then to the court of claims.[105] Control was to last during the period of the war and "for a reasonable time" thereafter.[106]

LEGAL PROFILES

Walker D. Hines was the assistant director general of railroads. He was born in Kentucky in 1870 and started his legal practice there. He worked for the Louisville and Nashville railroad from 1893 to 1903. After private practice, he became general counsel and eventually chairman of the Santa Fe railroad for over a decade (1906 to 1918). He then moved to a New York law firm and later returned to work for the railroads. When the Railroad Administration was created, he was appointed as the

---

101. Woodrow Wilson, Address to a Joint Session of Congress on Government Administration of Railways (Jan. 4, 1918).
102. Pub. L. No. 65-107, An Act to provide for the operation of transportation systems while under Federal control, for the just compensation of their owners, and for other purposes (1918).
103. *Id.* § 1.
104. *Id.* § 2.
105. *Id.* § 3.
106. *Id.* § 14.

assistant director general. In 1919 he became the director general. After the war, he first was appointed to arbitrate shipping disputes on rivers in Europe. He then returned to the United States to work for railroads and law firms specializing in railroad law. He died in 1934.[107]

2. War Industries Board

The Council of National Defense was established in 1916 to coordinate "industries and resources for the national security and welfare" and was to be composed of the secretaries of war, navy, interior, agriculture, commerce, and labor.[108] It was also to have an advisory commission of specialists in industry, resources, or public utilities. It had seven committees: transportation and communications; raw materials; munitions, manufacturing and industrial relations; supplies; engineering and education; labor; and medicine. Several sub-organizations were created, including the Munitions Standards Board (March 1917), for generating standards for the manufacturing of munitions, and the General Munitions Board (March–July 1917), for coordinating munitions purchases, assisting in acquiring raw materials and manufacturing facilities, and establishing order priorities. These were in turn subsumed, on July 28, 1917, by the creation of the War Industries Board (WIB).

This board had commissioners heading up raw material, finished products, labor, and production and delivery priorities. Unlike the Railroad Administration, the Food Administration, the Fuel Administration, the War Trade Board, and the Shipping Board,[109] which were established by acts of Congress, the WIB had remained part of a Council of National Defense, an advisory body, which meant that its price-fixing regulations for commodities and its production and delivery priority rules were also advisory. On May 28, 1918, the WIB became by executive order an independent agency (based on the Overman

---

107. See Walker D. Hines is Dead in Italy, N.Y. TIMES (Oct. 30, 1911).
108. Pub. L. No. 64-242, An Act making appropriations for the support of the Army for the fiscal year ending June thirtieth, nineteen hundred and seventeen, and for other purposes (1916), § 2.
109. Pub. L. No. 64-260, An Act to establish a United States Shipping Board for the purpose of encouraging, developing, and creating a naval auxiliary and naval reserve and a merchant marine to meet the requirements of the commerce of the United States with its Territories and possessions and with foreign countries; to regulate carriers by water engaged in the foreign and interstate commerce of the United States; and for other purposes (1916).

Act passed the previous week,[110] which allowed the president the wartime authority to reorganize executive agencies as necessary), referring to a letter sent by the president on March 4, 1918, asking board member Bernard Baruch to take over the role of chairman of the WIB. It was not directly authorized by Congress.

Two of the most important functions of the WIB were setting production and delivery priorities and setting prices for war-related materials. Strictly, Congress had not explicitly granted either of these powers, but there were a large number of incentives and voluntary cooperation that made it work, sitting on top of the president's already significant war powers. Among the incentives were the priorities provided to the industry, which actually benefitted them, and as the government-controlled railroads and the regulated fuel industry (see below) were earlier in the production cycle, it made sense for iron and steel producers, for example, to fall into line with these priorities. Price controls, although agreed to voluntarily, got some of their acceptance from the ability of the administration to take over any war-related plants and their outputs or a firm's goods and pay only what it determined to be "just" compensation. And lack of cooperation with WIB's price-fixing committee could lead to a less-than-enthusiastic response from the raw materials deliveries scheduled by the WIB's priorities division.

LEGAL PROFILES

Robert S. Lovett was the first priorities commissioner on the War Industries Board. He was born in Texas in 1860 and started his legal practice there in 1882. He worked as general counsel and president of railroads, including the Southern Pacific, from 1884. In 1904 he began working for the Union Pacific. He was chosen for the WIB priorities position in 1917, then worked for the Railroad Administration in 1918. He was succeeded in his priorities role by Edwin B. Parker (see Chapter

---

110. Pub. L. No. 65-152, An Act authorizing the President to coordinate or consolidate executive bureaus, agencies, and offices, and for other purposes, in the interest of economy and the more efficient concentration of the Government (1918).

2). After the war he returned to the railroad industry, becoming chairman of the Union Pacific. He died in 1932.[111]

Albert C. Ritchie was the general counsel of the War Industries Board. He was born in Virginia in 1876, the son of a judge, but started his legal practice in Maryland. From 1903 he was appointed assistant solicitor for the city of Baltimore. From 1907 he started teaching at law school. In 1910 he worked as assistant general counsel for the state public service commission. He was then the attorney general for the state of Maryland from 1915 to 1919. He took a leave to serve as general counsel at WIB. He was elected governor of Maryland in 1920. He served four terms, until 1934, when he lost a bid for a fifth term. He had tried for the Democratic nomination for president in 1932. He died in 1936.[112]

3. Food and Fuel

Besides the commodities feeding into the war materials production, the sources of energy—fuel and food—for those machines and for the people running them and fighting the war were the other key resources. To protect, conserve, and encourage further supply, Congress passed the Food and Fuel Control Act in August 1917[113] (a.k.a. the Lever Act). The goal was "to assure an adequate supply and equitable distribution, and to facilitate the movement, of foods, feeds, fuel including fuel oil and natural gas, and fertilizer and fertilizer ingredients, tools, utensils, implements, machinery, and equipment required for the actual production of foods, feeds, and fuel, ('necessaries'); to prevent, locally or generally, scarcity, monopolization, hoarding, injurious speculation, manipulations, and private controls, affecting such supply, distribution, and movement; and to establish and maintain governmental control of such necessaries during the war."[114]

---

111. See *R.S. Lovett Dead; Union Pacific Head*, N.Y. TIMES (June 20, 1932).
112. See *Ex-Governor Ritchie is Dead*, N.Y. TIMES (Feb. 24, 1936).
113. Pub. L. No. 65-41, An Act to provide further for the national security and defense by encouraging the production, conserving the supply, and controlling the distribution of food products and fuel (1917).
114. *Id.* § 1.

It was unlawful to destroy necessaries in order to increase the price or restrict the supply; to commit waste or preventable deterioration of necessaries during production, manufacture, or distribution; to hoard or monopolize necessaries; to engage in discriminatory, unfair, deceptive or wasteful practices or charge unjust or unreasonable rates for necessaries; to conspire to limit transporting, producing, harvesting, manufacturing, supplying, and storing facilities of necessaries; to restrict the supply or distribution of necessaries, to limit the manufacture or production of necessaries to increase the price, or to exact excessive prices for necessaries; or to aid or abet any of these acts.[115]

The president was authorized to take over necessaries as required for the armed forces and public use while paying a just compensation;[116] to buy wheat, flour, meal, beans, and potatoes;[117] and to take over and operate factories, packing houses, oil pipelines, mines or other plants involved in the production of necessaries while paying a just compensation.[118] Additionally, the "evil practices" of financial speculation of necessaries were to be banned or regulated;[119] the use of "foods, fruits, food materials, or feeds" in the distillation of alcoholic beverages was forbidden;[120] and the president could set prices for and take over and operate businesses and mines dealing with coal and coke.[121] The act was only to last while the war was engaged.

Subsequently, the president appointed food[122] and fuel administrators[123] and also created the Food Administration Grain Corporation (U.S. Grain Corporation)[124] and the U.S. Sugar Equalization Board, Inc., to buy and sell wheat and sugar. The Food Administration was to address, among other things, the supply, distribution, and conservation of food by voluntary agreements, licensing, and buying and selling food. Many well-known supply and conservation ideas came from this agency, including "victory gardens" with the slogans "Sow the seeds of Victory!" and "It's Thrifty! It's Patriotic!"; food-conservation

---

115. *Id.* § 4.
116. *Id.* § 10.
117. *Id.* § 11.
118. *Id.* § 12.
119. *Id.* § 13.
120. *Id.* § 15.
121. *Id.* § 25.
122. Exec. Order No. 2679-A, Appointment of Food Administrator (Aug. 10, 1917).
123. Exec. Order No. 2690, Appointment of Fuel Administrator (Aug. 23, 1917).
124. Exec. Order No. 2681, Authority to Organize Food Administration Grain Corporation (Aug. 14, 1917).

days such as "wheatless Mondays," "meatless Tuesdays," and "sweetless Saturdays"; and posters encouraging conservation, such as "Food Will Win the War" (waste nothing), "Be Patriotic" (save the food), and "Eat More (corn, oats, and rye), Eat Less (wheat, meat, and sugar)." The Fuel Administration had a similar purview in fuel and took up similar slogans, such as for "heatless Mondays" and "gasless Sundays," and daylight savings time was initiated to save fuel.[125]

LEGAL PROFILES

Asbury F. Lever was the sponsor of this act. He was born in South Carolina in 1875 and started his legal practice in 1899. He was first elected to the state legislature in 1900 but resigned to be elected to the U.S. Congress in 1901, where he served until 1919. Besides the Lever Act, he also sponsored the Smith-Lever Farm Act and other agricultural laws. During the war he was chairman of the House agricultural committee. He then resigned from Congress to take a position with the Federal Farm Loan Board until 1922. He later worked for the Farm Credit Administration. He died in 1940.[126]

Harry Augustus Garfield was the fuel administrator. He was born in Ohio in 1863, the son of future U.S. president James A. Garfield, and started his legal practice there in 1888. He taught contract law from 1891 to 1897 and then taught politics at Princeton University from 1903 to 1908. In 1908 he taught law and became president of Williams College. He was involved in the reorganization of the consular services. During the war, he was a member of the WIB price-fixing committee and chairman of the Food Administration's price-fixing committee before being named as fuel administrator. He returned to the college after the war. He died in 1942.[127]

---

125. Pub. L. No. 65-206, An Act to save daylight and provide standard time in the United States (1918).
126. *See Lever, Asbury Francis*, BIOGRAPHICAL DIRECTORY OF THE UNITED STATES CONGRESS.
127. *See H.A. Garfield Dies; Williams Ex-Head*, N.Y. TIMES (Dec. 13, 1942).

4. Labor

The American labor movement agreed early to support the war effort by avoiding strikes, and as such there were few significant labor issues that arose during the war. This strategy worked well, with organized labor adding significantly to the members during the war. Cooperation was the key to this success, and to ensure that result, several federal organizations were created through the Department of Labor and its secretary, who was named the war labor administrator. These included the National War Labor Board (NWLB), created in March–April 1918, and the War Labor Policies Board (WLPB), which was created in May 1918.

The secretary of labor created the War Labor Policies Board, which included representatives from the departments of labor, agriculture, navy, and war, the boards of war industries and shipping, the public information committee, and the administrations of railroad, food, and fuel to promulgate appropriate labor policies. Its purpose was to determine solutions for war industries (implemented through the board constituents) and for nonwar industries (implemented through the WIB), for the distribution of labor, wages, hours, and working conditions, and for housing, transportation, and employee turnover.

The NWLB was created by the secretary of labor in late March 1918 on recommendation of the War Labor Conference Board (WLCB) and by presidential proclamation[128] in April, to be co-chaired by former president William Howard Taft (see Chapter 1). It included two public members leading the board, five representatives of labor, and five others from industries, such as manufacturing and transportation, vital to the war effort (the same twelve members as the WLCB). Umpires were appointed to deal with the actual disputes. The NWLB was to follow principles laid down by the WLCB, including no strikes or lockouts during the war, the right to organize, equal pay for women, eight-hour workdays, maximum production, and a living wage.[129] It was to keep labor peace by adjusting labor disputes in a manner acceptable to both employees and employers. As with the WIB, it did not have explicit powers of legal enforcement for its decisions, but the war powers of the president, the pressure not to impact military and naval procurement, and the cooperative

---

128. Pub. Proclamation, Creating the National War Labor Board (Apr. 8, 1918).
129. War Labor Conference Board, Principles and Policies to Govern Relations between Workers and Employers in War Industries for the Duration of the War (Mar. 29, 1918).

nature of jointly submitted disputes all ensured that its decisions were, on the whole, obeyed.

The president, while urging that there be "no discontinuance of industrial operations which would result in curtailment of the production of war necessities," proclaimed the NWLB's specific charter to:

> settle by mediation and conciliation controversies arising between employers and workers in fields of production necessary for the effective conduct of the war, or in other fields of national activity, delays and obstructions in which might, in the opinion of the national board, affect detrimentally such production; to provide, by direct appointment or otherwise, for committees or boards to sit in various parts of the country where controversies arise and secure settlement by local mediation and conciliation; and to summon the parties to controversies for hearing and action by the national board in event of failure to secure settlement by mediation and conciliation.

LEGAL PROFILES

Frank P. Walsh was the co-chairman of the NWLB. He was in Missouri in 1864 and started his legal practice there in 1889. He was named in 1913 by President Wilson to head the Commission on Industrial Relations, which he ran through 1918 and produced several reports investigating the conditions of labor throughout the country. He then co-led the NWLB. After the war he continued to be involved in the labor movement. He was chairman of the New York Power Authority from 1931. He died in 1939.[130]

Felix Frankfurter was the chairman of the WLPB and was assistant labor administrator during the war. He was born in Austria in 1882 but moved to New York as a teenager, starting his legal practice there in

---

130. See *Frank Walsh Dies; Lawyer for Labor*, N.Y. TIMES (May 3, 1939).

1906. He was an assistant U.S. attorney from 1906 to 1909. In 1911 he joined the Bureau of Insular Affairs, remaining there until 1914. In 1914 he joined the faculty at Harvard Law School, where he would remain until 1939, except for his war service. For his service he took a leave in 1917 and first joined the JAG Corps, was counsel to the president's Mediation Committee on resolving strikes, and represented labor on the WIB priorities boards. He returned to teaching after the war. In 1939 he was nominated by President Roosevelt for the U.S. Supreme Court. He served on the court until 1962 before resigning. He died in 1965.[131]

B. Cases

In addition to cases under those agencies, like the NWLB, that operated in a quasi-judicial role, each of these agencies regulating an area of supply to the wartime economy had cases that reached the Supreme Court. The first case concerned a state utility commission's rate-setting power vs. the Railroad Administration. The second case involved the legal responsibility of railroads and the Railroad Administration for compensation and penalties. The third case covered whether price-fixing changes could be used for previous commitments. The fourth case involved the setting of market rates for commodities. The fifth case discussed reasonable rates for food. The sixth case was whether fuel should use domestic or export rates in setting just compensation. The seventh case showed the impact of an NWLB decision.

1. Railroad Administration—Rates

In *Northern Pacific*,[132] the state of North Dakota had resisted an order by the director general of railroads in May 1918 setting federal railroad rates, wanting instead to utilize rates set by the state utilities commission for intrastate traffic. It acquired a court order requiring the director general to pay the state's rate levels, calling attention to section 15 of the act about not disturbing existing state law. The Supreme Court instead focused on section 10 of the act, which provided for the director general, acting for the president, to set rates, as "That

---

131. *See Frankfurter, Felix*, FED. JUDICIAL CTR., BIOGRAPHICAL DIRECTORY OF FEDERAL JUDGES.
132. N. Pac. R. Co. v. N. D. ex rel. Langer, 250 U.S. 135 (1919).

during the period of Federal control, whenever in his opinion the public interest requires, the President may initiate rates, fares, charges, classifications, regulations, and practices."[133]

Regarding the state's having the ability to retain control over rates in the face of this statutory declaration, the Court said, "although authority to regulate within a given sphere may exist in both the United States and in the States, when the former calls into play constitutional authority . . . to the extent that any conflict arises the state power is limited."[134] Noting also the "complete and undivided character of the war power of the United States,"[135] the Court held that the lower court's ruling was erroneous and so reversed.

LEGAL PROFILES

John Barton Payne was counsel for the director general of railroads. He was born in West Virginia in 1855 and started his legal practice there in 1876. He was a special judge and was elected mayor. He moved in 1883 to Chicago and was elected as a superior court judge in 1893, serving in that role until 1898. He turned down an offer of being U.S. solicitor general in 1913, but during the war he was appointed counsel to both the Railroad Administration and the Emergency Fleet Corporation under the U.S. Shipping Board. After the war, he was appointed chairman of the U.S. Shipping Board. He also was the U.S. secretary of the interior from 1920 to 1921. In that year, he became chairman of the American Red Cross, where he served until his death in 1935.[136]

---

133. *Id.* at 148.
134. *Id.* at 151.
135. *Id.* at 149.
136. *See John B. Payne Dies in Washington*, 79, N.Y. TIMES (Jan. 24, 1935).

2. Railroad Administration—Penalties

In *Ault*,[137] a railroad employee was discharged in July 1918 but did not receive all of his wages and so, under Arkansas law, was due an additional penalty amount. In subsequent litigation, the railroad claimed that it was not liable for the separation wages or the penalty imposed by the court, as the Railroad Administration now controlled the railroad. The Court said that railroads, until the act, were operated and managed by the director general, not through supervising the railroad companies, but with the officers acting as agents of the federal government. It was alleged that the railroad company here could be sued because under section 10 of the act "carriers while under Federal control shall be subject to all laws and liabilities as common carriers," but the Court interpreted that as meaning the transportation systems themselves that were taken over and not the railroad companies.[138] As the railroad companies were no longer operating the transportation systems, it dismissed the claim against this railroad company.

The director general, however, was operating the transportation systems and was liable for the wages of the dismissed employee, which the government freely admitted. What the government did not agree to was that a penalty could be imposed on it. The plaintiff had argued that, under section 10 and also section 15 of the act, the regulations of the states should continue unimpaired, so the Arkansas penalty should apply. But the Court ruled that the government had allowed itself to be sued "for compensation but not punishment."[139] Even though a lower court had characterized the penalty as compensation for delay, the Court disagreed, stating that "the element of punishment clearly predominates and Congress has not given its consent that suits of this character be brought against the United States."[140] It dismissed the penalty against the director general of railroads as erroneous.

3. War Industries Board—Price Changes

In *American Smelting*,[141] the plaintiff had agreed in April 1918 to sell copper to the government at a price of 23.5 cents/pound, which was the rate fixed by

---

137. Mo. Pac. R. Co. v. Ault, 256 U.S. 554 (1921).
138. *Id.* at 558.
139. *Id.* at 564.
140. *Id.* at 565.
141. Am. Smelting and Refining Co. v. United States, 259 U.S. 75 (1922).

WIB's price-fixing committee. Delivery of about one-third of the order was delayed until after the stipulated delivery date of June 1, 1918. On July 2, the rate paid for copper was increased by WIB to 26 cents/pound. The plaintiff sought to receive these additional amounts for the copper delivered after that date. The Court ruled that, far from being a taking under the Fifth Amendment, the company had voluntarily agreed to sell its copper and that, while the government's not sending a shipping order may have been one of the reasons for the delayed performance, the plaintiff was still entitled only to the rate stipulated at the time it entered into the agreement with the government.

4. War Industries Board—Market Rates

In *Vogelstein*,[142] copper rates were again the focus, but here, the claimant was alleging that the just compensation that the United States promised to pay was other than the market price set by the WIB. The copper producers took orders from the army and navy through their United Metals Selling Company, which would then contract with producers. The appellant/claimant instead said the market price was that which it had to pay to fulfill mandatory orders from the government. The appellant argued that the price that it had to pay under long-term contracts to acquire copper (it was not a producer) was a better proxy for market price than that set by the government. The Court disagreed, holding that the price set by WIB was the prevailing market price and so just compensation to the claimant. The Court closed by noting that "The United States is under no obligation to make good the loss. Appellant would be entitled to the gain if it had purchased at less than the market price at the time of taking."[143]

LEGAL PROFILES

Alfred A. Wheat was counsel for the United States in this case. He was born in New Hampshire in 1867 but started his legal practice in New York in 1893. He remained in private practice until 1922, when he started working as a special assistant for the U.S. attorney general and then the solicitor general, until 1929. In that year, President Hoover

---

142. L. Vogelstein & Co. v. United States, 262 U.S. 337 (1923).
143. *Id.* at 340.

nominated him for a seat on the district court for the District of Columbia, where he served as chief justice from 1930. He served in this position until he retired in 1941. He died in 1943.[144]

5. Food and Fuel Administrations—Reasonable Rates

In *L. Cohen Grocery*,[145] the Supreme Court was reviewing section 4 of the Lever Act. This section made it illegal to set unreasonable rates for necessaries. It was charged in court with setting the following prices for sugar: $10.07 for about 50 lbs. and $19.50 for a 100-pound bag. The Court needed to answer the question of whether the text of section 4—"That it is hereby made unlawful for any person willfully . . . to make any unjust or unreasonable rate or charge in handling or dealing in or with any necessaries"—was sufficient to ascertain when someone had violated it and to inform such people "of the nature and cause of the accusation against them."[146]

Because of a lack of standards and other deficiencies in what and how to measure regarding what constituted a reasonable price for necessaries, the Court agreed with the lower court's wording "because the law is vague, indefinite, and uncertain, and because it fixes no immutable standard of guilt, but leaves such standard to the variant views of the different courts and juries which may be called on to enforce it, and because it does not inform defendant of the nature and cause of the accusation against it"[147] and held that that part of the statute was not constitutional.

LEGAL PROFILES

William D. Guthrie filed an amicus curiae brief in this case. He was born in California in 1859, raised partly in France and England, and started his legal practice in New York in 1880. He was involved in a number of well-known cases, including those involving income tax, inheri-

---

144. *See Wheat, Alfred Adams*, FED. JUDICIAL CTR., BIOGRAPHICAL DIRECTORY OF FEDERAL JUDGES.
145. United States v. L. Cohen Grocery Co., 255 U.S. 81 (1921).
146. *Id.* at 89.
147. *Id.* at 87-88.

tance tax securities, telegraphs, railroads, and Prohibition. He was also involved in many cases based on canonical law. During the war he helped in funding relief work for French war orphans. He taught law at Yale University and Columbia between 1907 and 1922. He died in 1935.[148]

6. Food and Fuel Administrations—Export v. Domestic Prices

In *New River Collieries*,[149] the company had a lucrative market for its coal, more so in the export market than the domestic market. The United States had requisitioned coal from the company for use by the navy. The just compensation set by the government for this requisitioned coal was not acceptable to the company, who accepted 75 percent of that amount and then sued for the balance. The trial court used the spot export prices for coal to determine just compensation, which the government claimed was an error, in addition to the exclusion of considering the market price for domestic coal.

The Court said that the owner was entitled to full compensation for the property, to be "put in as good position pecuniarily as it would have occupied if its property had not been taken."[150] The Court further explained that "Where private property is taken for public use, and there is a market price prevailing at the time and place of the taking, that price is just compensation . . . More would be unjust to the United States and less would deny the owner what he is entitled to."[151] It concluded that the lower courts were correct in using the market price "prevailing at the time and place of the taking" to determine the just compensation[152] and affirmed the lower court's ruling for the claimant.

7. NWLB—Impact of Wage Decisions

In *Columbus Railway*,[153] the Court was dealing with the impact of a ruling by the NWLB. The NWLB made decisions in over a thousand cases, mostly dealing with wages, hours, and working conditions, but here its ruling resulted in a more significant impact. Columbus, Ohio, was a town with 25,000 muni-

---

148. *See W.D. Guthrie Dies Suddenly at 76*, N.Y. Times (Dec. 10, 1935).
149. United States v. New River Collieries Co., 262 U.S. 341 (1923).
150. *Id.* at 343.
151. *Id.* at 344.
152. *Id.* at 345.
153. Columbus Ry., Power & Light Co. v. City of Columbus, Ohio, 249 U.S. 399 (1919).

tions workers plus many others in railroad repair and other necessary war industries. The city railway surrendered its franchise in August 1918, after the NWLB provided its workers with a 50-plus percent increase in wages in late July 1918. This was after the railway determined that it would not only suffer a loss for the next fiscal year, it would not be able to pay interest on its debt. The city had also refused the railway's request to raise ticket prices and insisted it maintain the discount ticket and transfer policies in its franchise agreement. The matter had been referred to the NWLB after a two-day strike in June for higher wages.

The Court considered if there was anything that had happened that would release the railroad company from its franchise agreement. It said that there was no claim of impossibility and that it was not clear that the contract would be unprofitable over its whole twenty-five-year term. Viewing the act of the NWLB as an unforeseen event, the Court said, "Unforeseen difficulties will not excuse performance. Where the parties have made no provision for a dispensation, the terms of the contract must prevail."[154] Noting the "equity does not relieve from hard bargains simply because they are such,"[155] the Court could find no reason in the ruling of the NWLB to relieve the company of its obligations under the franchise agreement.

LEGAL PROFILES

Joseph Sill Clark Sr. was the counsel for the appellant. He was born in Pennsylvania in 1861 and started his legal practice there in 1885. He brought many cases before the Supreme Court and served as counsel to his family's investment firm. Besides law, he was a noted tennis player and served as the president of the U.S. Lawn Tennis Association and member of the tennis hall of fame. His son was the mayor of Philadelphia, a U.S. Senator, and a lawyer. He died in 1956.[156]

---

154. *Id.* at 412.
155. *Id.* at 414.
156. See *Joseph Clark Sr., An Attorney, Dies*, N.Y. TIMES (Apr. 16, 1956).

C. Subsequent Events

The Transportation Act of 1920,[157] also called the Esch-Cummins Act, ended the federal operation of the railroads but simultaneously increased regulatory oversight of the Interstate Commerce Commission by amending the Interstate Commerce Act. It also provided several mechanisms for resolving disputes between the railroads and the government, especially financial ones, and for disputes between the common carriers and their employees. The WIB was decommissioned after the war, but the question of war profiteering went on for much longer, with the 1934 report of the Nye committee (led by Senator Gerald Nye) feeding the neutrality movement in the United States between the wars.[158]

Both the Food Administration and Fuel Administration ended after the war, but the Food and Fuel Control Act was invoked by the attorney general to help break the 1919 railroad and coal strikes. Food Administrator Herbert Hoover was to take on the role of leading the American Relief Administration in Europe after the war to feed the hungry displaced by the conflict. This administration was funded with $100 million by an act of Congress.[159] The NWLB was decommissioned after the war, and its remaining functions were moved to the department of labor. There were numerous postwar labor activities, including the unsuccessful four-month steel strike in 1919. The NWLB was to be restarted again and have a larger role in WWII.[160]

LEGAL PROFILES

John Jacob Esch was one of the co-sponsors of the Transportation Act. He was born in Wisconsin in 1861 and started his legal practice there in

---

157. Pub. L. No. 66-152, An Act to provide for the termination of Federal control of railroads and systems of transportation; to provide for the settlement of disputes between carriers and their employees; to further amend an Act entitle "An Act to regulate commerce," approved Feb. 4, 1887, as amended, and for other purposes (1920).
158. *See* WWII LAW AND LAWYERS, ch. 1.
159. Pub. L. No. 65-274, An Act providing for the relief of such populations in Europe, and countries contiguous thereto, outside of Germany, German-Austria, Hungary, Bulgaria, and Turkey, as may be determined upon by the President as necessary (1919).
160. *See* WWII LAW AND LAWYERS, ch. 3.

1887. He was a judge advocate general from 1894 to 1896. In 1898 he was elected to Congress, where he remained a member of the House until 1921. During the war he chaired the Interstate and Foreign Commerce committee. In 1921 he was appointed to the Interstate Commerce Commission and was elected its chairman from 1927. In 1928 he resigned and returned to private practice. He died in 1941.[161]

5.4 FUNDING THE WAR

A. Statutes

To pay for all of the military buildup and programs described in this chapter, the United States needed to find a new way to fund them. Total expenditures in the year before the start of the war were less than $1 billion. Yet, estimates of the total amounts spent by America for the war exceeded $30 billion. This immense funding gap needed to be made up, and it could only be done by one of three techniques: increasing federal government revenues through taxation, increasing the money supply ("printing money"), or increasing government borrowings (and then hopefully having the power of inflation repay these borrowings in cheaper future dollars).

In 1913 the Sixteenth Amendment, passed by a 1909 joint resolution of Congress, was finally ratified, allowing Congress to directly tax income without apportionment (through the states). The amendment was required due to two Supreme Court decisions in 1895[162] that voided a tax on real estate rents included as part of 1894 tariff legislation. The two rather lengthy opinions from a divided Court held that, while the states and the federal government both had the right to implement direct taxation, considering the history of the conflict with the former king (i.e., no taxation without representation) and the compromises made in arriving at the final text of the Constitution, federal direct taxes had to be apportioned among the states. This meant that the

---

161. *See Esch, John Jacob*, BIOGRAPHICAL DIRECTORY OF THE UNITED STATES CONGRESS.
162. Pollock v. Farmers' Loan & Trust Co., 157 U.S. 429 (1895); Pollock v. Farmers' Loan & Trust Co., 158 U.S. 601 (1895).

federal government taxed the states and that the states would determine how to collect the tax from their citizens. Indirect taxes on citizens, such as excise taxes and import duties, were available to the federal government if uniformly applied, but direct taxes were not.

The Revenue Act of 1916[163] passed in September of that year taxed individuals at a base rate of 2 percent of income after deductions and then added an additional tax in a graduated system from 1 to 13 percent,[164] with the highest rate on net income exceeding $2 million. Corporate tax was 2 percent of net income,[165] while estates were taxed on a graduated scale based on the size of the estate from 1 to 10 percent, with the highest rate applying to estates worth over $5 million.[166] There was also a munitions manufacturer's tax of 12.5 percent of net profits, which was to last until one year after the end of the war.[167] Another act in March 1917[168] added an extra tax of 8 percent on the net income of corporations and partnerships.[169] It also modified the rate schedule for estate taxes over the same graduated estate valuations to be from 1.5 percent to 15 percent.[170]

The War Revenue Act of 1917,[171] passed in October of that year, started to label each tax with the prefix "war." The war income tax was a base rate of 2 percent of income after deductions and an additional tax of from 1 to 50 percent of income, with the highest rate on net income exceeding $1 million.[172] The war excess profits tax on corporations and partnerships started at 20 percent of net income in excess of a special deduction of 7 to 9 percent of invested capital, not to exceed 15 percent of invested capital.[173] This rose up to a top level of 60 percent of net income in excess of 33 percent of invested capi-

---

163. Pub. L. No. 64-271, An Act to increase the revenue, and for other purposes (1916).
164. *Id.* Title I.
165. *Id.*
166. *Id.* Title II.
167. *Id.* Title III.
168. Pub. L. No. 64-377, An Act to provide increased revenue to defray the expenses of the increased appropriations for the Army and Navy and extensions of fortifications, and for other purposes (1917).
169. *Id.* Title II.
170. *Id.* Title III.
171. Pub. L. No. 65-50, An Act to provide revenue to defray war expenses, and for other purposes (1917).
172. *Id.* Title I.
173. *Id.* Title II.

tal. There were war taxes on beverages,[174] cigars, and tobacco,[175] on transportation, insurance, telephone and telegraph messages,[176] and on admissions and dues.[177] There were war excise taxes on the sales of automobiles, player pianos, phonographs, cameras, motion pictures, jewelry, sports equipment, toiletries, medicines, and chewing gum,[178] as well as war stamp taxes.[179] There was also a surtax of 0.5 to 10 percent to be applied to estates.[180]

The Revenue Act of 1918,[181] passed in February 1919, terminated the previous revenue acts.[182] It taxed individuals at 12 percent for the 1918 calendar year and at 8 percent thereafter. A surtax of from 1 to 65 percent was to be charged, with the top rate for incomes over $1 million.[183] Corporations were to be taxed at 12 percent of net income for the 1918 calendar year and at 10 percent thereafter.[184] War profits and excess-profit taxes for the 1918 calendar year were to be in the brackets of 30 percent of net income but not over 20 percent of invested capital, 65 percent on income in excess of 20 percent of invested capital, and 80 percent of income over the limits in the first two brackets, reduced to two brackets—20 and 40 percent—thereafter.[185] Estate tax rates were from 1 to 25 percent, with the top rate on estates worth over $10 million.[186] There were taxes on varying types of transactions, including the sale of certain items over a fixed price, and a tax on the employment of child labor.[187]

The second method of war financing was the increase in the money supply. The Federal Reserve had been created only just before the war by the Federal Reserve Act of 1913,[188] but it facilitated a key method for war financing.

---

174. *Id.* Title III.
175. *Id.* Title IV.
176. *Id.* Title V.
177. *Id.* Title VII.
178. *Id.* Title VI.
179. *Id.* Title VIII.
180. *Id.* Title IX.
181. Pub. L. No. 65-254, An Act to provide revenue, and for other purposes (1918).
182. *Id.* Title XIV.
183. *Id.* Title II, Part II.
184. *Id.* Title II, Part III.
185. *Id.* Title III.
186. *Id.* Title IV.
187. *Id.* Title XII.
188. Pub. L. No. 63-43, An Act to provide for the establishment of Federal reserve banks, to furnish an elastic currency, to afford means of rediscounting commercial paper, to establish a more effective supervision of banking in the United States, and for other purposes (1913).

Through selling government securities or by lowering bank reserve requirements, the Federal Reserve makes more money available to commercial banks, who can then loan this out to other banks (thereby creating more money than was available from the first loan) or to companies and individuals. In WWI, the credit that came from this type of financing operation was around one-fifth of the amounts spent on the war (taxation was also about one-fifth, and debt sales were about three-fifths).[189]

Just prior to the Federal Reserve's becoming fully operational in late 1914, there occurred a crisis when the European belligerents began to liquidate their large holdings of U.S. stocks, especially in the railroads, and convert them into gold to help pay for the cost of the war. In response, the U.S. treasury closed the New York Stock Exchange at the end of July 1914, making it impossible to liquidate these stock shares. It remained closed until mid-December 1914. There was a second crisis in 1914 where the Aldrich-Vreeland Act[190] (also a starting point for the creation of the Federal Reserve by initiating the National Monetary Commission[191]) was utilized. To avoid a run on the banks similar to the Panic of 1907, the treasury allowed the banks to deposit any securities, not just federal government obligations, with the comptroller of the currency, so that the banks could issue new emergency currency to their customers. As the Federal Reserve got up and running, these measures were withdrawn, and significant export sales to the belligerents reversed the need to export gold.

The third method of war financing was the sale of government bonds. Deemed the "Liberty" bonds, these were sold with lots of glitz (by Hollywood stars) and social pressure (to not be the only ones not contributing financially to the war effort). The social pressure was even targeted at children, including Boy and Girl Scouts, with small denomination certificates available for children to purchase from their allowances. The first sale of the bonds was authorized by Congress in April 1917.[192] This first of four sales during the war (one more happened after the war) allowed up to $5 billion of bonds issued at par, at an interest of 3.5 percent, with interest received free of income tax (though

---

189. M. FRIEDMAN & A. SCHWARTZ, *A MONETARY HISTORY OF THE UNITED STATES*, 1867–1960 (1963).
190. Pub. L. No. 60-169, An Act to amend the national banking laws (1908).
191. *Id.* §§ 17-19.
192. Pub. L. No. 65-3, An Act to authorize an issue of bonds to meet expenditures for the national security and defense, and, for the purpose of assisting in the prosecution of the war, to extend credit to foreign governments, and for other purposes (1917).

the principal was not free of estate or inheritance taxes).[193] If subsequent bonds were offered at a higher rate before termination of the war, then this series of bonds could be converted to the higher coupon rate.[194]

Succeeding legislation authorized $3 billion in bonds in September 1917 at 4 percent,[195] $3 billion in bonds in April 1918 at 4.25 percent,[196] and $6 billion in September 1918 at 4.25 percent.[197] Beyond merely the coupon interest rates, there were many other features of these bond issuances that varied, such as the taxability of the interest payments (only the first was completely exempt), the maturity date of the bonds, and the ability of the government to call the bond (repay it at its convenience or on a specified date). All of the bond issuances were oversubscribed, giving a positive support to the feeling of patriotism, although it is not clear whether patriotism or standard capitalism were at play in these purchases.

Beyond funding the government was providing credit to businesses in industries supporting the war effort. The War Finance Corporation was created by an act of Congress in April 1918.[198] This act created the corporation, financing it at $500 million,[199] and provided for a board of the secretary of the treasury and four others to be named by the president. The objective of the War Finance Corporation was to make advances directly to established businesses "whose operations shall be necessary or contributory to the prosecution of the war"[200] or to banks who were loaning money to such businesses

---

193. *Id.* § 1.
194. *Id.* § 5.
195. Pub. L. No. 65-43, An Act to authorize an additional issue of bonds to meet expenditures for the national security and defense, and, for the purpose of assisting in the prosecution of the war, to extend credit to foreign governments, and for other purposes (1917).
196. Pub. L. No. 65-120, An Act to amend an Act approved September twenty-fourth, nineteen hundred and seventeen, entitled "An Act to authorize an additional issue of bonds to meet expenditures for the national security and defense, and, for the purpose of assisting in the prosecution of the war, to extend credit to foreign governments, and for other purposes (1918).
197. Pub. L. No. 65-192, An Act to authorize an additional issue of bonds to meet expenditures for the national security and defense, and, for the purpose of assisting in the prosecution of the war, to extend credit to foreign governments, and for other purposes (1918).
198. Pub. L. No. 65-121, An Act to provide further for the national security and defense, and, for the purpose of assisting in the prosecution of the war, to provide credits for industries and enterprises in the united States necessary or contributory to the prosecution of the war, and to supervise the issuance of securities, and for other purposes (1918).
199. *Id.* § 2.
200. *Id.* § 9.

essential to the war effort.[201] Limitations included that the businesses had to be doing business in the United States and that the advances to a business could not exceed 10 percent of its corporate capital. Liberty bonds could be used for these transactions.[202]

LEGAL PROFILES

William Gibbs McAdoo was the secretary of the treasury during the war and the force behind the Liberty bonds. He was born in Georgia in 1863 and started his legal practice in Tennessee in 1885. He was involved in public transportation systems in Tennessee, and in New York he developed and operated a series of rapid transit tunnels, from 1902 to 1913. In 1913 he was named secretary of the treasury, where he oversaw the start of the Federal Reserve System. In 1918 he moved to head the Railroad Administration until the end of the war. After the war he returned to private practice. In 1914 he married the daughter of President Wilson. He unsuccessfully ran for the Democratic nomination for U.S. president in 1920 and 1924. In 1932 he was elected to the U.S. Senate from California, where he served a single term. He died in 1941.[203]

B. Cases

There were no major cases involved with the funding of the war, but there were a few Supreme Court cases that were decided after the war. In the first case, the constitutionality of the excess profits tax was in question, as were the methods used to calculate it. The second case reviewed the tax-exempt status of Liberty bonds and the constitutionality of state excise taxes that used their interest payments for valuation purposes.

---

201. *Id.* § 7.
202. *Id.* § 11.
203. *See McAdoo, William Gibbs*, BIOGRAPHICAL DIRECTORY OF THE UNITED STATES CONGRESS.

1. Excess Profits Tax

In *LaBelle Iron Works*,[204] the Supreme Court was reviewing the constitutionality and methodology in the excess profits tax implemented for the war funding. The appellants had sought a claim for what it said was an improper calculation of its invested capital. The company had taken the increase in the value of land containing ore and declared a stock dividend of almost $10 million, which it used to increase the invested capital in its calculation of the excess profits tax. The Court noted that "the manufacture and export of war supplies . . . resulting in large profits . . . as compared with ordinary returns upon the capital embarked . . . so that the unusual gains derived therefrom formed a natural subject of special taxation."[205]

The Court stated that Congress deliberately created a special term, "invested capital," and a definition for it to prevent inflated valuations based on inflated market values. The definition only allowed for cash or tangible property contributed as invested capital but not for any surplus. Congress intended to limit the invested capital "to something approximately representative of the risks accepted by investors in embarking their means in the enterprise."[206] The Court rejected both the increased market value of the ore lands and the stock dividend as being within the definition of invested capital. Turning down a due process challenge because it affected this corporation differently than others, the Court said that "this is due to differences in their circumstances, not to any uncertainty or want of generality in the test applied."[207] It affirmed the Court of Claims calculation of the tax, noting that "from every point of view, the tax in question must be sustained."[208]

LEGAL PROFILES

Mahlon Pitney delivered the opinion of the Court. He was born in New Jersey in 1858 and started his legal practice there in 1882. He was in private practice until 1894, when he was elected to Congress, where

---

204. LaBelle Iron Works v. United States, 256 U.S. 377 (1921).
205. *Id.* at 386-87.
206. *Id.* at 390.
207. *Id.* at 393.
208. *Id.* at 394.

he served until 1899. From 1899 to 1901 he served as state senator. In 1901 he became an associate justice on the New Jersey supreme court, serving until 1908. From 1908 until 1912, he was chancellor of New Jersey. In 1912 he was appointed by President Taft to the U.S. Supreme Court, where he served until resigning in 1922. He died in 1924.[209]

2. Tax on Liberty Bonds

In *Macallen*,[210] the State of Massachusetts was trying to collect taxes on income paid to a corporation that owned Liberty bonds. In determining its 1926 income for state tax purposes, the company was assessed for the interest received from its Liberty bonds. The state supreme court had determined that it was an excise tax, not an income tax, on the Liberty bond interest payments received by the corporation, with the interest received only helping to set the valuation for the excise tax. The Court said, "what cannot be done directly because of constitutional restriction cannot be accomplished indirectly by legislation that accomplishes the same result."[211] Although the state's purported purpose in creating the excise tax rules was to avoid discrimination against national banks, the Court ruled the state act was void, as it must use "some method which does not involve the imposition of a tax which uniformly for a century has been condemned by this Court as unconstitutional."[212]

C. Subsequent Events

As expected, after the massive stimulus to the economy from government spending stopped, the U.S. economy at first slowed down. This created some concern over government receipts and the ability to redeem all of the Liberty bonds it had issued, but they were eventually redeemed by being called and redeemed before their stated maturity dates. As they were called, two contentions arose. One involved what species was to be used to pay the redeemed bondholder, which led to a court case in the mid-1930s that eventually went

---

209. *See* Pitney, Mahlon, BIOGRAPHICAL DIRECTORY OF THE UNITED STATES CONGRESS; Pitney, Mahlon, FED. JUDICIAL CTR., BIOGRAPHICAL DIRECTORY OF FEDERAL JUDGES.
210. Macallen Co. v. Massachusetts, 279 U.S. 620 (1929).
211. *Id.* at 629.
212. *Id.* at 634.

to the Supreme Court.[213] The central issue was that the owner of the bond had the option to be paid in gold coin when the bond was called in 1934, at the 1918 rate of 25.8 grains of gold per gold dollar (instead of the 1934 rate of 15.24). The government refused, offering only to pay the bond's value of $10,000 in currency. The Court said that while the government could not repudiate its obligation to pay, the claimant had not suffered a loss, but in fact would be unjustly enriched if he was paid in legal tender at the new conversion rate, due to limitations in the domestic gold coin market. So he only had to be paid the $10,000 in legal tender currency. The other contention was that interest was due on an unredeemed bond after the redemption date, but the Court ruled that interest was only due to be paid until the notified redemption date, not the original maturity date of the bond.[214]

LEGAL PROFILES

Charles Evans Hughes delivered the opinion of the Court in this case and also filed an amicus curiae brief in the *LaBelle Iron Works* case (above). He was born in New York in 1862 and started his legal practice there. He taught briefly at a law school from 1891 to 1893, returning afterward to his New York law practice. He was elected governor of New York in 1906, serving until 1910. In that year, he was nominated to the Supreme Court by President Taft but resigned in 1916 to run unsuccessfully for U.S. president. In 1921 he was appointed as the secretary of state, where he served until 1925. From 1926 to 1930, he served on the Permanent Court of Arbitration at the Hague. In 1930 he returned to the Court, named by President Hoover as the chief justice to succeed the man who had originally nominated him, William Howard Taft. He served as chief justice until 1941 and died in 1948.[215]

---

213. Perry v. United States, 294 U.S. 330 (1935).
214. Smyth v. United States, 302 U.S. 329 (1937).
215. *See Hughes, Charles Evans*, FED. JUDICIAL CTR., BIOGRAPHICAL DIRECTORY OF FEDERAL JUDGES.

5.5 WOMEN AND THE WAR

A. Statutes

The impact of this war on the widely varying situations of women both within and across national boundaries was simultaneously diverse and complex, unique and common. There were several general impacts of this war on women, such as the changing dynamics in women's employment opportunities, both paid and unpaid, in their rights to participate in choosing their nations' governments, and in social causes that had been led by women. The result of the carnage of the war and its aftermath also significantly affected women in the belligerent nations. This section addresses the impact of the war on employment, women's suffrage, and Prohibition, and on the time period after the conflict ended, primarily from the experiences of women in the United States but also somewhat from experiences of women in the United Kingdom.

1. Employment

One way in which women impacted the war and the war impacted women directly was in the workforce. This had two components—the paid and the unpaid workforce. Women in very large numbers served as volunteers of all stripes: from preparing bandages for soldiers at the front to caring for soldiers who had returned home, from continuing to take care of families to helping to raise money through Liberty bond drives, from growing food to conserving food and fuel, from knitting socks for soldiers to volunteering at the Red Cross. The Women's Land Army stepped into agricultural roles vacated by men. The unpaid contributions of women made the paid part of the war possible. Yet many of these roles were ones women had had before, in other conflicts. What was new were the types of paid employment that women were able to take on.

With the large numbers of men leaving for either the front lines or other military-related work, and with the demand for war materials also skyrocketing, the only way to make up for the paid manpower shortage was to tap resources not commonly used. African Americans in large numbers moved from the South to the North to take factory jobs. Even then, more employees were needed, and it was from the female population that this labor arose. Women worked not only because they were needed in the war effort but because they needed to make money to support their families. While some of the labor was in what had been traditionally "women's work," like nursing and textiles/clothing, more was in manufacturing and farming, previously a male domain. Labor unions, aware of the potentially dilutive effect on all wages of women entering factory jobs and being paid lower wages, encouraged equal pay for women (and that their positions end when the war ended). The military employed women not only as nurses but in clerical roles and as "Hello Girls" (bilingual telephone operators sent to work in France).

Just as the conditions of soldiers in the trenches was far different from the patriotic but controlled public message put out by governments, so the reality of women's work during the war was far from the happy, patriotic experience depicted in the propaganda. Women working as nurses near the front lines were often killed or wounded. Women working in munitions plants were exposed to unsafe working conditions with dangerous component materials and potential health issues. (The British unofficially called munitionettes the "canary girls," due to their jaundiced yellow skin produced by sulfurous munitions components.) This was in addition to being the targets of sabotage (see Chapter 4). Women working in agriculture, factories, or mills worked very long hours at extremely monotonous, repetitive tasks in unheated and noisy or extremely hot environments, with little training and for low pay.

The impact of women directly supporting the military should not be minimized. It is estimated that upwards of 100,000 women were working in support positions with the military, in everything from running kitchens to performing administrative functions. But there were numerous women who insisted that, following the models of Florence Nightingale and Clara Barton in the nineteenth-century conflicts, they could provide better health care to wounded soldiers closer to the front lines. As such, numerous hospitals and aid stations were set up in the European theater by women nurses, doctors, and benefactresses. And women were also significant wartime victims (see Chapter 6), not only those working in countries overrun by belligerents but also those who, for economic and possibly social reasons, were providers of sexual and entertainment services to the military.

Women were mentioned explicitly only a few times in the U.S. federal laws passed during the war, beyond the frequent mentions of funding for charwomen and nurses. One act in September 1918 was to investigate, hold hearings on, and set a minimum wage for women in Washington, DC.[216] This

---

216. Pub. L. No. 65-215 (1918). An Act to protect the lives and health and morals of women and minor workers in the District of Columbia, and to establish a Minimum Wage-Board, and define its powers and duties, and to provide for the fixing of minimum wages for such workers, and for other purposes.

District of Columbia minimum-wage law was to set a wage at a level to "maintain their health and protect their morals."[217] An agriculture-stimulation act[218] in August 1917 required the secretary of agriculture "so far as practicable" to utilize women for the work specified (e.g., procuring seeds, conserving animal products, eradicating livestock disease, participating in food conservation demonstrations, certifying the condition of fruit).[219] In June 1918, Congress gave to the legislature of the territory of Hawaii—or, if the legislatures so chose, to the current voters—the power to decide "whether or not the female citizens of the Territory shall be empowered to vote at elections held under the laws of the Territory of Hawaii."[220] A July 1918 sundry appropriation bill stated that the secretary of labor, as the war labor administrator, was to render assistance in the employment of wage earners "as may be necessary in the prosecution of the war and to aid in the standardization of all wages paid by the Government," which included gathering information on the "employment of women in industry."[221]

LEGAL PROFILES

Belva Ann Lockwood was the first female lawyer to bring a case before the Supreme Court. She was born in New York in 1830 and started her legal practice in Washington, DC. After the death of her husband, she went back to college and then taught school for many years. She eventually was able to complete her legal training and overcome the unwillingness of the law school to give her the diploma she had earned, and she was finally admitted to the bar at the age of 43. She advocated for women's suffrage and equal pay. She also pushed for an

---

217. *Id.* § 10.
218. Pub. L. No. 65-40, An Act to provide further for the national security and defense by stimulating agriculture and facilitating the distribution of agricultural products (1917).
219. *Id.* § 8.
220. Pub. L. No. 65-168, An Act granting to the Legislature of the Territory of Hawaii additional powers relative to elections and qualification of electors (1918).
221. Pub. L. No. 65-181, An Act making appropriations for sundry civil expenses of the Government for the fiscal year ending June thirtieth, nineteen hundred and nineteen, and for other purposes (1918).

anti-discrimination bill that allowed women attorneys (with three years of experience, good standing, and good moral character) to practice in any federal court.[222] Under her own bill, which passed in early 1879, she became the first female member of the Supreme Court bar. She ran for U.S. president in the 1884 and 1887 elections as the nominee of the National Equal Rights Party (this was before women's suffrage). She also advocated peace and attended peace conferences but died as the United States was entering the war in 1917.[223]

Belle Case La Follette was a long-time activist in the progressive and suffrage movements. She was born in Wisconsin in 1859 and obtained her legal license there in 1885. She did not actively practice but had worked closely on legal (writing briefs) and social matters with her husband, progressive politician senator and presidential candidate Bob La Follette. They teamed up to put out a periodical, and she was involved in pushing women's suffrage up until its national passage. During the war she was a supporter of the peace movement. She turned down the opportunity to succeed her deceased husband to the U.S. Senate in favor of one of her sons (another son was the elected governor of the state). She died in 1931.[224]

---

2. Suffrage

Women's suffrage had been a battle long waged, in the United States and in other countries like the United Kingdom, that only came to fruition as the war was at or near the end. In the United States, though Congress had not yet approved the suffrage of women, many states had already acted. By the time the war started, the U.S. states that had women's suffrage of some measure included Wyoming, Colorado, Idaho, Utah, Washington, California, Oregon, Arizona, Kansas, and Montana. These states were all among those that had been settled later, so their flexibility in providing voting rights to women was due to several

---

222. Pub. L. No. 45-c. 91, An act to relieve certain legal disabilities of women (1879).
223. *See Belva Lockwood, Lawyer, Dies at 85*, N.Y. TIMES (May 20, 1917).
224. *See Wisconsin's Matriarch*, N.Y. TIMES (Aug. 20, 1931).

factors, including the dynamics of the transition from territory to statehood and the desire of these western states to attract women settlers to help populate the wide open spaces within their borders. Illinois was the first state east of the Mississippi to give women the right to vote and the last state to do so before the war started in Europe. New York finally passed women's suffrage in 1917.

In the United Kingdom, the battle had gone on for a long time, but through the leadership of Millicent Fawcett, Emmeline Pankhurst, and Emily Davison, women in the United Kingdom (over the age of thirty) were granted the right to sit in Parliament and vote under the Qualification of Women Act of 1918[225] and the Representation of the People Act of 1918.[226] Several other countries in the British Empire, such as New Zealand (enacted the Electoral Bill in 1893) and Australia (federally in 1902[227]), had already granted women the franchise. Canada was to follow in 1917[228] and 1918.[229] The Scandinavian countries had allowed it: Finland (in 1906), Norway (in 1913), Denmark and Iceland (in 1915), and Sweden (in 1919). The Netherlands and Russia (in 1917) and Germany (in 1918) had empowered women with the vote. Strangely, republican France (along with Italy) did not do so until after WWII.

Women's suffrage was legally initiated through joint resolution of Congress in June 1919 and passed by two-thirds of each house.[230] The proposed text was "The right of citizens of the United States to vote shall not be denied or abridged by the United States or by any State on account of sex. Congress shall have power to enforce this article by appropriate legislation." There being forty-eight states at that time (Hawaii and Alaska joined as states after WWII), the required three-fourth majority required for ratification meant thirty-six states had to approve this measure. The thirty-sixth and final state necessary for ratification (Tennessee) voted its approval in August 1920, adding the Nineteenth Amendment to the Constitution.

---

225. An Act to Amend the Law with respect to the Capacity of Women to sit in Parliament, 8 & 9 Geo. 5, c. 47 (U.K.).
226. An Act to Amend the Law with respect to Parliamentary and Local Government Franchises, and the Registration of Parliamentary and Local Government Electors, and the conduct of elections, and to provide for the Redistribution of Seats at Parliamentary Elections, and for other purposes connected therewith, 8 & 9 Geo. 5, c. 64, art. 4 (U.K.).
227. An Act to provide for an Uniform Federal Franchise, No. 8 of 1902 (Australia).
228. War-time Elections Act, S.C. 1917, c. 39; Military Voters Act, S.C. 1917, c. 34 (Canada).
229. An Act to confer the Electoral Franchise upon Women, S.C. 1918, c. 20 (Canada).
230. H.J. Res. 1, 66th Cong. Proposing an amendment to the Constitution extending the right of suffrage to women (1919).

Thanks to the exhaustive and committed efforts over so many decades by women including Elizabeth Cady Stanton, Susan B. Anthony, Lucretia Mott, Lucy Stone, Carrie Chapman Catt, Alice Paul, Lucy Burns, Victoria Woodhull, and thousands of lesser-known suffragists and suffragettes, including the first American female lawyer Arabella Mansfield,[231] working independently and with leading organizations like the National American Woman Suffrage Association (later the League of Women Voters), American women were now eligible to vote in elections nationwide. Representation in elective offices had preceded the franchise, as women were already serving in Congress; Rep. Jeanette Rankin of Montana had been in Congress since 1916, voting against this war and later against WWII.[232]

LEGAL PROFILES

Catherine Waugh McCulloch was involved in the suffragist movement during the war. She was born in Illinois in 1862 and started her legal practice there in 1886. In 1890 she started a legal partnership with her husband. From 1904 to 1911, she was legal counsel to the National American Woman Suffrage Association (NAWSA) and for almost a dozen years led the legislative activities of the Illinois Equal Suffrage Association. From 1905 she worked as a justice of the peace, perhaps the first American woman to have this role. She worked on a number of laws related to legal rights for women in Illinois, from jury duty to marriage and guardianship. In 1917 she was appointed to be a master in chancery, the first woman to do so in the country. She authored numerous books and articles on women's suffrage. She died in 1945.[233]

Inez Milholland was involved in the suffragist movement during the war. She was born in New York in 1886 and completed her legal training there in 1912, after being denied, as a woman, admission to Oxford,

---

231. *See First Woman Lawyer Dies*, N.Y. TIMES (Aug. 3, 1911).
232. *See* WWII LAW AND LAWYERS, ch. 2.
233. *See Mrs. M'Culloch, 82, Legal Figure, Dies*, N.Y. TIMES (Apr. 21, 1945).

Cambridge, or Harvard. She had organized suffrage groups during college and helped to organize the 1913 Suffrage Parade planned to coincide with the inauguration of President Wilson. She was involved in Henry Ford's 1915 Peace Ship to Europe and, with the outbreak of the war, traveled as a journalist to Europe to observe the front-line conditions. She was also involved with NAWSA and supported the cause of the offshoot National Woman's Party. She died in 1916 while on a political speaking tour.[234]

Etta H. Maddox was an advocate of women's suffrage but also a victim of the lack of it. She was born in Maryland in 1860, the daughter of a lawyer. After completing law school in 1901, she was refused permission to take the Maryland bar exam, based on her gender (Maryland being one of seven states that expressly refused women lawyers). She then advocated for a bill allowing women to become lawyers, bringing in other women lawyers from around the country (Ellen Foster of Iowa, Gail Laughlin of New York), which was successfully passed in 1902. That year she then passed the bar and became the first licensed woman attorney in the state. A long-time advocate in women's suffrage, she authored a suffrage bill for the state in 1910, which was not acted upon after hearings on suffrage. After spending a career advocating for women's rights, she died in 1933.[235]

---

3. Prohibition

Long closely aligned with the women's suffrage movement were the temperance and Prohibition movements. This was such that the funding for the opposition to women's suffrage often came from the brewing and saloon industries, which feared that women voters would take the country "dry." Going as far back as the Whiskey Rebellion (over a tax on whiskey) in the 1790s, various religious and social forces were in support of temperance (moderating alcohol intake) and Prohibition (banning it). From women's perspective, alcohol was a

---

234. *See Mrs. Inez Boissevain Dies in Los Angeles*, N.Y. TIMES (Nov. 26, 1916).
235. *See Women as Lawyers*, N.Y. TIMES (Feb. 23, 1902).

destructive influence on families and directly related to domestic violence and other crimes. After the Civil War, the Women's Christian Temperance Union (WCTU) and the Peace Party arose, with alcohol as a main focus.

Various states and counties had tried different measures to lessen the sales of alcohol, but it was the start of the war that brought both existing and new dynamics into play that were to lead to Prohibition. One was the war's needs for grain, as was discussed in the various efforts to increase production and conservation of food, particularly grains. Another was that the opposition to Prohibition had long been led by the brewers' industry, predominantly German-American; during the war, however, German opinion was given little effect. Taken together with the women's suffrage movement, the WCTU's Anna Adams Gordon's influence on President Wilson to soften his opposition in light of the war, and the lobbying of the Anti-Saloon League, Prohibition finally had sufficient backing to get Congress to act.

Congress already had recently placed bans on alcohol in those places where it had direct control: at or near army camps[236] and navy facilities,[237] in Alaska,[238] in Washington, DC,[239] in Hawaii for the period of the war,[240] and in the Indian territories.[241] The federal government had also banned the advertising of liquor via the postal mails: "That no letter, postal card, circular, newspaper, pamphlet, or publication of any kind containing any advertisement of spirituous, vinous, malted, fermented, or other intoxicating liquors of any kind, or containing a solicitation of an order or orders for said liquors, or any of them, shall be deposited in or carried by the mails of the United States, or be delivered by any postmaster or letter carrier, when addressed or directed to any person, firm, corporation, or association, or other addressee, at any place or point in

---

236. Pub. L. No. 65-12, An Act to authorize the President to increase temporarily the Military Establishment of the United States, § 12 (1917).
237. Pub. L. No. 65-77, An Act to promote the efficiency of the United States Navy (1917).
238. Pub. L. No. 64-308, An Act to prohibit the manufacture or sale of alcoholic liquors in the Territory of Alaska, and for other purposes (1917).
239. Pub. L. No. 64-383, An Act to prevent the manufacture and sale of alcoholic liquors in the District of Columbia, and for other purposes (1917).
240. Pub. L. No. 65-157, An Act to prohibit the sale, manufacture, and importation of intoxicating liquors in the Territory of Hawaii during the period of the war, except as hereinafter provided (1918).
241. Pub. L. No. 65-161, An Act to authorize the establishment of a town site on the Fort Hall Indian Reservation, Idaho (1918).

any State or Territory of the United States at which it is by the law in force in the State or Territory at that time unlawful to advertise."[242]

Prohibition was started nationally through a joint resolution of the two houses of Congress in December 1917.[243] It said that one year after ratification, "the manufacture, sale or transportation of intoxicating liquors, within, the importation thereof into, or the exportation thereof from the United States and all territory subject to the jurisdiction thereof for beverage purposes is hereby prohibited. The Congress and the several States shall have concurrent power to enforce this article by appropriate legislation."[244] While awaiting ratification, Congress passed, as part of the act stimulating agriculture,[245] the Wartime Prohibition Act, which prohibited, until after the war's termination and demobilization, importing or selling distilled spirits, beer, or wine, except for export, or using grains, cereals, fruit, or other food products in beer, wine, or other intoxicating liquors. This was "for the purpose of conserving the manpower of the Nation, and to increase efficiency in the production of arms, munitions, ships, food and clothing for the army and navy."[246]

Even though it was ratified by three-fourths of the states and proclaimed as part of the Constitution in January 1919, enabling legislation was not passed by Congress until October 1919 in the form of the National Prohibition (a.k.a. Volstead) Act.[247] This act provided for the prosecution of anyone who had violated any of the wartime prohibition acts (mentioned above),[248] and prohibited the manufacture, sale, barter, transport, import, export, delivery, furnishing, or

---

242. Pub. L. No. 64-380, An Act making appropriations for the service of the Post Office Department for the fiscal year ending June thirtieth, nineteen hundred and eighteen, and for other purposes, § 5 (1917).
243. S.J. Res. No. 65-17 Proposing an amendment to the Constitution to the United States (1917).
244. *Id.* § 1.
245. Pub. L. No. 65-243, An Act to enable the Secretary of Agriculture to carry out, curing the fiscal year ending June thirtieth, nineteen hundred and nineteen, the purposes of the Act entitled "An Act to provide further for the national security and defense by stimulating agriculture and facilitating the distribution of agricultural product," another purposes (1918).
246. *Id.* § 1.
247. Pub. L. No. 66-66, An Act to prohibit intoxicating beverages, and to regulate the manufacture, production, use, and sale of high-proof spirits for other than beverage purposes, and to insure an ample supply of alcohol and promote its use in scientific research and in the development of fuel, dye, and other lawful industries (1919).
248. *Id.* Title I.

possession of an intoxicating liquor,[249] except for medicinal or sacramental use, or for industrial use.[250] It was also unlawful to advertise liquor.[251] Lawsuits for injuries caused by intoxicated people could be filed, including exemplary damages, against any who assisted in procuring liquor.[252] Possession for personal use was not illegal.[253] This act was vetoed by President Wilson but then passed by two-thirds of the members of Congress.

LEGAL PROFILES

Morris Sheppard was a sponsor of several of the Prohibition laws. He was born in Texas in 1875, the son of a lawyer, and started his legal practice there in 1898. He was elected to Congress in 1902, where he served until 1913. In that year, he was elected to fill a vacancy in the Senate, where he served until 1941. Besides sponsoring Prohibition laws (the DC law, the Nineteenth Amendment, and the Volstead Act, plus an earlier law to limit interstate shipments of alcohol), he also was a supporter of women's suffrage and co-sponsored legislation on maternal and infancy mortality. He died still in office in 1941.[254]

Wayne Wheeler was the primary drafter of the Prohibition Act. He was born in Ohio in 1869 and started his legal practice there in 1898. He had been involved in the temperance movement even in college and soon after joined the Anti-Saloon League. He eventually rose to be the general counsel and the political voice of this organization, which overtook the WCTU in political influence on Prohibition. The Anti-Saloon League worked at the grass-roots levels to defeat candidates who did not follow its Prohibition mandate, resulting eventually in a Congress

---

249. *Id.* Title II, § 3.
250. *Id.* Title III.
251. *Id.* Title II, § 17.
252. *Id.* Title II, § 20.
253. *Id.* Title II, § 33.
254. *See Sheppard, Morris*, BIOGRAPHICAL DIRECTORY OF THE UNITED STATES CONGRESS.

that had sufficiently motivated members to pass Prohibition. He also appeared numerous times before the Supreme Court on saloon issues. He died in 1927 just after the death of his wife.[255]

B. Cases

There were of course many cases that arose during the war that impacted women, but this section focuses on those that had to do with the statutes discussed above. The first case was a challenge to the law passed in support of women and their minimum wages for employment in Washington, DC. The second case involved challenges to women's suffrage after the passing of the Nineteenth Amendment. The third case concerned challenges made to the Eighteenth Amendment.

1. Minimum Wage for Women

In *Adkins*,[256] the Supreme Court was reviewing two cases: The first dealt with a corporation that ran a hospital for children and employed women, some below the minimum wage set by the wage board under the act. The second dealt with a woman employed as an elevator operator in a hotel who had lost her job due to an order of the wage board. She wanted it back, as she could not find another position with "as good physical and moral surroundings, and earn as good wages."[257] The act was being attacked on Fifth Amendment due process grounds, in that it interfered with the liberty that included the right to contract for the employment of one's labor. The Court noted that freedom of contract, as upheld in several prior Court cases, was the general rule and only "exceptional circumstances"[258] allowed Congress to restrict it.

Looking back to previous decisions where such restrictions were allowed, the Court listed these types as being: (1) Those dealing with statutes fixing rates and charges to be exacted by businesses impressed with a public interest; (2) Statutes relating to contracts for the performance of public work; (3) Statutes prescribing the character, methods, and time for payment of wages;

---

255. *See W.B. Wheeler Dies of Heart Attack*, N.Y. TIMES (Sept. 6, 1927).
256. Adkins v. Children's Hosp. of D.C., 261 U.S. 525 (1923).
257. *Id*. at 543.
258. *Id*. at 546.

and (4) Statutes fixing hours of labor.[259] It was the last that attracted the most attention during arguments. The Court quoted from its decision in *Lochner*,[260] "The mere assertion that the subject relates though but in a remote degree to the public health does not necessarily render the enactment valid. The act must have a more direct relation, as a means to an end, and the end itself must be appropriate and legitimate, before an act can be held to be valid which interferes with the general right of an individual to be free in his person and in his power to contract in relation to his own labor."[261]

The Court then turned to its own prior decisions regarding the working hours for women. It had upheld limited working hours, such as in *Muller*,[262] where the differences in the genders were described as "differences of physical structure, especially in respect of the maternal functions, and also in the fact that historically woman has always been dependent upon man, who has established his control by superior physical strength."[263] Then pointing to the "great—not to say revolutionary—changes which have taken place since that utterance, in the contractual, political and civil status of women, culminating in the Nineteenth Amendment," the Court found that women were no longer in need of such special protections that were not available to men.

With the assumed equality of women to contract for their own labor, and noting the vagueness of a standard that was based upon fixing wages that are "sufficient to supply the necessary cost of living for a woman worker and maintain her in good health and protect her morals,"[264] and that "The relation between earnings and morals is not capable of standardization,"[265] the Court ruled that there was no connection between the labor being performed and the wages being set, as "solely with relation to circumstances apart from the contract of employment, the business affected by it and the work done under it."[266] The statute was held to be unconstitutional under the Fifth Amendment, with Justices Holmes and Sanford and Chief Justice Taft dissenting.

---

259. *Id.* at 546-47.
260. Lochner v. New York, 198 U.S. 45 (1905).
261. *Id.* at 549.
262. Muller v. Oregon, 208 U.S. 412 (1908).
263. *Id.* at 552-53.
264. *Id.* at 555.
265. *Id.* at 556.
266. *Id.* at 559.

LEGAL PROFILES

Wade H. Ellis was the counsel for the appellees. He was born in Kentucky in 1866 and started his legal practice in Ohio in 1897. He had previously served as editor of a Cincinnati newspaper. In 1897 he started as counsel for the city of Cincinnati. In 1903 he was elected attorney general for Ohio. In 1908 he became an assistant to the U.S. attorney general. From 1910 he was in private practice in Washington, DC, including as a special master for the Supreme Court. He died in 1948.[267]

2. Suffrage

In *Leser*,[268] shortly after the ratification of the Nineteenth Amendment, two women, Cecilia Streett Waters and Mary D. Randolph, registered to vote in Maryland. Suit was brought to strike them from the rolls of eligible voters, as Maryland had not ratified the amendment, and its constitution did not allow women to vote. Even though the amendment had been proclaimed on August 26, 1920, the appellants made several contentions, the first being that such a significant change to the electorate destroys a state's autonomy. The Court stated that the Nineteenth Amendment was the same character as theFifteenth Amendment, which had prohibited refusal of the franchise based on race. Noting that Maryland had rejected the the Fifteenth as well as the Nineteenth Amendments, the Court stated, as the theFifteenth Amendment had been accepted law for half a century, "One cannot be valid and the other invalid."[269]

The second allegation was that the constitutions in some of the ratifying states did not allow women to vote. The Court replied that, based on recent Court cases dealing with Prohibition[270] (see below), the ratification of a federal amendment was based on federal law and so actions taken to do so by a state legislature override state law. The third contention was that the ratifications of Tennessee and West Virginia violated their rules of procedure and were thus

---

267. *See Wade H. Ellis, 82, Lawyer, Ex-Editor*, N.Y. TIMES (July 6, 1948).
268. Leser v. Garnett, 258 U.S. 130 (1922).
269. *Id.* at 136.
270. *See, e.g.*, Hawke v. Smith, *No. 1,* 253 U.S. 221 (1920).

invalid. The Court first pointed out that Connecticut and Vermont had since ratified the amendment and so could substitute for Tennessee and West Virginia but more generally, the official authenticated notice from Tennessee and West Virginia was sufficient for the proclamation. As such the Court unanimously affirmed the lower courts' dismissal of this suit and its attack on the constitutionality of the Nineteenth Amendment. The same day, the Court dismissed another suit that was trying to prevent the secretary of state from proclaiming the Nineteenth Amendment.[271]

LEGAL PROFILES

Oscar Leser was the plaintiff in this case. He was born in Missouri in 1870 and started his legal practice in Pennsylvania in 1891. He was appointed to the tax court of appeals in 1901. Afterward he was involved in private practice, including in tax commissions and policy and was a justice on a Baltimore court from 1937 to 1939. He resigned to run unsuccessfully for the U.S. Senate. He died in 1960.[272]

3. Prohibition

In the *National Prohibition Cases*,[273] the Supreme Court decided seven related challenges to Prohibition from several states. The Court simply listed eleven rulings that it made based on the challenges received. First, the Court ruled that, for the Article V phrase "whenever two thirds of both Houses shall deem it necessary," passing a joint resolution sufficiently implied that the members thought it was necessary, without an express declaration about that necessity. Second, two-thirds of each chamber meant those present, not the total membership. Third, state referendum laws were overruled by federal rules for constitutional amendments. Fourth, the prohibition on certain activities regarding

---

271. Fairchild v. Hughes, 258 U.S. 126 (1922).
272. *See Tydings is Winner by Mounting Lead*, N.Y. TIMES (Sept. 14, 1938).
273. *National Prohibition Cases*, 253 U.S. 350 (1920).

liquor was within the Fifth Amendment power to amend. Fifth, the Eighteenth Amendment had lawfully become part of the Constitution.

Sixth, Prohibition was operative through the United States, bound all legislative bodies, courts, police and people, and invalidated any contrary state or territorial laws. Seventh, the amendment's section about Congress's power gave the power only to enforce, not to defeat, Prohibition. Eighth, the power did not mean joint power with the states or their approval of federal legislation or a breakdown along the lines of intra- and interstate commerce. Ninth, the power of Congress to enact legislation covered both inter- and intrastate and did not require any action (or inaction) by the states. Tenth, Prohibition may be enforced against liquor manufactured before the amendment was ratified. Eleventh, the Volstead Act did not exceed the powers of Congress under the amendment.

With these rulings, the Court dismissed all of these challenges to the Eighteenth Amendment. In its decision, the Court referred to several of its own decisions for support. In *Hawke*,[274] announced the same day, the Court ruled that the fact that the state now required constitutional questions to be settled by a direct vote of the people instead of by the legislature was not the key, as federal not state law was operative in the ratification of constitutional amendments. In *Jacob Ruppert*,[275] the Court had affirmed the constitutionality of the Wartime Prohibition Act, based on the war powers of Congress.

That case in turn had referred to *Kentucky Distilleries and Warehouse*,[276] where the Court had ruled on several points regarding the Wartime Prohibition Act. First, the Act's regulations did not amount to a Fifth Amendment taking, as it gave a grace period to dispose of alcohol, alcohol could be exported, and it could be sold for other than beverage purposes. Second, the act was not terminated when the armistice was announced, as the war emergency had not ceased. It was continued for many reasons, including the extension of wartime controls on the railroads, food, and fuel; the posting of part of the army overseas; the lack of a peace agreement with Germany; that the Wartime Prohibition Act was not repealed by the Eighteenth Amendment; and that the period of war would last until there was ratification of a treaty of peace.

---

274. Hawke v. Smith (No. 1), 253 U.S. 221 (1920).
275. Jacob Ruppert v. Caffey, 251 U.S. 264 (1920).
276. Hamilton v. Ky. Distilleries & Warehouse Co., 251 U.S. 146 (1919).

LEGAL PROFILES

William L. Frierson was the assistant U.S. attorney general for the defense in these cases. He was born in Tennessee in 1868 and started his legal practice there in 1889. In 1905 he was elected mayor of Chattanooga and in 1912 became city attorney. In 1917 he was appointed assistant U.S. attorney general, a role he held until 1920. In that year, after these cases were announced, he was appointed as solicitor general for the United States. The following year he returned to private practice. He died in 1953.[277]

C. Subsequent Events

After the war, the franchise for women was enhanced in the United Kingdom, when universal suffrage was permitted by the Representation of the People (Equal Franchise) Act of 1928.[278] In the United States, the right to vote was already available, though the last state to approve the Nineteenth Amendment (Mississippi) did so as late as 1984. Prohibition in America, unequally enforced in the various states and with crime possibly worse without truly achieving the goals of temperance, was repealed in three steps at the very beginning of the new Roosevelt administration in 1933. Congress proposed the Twenty-First Amendment in February 1933.[279] The Cullen-Harrison Act in March 1933[280] amended the Volstead Act by legalizing lower-content alcoholic beverages. In late 1933, the Twenty-First Amendment was ratified by state conventions, thereby repealing the Eighteenth Amendment but continuing the regulation of the alcohol industry.

One significant impact of the war on women was felt after the war, especially in those European countries, like France, Russia, Germany, Austria-Hun-

---

277. *See William Frierson, Aide of Wilson*, 83, N.Y. TIMES (May 27, 1953).
278. 18 & 19 Geo. 5, c. 12 (U.K).
279. S.J. Res. No. 72-211, Proposing an amendment to the Constitution of the United States (Prohibition Repeal) (1933).
280. Pub L. No. 73-3, An Act to provide revenue by the taxation of certain nonintoxicating liquor, and for other purposes (1933).

gary, and the United Kingdom, that had lost so many young men. Clearly there was now a shortage of men of marriageable age available, both to war widows and to women who had never married. In Great Britain, although there had historically been more women than men, there were now significantly more "surplus women," mainly as a result of over 700,000 British men dying in the war.[281] As measured by the 1911 census, women aged twenty to forty made up from 51.6 to 53.2 percent of the population of England and Wales, but in the 1921 census, women aged twenty to forty made up from 52.5 to 55.3 percent of the population. That year the total number of women aged twenty to forty—approximately 6.6 million—was fully one million more than the number of men aged twenty to forty.

Not being able to find a spouse was one problem, but not being able to find work was another. With the return of soldiers to the workforce and with the economy suffering from the postwar drop in government spending on the military, women who had entered the workforce and gained new skills now became unemployed. As a response to this, the British government set up in late 1919 the Society for the Overseas Settlement of British Women. This was established as a way for British women to find work (and perhaps a spouse) somewhere in the British Empire (e.g., Canada, Australia, New Zealand, South Africa). At the same time, it could help develop the rest of the Empire along the lines of the British social and economic model and further strengthen ties (creating more British families across the Empire) and increase export markets (decreasing unemployment in Britain and the Empire countries). To facilitate overseas emigration for not only these women but also unemployed returning soldiers and their families, the government passed the Empire Settlement Act in 1922,[282] which allowed for funding the cost of the passage, training those who emigrated, and even providing land in the countries of the Empire.

---

281. All numbers in this section are derived from census information from the U.K. Office of National Statistics.
282. Empire Settlement Act of 1922, 12 & 13 Geo. 5, c. 13 (U.K.).

LEGAL PROFILES

Annette Abbott Adams was the first woman to be named assistant attorney general of the United States. She was born in California in 1877 and started her legal practice there in 1912. In 1914 she was named the assistant U.S. attorney for Northern California, where she served until 1920, becoming U.S. attorney there in 1918. During the war she prosecuted people under both the Espionage and Wartime Prohibition Acts, as well as prosecuting the German consul for violating U.S. neutrality laws (see Chapter 4). In 1920 she was named the assistant attorney general of the United States. At the end of the Wilson administration, she returned to private practice. In 1935 she was appointed assistant special counsel on federal oil litigation. In 1942 she was appointed to the California court of appeals. She retired in 1952 and died in 1956.[283]

---

283. *See Woman Prosecutor Named Palmer Aid*, N.Y. TIMES (May 30, 1920).

CHAPTER 6

EUROPE & ELSEWHERE: WAR CRIMES, UPRISINGS & HORSES

There were actions taken by both nations and individuals during this war that shocked the civilized world. Although for the most part these acts were not unknown in the history of warfare, international conventions and human conscientiousness had changed. So, during the war and when it was coming to an end, there was an outcry for justice and the holding of war crimes trials. What was considered a war crime was still evolving, and the war crime trials that did occur were often under quite disparate rules. To a large extent, as is always the case in postwar trials, the victors set the agenda for the trials, but in this situation, because the war ended without an unconditional surrender, the vanquished were able to modify that agenda and so dilute it. So while it was Germans who were tried for their alleged crimes and, to a lesser extent, Turks who were tried for theirs, the results of these trials were far from conclusive.

The war also brought to a head many long-simmering causes of independence. Mostly from within the British Empire, there were pushes for independence from India and Ireland. From the Middle East, independence of a different sort arose, with the Jewish diaspora desiring a homeland while a new Arab nationalism was also taking hold in the region. Russia had its own long-percolating need for change, which led to revolution impacting the war. Yet there were also softer types of uprisings within the British Empire, of those dominion members who wanted not only national control of their troops on the front lines and postwar recognition for their contributions to the war effort but also to have their own voice in matters such as foreign affairs, which Canada, Australia, New Zealand, and South Africa sought in varying degrees.

The most essential but silent participants in warfare did not seek additional rights but merely the loving acknowledgment from their caretakers. Animals have been used in battle from time immemorial, but importantly so in this conflict. Perhaps in their last significant role in active combat before mechanization and electronic mediums took over permanently, horses, dogs, and birds played important roles during the war, supporting the functions of the military in transporting men and supplies, relaying messages, and identifying the wounded. With this war, they passed from primary to very secondary roles in military affairs but made significant contributions along the way.

This chapter focuses first on the acts that were considered to be war crimes, on land and sea, and the trials that did (or did not) take place after the war to try those crimes. Next discussed are the uprisings that occurred against empires, followed by the dynamics of change among the countries that were part of the British Empire. The chapter closes by looking at the role that animals played in this war. The chapter covers the issues of war crimes against civilians and POWs, the use of poisonous gases, deportations and massacres/genocide of civilians, uprisings for independence, postwar territorial mandates, the dividing of regions of postwar influence, the impact of political revolutions on the war, the seeking of parity within the British Empire, the role of animals in this war, the use of bacterial warfare, and the impacts on war animals after the conflict was over.

PROMINENT LAWYERS AND JUDGES IN THIS CHAPTER

War Crimes:
- James Bryce (head of the atrocities committee)
- Charles Willie Mathews (director of public prosecutions)
- Ellis Hume-Williams (British mission to Leipzig trials)
- Alfred Herbert John Andrews (poison gas noncommissioned officer)
- Krikor Zohrab (member of the Ottoman parliament)
- Henry Morgenthau Sr. (U.S. ambassador to Ottoman Empire)
- Kenelm Edward Digby (member of Bryce committee)

- Edward Grimwood Mears (secretary of Bryce committee)
- Heinrich Schmidt (president of the Leipzig court)
- Ludwig Ebermayer (state attorney)
- Jonathan Mayhew Wainwright (advisory committee)
- Jasper Y. Brinton (mission member)

Uprisings:

- John Redmond (Irish parliamentary leader)
- Mohandas K. Gandhi (independence leader)
- Alfred Milner (declaration drafter)
- Vladimir Ilyich Lenin (revolutionary)
- Patrick Pearse (defendant)
- A. M. Sullivan (lead defense counsel)
- John H. Morgan (defense counsel)
- Horace Avory (trial judge)
- Thomas Horridge (trial judge)
- Shiv Narayan Raina (special commissioner)
- Robert Finlay (international court justice)
- Alexander Kerensky (prime minister)
- Eamonn Duggan (treaty negotiator)
- George Gavan Duffy (treaty negotiator)

Parity in the Empire:

- Robert L. Borden (Canadian prime minister)
- Wilfrid Laurier (opposition leader)
- Donald Mackinnon (director general of recruiting)
- Jan Smuts (minister of defence)
- Robert Garran (solicitor general)
- Henry N. MacLaurin (brigade commander)

Animals in War:

- Andrew Barton Paterson (horse veterinarian)
- George Harold Baker (unit commander)
- Charles White Whittlesey (battalion commander)
- John Butcher (member of Parliament)

6.1 WAR CRIMES

A. Statutes

At the start of the war, there were both international conventions and national regulations that addressed behaviors that could be considered war crimes. For example, 1899 Hague Convention IV Declaration II (see Chapter 1) stated that those ratifying this agreement should "abstain from the use of projectiles the object of which is the diffusion of asphyxiating or deleterious gases."[1] The 1907 Hague Convention IV stated that "it is especially forbidden – To employ poison or poisoned weapons . . . To employ arms, projectiles, or material calculated to cause unnecessary suffering . . . To destroy or seize the enemy's property, unless such destruction or seizure be imperatively demanded by the necessities of war."[2] The Geneva Convention of 1906 required, inter alia, that the sick and wounded be cared for by whichever army was holding them[3] and were protected under the rules of international law for prisoners of war,[4] that medical units were to be "protected and respected by belligerents,"[5] and that the contracting parties make their armies aware of the convention.[6]

Each nation had its own military regulations and manuals based on these conventions, such as the British "Law and Usages of War on Land" or the American "Rules of Land Warfare." The Germans had their version,[7] several of whose provisions which would seem to be at odds with international law. Excerpts from some of the problematic passages included claims that international law may conflict with the necessities of warfare and so should be objected to by the military. Additionally, that respect for the people and property of belligerents was secondary to the military objectives, such that destruction of the enemy's "material and moral resources" (i.e., home, family, etc.) was to be considered an acceptable technique to use in achieving military goals.[8]

---

1. Hague IV, Declaration II on the Use of Projectiles the Object of Which is the Diffusion of Asphyxiating or Deleterious Gases (July 29, 1899).
2. Hague IV, Convention Respecting the Laws and Customs of War on Land (Oct. 18, 1907), art 23.
3. Geneva Convention on the Amelioration of the Condition of the Wounded and Sick in the Armies in the Field (July 6, 1906), art. 1.
4. *Id.* art. 2.
5. *Id.* art. 6.
6. *Id.* art. 26.
7. Kriegsbrauch im Landkriege (1902).
8. *Id* at 3.

While the postwar peace conference (see Chapter 7) was in process, the major powers in January 1919 appointed the Commission on the Responsibility of the Authors of the War and on Enforcement of Penalties. Among its charges was to determine the degree of responsibility for breaches of the laws and customs of war committed by the Central Powers and high-ranking officials. In March the committee issued its report[9] with several major sections, one involving responsibility for the war, discussed in Chapter 7, and a second involving war crimes. For the latter section, three major points were that there were innumerable acts of violations of the laws and customs of war, that those responsible anywhere in the chain of command must be responsible for them, and that military tribunals must be set up to try them.

On the first point, the report categorized the violations of the laws and customs of war as:

(1) Murders and massacres; systematic terrorism
(2) Putting hostages to death
(3) Torture of civilians
(4) Deliberate starvation of civilians
(5) Rape
(6) Abduction of girls and women for the purpose of enforced prostitution
(7) Deportation of civilians
(8) Internment of civilians under inhuman conditions
(9) Forced labor of civilians in connection with the military operations of the enemy
(10) Usurpation of sovereignty during military occupation
(11) Compulsory enlistment of soldiers among the inhabitants of occupied territory
(12) Attempts to denationalize the inhabitants of occupied territory
(13) Pillage
(14) Confiscation of property
(15) Exaction of illegitimate or of exorbitant contributions and requisitions
(16) Debasement of the currency, and issue of spurious currency
(17) Imposition of collective penalties

---

9. Commission on the Responsibility of the Authors of the War and on Enforcement of Penalties, Report Presented to the Preliminary Peace Conference (Mar. 29, 1919).

(18) Wanton devastation and destruction of property
(19) Deliberate bombardment of undefended places
(20) Wanton destruction of religious, charitable, educational, and historic buildings and monuments
(21) Destruction of merchant ships and passenger vessels without warning and without provision for the safety of passengers or crew
(22) Destruction of fishing boats and of relief ships
(23) Deliberate bombardment of hospitals
(24) Attack on and destruction of hospital ships
(25) Breach of other rules relating to the Red Cross
(26) Use of deleterious and asphyxiating gases
(27) Use of explosive or expanding bullets, and other inhuman appliances
(28) Directions to give no quarter
(29) Ill-treatment of wounded and prisoners of war
(30) Employment of prisoners of war on unauthorized works
(31) Misuse of flags of truce
(32) Poisoning of wells[10]

On the second point regarding personal responsibility, the committee concluded that: "All persons belonging to enemy countries, however high their position may have been, without distinction of rank, including Chiefs of States, who have been guilty of offences against the laws and customs of war or the laws of humanity, are liable to criminal prosecution."[11] But it clearly defined the concept of superior orders, in that "civil and military authorities cannot be relieved from responsibility by the mere fact that a higher authority might have been convicted of the same offence. It will be for the court to decide whether a plea of superior orders is sufficient to acquit the person charged from responsibility."[12]

On the third point, the committee noted that while nations could try individuals who had fallen into their grasp, there should be international tribunals to try the following types of violations of the laws and customs of war:

---

10. *Id.* ch. II.
11. *Id.* ch. III.
12. *Id.*

(a) Against persons belonging to enemy countries who have committed outrages against a number of civilians and soldiers of several Allied nations, such as outrages committed in prison camps where prisoners of war of several nations were congregated or the crime of forced labor in mines where prisoners of more than one nationality were forced to work

(b) Against persons of authority, belonging to enemy countries, whose orders were executed not only in one area or on one battle front, but whose orders affected the conduct of operations against several of the Allied armies

(c) Against all authorities, civil or military, belonging to enemy countries, however high their position may have been, without distinction of rank, including the heads of states, who ordered, or, with knowledge thereof and with power to intervene, abstained from preventing or taking measures to prevent, putting an end to or repressing, violations of the laws or customs of war (it being understood that no such abstention should constitute a defence for the actual perpetrators)

(d) Against such other persons belonging to enemy countries as, having regard to the character of the offence or the law of any belligerent country, it may be considered advisable not to proceed before a court other than the high tribunal hereafter referred to.[13]

The final peace treaty signed with Germany[14] included variously purposed tribunals. It was contained in four articles, the first of which was targeted at Kaiser Wilhelm himself, which required a special tribunal of five judges, each drawn from one of the Allied or Associated Powers, for "a supreme offence against international morality and the sanctity of treaties."[15] Anyone accused of committing acts that violated the laws and customs of war was to be tried

---

13. *Id.* ch. IV.
14. Treaty of Peace Between the Allied and Associated Powers and Germany, June 28, 1919 [hereinafter Versailles Treaty].
15. *Id.* art. 227.

before a military tribunal in Germany.[16] Those who were guilty of crimes against the nations of one of the Associated or Allied Powers could be brought to trial before a military tribunal composed of members of that nation, but if against multiple nations, then the tribunal would have members of each such country.[17] The German government was to furnish all available documents and details about the specified acts.[18]

Despite the extensive definitions of what was considered a war crime, most of the war crimes were not prosecuted by tribunals but were addressed in other forums. The following types of war crimes are discussed: the atrocities committed by German troops in Belgium in the early parts of the war; crimes committed by German forces on the land and sea, including against clearly identified hospital ships and against POWs; the use of poisonous gases eventually used by all sides in the European theater; and the massacre/genocide by the Ottoman Empire of up to one million or more Armenians.

1. Atrocities in Belgium

These events were not tried in court as much as they were tried through evidence collected and reports produced by Britain, Germany, and Belgium. When the German army passed through Belgium at the start of the war, contrary to their expectations, the Belgian army put up a significant resistance, slowing down the German advance enough to make an early capture of Paris impossible. The Belgians, both citizens and partisans, then became the victims of German frustration. Stories of the events that occurred in the early days of the war and later in Belgium came to England with many of the Belgian refugees who fled to Britain. Prime Minister Asquith set up a commission, called the Committee on Alleged German Outrages and headed by James Bryce, to investigate these allegations. Run principally by lawyers, this commission took over a thousand depositions from Belgians who had escaped but who were witnesses under the oversight of the director of public prosecutions. War diaries of captured or killed German soldiers were sent to England and translated, and testimony from others such as British and Belgian soldiers was added to produce their report. Hearsay evidence was mostly omitted, as that

---

16. *Id.* art. 228.
17. *Id.* art. 229.
18. *Id.* art. 230.

testimony was considered unreliable. This was to be followed by reports from the governments of Germany and Belgium, all trying this case in the court of public opinion instead of in a courtroom.

LEGAL PROFILES

James Bryce was head of the commission on German atrocities in Belgium. He was born in Ireland in 1838 and obtained his legal training in Great Britain. After being called to the bar in 1867, he became a professor of law at Oxford in 1870, retaining this role until 1893. In 1880 he was elected to Parliament, where he served until 1907, his last role there being chief secretary for Ireland. In that year he was appointed as the ambassador to the United States, which he held until 1913. Upon returning to the United Kingdom, he ran not only this committee but also was responsible for reporting on the Armenian situation (see the following section), where he had spent time decades before. He was the author of numerous books throughout his lifetime and died in 1922.[19]

Charles Willie Mathews was director of public prosecutions, under whose responsibility the depositions were taken in this case. He was born in New York in 1850 and obtained his legal training in England. He started his career in criminal law in 1872. In 1886 he moved to the British treasury department, becoming senior counsel in 1888. He was appointed as the director for the office of public prosecutions (previously part of the treasury solicitor's office) and became its first independent director in 1908. He held this post until his death in 1920.[20]

---

19. *See James Bryce*, OXFORD DICTIONARY OF NATIONAL BIOGRAPHY 101032141.
20. *See Charles Mathews*, OXFORD DICTIONARY OF NATIONAL BIOGRAPHY 101034935.

2. War Crimes on Land and Sea

As explained in Chapter 3, Kaiser Wilhelm was never tried as a war criminal, even though this was called for in the Versailles Treaty, nor were any of the architects of the war. Instead, only a small number of lower ranking defendants were brought to trial. The evidence was gathered by the Belgians, English, and French against those who sunk hospital ships, mistreated POWs, and mistreated civilians. In addition, there were other crimes alleged against Germany that were not tried, involving the deportations of Belgian civilians for use as forced labor in Germany (which freed up German laborers for military service) and the forced deportation of French civilians in Lille to the surrounding countryside to work as agricultural laborers. The latter of these two may have been difficult to win a conviction for, due to the recognition of the requisitioning of services to support armies of occupation as allowed under the Hague Convention.[21]

From an initial list of around 3,000, the Allied and Associated Powers had originally provided a list of about 900 possible defendants to Germany to be tried, including war leaders von Hindenburg, Bismarck, and the Crown Prince, but this was rejected by the Germans as potentially destabilizing to the new postwar government. The German government had passed a law in December 1919[22] (which was subsequently twice amended[23]), that allowed for the trying of war criminals in Germany, so the government proposed instead that a much-reduced number of defendants be tried there. The Allies agreed to this, with the stipulation that they reserved the right to try the defendants themselves if the trial proved unsatisfactory.

There was a delay of over two years from the signing of the armistice until the start of the trial, and this led to a significant attenuation of evidence and defendants. Of the forty-five men on the reduced list of defendants—for reasons including the inability to find the accused in Germany, as some had left the country or moved to the free city of Danzig (technically non-German now), the inability to acquire evidence sufficient for the typical standards of a criminal court, and the difficulty in locating witnesses who returned to

---

21. Hague IV, art. 52.
22. RGBl 1919, No. 247 (Germany).
23. RGBl 1920, No. 53; RGBl 1921, No. 51 (Germany).

their home countries after the war, such as to Dominion countries outside Europe—just twelve defendants were finally brought to trial in 1921.

LEGAL PROFILES

Ellis Hume-Williams was part of the British mission to the Leipzig War Crimes Trials. He was born in England in 1863 and obtained his legal training there, called to the bar in 1881. He became a king's counsel in 1899. After three unsuccessful attempts, he was elected to Parliament in 1910, where he served until 1929. He then was appointed as a privy counselor. He was the prosecutor in the Noel Pemberton Billing libel trial involving the supposed "Unseen Hand" (a pro-German influence in the country and in the British government). During the war, he served in the ambulance service and dealt with interned and returning prisoners. He died in 1947.[24]

3. Use of Poisonous Gases

This war is well remembered as the start of the significant use of chemical weapons, especially poisonous gases. First introduced were nonpoisonous gases, such as tear gas, by the French and then the Germans after trench warfare had commenced, but it was ineffective. The first use of poisonous gas on any significant scale and to significant result was deployed by the Germans in April 1915 at the Second Battle of Ypres. Chlorine was released via cylinders in the German trenches and, following the wind, descended upon the Allied trenches. Because it was not deployed using projectiles, as the 1899 Hague Convention declaration specified, Germany could temporarily find some legal cover for its use of this gas.

Later in the year, the deadlier and less visible phosgene gas was developed by the French and deployed initially via cylinders, where the direction of the prevailing wind was always a key consideration (to avoid the gas com-

---

24. *See Sir Ellis Hume-Williams, K.C.,* THE TIMES (Feb. 7, 1947).

ing back upon the troops who released it). To overcome this limitation, they tested deploying the gas via artillery shells. In 1917 mustard gas, less deadly but more likely to disable, was deployed via shells. Although various defensive techniques, including the gas masks, were developed and deployed sufficiently to decrease the effectiveness of poisonous gas attacks, perhaps over one million soldiers became casualties of poisonous gas used during the war, leading to upwards of 100,000 deaths.

LEGAL PROFILES

Alfred Herbert John Andrews was responsible for poisonous gas defenses in part of the Canadian trenches and was also a lawyer. He was born in Saskatchewan, Canada, in 1888 and obtained his legal training there. He enlisted in September 1914, at the age of almost twenty-six. During the war he was involved with gas units. He kept a diary of his war years, which was discovered after his death and later published. He died in 1935.[25]

4. Armenian Massacre

The Ottoman Empire, made up of many disparate cultures spread over a wide geographic area, had long been generally tolerant of these cultures and their religions. As with all of the other empires that started this war (British, French, German, Russian, Austro-Hungarian), the Ottomans saw their culture as ascendant and treated as second-class citizens those from other cultures dwelling within their borders. But the general tolerance began to change within the Ottoman Empire in the decades before the war, as there were several massacres of Armenians. These were met with European demands for protection of minorities like the Armenians. Although safeguards were committed to in agreements like the Treaty of Berlin (see Chapter 1), they were not generally implemented.

---

25. *See Herbert Andrews*, LIBRARY AND ARCHIVES CANADA, Soldiers of the First World War.

With part of Armenian territory lying within the Russian Empire and also being co-religionists, Russia was looked upon as a protector of Armenian rights. When the Ottoman Empire allied with the Central Powers at the start of this war (see Chapter 2), the fear of an enemy within the empire became widespread. Armenian units were demobilized from the armed forces and their weapons taken away. In April 1915 arrests and subsequent murders of Armenians began within the Ottoman Empire. At the time, the empire was run by the Young Turks who had overthrown the sultan and ran things under the Committee of Unity and Progress. With instructions from the ministry of the interior, a member of the Committee of Unity and Progress, hundreds of Armenian intellectuals were arrested in Constantinople, including a number of lawyers, who later were deported and killed, often extra-judiciously. Some of those detained managed to be freed, often because of the intercession of foreign diplomats such as the American ambassador, but this was not the most common fate.

The empire's parliament then passed the Tehcir Law[26] in late May 1915 to allow for "temporary" deportations. This law allowed the government and, if necessary, the military to move people who were security risks out of the war zones contiguous to Russia. It could relocate those engaged in espionage or treason, either as individuals or entire towns and villages. Although an order in May 1915 stated that property of those so relocated would be inventoried and held for them (except for perishables, which would be sold and the money held in trust), in September 1915 the Abandoned Properties Law[27] allowed for the confiscation of the property of the Armenians who had been deported and were most likely dead. This latter law was declared by parliamentarian Ahmed Riza to be illegal under the Ottoman constitution. The Tehcir Law was to eventually expire in February 1916, as it was only a temporary measure, but by that time, the damage had already been done.

As discussed further in the following section on cases, hundreds of thousands of Armenians were taken not only from war zones but from all across Anatolia and were relocated to other places within the Ottoman Empire, many to eventually suffer death. Many of the men were executed, and the women,

---

26. Law on Dispatchment and Settlement of 1915, *Sevk ve İskân Kanunu* (Ottoman).
27. Law Concerning Property, Debts and Assets Left Behind by Deported Persons of 1915 (Ottoman).

children, and elderly were driven into the desert or the sea. According to estimates, before the war more than two million Armenians were living in the Ottoman Empire, but by 1922, there were only around 400,000.[28] More than one million Armenians had disappeared. At the time, officials of different governments filed numerous reports documenting these events. Viscount Bryce, in his report to the British government, said "It would seem that three-fourths or four-fifths of the whole nation has been wiped out, and there is no case in history, certainly not since the time of Tamerlane, in which any crime so hideous and upon so large a scale has been recorded."[29]

LEGAL PROFILES

Krikor Zohrab was a member of the Ottoman parliament and a victim of the massacre of Armenian intellectuals. He was born in the Ottoman Empire in 1861 and obtained his legal training there. He became a law professor while also defending various minority defendants, one of which led to his disbarment and deportation. After the 1908 revolution, he was returned to the Empire and became a member of the parliament. He used his parliament position to try to stop the deportations in April 1915 but was himself deported to Aleppo, and after unsuccessful attempts by the governor there to have him returned to his home, Zohrab was murdered in July 1915.[30]

Henry Morgenthau Sr. was U.S. ambassador to the Ottoman Empire during the war. He was born in Germany in 1856 but immigrated to the United States and started his legal practice in New York in 1877. He practiced until 1899 then went into real estate. He became involved in politics and was appointed the ambassador to the Ottoman Empire in the new Wilson administration in 1913. He served in this role until 1916, where he represented the Allied Powers, led the efforts to stop the

---

28. *Armenian Genocide of 1915: An Overview*, N.Y. TIMES.
29. British Government Report on the Armenian Massacres April–December 1915 (1915).
30. *See Wholesale Murder in Armenia*, THE TIMES (Sept. 30, 1915).

deportations and massacres, and raised funds for Armenians. A founder of the American National Red Cross, he was involved with relief activities in the near east between 1919 and 1921 and then chaired the Greek Refugee Settlement Commission under the League of Nations in 1923. His descendants included a U.S. secretary of the treasury, a Manhattan district attorney, and a renowned historian. He died in 1946.[31]

B. Cases

There were few proper war crimes trials after the war, so the trying of the alleged war crimes was done in several different forums. For the atrocities committed in Belgium, the reports of the Bryce commission, the response by the Germans, and the reply by the Belgium government provided the arguments in that case. After the war, the Leipzig War Crimes Trials tried the German military abuse of POWs on land and the sick and injured at sea. The use of poisonous gas was never tried as a crime, as it was used by all the major belligerents, but it did lead to several agreements, including the Geneva Protocol in 1925. The Armenian massacre was tried several times after the war and was supplemented by reports from U.S. officials on the ground there.

1. Bryce Report

The crimes alleged to have occurred in Belgium as described in the Bryce report had many sensational entries based on witness testimony. The German army, frustrated by the fighting, occasional reverses, and the feeling that it was being targeted by Belgian civilians (*francs-tireurs*), began to turn its frustrations on the local populations. Based on an entry found in the diary of a German soldier about what occurred in the town of Dinant, the report stated: "[The] diary confirms what is clear from the evidence as a whole both as regards these and other districts, that civilians were constantly taken as prisoners, often dragged from their homes and shot under the direction of the authorities without any charge being made against them. An event of the kind is thus referred to in a diary entry: 'Apparently 200 men were shot. There must have

---

31. *See H. Morgenthau, Sr. Dies in Home at 90*, N.Y. TIMES (Nov. 26, 1946).

been some innocent men amongst them. In future we shall have to hold an inquiry as to their guilt instead of shooting them.'"[32]

Later the report, while acknowledging individual acts of moral behavior by German soldiers, tried to differentiate immoral acts of individuals from the systematic acts of the German army.

> Here let a distinction be drawn between two classes of outrages. Individual acts of brutality treatment of civilians, rape, plunder, and the like were very widely committed. These are more numerous and more shocking than would be expected in warfare between civilised Powers, but they differ rather in extent than in kind from what has happened in previous though not recent wars. In all wars many shocking and outrageous acts must be expected, for in every large army there must be a proportion of men of criminal instincts whose worst passions are unloosed by the immunity which the conditions of warfare afford . . .
>
> In the present war, however—and this is the gravest charge against the German army—the evidence shows that the killing of non-combatants was carried out to an extent for which no previous war between nations claiming to be civilized . . . furnishes any precedent. That this killing was done as part of a deliberate plan is clear from the facts herein before set forth regarding Louvain, Aerschot, Dinant, and other towns. The killing was done under orders in each place. It began at a certain fixed date, and stopped (with some few exceptions) at another fixed date. Some of the officers who carried out the work did it reluctantly, and said they were obeying directions from their chiefs. The same remarks apply to the destruction of property. House burning was part of the programme; and villages, even large parts of a city, were given to the flames as part of the terrorising policy.
>
> Citizens of neutral states who visited Belgium in December and January report that the German authorities do not deny that non-combatants were systematically killed in large numbers during the first weeks of the invasion, and this, so far as we know, has never been officially denied. If it were denied, the flight and continued voluntary exile of thousands of Belgian refugees would go far to contradict a denial . . . The Ger-

---

32. Report of the Committee on Alleged German Outrages (Bryce Commission), Part I.

man Government have, however, sought to justify their severities on the grounds of military necessity, and have excused them as retaliation for cases in which civilians fired on German troops. There may have been cases in which such firing occurred, but no proof has ever been given, or, to our knowledge, attempted to be given, of such cases, nor of the stories of shocking outrages perpetrated by Belgian men and women on German soldiers.

The inherent improbability of the German contention is shown by the fact that after the first few days of the invasion every possible precaution had been taken by the Belgian authorities, by way of placards and hand-bills, to warn the civilian population not to intervene in hostilities. Throughout Belgian steps had been taken to secure the handing over of all firearms in the possession of civilians before the German army arrived. These steps were sometimes taken by the police and sometimes by the military authorities. The invaders appear to have proceeded upon the theory that any chance shot coming from an unexpected place was fired by civilians. One favourite form of this allegation was that priests had fired from the church tower.[33]

It then discussed the types of murders that had taken place:

Two classes of murders in particular require special mention, because one of them is almost new, and the other altogether unprecedented. The former is the seizure of peaceful citizens as so-called hostage to be kept as a pledge for the conduct of the civil population, or as a means to secure some military advantage, or to compel the payment of a contribution, the hostages being shot if the condition imposed by the arbitrary will of the invader is not fulfilled.

Such hostage taking, with the penalty of death attached, has now and then happened . . . but it is opposed both to the rule of war and to every principle of justice and humanity. The latter kind of murder is the killing of the innocent inhabitants of a village because shots have been fired, or are alleged to have been fired, on the troops by someone in the village. For this practice no previous example and no justification have been or

---

33. *Id.*

can be pleaded. Soldiers suppressing an insurrection may have sometimes slain civilians mingled with insurgents, and Napoleon's forces in Spain are said to have now and then killed promiscuously when trying to clear guerrillas out of a village.

But in Belgium large bodies of men, sometimes including the burgomaster and the priest were seized, marched by officers to a spot chosen or the purpose, and there shot in cold blood, without any attempt at trial or even inquiry, under the pretence of inflicting punishment upon the village, though these unhappy victims were not even charged with having themselves committed any wrongful act, and though, in some cases at least, the village authorities had done all in their power to prevent any molestation of the invading force. Such acts are no part of war, for innocence is entitled to respect even in war. They are mere murders . . . and not an act of war.[34]

The charges the commission made fell into two groups. The first was related to the treatment of noncombatants: killing them, using them as human shields, mistreating women and children, and looting, burning, and destroying their property. The second charges were over violations of the Hague Convention IV, including killing wounded soldiers or prisoners of war or firing on ambulances, hospitals, and their workers. After giving even more examples (the depositions and diaries used as evidence were appendices to the report) of each of these charges, the report concluded that it had proven the following:

(i) That there were in many parts of Belgium deliberate and systematically organised massacres of the civil population, accompanied by many isolated murders and other outrages.

(ii) That in the conduct of the war generally innocent civilians, both men and women, were murdered in large numbers, women violated, and children murdered.

---

34. *Id.*

(iii) That looting, house burning, and the wanton destruction of property were ordered and countenanced by the officers of the German Army, that elaborate provisions had been made for systematic incendiarism at the very outbreak of the war, and that the burnings and destruction were frequent where no military necessity could be alleged, being indeed part of a system of general terrorisation.

(iv) That the rules and usages of war were frequently broken, particularly by the using of civilians, including women and children, as a shield for advancing forces exposed to fire, to a less degree by killing the wounded and prisoners, and in the frequent abuse of the Red Cross and the White Flag.[35]

In response to the May 1915 Bryce report, which some felt was too sensationalistic and reliant upon depositions (although taken by lawyers, they were not under oath), the German government issued in response their own "White Book" in May 1915.[36] This placed the blame instead on the civilian *francs-tireurs* (free shooters) who were not following the accepted rules of warfare, and so the responses were appropriate. It used a number of its own depositions from German and local personnel. Several years later, and in great detail, the Belgian government replied to and disavowed the White Book[37] regarding the depicted role of the Belgian people and the Belgian government in the early days of the war. It listed the facts of each of the major locations where atrocities were alleged to have occurred, quoting at length from fully named individual witnesses, many holding leading positions in Belgian society. It provided a more detailed basis to support the deaths of more than 5,000 Belgians and the destruction of more than 20,000 homes during this period in the war and accused the German military of significant war crimes and violations of the Geneva Convention.

---

35. *Id.* Part II.
36. *Die volkerrechtswidrige Filhrung des belgischen Volkskriegs* (1915).
37. Government of Belgium, Reply to the German White Book of May, 1915 (1918).

LEGAL PROFILES

Kenelm Edward Digby was another member of the Bryce committee. He was born in England in 1836, obtained his legal training there, and was called to the bar in 1865. From 1892 to 1894 he was a county court judge. He became a king's counsel in 1904. He was home office undersecretary from 1895 to 1903. He also taught law at Oxford and published a legal textbook on real property. He died in 1916.[38]

Edward Grimwood Mears was the secretary of the Bryce committee. He was born in England in 1869 and obtained his legal training there. After serving on this committee, he authored "The Destruction of Belgium—Germany's Confession and Avoidance" in 1916, as a reply to the German White Book. From 1917 to 1919 he served on the Dardanelles Commission. From 1919 until 1932 he served as the chief justice on the high court in India (Allahabad). He died in 1963.[39]

2. Leipzig War Crimes Trials

The evidence submitted by Belgium, France, and Germany was taken to Germany to be used before the German Imperial Court of Justice (*Reichsgericht*) sitting at Leipzig. The twelve defendants who were brought to trial starting on May 23 to July 16, 1921, were:

- Sgt. Karl Heynen, charged with cruelty to POWs, such as those who reported sick or refused to work in the mines, convicted on eighteen counts, and sentenced to ten months' imprisonment.
- Capt. Emil Müller, charged with cruelty to POWs in a camp he led (see below).
- Pvt. Robert Neumann, charged with cruelty to POWs, convicted on twelve counts, and sentenced to six months' imprisonment.

---

38. *See Kenelm Digby*, OXFORD DICTIONARY OF NATIONAL BIOGRAPHY 101050587.
39. *See Deaths—Mears*, THE TIMES (June 1, 1963).

- Lt.-Capt. Karl Neumann, charged with sinking hospital ship *Dover Castle* (see below).
- First-Lt. Ludwig Dithmar, charged with sinking hospital ship *Llandovery Castle* (see below).
- First-Lt. John Boldt, charged with sinking hospital ship *Llandovery Castle* (see below).
- Max Ramdohr, a former law student, charged with cruelty to civilian children, by arresting them on connection with suspected sabotage but found innocent due to the contradictions in the children's testimonies.
- Lt.-Gen. Karl Stenger, charged with ordering the killing of POWs but acquitted due to a lack of evidence presented.
- Maj. Benno Crusius, charged with the killings of POWs, found guilty of killing through negligence, and sentenced to two years' imprisonment.
- First-Lt. Adolph Laule, charged with killing an escaping French POW but acquitted since no evidence of his ordering or killing the POW was presented.
- Lt.-Gen. Hans von Schack, charged with deliberately or negligently allowing typhus to infect POWs, leading to deaths of thousands of men, but acquitted as the court found the outbreak a misfortune but not deliberate or negligent.
- Maj.-Gen. Benno Kruska, also charged with deliberately or negligently allowing typhus to infect POWs at the same camp until von Schack was acquitted when the court found the outbreak a misfortune but not deliberate or negligent.

a. Müller

The case of Captain Emil Müller is of special note, as he was a lawyer in civilian life and this involved a case of command responsibility, among the first so tried. As commander responsible for just over a month for a section of a prison camp close to the front lines, his duties included supervising the prisoners' daily lives and providing them for outside labor under the control of another commander. The camp was built for three hundred and housed more than three times that many, with no sanitary or cooking facilities, beds, or sufficient food or clothing, and only a mud floor in the primitive huts housing the POWs. Many men in the crowded huts could not lie down at night. More than half the men came down with dysentery but were still forced to work, and some men died.

The court did not condemn Müller for the condition of the camp, which he had inherited from the British and had taken some steps to fix, including sinking wells, installing stoves, providing washing facilities, and getting additional medicine, food, and clothes. He was, however, convicted for individual acts of brutality to prisoners, including beating prisoners, tying them to stakes, and forcing sick POWs to work. This conviction was not only for what he did personally but for what he instructed his subordinates to do or what he tolerated them doing under his command. As the court noted in its decision, "the accused never had any right to get over these difficulties by means of endless acts of violence,"[40] and "he had no eyes for their obvious sufferings: he cared little for the individual." For sixteen proven counts, he was sentenced to six months' imprisonment.

b. Neumann

Lt. Captain Karl Neumann was the commander of the U-boat UC-67, which in May 1917 torpedoed and sank the hospital ship HMHS *Dover Castle*. Six sailors lost their lives, but the remaining crew and all of the wounded were rescued. The issue was one of whether the order to sink the ship was legal. The German government had issued orders that hospital ships in the blockade zone could be carrying munitions or troops and, as such, were not protected by international law and could be treated as vessels of war. Neumann had waited for all of the wounded to be loaded onto a destroyer that was escorting it before sinking it with a second torpedo. Because he was following orders and did not carry out an act that involved a crime, the court found him not guilty.

c. Dithmar/Boldt

First-Lts. Ludwig Dithmar and John Boldt were being tried because the commander of their U-boat, Helmut Patzig, could not be found. In June 1918 HMHS *Llandovery Castle* was transporting wounded from Canada to England but was torpedoed and sunk by Patzig's U-boat, U-86. The *Llandovery Castle* was far outside the blockade area, so there should have been no interpretation of this being a legitimate target under international law. The U-boat stuck around, interrogating the survivors in lifeboats who were trying to rescue their shipmates. The Germans were looking for proof of munitions or troops to

---

40. Judgment in the Case of Emil Müller, I. *Ill Treatment* (May 30, 1921).

justify the sinking. When none was found, most men on the submarine were ordered below, and the U-boat began firing on the survivors in the lifeboats.

The two defendants refused to testify, and the captain had refused to log the incident. Of the three lifeboats that had survived the torpedoing, only one survived the gunfire, with an unknown number of people (men and the female nurses on board the hospital ship) killed. The court found them guilty of manslaughter, not murder, as this was a crime of emotion, committed after not finding evidence of troops. Because Dithmar and Boldt did not refuse to cooperate with what was clearly an illegal order, both were sentenced to four years' imprisonment.

In summary, of the twelve men who were tried, six were on British evidence and six on French or Belgian evidence. Six of these were convicted. The sentences ranged from six months to four years' imprisonment. Not satisfied with this test of using the German courts, the Commission of Allied Jurists reviewed the verdicts and declared in January 1922 that further use of the German courts would be of little value and an international tribunal should be undertaken. This never happened, and although there were hundreds of other cases reviewed by the German court, no further significant convictions were obtained. It was generally felt, outside of Germany, that the war crimes trials were a failure. The next time that major war crimes trials were called for, they were held much more rapidly and in a completely different manner, at Nuremberg and elsewhere, after WWII (see below).

LEGAL PROFILES

Heinrich Schmidt was the president of the Leipzig court. He was born in Germany in 1856 and obtained his legal training there. He served the judicial service in the state of Hesse-Darmstadt. He then served as a prosecutor and judge, becoming the chief prosecutor in Mainz in 1897. In 1905 he moved to the criminal division of the Reichsgerichtsrat, becoming its president in 1921. In 1923 he became president of the constitutional court. He retired the following year and died in 1927.[41]

---

41. See *Schmidt, (Karl Ludwig Theodor) Heinrich*, Das Bundesarchiv.

Ludwig Ebermayer was the state attorney (prosecutor) of the Leipzig court. He was born in Germany in 1858 and obtained his legal training there. From 1883 until 1902 he worked in the state of Bavaria's judicial service. He then moved to the Reichsgerichtsrat, becoming its president in 1918. From 1921 to 1926 he was the senior prosecutor there. He then retired and taught law. He died in 1933.[42]

3. Poisonous Gas Protocols

There were no trials of Fritz Haber, the leading German poisonous gas scientist, or of Victor Grignard, the leading French poisonous gas scientist, for the creation and deployment of the gases first used during this war. Instead, both were Nobel laureates (in 1918 and 1912, respectively). Neither were there trials for the military men who deployed these poisonous gases. There were, however, repeated efforts made after the war to ban their further use. Although all major powers eventually used poisonous gases, Germany deployed these weapons most heavily. As such, the Versailles Treaty stated that "The use of asphyxiating, poisonous, or other gases and of analogous liquids, materials or devices being prohibited, their manufacture and importation are strictly forbidden to Germany."[43] Such language was also incorporated into peace treaties between the United States and Germany, Austria, Bulgaria, and Hungary (see Chapter 7).

In 1922 the participants of the Washington Naval Conference (see Chapter 7) agreed to a treaty prohibiting such gases. This agreement prohibited "The use in war of asphyxiating, poisonous or other gases, and all analogous liquids, materials, or devices, having been justly condemned by the general opinion of the civilized world and a prohibition of such use having been declared in treaties to which a majority of the civilized Powers are parties. The Signatory Powers, to the end that this prohibition shall be universally accepted as part of international law binding alike the conscience and practice of nations, declare

---

42. *See Ebermayer Peter Friedrich Ludwig*, NEUE DEUTSCHE BIOGRAPHIE.
43. Versailles Treaty, art. 171.

their assent to such prohibition, agree to be bound thereby as between themselves and invite all other civilized nations to adhere thereto."[44]

In 1925 the more globally inclusive Geneva Protocol[45] was signed and ratified in 1928, although many of the ratifiers reserved the right to use such weapons in response to the first use by other nations. It stated that:

> Whereas the use in war of asphyxiating, poisonous or other gases, and of all analogous liquids materials or devices, has been justly condemned by the general opinion of the civilized world; and
>
> Whereas the prohibition of such use has been declared in Treaties to which the majority of Powers of the world are Parties; and
>
> To the end that this prohibition shall be universally accepted as a part of International Law, binding alike the conscience and the practice of nations;
>
> Declare:
>
> That the High Contracting Parties, so far as they are not already Parties to Treaties prohibiting such use, accept this prohibition, agree to extend this prohibition to the use of bacteriological methods of warfare and agree to be bound as between themselves according to the terms of this declaration.
>
> The High Contracting will exert every effort to induce other States to accede to the Present Protocol.

---

44. Treaty Relating to the Use of Submarines and Noxious Gases in Warfare, art. 5, U.S.-Brit.-Fr.-It.-Japan, Washington (1922).
45. Protocol for the Prohibition of the Use in War of Asphyxiating, Poisonous or Other Gases, and of Bacteriological Methods of Warfare, Geneva (1925).

LEGAL PROFILES

Jonathan Mayhew Wainwright was part of an advisory committee for the 1922 treaty that supported its approval in the U.S. Congress. He was born in New York in 1864 and started his legal practice there in 1886. He was elected to the New York legislature from 1902 to 1913. Having previously served in the Spanish-American War and as part of the National Guard on the Mexican border in 1916, he served again in the military when America entered the war. After the war, he was appointed assistant secretary of war in 1921, serving until 1923. In that year, he was elected to Congress, serving there until 1931. He returned to private practice and died in 1945.[46]

4. Ottoman Trials

On May 24, 1915, the Allied Powers of France, Great Britain, and Russia issued an ultimatum to the Ottoman government through the neutral American embassy in Constantinople, stating that "in view of these new crimes of Turkey against humanity and civilization, the Allied governments announce publicly to the Sublime-Porte [see Chapter 1] that they will hold personally responsible [for] these crimes all members of the Ottoman government and those of their agents who are implicated in such massacres."[47] After the war, two sets of trials, one Turkish and one international, were to be held to try those responsible for the massacres. The postwar U.S. military mission in Armenia issued a report on the matter to the U.S. Congress.

In the first trial, the postwar Turkish government, during the occupation by the Allied Powers after the armistice of Mudros (see Chapter 7), brought charges against the "Three Pashas" and others in power during the massacres. The Three Pashas were the leading members of the Committee of Unity and Progress and ran the empire during the war: war minister Enver Pasha, minister

---

46. *See Wainwright, Jonathan Mayhew*, BIOGRAPHICAL DIRECTORY OF THE UNITED STATES CONGRESS.
47. Telegram sent from Department of State in Washington to the U.S. Embassy in Constantinople to be given to the Turkish Government (May 24, 1915).

of the interior Talaat Pasha, and minister of the navy Djemal Pasha. They were tried and convicted by a court-martial under the Ottoman Criminal Code for premeditated murder for masterminding the massacres of the Armenians and Greeks and were sentenced to death in absentia (all had fled Turkey). With the political upheaval in postwar Turkey, the war of independence from the Allied occupation raging, and the uncertainty about procedural aspects of the trials, these sentences were not carried out, and instead the focus switched to a British trial in Malta.

The British, who had, after the armistice, seized and held more than one hundred Turkish prisoners on Malta with the hopes of trying them, first ran into the difficulties of obtaining sufficient evidence to prove the defendants' guilt needed for criminal trials. After holding these defendants for several years, the British government was finally forced to exchange its Turkish prisoners for British citizens captured by the nationalists in the war. The postwar Treaty of Sèvres[48] had allowed for an international tribunal to "hand over . . . persons . . . responsible for the massacres committed,"[49] but it was rejected by the nationalists and so was never ratified. Instead, the Treaty of Lausanne[50] was signed, which did not allow for international tribunals. Through all of these legal machinations that ended with the 1915 Ottoman leaders still being free, the Armenians felt that justice had not been served and set about enforcing the sentences of the original Turkish courts-martial. As part of Operation Nemesis (named for the Greek goddess of divine retribution), the Armenian Revolutionary Federation assassinated Talaat Pasha, Djemal Pasha, and others who had been in power during the massacres.

In 1920 the American Military Mission to Armenia issued a report[51] to the U.S. Secretary of State (and Congress) about the situation in Armenia. This report, which concerned the best way to resolve the many issues remaining in the region after the war, was based on interviews with varying nationalities of people there and onsite investigations in the region. It discussed first the history of the Armenians, noting that they had lived in the same area for 2,500

---

48. Treaty of Peace Between the Allied and Associated Powers and Turkey, Sèvres (Aug. 10, 1920).
49. *Id.* art. 230.
50. Treaty of Peace with Turkey, Lausanne (July 23, 1923).
51. Conditions in the Near East, Report of the American Military Mission to Armenia (Apr. 13, 1920).

years. Its recent history had turned significantly worse when the Ottomans under sultan Abdul Hamid started to massacre Armenians, killing 100,000 in 1895 and 30,000 in 1909. The report stated, "The official reports of the Turkish Government show 1,100,000 as having been deported [in 1915] . . . The dead from this wholesale attempt on the race are variously estimated from 500,000 to more than a million, the usual figure being about 800,000."[52]

It did note that a number of Ottoman officials had refused to carry out central government dictates to participate in the deportations and massacres but were then removed from their positions for taking a stand. Before moving on to its recommendations on how to deal best with the political situation in the region in the post-Ottoman period, the report, while discussing the impacts of these events on deported Armenian women and girls, said, "Mutilation, violation, torture, and death have left their haunting memories in a hundred beautiful Armenian valleys, and the traveler in that region is seldom free from the evidence of this most colossal crime of all the ages."[53]

LEGAL PROFILES

Jasper Y. Brinton was a judge advocate and member of the American Military Mission to Armenia. He was born in Pennsylvania in 1879 and started his legal training there in 1904. He worked in admiralty law and served as an assistant U.S. attorney. During the war he served as a judge advocate. He was then appointed to the Mixed Courts in Egypt in 1921, which headed cases involving foreign nationals there. He was eventually named president of the court from 1943 to 1948. He then served as an attorney for the U.S. embassy in Egypt. He died in 1973.[54]

---

52. *Id.* at 7.
53. *Id.*
54. *See Japser Yates Brinton Dead; Headed Mixed Courts of Egypt*, N.Y. TIMES (Aug. 13, 1973).

C. Subsequent Events

The use of war crimes trials differed substantially after WWII. Perhaps discovering what they did not do correctly after WWI, the surviving architects of the war in Europe were tried by the International Military Tribunal at Nuremberg, with exhaustive testimony and documentary evidence presented.[55] Following that would be twelve Nuremberg Military Tribunals held against a variety of different defendants, including jurists. Then there were numerous trials by the various nations under their military and civil justice systems, including for concentration camp offenses. This was replicated in Asia by the International Military Tribunal for the Far East.[56] This set the precedent of trying not only the lower level offenders for crimes against humanity and war crimes but also the architects of prosecuting aggressive war and crimes against peace. Asserting that one was just following orders was no longer considered to be a defense to committing war crimes or crimes against humanity. Additionally, the rules of evidence were to be more loosely applied, in order to allow all relevant evidence, considering courts had to deal with significant destruction of documents by nations. Finally, the treatment of POWs was aided by the Geneva Convention of 1929,[57] which required that POWs "must at all times be humanely treated and protected, particularly against acts of violence, insults and public curiosity. Measures of reprisal against them are prohibited."[58]

D. Modern Applicability

The trying of war crimes continues to this day, with war crimes tribunals still sitting in the Hague as the International Criminal Tribunal for the Former Yugoslavia and International Criminal Tribunal for Rwanda. The term "genocide" was coined by Raphael Lemkin,[59] literally meaning the killing of a race or group and further defined as the "denial of the right of existence of entire human groups."[60] It includes acts intended to destroy a group, such as killing members of the group or "deliberately inflicting on the group conditions of

---

55. *See* WWII Law and Lawyers, ch. 6.
56. *See* WWII Law and Lawyers, ch. 7.
57. Convention Relative to the Treatment of Prisoners of War, July 27, 1929.
58. *Id.* art. 2.
59. *See* WWII Law and Lawyers, ch. 6.
60. United Nations, The Crime of Genocide, GA Res. 96(1) (Dec. 11, 1946).

life calculated to bring about it physical destruction."[61] Its applicability to the deportations and massacres within the Ottoman Empire in 1915 continues to be a hotly contested issue between the government of Turkey, where it is a crime to insult the Turkish nation, and the Armenian government and supporters of the Armenian diaspora. Several dozen countries have accepted that these events constituted genocide, and U.S. presidents have stated that it was genocide.[62] Attempts are still being made in the U.S. Congress to achieve government recognition of these events as genocide.[63]

In 1997 the Chemical Weapons Convention[64] went into effect and addressed the poisonous gases utilized in WWI. It considered not only chlorine and phosgene (choking agents) and mustard gas (a blistering agent) but also blood and nerve agents like sarin gas. It declared the use and production of this group of weapons of mass destruction to be prohibited, and it included an inspection mechanism to verify their destruction. The regime of Saddam Hussein used poison gas in its wars in the 1980s, giving further cause to the implementation of this convention. The convention has been ratified by almost all nations in the world, except for a handful. One of the nations that has not yet ratified this convention is Syria, where poison gas has purportedly been used in the battle between the regime and rebel forces,[65] and the Syrian government agreed to destroy its stockpile of chemical weapons.[66]

6.2 UPRISINGS

A. Statutes

Across the British Empire were a number of uprisings that occurred during the war. As discussed previously (see Chapter 5), Germany was trying to

---

61. United Nations, Prevention and Punishment of the Crime of Genocide, GA Res. 260 (III) (Dec. 9, 1948), art. II.
62. Pub. Proclamation No. 4838, Ronald Reagan, Days of Remembrance of Victims of the Holocaust (Apr. 22, 1981).
63. H. Res. 227, 113th Congress, Calling on the President to work toward equitable, constructive, stable, and durable Armenian-Turkish relations based upon the Republic of Turkey's full acknowledgment of the facts and ongoing consequences of the Armenian Genocide, and a fair, just, and comprehensive international resolution of this crime against humanity (May 20, 2013).
64. Convention on the Prohibition of the Development, Production, Stockpiling and Use of Chemical Weapons and on their Destruction, Jan. 13, 1993.
65. *France Offers Evidence of Multiple Use of Nerve Gas in Syria*, N.Y. TIMES (June 4, 2013).
66. *Syria submits plan to destroy its chemical weapons: OPCW*, REUTERS (Oct. 27, 2013).

foment rebellion in those parts of the empire where long-suppressed people were ready to move forward. These areas included both Ireland and India. While officially India had proclaimed her support and provided significant numbers of troops throughout the war, certain political movements wished to take advantage of the British's efforts and attention being diverted elsewhere to make a push for independence. In Ireland, the island provided significant voluntary manpower for the British war effort, but the lack of definitive progress on independence led to an uprising there in 1916.

In the Middle East, the colonial positioning of the British, French, Germans, Italians, and Ottomans was complex. To keep control, the colonial overlords often used uprisings to bring in a more pliant regime when the current regime became too independent. In the war, similar uprisings were used to destabilize enemies. Furthermore, against the backdrop of the uprisings in the Middle East was the long-standing Jewish desire for a return to its homeland of several millennia prior. The Zionist movement wanted to secure a homeland and again saw the war as the catalyst that could make that happen, or at least begin the process.

In Russia, the czar's grip on power was fading, and a new dynamic was in play, with the Bolsheviks leading a complete revolution that was different from the ones proceeding in other places. This revolution was less about replacing a tottering empire with a slimmed-down core nation still holding to its principal culture, as would occur to Germany, Austria-Hungary, the Ottomans, and Bulgaria. Instead, it was more of a complete change in ruling style and culture, moving from a small ruling elite oppressing a significant peasantry to a supposedly egalitarian state based on comradeship of all. To make this occur, the uprising was planned again by Germany, who hoped to take Russia out of the war.

1. Ireland

The British had been in Ireland seemingly forever, but it was the Act of Union of 1800 that brought the Kingdoms of Ireland and Great Britain together as the United Kingdom. With a land mass slightly greater than a third of Great Britain's, the Irish population at the start of the war was only 10 percent of that of Great Britain. Devastated by the great famine in the 1840s and the subsequent massive emigration, and not anywhere near the leader in the industrial revolution, trade, finance, or empire that Great Britain was, Ireland had always been the weaker state. But the Irish began to demand more, at least the right to home rule within the United Kingdom.

Two attempts at getting a home rule bill through Parliament failed in the era of Prime Minister William Gladstone in the second half of the nineteenth century. The second time it was the House of Lords that refused to advance the home rule bill passed by Commons. Later, the Parliament Act in 1911 gave Commons the right (being the only elected body of the two in Parliament) to pass legislation without the approval of the House of Lords (vetoes were only temporary). But, although the stage was finally set to pass a home rule law for Ireland, problems with the Ulster bloc, led by Edward Carson (see Chapter 2), were making passage difficult. At last, the start of the war changed the dynamics, and in September 1914, the Irish Home Rule Act was passed.[67] Unfortunately, it was passed the same day as the Suspensory Act,[68] which blocked implementation of home rule during the war or for a year, whichever was longer. Orders in council were subsequently issued that suspended this act for six months at a time.

LEGAL PROFILES

John Redmond was the leader of the Irish independence movement in Parliament when the Home Rule Act was passed. He was born in Ireland in 1856 and obtained his legal training there, being called to the Irish bar in 1887 and the English bar in 1888. He was first elected to the British Parliament in 1881, where he would serve for the remainder of his life. He led the Irish Parliamentary Party during much of that time, with the leading achievement of finally passing the Irish Home Rule Act in 1914. He died in 1918.[69]

---

67. Government of Ireland Act of 1914, 4 & 5 Geo. 5, c. 90 (U.K.).
68. Suspensory Act of 1904, 4 & 5 Geo. 5, c. 88 (U.K.).
69. *See John Redmond Dies; Many Pay Tribute*, N.Y. TIMES (Mar. 7, 1918).

2. India

Like in Ireland, Great Britain in different forms had been in India for some time though initially as a trading venture, through the East India Company. This changed as the company took over or aligned with numerous Indian states. After the Indian (or Sepoy—soldier) Rebellion started in 1857, the British government decided to take direct control of the country and passed the Government of India Act[70] the following year. This transferred all ruling powers of the East India Company to the Queen, the new Empress of India. After the start of the war, the rule of India was consolidated under the Government of India Act in 1915[71] and amended the following year.[72] It allowed for a secretary of state for India[73] presiding over a council of India[74] and a governor-general with an executive council.[75] Although India was in some ways similar to Canada, Australia, New Zealand, and South Africa in having a governor-general who represented the monarch while running the administration of the country, it also uniquely had a secretary of state for India who controlled the governor-general and the country's revenues.

When the war started, the Congress Party, the biggest political party in India, determined that it would be in its interests to support the war effort, which in turn would lead to independence after the war was over. But not all citizens of India, a country of so many languages, cultures, and religions, agreed with this direction. In particular, some of the Indian diaspora looked for ways to accelerate independence and remove the British. To deal with security threats in the country, the Defence of India Act (modeled on DORA, see Chapter 3) was passed by the governor-general in council in March 1915.[76] It was to be in force for the duration of the war plus six months[77] and allowed the governor-general to make rules "for the purposes of securing the public safety

---

70. Government of India Act of 1858, 21 & 22 Vict., c. 106 (U.K.).
71. Government of India Act of 1915, 5 & 6 Geo. 5, c. 61 (U.K.).
72. Government of India (Amendment) Act of 1916, 6 & 7 Geo. 5, c. 37 (U.K.).
73. *Id.* § 2.
74. *Id.* § 3.
75. *Id.* § 33 et seq.
76. Defence of India (Criminal Law Amendment Act) No. 4 of 1915. An Act to provide for special measures to secure the public safety and the defence of British India and for the more speedy trial of certain offences (British India).
77. *Id.* § 1(4).

and the defence of British India."[78] It could appoint three-commissioner panels to hold trials under the act.[79] Judgments were to be "final and conclusive," neither requiring confirmation of sentences[80] nor allowing appeals.[81]

LEGAL PROFILES

Mohandas K. Gandhi was one of the Indian leaders who believed in supporting the war effort, despite his personal pacifism. He was born in India in 1869, obtained his legal training in England, and was called to the bar in 1891. In 1894 he relocated to South Africa, where he assisted Indians whose rights were being suppressed, and he began to take part in both nonviolent protests and direct negotiations with government officials. He also supported British war efforts in the Second Boer War and the Zulu War by forming Indian ambulance crews. He returned to India in 1915 to become involved in and soon to lead the independence movement through the Indian National Congress Party. Under principles of nonviolence and noncooperation, leading actions such as the Salt March, suffering imprisonment, and traveling to England, he negotiated (and pulled back from negotiating) with the British to achieve independence. He continued his vigorous support for all of the oppressed people in India. Jailed again for not supporting the war effort during WWII and instead demanding that the British quit India now, he lived to see independence given to his people after the passing of the Indian Independence Act. He was assassinated in 1948.[82]

3. Middle East

In contrast to being the target of uprisings, the British could also assist those who were working against its enemies. In the Middle East, the British had

---

78. *Id.* § 2(1).
79. *Id.* § 4.
80. *Id.* § 6(1).
81. *Id.* § 8(1).
82. *See Mohandas K. Gandhi, The Indian Leader at Home and Abroad*, N.Y. TIMES (Jan. 31, 1948).

several strategic interests, primarily the Suez Canal and the Anglo-Persian pipeline. The Suez Canal, originally built in an Egyptian partnership with the French, incurred such debts that the Egyptians sold their share to the British, who were then involved in the government to ensure proper running and revenue from the canal. The pipeline transported oil critical to the war effort, especially with the new oil-burning (instead of coal-burning) warships in the Royal Navy. Although Egypt was part of the Ottoman Empire, after the start of the war, the British overthrew the khedive and replaced him with a sultan. After the Germans tried and failed to incite an insurrection in Egypt, Britain responded by encouraging a revolt against the Ottoman Empire throughout the Arab world. Inspired by T. E. Lawrence (Lawrence of Arabia), the British and their allies were able to eventually take over enough territory in the region, including Jerusalem in December 1917, to drive the Ottomans from the war.

The British and the French had made an agreement, in May 1916, to deal with the Middle East after the expected fall of the Ottomans. Written by diplomats Francois Georges-Picot and Mark Sykes and signed by foreign ministers Edward Grey and Paul Cambon (see Chapter 1), the agreement divided the Middle East into spheres of influence.[83] Essentially, it divided Iraq, Syria, Lebanon, Transjordan, and Palestine into areas that would be controlled or influenced by the British (part of Iraq and Transjordan), by France (part of Iraq, Syria, and Lebanon), and under international control (Palestine), with several free ports, limits in railways, and access to the sea. Although the agreement provided for independent Arab states or a confederation of such states, it did not allow other powers into the region, and all advisers were to come from France or Great Britain respectively. This agreement was to be secret and was to include Russia, which after the ascendancy of the Bolsheviks exposed the agreement to the world.

Several weeks prior to the exposure, the British had signaled support for the creations of a Jewish state. The Balfour Declaration,[84] a letter from the foreign minister of the United Kingdom Arthur Balfour, for publication to the British Jewish community, stated the British government's sympathy to the aspirations of Jewish Zionists. It stated, "His Majesty's Government view with favour the establishment in Palestine of a national home for the Jewish people, and will

---

83. Sykes-Gambon Agreement (May 16, 1916).
84. Letter from Arthur Balfour to Walter Rothschild, Balfour Declaration (Nov. 2, 1917).

use their best endeavours to facilitate the achievement of this object, it being clearly understood that nothing shall be done which may prejudice the civil and religious rights of existing non-Jewish communities in Palestine, or the rights and political status enjoyed by Jews in any other country." This declaration was incorporated into the Treaty of Sèvres[85] in 1920 and the San Remo Resolution of April 25, 1920. British control of Palestine would be confirmed with a League of Nations mandate following the war (see Chapter 7), which again would refer to this declaration.

LEGAL PROFILES

Alfred Milner was one of the drafters of the Balfour Declaration. He was born in Germany in 1854 but was raised and obtained his legal training in England, being called to the bar in 1881. After several years in journalism and an unsuccessful run for Parliament, he became involved in finance, working for the chancellor of the exchequer, then as undersecretary of finance in Egypt. After four years in Egypt, he was chairman of Inland Revenue from 1892 to 1897. In that year, he was posted to South Africa as high commissioner. He served in this role through 1905, including during the Second Boer War. In 1916 he joined the coalition's War Cabinet. In 1918 he was appointed war secretary, then after the armistice, colonial secretary. He died in 1925.[86]

4. Russia

The Eastern Front was as much of a stalemate as the Western Front, though along a much longer distance. Both Germany and Russia were hurting through loss of people and money, but Russia, although having a larger population but a smaller economy not as heavily industrialized, was hurting more. Heavy losses

---

85. Treaty of Peace Between the Allied and Associated Powers and Turkey, Sèvres, art. 95 (Aug. 10, 1920).
86. *See Alfred Milner*, OXFORD DICTIONARY OF NATIONAL BIOGRAPHY 101035037.

in troops, poor harvests, the inability to get food and other imports past the German blockade, devastation due to battles from the war, poor industrial working conditions, lack of sustained political liberalization, loss of esteem from more than a decade of military setbacks, and the long-standing disenchantment with the czar-led feudal system still prevalent in much of Russia led to a strong movement to overthrow the government. The February 1917 revolution led to the March 1917 abdication of the czar.

A provisional government was created to take over and keep the war effort going. Wanting to further cripple their enemy at a time of extreme weakness, the Germans provided safe passage (in a sealed train) from Switzerland through Germany to Russia for Vladimir Lenin, who hit the ground running by forming soldier and worker councils (soviets) as the supposed key decision-making apparatus. A civil war broke out between the Red Army of the Bolsheviks and the White Army (and others including the Allied Powers), made up of those opposed to the Bolsheviks. By November (October on the old Julian calendar Russia was still using), the Bolsheviks had taken over the government (the "October" Revolution). Lenin immediately sued for peace to exit from the war, but the negotiations made by the inexperienced Bolsheviks did not proceed the way they had planned. Eventually, through threat of force from the Central Powers, the Bolsheviks agreed to a peace deal on terms they would not have otherwise wanted.

The resulting Treaty of Brest-Litovsk[87] was beneficial for both Russia and Germany. The former got to spend all of its resources on fighting its civil war, while the latter was able to redeploy men and materials from the Eastern to the Western Front, leading to the Spring Offensive of 1918. On the other hand, Russia was to lose control over the soon-to-be-independent countries of the Ukraine, Finland, Estonia, Latvia, Lithuania[88] and its territory in the Ottoman Empire,[89] and Poland.[90] And the civil war that was about to become fully engaged in Russia would leave millions of Russian soldiers and civilians dead before the Bolsheviks finally had firm control of the country. The Treaty

---

87. Treaty of Peace between Germany, Austria-Hungary, Bulgaria, and Ottoman Empire and Russian SFSR, Mar. 3, 1918.
88. *Id.* arts. 3 & 6.
89. *Id.* art. 4.
90. Treaty (Peace) of Riga, Rus.-Pol. (Mar. 18, 1921).

of Brest-Litovsk was to be short-lived, with the armistice ending the fighting and with Germany then abandoning the treaty.[91]

LEGAL PROFILES

Vladimir Ilyich Lenin was one of the founders of the Communist state in Russia. He was born in the Russian Empire in 1870 and obtained his legal training there. He worked for a local court and lawyer around his involvement in radical politics and the works of Marx and Engels. He continued to move in Socialist and radical circles, traveling abroad and defining the roles of the proletariat. He was imprisoned and exiled from 1895 to 1900, the last several years in Siberia. He spent most of his life, from 1900 to 1917, living in western Europe and, during the war, in neutral Switzerland. On his return to Russia in 1917, he led the Soviet revolution to the October Revolution and then, after dropping out of WWI, led the Bolsheviks in the civil war inside the country. The Soviets were successful in the civil war, but Lenin had been the victim of assassination attempts, which, combined with other illnesses, forced his retirement in late 1922. He died in early 1924.[92]

B. Cases

This group of cases had to do with the uprisings against the ruling powers, the first four cases involving the British Empire in various locations around the globe and the fifth the Russian Empire. In the first case, the leaders of the 1916 Irish uprising were brought to trial. In the second case, Sir Roger Casement was tried for treason surrounding the same events. The third case discussed the many conspiracy trials resulting from the Ghadar uprisings in India in 1915. The fourth trial addressed the validity of the mandate over Palestine given to

---

91. Terms of Armistice Signed by Germany, Point 15 (Nov. 11, 1918).
92. *See Lenin, Dictator of Soviet Russia*, THE TIMES (Jan. 23, 1924).

Great Britain. The fifth trial was an early challenge by the Bolsheviks against the ruling elite of the Russian nobility.

1. Ireland
a. Leaders of the Uprising

The lack of progress in implementing home rule led to some members of the Irish independence movement taking matters into their own hands. One of the independence groups, the Irish Republican Brotherhood, decided after the start of the war to stage an uprising. Using its armed unit, the Irish Volunteers, plus other similarly minded groups, took over various locations in Dublin and elsewhere in the country on Easter Sunday of 1916 (April 24). One of the leaders of the uprising, Patrick Pearse, declared that day from the steps of the commandeered General Post Office building in Dublin, "Standing on that fundamental right and again asserting it in arms in the face of the world, we hereby proclaim the Irish Republic as a Sovereign Independent State. And we pledge our lives and the lives of our comrades-in-arms to the cause of its freedom, of its welfare, and of its exaltation among the nations."[93]

The British, focused elsewhere, were not initially prepared to respond but soon brought in sufficient troops and weaponry to overwhelm the uprising in less than a week. The rebels were already plagued by insufficient weapons and conflicting orders, as not all Irish nationalists agreed with the timing. Hundreds of military personnel and civilians were killed and thousands wounded. Martial law was declared. After the surrender, several thousand people were arrested in Ireland and many others interned in Britain. The leaders of the uprising in Ireland were captured and taken before courts-martial starting immediately, including the seven men who had signed the proclamation. Almost two hundred were tried in the weeks after the uprising was crushed.

The trials took place in military instead of civilian courts, as provided for under the Defence of the Realm Act[94] (DORA) § 1 (see Chapter 3). Even though DORA now allowed for trial by civil courts,[95] the British did not believe Irish civil court would convict[96] (and had suspended jury trials after the

---

93. Poblacht Na H Eireann, The Provisional Government of the Irish Republic to the People of Ireland, Proclamation of the Irish Republic, Apr. 24, 1916.
94. Defence of the Realm Consolidation Act of 1914, 5 Geo. 5, c. 8 (U.K.).
95. Defence of the Realm (Amendment) Act of 1915, 5 Geo. 5, c. 34, § 1.1 (U.K.).
96. Royal Commission on the Rebellion in Ireland, Report of Commission, at 7 (1916).

uprising, as DORA allowed). The charges under DORA were that the rebels took part in an armed rebellion and were waging war against the country with the intent that it would assist their enemy.[97] Civilians could be tried by court-martial and sentenced to death for assisting the enemy.[98] Secret trials began on May 2, 1916, for the following uprising leaders (in their leadership roles): Thomas Clarke (planning), Patrick Pearse (military organization), James Connolly (Irish Citizens Army), Eamonn Ceannt (communications), Joseph Plunkett (military operations), Sean Mac Diarmada (a.k.a. McDermott, planning), and Thomas MacDonagh (training). The seven leaders and eighty-three others were convicted on this charge and received death sentences, but only fourteen of the men (the seven leaders and seven others who had led the uprising) were executed for the uprising, in early May 1916.

LEGAL PROFILES

Patrick Pearse was a leader of the uprising and a lawyer. He was born in Ireland in 1879 and obtained his legal training there, being called to the bar in 1901. A strong believer in the Irish language, he founded a school for bilingual education for Irish children. He was a leader in the Irish Volunteers, who had split into a majority of the men who volunteered to fight overseas in the war and those men who chose not to fight overseas. He also was a leader in the Irish Republican Brotherhood. In reading and signing the proclamation at the start of the uprising, he had committed himself fully, and after his capture, trial, and conviction, he was executed in 1916.[99]

---

97. Defence of the Realm Consolidation Act of 1914, § 1.1(e).
98. *Id.* § 1.4.
99. *See Pearse's Last Letter*, N.Y. TIMES (May 27, 1916).

b. Roger Casement

One of the reasons for the failure of the uprising was a lack of weapons. The delivery of weapons for the uprising had been arranged by Sir Roger Casement, who had spent time negotiating with the Germans and had a ship sent to Ireland to aid the uprising. The ship was, however, intercepted, and Casement, on landing in Ireland from a U-boat, was himself captured and brought to trial.

Roger Casement had been involved, while working for the British consular service, in documenting human rights abuses in both Africa and South America. On return to Europe, he got heavily involved in the cause of Irish independence. He traveled to the United States to raise funds and, while there, met with the German ambassador Bernstorff (see Chapter 5) to try to coordinate a swap of German arms for an Irish uprising to distract the British during the war. To further these plans, he then traveled to Germany to gather uprising troops from among Irish POWs in Germany and to further solidify the arms deal. He was unsuccessful in the former and while he did receive some weapons, they were older and fewer than requested.

He and the weapons then sailed separately from Germany, with Casement making landfall in Ireland several days before the start of the uprisings, where he was quickly arrested. He was charged with high treason under the Treason Act of 1351 (see Chapter 3). Originally written in Normal French, the translated and operative phrasing of import to this case was "if a Man do levy War against our Lord the King in his Realm, or be adherent to the King's Enemies in his Realm, giving to them Aid and Comfort in the Realm, or elsewhere, and thereof."[100] The facts were not in dispute, as he had been giving aid to the enemy of the United Kingdom during a time of war. What could be disputed by the defense, in the trial[101] and the appeal,[102] was that the Treason Act only applied to treasons committed within England or the United Kingdom, not outside.

The prosecution detailed in its opening statement how the Germans had, between December 1914 and February 1915, taken geographically distributed Irish POWs and assembled them in a single camp, for the purpose of being turned by Casement. He then tried forming an Irish Brigade, with the under-

---

100. Treason Act of 1351, 25 Edw. 3, Stat. 5, c. 2 (U.K.).
101. R v. Casement, 32 TLR 601, K. B. (1916).
102. R v. Casement, 32 TLR 667, C.C.A. (1916).

standing that "everything was to be gained for Ireland by Germany winning the war."[103] If Germany lost the war, each POW would be given a bonus and free passage to America. Those who did not concur with this message were put on short rations. The prosecution also presented evidence of a code, captured on Casement, that included phrases about men, communications, railways, arms, ammunition, cannons, and vessels, as well as how the ship with arms intended for the Irish uprisings was sent from Germany with German sailors, though it was intercepted.

The defense made a motion to quash the indictment, using the following very creative arguments. Going from the reigns of Edward III (the original Treason Act) to Henry VIII (when the Treason Act was expanded), the defense contended that there was no treason (i.e., the crime was not triable) if done outside the realm because there was no venue, but famed English law authority Lord Coke later interpreted it otherwise to find a venue. The defense tried to show that Coke's cited supporting cases were not valid. From the time of Henry VIII (he died in 1547) until a statute passed in 1745, an offense committed abroad by an offender who returned to the realm of the English king could not be prosecuted. It quoted from a mid-sixteenth century case overruling the Henry VIII statute, "No offence of treason committed out of the 'realm was triable here by the course of the common law.'"[104] That meant that only the treason statute and its wording were important. In the original Treason Act, in the phrase "adherent to the King's Enemies in his Realm, giving to them Aid and Comfort in the Realm or elsewhere," the last word "elsewhere" was proposed to modify the location of the king's enemies. The defense insisted that the statute be read literally.

The court looked even at the original Normal French for guidance and the statute of 35 Henry VIII, which allowed the King's Bench to try overseas crimes. It also reviewed past legal authorities and a 1903 case (*The King v. Lynch*) and construed "or elsewhere" to modify the location of the performance of the treasonous acts, not the location of the enemy, meaning that aid and comfort given to the enemy "elsewhere" (i.e., outside the United Kingdom) still qualified as a treasonable act. As Casement had committed his treasonous acts in Germany, the United States, and elsewhere outside the United

---

103. R v. Casement, 32 TLR 601, K. B., Opening Speech for Prosecution.
104. *Id.* Motion to Quash Indictment.

Kingdom, but not in the short time he was ashore in Ireland before being captured, this interpretation was vital for his conviction. The English jury did convict him, and the court gave him the only available sentence, that of death. Casement read a statement, protesting the court did not have jurisdiction over an Irishman and that a jury of Englishmen was not a jury of his peers. After the dismissal of his appeal ("he may violate his allegiance in a foreign country just as well as he may violate it in this country"[105]), Casement was then executed on August 3, 1916.

LEGAL PROFILES

A. M. Sullivan was the lead defense counsel for Casement. He was born in Ireland in 1871 and obtained his legal training there, being called to the Irish bar in 1892 and the English bar in 1899. He became an Irish king's counsel in 1906 and English king's counsel in 1919. He was appointed as a king's serjeant at law in Ireland, giving advice to the crown, the last first serjeant appointed. He relocated to England after the Irish War of Independence but returned to Ireland in 1949. He died in 1959.[106]

John H. Morgan was another defense counsel for Casement, discussing the importance of older caselaw. He was born in England in 1876 and obtained his legal training there, being called to the bar in 1913. He had previously worked in journalism and had an extensive academic career, including study in Germany. In 1908 he was appointed to a constitutional law chair and in 1913 a chair on law of the empire. During the war he served on the adjutant general staff and then attended the Paris Peace Conference in 1919. He worked as adjutant-general for the inter-allied military commission in Berlin from 1919 to 1923. In 1926 he was appointed reader in constitutional law and became a king's counsel. He also worked as a legal editor for the Encyclopædia Britannica and again

---

105. R v. Casement, 32 TLR 667, C.C.A, Judgment.
106. *See Serjeant A. M. Sullivan*, THE TIMES (Jan. 10, 1959).

as a law professor and practiced international law. After WWII he served on the UN War Crimes Commission and was a witness at the Nuremberg trials. He died in 1955.[107]

Horace Avory was one of the three judges at this trial. He was born in England in 1851 and obtained his legal training there, being called to the bar in 1875. He was involved in many well-known criminal cases at the Old Bailey, both prosecuting and defending. In 1889 he was appointed as junior treasury counsel and in 1899 as senior treasury counsel. In 1901 he went into private practice and became a king's counsel. In 1910 he was appointed judge in the King's Bench division of the High Court, becoming senior judge in 1924. He was appointed privy councilor in 1932. He died in 1935.[108]

Thomas Horridge was another of the three judges at this trial. He was born in England in 1857 and obtained his legal training there. After starting out as a solicitor in 1879, he was called to the bar in 1884. He became a king's counsel in 1901. In 1906 he was elected to Parliament, where he served until 1910. He then was appointed judge in the King's Bench division of the High Court. He served there, also working in the bankruptcy and divorce courts, until retiring in 1937. He died in 1938.[109]

2. India

The Ghadar (literally "mutiny") Party was made up of Indian expatriates who decided to return to India and free it from British rule. As discussed in Chapter 5, they were involved with the Germans who wanted to foment trouble in the British Empire and also had ties to Irish nationalists with similar ambitions. Knowing that the British army in India had been reduced to transfer troops to the war, the timing was right for a rebellion. With members of the

---

107. *See John Morgan*, Oxford Dictionary of National Biography 101035105.
108. *See Horace Avory*, Oxford Dictionary of National Biography 101030506.
109. *See Thomas Horridge*, Oxford Dictionary of National Biography 101033996.

diaspora returning from overseas locations such as the United States, Canada, Japan, China, Germany, and the Philippines, thousands converged on India and, in February 1915, started an uprising, primarily in the Punjab. But due to intelligence received and agents inside the movement, the British were able, in conjunction with local intelligence officials and soldiers, to arrest the leaders and many of the followers of the movement and disarm other potential army mutineers.

Starting in April almost three hundred were brought to trial in Lahore before the special commissioners and were charged with violating the Defence of India Act. Of those convicted in September 1915, forty-two were sentenced to death and 114 to transportation (sent to imprisonment overseas) for life. One of the leaders of the Ghadar movement, Sohan Singh Bhakna, was convicted and sentenced to death, which was commuted to transportation for life. Kartar Singh Sarabha, who published a newsletter for the movement, was convicted, sentenced to death, and executed at the age of nineteen. Ras Bihair Bose escaped back to Japan. Although many army units that were requested to rebel chose in the end not to do so, in Singapore one unit did mutiny when it was to ship out for redeployment, though not for the same reasons of Indian nationalism as the potential mutineers in other locations. More than one hundred men there were put on trial; of those, thirty-seven were sentenced to death and forty-one to transportation for life. Other conspiracy trials went on in Lahore through 1917, with the number of those convicted in total exceeding five hundred.

LEGAL PROFILES

(Rai Bahadur Pandit) Shiv Narayan Raina (Shameem) was the one Indian commissioner on the panel of three commissioners trying the first Lahore conspiracy trial. He was born in India in 1859 and obtained his legal training there. Besides being a leading lawyer for the Lahore bar (the Punjab Chief Court until 1919, then the Lahore High Court[110]), he was a primary mover in the drafting of the Sikh Gurdwaras

---

110. Government of India Act of 1915, 5 & 6 Geo. 5, c. 61, § 101 et seq. (U.K.).

Act of 1925[111] and authored the treatise "Pleadings in India Courts." He was also a poet and novelist. He died in 1936.[112]

3. Middle East

The British mandate to control arose out of an article specified in the League of Nations covenant.[113] This article 22 said, in part:

> To those colonies and territories which as a consequence of the late war have ceased to be under the sovereignty of the States which formerly governed them and which are inhabited by peoples not yet able to stand by themselves under the strenuous conditions of the modern world, there should be applied the principle that the well-being and development of such peoples form a sacred trust of civilisation and that securities for the performance of this trust should be embodied in this Covenant.
>
> The best method of giving practical effect to this principle is that the tutelage of such peoples should be entrusted to advanced nations who by reason of their resources, their experience or their geographical position can best undertake this responsibility, and who are willing to accept it, and that this tutelage should be exercised by them as Mandatories on behalf of the League.
>
> The character of the mandate must differ according to the stage of the development of the people, the geographical situation of the territory, its economic conditions and other similar circumstances. Certain communities formerly belonging to the Turkish Empire have reached a stage of development where their existence as independent nations can be provisionally recognized subject to the rendering of administrative advice and assistance by a Mandatory until such time as they are able to stand alone. The wishes of these communities must be a principal consideration in the selection of the Mandatory.

---

111. Sikh Gurdwaras Act of 1925, Punjab Act No. 8 (British India).
112. *See High Court of Punjab and Haryana*, CDJ Law Journal.
113. Covenant of the League of Nations, art. 22 (June 28, 1919).

In 1922 the League of Nations Council gave the United Kingdom the mandate for Palestine.[114] This legal mandate (meaning that the power had mandatory responsibilities beyond those involved in managing protectorates) gave the Mandatory (the supervising country) control of the legislative and executive functions[115] and foreign relations;[116] the authority to set up self-governing institutions,[117] a judicial system,[118] and local autonomy;[119] and the power to protect and provide access to "Holy Places."[120]

The mandate gave significant encouragement for a Jewish homeland in Palestine, as "The Mandatory shall be responsible for placing the country under such political, administrative and economic conditions as will secure the establishment of the Jewish national home, as laid down in the preamble."[121] For the Jewish representations, "An appropriate Jewish agency shall be recognised as a public body for the purpose of advising and co-operating with the Administration of Palestine in such economic, social and other matters as may affect the establishment of the Jewish national home and the interests of the Jewish population in Palestine."[122]

The preamble of the mandate further clarified the responsible party and the intention for a Jewish presence there:

> Whereas the Principal Allied Powers have agreed, for the purpose of giving effect to the provisions of Article 22 of the Covenant of the League of Nations, to entrust to a Mandatory selected by the said Powers the administration of the territory of Palestine, which formerly belonged to the Turkish Empire, within such boundaries as may be fixed by them; and
>
> Whereas the Principal Allied Powers have also agreed that the Mandatory should be responsible for putting into effect the declaration originally

---

114. League of Nations, Mandate for Palestine (Sept. 16, 1922).
115. *Id.* art. 1.
116. *Id.* art. 12.
117. *Id.* art. 2.
118. *Id.* art. 9.
119. *Id.* art. 3.
120. *Id.* art. 13.
121. *Id.* art. 2.
122. *Id.* art. 4.

made on November 2nd, 1917, by the Government of His Britannic Majesty, and adopted by the said Powers, in favour of the establishment in Palestine of a national home for the Jewish people, it being clearly understood that nothing should be done which might prejudice the civil and religious rights of existing non-Jewish communities in Palestine, or the rights and political status enjoyed by Jews in any other country; and

Whereas recognition has thereby been given to the historical connection of the Jewish people with Palestine and to the grounds for reconstituting their national home in that country; and Whereas the Principal Allied Powers have selected His Britannic Majesty as the Mandatory for Palestine.[123]

The authority of this article was challenged in court in cases such as *Greece v. Britain* in 1924.[124] In this case, a Greek national was seeking redress against the British Mandatory for not honoring contracts (signed when the Ottoman Empire ruled in Palestine) for the construction of electric tramway systems and utilities supply in two cities (Jerusalem and Jaffa). In ruling on whether it had jurisdiction to hear this case, as it was between a nation and a nation who intervened for an individual, the court accepted, as did the parties, the legal position of the Mandatory for Palestine to act as the successor to the Ottoman Empire in these obligations and its ability to avoid these prior obligations. One such example of this support was stated in a dissenting opinion, "A State which has undertaken a Mandate under the League of Nations has gratuitously taken upon itself a very arduous task and full effect must be given to the provisions of the Mandate."[125]

---

123. *Id.* Preamble.
124. Greece v. Britain, The Mavrommatis Palestine Concession, Permanent Court of International Justice, Judgment No. 2 (Aug. 30, 1924)
125. *Id.* Dissenting Opinion by Lord Finlay, [112].

LEGAL PROFILES

Robert Finlay was one of the judges on this court who wrote the dissenting opinion. He was born in Scotland in 1842 and obtained his medical training there. He did not practice medicine but instead was called to the bar in 1867 and became a queen's counsel in 1882. In 1885 he was elected to Parliament, serving until 1892 but returning twice, from 1895 to 1906 and from 1910 to 1916. In 1895 he was appointed solicitor general for England and in 1900 attorney general until 1905. From 1916 to 1919 he served as lord chancellor. In 1920 he was appointed to the International Court of Arbitration and in 1921 joined the Permanent Court of International Justice. He died in 1929.[126]

4. Russia

As a token first show trial that in the following decades would become common, the trial of Countess Sofia Panina occurred during the war and was an attempt by the Bolsheviks to take on the existing order through legal means. Sofia Panina was an assistant to the education minister in the provisional government that had taken over after the abdication of the czar. She was also a wealthy aristocrat, well known for her charitable work. She had been elected to the Petrograd Duma and was also a member of a now-outlawed political party (Constitutional Democratic Party). This trial could demonstrate how the Bolshevik's new Revolutionary Tribunal of the Petrograd Soviet could utilize the power of the peasants, workers, and soldiers to dole out appropriate justice.

Starting on December 10, 1917, she went on trial, charged with stealing money from the ministry of education. She admitted that she had the money, had deposited it in the bank under the name of the education ministry, had deliberately withheld it because she did not recognize the validity of the Bolshevik government, and would not return it except to the proper authorities. A number of witnesses testified to her charitable works. The tribunal of seven

---

126. *See Robert Finlay*, Oxford Dictionary of National Biography 101033132.

workers and soldiers found her guilty, but her punishment was public censure and to remain in prison until she returned the "people's money." The monies were eventually repaid by her friends (she continued to refuse to do so), and so she was able to leave prison. This was the first of many of the show trials put on by the Soviet regime, reaching a high point in the great purges of the Stalin-led 1930s.

LEGAL PROFILES

Alexander Kerensky was the prime minister in the provisional government overthrown by the Bolsheviks. He was born in the Russian Empire in 1881 and obtained his legal training there. After being called to the bar in 1904, he defended revolutionaries from the 1905 revolution. He then defended workers, peasants, soldiers, and intellectuals. He was elected to the Duma in 1912. After the February Revolution in 1917, he became justice minister in provisional government and was also a leader in the Petrograd Soviet. He then became minister of war and, in the very fluid political environment, soon the prime minister. After the October Revolution, he escaped the country and spent the remainder of his life outside Russia. He died in 1970.[127]

C. Subsequent Events

The difficulties in trying a person under the centuries-old treason statute in England were to arise again in WWII. To get around this problem, a new law on treachery was created early in the war before the Treason Act itself was finally modernized in the last year of the war.[128] That crime was to be more heavily prosecuted, especially on those who worked with the enemy to put out false information and propaganda. After the 1916 uprising, the Irish independence movement was to hit quickly several milestones: the conscription

---

127. See *Alexander Kerensky Dies Here at 89*, N.Y. TIMES (June 12, 1970).
128. *See* WWII LAW AND LAWYERS, ch. 5.

crisis of 1918 when the British tried to extend the conscription laws to Irish men (see Chapter 3), the landslide win by Sinn Féin in the 1918 Parliamentary elections for Irish seats and their declaration of independence, the 1920 Home Rule Bill,[129] the Irish War of Independence from 1919 to 1921, and finally the Anglo-Irish Treaty of late 1921,[130] which provided for an independent Ireland.

The cause of Indian independence would take longer to come to fulfillment. It was not until after WWII that India would again become a separate nation. It started right after the war with the new Government of India Act in 1919,[131] where many internal functions (excepting defense and foreign affairs) were to become shared responsibilities between British and Indian officials. Acts such as the Rowlatt Act, extending the Defence of India Act, were to be short-lived, although it was a precipitating cause of the Amritsar massacre in 1919. The nonviolence movement of Gandhi, Congress leaders such as Jawaharlal Nehru, and Muslim League leaders like Muhammad Ali Jinnah were to dominate the activities in the subcontinent until peace was achieved. Another Government of India Act was passed in 1935,[132] leading (after the interval of WWII) to the Indian Independence Act in 1947[133] and full independence the following year.

LEGAL PROFILES

Eamonn Duggan was one of the Irish delegates to the Anglo-Irish treaty talks. He was born in Ireland in 1874 and obtained his legal training there. He worked as a solicitor and was imprisoned after the 1916 uprising but later amnestied. After Ireland's independence, he worked in the new government as home affair minister. He died in 1936.[134]

---

129. Government of Ireland Act of 1920, 10 & 11 Geo. 5, c. 67 (U.K.).
130. Articles of Agreement for a Treaty Between Great Britain and Ireland, Dec. 6, 1921.
131. Government of India Act of 1919, 9 & 10 Geo. 5, c. 101 (U.K.).
132. Government of India Act of 1935, 26 Geo. 5 & 1 Edw. 8, c. 2 (U.K.).
133. Indian Independence Act of 1947, 10 & 11 Geo. 6, c. 30 (U.K.).
134. *See British Turn Over Control of Ireland to Michael Collins*, N.Y. TIMES (Jan. 27, 1922).

George Gavan Duffy was one of the Irish delegates to the Anglo-Irish treaty talks. He was born in England in 1882 and obtained his legal training there, after being raised in France. He started as a solicitor in 1906. He assisted in the Roger Casement trial and then returned to Ireland in 1917, being called to the local bar. He was elected to Parliament in 1918. After Ireland's independence, he returned to private practice, becoming senior counsel in 1930, a high court judge in 1936, and president of the court in 1946. He also acted as legal adviser to the drafting of the 1937 Irish Constitution. He died in 1951.[135]

D. Modern Applicability

Uprisings still occur whenever warfare weakens a state holding back independence from one of its constituent members. Slovenia broke away from Yugoslavia in 1991 when the civil war was raging, and the other provinces in that country began to follow. South Sudan was created as an independent state after the civil wars broke apart that country. Revolutions overthrew many of the old Communist countries in Eastern Europe from 1989 and then came to many countries in the Arab world, like Libya, where the fighting there in 2011 led to a new order.

The question of which state controls what in Palestine, based initially on the Balfour Declaration and the subsequent actions that led to the creation of the state of Israel but not the state of Palestine, currently remains a major issue.[136] The British Mandate suffered through the Arab Revolt and terrorist activity from Jewish groups, leading it to seek to end the Mandate after WWII. The new United Nations passed a resolution in 1947,[137] partitioning the Mandate of Palestine into Arab and Jewish states. In the previous year, Transjordan had become independent and left the Mandate. Britain then announced its withdrawal from the remainder of the Mandate on May 14, 1948, following the passage of the Palestine Act.[138] On that date, the state of Israel was declared,

---

135. *See Mr. Justice Gavan Duffy*, THE TIMES (June 11, 1951).
136. *Israel-Palestinian Peace Talks Could Begin in Washington Next Week*, THE INDEPENDENT (July 25, 2013).
137. United Nations Plan of Partition with Economic Union, GA Res. 181 (II) (Nov. 29, 1947).
138. Palestine Act of 1948, 11 & 12 Geo. 6, c. 27 (U.K.).

and the first Arab-Israeli war began. This was followed by additional wars in 1967 (the Six-Day War, where Israel captured the West Bank from Jordan and Golan Heights from Syria) and 1973 (the Yom Kippur War).

While there are no absolutes in this long-standing dispute, in essence the Israeli position is likely based on a modified version of the current realties, while the Palestinian position may have best been stated in the first sections of the 1967 UN Security Council resolution:[139]

> *1. Affirms* that the fulfilment of Charter principles requires the establishment of a just and lasting peace in the Middle East which should include the application of both the following principles:
> (i) Withdrawal of Israeli armed forces from territories occupied in the recent conflict;
> (ii) Termination of all claims or states of belligerency and respect for and acknowledgment of the sovereignty, territorial integrity and political independence of every State in the area and their right to live in peace within secure and recognized boundaries free from threats or acts of force;
> 2. *Affirms further* the necessity
> (a) For guaranteeing freedom of navigation through international waterways in the area;
> (b) For achieving a just settlement of the refugee problem;
> (c) For guaranteeing the territorial inviolability and political independence of every State in the area, through measures including the establishment of demilitarized zones.

6.3 PARITY IN THE EMPIRE

A. Statutes

The main dominions in the British Empire were Australia, South Africa, and Canada. (As its population was significantly smaller and its laws during wartime generally followed Australia or the United Kingdom, New Zealand laws are not discussed separately). Each had at one time been tightly under the

---

139. UN Sec. Res. 242 (Nov. 22, 1967).

control of London, but had been consolidated and achieved a measure of independence via the Constitution Act (a.k.a. the British North America Act) in 1867 for Canada[140] (combining New Brunswick, Nova Scotia, Ontario, and Quebec; other provinces joined later), the Commonwealth of Australia Constitution Act in 1900[141] (combining the states and territories), and the South Africa Act of 1909[142] (combining four British colonies). Canada and Australia became federations while South Africa did not, having a single national government. But the foreign policy, especially regarding foreign war powers, was controlled from London.

Upon the outbreak of war, the declarations of war on Germany were in essence made for them through British control of their aired forces through the governor-generals, who were the crown's representative in each country. For example, the governor-general of Australia was the executive power in the country and was considered the commander-in-chief of the military.[143] It was the same in Canada[144] and in South Africa.[145] In addition, these countries all had, to varying degrees, supplied troops and resources to the war. During the war, Australia provided more than 400,000 men to the war, Canada more than 600,000 men, South Africa more than 140,000 men, and New Zealand more than 100,000 men. These numbers ranged from 8 to 12 percent of the total populations of each of these countries. They provided to the war effort not only men but also natural resources (e.g., ores and timber), foodstuffs (e.g., wheat and dairy products), animals (e.g., horses), and animal products (e.g., wool).

These countries generally passed laws similar to the British Defence of the Realm Act (see Chapter 3). In Canada, the War Measures Act[146] gave the governor in council the power for the "security defence, peace, order, and welfare" of the country to implement censorship, arrest and deport, control transportation by any means, regulate trading, import, export, manufacture, and appropriate and use property.[147] In Australia, the War Precautions Act[148] authorized

---

140. An Act of the Imperial Parliament for the Union of Canada, Nova Scotia and New Brunswick (Constitution Act) of 1867, 30 Vict., c. 3 (U.K.).
141. An Act to constitute the Commonwealth of Australia of 1900, 63 & 64 Vict., c. 12 (U.K.)
142. An Act to constitute the Union of South Africa of 1909, 9 Edw. 7, c. 9 (U.K.).
143. Constitution of the Commonwealth of Australia, art. 68.
144. Constitution Act, § 15 (U.K.).
145. Act of Union, § 17 (U.K.).
146. War Measures Act of 1914, 5 Geo. 5, c. 2 (Canada).
147. *Id.* art. 6.
148. War Precautions Act, No. 10 of 1914, An Act to enable Governor-General to make Regulations and Orders for the safety of the Commonwealth during the present state of war (Australia).

court-martial for communicating with the enemy or obtaining information to do so; impairing the safety of communications or railways, docks, or harbors; or spreading reports that would cause alarm.[149] The governor-general had the power to restrict the movement of or deport aliens or naturalized persons, prevent money or goods from being exported, and arrest and detain.[150] South Africa was attacked by German forces in South-West Africa and, for this reason and a rebellion within the country (see below), declared martial law.

But where they showed the differences in their national characters was in their responses to the call for more men. With the high attrition rates on the front lines and in disasters like the landing in Gallipoli, there was significant pressure on each of the dominion's countries to come up with more manpower. In South Africa, there was among the Boer populations great resistance to fighting against Germany, and this led to a rebellion. In Canada, the Military Service Act[151] made men aged twenty to firty-five liable for military service during the war, but not all Francophone people supported the war, leading to a crisis in upholding this law. In Australia, the Defence Act[152] provided for universal military training for men from eighteen to fifty-nine years old, but it did not require those trained to serve, so Australia held referendums to get consensus on mandatory military service.

LEGAL PROFILES

Robert L. Borden was the Canadian prime minister during the war. He was born in Nova Scotia (soon to be part of Canada) in 1854 and started his legal practice there. In 1896 he was elected to Parliament. In 1911 he was elected as the prime minister of Canada, a role he would maintain during the entire war. He led Canada until 1920. After that he became chancellor of Queen's University in 1924, where he remained until 1930. He died in 1937.[153]

---

149. *Id.* § 4(2).
150. *Id.* § 5.
151. Military Service Act of 1917, 7 & 8 Geo. 5, c. 19 (Canada).
152. Defence Act, No. 15 of 1911, An Act relating to Naval and Military Defence (Australia).
153. *See Sir Robert Borden is Dead in Ottawa*, N.Y. TIMES (June 11, 1937).

B. Cases

As the casualties in the trenches in France and Belgium mounted, the all-volunteer nature of military service in these countries became an issue. The first case describes how Canada handled its conscription crisis. The second case discusses Australia's use of public referendums of the electorate to solve its conscription crisis. The third case involves South Africa's response to those who did not want to serve in a war on the side of the British Empire.

1. Canada

When conscription was introduced in Canada by the Military Service Act, it caused significant resistance among the Quebec Francophone population, despite the war being fought primarily in French-speaking countries. At the start of the war, Francophones were more than one-third of the Canadian population[154] but less than 5 percent of the voluntary enlistments in the Canadian military during the war.[155] The lack of sufficient Francophone units in the military was one reason, another was the lack of French language used in the military hierarchy, while a third was the Francophones feeling a bigger disconnect from the country of their linguistic roots than did Anglophones. In any event, the government, with an electoral triumph behind them, moved to enforce conscription under the Military Service Act from the start of 1918.

The government called up more than 400,000 men, but of these, 95 percent qualified for some kind of exemption. Subsequently, an order in council in mid-April was issued to eliminate most of these exemptions. In the interim, large-scale rioting broke out in Quebec at the end of March and beginning of April, in part based on a rejection of conscription and in part based on long-standing linguistic tensions. After several deaths and large-scale property destruction, the government issued an order-in council authoring the suspension of the writ of habeas corpus for prisoners in military custody and implemented courts-martial of civilians for those interfering with the Military Service Act. Order was eventually restored, and conscription did end up enlisting over 100,000 Canadians, but the war ended before most of those were deployed to the front lines.

---

154. *The Role of Francophones*, Canadian Military History Gateway, Government of Canada.
155. *The Conscription Crisis*, CBC.

LEGAL PROFILES

Wilfrid Laurier led the national opposition to conscription in Canada. He was born in England in 1841 and obtained his legal training there. He was elected to the Quebec legislature in 1871 and the federal Parliament in 1874, where he would serve for the remainder of his life. He was prime minister of Canada from 1896, serving in this role until 1911, overseeing important issues such as the addition of the provinces of Alberta and Saskatchewan to Canada. He was one of the longest-serving Canadian prime ministers and the first French-Canadian in the role. During the war he led the opposition party (the Liberals). He died in 1919.[156]

2. Australia

With incessant requests from London for more men, from the losses suffered starting with the Battle of the Somme, but without sufficient ability to pass a conscription law through the Australian Parliament, the government of Australia decided to put conscription to a vote of the people. The Parliament first passed the Military Service Referendum Act[157] in September 1916. There was much fierce debate inside the country in the interim, with organized labor opposed. The government, confident of victory, began requiring men to register for military service inside Australia, but this and the process of applying for exemptions turned many against conscription. When the referendum was held in late October 1916, it asked the following Yes or No question: "Are you in favour of the Government having, in this grave emergency, the same compulsory powers over citizens in regard to requiring their military service, for the term of this war, outside the Commonwealth, as it now has in regard to military service within the Commonwealth?" A slim majority voted "No."

---

156. *See Sir W. Laurier Dies; Premier 15 Years*, N.Y. TIMES (Feb. 18, 1919).
157. Act No. 27 of 1916, An Act to submit to a Referendum a question in relation to Military Service Abroad (Australia).

While the threat of the referendum had helped to drive up voluntary enlistments after the vote, voluntary enlistment numbers fell significantly. A nonmilitary director general of recruiting was brought to oversee efforts to encourage voluntary enlistment and to keep up the manpower of the five Australian divisions in the war. As had other countries (see Chapters 3 and 5), the government also tried to silence some of the voices of those against conscription, including newspaper editors and Wobblies (see Chapter 5), using censorship under the War Precautions Act and the provisions of the Crime Act for unlawful associations[158] that encouraged treachery that assisted the enemy or sedition. With the pressing need for recruits, the government in December 1917 returned to a vote of the people. This referendum simply asked, "Are you in favour of the proposal of the Commonwealth Government for reinforcing the Australian Imperial Forces overseas?" By a larger majority this time, the "No" vote prevailed again, and the cause of mandatory overseas conscription during the war for Australians perished.

LEGAL PROFILES

Donald Mackinnon was the Australian director general of recruiting during the war. He was born in Australia in 1859 and obtained his legal training England. He was called to the English bar in 1883 and the Australian bar in 1884. In 1900 he was elected to Parliament, where he served until 1920. He then served as solicitor general and attorney general. He took on the national recruiting role in late 1916 after leading recruiting in the state of Victoria. From 1923 he served in the United States. He died in 1932.[159]

---

158. Crimes Act, No. 12 of 1914, An Act relating to Offences against the Commonwealth, § 30A (Australia).
159. See *Mackinnon, Donald*, AUSTRALIAN DICTIONARY OF BIOGRAPHY.

3. South Africa

South Africa had both German South-West Africa (modern Namibia) and German East Africa (modern Tanzania plus parts of Rwanda and Burundi) among its neighbors. With its dual European heritage of both German/Dutch and English settlers, it had inbred conflicts on which side to support. While the leadership of the country immediately joined the cause of the British and the Allied Powers, many of the Boer settlers remembered all too well the tactics of the British in winning the Second Boer War of the previous decade. As such, there was significant resistance from Boers to support the British and to move against the neighboring German colony of South-West Africa, as London desired. Previously, at the end of the Second Boer War in 1902, the government had deported those Boers who would not pledge to support the new government. Some had since returned, but there was still a feeling of wanting to take back from the British at least the Boer colonies.

The South African role at the beginning of the war was to defend itself, so that its British Empire troops could depart for Europe, and to take on these two German colonies. As such, South African troops were deployed to the border between South Africa and South-West Africa. The second-in-command of the South African troops, Lt. Col. Manie Maritz, rebelled and joined the German side with over 10,000 troops following. This led the South Africans to declare martial law in the country on October 14, 1914, and then set out with over 30,000 troops, a majority of whom were Afrikaners, to crush the Maritz rebellion, which it did in several battles through February 1915. Those who had joined the rebellion included generals Christiaan de Wet and Christian Beyers, who resigned his leading position in the military to join the rebellion.

Beyers drowned while trying to escape, and Maritz and rebel leader Jan Kemp fled the country, but forty-eight others, including surviving leaders of the rebellion, were brought to trial from March to June 1915, charged with high treason, convicted, and sentenced. For what could have been sentences of death, there was only a single leader executed, while the remaining were given rather short prison terms in the interests of national conciliation. Those convicted were all released within a few years. Christiaan de Wet was sentenced to six years but served only six months due to ill health. Josef Fourie, on the other hand, was executed for leading a rebel group without first resigning his commission and for causing significant casualties among the government forces.

LEGAL PROFILES

Jan Smuts was the South African leader during the war. He was born in South Africa (Cape Colony) in 1870 but obtained his legal training in England. He returned to South Africa to start legal practice and then worked as a state attorney. But events soon overtook his legal practice, as the Second Boer War began. He became not only a military leader for the Boers but also a negotiator at peace talks before and after the war. From 1905 he helped negotiate an independent Transvaal, where he served in several roles. He then worked with the other three colonies to organize the union of South Africa, approved in late 1909. During the war he led offensives into the German colonies of South-West Africa and East Africa. In 1917 he joined the Imperial War Cabinet and in 1919 the Paris Peace Conference. In that year he became prime minister of South Africa until 1924 and then again from 1939 to 1948. He died in 1950.[160]

C. Subsequent Events

During the war, the dominions had tried to keep their soldiers under the direct command of their compatriots, so Australians fought under Australian leadership and Canadians under Canadian leadership. After the war, the dominions demanded a place at the Paris Peace Conference and were recognized as separate countries, signing the Treaty of Versailles as such (see Chapter 7). A decade after that, the Statute of Westminster in 1931[161] finally provided the equality the dominions had sought. Applying to Canada, Australia, New Zealand, South Africa, Ireland, and Newfoundland (still not yet part of Canada), it stated, "No Act of Parliament of the United Kingdom passed after the commencement of this Act shall extend, or be deemed to extend, to a Dominion as part of the law of that Dominion, unless it is expressly declared in that Act that that Dominion has requested, and consented to, the enactment thereof."[162]

---

160. *See Smuts Dies at 80 on African Farm; Statesman Dead*, N.Y. TIMES (Sept. 12, 1950).
161. An act to give effect to certain resolutions passed by Imperial Conferences in the years 1926 and 1930 of 1931, 22 Geo. 5, c. 4 (U.K.).
162. *Id.* § 4.

LEGAL PROFILES

Robert Garran was the Australian solicitor general during the war, responsible for prosecuting offenses under the various wartime acts. He was born in Australia in 1867 and obtained his legal training there, being called to the bar in 1891. He was heavily involved in the movement to commonwealth status for the country. In 1901 he was appointed head of the attorney general's department where, among other duties, he was a draftsman for legislation and also had to organize the first elections for the new Parliament. In 1916 he was appointed as the first solicitor general of Australia. In 1919 he attended and participated in drafting provisions of the Versailles Treaty. He retired in 1932, returned to private practice, and was made a king's counsel. He died in 1957.[163]

Henry N. MacLaurin was an Australian lawyer who was involved in the fighting and was killed leading troops at Gallipoli. He was born in Australia in 1878 to a well-known physician father and obtained his legal training there, being called to the bar. He had volunteered for military service years before and was serving as a colonel serving as brigade commander on the Gallipoli campaign. He was shot and killed on April 27, 1915. He was posthumously promoted to brigadier general.[164]

6.4 ANIMALS IN WAR

A. Statutes

Animals have been used in warfare since the earliest battles: the cavalry of Alexander the Great facing off against the chariots of Darius III at the Battle of Gaugamela; the war elephants of Hannibal Barca deployed in Europe and the war pigs sent to counteract them; the war horses of armored French knights

---

163. *See Garran, Sir Robert Randolph*, AUSTRALIAN DICTIONARY OF BIOGRAPHY.
164. *See Henry Normand MacLaurin*, AUSTRALIAN WAR MEMORIAL.

in the Middle Ages and the steppe ponies of the far-ranging Mongolians; the primary roles of horses in the American Civil and Indian wars; the camels used by T. E. Lawrence in this war to spring an unexpected attack out of the desert. During WWI, animal deployment probably reached its penultimate use, for messaging, transport, and support. More than just as a beast of burden substitute for manpower, this war featured animals performing roles that were suited to their unique capabilities, and so they added significantly to the mobility and communications of armies. The animals in service to their countries most prominently during WWI were horses, dogs, and pigeons.

Horses, used for human transportation and also as a pack animal, were the predominant animal used in the war. Equestrian animals of all types were shipped from all over the dominions of the British Empire and from neutral powers into Europe. Spending on horses was still something near and dear to the United States' military. In federal appropriations bills from 1916 to 1918, monies allotted for horses were included in every funding for the military,[165] for such purposes as hiring veterinary surgeons, for blacksmith tools and materials, for horseshoes, and for the horses themselves, for their equipment, forage, salt, vinegar, bedding, shoeing, picket ropes, medicines, and veterinary services. There were very specific instructions on the acquiring of such animals, such as:

---

165. Pub. L. No. 64-41, An Act making appropriations to supply urgent deficiencies in appropriations for the Military Establishment for the fiscal year nineteen hundred and sixteen (1916); Pub. L. No. 64-85, An Act for making further and more effectual provision for the national defense, and for other purposes (1916); Pub. L. No. 64-242, An Act making appropriations for the support of the Army for the fiscal year ending June thirtieth, nineteen hundred and seventeen, and for other purposes (1916); Pub. L. No 65-2, An Act making appropriations to supply deficiencies in appropriations for the fiscal year ending June thirtieth, nineteen hundred and seventeen, and prior fiscal years, end for other purposes (1917); Pub. L. No. 65-11, An Act making appropriations for the support of the Army for the fiscal year ending June thirtieth, nineteen hundred and eighteen, and for other purposes (1917); Pub. L. No. 65-28, An Act making appropriations to supply urgent deficiencies in appropriations for the Military and Naval Establishments on account of war expenses for the fiscal year ending June thirtieth, nineteen hundred and seventeen, and for other purposes (1917); Pub. L. No. 65-64, An Act making appropriations to supply urgent deficiencies in October 6, 1917 appropriations for the fiscal year ending June thirtieth, nineteen hundred and eighteen, and prior fiscal years, on account of war expenses, and for other purposes (1917); Pub. L. No 65-109, An Act making appropriations to supply urgent deficiencies in appropriations for the fiscal years ending June thirtieth, nineteen hundred and eighteen, and prior fiscal years, on account of war expenses, and for other purposes (1918); Pub. L. No. 65-191, An Act making appropriations to supply deficiencies in appropriations for the fiscal year ending June thirtieth, nineteen hundred and eighteen, and prior fiscal years, on account of war expenses, and for other purposes (1918); Pub. L. No. 65-193, An Act making appropriations for the support of the Army for the fiscal year ending June thirtieth, nineteen hundred and nineteen (1918).

purchase of horses of ages, sex, and size as may be prescribed by the Secretary of War for remounts, for officers entitled to public mounts for the Cavalry, Artillery, Signal Corps, and Engineers, the United States Military Academy, service schools, and staff colleges, and for the Indian scouts, and for such Infantry and members of the Hospital Corps in field campaigns as may be required to be mounted, and the expenses incident thereto, and for the hire of employees: *Provided*, That the number of horses purchased under this appropriation, added to the number now on hand, shall be limited to the actual needs of the mounted service, including reasonable provisions for remounts, and, unless otherwise ordered by the Secretary of War, no part of this appropriation shall be paid out for horses not purchased by contract after competition duly invited by the Quartermaster Corps and an inspection under the direction and authority of the Secretary of War.

When practicable, horses shall be purchased in open market at all military posts or stations, when needed, at a maximum price to be fixed by the Secretary of War: *Provided further*, That no part of this appropriation shall be expended for the purchase of any horse below the standard set by Army Regulations for Cavalry and Artillery horses, except when purchased as remounts or for instruction of cadets at the United States Military Academy: *And provided further*, That no part of this appropriation shall be expended for polo ponies except for West Point Military Academy, and such ponies shall not be used at any other place.[166]

Pigeons were used primarily for communications but also, amazingly, to help rescue downed flyers on the seas, by pecking on a button when, sitting in a box under a spotter aircraft, they sighted the airman's orange-colored jacket. There were laws concerning carrier pigeons,[167] making it unlawful to "knowingly entrap, capture, shoot, kill, possess, or in any way detain an Antwerp, or homing pigeon, commonly called carrier pigeon."[168] These pigeons were

---

166. Pub. L. No. 64-242, An Act making appropriations for the support of the Army for the fiscal year ending June thirtieth, nineteen hundred and seventeen, and for other purposes (1916).
167. Pub. L. 65-134, An Act to prevent interference with the use of homing pigeons by the United States, to provide a penalty for such interference, and for other purposes (1918).
168. *Id.* § 1.

owned by the country, shown by bands on their legs with "USA" or "USN" designations and a serial number. Prima facie evidence that proved a violation of this act, which could result in imprisonment, was possessing or detaining without notice a government-owned pigeon in "any loft, house, cage, building, or structure."[169]

LEGAL PROFILES

Andrew Barton Paterson was an Australian horseman and solicitor. He was born in Australia in 1864 and obtained his legal training there, starting as a solicitor in 1886. He also wrote poetry under the pen name "The Banjo," leading to the publication of *The Man From Snowy River, and Other Verses* in 1895. The same year, he penned the poem for the famous Australian song *Waltzing Matilda*. He traveled to South Africa to cover the Second Boer War as a journalist. He tried to do the same when WWI broke out, but instead ended up working as a veterinarian on several voyages of horses transported on ships for the war. He also ended up leading a mounted unit and was injured. After the war he returned to journalism and writing. He died in 1941.[170]

B. Cases

There were not as many legal trials as there were many different cases of deploying animals in varying roles in this war, with the feats of these animals becoming legendary. The first case describes the use of horses during the war and a Supreme Court case involving a military horse. The second case was an attempt by the Germans to utilize bacterial warfare to kill U.S. horses and thereby impede the Allied war effort and its disclosure decades later in a trial. The third case is about the several roles of dogs during the war and the regu-

---

169. *Id.* § 2.
170. *See Paterson, Andrew Barton (Banjo)*, AUSTRALIAN DICTIONARY OF BIOGRAPHY.

lations against interfering with them. The fourth case is about the tasks performed by carrier pigeons.

1. Horses in Wartime

The use of horses was incredibly diverse during the war. Literally millions of horses were used in Europe during the war, taking supplies to the trenches from the railheads at the back, transporting people, artillery, and loads of all kinds, pulling ambulances, going on reconnaissance missions, and, at least at the very start of the war, in their traditional role of leading the cavalry charge. But the lethality of fixed trench warfare on the Western Front limited their use there in direct charges, but in the more mobile Middle East and on the Eastern Front, horses retained much of their value. Unfortunately, the war took a terrible toll on these animals. Estimates are that upwards of eight million horses died during the war,[171] almost as many as soldiers who died in the war. Some horses died in battle, others from disease and starvation, and still others from overwork and lack of care. Fortunately (or not), horses that were injured were treated by veterinarians, within both government and private relief organizations, and returned to work. From this equine tragedy come several more hopeful tales.

Morning Glory was a horse from Quebec, Canada, who went to France in 1915 along with her owner, Harry Baker, in a mounted rifle unit Baker led. Upon arrival, the cavalry unit was shifted to an infantry unit, due to the trench conditions. Horse and owner were separated although able periodically to see each other. In June 1916, Baker was killed. Morning Glory avoided battle, survived the war, and was, quite unusually, repatriated to Canada. She was able to live out the rest of her life in Quebec, living until the age of twenty-six in 1936.[172] Another horse on the front lines was Warrior, who took part in the first and last cavalry charges of the war in 1914 (Mons) and 1918 (Moreuil Wood) and then, upon returning home, was able to live out his life until the next world war, dying at the age of thirty-three in 1941.[173]

---

171. *See Unshakeable Courage of the Real War Horses: The Eight Million Forgotten Animals Who Were Killed on the Frontline,* DAILY MAIL (Oct. 6, 2011).
172. *See Morning Glory: Canada's own WWI war horse,* CBC (Nov. 9, 2012).
173. *See Warrior, the REAL 'War Horse' the Germans Couldn't Kill—Who Braved the Bullets, Barbed Wire and Shell Fire of World War I* DAILY MAIL (Jan. 3, 2012).

Just as the war was ending, the U.S. Supreme Court issued an opinion regarding horses in the military. An officer who was using his personal horse in the military had submitted a claim to the government regarding the death of the war horse.[174] The owner had lost his horse because the barley he was using as feed still had the awns (beardlike coverings) in it. The war department had originally disallowed the claims because "the death of officer's horse was not caused by any exigency of the service, nor from a cause incident to or produced by the military service."[175] The officer appealed to the Court of Claims, where he was awarded $200 for the loss of his horse. The Supreme Court reversed that award, saying that while it may be the right value of the horse, the Treasury Department was authorized by statute to be the final forum for such claims, and because the Comptroller of the Treasury had concurred in the opinion denying the claim, the Court of Claims had no jurisdiction to hear the matter and award against the claims.

LEGAL PROFILES

George Harold Baker was the owner of Morning Glory, a member of Parliament (MP), and a lawyer. He was born in Quebec, Canada, in 1877, the son of a senator and MP, and obtained his legal training there. He was elected to Parliament in 1911. He volunteered to join the war in Europe, leading a mounted unit. He was killed fighting at Ypres in June 1916, the only Canadian MP killed in the war.[176]

2. Bacterial Warfare and Horses

Due to the large number of horse injuries and fatalities, the demand outstripped the European supply, so horses were shipped from Australia, New Zealand, Argentina, America, and Canada. Because of the vital role of horses

---

174. United States v. Babcock, 250 U.S. 328 (1919).
175. *Id.* at 329.
176. *See Baker, Lt. Col. George Harold*, PARLIAMENT OF CANADA.

in logistics, harming them would harm the enemy. So Germany, as briefly introduced in Chapter 5, initiated a program to infect with diseases the horses being sent from America to the Allied Powers in Europe. Anton Dilger, a German-American physician born in the United States but educated mostly in Germany, and the son of the U.S. Medal of Honor winner from the Civil War, had returned to the U.S. in 1915 from Germany, with cultures for both anthrax (can be fatal to horses and people) and glanders (an infectious disease affecting horses). His intent, as disclosed in the postwar Mixed Claims Commission cases involving German sabotage of U.S. munitions plants (see Chapter 4), was to sabotage horses and mules headed for Europe.

To do so, he enlisted some German-sympathizing stevedores in the Baltimore area to infect horses and mules that were scheduled to be shipped from America to Europe. They were to paint the *burkholderia (pseudomonas) mallei* (glanders agent) into the noses of the horses and inject the *bacillus anthracis* (anthrax agent) into the horses or put it into their food. In the result, his scheme appeared to be arguably successful by infecting a few thousand horses and mules (and some humans). Dilger ended up leaving the United States under suspicion, going to Mexico, and ending up in Spain. As fate would have it, he died before the war even ended as an early victim of the Spanish flu (see Chapter 7). But he had set the troubling precedent of a doctor's weaponizing diseases, which would arise again in the next world war.[177]

3. Dogs in Wartime

Dogs carried out some surprising tasks during the war. In addition to being man's best friend and undoubtedly mascots of numerous camps, dogs were involved in detecting artillery and gas, in providing emergency ambulance services, in running communications, acting as sentinels, being taken out on patrols, and serving in guard positions. "Trench" dogs were used as messengers due to their relatively greater speed, their physically smaller target area for snipers, their ability to function where communications lines had been cut, and their agility in running through difficult terrain such as shell holes and mud. "Liaison" dogs traveled in both directions with inbound and outbound messages, but as that required trainers on both ends, these were not as frequently deployed. The roles of sentinel, patrol, and guard dog were based on the dogs'

---

177. *See* WWII Law and Lawyers, ch. 6 & 7.

innately superior senses of smell and hearing and their sense of loyalty to their owners.

Ambulance dogs performed the role of finding wounded soldiers stuck in "no-man's land," some of them buried by explosions or hiding to avoid capture. These dogs were taught to differentiate between the still-living wounded and the dead soldiers. A dog that found a wounded soldier would deliver comfort and a small first-aid kit, then either return to the trenches with some part of the wounded man's clothing or personal articles or put a strap tied around its neck in its mouth. Either of these signals would indicate to the stretcher-bearers that wounded men were there, and the dog would then lead medics back to the wounded men. They were even known to drag men back to safety into a trench or depression in the ground and could also work at night, without the danger of using lights.

Lt. Col. E. H. Richardson, the leading trainer of war dogs during WWI in the United Kingdom, published a training manual, dedicating it to "the brave dogs of Britain, who helped their country in her hour of need—Faithful unto Death."[178] Noting that British army regulations specified that "Messenger dogs are not to be hindered [by troops] when on a run,"[179] he included a report on the first two messenger dogs sent to front: "Both dogs reached brigade headquarters, travelling a distance as the crow flies of 4,000 yards over ground they had never seen before and over an exceptionally difficult terrain. The dog dispatched at 12:45 p.m. reached his destination under the hour, bringing in an important message, and this was the first message which was received, all visual communication having failed."[180] In his final dispatch of the war, English commander Gen. Douglas Haig said, "In 1917 a Messenger Dog Service was started [as an alternative method of communication with front line troops] and did good work on a number of occasions.[181]

Many dogs from the war became well known, and their stories demonstrate their added value to military units. "Rin Tin Tin," the famous German Shepherd movie idol of the 1920s and '30s, was found as a one-week-old puppy on the battlefield during WWI, from an abandoned German war dog position. He was brought back to America and eventually taken to Hollywood. "Satan"

---

178. E.H. Richardson, BRITISH WAR DOGS, THEIR TRAINING AND PSYCHOLOGY (1920).
179. *Id.* at 133.
180. *Id.* at 56.
181. Douglas Haig, Final Despatch (Apr. 8, 1919).

was a dog who was with the French forces at Verdun. One unit that had been cut off was out of shells and food, and it had lost its remaining carrier pigeons and had no manner to signal for help. Satan was sent, a gas mask over his snout, with a message and two carrier pigeons in wicker baskets on his back. Upon arrival and full of bullet wounds, Satan delivered his message but then died. The unit used the two pigeons, one of which was immediately shot down, to send the message to the rear to shell the positions near them, allowing them to survive.

"Rags" was an abandoned dog adopted by a U.S. infantry division while they were in France in 1918. His new duties included running messages when the communication lines were downed, and several times he saved units with his messages. He also purportedly could sense the arrival of artillery shells before humans could, acting as an early warning device. Both he and his owner James Donovan were caught in an artillery and gas barrage toward the end of the war. Donovan eventually died from his wounds, but Rags survived, becoming the mascot of the First Infantry Division, until his own death at the age of twenty in 1936.

"Sgt. Stubby" was the most famous of the American war dogs, even decorated by General Pershing.[182] He was adopted as a puppy watching military drills in America and was smuggled aboard the troop ship for Europe. He was deployed with his owner (and future law student) J. Robert Convoy into the trenches, where he lived through over a dozen battles, was injured by shrapnel, helped warn his compatriots of poison gas and artillery attacks, helped find wounded men, and was able to capture a German spy. He was made a noncommissioned officer for the latter act. He returned to fame in the United States, meeting three presidents. Upon his death in 1926, his playfully written obituary was longer than that of most well-known people.[183]

4. Pigeons in Wartime

Carrier pigeons provided a reliable secure message transmission technique, as the vast majority of these birds delivered their messages during the war. This made them common targets for enemy fire, so much so that they eventually were painted black to camouflage them. After artillery had destroyed and inter-

---

182. *See Pershing Honors Dog Mascot of A.E.F.*, N.Y. TIMES (July 7, 1921).
183. *See Stubby of A.E.F. Enters Valhalla*, N.Y. TIMES (Apr. 4, 1926).

rupted the physical lines of wired communications, the goal of the sharpshooters was to interrupt their enemies' lone remaining long-range communications abilities by killing these pigeons. Pigeons were introduced as a separate branch of the British Signal Service in 1915, which ultimately deployed 20,000 birds. Not only were they used on land, but also boats that had been sunk by torpedo often relied on pigeons dispatched at the last minute to initiate a rescue of the remaining crew. These birds were so important to communications that a regulation in DORA (see Chapter 3) was dedicated to them:

> If any person—(a) without lawful authority or excuse kills, wounds, molests, or takes any carrier or homing pigeon not belonging to him ; or (b) having found any such carrier or homing pigeon dead or incapable of flight, neglects forthwith to hand it over or send it to some military post or some police constable in the neighbourhood, with information as to the place where the pigeon was found; or (c) having obtained information as to any such carrier or homing pigeon being killed or found incapable for flight, neglects forthwith to communicate the information to a military post or to a police constable in the neighbourhood; he shall be guilty of a summary offence against these regulations.[184]

Among the most well-known pigeons of the war was one named "Cher Ami," who was provided to the U.S. Signal Corps from pigeon devotees in Great Britain. In one fierce battle in the Argonne Forest in October 1918, after delivering a dozen messages, she was able, despite grievous wounds, to fly for more than an hour to deliver a message to the rear, ultimately saving a "lost battalion" of several hundred men. She lost her leg but did recover enough to return to America as a hero, saluted even by General Pershing. She eventually died of those battle wounds in 1919. Another was "President Wilson," a bird that had already lost a leg in service but who continued to serve on tanks, as a form of wireless communication, relaying messages back to the artillery to take out hidden machine gun nests.

---

184. DORA Regulation 21A, Prohibition on killing, or neglecting to hand over or give information as to, disabled Carrier pigeons (Jan. 27, 1916).

LEGAL PROFILES

Charles White Whittlesey was the commander of the "lost battalion" and a lawyer. He was born in Wisconsin in 1884 and started his legal practice in New York in 1909. He left his legal practice and volunteered for service after America entered the war in 1917. It was in October 1918 that his unit, though cut off for five days and out of food, did not surrender even after a demand from the enemy, until they were relieved after the flight of Cher Ami. Whittlesey returned to the United States a Medal of Honor winner and a hero, but the pressure of this sudden fame after the stress of this battle seemed to be overwhelming. In 1921 he went overboard from a ship, and, based on the notes left behind, it was assumed to be a suicide.[185]

C. Subsequent Events

Of the surviving horses belonging to the Allied Powers after the war, the dilemma arose on what to do with them. The new secretary of war, Winston Churchill, was asked in Parliament in 1919 about the plan of the War Office in regards to "the disposal of horses and mules recently used on the various battle fronts, specifying which class of animals are to be retained for use in the Army and which are to be sold either in this country or abroad?"

To this Churchill replied,

> It has been decided, after consultation with the Board of Agriculture, not to bring to this country any horses and mules from theatres of operations other than France owing to the risk of importing disease. In Mesopotamia, Egypt, Salonika, and Italy surplus animals are therefore disposed of by sale to the inhabitants who are in urgent need of them, or by destruction, as to which generals commanding are authorised to use the most

---

185. *See Col. Whittlesey, of the Lost Battalion, Vanishes from Ship*, N.Y. TIMES (Nov. 29, 1921).

liberal discretion. In France the animals have been divided into four classes for disposal:—

1st. Those required for the Army of Occupation.

2nd. Those which are considered suitable for sale in Great Britain.

3rd. Those which it is not desirable to repatriate but which are well fitted for work in civil life.

4th. Those which it is considered better to destroy.

The animals in class (3) are being sold both in Belgium and France, where they are much required by the inhabitants.[186]

The reality was that most of the horses were sold either to butchers or, often, into worse conditions into local markets across the world. Almost all of the Allied war horses met a poor fate, except the very few who belonged to top people who were allowed to ship them home, such as Gen. Pershing's horse Kidron. Of the tens of thousands of horses that were shipped to the war, only one horse was allowed to return to Australia (Sandy) and one to New Zealand (Bess). In the 1930s, Dorothy Brooke, the wife of a cavalry officer, took it upon herself, while living in Egypt and finding former war horses living in abysmal conditions, to purchase 5,000 of these Allied horses and then founded the Old War Horse Memorial Hospital in Cairo. She helped raise the funds by appealing to her fellow citizens in a letter she sent to a newspaper.[187] Churchill himself, to ensure that more British horses returned home over the relatively short distance from France, strongly criticized the quartermaster of the British Army to speed up the shipments and got the quota increased from 4,000 to 9,000 horses shipped home weekly.

The use of animals faded from WWI to WWII. Trucks and airplanes could now provide the pack animal function. Tanks, cars, and railways could provide

---

186. *See* Hansard HC Deb 13 Feb. 1919 vol. 112 cc296-7W.
187. *Our War Horses Once—Nearly Skeletons Now*, Letter to the Editor of MORNING POST (Apr. 16, 1931).

the transportation functions. Without the trench warfare, trench dogs were no longer required, but K-9 corps were formed to train dogs as sentries, patrols, and mine detection. Communications were sent over more secure lines, but carrier pigeons did still find a place in certain situations in WWII, as the recent discovery of a wartime carrier pigeon and his message in an attic in England has aroused great curiosity.[188] Combining the need for secrecy (see Chapter 5) with a reliable medium, this homing pigeon was dispatched during the war with a confidential message most likely from behind enemy lines in France. Due to both the tenacity of this bird in reaching England, likely while wounded, but the inability of even today's code breakers to determine the cipher used, the contents of this war message still remain unknown.[189]

LEGAL PROFILES

John Butcher was the member of the House of Commons who had asked Churchill about war horses in 1919. He was born in England in 1853 and received his legal practice there, being called to the bar in 1878. He was elected to Parliament in 1892, where he served until 1906 and again from 1910 to 1923. He became a queen's counsel in 1897. He died in 1935.[190]

D. Modern Applicability

Bacterial weapons production, possession, transfer, and use were banned when the Biological Weapons Convention entered into force in 1975.[191] Signed by most countries in the world, with the commitment that the parties would never be allowed "in any circumstance to develop, produce, stockpile or other-

---

188. Skeleton of Hero World War II Carrier Pigeon Found in Chimney with Secret Message Still Attached to its Leg, DAILY MAIL (Nov. 1, 2012).
189. *Government's Top Code-Breakers Left Stumped by Wartime Carrier Pigeon's Secret Note Appeal for Public's Help to Decipher Message*, DAILY MAIL (Nov. 23, 2012).
190. *See John Butcher*, OXFORD DICTIONARY OF NATIONAL BIOGRAPHY 1010101351.
191. Convention on the Prohibition of the Development, Production and Stockpiling of Bacteriological (Biological) and Toxin Weapons and on their Destruction, Apr. 10, 1972.

wise acquire or retain: Microbial or other biological agents, or toxins whatever their origin or method of production, of types and in quantities that have no justification for prophylactic, protective or other peaceful purposes; Weapons, equipment or means of delivery designed to use such agents or toxins for hostile purposes or in armed conflict."[192] Unlike the Chemical Weapons Convention, this convention does not have a corresponding verification mechanism to determine that biological weapons stocks are being destroyed as committed.

Animals continue to be used in war, although in different roles. Horses still serve a function, although largely ceremonial. Dolphins and sea lions are deployed by the modern military to detect underwater mines and enemy frogmen. And dogs continue in their role as the best friend of man both during and after conflicts, now that laws have been passed to ensure that a proper life in retirement is provided for these animals that served their country. The U.S. Congress in 2000 passed a law that allowed retired military dogs to be adopted rather than euthanized.[193] The provisions of this statute required that the Defense Department make any suitable military working dog available for adoption either at the end of the dog's useful working life or when the dog is no longer required by the department.

---

192. *Id.* art. 1.
193. Pub. L. No. 106-446, To require the immediate termination of the Department of Defense practice of euthanizing military working dogs at the end of their useful life and to facilitate the adoption of retired military working dogs by law enforcement agencies, former handlers of these dogs, and other person capable of caring for these dogs (2000).

CHAPTER 7

AFTER THE WAR

Various factors brought about the end of the war in late 1918. Russia had left the conflict (see Chapter 6), but new nations, including the United States and its allies, had joined in declaring war on the Central Powers. The original participants were all near exhaustion in both material and manpower but more so the Central Powers, with their smaller resource bases. Although both the British blockade on Germany and the unrestricted German submarine warfare (see Chapter 2) had had significant impacts on both nations, the Germans had been blockaded longer and had fewer alternate sources of materials. Civilian populations, especially in the Central Powers, were no longer in support of aggressive war. Then the added strength of the newly joined nations began to have an impact on the battlefield, and one by one the Central Powers began to request cessations of hostilities.

First was Bulgaria. Offensives by the Serbs, Greeks, British, and French brought Bulgaria into an untenable position, and so they requested and signed an armistice. Next was the Ottoman Empire, where British, Arab, Italian, Jewish, Greek, and other forces had largely taken over many of the colonies of the empire, and so the government finally requested an armistice. After that, Austria-Hungary, long blockaded by the French fleet and now dealing with revolts among the many constituent parts of its empire and losses on the battlefield, called a halt to hostilities. Finally, Germany, facing significant internal pressures at home, the folding of its Central Power allies, and with the Allied and Associated Powers moving forward on the battlefield almost everywhere, requested its own armistice.

The war devastated, in a scale unseen in modern human history, combatants and noncombatants alike, their people, economies, political structure, and the very souls of the nations involved. As explained in Chapter 5, the loss of men made it difficult for women to find husbands. The toll on animals was explained in Chapter 6. For the soldiers and sailors who did return, war wounds, psychological and physical, took a toll beyond simple statistical measure. The economies and finances of the European combatants were in poor shape for years. Empires crumbled as well, with the heads of five different empires changing as a result of the war, and territory changed hands on a massive scale. The efforts to balance the demands and needs for reparations and restitution with the stability of the defeated nations and international commerce went on for many years after the conflict ended.

This chapter focuses on the end of the war and the agreements that were reached to first stop the war and then solidify the peace. This included the impacts on the boundaries and independence of nations, the limitations on military capabilities, and the needs to compensate nations injured by the war. It also discusses the other impacts, including how disease affected war-weakened populations, the lives of returning and disabled soldiers, and dealing with unneeded war materials.

PROMINENT LAWYERS AND JUDGES IN THIS CHAPTER

Armistice and Peace Treaties:
- Karl Liebknecht (antiwar leader)
- David Hunter Miller (member of The Inquiry)
- James Brown Scott (conference legal adviser)
- Cecil Hunt (co-drafter of the League of Nations covenant)
- Léon Bourgeois (conference delegate)
- Henry Cabot Lodge (senator)
- Paul Hymans (Versailles conference delegate-Belgium)
- Emile Vandervelde (Versailles conference delegate-Belgium)

- Eduard Beneš (Versailles conference delegate-Czechoslovak Republic)
- Otto Landsberg (Versailles conference delegate-Germany)
- Carl Melchior (Versailles conference delegate-Germany)
- Milenko Radomar Vesnić (Versailles conference delegate-Serb-Croat-Slovene)
- Vittorio E. Orlando (Versailles conference delegate-Italy)
- Charles Joseph Doherty (Versailles conference delegate-Canada)
- Rodrigo Octavio (Versailles conference delegate-Brazil)
- Antonio Sanchez de Bustamante (Versailles conference delegate-Cuba)
- Ellis Loring Dresel (peace treaty signatory)
- John Johnston Parker (court of appeals judge)
- Lucius Franklin Robinson (counsel for appellee)
- Roland W. Boyden (commission representative)
- John Foster Dulles (reparations commission)
- Charles G. Dawes (commission chairman)
- Owen D. Young (commission chairman)

Other Impacts of the War:
- Max Weber (sociologist)
- Mark Sykes (justice of the peace)
- Charles Allen Prosser (head of Board for Vocational Education)
- Stanley Hubert Dent Jr. (legislation sponsor)
- Robert E. Lewis (court of appeals judge)
- Susan Brandeis (petitioner's attorney)
- John William Wright Patman (sponsor of veterans' bills)
- Merrill E. Otis (special assistant to attorney general)
- Harry Colmery (GI bill drafter)

Afterword:
- Robert Schuman (president of European Parliament)

7.1 ARMISTICE AND PEACE TREATIES

A. Statutes
1. Armistices

The war ended at different times for different nations. As discussed in Chapter 6, Russia withdrew from the war in early 1918. Bulgaria proposed an armistice on September 24, 1918, and signed the Armistice of Thessalonica with the Allied Powers on September 29, 1918.[1] The terms of the armistice, in addition to requiring that Bulgarian forces be demobilized, required Bulgaria to give up all territory in Greece and Serbia that it had taken during the war. It was also to give up all means of transportation, including boats, and to allow passage through the country by the Allied forces. French, Italian, and British forces were to occupy Bulgaria proper. On October 4, Tsar Ferdinand of Bulgaria abdicated.

The Ottoman Empire signed the Armistice of Mudros on October 30, 1918, with the British.[2] This required that the Ottoman's military forces were to be demobilized and to withdraw inside Anatolia to the west and south (including its Arab colonies) and its prewar borders in the north and east. Ottoman territory could be utilized to continue the war effort, including the means of transportation, against the remaining Central Powers. The Bosporus Strait (from the Black Seas to the Sea of Marmara) and the Dardanelles Strait (from the Sea of Marmara to the Aegean Sea and the Mediterranean Sea) were to come under control of the Allied Powers, and the positions of mines were to be indicated. Oil and coal were not to be exported. POWs were to be handed over unconditionally. All German and Austrian military and naval personnel and civilians were to leave within a month. Turkey was to cease relations with the Central Powers.

Austria-Hungary, after losses to the Italian and British forces at Vittorio Veneto in October 1918, sought an armistice.[3] The terms of the Armistice of Villa Giusti, signed with the Italians on November 3, 1918, required Austria-Hungary to demobilize its forces down to a prewar strength inside its territories, giving up munitions and equipment, and to withdraw from any territory

---

1. Armistice with Bulgaria, Sept. 30, 1918.
2. Armistice with Ottoman Empire (Turkey), Oct. 30, 1918.
3. Armistice between the Allied and Associated Powers and Austria-Hungary, Nov. 3, 1918.

it had gained during the war. The Allied Powers were to be granted freedom of access through Austro-Hungarian territory, including the Adriatic Sea and Danube River freed of mines, and use of the necessary means of transportation. German troops were to be evacuated within fifteen days from all Austro-Hungarian territory or face internment. POWs and Allied merchant ships were to be repatriated immediately. The blockade was to continue unchanged. Austria-Hungary's Emperor Karl abdicated on November 11, 1918.

Germany's military leaders, recognizing the difficulty of its situation, had told the Reichstag in early October that the loss of Bulgaria in the south, the superior deployment of tanks by the Allied Powers, and the Allies' larger reserves bolstered by the influx of American troops, meant that it was now time to seek a peace. Germany changed chancellors, released political prisoners, and opened talks on the armistice. Social revolution and labor strikes were breaking out in Germany, and a few military units were in mutiny. Germany had appealed to President Wilson for a peace based on his Fourteen Points (see next section), which over a series of exchanges included the insistence that the emperor step down. The government announced on November 9, 1918, that Kaiser Wilhelm had abdicated (although he did not do so until November 28, stepping down from both the imperial throne and that of Prussia). On November 11, 1918, the Armistice of Compiegne with Germany was signed,[4] and the hostilities had all but concluded.

The terms of this armistice included Germany's evacuation of countries it had invaded in the west (France, Belgium, Alsace-Lorraine, and Luxembourg) and repatriation of those countries' citizens within two weeks. It was also to evacuate the left and right banks of the Rhine within thirty-one days, with a ten-kilometer demilitarized zone on the right bank. Germany was to take no inhabitants, food, or military materials from the territories it evacuated, and it was not to damage property, people, or businesses. Roads and communications were to remain unimpaired, control of railways and locomotives turned over, and barges returned. All POWs were to be immediately returned and the location of mines disclosed. Germany was to withdraw from Russia, Romania, and East Africa.

---

4. Armistice between the Allied Government and Germany, Nov. 11, 1918.

Additionally, Germany was to repatriate interned civilians and make reparations "for damages done,"[5] removing no public securities that could be used to facilitate the payment of reparations for war losses. It was to return cash that it had taken from the government of Belgium and gold from Russia and Romania. Submarines were to be surrendered, naval ships interned, and Allied merchant ships returned. Freedom of access was to be available in the Baltic, with mines removed. The blockade was to remain in place, with the Allied Powers giving "consideration to the provisioning of Germany during the armistice to the extent recognized as necessary."[6] Germany was also to renounce treaties with Russia and Romania. The armistice had only an initial duration of thirty days, although it was renewed several times until the peace treaty became effective in January 1920.

LEGAL PROFILES

Karl Liebknecht was a German antiwar leader who tried to lead a revolution after the war. He was born in Germany in 1871 and obtained his legal training there, starting his practice in 1899. Liebknecht's father was a cofounder of the Social Democratic Party, so he was involved in defending Socialists and was heavily involved in the movement, including the Second International. He was elected to the Berlin city council in 1901, the Prussian parliament in 1908, and the Reichstag in 1912. He was part of the antiwar Spartacus League from 1914, which led to his arrest in May 1916 for the balance of the war. When he was released in the general amnesty in October 1918, he tried to lead a Communist revolution in Germany but was abducted and then executed by right-wing militia in January 1919.[7]

---

5. *Id.* art. 19.
6. *Id.* art. 26.
7. *See Karl Liebknecht*, Deutsches Historisches Museum.

2. Peace Treaties

After the armistice, the negotiations for peace treaties began. The conditions of peace had been laid out sometime before this. From the American perspective, President Wilson had directed Col. Edward House, his foreign policy adviser, to assemble "The Inquiry," a group of eventually more than one hundred mostly academics to research the problems with European history, geography, ethnicity, economics, and politics, as a basis for making recommendations. He then addressed Congress in January 1918, discussing the possible terms of peace, where he first publicly laid out the Fourteen Points.[8]

a. Fourteen Points

Wilson referred to Germany's "military and imperialistic minority which has so far dominated their whole policy" in the negotiations for the Treaty of Brest-Litovsk, believing that there was, he said, "a voice calling for these definitions of principle and of purpose which is, it seems to me, more thrilling and more compelling than any of the many moving voices with which the troubled air of the world is filled . . . It is that the world be made fit and safe to live in; and particularly that it be made safe for every peace-loving nation." He then laid out the program of the world's peace in fourteen points:

    I.   Open covenants of peace, openly arrived at, after which there shall be no private international understandings of any kind, but diplomacy shall proceed always frankly and in the public view.

    II.   Absolute freedom of navigation upon the seas, outside territorial waters, alike in peace and in war, except as the seas may be closed in whole or in part by international action for the enforcement of international covenants.

    III.   The removal, so far as possible, of all economic barriers and the establishment of an equality of trade conditions among all the nations consenting to the peace and associating themselves for its maintenance.

    IV.   Adequate guarantees given and taken that national armaments will be reduced to the lowest point consistent with domestic safety.

---

8. Woodrow Wilson, Address to Joint Session of Congress, Jan. 8, 1918.

V. A free, open-minded, and absolutely impartial adjustment of all colonial claims, based upon a strict observance of the principle that in determining all such questions of sovereignty the interests of the populations concerned must have equal weight with the equitable claims of the government whose title is to be determined.

VI. The evacuation of all Russian territory and such a settlement of all questions affecting Russia as will secure the best and freest cooperation of the other nations of the world in obtaining for her an unhampered and unembarrassed opportunity for the independent determination of her own political development and national policy and assure her of a sincere welcome into the society of free nations under institutions of her own choosing; and, more than a welcome, assistance also of every kind that she may need and may herself desire. The treatment accorded Russia by her sister nations in the months to come will be the acid test of their good will, of their comprehension of her needs as distinguished from their own interests, and of their intelligent and unselfish sympathy.

VII. Belgium, the whole world will agree, must be evacuated and restored, without any attempt to limit the sovereignty which she enjoys in common with all other free nations. No other single act will serve as this will serve to restore confidence among the nations in the laws which they have themselves set and determined for the government of their relations with one another. Without this healing act the whole structure and validity of international law is forever impaired.

VIII. All French territory should be freed and the invaded portions restored, and the wrong done to France by Prussia in 1871 in the matter of Alsace-Lorraine, which has unsettled the peace of the world for nearly fifty years, should be righted, in order that peace may once more be made secure in the interest of all.

IX. A readjustment of the frontiers of Italy should be effected along clearly recognizable lines of nationality.

X. The peoples of Austria-Hungary, whose place among the nations we wish to see safeguarded and assured, should be accorded the freest opportunity of autonomous development.

XI. Rumania, Serbia, and Montenegro should be evacuated; occupied territories restored; Serbia accorded free and secure access to the sea; and the relations of the several Balkan states to one another determined by friendly counsel along historically established lines of allegiance and nationality; and international guarantees of the political and economic independence and territorial integrity of the several Balkan states should be entered into.

XII. The Turkish portions of the present Ottoman Empire should be assured a secure sovereignty, but the other nationalities which are now under Turkish rule should be assured an undoubted security of life and an absolutely unmolested opportunity of autonomous development and the Dardanelles should be permanently opened as a free passage to the ships and commerce of all nations under international guarantees.

XIII. An independent Polish state should be erected which should include the territories inhabited by indisputably Polish populations, which should be assured a free and secure access to the sea, and whose political and economic independence and territorial integrity should be guaranteed by international covenant.

XIV. A general association of nations must be formed under specific covenants for the purpose of affording mutual guarantees of political independence and territorial integrity to great and small states alike.

LEGAL PROFILES

David Hunter Miller was a leading member of The Inquiry. He was born in New York in 1875 and obtained his legal training there, after serving in the Spanish-American War. From 1911 to 1929 he was in private practice in New York. From his membership in The Inquiry, he then became a legal adviser to the U.S. delegation at the peace conference in Paris, where he helped draft the covenant of the League of Nations. After the war he was involved in helping Germany settle their border with Poland and in drafting what would become the Geneva Protocol. From

1929 to 1948 he worked for the U.S. Department of State, where he was the editor for treaties and also involved in 1930 in the Hague Conference on codification of international law. He died in 1961.[9]

James Brown Scott was a legal adviser to the U.S. delegation at the peace conference in Paris. He was born in Ontario, Canada, but was educated in the United States and Europe. He started practice in 1894 in Los Angeles, including the founding and heading of the law school at the University of Southern California. He was also involved in the Spanish-American War. From 1899 to 1906 he taught at other law schools before attending the 1907 Hague Conference. In 1906 he was appointed solicitor for the state department, where he remained until 1910. He continued to teach law and was secretary and trustee for the Carnegie Endowment for International Peace from 1910 to 1940. During the war he was a judge advocate in the army and afterwards an adviser to the peace conference and a delegate to the Washington Naval Conference. He also helped to resolve numerous disputes between countries and was a leading member of international law organizations. He died in 1943.[10]

---

b. Treaty of Versailles

Although for Germany these may have been the starting points for a peace treaty, for Britain and France, who had been involved from the beginning and had lost significantly more people and resources in the conflict, there was a different agenda, centered on reparations and guarantees against future aggressions. The negotiations of the peace treaty opened in mid-January 1919 and were to stretch out until the end of June. Although many countries were initially involved, the essential negotiators were whittled down to the leaders of the United Kingdom (Lloyd George), France (Clemenceau), and the United States (Wilson). In the end, perhaps quite expectedly because of their significantly greater losses, the desires of France and the United Kingdom were reflected in the final treaty. Germany was given little time to respond, as it was

---

9. *See David H. Miller, Ex-U.S. Aide, Dies, Co-Author of Covenant of League of Nations was 86*, N.Y. TIMES (July 24, 1961).
10. *See Dr. James B. Scott, Law Expert, Dead; State Department Ex-Solicitor Took Part in the Hague and Paris Peace Conferences*, N.Y. TIMES (June 27, 1943).

presented with the treaty on May 7 and was able to get only minimal changes included before the Allied and Associated Powers finalized the treaty on June 16 and signed it on June 26. The treaty was ratified by Germany on July 12.

The Treaty of Versailles[11] contained 440 articles. It is most easily understood as groups of articles in fifteen parts. Starting from the beginning, articles 1–26 in Part I cover the Covenant of the League of Nations. The preamble to this covenant states, "in order to promote international co-operation and to achieve international peace and security by the acceptance of obligations not to resort to war, by the prescription of open, just and honourable relations between nations, by the firm establishment of the understandings of international law as the actual rule of conduct among Governments, and by the maintenance of justice and a scrupulous respect for all treaty obligations in the dealings of organized peoples with one another, Agree to this Covenant of the League of Nations."[12]

The first article allowed the signatories and any self-governing state accepted by two-thirds of existing members who accept its international obligations and regulations on its military to join. Sixty-two nations did join, including Austria and Bulgaria in 1920, Hungary in 1922, and Germany in 1926. Thirty-two were signatories and another thirteen were invited to join originally. The United States, where Senate Republicans' opposition to this part of the Versailles Treaty (and a few other sections on international organizations) killed the passage of the treaty (the United States signed separate peace treaties; see U.S. Treaties section), never became a member of the League of Nations. Several of the countries that would form the Axis powers in WWII left the League in the 1930s.[13]

Other articles, as revised during the life of the League, include article 2, which specified that there was to be both an assembly and a council, and article 8 provided for reduction in national armaments. Article 10 required members to "respect and preserve as against external aggression the territorial integrity and existing political independence of all Members of the League." Article 12 required any threat of conflict to be submitted either to the Council or to arbitration or, under article 13, to the Permanent Court of International Justice, which was established under article 14. Any declaration of war was deemed

---

11. Treaty of Peace Between the Allied and Associated Powers and Germany, June 28, 1919.
12. Versailles Treaty, League of Nations Preamble.
13. *See* WWII LAW AND LAWYERS, ch. 1.

to be against all other members of the League under article 16, leading to the severing of trade, financial, and "personal intercourse" between the belligerent and other members, and to the Council's recommending what military forces were necessary to "protect the covenants of the League." Those violating these covenants could be voted out of the League, which is what happened to the USSR in 1939 after its invasion of Finland.

Article 22 explained the Mandatory system (see Chapter 6). Group A countries were part of the Ottoman Empire and could stand on their own, needing only administrative assistance from the Mandatory country. Group B countries in Central Africa required administration by the Mandatory country. Group C countries were to be administered by the Mandatory country as an integral part of its territory. In Group A, the United Kingdom was the Mandatory for Palestine, Transjordan, and Mesopotamia, and France for Syria and Lebanon. In Group B, France and the United Kingdom were Mandatories for Togoland and Cameroon, while Belgium, as part of the Belgian Congo, took on part of the German East Africa; the United Kingdom was Mandatory for the remainder. In Group C, Australia got New Guinea and New Zealand got Western Samoa, while Japan got the islands in the North Pacific, and South Africa got South-West Africa.

Article 23 had the League aspiring to take on many human rights issues, such as "fair and humane conditions of labor," the "just treatment of native inhabitants," arms control, the trafficking of women, children, and dangerous drugs, the prevention and control of disease, and the freedom of communications and transit and equitable treatment in commerce.

LEGAL PROFILES

Cecil Hurst was the co-drafter (along with David Hunter Miller) of the covenant of the League of Nations. He was born in England in 1870 and obtained his legal training there, being called to the bar in 1893. In 1902 he was the assistant legal adviser to the British foreign office, and from 1918 to 1929 the principal adviser. Besides the peace conference, he was also a delegate to the 1907 Hague Conference and the 1908 London naval conference. He became a king's counsel in 1913, was the

British agent to the Anglo-American claims arbitration tribunal from 1912, and was involved in the Locarno treaties.[14] From 1929 to 1945, he was on the Permanent Court of International Justice, where he was vice president and then president of the court. He died in 1963.[15]

Léon Bourgeois was a delegate at the conference and became the president of the first council session of the League of Nations. He was born in France in 1851 and obtained his legal training there, interrupted by his service in the Franco-Prussian war. He then entered the French civil service, working as prefect in several departments across the country. In 1888 he was elected to the Chamber of Deputies. He served in several cabinets, including as the ministers of justice, foreign affairs, and the interior and briefly as the prime minister. In 1902 he was elected president of the chamber and in 1905 to the Senate, where he would later be elected president of that body. He was a delegate to both the 1899 and 1908 Hague Conferences. At the Paris Peace Conference in 1919, he advocated for a permanent court of international justice. In 1920 he won the Nobel Peace Prize for his long commitment to international peace. He died in 1925.[16]

Henry Cabot Lodge led the opposition to the Versailles Treaty in the U.S. Senate. He was born in Massachusetts in 1850 and started his legal practice there in 1875. He taught history from 1876 to 1879. In 1880 he was elected to the state legislature in Massachusetts. In 1886 he was first elected to Congress, after two unsuccessful attempts, where he would remain for the rest of his life. In 1892 he was elected to the U.S. Senate. His opposition to the League of Nations was later reflected in the ability of the UN Security Council vetoes of security actions. He was also a delegate to the Washington Naval Conference on arms limitation in 1922. He died in 1924.[17]

---

14. *See* WWII LAW AND LAWYERS, ch. 1.
15. *See Cecil Hunt*, OXFORD DICTIONARY OF NATIONAL BIOGRAPHY 101034069.
16. *See Léon Bourgeois*, ASSEMBLÉE NATIONALE, LES PRÉSIDENTS DE L'ASSEMBLÉE NATIONALE.
17. *See Lodge, Henry Cabot*, BIOGRAPHICAL DIRECTORY OF THE UNITED STATES CONGRESS.

Part II of the treaty dealt with the boundaries of Germany and East Prussia in articles 27–30. Part III (articles 31–117) dealt with political status in Europe, such as articles 31–39 on Belgium and 40–41 on Luxembourg, and articles 42–44 demilitarized the left bank of the Rhine (no fortifications or troops). Articles 45–50 provided France with the coal mines in the Saar region to replace those in Northern France destroyed by Germany during its withdrawal. It also provided the League of Nations with guardianship of that territory for fifteen years, when its inhabitants could then vote in a plebiscite on its affinity to France or Germany, which, when voted on in 1935, the half million or so eligible voters cast their ballots almost entirely for returning to German sovereignty. The mines were repurchased by Germany, both in cash and in coal supplied to France.

LEGAL PROFILES

Paul Hymans was part of the delegation from Belgium and president of the first assembly of the League of Nations. He was born in Belgium in 1865 and obtained his legal training there. He taught law and was elected to the Chamber of Deputies in 1900. He served in the Belgian cabinet as minister of foreign affairs (four times from 1918 to 1935) and justice. He had to draft the response to the German ultimatum at the start of the war and then traveled to the United States to get political, financial, and humanitarian support, relaying to his audiences accounts of atrocities that had occurred in Belgium. He was then appointed ambassador to the United Kingdom until 1917. In addition to his involvement in the peace conference, he was president of the council of the League of Nations in 1922, was involved in the Dawes Plan (discussed later in this chapter) and the Kellogg-Briand Pact in 1928.[18] He again served as president of the assembly of the League of Nations in 1932. He died in 1941.[19]

---

18. *See* WWII LAW AND LAWYERS, ch. 1.
19. *See Paul Hymans Dies; Belgian Leader*, N.Y. TIMES (Mar. 9, 1941).

Emile Vandervelde was part of the delegation from Belgium. He was born in Belgium in 1866 and obtained his legal training there. He was elected to the Belgian parliament in 1894. He served in the cabinet as minister of justice and of foreign affairs and taught law. During the war he was minister of state and traveled to America with Paul Hymans. He was a signer of the Treaty of Locarno and was involved in getting Germany admitted to the League of Nations in 1926. He was involved in international Socialist causes but was also a staunch defender of Belgian's national interests. He died in 1938.[20]

Articles 51–79 in Part III concerned the return to France of the Alsace-Lorraine region taken in the 1871 war (see Chapter 1), which was from the armistice date of November 11, 1918, not the treaty effective date. Germany wanted a plebiscite by the inhabitants of the region to determine their affinity to France or Germany, even though it had not been granted one in 1871, but this was refused. Article 80 stated that Germany would "respect strictly the independence of Austria . . . this independence shall be inalienable." There was a similar clause in the Allies peace treaty with Austria (see Other Treaties section) prohibiting such a union with Germany, but that did not stop the Anschluss from occurring in 1938.[21]

Articles 81–86 provided for an independent Czechoslovakia, including the right of German nationals there to opt for German citizenship instead. The rights of this group were used by Nazi Germany as a reason to invade Czechoslovakia in 1938 and 1939. Articles 87–93 dealt with the creation of an independent Poland, including a right of free passage across it between Germany and East Prussia and the right of German nationals to opt for German citizenship instead. Again, the rights of these German nationals were used as a pretext by Nazi Germany for the 1939 invasion of Poland. Article 94 dealt with East Prussia, as a German political entity not contiguous to Germany proper, whose physically separated nature the Allied Powers justified both with the free passage through Poland and that the majority of trade between East Prussia and Germany was seaborne. A plebiscite confirmed the inhabitants' desire to be

---

20. *See E. Vandervelde, 72, Belgian Socialist*, N.Y. TIMES (Dec. 28, 1938).
21. *See* WWII LAW AND LAWYERS, ch. 5.

part of East Prussia instead of Poland. Articles 100–117 were about areas in the Baltic Sea, including Denmark and the free city of Danzig, used as a port by both Poland and Germany and also Russia.

LEGAL PROFILES

Eduard Beneš was part of the delegation from the Czechoslovak Republic. He was born in the Austro-Hungarian Empire in 1884 and obtained his legal training there and in France. During the war he advocated for an independent Czechoslovakia and worked in its provisional government. He then became foreign minister for the independent Czechoslovakia, until 1935, where he was involved in many of the key international conferences. He served on the council of the League of Nations from 1923 to 1927. He was also a member of the national parliament until 1935, serving as prime minister from 1921. In 1935 he became president of the country, serving until the Sudetenland crisis of 1938. After living in exile, he returned as president of the country from 1945 until resigning in 1948 and dying later that year.[22]

Part IV, articles 118–158 concerned German interests outside of Germany proper. Article 118 starts by renouncing Germany's right to territory it held outside Europe (as defined in Parts II and III), including in article 119 its overseas possessions and in China, Siam, Liberia, Morocco, Egypt, Turkey, and Bulgaria. Articles 156–158 ceded the German rights in Shantung and Kiaochow provinces in China including the railway, submarine cables, and mines, to Japan, instead of directly to China. Insisted on by the Japanese and supported by the British (at the time an ally), these were the reasons that China did not sign the Treaty of Versailles.

Part V, articles 159–213 dealt with Germany's military. In particular, Germany was to reduce the size of its army, arms, and munitions, and weapons were to be produced only in identified factories, importation being banned. Article 171 banned the use, manufacture, or importing of asphyxiating or poi-

---

22. See *Benes Dies in Coma at 64*, N.Y. TIMES (Sept. 4, 1948).

sonous gases. Universal military training was to be abolished, as were university or shooting clubs dedicated to military matters and the creation of mobilization plans. Naval ships were limited by type and quantity, and submarines were banned. Air forces were prohibited. The Inter-Allied Commissions of Control were to monitor the implementation of these military clauses. In the years that followed, these clauses were not closely adhered to, allowing for an eventual rearmament of Germany in the 1920s and 1930s.[23] Part VI, articles 214–226 dealt with POWs and graves.

Part VII involved the penalties previously discussed, including article 227 calling for the trial of Kaiser Wilhelm. As discussed in Chapter 2, he had fled Germany to the Netherlands, where he remained for the rest of his life, with the Netherlands claiming it would be an infringement on neutrality to give him up. Article 228 allowed military tribunals for those accused of war crimes and article 229 for crimes against Allied and Associated nationals, as discussed in Chapter 5.

Part VIII covered reparations in articles 231–247. Under article 231, Germany and its Allies accepted responsibility "for causing all loss and damage to which the Allied and Associated Governments and their nationals have been subject as a consequence of the war imposed upon them by the aggression of Germany and her allies." Germany undertook to make complete reparations to all of the damages to people and property under the Allied and Associated governments, with the amount of such damages set by a reparations commission. Restitution was to be for cash, animals, works of art, industrial materials, and rolling stocks taken. Germany also committed to restocking the burned library of Louvain.

LEGAL PROFILES

Otto Landsberg was part of the delegation from Germany. He was born in Germany in 1869 and obtained his legal training there, starting practice in 1895. He was a city councilor from 1903 to 1909. He was elected to the Reichstag, on his second attempt, in 1912, serving until 1920. He served in the cabinet as minister of justice. In 1920 he

---

23. *See* WWII LAW AND LAWYERS, ch. 7.

was appointed as ambassador to Belgium from 1920 to 1923. He then returned to serve in the Reichstag from 1924 to 1933. He was the counsel for President Friedrich Ebert at his 1925 "stab in the back" civil trial against a right-wing editor who declared as treasonous the then-chancellor Ebert's actions at the end of the war in forcing the abdication of the kaiser. After the coming to power of the Nazi Party, Landsberg immigrated to the Netherlands. He died in 1957.[24]

Carl Melchior was part of the delegation from Germany. He was born in Germany in 1871 and obtained his legal training there. He served as an assessor and magistrate from 1897 and as legal counsel for a bank from 1902. During the war he served in the military before being injured and working on procurement. He was involved in the financial aspects of the armistice and peace negotiations. After the conference, he was involved in and eventually headed the finance committee of the League of Nations, becoming its chairman in 1930, was involved in the Young Plan in 1929, and was on the board of the Bank of International Settlements from 1930 to 1933. He died in 1933.[25]

Part IX detailed the financial clauses in articles 248–263. Reparations payments were to be prioritized: Germany was to pay for the cost of occupation—with occupations costs at the highest priority, then reparations payments, then all other obligations under the treaty. Enemy assets within the jurisdiction of each Allied and Associated Power were not affected by this priority. Payments due to Germany were to be transferred to the Allied and Associated Powers. The actual funding of reparations is discussed in greater detail below, as this was the focus of several post-treaty working groups. Germany was liable for damages to injured persons, to surviving dependents, for acts of maltreatment or violence to civilians, for maltreatment of POWs, for seized property, unpaid labor, exactions, and government pensions and compensation for injured and dependents, among others. It could pay in cash or gold, or in kind via merchant ships, securities, commodities (e.g., timber, coal, dyestuffs), reconstruction

---

24. See *Landsberg, Otto*, Neue Deutsche Biographie.
25. See *Melchior, Carl*, Neue Deutsche Biographie.

materials, and tools. Another way to pay reparations was through the confiscation of assets or revenues. Certain assets were expropriated (e.g., submarine cables), and others came as taxes on amounts due to German companies for sales made in Allied countries (e.g., 26 percent export tax in the United Kingdom[26]). Germany was also liable for restitution of cash, securities, specifically identifiable objects of any kind (e.g., artworks, industrial materials, agricultural materials), rolling stock, river craft, and animals.

Part X, articles 264–312 covered customs duties and the status of most favored nations, unfair competition, shipping, and the protection of Allied and Associated Powers citizens' interests. It also dealt with treaties, including abrogating all treaties between Germany and its fellow Central Power allies or with Russia that were entered into since the start of the war. Contracts between enemies, except for payments for executed agreements, were cancelled. A mixed arbitral tribunal was to be established between each power and Germany. Each tribunal would be made up of three members, one from each country and the third person mutually agreed to (see Chapter 2), addressing disputes over industrial, literary and artistic properties, contracts, debts, and property.

Part XI, articles 313–320 dealt with air navigation, and Part XII, articles 312–386 with ports, waterways, and railways, generally looking to freedom of navigation and minimal restrictions. Part XIII, articles 387–427 addressed the creation of the International Labor Organization, because "conditions of labour exist involving such injustice, hardship and privation to large numbers of people to produce unrest so great that the peace and harmony of the world are imperiled; and an improvement in those conditions is urgently required." Part XIV, articles 428–433 concerned guarantees, such as occupation of the Rhineland for fifteen years, or fewer if Germany complied completely, or a reoccupation in the event of a lack of compliance. Part XV, articles 434–440 contained miscellaneous provisions, such as Germany respecting agreements reached by the powers and made with its former allies.

c. Other Treaties

The other Central Powers signed peace treaties with the Allied and Associated Powers as follows: Austria—Treaty of Saint-Germain-en-Laye (SG) on September 10, 1919; Bulgaria—Treaty of Neuilly-sur-Seine (N) on November 27,

---

26. *See* German Reparation (Recovery) Act of 1921, 11 & 12 Geo. 5, c. 5 (U.K.).

1919; Hungary—Treaty of Trianon (T) on June 4, 1920; and Turkey—Treaty of Sèrves on August 19, 1920 (S), which was never ratified and was superseded by Treaty of Lausanne on July 24, 1923. These treaties were all similarly constructed, except for the last. The Treaty of Saint-Germain-en-Laye, mirrored in the other subsequent treaties, recognized the new Serb-Croat-Slovene state.

LEGAL PROFILES

Milenko Radomar Vesnić was part of the delegation from the Serbs, Croats, and Slovenes. He was born in Serbia in 1863 and obtained his legal training there and in Germany and France. He served in the diplomatic service, taught law, and was elected into the national parliament. He was the Serbian minister in Rome from 1901 and in Paris from 1904 to 1920, interrupted by serving as the minister of justice in Serbia. He was involved in the negotiations after the Balkan Wars in 1912 and 1913 (see Chapter 1). In 1917 he headed the Serbian mission to the United States. At the peace conference, he was also involved in the drafting of the covenant of the League of Nations. He became Serbian prime minister in 1920 while also serving as foreign minister. He died in 1921.[27]

d. Fourteen Points and the Peace Treaties

One criticism of these treaties is that they strayed too far from or completely ignored Wilson's Fourteen Points. The following is a mapping of the Fourteen Points to armistice and treaty articles that addressed some part of the letter, and sometimes the spirit, behind Wilson's points. As these treaties were similar, only the most relevant treaty is noted:

---

27. See Dr. Milenko Vesnitch, Envoy, Dies in Paris, N.Y. TIMES (May 21, 1921).

Fourteen Points	Treaty Articles
Open covenants	Not included
Free navigation of the seas	Applied only to Central Powers
Removal of economic barriers	Applied only to Central Powers
Minimization of armaments	Applied only to Central Powers
Self-determination including colonies	V/SG/T/N/S22 (Mandatory system)
Evacuation/independence of Russia	G Armistice (12), V116
Evacuation/independence of Belgium	G Armistice (2), V31
Return of Alsace-Lorraine	V51—V79
Italian borders	SG27, SG36
Autonomy within Austro-Hungarian Empire	SG46, SG53, T41, T48
Evacuation/autonomy in Balkans	AH Armistice (3), SG46, T41, N36, S134
Autonomy in non-Turkish Ottoman Empire	S88, S94, S98, S101, S121, S139
Independent Poland	V87—V93
Association of nations (League of Nations)	V1-26

The peace treaties did not address the issue of making secret agreements, which would continue as a practice into WWII. Although there were to be a number of subsequent disarmament conferences that led to agreements, especially regarding on naval ships such as in Washington (1922) and London (1930 and 1936),[28] the peace treaties did not address general arms reductions for all of the belligerents, only the Central Powers. Self-determination was provided for newly independent states such as Czechoslovakia, Poland, and the Serb-Croat-Slovene State, but not immediately for states under the Mandatory system, especially those classified as groups B or C (see Chapter 6), who were former colonies of Germany or were within the Ottoman Empire.

---

28. See WWII LAW AND LAWYERS, ch. 1.

LEGAL PROFILES

Vittorio E. Orlando was part of the delegation from Italy. He was born in Italy in 1860 and obtained his legal training there. In 1897 he was first elected to the national Chamber of Deputies, where he served until 1925. He was in the cabinet, serving as ministers of justice, the interior, and education. In late 1917 he became prime minister until June 1919. During that time he represented Italy at the peace conference but left early when he could not obtain requested territory. He then became president of the Chamber of Deputies until 1925, when he departed political life during the time of the Fascists. He returned after WWII and died in 1952.[29]

Charles Joseph Doherty was part of the delegation from Canada. He was born in Quebec, Canada, in 1855, the son of a judge, and obtained his legal training there. He became a king's counsel in 1887 and was a superior court judge in Quebec from 1891 to 1906. After unsuccessful attempts, he was elected to the national parliament in 1908 and joined the cabinet as justice minister in 1911. After the peace conference he was Canada's representative to the League of Nations from 1920 to 1922. He remained minister of justice and attorney general until 1921. He died in 1931.[30]

Rodrigo Octavio de Menezes Langgaard was part of the delegation from Brazil. He was born in Brazil in 1866 and obtained his legal training there. In 1888 he was appointed as a municipal judge and in 1890 as federal district attorney. From 1911 he was appointed consulate general, a role he held until 1929. After the peace conference he was the representative of Brazil at the League of Nations. He was appointed to the Supreme Court in 1929, serving there until retiring in 1934. He

---

29. See *Orlando, 92, Dies; Last of Big Four*, N.Y. TIMES (Dec. 2, 1952).
30. See *Charles Joseph Doherty*, PROMINENT PEOPLE OF THE PROVINCE OF QUEBEC 1923-24.

taught law and represented Brazil in many international commissions and conferences and arbitration panels. He died in 1944.[31]

Antonio Sanchez de Bustamante was part of the delegation from Cuba. He was born in Cuba in 1865 and obtained his legal training there and in Spain and started practice in 1884. He taught law from 1891 in Cuba, developed the "Bustamante code" of private international law, used in the Latin American region, and also presided over international law conferences. He served in the Cuban Senate from 1902 to 1916. He attended the 1907 Hague Conference and joined the International Court of Arbitration in 1908. He was Cuba's delegate to the League of Nations. In 1921 he was elected as a judge in the new Permanent Court of International Justice. He died in 1951.[32]

---

e. U.S. Treaties

The United States did not ratify these agreements, due primarily to the League of Nations and International Labour Organization provisions. Instead, it signed separate agreements with Austria,[33] Germany,[34] and Hungary[35] in August 1921. The month prior, Congress had passed a joint resolution terminating the state of war between the United States and Germany and between the United States and Austria-Hungary.[36] This resolution reserved the "rights, privileges, indemnities, reparations, or advantages"[37] from the armistices with Germany or Austria-Hungary, from the Versailles or Saint Germain-en-Laye treaties, as a participant in the war, as a principal Allied or Associated power, or by law.

---

31. See Rodrigo Octavio, BRASIL SUPREMO TRIBUNAL FEDERAL – REPUBLICA.
32. See Dr. De Bustamante, Noted Jurist, Dead, N.Y. TIMES (Aug. 26, 1951).
33. A Treaty Between the United States and Austria To Establish Securely Friendly Relations Between the Two Nations, Aug. 24, 1921.
34. A Treaty Between the United States and Germany To Restore Friendly Relations Existing Between the Two Nations Prior to the Outbreak of War, Aug. 25, 1921
35. A Treaty Between the United States and Hungary To Establish Securely Friendly Relations Between the Two Nations Aug. 29, 1921
36. Pub. Res. No. 67-8, Joint Resolution Termination the state of war between the Imperial German Government and the United States of America and between the Imperial and Royal Austro-Hungarian Government and the United States of America (July 2, 1921).
37. Id. § 2.

It also retained property belonging to these two nations, which it held until claims could be resolved.

The peace treaty with Germany (the Treaty of Berlin) accepted parts V, VI, VIII, IX, X, XI, XIII, XIV, and XV of the Treaty of Versailles. It was not bound by Part I (League of Nations), and it assumed no obligations under Part II (boundaries of Germany), Part III (political settlements of other parts of Europe), Part IV (rights outside Germany) except for section I, which renounces rights to its overseas possessions, and Part XIII (International Labour Organisation). While the United States could participate in the reparations commission (Part VIII), it was not obligated to do so. There was no mention of Part VII (penalties). Its peace treaties with Austria and Hungary followed the same pattern of referencing the main treaty those countries had signed and then excluding these parts of it.

LEGAL PROFILES

Ellis Loring Dresel was the U.S. signer of the peace treaty with Germany. He was born of German heritage in Massachusetts in 1865 and started his legal practice there in 1893. He happened to be in Berlin when the war started and volunteered his services to the U.S. embassy there. He was thus made attaché for the U.S. embassy in Germany from 1915 to 1917. When America declared war, he relocated to the U.S. embassy in Vienna to close it down. He then moved to Switzerland to assist the American Red Cross in dealing with American POWs in Germany, having previously looked after English POWs while in Germany. While in Switzerland, he also represented the War Trade Board. After the war, from 1919 to 1922, he was the U.S. commissioner and chargé d'affaires to Germany. He died in 1925.[38]

---

38. See *Ellis L. Dresel, Diplomatist, Dead*, N.Y. TIMES (Sept. 21, 1925).

B. Cases

Most of the postwar trials covered the areas of war crimes, claims by private parties against the belligerents, claims on the return of assets seized during the war, and claims by the states against the belligerents for reparations. Most of these have already been discussed: Chapter 6 discussed the war crimes trials called for under the Treaty of Versailles and related treaties. Chapter 2 discussed the work of the Mixed Claims Commission for private claims against Germany, and Chapter 5 discussed the claims for return of assets or liquidated funds seized by the Alien Property Custodian. The reparations claims are covered in the following sections. A few other trials related specifically to the interpretation of the treaties vis-à-vis the reclaiming of assets after the war. The first case dealt with the obsolescence of provisions from the Treaty of Versailles as adopted under the Treaty of Berlin. The second case dealt with how claims made to return property seized under the Trading with the Enemy Act were addressed in the Treaties of Versailles and Berlin.

1. Duration of Provisions

In *Robertson*,[39] the court of appeals was reviewing a patent filing to determine if the American filing, which occurred several years after the foreign patent was filed, was filed within the allotted timeframe. The appellee had filed the application in 1915 in Germany, but it was not granted until October 1919. The patent was not filed in the United States until May 1922. Article 308 of the Treaty of Versailles, acknowledging the difficulties of patent filings during the war, allowed such applications to be filed within six months after the effective date of the treaty's coming into force. The treaty came into force in America in November 1921, after the ratifications of the Treaty of Berlin. After rejecting the Treaty of Versailles, Congress had passed the Nolan Act[40] in March 1921 to protect those who could not file their patent applications after August 1914, providing them an additional six months from the effective date of this act (to September 1921). It contained the same language as article 308, except that the treaty said "should" and the statute "shall."

---

39. Robertson v. Gen. Elec. Co., 32 F. 2d 495 (4th Cir. 1929).
40. Pub. L. No. 66-366, An Act to extend temporarily the time for filing applications for letters patent, for taking actions in the United States Patent Office with respect thereto, for the reviving and reinstatement of applications for letters patent, and for other purposes (1921).

The appellant argued that the latter (November 1921) was the appropriate date to determine whether a filing was too late, and the appellee believed it was the former date (September 1921). The court of appeals ruled that, for two reasons, the former date based upon the U.S. statute (Nolan Act) was the appropriate date. First was that the Nolan Act had already addressed these rights within the United States, and second was that the treaty provision was not self-executing and so required domestic legislation. The court said that because the Treaty of Versailles had been in effect for nearly two years by the time the Treaty of Berlin was ratified, many of its provisions had already been dealt with and were obsolete. The court said that article 308 was one of those provisions, already being obsolete before the Treaty of Berlin's ratification.

Even if the Treaty of Berlin had somehow brought article 308 to life, the court said that it still would not provide the expiration date for patent filing because it was not self-executing. Quoting John Marshall, the court said, "A treaty is, in its nature, a contract between two nations, not a legislative act. It does not generally effect, of itself, the object to be accomplished, especially so far as its operation is infraterritorial, but is carried into execution by the sovereign power of the respective parties to the instrument. In the United States, a different principle is established. Our Constitution declares a treaty to be the law of the land. It is, consequently, to be regarded in courts of justice as equivalent to an act of the Legislature, whenever it operates of itself, without the aid of any legislative provision. But when the terms of the stipulation import a contract—when either of the parties engages to perform a particular act, the treaty addresses itself to the political, not the judicial department; and the Legislature must execute the contract, before it can become a rule for the court."[41] As there was no act other than the Nolan Act and the time for filing under it had passed, the patent application was properly denied.

LEGAL PROFILES

John Johnston Parker was the judge delivering the opinion in this case. He was born in North Carolina in 1885 and started his legal prac-

---

41. *Id.* at 500.

tice there in 1908. After several unsuccessful runs at elected office, he served as a special assistant to the U.S. attorney general from 1923 to 1924. In 1925 he was appointed to the Court of Appeals for the Fourth District. He served as chief judge there from 1948 to 1958. In 1930 he was nominated to the U.S. Supreme Court, but the Senate rejected him by a single vote. He also served as an alternative judge at the post-WWII International Military Tribunal at Nuremberg.[42] He died in 1958.[43]

2. Alien Claims

In *Munich Reinsurance Co.*,[44] the court of appeals was dealing with a demand for an accounting of shares of a German corporation whose stock owned by an American corporation was seized and sold by the Alien Property Custodian under the Trading with the Enemy Act (see Chapter 5) to liquidate a claim against it. In taking judicial notice of the Treaty of Berlin, the court noted that this treaty gave the United States the rights and privileges available to the Allied Powers under the Treaty of Versailles, even though the United States did not ratify it.

The court extracted and summarized those pertinent rights under article 297 of the Treaty of Versailles as:

> Germany undertakes to compensate her nationals in respect of the sale or retention of their property, rights or interests in Allied or Associated States . . . that there was reserved to the United States, being one of the Allied Powers, the right to retain and liquidate all property, rights and interests belonging . . . to German nationals or companies controlled by them . . . all exceptional war measures, or measures of transfer, or acts done or to be done in execution of such measures . . . shall be considered as final and binding upon all persons . . . No question shall be raised as to the regularity of a transfer of any property, rights or interests dealt with in pursuance of any such order, direction, decision or instruction . . . the

---

42. *See* WWII LAW AND LAWYERS, ch. 6.
43. *See Parker, John Johnston*, FED. JUDICIAL CTR., BIOGRAPHICAL DIRECTORY OF FEDERAL JUDGES.
44. Munich Reinsurance Co. v. First Reinsurance Co., 6 F. 2d 742 (2nd Cir. 1925).

property, rights, and interests of German nationals will continue to be subject to exceptional war measures that have been or will be taken with regard to them.[45]

The court then ruled, "Those provisions clearly contemplate that no question shall be raised by a German national in the courts of the United States as to the regularity or validity of the proceedings taken by the Alien Property Custodian in the sale and transfer of any property rights or interest owned by a German national and dealt with as enemy property under the war legislation of Congress. The treaty, in our opinion, bars the assertion in our courts of any such claim as that put forward by the complainant herein."[46]

LEGAL PROFILES

Lucius Franklin Robinson was the counsel for the appellee in this case. He was born in Connecticut in 1863, the son of a lawyer, and started his legal practice there in 1887. He served in the family firm and was a member of the Hartford city council and numerous other local organizations. During the war he served in the state guard. He died in 1941.[47]

C. Subsequent Events

The repercussions from the Treaty of Versailles were to be quite significant.[48] A part of German society never accepted that Germany had lost the war on the battlefield but instead believed it had been sold out by certain individuals. What was viewed as a punitive peace treaty, a "diktat," burned as smoldering embers long enough during the political and economic upheavals of the 1920s and early 1930s to finally lead to the Nazi Party's taking power legally in 1933. There was perhaps no demonstration of this resentment shown more clearly than the

---

45. *Id.* at 748.
46. *Id.* at 749.
47. See *Robinson*, N.Y. TIMES (June 13, 1941).
48. See WWII LAW AND LAWYERS, ch. 6.

retrieval and use of the same French railway car that hosted the signing of the armistice in 1918 to then host the 1940 signing of the armistice between France and Nazi Germany. Alsace-Lorraine was retaken and for the third time in seventy years, Germany and France were involved in a major war against each other.

The issue that took probably the largest amount of diplomatic time after the peace treaty was the issue of reparations payments. Because the Treaty of Versailles did not set the actual amount of reparations due, the reparations commission was required to take in all claims and determine the appropriate amount per Part VIII. In Annex II, as initial payment of its uncalculated damages, Germany was to pay 20 billion gold marks by May 1921 and issue two sets of bonds, each valued at 40 billion gold marks. This amount of reparations was determined by the commission to be 132 billion gold marks, to be funded by issues of bonds in categories of A (12 billion gold marks at 5 percent coupon interest amortized over 37 years), B (38 billion gold marks at 5 percent coupon interest amortized over 37 years), and C (82 billion gold marks without coupons or a defined maturity date, subject to subsequent adjustment). The Treaty of Versailles Part VIII, Annex II was subsequently amended in May 1921.[49] Of the reparations payments, over 50 percent were to go to France, over 20 percent to the British Empire, 10 percent to Italy, 8 percent to Belgium, and 5 percent to the Serb-Croat-Slovene State.

LEGAL PROFILES

Roland W. Boyden represented the United States at the reparations commission. He was born in Massachusetts in 1863 and started his legal practice in 1888. During the war he was appointed as a legal counsel for the Food Administration. After the armistice, he headed the American Relief Administration efforts to feed those in the areas overrun by war. He represented the United States at the reparations commission until 1923. He then returned to private practice, staying involved in some international forums. In 1930 he was appointed to the Mixed Claims

---

49. Protocol modifying Annex II of Part VIII of the Treaty of Versailles, May 5, 1921.

Commission (see Chapter 4) and then to the Permanent Court of Arbitration in 1930 to replace Charles Evans Hughes. He died in 1931.[50]

John Foster Dulles was legal counsel for the U.S. delegation at the Paris conference and was on the organizing committee for the reparations commission. He was born in Washington, DC in 1888 and started his legal practice in New York in 1911. Unable to enlist, he served on the War Industries Board during WWI. He joined his uncle, Robert Lansing, at the peace conference. After the peace conference and reparations commission work, he returned to private practice and was involved in setting up the Dawes Plan (see next section). He was involved in the post-WWII peace conference and was a U.S. delegate to the United Nations. He then served as U.S. secretary of state from 1953 to 1959, dying shortly thereafter.[51]

But Germany did not meet its obligations for paying reparations, in cash or in kind, leading to the reoccupation of the Rhineland areas of industry by French and Belgian troops and to hyperinflation in Germany as the government printed money. This crisis, along with requests by Germany for a moratorium on reparations payments, led to a commission under American Charles Dawes, focused on balancing the German budget and stabilizing the German currency, which included paying the reparations. The commission produced the Dawes Plan, which created a reparations annuity payment starting at 1 billion gold marks and rising to over 2 billion gold marks over several years, adjusted by an "index of prosperity." Part VIII of the Treaty of Versailles had been revised in May 1921[52] to allow the use of German customs and duties revenues and export taxes to service the underlying bonds and was revised again in August 1924[53] to allow for appeals to the Permanent Court of International Justice.

---

50. *See Roland W. Boyden Dies at Church*, N.Y. TIMES (Oct. 26, 1931).
51. *See An Inheritance of Diplomacy, John Foster Dulles*, N.Y. TIMES (Apr. 16, 1959).
52. Protocol modifying Annex II of Part VIII to the Treaty of Versailles of June 28, 1919, U.K.-Fr.-It.-Belg.-Jap., May 5, 1921.
53. Agreement between the Allied Governments and the German Government concerning the Agreement of Aug. 9, 1924 between the German Government and the Reparation Commission, Aug. 30, 1924.

This plan was eventually to be superseded by the Young Plan in 1929 to 1930, from a commission headed by American Owen D. Young that provided for the Bank of International Settlements to handle the movement of these funds, terminated the reparations commission, recommended winding down in-kind payments, removed political-economic controls from Germany, and reduced the amount of the reparations payments to be made. The reparations payments, given the onset of the Great Depression, were stopped temporarily under the Hoover moratorium in 1931 and then suspended and essentially eliminated under the Lausanne agreement of 1932. As the Allied Powers' ability to pay the large war debts to their chief creditors in America depended on receiving these reparations payments, the result of this suspension was to be borne in the United States. It is estimated that Germany paid just over 20 billion gold marks in reparations in the 1920s and 1930s. In 2010 Germany paid off the final interest on U.S. loans taken out to finance reparations payments.[54]

LEGAL PROFILES

Charles D. Dawes chaired the Dawes commission. He was born in Ohio in 1865 and started his legal practice in 1887 in Nebraska. From 1894 he started a utilities company. From 1897 to 1901 he served as the U.S. comptroller of the currency. He resigned to run unsuccessfully for the U.S. Senate and then founded a bank in Illinois. During the war he served with the U.S. Army, heading up its supplies needs and then working on the liquidation commission. In 1921 he was named director of the Bureau of the Budget and in 1923 appointed to the reparations commission that bore his name. His Dawes Plan won him the Nobel Peace prize in 1925. In 1924 he was elected vice president of the United States and served a single term. From 1929 to 1932 he was U.S. ambassador to the United Kingdom, when he then returned to his bank. He died in 1951.[55]

---

54. *Germany Ends World War One Reparations after 92 Years with £59m Final Payment*, THE MAIL (Sept. 29, 2010).
55. *See Charles G. Dawes Dies in Home at 85*, N.Y. TIMES (Apr. 24, 1951).

Owen D. Young chaired the Young commission. He was born in New York in 1874 and started his legal practice in Massachusetts in 1896. He stayed in private practice and taught law until 1912. In 1913 he became general counsel for General Electric and its president in 1922, retiring as chairman of the board in 1939. He was involved in starting America in key industries, founding in 1919 Radio Corporation of America (RCA) at the request of the government to keep American radio patents from falling into European possession, serving as its chairman until 1929, including the launching of its subsidiary the National Broadcasting Corporation (NBC). He was heavily involved in the Dawes commission by co-drafting its plan in 1924 and then chaired the Young commission in 1929, which included J. P. Morgan, who had been behind many of the loans of the Dawes Plan. He died in 1962.[56]

D. Modern Applicability

The proper use or lack of use of peace treaties after the end of conflicts often seems to define how the conflict is understood. Between North and South Korea, only an armistice exists for a conflict that principally ended sixty years ago. The lack of a peace treaty is a recurrent feature in those modern conflicts that seem to be never-ending. Between Palestine and Israel, a comprehensive peace treaty still does not exist, and so the conflict goes on decade after decade without resolution. A peace treaty between Israel and Egypt was reached to end their multi-decade conflict and allow constructive and joint efforts to be made. The geographic vagueness in certain parts of the peace treaty with Japan that ended WWII (Treaty of San Francisco in 1951)[57] continues to resonate in disputes among South Korea, China, and Japan over islands located between them, while the conclusive language in that same treaty about resolving all claims against Japan has made it impossible for those with valid claims, such as POWs who worked under slave-labor-like conditions, to recover damages.

---

56. *See Owen D. Young, 87, Industrialist, Dies,* N.Y. TIMES (July 12, 1962).
57. *See* WWII LAW AND LAWYERS, ch. 7.

7.2 OTHER IMPACTS OF THE WAR

A. Statutes

There were a number of impacts WWI had on the living beings involved that carried into the postwar era, many of which were already discussed in prior chapters, such as:

- Freedom of expression
- Women's employment and suffrage
- Women's ability to marry and have a family
- Social movements like Prohibition and desegregation
- Social revolutions as in Russia and elsewhere
- Independence and self-determination movements
- The lives of animals

There were other impacts of the war that mostly came about as the war was concluding or after it finished. These included the effect of disease on the human physical condition weakened from four years of intense war and crowded, unsanitary conditions, the struggles of veterans who were disabled in the war and needed medical and occupational assistance, the financial and employment difficulties of all veterans after the war through the onset of the Great Depression, and the impact to businesses of the cancellation of wartime contracts, when the country no longer needed the war materials they were producing.

1. Influenza Pandemic

The war had several impacts on the physical condition of humans. The war had brought together disparately situated troops and support personnel into small geographic areas, often crowded together in less than ideal sanitary conditions and living in the awful world of death and disease that lurked in the war's front line trenches. Then malnutrition and exhaustion were brought on by the blockades, rationing, uprooting of communities into refugee status, and the deprivations and stress of life in and out of war zones. As such, the physical stamina of populations had diminished, such that even those normally able to withstand disease were now more vulnerable to it. These conditions set the stage for the worst pandemic the world has ever experienced, the Spanish flu, which started killing people in early 1918.

Thought to have originated variously in China, Europe, and the United States, outbreaks of the flu hit military camps in the United States in the first half of 1918. This wave seemed to ebb, but with a million people still moving back and forth from the United States to the battlefields in Europe and living tightly confined in ships, trenches, hospital ships, and trains, a more virulent form of the virus arose between September and November of 1918 (there was a third wave in winter 1919). Coming back to the United States and then radiating out from the battlefronts of European camps, it rapidly spread around the world, infecting perhaps one billion people or more. The disease was to rage globally and leave fifty million or more dead in its wake. In the United States, nearly 700,000 people died (almost 200,000 in October 1918), including more than 50,000 soldiers, and the average life span decreased by more than ten years with the pandemic. With the need to isolate people with the disease working directly against the public volunteer and enlistment activities supporting the war effort, along with all of the transporting of soldiers and supplies across the country and world, the disease was carried everywhere.

Businesses shut down due to lack of staff or customers or both, and doctors and nurses were in desperate need but many had been shipped off to the war. Public meetings, movie theaters, bars, schools, and other places of gathering were closed, and quarantine/isolation was implemented based on the direction from the head of the U.S. Public Health Service. This direction was passed down to state and local health boards, with the police powers to implement locally as deemed appropriate (those localities that acted early and vigorously saved significant numbers of lives[58]). Disproportionately affecting the young and healthy, it reached into the world of sport, causing the cancellation of the 1919 Stanley Cup final and killing star player "Bad" Joe Hall. Congress, with all of the deaths, tried to help by passing a funding law in October 1918,[59] with one million dollars allocated to "combat and suppress Spanish influenza" by paying for medical personnel and medical supplies. The medical departments of the army and navy were to work with the federal public health service to deal with this outbreak.

---

58. *How (and How Not) to Battle Flu: A Tale of 23 Cities*, N.Y. TIMES (Apr. 17, 2007).
59. Pub. Res. No. 65-42, Joint Resolution To aid in combating "Spanish influenza" and other communicable diseases (1918).

LEGAL PROFILES

Max Weber was among the best-known victims of the Spanish flu. He was born in Germany in 1864, the son of a lawyer, and obtained his legal training there. He then joined the law faculty at the University of Berlin, then at Freiburg and then Heidelberg. He continued to teach and write, moving more into the field of sociology, where he authored tracts such as *The Protestant Ethic and the Spirit of Capitalism* and *Economy and Society* and became one of the founders of this emerging field. He volunteered to serve at the start of the war despite his age and later protested against certain military policies such as unrestricted submarine warfare (see Chapter 2). He attended the peace conference in Paris and was involved in drafting the Weimar constitution. He died in 1920.[60]

Mark Sykes was a justice of the peace and likely the most well known of the casualties from the Spanish flu. He was born in England in 1879. He spent significant amounts of time in his younger years traveling through the Ottoman Empire, including the Middle East, and published several travel books about the region. He served in the military, including two years during the Second Boer War. Due to his family's wealth and position, he served as the justice of the peace in the county seat. He was elected to the House of Commons in 1912. Upon the outbreak of the war, he left his reserve unit and served in the Arab Bureau in the Ministry of War. He was involved also with negotiating the Sykes-Picot Agreement with France, which defined spheres of influence in the post-Ottoman Middle East (see Chapter 6). He attended the Paris Peace Conference after the war, pushing the causes of Arab and Jewish nationalism. He caught the influenza virus and died in France in 1919.[61]

---

60. *See Max Weber*, DEUTSCHES HISTORISCHES MUSEUM.
61. *See Mark Sykes*, OXFORD DICTIONARY OF NATIONAL BIOGRAPHY 101036394.

2. Veterans' Issues

The impact of the war on returning veterans came in many forms, including physical and mental disabilities and vocational and financial issues. To address the former, Congress had passed several acts, including amendments to the War Risk Insurance Act (see Chapter 4) in June 1917[62] and October 1917.[63] The former amendment was still directed at merchant seamen and provided insurance for their loss of life, personal injury, or capture by enemies when involved in the wartime merchant force, in payment up to $5,000. The latter amendment reorganized the Bureau of War Risk Insurance into a division for merchant seaman insurance and a division for army and navy personnel insurance. If death resulted from active service, a widow and child would receive $35 a month. If the serviceman was totally disabled, the family with one child would receive $55 plus up to $20 per month for a nurse and up to $100 per month for severe disabilities (e.g., blindness). Vocational training was provided for those who became disabled. Every commissioned officer and enlisted man could also purchase up to $10,000 of death or permanent disability insurance.

Vocational training was further addressed in June 1918 under the Vocational Rehabilitation Act,[64] which created the Rehabilitation Division of the Federal Board for Vocational Education (later combined with the Bureau of War Risk Insurance and the Public Health Service's medical care of veterans into the Veterans Bureau,[65] the forerunner of the Veterans Administration). Any armed services member who was disabled and unable to carry on a gainful occupation was to be given vocational rehabilitation. This involved taking courses and being paid in the meantime, including for related medical expenses. To further address the financial issues, Congress passed the World War Adjusted Compensation Act in 1924[66] over a presidential veto. The law covered WWI

---

62. Pub. L. No. 65-20 (1917). An Act to amend an Act entitled "An Act to authorize the establishment of a Bureau of War Risk Insurance in the Treasury Department," approved September second, nineteen hundred and fourteen, and for other purposes.
63. Pub. L. No. 65-90 (1917). An Act to amend an Act entitled "An Act to authorize the establishment of a Bureau of War Risk Insurance in the Treasury Department," approved September second, nineteen hundred and fourteen, and for other purposes.
64. Pub. L. No. 65-178, An Act to provide for vocational rehabilitation and return to civil employment of disabled persons discharged from the military or naval forces of the United States, and for other purposes (1918).
65. Pub. L. No. 67-47, An Act to establish a Veteran's Bureau and to improve the facilities and service of such bureau, and further to amend and modify the War Risk Insurance Act (1921).
66. Pub. L. No. 68-130, An Act to provide adjusted compensation for veterans of the World War, and for other purposes (1924).

veterans and provided a bonus based on $1 per day for veterans who had served stateside and $1.25 per day for those who had served overseas between April 5, 1917, and July 1, 1919. It was to be paid in March 1925 if the total bonus was $50 or less but was issued as an adjusted service certificate if more than $50, which was payable twenty years later. The certificate could also be used as collateral for a loan.

LEGAL PROFILES

Charles Allen Prosser was a leader in vocational training and the executive director of the Federal Board for Vocational Education during the war. He was born in Indiana in 1871 and obtained his legal training in Kentucky. Not a practicing lawyer, he did later serve as a juvenile judge. He taught in high schools in New York and became superintendent. This would lead him to see the need for vocational training, and he led industrial education groups from 1910. He was instrumental in helping to pass the Smith-Hughes Act of 1917[67] to support vocational education. He then became director of the Federal Board for Vocational Education, until 1919, staying on further to help disabled veterans. He continued to work in vocational education until his death in 1952.[68]

3. War Contracts

The ending of the war meant that many of the agreements signed in support of the war would be providing materials no longer required. So Congress passed the War Contracts (or Dent) Act in March 1919.[69] This allowed the secretary of war to "adjust, pay or discharge" any agreement for any of the following: acquisition or use of lands, production of equipment, materials or supplies, or

---

67. Pub. L. No. 64-347, An Act to provide for the promotion of vocational education; to provide for cooperation with the States in the promotion of such education in agriculture and the trades and industries; to provide for cooperation with the States in the preparation of teachers of vocational subject; and to appropriate money and regulate its expenditure (1917).
68. *See Charles Prosser, Educator, 81, Dies*, N.Y. TIMES (Nov. 28, 1952).
69. Pub. L. No. 65-322, An Act to provide relief in cases of contracts connected with the prosecution of the war, and for other purposes (1919).

services that were connected to the prosecution of the war. It allowed only for profits on goods delivered and accepted any reasonable expenses in performing the contract. Appeals of the determinations by the secretary of war could be made to the Court of Claims. This included claims by foreign governments and nationals ending with the armistice. The secretary of the interior was to do the same for requests for raw materials from the War Industries Board, the War Trade Board, the Shipping Board, or the Emergency Fleet Corporations (see Chapter 5). No jurisdiction was given to any court for a suit against the United States.

LEGAL PROFILES

Stanley Hubert Dent Jr. was namesake of this act of Congress. He was born in Alabama in 1869 and started his practice there in 1889. From 1902 to 1909 he was a prosecuting attorney. He was elected to Congress in 1908, serving until 1921. He then returned to private practice and died in 1938.[70]

B. Cases

There were different types of cases involving these three areas. The first group of cases included those arising from the effect of the influenza pandemic on the lives of soldiers and businesses. The second group involved the claims of soldiers, their beneficiaries, or their lawyers for the soldier's benefits under the War Risk Insurance Acts. The third set of cases concerned the bonuses payable under the World War Adjusted Compensation Act. The fourth group of cases arose from the Dent Act and termination of war contracts.

1. Influenza Pandemic

In *Hooper*,[71] a soldier had entered the military in the autumn of 1918 and shortly thereafter died of the Spanish flu. He had applied for war risk insur-

---
70. See Dent, Stanley Hubert, Jr., BIOGRAPHICAL DIRECTORY OF THE UNITED STATES CONGRESS.
71. Hooper v. United States, 13 F.2d 19 (8th Cir. 1926).

ance, naming himself as beneficiary. Upon his death, three different parties claimed to be the legatee of his estate—adoptive parents, in loco parentis (legal guardians), and "true" biological parents—eligible to claim the $10,000 death benefit, which the court denied to all of the claiming parties. In *Bean*,[72] a soldier had been sent to France and there caught the Spanish flu. From this, he suffered a variety of different ailments, for which he spent time in various hospitals over the next five years. After he was discharged, he was paid a disability allowance under his war risk insurance policy for a 30 percent disability and was provided medical care. When he applied for total disability but could not provide medical evidence supporting his claim and had not paid his insurance premiums since discharge, the war risk bureau denied his claims, and the court affirmed that decision. In *Hettrick Mfg.*,[73] a company could not fulfill its contract due to staff absences during the outbreak of the Spanish flu. *Appeal of Frank-Sievers Undertaking Co.*[74] and *Jackson Casket & Manufacturing Co.*[75] showed that undertakers and casket makers, respectively, made extraordinary profits from the Spanish flu pandemic.

LEGAL PROFILES

Robert E. Lewis wrote the opinion of the court in *Hooper*. He was born in Missouri in 1857 and started his legal practice there in 1880. He was a county prosecutor from 1883 to 1887. From 1903 to 1906 he served as a district judge in Colorado. In 1906 President Roosevelt nominated him to the federal district court in Colorado. In 1921 President Harding appointed him to the Court of Appeals for the Eighth Circuit. He was reassigned in 1929 to the Tenth Circuit, where he retired in 1940. He died in 1941.[76]

---

72. Bean v. United States, 7 F.2d 393 (D. Kansas 1925).
73. Hettrick Mfg. Co. v. Waxahachie Cotton Mills, 1 F.2d 913 (6th Cir. 1924).
74. Appeal of Frank-Sievers Undertaking Co., 3 BTA 94 (BTA, 1925).
75. Jackson Casket & Mfg. Co. v. Comm'r of Internal Revenue, 7 BTA 1190 (BTA 1927).
76. *See Lewis, Robert E.*, FED. JUDICIAL CTR., BIOGRAPHICAL DIRECTORY OF FEDERAL JUDGES.

2. Veterans' Claims

a. Disability

In *Silberschein*,[77] a soldier had been injured while in service during the war and put on total temporary disability, which was later reduced to temporary partial disability. The question before the Supreme Court was whether the determinations of the director of the Veterans Bureau could be challenged in court. The director's decision was alleged to be arbitrary because "after allowing compensation he discontinued it, although petitioner's physical condition had not improved but had become worse, *being the same and resulting from the same causes for which compensation was originally allowed*"[78] The Court held that the decisions of the director were to be final and conclusive, meaning the courts could not review them, unless "the decision is wholly unsupported by the evidence, or is wholly dependent upon a question of law or is seen to be clearly arbitrary or capricious."[79]

b. Beneficiaries

In *White*,[80] a soldier had taken out a war risk insurance policy and died in October 1918. He had designated in the policy only his mother as beneficiary but by will on the same date had designated both his mother and his aunt as beneficiaries for the policy. At the time, the statute did not allow for aunts to be beneficiaries of these policies, but this was changed by the War Risk Insurance Act Amendments statute of December 1919,[81] with retroactive effect. The mother had been receiving the payments under the policy, but this was suspended and so she brought suit for being deprived of her property without due process, claiming that as the aunt could not receive the benefit as of the date of the will, it was void. The Court held otherwise, that the certificate of insurance was subject to the act and any subsequent amendments, and as these amendments allowed for his aunt to be a beneficiary, the intention stated in his will for his aunt to receive 50 percent of the payments should prevail.

---

77. Silberschein v. United States, 266 U.S. 221 (1924).
78. *Id.* at 224.
79. *Id.* at 225.
80. White v. United States, 270 U.S. 175 (1926).
81. Pub. L. No. 66-106, An Act to amend and modify the War Risk Insurance Act (1919), § 13.

c. Attorney Fees

In *Margolin*,[82] the Court reviewed a decision regarding attorney fees under the War Risk Insurance Act. Under the act, an attorney could receive compensation of only 10 percent for collecting claims for the death, personal injury, or detention of merchant seamen and only when proceedings had been initiated in a district court. This was modified later to 10 percent for the activities necessary to establish a right to benefits and still later modified to $3 for preparing the papers and 5 percent of the amount recovered after an action was initiated in district court. The petitioner attorney was found guilty under the act of a misdemeanor for receiving $1,500 to prepare an affidavit for a beneficiary in support of a claim and was fined $250. The petitioner claimed the $3 limit must have related to clerical work to prepare the forms, but the Court disagreed, holding that the plain language of the statute allowed for only $3 regardless of the extent of the attorney's work and, as such, upheld the conviction.

LEGAL PROFILES

Susan Brandeis was the attorney for the petitioner in *Margolin*. She was born in 1893 in Massachusetts, the daughter of a law professor (and later Supreme Court justice), and she started her legal practice in New York in 1921 and briefly worked as a special assistant to the district attorney in New York. An early supporter of women's suffrage, she could not get a job with a law firm, so she opened her own firm, which she later made into a partnership with her lawyer husband. When she brought this case before the Supreme Court, her father recused himself for obvious reasons. She died in 1975.[83]

---

82. Margolin v. United States, 269 U.S. 93 (1925).
83. *See Susan Brandeis Gilbert is Dead; Lawyer was Daughter of Jurist*, N.Y. TIMES (Oct. 9, 1975).

3. Veterans' Bonuses

a. Judicial Review

In *Bentley*,[84] a member of the National Guard who received a provisional commission in the regular army in November 1917 had been issued an adjusted service certificate of $1,246 under the World War Adjusted Compensation Act. Using this certificate as collateral, he borrowed $623 in 1935. Later that year, the secretary of war found that it had made a mistake in determining the benefits, as under section 202 there was no allowance to be made for holding a provisional commission, and so he should have been given a service certificate of only $371. The director of the Veterans Bureau then moved to recover the loan, but the defendant claimed that since all decisions of the director were to be considered final and conclusive under the act, the director could not adjust his certificate amount. The court of appeals ruled that the nonreviewability of decisions only applied to judicial review, not review within the bureau, as they had hundreds of thousands of claims and so needed the ability to increase them for those whom they had underpaid as well as seek a return from those they had overpaid. The court affirmed the secretary of war's decision.

b. March on Washington

With the onset of the Great Depression, veterans of WWI were among the many millions thrown out of work. As such, the need for money was acute, and veterans were clamoring for the ability to receive the amounts of the adjusted savings certificates granted under the World War Adjusted Compensation Act. Several bills were introduced in Congress to move forward the payments of the adjusted savings certificates from the 1945 payment date into the early 1930s, but after one bill that passed Congress was vetoed by President Hoover in 1931, many veterans were determined to go to Washington, DC, to be heard. In the spring and summer of 1932, upwards of 50,000 marched to the nation's capital, only to see the Senate refuse to pass an acceleration of payments of savings certificates. The camps in which the veterans had lived in since arriving in Washington, DC, were closed down by the military, led by future WWII commander Douglas MacArthur, and the veterans and their families were evicted. A different approach was used for a 1933 march after the 1932 election brought in President Roosevelt. He issued orders to find jobs for these

---

84. United States v. Bentley, 107 F.2d 382 (1939).

veterans in the Civilian Conservation Corps. And in 1936 Congress finally accelerated the payments of the veterans' bonuses to be awarded immediately by passing the Adjusted Compensation Payment Act in 1936.[85]

LEGAL PROFILES

John William Wright Patman initiated several bills supporting veterans. He was born in Texas in 1893 and started his legal practice there in 1916. He then served in the army during the war. In 1921 he was elected to the Texas state legislature. From 1924 to 1929 he was a district attorney. In 1928 he was elected to the U.S. Congress, where he would serve until his death in 1976.[86]

4. War Contracts

a. Implied Contracts

In *Baltimore & Ohio Railroad*,[87] the Supreme Court was asked to rule on the implicit contracts under the Dent Act. During the war the federal government had leased some piers in a larger yard owned by the plaintiff railroad. As there were acts of sabotage that destroyed two of the piers, the company asked the government to provide security for its leased piers. National Guard troops were assigned to provide this security. The troops ended up living in tents on the grounds through a bitterly cold autumn and winter, so after family members complained to the railroad, the company converted a transfer shed into barracks for the troops. But no agreement, oral or written, was ever reached, orders made, or compensation discussed over the building of this barracks between the government and the railroad company. Additionally, the Court found no implied agreement, as the quartermaster they dealt with had no

---

85. Pub. L. No. 74-425, An Act to provide for the immediate payment of World War adjusted service certificates, for the cancelation of unpaid interest accrued on loans secured by such certificates, and for other purposes (1936).
86. *See Patman, John William Wright*, BIOGRAPHICAL DIRECTORY OF THE UNITED STATES CONGRESS.
87. Baltimore & Ohio R. Co. v. United States, 261 U.S. 592 (1923).

authority to order such barracks, and the implied agreements under the act were to be implied in fact, not implied in law (quasi-contracts). The quartermaster had not ordered the barracks, which had been constructed voluntarily by the company. As such, the claim for compensation was properly denied.

b. Damages or Profits

In *Russell Motor Car Co.*,[88] the government had ordered plaintiff anti-aircraft gun mounts in spring 1918. Just after the armistice, the navy asked that the quantity of such mounts be significantly decreased and then stopped. The Court of Claims found the compensation for the termination of the contracts to be almost $500,000, even though the company would have earned almost $1 million if the contracts had been fully executed. The company first contended that the contracts that could be cancelled were only private contracts, not government contracts, but the Court of Claims and the Supreme Court did not agree. The company also alleged that just compensation should have included its anticipated profits. The Court answered that that confused a breach of contract damages with just compensation for a taking of private property by the government, saying it "must consider the value of the contract at the time of its cancellation, not what it would have produced by way of profits for the Car Company if it had been fully performed."[89] It affirmed the Court of Claims' decision.

c. Manganese Production

In *Work*,[90] the decision being challenged was that of the secretary of interior on damages awarded for claims related to manganese production. The plaintiff/relator claimed $55,000 in damages but was awarded only around $23,000. One of the excluded items was a $10,000 charge for the plaintiff to be released from contracts he had signed to buy land containing manganese (which had lost significant value after the war). The act had allowed payment for property purchased only for producing manganese during the war but not for speculation. Claims were to be based on ore on hand and machinery deployed but

---

88. Russell Motor Car Co. v. United States, 261 U.S. 514 (1923).
89. *Id.* at 523.
90. Work v. United States ex rel. Rives, 267 U.S. 175 (1925).

not for real estate or mining rights. The Court held that the secretary's decision was not "arbitrary or capricious or fraudulent or an abuse of discretion. The Secretary's view that it was not just or equitable to include loss by a land purchase within the gratuity of the Government as defined by the statute must therefore prevail against mandamus."[91] As such, the Court reversed the lower court's decision and let the secretary's decision stand.

LEGAL PROFILES

Merrill E. Otis was a special assistant to the attorney general in *Work*. He was born in Missouri in 1884 and started his practice there in 1911. He also worked as a city prosecutor from 1915 to 1918. From 1921 he was state assistant attorney general and in 1924 became assistant to the U.S. solicitor general. In 1925 he was appointed by President Coolidge to the federal district court in Missouri, where he served until his death in 1944.[92]

C. Subsequent Events

When WWII was coming to a close, President Roosevelt was still in office and, remembering the veterans' claims from WWI, looked to resolve these in advance. In 1944 Congress passed the Servicemen's Readjustment Act, popularly known as the GI Bill,[93] which Roosevelt signed. This act provided for postwar hospitalization for veterans, funding for education and vocational training, especially for those under the age of twenty-five when entering the service, and guarantees on home loans for up to 50 percent of the loan value (capped at $2,000) by the administrator of Veterans Affairs. Additionally, it provided guarantees on loans for farms and various types of business property,

---

91. *Id.* at 184.
92. *See Otis, Merrill E.*, Fed. Judicial Ctr., Biographical Directory of Federal Judges.
93. Pub. L. No. 78-346, An Act to provide Federal Government aid for the readjustment in civilian life of returning World War II veterans (1944).

job counseling, and job placement services, and a readjustment allowance of up to one year for veterans who were unemployed. Almost half of the sixteen million WWII veterans had used the education and training program by the end of the original act in 1956, and between 1944 and 1952 more than two million home loans had been guaranteed under it.[94]

LEGAL PROFILES

Harry Colmery was the original drafter of the GI bill of rights and a WWI veteran. He was born in Pennsylvania in 1890 and started his legal practice in Utah in 1916. Shortly thereafter, he volunteered to serve in the army during the war, working as a pilot, and then relocated to Kansas after the war to practice law. He was later the national commander of the American Legion. Between the wars he tried to get veterans treated at VA hospitals for illnesses unrelated to the service. He ran unsuccessfully for the U.S. Senate in 1950. He died in 1979.[95]

D. Modern Applicability

While renewals of the GI Bill continue to support veterans to this day, countries must now respond to pandemics and other large-scale health crises arising from concentrated and destructive wartime conditions or the intentional use of biological weapons as acts of war or terrorism. The legal response to pandemics and epidemics is based on the statutory authority provided. In WWI, with the federal government legally limited to affecting the federal institutions it controlled (army, navy, public health services) and to providing moral leadership and funding for a potential solution (none of which were effective against the virus they thought was a bacteria), the states responded in a noncoordinated and diverse manner to the influenza pandemic, with varying effective-

---

94. U.S. Dept. of Veterans Affairs, *The GI Bill's History*.
95. *See Harry W. Colmery, 88, A Former Legion Leader*, N.Y. TIMES (Aug. 25, 1979).

ness. Later flu epidemics, in 1957 and 1968, killed several million people, and the 2003 SARS epidemic spread globally in a matter of days. In the United States, a possible way toward a standardized state and local response is in the Model State Emergency Health Powers Act, which includes declaration of an emergency and special powers available during the emergency, including vaccination, isolation, and quarantine.

AFTERWORD

The early beginnings of the dynamics that would lead to WWII can be seen in how WWI's legal issues were addressed after the war. Perhaps more clearly than any other metric, the resolution to legal issues mirrored the nations' mindsets and therefore future actions. The most visible legal issue in exiting the conflict was the settling of peace treaties between the belligerents. The tenor for these agreements was set by those Allied Powers most injured by the war. Accordingly, the punitive aspects of the peace treaties went beyond the need for reasonable compensation and to a desire to keep Germany from initiating another conflict by reducing its military and economic capabilities. Germany not only lost its overseas colonies, Alsace-Lorraine, and other territory in Europe, it (along with Austria-Hungary) was held responsible for starting the war and was demilitarized, made to pay perhaps outsized compensatory reparations, and kept out of international institutions where it could debate these matters.

Numerous international agreements were reached in the 1920s and 1930s to try to avoid another conflict, by reducing the reparations payments, by limiting the number and types of armaments and naval ships, by creating conventions addressing the use of poison gas and other offensive weapons, and by renouncing war as a solution to the disputes between countries.[1] It was all to naught, as national rivalries, imperial ambitions, militaristic and racial policies, the weakness in the security function of the League of Nations, the Allied Powers' utter political and psychological exhaustion from WWI, the neutrality of the United States, the transfer of Germany's China concessions not back to China but to Japan, and the bitter feelings in Germany (over the Treaty of Versailles and its subsequent enforcement activities) and Italy (over the lack of territorial acquisition at Versailles) all combined to create a new

---

1. *See* WWII Law and Lawyers, ch. 1.

axis of power that would bring the world into an even wider ranging and more terrible global conflict.

Eighty legal issues from WWI have been presented here, originating from countries all across the geography of this conflict. Some of the issues were unique to a country's situation, others happened to all major countries involved in the war. The issues ranged from matters of life and death to matters of dollars and cents, from ancient royal powers to modern technologies, from emancipation of nations and genders to the freeing of chemical and biological warfare. With so many issues, they are perhaps easier understood if categorized in some manner. One way to do so is to classify the issues as those that were a necessary action or inevitable result of waging war (i.e., those that arise whenever there is a serious enough conflict requiring a reordering of national priorities) versus those that were particular to the political, military, social, or economic circumstances of this war. An example of the first category would be the special war powers devolved on the national executive branch to prosecute the war, including official secrecy and seizure of alien citizens and assets. Examples of the second category would be the closure of the U.S. stock exchanges to prevent the outflow of capital from America to Europe, the enacting of women's suffrage, the significant use of animals on the battlefield, and the assigning of country mandates to the former colonies of broken-up empires.

There were a number of issues that should have been consigned to this second category, but because society or the military reflecting society did not progress sufficiently in the twenty years that followed, the issue was to rise again, in a different setting and to different players but with the same core legal issue. An example of this was the segregation of troops by race. To a large extent this was a reflection of a racially segregated society. When General Pershing had brought the American Expeditionary Forces to Europe, he had notions of using all races in the fight (he had previously commanded regiments of the Buffalo Soldiers, comprised of African American troops), but he was prevented from doing so by the social and political landscape of America. By WWII, society still had not solved this problem, and so African Americans were disproportionately given menial tasks, leading to further incidents.[2] It was

---

2. *See* WWII LAW AND LAWYERS, ch. 2.

not until after WWII that the military, perhaps showing the way for society, desegregated and integrated.

In addition to the legal issues were the legal players involved with framing those issues into laws, prosecuting, defending, or adjudicating cases based on those laws, occasionally being a defendant in one of these trials, or carrying out these laws in an executive, diplomatic, or military function. It was through these roles that lawyers and judges and those trained in the law were able to have a significant impact on the events composing this war and the many conferences following it. Because the rule of law stayed mostly intact within the political systems of the major belligerents of this war, it was the lawyers and judges from so many disparate legal traditions, more than the better-known military leaders, who were involved in addressing the many diverse but interwoven threads in the broad tapestry of this global conflict.

LEGAL PROFILES

Robert Schuman was perhaps the embodiment of all the cultures from this global war and the next, and the hope for no more such conflicts. He was born in Luxembourg to a father from Alsace-Lorraine (then part of Germany) in 1886 and obtained his legal training in Germany. He opened a legal office in Metz (in Lorraine) in 1912. At the start of the war, he performed noncombatant duties and then worked as a civil administrator. With the return of Alsace-Lorraine to France after the war, he became a French citizen and was elected to the French national assembly, where he remained in its different forms until 1962, often serving as finance minister. At the start of WWII, he was arrested by the Nazis but later escaped and joined the resistance, remaining in Europe at personal risk despite being called to London by De Gaulle. After the war, he was elected prime minister of France in 1947, as foreign minister from 1948 to 1953, and later as justice minister. His declaration in 1950 was the start of the pan-European institutions, such as the European Coal and Steel Community. He was the president of the first European Parliamentary Assembly from 1958 and honorary president from 1960.

He died in 1963.[3] A deeply religious man, he was beatified by Pope John Paul II in 1995.

The results of this war are known to have prepared the ground of the next global war, even though there was hope then that addressing its causes and symptoms could preclude such a future. Yet given the significant number of examples of modern applicability of these legal issues, the lessons to be learned from this war can still be used to avoid or mitigate problems today. With a base understanding that much of the current political geography and some of the legal issues have their origin in this conflict, this foundation can assist in comprehending and tackling those issues still bedeviling a new century. It is only with a complete understanding of the failure and successes of prior generations can we hope to set the direction for future generations. As our grandparents set that course almost a century ago and our parents did again some seventy years ago, so must we, standing upon the quarterdeck of the ship built of their collective wisdom, set a truer course, shorn of global conflict, for our own children and their descendants.

---

3. *See Shuman Dies at 77; Led European Unity*, N.Y. TIMES (Sept. 5, 1963).

APPENDIX

LIST OF LAWYERS AND JUDGES PROFILED[1]

CHAPTER 1

- Mineichirō Adachi — Japan
- Felipe Agoncillo — Philippines
- Cayetano Arellano — Philippines
- Otto von Bismarck — Germany
- Jules Cambon — France
- Paul Cambon — France
- Henry A. Cooper — United States
- William Nelson Cromwell — United States
- William R. Day — United States
- Ferenc Deák — Hungary
- Edgar Demange — France
- Benjamin Disraeli — United Kingdom
- Jules Favre — France
- William Ewart Gladstone — United Kingdom
- Samuel R. Gummere — United States
- John M. Hay — United States
- Heinrich VII — Germany
- Charles Merrill Hough — United States

---

[1]. Each country is that which the lawyer or judge profiled is most closely associated. Modern political units are typically used (e.g., Germany includes Prussia, Turkey includes the Ottoman Empire, Ireland is broken out from the United Kingdom but Scotland and Wales are not).

- Philander C. Knox — United States
- Jutarō Komura — Japan
- Fernand Labori — France
- Heinrich Lammasch — Austria
- Titu Maiorescu — Romania
- Frederick de Martens — Russia
- Giuseppe Mazzini — Italy
- Joseph McKenna — United States
- William McKinley — United States
- Safvet Pasha — Turkey
- Joseph Pulitzer — United States
- Louis Renault — France
- Eugenio Montero Ríos — Spain
- Elihu Root — United States
- Alfons Mumm von Schwarzenstein — Germany
- John Sherman — United States
- William Howard Taft — United States
- Adolphe Thiers — France
- James Francis Thomas — Australia
- Sylvain Van de Weyer — Belgium
- Edward Douglass White — United States

CHAPTER 2

- Henry Herbert Asquith — United Kingdom
- Tobias Asser — Netherlands
- Louis Barthou — France
- Lucius H. Beers — United States
- Leopold Berchtold — Austria
- Theobald von Bethmann-Hollweg — Germany
- John Bigham — United Kingdom
- Thomas Bloomfield — United States
- Alfred de Bathe Brandon — New Zealand
- William Jennings Bryan — United States
- Edward Carson — United Kingdom
- George Cave — United Kingdom

- Robert Cecil — United Kingdom
- René Coty — France
- Alois Curinaldi — Bosnia
- Samuel Thomas Evans — United Kingdom
- David Lloyd George — United Kingdom
- James W. Gerard — United States
- Félix Gouin — France
- Henri Guernut — France
- Richard Haldane — United Kingdom
- Timothy Michael Healy — Ireland
- Joseph Chappell Hutcheson Jr. — United States
- Wilhelm Kiesselbach — Germany
- Julius M. Mayer — United States
- Alexandre Millerand — France
- John Bassett Moore — United States
- Philip Morrell — United Kingdom
- Louis Nail — France
- Edwin B. Parker — United States
- Robert John Parker — United Kingdom
- Raoul Péret — France
- Robert George Raper — United Kingdom
- Antonio Salandra — Italy
- Walther Schücking — Germany
- Frank D. Slee — Australia
- F. E. (Frederick Edwin) Smith — United Kingdom
- István Tisza — Hungary
- René Viviani — France

CHAPTER 3

- Max Aitken — United Kingdom
- James Atkin — United Kingdom
- Edward Tindal Atkinson — United Kingdom
- Adolf von Batocki — Germany
- Charles Ruijs de Beerenbrouck — Netherlands
- Archibald Bodkin — United Kingdom

- Pierre Bouchardon — France
- Léon Bourgeois — France
- Aristide Briand — France
- John Buchan — United Kingdom
- Stanley Buckmaster — United Kingdom
- Joseph Caillaux — France
- Felix Cassel — United Kingdom
- Edouard Clunet — France
- Charles Darling — United Kingdom
- Charles Swinfen Eady — United Kingdom
- Thomas A. Fyfe — United Kingdom
- William Gloag — United Kingdom
- Seerp Gratama — Netherlands
- Henry Holman Gregory — United Kingdom
- John Hamilton — United Kingdom
- Theo Heemskerk — Netherlands
- Gordon Hewart — United Kingdom
- Travers Humphreys — United Kingdom
- Rufus Isaacs — United Kingdom
- Sadi Kirschen — Belgium
- Gaston de Leval — Belgium
- Merton E. Lewis — United States
- John Loudon — Netherlands
- Reginald McKenna — United Kingdom
- Daniel Mérillon — France
- Georg Michaelis — Germany
- Rosslyn Mitchell — United Kingdom
- Anatole de Monzie — France
- André Mornet — France
- Vincent de Moro-Giafferri — France
- John Fletcher Moulton — United Kingdom
- Robert Munro — United Kingdom
- Andrew Murray — United Kingdom
- Fridtjof Nansen — Norway
- Raymond Poincaré — France
- Ernest Pollock — United Kingdom

- Henri Robert — France
- Albert Salle — France
- Leslie Frederic Scott — United Kingdom
- John Simon — United Kingdom
- A. A. H. Struycken — Netherlands
- Pieter Cort van der Linden — Netherlands
- Wilhelm von Waldow — Germany
- Brand Whitlock — United States

CHAPTER 4

- Heinrich Albert — Germany
- Henry W. Anderson — United States
- Samuel T. Ansell — United States
- Eliseo Arredondo — Mexico
- Newton D. Baker — United States
- James M. Beck — United States
- Alexander Bruce Bielaski — United States
- Louis D. Brandeis — United States
- Luis Cabrera — Mexico
- William W. Canada — United States
- George E. Chamberlain — United States
- John Hessin Clarke — United States
- Enoch Crowder — United States
- Willis van Devanter — United States
- William van Fleet — United States
- James A. Fowler — United States
- Patrick Garvan — United States
- John M. Hay — United States
- Louis T. Hengstler — United States
- Julier Clyde Hizar — United States
- Oliver Wendell Holmes — United States
- Edwin Hubble — United States
- John A. Hull — United States
- George Langham Ingraham — United States
- Hugh S. Johnson — United States

- Frederick William Lehmann — United States
- William H. Lewis — United States
- Louis Marshall — United States
- James B. Morris — United States
- Walter Nelles — United States
- A. Mitchell Palmer — United States
- John J. Pershing — United States
- Frank L. Polk — United States
- John W. Preston — United States
- Franklin Delano Roosevelt — United States
- Edward Terry Sanford — United States
- George Sutherland — United States
- Robert Szold — United States
- Woodrow Wilson — United States
- John M. Woolsey — United States
- Arthur Zimmermann — Germany

CHAPTER 5

- John William Abercrombie — United States
- Annette Abbott Adams — United States
- Alfred Bettman — United States
- Benjamin Franklin Bledsoe — United States
- Zechariah Chafee Jr. — United States
- Joseph Sill Clark Sr. — United States
- Charles Allen Culberson — United States
- Josephus Daniels — United States
- William Paul Dillingham — United States
- Wade H. Ellis — United States
- John Jacob Esch — United States
- Isaac Edward Ferguson — United States
- Felix Frankfurter — United States
- William L. Frierson — United States
- Harry Augustus Garfield — United States
- Thomas Watt Gregory — United States
- William D. Guthrie — United States
- Learned Hand — United States

- Walker D. Hines — United States
- J. Edgar Hoover — United States
- Charles Evans Hughes — United States
- John E. Joyce — United States
- Belle Case La Follette — United States
- William H. Lamar — United States
- Kenesaw Mountain Landis — United States
- Oscar Leser — United States
- Asbury F. Lever — United States
- Belva Ann Lockwood — United States
- Robert S. Lovett — United States
- Etta H. Maddox — United States
- William Gibbs McAdoo — United States
- Catherine Waugh McCulloch — United States
- Kenneth Douglas McKellar — United States
- James C. McReynolds — United States
- Inez Milholland — United States
- Thomas G. Patten — United States
- John Barton Payne — United States
- Mahlon Pitney — United States
- Albert C. Ritchie — United States
- Seth Shepard — United States
- Morris Sheppard — United States
- Seymour Stedman — United States
- Frank P. Walsh — United States
- Edwin Y. Webb — United States
- Alfred A. Wheat — United States
- Wayne Wheeler — United States

CHAPTER 6

- Alfred Herbert John Andrews — Canada
- Horace Avory — United Kingdom
- George Harold Baker — Canada
- Robert L. Borden — Canada
- Jasper Y. Brinton — United States
- James Bryce — United Kingdom

- John Butcher — United Kingdom
- Kenelm Edward Digby — United Kingdom
- George Gavan Duffy — Ireland
- Eamonn Duggan — Ireland
- Ludwig Ebermayer — Germany
- Robert Finlay — United Kingdom
- Mohandas K. Gandhi — India
- Robert Garran — Australia
- Thomas Horridge — United Kingdom
- Ellis Hume-Williams — United Kingdom
- Alexander Kerensky — Russia
- Wilfrid Laurier — Canada
- Vladimir Ilyich Lenin — Russia
- Donald Mackinnon — Australia
- Henry N. MacLaurin — Australia
- Charles Willie Mathews — United Kingdom
- Edward Grimwood Mears — United Kingdom
- Alfred Milner — United Kingdom
- Henry Morgenthau Sr. — United States
- John H. Morgan — United Kingdom
- Andrew Barton Paterson — Australia
- Patrick Pearse — Ireland
- Shiv Narayan Raina — India
- John Redmond — Ireland
- Heinrich Schmidt — Germany
- Jan Smuts — South Africa
- A. M. Sullivan — Ireland
- Jonathan Mayhew Wainwright — United States
- Charles White Whittlesey — United States
- Krikor Zohrab — Armenia

CHAPTER 7

- Eduard Beneš — Czechoslovakia
- Léon Bourgeois — France
- Roland W. Boyden — United States

- Susan Brandeis — United States
- Antonio Sanchez de Bustamante — Cuba
- Harry Colmery — United States
- Charles G. Dawes — United States
- Stanley Hubert Dent Jr. — United States
- Charles Joseph Doherty — Canada
- Ellis Loring Dresel — United States
- John Foster Dulles — United States
- Cecil Hurst — United Kingdom
- Paul Hymans — Belgium
- Otto Landsberg — Germany
- Robert E. Lewis — United States
- Karl Liebknecht — Germany
- Henry Cabot Lodge — United States
- Carl Melchior — Germany
- David Hunter Miller — United States
- Rodrigo Octavio — Brazil
- Vittorio E. Orlando — Italy
- Merrill E. Otis — United States
- John Johnston Parker — United States
- William Wright Patman — United States
- Charles Allen Prosser — United States
- Lucius Franklin Robinson — United States
- James Brown Scott — United States
- Mark Sykes — United Kingdom
- Emile Vandervelde — Belgium
- Milenko Radomar Vesnić — Serbia
- Max Weber — Germany
- Owen D. Young — United States

AFTERWORD

- Robert Schuman — France/Germany/Luxembourg/Europe

INDEX

A

ABA. *See* American Bar Association (ABA)
Abandoned Properties Law, 381
Abd al-Aziz, Mulai, 35
Abercrombie, John William, 297, 321–322
Abraham Lincoln: A History (Nicolay & Hay), 35
Abrams v. United States, 250 U.S. 616 (1919), 320–321
Absolutist conscientious objectors, 90–91
Act to Regulate Radio Communication, 243
Adachi, Mineichirō, 4, 62–63
Adams, Annette Abbott, 298, 367
Adkins v. Children's Hosp. of D.C., 261 U.S. 525 (1923), 360
Aehrenthal, Alois von, 36
Aerial bombardment, 141–146
Afghanistan, 2, 20
Africa, 27–28
African Americans, 292, 350, 492
Agadir Crisis, 33–34
Agoncillo, Felipe, 4, 43
Agriculture-stimulation act, 352
Aguinaldo, Emile, 49

Ahlers, Nicholaus, 203, 218–220
Air power
    cases, 143–144
    modern applicability, 147–148
    statutes, 139–142
    subsequent events, 145–146
    use of, 69–70, 139–148
Air reconnaissance, 140–141
Aitken, Jonathan, 175
Aitken, Max, Lord Beaverbrook, 151, 173, 174–175
Alaska Purchase, 39
Albania, 3, 37
Albanian crises, 37
Albert, Heinrich, 225, 257
Aldrich-Vreeland Act, 344
Algeciras Conference, 35, 62
Alien claims, 469–470
Alien Property Custodian, 469
Alien property custodian (APC), 260, 261, 264–265
Alien Restriction Act, 219
All Quiet on the Western Front (Remarque), 96
Allen, Clifford, 90
Allied Powers, 1, 19, 67–68, 75–76, 187, 192, 229–230, 439
Almereyda, Miguel, 217

505

Alsace-Lorraine, 9, 68
Am. Smelting and Refining Co. v.
    United States, 259 U.S. 75 (1922),
    335–336
Ambulance dogs, 436
American Bar Association (ABA), 237,
    293
American Civil Liberties Union, 276
American Civil War, 2, 39, 430
American Expeditionary Forces, 492
American Military Mission to
    Armenia, 395
American National Red Cross, 381
American Red Cross, 226, 466
American Relief Administration, 198,
    340
Anarchists
    cases, 319–321
    statutes, 316–319
    subsequent events, 322
Ancient Regime, 7
Anderson, Henry W., 225, 269
Andrews, Alfred Herbert John, 370,
    380
Anglo-Irish Treaty, 94, 419
Anglo-Persian pipeline, 403
Anglo-Russian Entente, 19–20
Animals in war
    cases, 432–438
    dogs, 430, 435–437, 442
    horses, 429–431, 433–435,
        439–440, 442
    modern applicability, 441–442
    pigeons, 430, 431–432,
        437–438, 441
    statutes, 429
    subsequent events, 439–441

Ansell, Samuel T., 225, 288, 290
Anthony, Susan B., 355
Anti-Saloon League, 357, 359
Anton and Carl Dilger, 258
Appeal of Frank-Sievers Undertaking
    Co., 3 BTA 94 (BTA, 1925), 481
ARA *General Belgrano* (warship), 139
Arab-Israeli war, 421
Arellano, Cayetano, 4, 50
Argentina, 139
Armed Ship Bill, 233
Armenian massacre, 380–382, 398
Armistice of Compiegne, 447
Armistice of Mudros, 394, 446
Armistice of Thessalonica, 446
Armistice of Villa Giusti, 446–447
Armistices, 446–448
Armstrong v. United States, 182 U.S.
    243 (1901), 51
Army Act, 91
Arredondo, Eliseo, 224, 250
Article I, U.S. Constitution, 275
Article III, U.S. Constitution, 313
Articles of War
    cases, 281–290
    Houston riot trials, 289–290
    modern applicability, 293–294
    statutes, 278–280
    subsequent events, 291–292
Artillery, 139
Asia, 27
Asquith, Henry Herbert (H. H.), 70,
    78–79, 89, 185, 376
Asser, Tobias, 71, 144
Assets, reclaiming of, 467–470
Associated Powers, 1
Atkin, James, 151, 171

Atkinson, Edward Tindal, 151, 171
Atkinson, John, Lord Atkinson, 160
Atrocities, 376–377, 383–387
Attorney Fees, 483
Aubrey, Crispin, 175
Australia, 28, 401, 421–423, 425–426, 428, 440
Austria, 7, 8, 16–17, 461, 465
Austria-Hungary, 15, 16–17, 21, 47
    Armistice of Villa Giusti, 446–447
    cessations of hostilities, 443
    civilian supply, 176
    declarations of war, 74–77
    Italy declares war on, 83
    July Crisis, 71–73
    military plans, 68
    reasons for starting war, 82
    role in Bosnia crisis, 36
    shelling of Belgrade by, 69
    significant impact of war on women in, 365–366
Austrian Empire, 11
Austro-Hungarian Compromise, 16, 17
Austro-Hungarian Empire, 16, 29, 95
Austro-Prussian War, 8
Avory, Horace, 371, 412

B

Bacterial warfare, 434–435, 441
Baer, Elizabeth, 301
Baker, George Harold, 371, 434
Baker, Harry, 433
Baker, Newton D., 225, 281
Baldwin, Roger, 276
Balfour, Arthur, 403
Balfour Declaration, 403, 420
Balkan League, 38
Balkan states, 3
Balkan Wars of 1912–13, 3, 37–38
Baltimore & Ohio R. Co. v. United States, 261 U.S. 592 (1923), 485
Baltimore, Charles, 289
Bangladesh, 106–107
Barrie, J. M., 133, 173
Barthou, Louis, 70, 89
Barton, Clara, 351
Baruch, Bernard, 327
Batocki, Adolf von, 151, 180
Battle of Ambos Nogales, 257
Battle of Chemin des Dames, 209, 210
Battle of Gaugamela, 429
Battle of Mohács, 16
Battle of the Falklands, 119
Battle of the Little Bighorn, 12
Battle of the Somme, 91, 106, 166, 425
Battles of the Aisne, 102
Bazeries, Étienne, 174
Bean v. United States, 7 F.2d 393 (D. Kansas 1925), 481
Beck, James M., 224, 240
Beers, Lucius H., 71, 130
BEF. *See* British Expeditionary Force (BEF)
Belgium
    atrocities in, 376–377, 383–387
    Edith Cavell case, 206–207
    hunger situation in, 198
    invasion of, 192
    neutrality of, 18
    reparations payments to, 471

Belgium, *continued*
  return of cash, 448
  Schlieffen Plan, 75, 85
  smuggling, 195
  use of zeppelins for strategic bombing, 142
  Wire of Death, 190
Beneficiaries, 482
Beneš, Eduard, 445
Benevolent neutrality, 21
Berchtold, Leopold, 70, 73
Berger, Victor L., 308
Bernard, Simon, 13
Bernstorff, Johann Heinrich von, 215, 409
Bess (horse), 440
Bethmann-Hollweg, Theobald von, 70, 77–78
Bettany, Michael, 175
Bettman, Alfred, 296, 302
Beyers, Christian, 427
Bhakna, Sohan Singh, 413
Bidwell, George, 51
Bielaski, Alexander Bruce, 225, 258–259
Bigham, John, Lord Mersey, 71, 125, 127
Biological warfare, 258, 434–435, 441–442
Biological Weapons Convention, 441
Birth of a Nation (film), 308
Bishop, Billy, 141
Bismarck, Otto von, 4, 378
  attempted assassination of, 13
  legal profile, 10
  role in Congress of Berlin, 15, 17
  Treaty of Frankfurt and, 9

Black Hand (Crna Ruka) Society, 79, 80, 81
"Black Sox" scandal, 308
Black Tom Terminal, 254–257
Blake, George, 175
Blanchard, Jean, 99
Bledsoe, Benjamin Franklin, 296, 309
Blockade
  cases, 112–116
  impact on Russia and Germany, 443
  modern applicability, 118–119
  statutes, 107–111
  subsequent events, 116–117
Bloomfield, Thomas, 71, 134
Bloomsbury Set, 93
Board of Relief, 227
Bodkin, Archibald, 151, 171
Boer War, 2, 29, 31
Boers, 29–30, 427
Boldt, John, 389, 390–391
Bolo, Paul, 202, 214, 215–216
Bolsheviks, 405
Bonaparte, Louis-Napoléon, 7, 9, 12
Bonaparte, Napoléon, 5, 7, 11
Bopp, Franz, 252
Borden, Robert L., 371, 423
Bose, Ras Bihair, 413
Bosnia, 79–81, 84
Bosnia crisis, 36
Bosnia-Herzegovina, 3, 15, 17, 36
Botany Worsted Mills, 262
Bouchardon, Pierre, 152, 205–206
Bourgeois, Léon, 152, 213, 444
Boxer Protocol, 47, 48
Boxer Rebellion, 3, 46–48
Boy-Ed, Karl, 258

Boyden, Roland W., 445, 471–472
Brandeis, Louis D., 224, 239, 320, 322
Brandeis, Susan, 445, 483
Brandenburg v. Ohio, 395 U.S. 444 (1969), 322
Brandon, Alfred de Bathe, 71, 142
Breaker Morant (film), 30
Briand, Aristide, 78, 97, 152, 221–222
Brinton, Jasper Y., 371, 396
British Admiralty, 135
British Board of Trade, 125
British Corn Production Act of 1917, 177
British Empire, 28
British Expeditionary Force (BEF), 68, 85, 141, 171
British Signal Service, 438
British Wreck Commissioners Court, 128
Brocklesby, Bert, 91–92
Brocklesby, Philip, 91–92
Brockway, Archibald Fenner, 90
Brooke, Dorothy, 440
Browne, Desmond, 107
Bryan, Williams Jennings, 41, 71, 124, 229, 242
Bryce commission, 383
Bryce, James, 370, 376, 377, 381
Bryce report, 383–387
Buchan, John, 151, 167
Buckmaster, Stanley, 152, 220–221
Buffalo Soldiers, 492
Bulgaria, 3, 13, 15, 21, 37–38, 443, 447, 462
Bureau of the Conference for the Reduction and Limitation of Armaments, 146
Bureau of War Risk Insurance, 478
Burma, 28, 162
Burns, Lucy, 355
Bushveldt Carbineers, 29
Bustamante, Antonio Sanchez de, 445, 465
Bustamante code of private international law,, 465
Butcher, John, 371, 441

C

Čabrinović Nedeljko, 80–81
Cabrera, Luis, 224, 248
Caillaux, Joseph, 152, 202, 210–215, 220
Cambon, Jules, 4, 21, 204
Cambon, Paul, 4, 20–21, 403
Camels, 430
Campbell, Duncan, 175
Canada, 28, 93, 354, 401, 421–423, 424, 428
Canada, William W., 224, 246–247
Capitulation, 103
Carbonari secret society, 11
Carnegie Endowment for International Peace, 64
Carranza, Venustiano, 246, 249
Carson, Edward, 71, 117, 400
Casement, Roger, 203, 406, 409–411
Cassel, Felix, 152, 222
Catherine the Great, 14
Catt, Carrie Chapman, 355
Cave, George, 70, 92
Cavell, Edith, 86, 202, 206–208, 220
Ceannt, Eamonn, 408
Cecil, Robert, 71, 111–112

Censorship. *See* Official secrets/
 Censorship
Central Powers, 1, 19, 67–68, 75–76,
 111, 187, 192
Chafee, Zechariah, Jr., 297, 322–323
Chakravarty, C. K., 252
Chamberlain, George E., 225, 283
Chapelant, Jean Jacques, 103
Charlemagne, King of the Franks, 7,
 11
Chemical Foundation, 268–269, 271
Chemical Weapons Convention, 398,
 442
"Cher Ami" (pigeon), 438
China, 3, 36, 46–48, 66, 476, 491
Chinese embassy, 139
Choctaw code talkers, 174
Christian IX, King of Denmark, 77
Churchill, Winston, 439–440
Civilian and military supply
 cases, 181–184
 food hoarding, 182
 munitions tribunals, 183–184
 statutes, 175–180
 subsequent events, 185–187
Cixi, Empress Dowager, 47
Claims, for loss or damage, 131–133
Clark, Joseph Sill, Sr., 297, 339
Clarke, John Hessin, 225, 251
Clarke, Thomas, 408
Clayton-Bulwer Treaty, 56
Clemenceau, Georges, 211
Cleveland, Grover, 313
Clunet, Edouard, 152, 205
Clyde Workers Committee, 184
Cocaine, 163
Colmery, Harry, 445, 488

Colombia, 56–57
Colonies, 27–30
Columbus Ry., Power & Light Co. v.
 City of Columbus, Ohio, 249 U.S.
 399 (1919), 338–339
Commercial Trust Co. of N.J. v. Miller,
 262 U.S. 51 (1923), 264–265
Commission for the Relief of
 Belgium (CRB), 198, 209
Commission of Allied Jurists, 391
Commission on the Responsibility
 of the Authors of the War and on
 Enforcement of Penalties, 373
Committee for Public Information,
 314
Committee of Unity and Progress,
 381
Committee on Alleged German
 Outrages, 376
Committee on Military Affairs, 248
Congress of Berlin, 15, 17
Congress of Vienna, 8
Connolly, James, 408
Conscientious objectors, 89–92, 272
Conscription
 in Australia, 425–426
 cases, 89–92
 crisis of 1918, 93, 419
 exemption from, 87–88
 introduced in Canada, 424
 statutes, 85–88
 subsequent events, 93
Le conseil de guerre, 96
Les conseils de guerre spéciaux, 97
Constitution Act (a.k.a. the British
 North America Act), 421
Le Consulat et l'Empire (Thiers), 8

Convention of Constantinople, 56
Convoy, J. Robert, 437
Cooper, Henry A., 4, 50
Cort van der Linden, Pieter, 151, 191–192
Coty, René, 70, 105
Council for National Defense, 243
Council of National Defense, 326
Councils of war, 96, 215
Cours martiales, 97
Court of Claims, 434
Court of Special Military Justice, 101, 104
Courts-martial, 278–279
CRB. *See* Commission for the Relief of Belgium (CRB)
Creel, George, 314
Crime Act, 426
Crimean War, 2, 6
Crimes and offenses against military duty, 97
Cripps, Charles, Lord Parmoor, 161
Crisp, Albert Hennington, 168–169
Croatia, 17, 84
Cromwell, William Nelson, 4, 57, 65
Crowder, Enoch, 225, 274
Crusius, Benno, 389
Cryptography, 174
Cuba, 41–42, 59, 64, 245, 272
Cuban missile crisis, 118
Culberson, Charles Allen, 296, 300
Cullen-Harrison Act, 365
Cunard Steamship Company, 128
Curinaldi, Alois, 70, 81–82
Custer, George Armstrong, 12
Czech Republic, 17
Czechoslovakia, 463

D

Dangerous Drugs Act of 1920, 163
Daniels, Josephus, 296, 315
Darius III, King of the Achaemenid dynasty of Persia, 429
Darling, Charles, 151, 183
Darrow, Clarence, 124
Daudet, Léon, 209
Davison, Emily, 354
Dawes, Charles G., 445, 472, 473
Dawes Plan, 472–473
Day, William R., 4, 42–43
De Lima v. Bidwell, 182 U.S. 1 (1901), 51–53, 55
de Wet, Christiaan, 427
Deák, Ferenc, 4, 17–18
Debs, Eugene, 304–305
Debs v. United States, 249 U.S. 211 (1919), 304–305
Defence Act, 423
Defence Act of 1842, 157, 158
Defence of India Act, 401, 419
Defence of the Realm Act (DORA)
    amended to regulate workers in munitions plants, 179
    conscientious objectors, 90
    De Keyser's Royal Hotel and, 156–161
    Defence of India Act and, 401
    leaders of Irish uprising and, 407–408
    overview of, 152–154
    Regulation 40B, 163
    use to control food, 177–178
    violations, 155–156
    War Measures Act and, 422

Defence of the Realm Consolidation Act (DORA Consolidation Act), 152
Defence of the Realm Losses Commission, 157
Demange, Edgar, 22, 24
Denmark, 77, 110, 187, 354
Dent Act, 485
Dent, Stanley Hubert, Jr., 445
Derby Scheme, 86
Dereliction of duty, 98–100
Desertion, 97, 103
Desertion and Capitulation, 103
DeSilver, Albert, 276
di Rudio, Carlo, 12
Diaz, Porfirio, 249
Digby, Kenelm Edward, 370, 388
Dilger, Anton, 435
Dillingham, William Paul, 297, 319
Dimitrijević, Dragutin, 79
Dirigibles, 141–142
Disability, 482
disobedience in the face of the enemy, 100–102
Disraeli, Benjamin, 4, 15–16
Distance neutrality
    cases, 235–242
    statutes, 226–234
    subsequent events, 243
Dithmar, Ludwig, 389, 390–391
Djemal Pasha, 395
Dogs, 430, 435–437, 441, 442
Doherty, Charles Joseph, 445, 464
Dolphins, 442
Dominican Republic, 65, 245, 258
Dooley v. United States, 182 U.S. 222 (1901), 51

DORA. *See* Defence of the Realm Act (DORA)
DORA Consolidation Act. *See* Defence of the Realm Consolidation Act (DORA Consolidation Act)
Douglas, Kirk, 101
Downes, Samuel, 53
Downes v. Bidwell, 182 U.S. 244 (1901), 51, 53–54, 55
Doyle, Arthur Conan, 173
Dred Scott v. Sandford, 60 U.S. 393 (1857), 54
Dresel, Ellis Loring, 445, 466
Dreyfus, Alfred, 22–23
Dreyfus trial, 22–23
Dual Alliance agreement, 17
Duffy, George Gavan, 371, 420
Duggan, Eamonn, 371, 419
Dulles, John Foster, 445, 472
Durantet, Francisque, 99
Duval, Emile Joseph, 217
Dyal, Har, 251

E

Eady, Charles Swinfen, 151, 158
East India Company, 401
Eastern Rumelia, 15
Ebermayer, Ludwig, 371, 392
Economy and Society (Weber), 477
Edward III, King of England, 410
Edwards, Alonzo, 289
Edwards, Rose, 155–156
Egypt, 20, 28, 403, 474
Eight-Nation Alliance, 47
Eighteenth Amendment, U.S. Constitution, 364, 365

Eighth Amendment, U.S.
    Constitution, 313
Electoral Bill, 354
Elephants, 429
Eliot, T. S., 93
Ellis, Wade H., 297
Emergency powers
    cases, 155–161
    statutes, 152–154
    subsequent events, 162–164
Empire Settlement Act, 366
Enemy Alien Registration Section,
    319
Enemy aliens
    cases, 319–321
    statutes, 316–319
    subsequent events, 322
Enemy asset and export controls
    cases, 261–269
    enemy ownership of shares,
        261–263
    import restrictions, 267
    joint account with nonenemy,
        264–265
    modern applicability, 271–272
    partnership valuation, 265–266
    sale of seized enemy intellectual
        property, 268–269
    statutes, 259–260
    subsequent events, 270–271
Enemy ownership of shares,
    261–263
English Service Act, 275
Enlisted Reserve Corps, 247
Entente Cordiale, 19, 21, 33
Enver Pasha, 394
Erie doctrine, 239

Esch-Cummins Act. *See*
    Transportation Act of 1920
Esch, John Jacob, 297, 340–341
Espionage, 97
    cases, 300–313
    modern applicability, 315
    statutes, 298–299
    subsequent events, 314
Espionage Act, 260
    cases that arose out of, 300–313
    free speech in motion pictures,
        308–309
    free speech in public speaking
        and, 304–305
    free speech in publications and,
        301–303
    modern applicability, 315
    nonmailable items, 310–311
    postal system privileges,
        312–313
    subsequent events, 314
    titles of, 298–299
    Wobblies, 306–307
Esterhazy, Ferdinand, 23
Estonia, 405
Evans, Samuel Thomas, 71, 114
Excess profits tax, 347
Execution of soldiers
    cases, 98–103
    dereliction of duty, 98–100
    desertion and capitulation, 103
    disobedience in the face of the
        enemy, 100–102
    mutiny, 97, 102–103
    process of, 97
    statutes, 94–97
    subsequent events, 104–105

F

Falkland Islands, 139
Falklands War, 118, 139
Favre, Jules, 4, 10–11
Fawcett, Millicent, 354
Febvre, Lucien, 214
Federal Reserve Act of 1913, 343
Federal Reserve System, 343–344, 346
Federal Reserve System Act, 239
Federal Trade Commission, 260
Federal Trade Commission Act, 239
Ferdinand, Franz, 69, 79–80
Ferdinand I, Tsar of Bulgaria, 446
Ferguson, Isaac Edward, 296, 306
Fifteenth Amendment, U.S. Constitution, 362
Fifth Amendment, U.S. Constitution, 313, 364
Finding Neverland (movie), 133
Finland, 354, 405
Finlay, Robert, 371, 417
First Amendment, U.S. Constitution, 301, 303, 313, 321
First Battle of Marne, 85, 141
First Battle of Ypres, 85
First French Republic, 7
First Philippine Commission, 49
First Violations of International Law by Germany (Renault), 27
First War Powers Act, 270
Fleming v. Page, 50 U.S. 603 (1850), 52–53
Floch, Paul-Henri, 99, 100
Florida Purchase, 39
Fonck, René, 141
Food, 328–330
Food Administration, 326, 337, 338, 340
Food Administration Grain Corporation (U.S. Grain Corporation), 329
Food and Fuel Control Act, 328, 340
Food Control Committee, 182
Food hoarding, 182
Forster, E. M., 93
Foster, Ellen, 356
Fourie, Josef, 427
Fourteen points, 449–451, 462–463
Fowler, James A., 225, 265
France, 7, 13, 85
    Agadir Crisis, 33–34
    China and, 66
    civilian supply, 176
    conscription laws, 86
    councils of war, 96–97, 200
    declarations of war, 74–77
    Eight-Nation Alliance, 47
    horses in wartime, 440
    Plan XVII, 68
    reasons for starting war, 82
    relative position of before start of war, 67–68
    reparations payments to, 471
    secret agreements with Italy, 22
    significant impact of war on women in, 365–366
    Tangier Crisis, 32–33
    treason statutes, 96–97, 200
    Treaty of Berlin, 34
    Treaty of Fez, 34
    Treaty of Frankfurt, 9–10
    Treaty of London, 83
    Triple Entente, 19
    use of poisonous gases, 379

Franco-Prussian War, 2, 11, 21, 74
Franco-Russian Alliance of 1894, 19
Frankfurter, Felix, 297, 332–333
Freedom of expression
    cases, 300–313
    modern applicability, 315
    statutes, 298–299
    subsequent events, 314
Freedom of Speech (Chafee), 322
French Revolution, 7
French Supreme Court of Appeals, 23
Friday, Frank, 246
Frierson, William L., 298, 365
Frohman, Charles, 133
Frohwerk, Jacob, 303
Frohwerk v. United States, 249 U.S. 204 (1919), 303
Fryatt, Charles, 134
Fuel, 328–330
Fuel Administration, 326, 330, 337, 338, 340
Fyfe, Thomas A., 151, 185

G
Gadsden Purchase, 39
Gallacher, Willie, 184
Galleani, Luigi, 319
Gandhi, Mohandas K., 371, 402, 419
Garfield, Harry Augustus, 297, 330
Garibaldi, Giuseppe, 12
Garran, Robert, 371, 429
Garvan, Patrick, 225, 271
Gay, Pierre, 99
General Munitions Board, 326
Geneva Convention IV, 147
Geneva Convention of 1906, 24, 26, 206, 372

Geneva Convention of 1929, 397
Geneva Convention of 1949, Additional Protocol to, 148
Geneva Conventions, 190
Geneva Protocol on poisonous gas, 392
Genocide, 397–398
Geoffrey Prime,, 175
George, David Lloyd, 70, 79, 88–89, 178
George V, King of the United Kingdom and the British Dominions, 77
Georges-Picot, Francois, 403
Gerard, James W., 71, 124–125
German Confederation, 8, 10
German Empire, 9
German Imperial Court of Justice, 388
German-Indian conspiracy, 251–252
Germany, 8–10, 17, 19, 21, 28
    Agadir Crisis, 33–34
    Armistice of Compiegne, 447
    atrocities in Belgium, 376–377, 383–387
    cessations of hostilities, 443–444
    China and, 66
    civilian supply, 176
    Declaration of Blockade around United Kingdom, 119
    declarations of war, 74–77
    declarations of war on, 422
    desertions, 95
    effect of the blockade on, 117
    Eight-Nation Alliance, 47

Germany, *continued*
   final peace treaty signed with, 375
   Hindenburg Program, 179–180
   impact of blockade, 443
   incursions by, 69
   involvement in schemes/attacks on U.S. soil, 244–258
   Leipzig war crimes trials, 388–391
   military tribunals, 375–376
   Mixed Claims Commission, 131–133
   modified Schlieffen Plan, 85
   peace treaty with U.S., 466
   poisonous gas protocols, 392
   rationing, 176–177, 185–186
   reasons for starting war, 82
   refunds for war risk insurance premiums, 241–242
   relative position of before start of war, 67–68
   reparations payments, 471–473
   repercussions from the Treaty of Versailles, 470–471
   role in Bosnia crisis, 36
   significant impact of war on women in, 365–366
   sinking of passenger ships, 122
   sinking of RMS *Lusitania*, 121–122
   smuggling, 194–195
   state of war declared by United States, 231–234
   Tangier Crisis, 32–33
   treason statutes, 201–202
   Treaty of Berlin, 15, 17, 34
   Treaty of Brest-Litovsk, 405
   Treaty of Fez, 34
   Triple Alliance agreement, 83
   United Kingdom blockade, 110, 116–117
   unrestricted submarine warfare by, 119–138
   U.S. Treaties, 465
   use of poisonous gases, 379–380
   use of zeppelins for strategic bombing, 142
   Venezuela blockade, 59, 60
   war crimes on land and sea, 378–379
   withdrawal from war, 447–448
Ghadar Party, 251
Ghadar uprisings, 251–252, 406, 412–413
GI Bill. *See* Servicemen's Readjustment Act
Gibson, Hugh, 207
Giovane Italia organization, 12
Girard, Louis, 101
Gladstone, William Ewart, 3, 6, 16, 400
Gloag, William, 151, 184–185
Goering, Hermann, 147
Goldman, Emma, 319
Goldstein, Robert, 308
Gomez, Antonio, 12
Gompers, Samuel, 277
Goodbye to All That (Graves), 96
Gordon, Anna Adams, 357
Gouin, Félix, 70, 105–106
Government bonds, 344–345
Government of India Act, 401, 419

Grabež, Trifko, 80
Gratama, Seerp, 152, 196
Great Britain, 139
Great white fleet, 63
Greater Serbia, 84
Greco-German Mixed Arbitral Tribunal, 143
Greece, 38
Greece v. Britain, The Mavrommatis Palestine Concession, Permanent Court of International Justice, Judgment No. 2 (Aug. 30, 1924), 416
Greek Refugee Settlement Commission, 383
Gregory, Henry Holman, 151, 182–183
Gregory, Thomas Watt, 296, 304
Grey, Edward, 403
Grier, Harry S., 289
Griffiths, D.W., 308
Grignard, Victor, 392
Guam, 41–42
Guernut, Henri, 70, 103–104
Gulflight, 121
Gummere, Samuel R., 4, 34, 35
Guthrie, William D., 297, 337–338
Gwynne, Howell Arthur, 171

H

Haber, Fritz, 392
Hague Convention I, Pacific Settlement of International Disputes, 25
Hague Convention II
    Laws and Customs of War on Land, 25
    Limitation of Employment of Force for Recovery of Contract Debts, 25
Hague Convention III
    Adaptation to Maritime Warfare of Principles of Geneva Convention of 1864, 25
    Opening of Hostilities, 25
Hague Convention IV
    Annex article 25, 144
    Annex article 26, 143, 144
    consignments of hides, 249
    Declaration extending Declaration I from 1899 Conference, 26
    Declaration on the Launching of Projectiles and Explosives from Balloons, 25
    Declaration on the Use of Bullets Which Expand or Flatten Easily in the Human Body, 25
    Declaration on the Use of Projectiles the Object of Which Is the Diffusion of Asphyxiating or Deleterious Gases, 25, 139, 372
    Respecting the Laws and Customs of War on Land, 25, 372
    rules for land warfare bombardments, 143
Hague Convention IX
    article 6, 144
    Bombardment by Naval Forces in Time of War, 25

Hague Convention of 1899, 24, 26, 30, 139, 379
Hague Convention of 1907, 24, 35, 108, 140
Hague Convention V, 188, 189
Hague Convention V, Rights and Duties of Neutral Powers and Persons in Case of War on Land, 25
Hague Convention VI, Status of Enemy Merchant Ships at the Outbreak of Hostilities, 25
Hague Convention VII, Conversion of Merchant Ships into War-Ships, 25
Hague Convention VIII, Laying of Automatic Submarine Contact Mines, 25
Hague Convention X, Adaptation to Maritime War of the Principles of the Geneva Convention, 25
Hague Convention XI, Certain Restrictions with Regard to the Exercise of the Right of Capture in Naval War, 26
Hague Convention XII, Creation of an International Prize Court, 26, 108
Hague Convention XIII, 236
    Respecting the Right and Duties of Neutral Powers and Persons in Case of War, 230
    Rights and Duties of Neutral Powers in Naval War, 26, 188, 230
Hague Draft Convention, Relative to the Creation of a Judicial Arbitration Court, 26
Hague Draft Convention, Rules of Air Warfare, 145
Hague International Opium Convention, 163
Hague Tribunal of Arbitration, 64
Haig, Douglas, 436
Haiti, 65, 245
Haldane, Richard, 71, 141
Hall, "Bad" Joe, 476
Hamas, 118
Hamid, Abdul, 396
Hamilton, John, 151
Hamilton, John, Lord Sumner, 163
Hamilton v. Ky. Distilleries & Warehouse Co., 251 U.S. 146 (1919), 364
Hand, Learned, 296, 322
Handcock, Peter, 29, 31
Hannibal Barca, 429
Hapsburg rule, 16
Harding, Warren G., 267, 268, 305
Hardy, Thomas, 173
Hawaii, 42, 352, 357
Hawke v. Smith (No. 1), 253 U.S. 221 (1920), 364
Hay, John M., 4, 34–35, 46, 224, 248
Hay-Pauncefote Treaty, 56
Haywood, William "Big Bill," 306–307
Healy, Timothy Michael, 70, 94
Hearst, William Randolph, 41
Heemskerk, Theo, 151, 191
Heinrich VII, Prince Reuss of Köstritz, 4, 21

Hengstler, Louis T., 225, 253
Henry, Vida, 289
Henry VIII, King of England, 410
Herbert, Henry, 70
Herrmann, Frederick, 255–256
Herzegovina, 84
Hettrick Mfg. Co. v. Waxahachie Cotton Mills, 1 F.2d 913 (6th Cir. 1924), 481
Hewart, Gordon, 151, 157
Heynen, Karl, 388
Hezbollah, 118, 272
High Contracting Party, 148
Hilken, Paul, 255–256
Hilmi, Abbas, 215
Hindenburg Program, 179–180
Hines, Walker D., 297, 325–326
Hinsch, Friedrich, 256
Histoire de la Revolution (Thiers), 7
Hitler, Adolf, 82
Hitt, Parker, 174
Hizar, Julier Clyde, 225, 253
HMHS *Dover Castle* (hospital ship), 390
HMHS *Llandovery Castle* (hospital ship), 390
Hoffman, Dustin, 133
Holland, 354
Holmes, Oliver Wendell, Jr., 224, 240, 320, 322
Holy Roman Empire, 8, 16
Home Office Scheme, 90
Home Rule Bill, 419
Homestead Act of 1862, 39
Homewood, Arthur J., 168–169
Honduras, 65
Hong Kong, 28

Hooper v. United States, 13 F.2d 19 (8th Cir. 1926), 480–481
Hoover, Herbert, 198, 336, 340, 349, 484
Hoover, J. Edgar, 297, 321
Hopkins, Albert, 132
Horridge, Thomas, 371, 412
Horses, 429–431, 433–435, 439–440, 442
Hough, Charles Merrill, 4, 58
Houghton, James T., 132
Houghton, Warren, 132
House, Edward, 449
Houston riot trials, 289–290
Hubble, Edwin, 224, 244
Hubble Space Telescope, 244
Huerta, Victoriano, 245, 246, 249
Hughes, Charles Evans, 297, 349
Hull, John A., 225, 290–291
Humbert, Charles, 215
Hume-Williams, Ellis, 370, 379
Humphreys, Travers, 151, 171–172
Hungarian Revolution, 18
Hungary, 16, 465
Hunt, Cecil, 444
Hunt, Percy, 29
Hussein, Saddam, 84
Hutcheson, Joseph Chappell, Jr., 71, 116
Huxley, Aldous, 93
Hymans, Paul, 444

I

ICC. *See* Interstate Commerce Commission (ICC)
Iceland, 354
Ilić, Danilo, 80

Immigration Act of 1918, 317
Implicit contracts, 485–486
Import/export controls, 272
Import restrictions, 267
Indemnity Act of 1920, 162
India, 2, 28, 401–402, 412–413
Indian Independence Act, 419
Influenza pandemic, 475–476
Ingraham, George Langham, 225, 264
Insubordination, 97
Insular Cases, 50–54
Intellectual property, sale of seized enemy, 268–269
International conventions, 24–26
International Criminal Tribunal, 84, 148
International Criminal Tribunal for Rwanda, 397
International Criminal Tribunal for the Former Yugoslavia, 397
International Labour Organization, 465, 466
International Law of Civilised Nations (Martens), 27
International Military Tribunal at Nuremberg,, 397
International Military Tribunal at Nuremberg, 469
International Military Tribunal for the Far East, 397
Interocean Transportation Company of America,, 114–115
Interstate Commerce Act, 340
Interstate Commerce Commission (ICC), 324, 325, 340
Iran, 272
Iran-Iraq War, 139

Iraq, 84, 272, 403
Iraq War, 118
Ireland, 93, 399–400, 407–408, 428
Irish Anti-Conscription Committee, 93, 94
Irish Free State, 28
Irish home rule, 94, 118
Irish Home Rule Act, 400
Irish Republican Brotherhood, 407, 408
Irish War of Independence, 419
Isaacs, Rufus, 151, 171
Israel, 421, 474
Italy
    Austria-Hungary empire, 17
    changes alliances, 83
    as colonizers, 28
    Eight-Nation Alliance, 47
    Orsini trial, 12–13
    Treaty of London, 83
    Triple Alliance agreement, 21, 83
    Turko-Italian War, 37
    Venezuela blockade, 59, 60
    wars of independence, 11–12
Izvolsky, Alexander, 36

J

Jackson Casket & Mfg. Co. v. Comm'r of Internal Revenue, 7 BTA 1190 (BTA 1927), 481
Jackson, Richard, 175
Jacob Ruppert v. Caffey, 251 U.S. 264 (1920), 364
Japan, 46, 47, 66, 474
Japan-Korea Annexation Treaty, 48
Jews, 403–404, 414–416

Jinnah, Muhammad Ali, 419
Johnson, Hugh S., 225, 277–278
Jonas, Joseph, 169
Joseph, Franz, 72, 79
Jospin, Lionel, 107
Joyce, John E., 296, 309
Judge advocate general (JAG)
    allegations against military
        justice system, 283–288
    specific cases cited by, 281–283
July Crisis, 71–73

K

Kalle, Arnold von, 203, 204
Kammgarnspinnerei Stoehr & Co.,
    AG, 262
Karl I, Emperor of Austria, 447
Kemp, Jan, 427
Kent, Tyler, 175
Kenya, 28
Keogh, David, 175
Kerensky, Alexander, 371, 418
Kidron (horse), 440
Kiesselbach, Wilhelm, 71, 134
King and Country (movie), 105
Kingsland munitions plant, 254–257
Kingsley, Horace Dennis, 155–156
Kipling, Rudyard, 173
Kirschen, Sadi, 152, 208
Kitchener, Horatio Herbert, 29–30,
    86, 91
Knox-Castrillo Convention, 65
Knox, Philander C., 5, 66
Komura, Jutarō, 4, 48
Kosovo, 37, 84, 139, 148
Kristoff, Michael, 256
Kroemer, Karl, 203, 204

Kruska, Benno, 389
Kuwait, 84

L

L. Richardson & Co. v. United States,
    266 U.S. 541 (1925), 267
L. Vogelstein & Co. v. United States,
    262 U.S. 337 (1923), 336
La Follette, Belle Case, 297, 353
LaBelle Iron Works v. United States,
    256 U.S. 377 (1921), 347
Labor, 331–332
Labor unions, 351
Labori, Fernand, 4, 24
Ladoux, Georges, 203, 204
Lamar, William H., 296, 313
Lammasch, Heinrich, 4, 61
Lancken, Baron von der, 207
Landis, Kenesaw Mountain, 296,
    307–308
Landsberg, Otto, 445
Lansbury, Edgar, 175
Lansing, Robert, 224, 242, 472
Latvia, 405
Laughlin, Gail, 356
Laule, Adolph, 389
Laurier, Wilfrid, 371, 425
Lawrence, D. H., 93
Lawrence, T. E. (Lawrence of Arabia),
    403, 430
Le Bonnet Rouge (newspaper), 203,
    210, 214, 217
Le Journal (newspaper), 215, 220
League of Nations, 84, 145, 146, 198,
    199, 251, 383, 414, 465, 491
League of Women Voters, 355
Lebanon, 118, 403

Lechat, Lucien, 101
Lefoulon, Louis, 101
Lehmann, Frederick William, 224, 237
Leipzig war crimes trials, 388–391
Lemkin, Raphael, 397
Lend-Lease program, 137
Lenin, Vladimir Ilyich, 371, 405, 406
Lenoir, Pierre, 220
Leser, Oscar, 298, 363
Leser v. Garnett, 258 U.S. 130 (1922), 362–363
Leval, Gaston de, 152, 208
Lever Act, 328
Lever, Asbury F., 297, 330
Lewis, Merton E., 152, 216
Lewis, Robert E., 445, 481
Lewis, William H., 225, 293
Leymarie, Jean, 217
Liaison dogs, 435
Liberty bonds, 344, 348–349
Libya, 37, 420
Liebknecht, Karl, 444, 448
Lincoln, Abraham, 35
Lithuania, 405
Lockwood, Belva Ann, 297, 352–353
Lodge, Henry Cabot, 444
Lody, Carl, 220
London Declaration, 108–111
London Naval Conference of 1930, 137
Loudon, John, 152, 195–196
Loughborough v. Blake, 18 U.S. 317 (1820), 54
Louisiana Purchase, 39
Lovett, Robert S., 297, 327–328
Lt. Paulaud, 98–99
Luxembourg, 9, 18, 75, 85, 187, 192

M

Mac Diarmada, Sean (a.k.a. McDermott), 408
Macallen Co. v. Massachusetts, 279 U.S. 620 (1929), 348
MacDonagh, Thomas, 408
Macedonia, 15, 38, 84
Machine guns, 85, 95, 139
Mackinnon, Donald, 371, 426
MacLaurin, Henry N., 371, 429
Maclean, John, 155
Maddox, Etta H., 297, 356
Madero, Francisco I., 248
Maiorescu, Titu, 4, 39
Malvy, Louis-Jean, 202, 209–210, 220
Manchuria, 66
Manganese production, 486–487
Manning, Bradley, 315
Mannock, Mick, 141
Mansfield, Arabella, 355
Manual for Courts-Martial, 294
March on Washington, 484–485
Margolin v. United States, 269 U.S. 93 (1925), 483
Maritz, Manie, 427
Mark Cross Company, 132
Marshall, John, 52, 54
Marshall, Louis, 225, 263–264
Martens, Frederick de, 4, 26–27
    International Law of Civilised Nations, 27
    (Right) *The Right of Private Property in War*, 27
Marx, Mannheim, 217
Maryland, 362–363
Masses Publ'g Co. v. Patten, 244 F. 535 (S.D.N.Y. 1917), 310–311

Massloff, Vladimir de, 203
Mata Hari, 202, 203–205, 215, 220
Mathews, Charles Willie, 370, 377
Maupas, Blanche, 101, 102
Maupas, Théophile, 101
Mayer, Julius M., 71, 130
Mayo, Henry, 245
Mazzini, Giuseppe, 4, 11–12
McAdoo, William Gibbs, 297, 324, 346
McCulloch, Catherine Waugh, 297, 355
McKellar, Kenneth Douglas, 297, 319
McKenna, Joseph, 4, 55
McKenna, Reginald, 151, 154–155
McKinley, William, 4, 124
    assassination of, 41, 55
    legal profile, 40–41
    Philippine-American War, 49
    Spanish-American War, 41–42
    USS *Maine* board of inquiry, 44–45
McReynolds, James C., 296, 304
Mears, Edward Grimwood, 371, 388
Mehmedbašić, Muhamed, 80–81
Melchior, Carl, 445
Merchant ships, arming of, 228
Mérillon, Daniel, 152, 210–211
Mersey Court of Inquiry, 125
Messenger Dog Service, 436
Mexican-American War, 2
Mexican Revolution, 246, 249
Mexico, 65
    Pancho Villa raid, 247
    Tampico Incident, 245–246
Michaelis, Georg, 151, 180–181
Middle East, 402–404, 414–416

Milholland, Inez, 297, 355–356
Military Service Act, 86, 87, 88, 89, 90, 93, 423, 424
Military Service Referendum Act, 425
Military supply, 178–180
Military tribunals, 374–376
Miller, David Hunter, 444, 451–452
Millerand, Alexandre, 70, 104
Milner, Alfred, 371, 404
Milwaukee Leader (newspaper), 308, 314
Minimum wages, 352–353, 360–362
Ministry of Information, 173
Ministry of Munitions, 170–171
Ministry of Munitions Act, 178
Missouri Staats Zeitung (newspaper), 303
Mitchell, Edward Rosslyn, 151, 185
Mixed Claims Commission, 131–133, 137, 143, 241, 271, 435
Mo. Pac. R. Co. v. Ault, 256 U.S. 554 (1921), 335
Model State Emergency Health Powers Act, 489
Money supply, 343–344
Monroe Doctrine, 27, 41, 59
Monroe, James, 59
Montenegro, 13, 15, 17, 38, 84
Monzie, Anatole de, 152, 213–214
Moore, John Bassett, 71, 146–147
Morant court-martial, 29–30
Morant, Harry Harbord, 29–30
Morgan, John H., 371, 411–412
Morgenthau, Henry, Sr., 370, 382
Mornet, André, 152, 218
Morning Glory (horse), 433
Moro-Giafferri, Vincent de, 152, 214

Moroccan crises
    first crisis, 32–33, 62
    Perdicaris Incident, 34–35
    second crisis, 33–34
Morocco, 3, 20
Morrell, Ottoline, 92
Morrell, Philip, 70, 92
Morris, James B., 225, 293
Mott, Lucretia, 355
Moulton, John Fletcher, Lord Moulton, 151, 160, 161–162
Muir, John William, 184
Müller, Emil, 388, 389–390
Mumm von Schwarzenstein, Alfons, 4, 48
Munich Reinsurance Co. v. First Reinsurance Co., 6 F. 2d 742 (2nd Cir. 1925), 469–470
Munitions of War Acts, 87, 178–179, 181, 183–184
Munitions plants, 178–179, 183–184, 254–257, 320, 351, 435
Munitions sabotage, 254–257
Munitions Standards Board, 326
Munitions tribunals, 183
Munro, Robert, 151, 187
Murray, Andrew, 151, 161
Murray, Andrew, Lord Dunedin, 159–160
Mutiny, 97, 102–103
Mutiny Act of 1689, 105

N

N. Pac. R. Co. v. N. D. ex rel. Langer, 250 U.S. 135 (1919), 333–334
Nail, Louis, 70, 98
Nansen, Fridtjof, 152, 198, 199
Nansen International Office for Refugees, 199
Nansen passport, 198
Napoleon I. *See* Bonaparte, Napoléon
Napoleon III. *See* Bonaparte, Louis-Napoléon
Napoleonic Wars, 7, 8
National American Woman Suffrage Association (NAWSA), 355, 356
National Bar Association, 293
National Civil Liberties Union, 275–276
National Defense Act of 1916, 247, 248, 272, 273, 277
National Guard, 247, 272, 484
National Monetary Commission, 344
National Prohibition Act, 358–359
National Prohibition Cases, 253 U.S. 350 (1920), 363–364
National Registration Act, 87
National Security Agency, 315
National War Labor Board (NWLB), 331–332, 338–339
Native American soldiers, 174
NATO war on Serbia, 118, 148
Navajo code talkers, 174
Naval Agreement of 1912, 19
Navicert preapproval system, 116
Navy Articles of Justice, 292
NAWSA. *See* National American Woman Suffrage Association (NAWSA)
Nazi Party, 470
NCC. *See* Non-Combatant Corps (NCC)
NCF. *See* Non-Conscription Fellowship (NCF)

Nederlandsche Overzee Trustmaatschappij. *See* Netherlands Overseas Trust (NOT)
Nehru, Jawaharlal, 419
Nelles, Walter, 225, 275–276
Nesbit, William, 289
Netherlands, 7, 9, 28, 110
    interning submarines, 192–193
    proximate neutrality of, 187–199
    sinking of neutral ships, 193–194
    smuggling, 194–195
Netherlands Overseas Trust (NOT), 110, 114
Neumann, Karl, 388, 390
Neumann, Robert, 388
Neutral countries, 110
Neutrality
    of Belgium and Luxembourg, 18
    benevolent, 21
    contracts and, 237–238
    declaring, 226–230
    declaring war, 231–234
    distance, 226–243
    prizes and, 235–237
    proximate, 187–199
Neutrality Act of 1794, 236
New York Stock Exchange, 344
New York World (newspaper), 58
New Zealand, 2, 28, 354, 401, 421–422, 428, 440
Newfoundland, 28
News & Observer (newspaper), 315
Newspapers, 166–167, 214
Nicaragua, 65, 245

Nicholas II, Emperor and Autocrat of All the Russias, 24, 77, 95, 405
Nicolay, John, 35
Nigeria, 28
Nightingale, Florence, 351
Nineteenth Amendment, U.S. Constitution, 354, 359, 362–363, 365
Nivelle, Robert, 102
Nobel Peace Prize, 27, 62, 64, 112, 144, 199, 213, 221, 473
Nolan Act, 467
Non-Combatant Corps (NCC), 90, 91, 93
Non-Conscription Fellowship (NCF), 90, 155
Nonmailable items, 310–311
North Africa, 20
North Asia, 84
North German Confederation, 9, 10
North Korea, 272, 474
Norway, 110, 187, 354
NOT. *See* Netherlands Overseas Trust (NOT)
Nuclear weapons, 147
Nye committee, 340

O

Obama, Barack, 315
Octavio de Menezes Langgaard, Rodrigo, 445, 464–465
October Revolution, 405, 406
Oetjen v. Central Leather Co., 246 U.S. 297 (1918), 249
Officer's Reserve Corps, 247
Official Secrets Act (OSA), 143, 169, 173, 175

Official secrets/Censorship
  cases, 168–171
  for communications sent outside the U.S., 243
  lord mayor case, 169
  Ministry of Munitions, 170–171
  modern applicability, 175
  neutral country citizen case, 170
  postal censors, 168
  publication assisting the enemy, 171
  statutes, 164–167
  subsequent events, 173–174
  War Office employees, 168–169
O'Hare, Kate Richards, 305
Old War Horse Memorial Hospital, 440
Olsson, Ernst Gustav Waldemar, 170
Open Door policy, 36, 66
Operation Nemesis, 395
Opium, 163
Organic Act of 1902, 49
Orlando, Vittorio E., 445, 464
Orsini, Felice, 12–13
Orsini trial, 12–13
OSA. *See* Official Secrets Act (OSA)
Otis, Merrill E., 445, 487
Ottoman Empire, 3, 5, 6, 95
  Albanian crises, 37
  Armenian massacre, 380–382, 398
  Armistice of Mudros, 446
  Balkan Wars of 1912–13, 37–38
  cessations of hostilities, 443
  colonies, 29
  declarations of war, 74–77
  reasons for starting war, 82
  role in Bosnia crisis, 36
  Treaty of San Stefano, 13–14
  Triple Alliance agreement, 21
  Turko-Italian War, 37
Ottoman Trials, 394–396
Owen, William, 175

P

Page, John, 132
Painlevé, Paul, 209
Painvin, Georges, 174
Palestine, 403–404, 414–416, 420, 474
Palestine Act, 420
Palmer, A. Mitchell, 225, 261
Panama, 56–57, 245
Panama Canal, 56–57, 58, 64, 228–229
Panama Canal Purchase Act, 56
Pancho Villa raid, 247
Panina, Sofia, 417–418
Pankhurst, Emmeline, 354
Papen, Franz von, 255, 258
Paris Commune movement, 8
Paris Peace Conference, 84, 163, 197, 242, 270, 428, 477
Parity in the empire
  cases, 424–427
  statutes, 421–423
  subsequent events, 428
Parker, Edwin B., 71, 138, 327
Parker, John Johnston, 445, 468–469
Parker, Robert John, 71, 114
Parliament Act of 1911, 400
Parnell, Charles Stewart, 94

Partnership valuation, 265–266
Pašić, Nikola, 72, 81
Paterson, Andrew Barton, 371, 432
Paths of Glory (movie), 101
Patman, John William Wright, 445
Patten, Thomas G., 296
Paul, Alice, 355
Payne, John Barton, 297, 334
Peace Party, 357
Peace treaties, 449–461
    Austria, 461
    Bulgaria, 461
    Fourteen points, 449–451, 462–463
    Hungary, 462
    Treaty of Versailles, 428, 452–461
    Turkey, 462
Pearse, Patrick, 371, 407, 408
Pencil bomb devices, 258
Perdicaris Incident, 34–35, 62
Perdicaris, Ion, 34
Péret, Raoul, 70, 97–98
Permanent Court of Arbitration at the Hague., 349
Permanent Court of International Arbitration, 60–61
Permanent Court of International Justice, 63, 64
Permanent Court of International Justice., 472
Pershing, John J., 225, 247, 280–281, 437, 438, 440, 492
Persia, 20
Personal responsibility, 374
Pétain, Philippe, 104, 221
Peter Pan (Barrie), 133

Peter the Great, 14
Petit, Gabrielle, 220
Pettelet, Claude, 99
Philippine-American War, 49
Philippine Supreme Court, 291
Philippines, 41–42, 64
Picquart, Georges, 23
Pieri, Giuseppe, 12
Pigeons, 430, 431–432, 437–438, 441
Pigs, 429
Pitney, Mahlon, 297, 347–348
Plan of Guadalupe, 248
Plan XIX, 68, 85
Plan XVII, 68
Platt Amendment, 42
Plunkett, Joseph, 408
Poincaré, Raymond, 152, 202, 209
Pointing, Clive, 175
Poisonous gases, 85, 95, 139
    Hague Convention IV, 25
    protocols, 392–393
    use of, 379–380
Poland, 17, 82, 405, 463
Political treason, 209–212
Polk, Frank L., 225, 268–270
Polk, James K., 269
Pollock, Ernest, 151, 159
Pope John Paul II, 494
Popović, Cetres, 80
Portsmouth Peace Conference, 62
Portugal, 28
Postal censors, 168
Postal system
    nonmailable items, 310–311
    privileges, 312–313
POWs. *See* Prisoners of war (POWs)

"President Wilson" (pigeon), 438
Press censorship, 166–167. *See also*
    Official secrets/Censorship
Preston, John W., 225, 253–254
Prewar conflicts, 31–38
    Albanian crises, 37
    Balkan Wars, 37
    Bosnia crisis, 36
    Moroccan crises, 32–35
    Turko-Italian War, 37
Prince William, Crown Prince of
    the Kingdom of Prussia and the
    German Empire, 197, 378
Princip, Gavrilo, 80–81
Prisoners of war (POWs), 189, 397,
    466, 474
Prohibition, 356–359, 363–364
Prosser, Charles Allen, 445, 479
Protected occupations, 87
The Protestant Ethic and the Spirit of
    Capitalism (Weber), 477
Proximate neutrality
    cases, 192–195
    statutes, 187–191
    subsequent events, 196–199
Prussia, 7, 8, 82
Puerto Rico, 41–42, 51–54
Pulitzer, Joseph, 4, 41, 45, 58
Pullman Strike, 305
Punishable crimes, 279–280

Q
Qing Dynasty, 47
Qualification of Women Act of 1918,
    354
Quien, Georges, 206
Quinault, Jean, 99

R
R. v. Hammick and Another, JJ. (*ex*
    parte Murdoch), K.B. Court of
    Appeal (1918), 182
"Rags" (dog), 437
Railroad Administration, 326,
    333–334, 335, 346
Railroad Control Act, 325
Railroads, 323–325
er Raisuli, Mulai Ahmed, 34
Ram Chandra, 252
Ram Singh, 252
Ramdohr, Max, 389
Randolph, Mary D., 362
Rankin, Jeanette, 355
Raper, Robert George, 70, 106
Rathenau, Walter, 179
Rationing, 176–178, 185
Rebellion, 97
Red Army, 405
Redmond, John, 371, 400
Refugees, 198
Renault, Louis, 4, 27
    First Violations of International
        Law by Germany, 27
    Traité de droit commercial, 27
Reparations payments, 471–473
Repington, Charles à Court, 171
Representation of the People Act of
    1918, 354
Representation of the People (Equal
    Franchise) Act of 1928, 365
Reserve Officers Training Corps
    (ROTC), 247
Revanchism, 9
Revenue Act of 1916, 342
Revenue Act of 1918, 342

Revolt, 97
Ribot, Alexandre, 217
Richardson, E. H., 436
Richmond 16, 91
Richthofen, Manfred von, 141
Right of angary, 190
Right of requisition, 113, 156–161
The Right of Private Property in War (Martens), 27
Righteous Harmony Society, 47
"Rin Tin Tin" (dog), 436
Ríos, Eugenio Montero, 4, 43
Ritchie, Albert C., 297, 328
Riza, Ahmed, 381
RMS *Empress of Ireland* (ocean liner), 127
RMS *Lusitania* (ocean liner), 207, 242
    British Court of Inquiry, 125–126
    Mixed Claims Commission, 131–133
    sinking of, 121–122, 138
    U.S. trial, 128–130
RMS *Titanic* (ocean liner), 127
Robert, Henri, 152, 222
Robertson v. Gen. Elec. Co., 32 F. 2d 495 (4th Cir. 1929), 467–468
Robinson, Lucius Franklin, 445, 470
Roman Empire, 11
Romania, 6, 13, 17, 38, 448
Roosevelt Corollary, 59–60
Roosevelt, Franklin D., 124, 225, 292, 487
Roosevelt, Theodore, 42, 264, 267, 280, 293
    foreign policy, 55–63
    great white fleet, 63
    legal action against the press, 58
    mediating global disputes, 61–62
    Panama Canal, 56–57
    Perdicaris Incident, 34–35
    role in Hague Convention of 1907, 25, 56
    Roosevelt Corollary, 59–60
    Spanish-American War, 41
Root, Elihu, 4, 63–64
Root-Takahira agreement, 48, 64
ROTC. *See* Reserve Officers Training Corps (ROTC)
Rough Riders, 41
Rowlatt Act, 419
Royal Prerogative, 77, 113, 156–161, 162–163
Ruijs de Beerenbrouck, Charles, 152, 197–198
Russell, Bertrand, 90, 93, 155
Russell Motor Car Co. v. United States, 261 U.S. 514 (1923), 486
Russia
    Anglo-Russian Entente, 19–20
    Boxer Rebellion, 46
    China and, 66
    declarations of war, 74–77
    Eight-Nation Alliance, 47
    German treaties, 448
    impact of blockade, 443
    Plan XIX, 68
    reasons for starting war, 82
    relative position of before start of war, 67–68
    role in Bosnia crisis, 36
    secret agreements with Italy, 22
    show trials, 417–418

Russia, *continued*
significant impact of war on women in, 365–366
Treaty of Paris, 6, 14–15
Triple Entente, 19
uprisings, 404–406
withdrawal from war, 231, 446
women's suffrage, 354
Russian Empire, 5, 14, 29
Russo-Japanese War, 3, 25, 26, 36, 61–62
Russo-Turkish War of 1877–78, 13
Ruthenberg, Charles Emil, 276, 306
Ruthenberg v. United States, 245 U.S. 480 (1918), 276, 305

S
Sabotage, 254–257, 435
Safvet Pasha, 4, 14
Salandra, Antonio, 70, 83–84
Salle, Albert, 152, 216
Sampson, William, 44
San Remo Manual, 118
San Remo Resolution, 403
Sandy (horse), 440
Sanford, Edward Terry, 225, 267–268
Sarabha, Kartar Singh, 413
Sarajevo, Bosnia, 79–80
Sardinia, 7
SARS epidemic, 489
"Satan" (dog), 436–437
Scapegoats of the Empire (Witton), 30
Schack, Eckhart von, 252
Scheele, Walter, 258
Schenck, Charles, 301
Schenck v. United States, 249 U.S. 47 (1919), 301–302

Scherbius, Arthur, 174
Schlieffen, Alfred von, 68
Schlieffen Plan, 68, 75, 85
Schmidt, Heinrich, 371
Schücking, Walther, 71, 136–137
Schue, Alphones, 276
Schuman, Robert, 445, 493–494
Scopes trial, 124
Scott, James Brown, 444, 452
Scott, Leslie Frederic, 151, 157–158
Sea lions, 442
Second Battle of Ypres, 379
Second Boer War, 2, 29, 230, 427
Second French Republic, 7
Second Philippine Commission, 49
Second War of Italian Independence, 13
Sedition
cases, 319–321
statutes, 316–319
subsequent events, 322
Sedition Act, 314, 316–317, 320–321, 322
Selective Service
cases, 274–276
statutes, 272–273
subsequent events, 277
Selective Service Act, 274, 301, 306–307
Serb-Croat-Slovene State, 463, 471
Serbia, 3, 68
Austria-Hungary empire, 15, 17
Balkan Wars of 1912–13, 37–38
declarations of war, 84
July Crisis, 71–73
NATO war on, 118

role in Bosnia crisis, 36
shelling of Belgrade, 69
Treaty of Paris, 6
Treaty of San Stefano, 13
Servicemen's Readjustment Act, 487–488
Settlement of War Claims Act, 270
Settlement of War Claims Act of 1928, 137
"Sgt. Stubby" (dog), 437
Shell Crisis, 171, 178
Shepard, Seth, 296, 313
Sheppard, Morris, 297, 359
Sheriff Court Act of 1908, 185
Sherman Antitrust Act, 40, 46
Sherman, John, 4, 45–46
Sherman, William Tecumseh, 46
Shipping Board, 326
Shiv Narayan Raina, 371, 413–414
Shoreham Aerodrome case, 156, 157
Show trials, 417–418
Siam, 20
Silberschein v. United States, 266 U.S. 221 (1924), 482
Simon, John, 151, 159
Singapore, 28
Sinn Féin, 419
Sino-Japanese War, 48
Sippe, Sydney, 194
Six-Day War, 421
Sixteenth Amendment, U.S. Constitution, 341
Sixth Amendment, U.S. Constitution, 313
Slee, Frank D., 71, 147
Slovakia, 17
Slovenia, 17, 84, 420

Smith, F. E. (Frederick Edwin), 71, 127
Smith, Michael, 175
Smuggling, 194
Smuts, Jan, 371, 428
Snowden, Edward, 315
Society for the Overseas Settlement of British Women., 366
South Africa, 2, 28, 31, 39, 401, 421–423, 427, 428
South Korea, 474
South Sudan, 119, 420
Spain, 20, 28, 41–42, 59, 187
Spanish-American War, 2, 21, 36, 41–42, 59, 124
Spanish Hapsburg Empire, 11
Spartacus League, 448
Spooner Act. See Panama Canal Purchase Act
SS *Annie Larsen* (schooner), 251–252, 253
SS *Appam* (merchant ship), 235
SS *Arabic* (passenger ship), 122
SS *Brussels* (merchant vessel), 134–136
SS *Falaba* (passenger ship), 120
SS *Gulflight* (tanker), 121
SS *Lisman* (ship), 114–116
SS *Llama* (tanker), 239
SS *Maverick* (tanker), 251
SS *Princess Melita* (merchant ship), 193
SS *Sussex* (ferry), 122
SS *Tubantia* (steamer ship), 193–194
SS *Zamora* (ship), 112–113, 156
Standard Oil Co. of N.J. v. United States, 267 U.S. 76 (1925), 239
Stanley, Edward, Lord Derby, 86
Stanton, Elizabeth Cady, 355

State Chronicle (newspaper), 315
Statute of Westminster, 428
The Steamship Appam, 243 U.S. 124 (1917), 235
Stedman, Seymour, 296, 306
Stenger, Karl, 389
Steppe ponies, 430
Stoehr & Sons, Inc., 262
Stoehr, Eduard, 263
Stoehr v. Wallace, 255 U.S. 239 (1921), 261
Stokes, Rose Pastor, 305, 306
Stone, Lucy, 355
Story, Joseph, 52
Strait of Gibraltar, 20
"Strict Accountability" warning, 119–120
Struycken, A. A. H., 152, 196
Submarine warfare, 119–139
Submarines, 69, 120–123, 125, 135, 192–194, 388–391, 448
Sudan, 119
Suez Canal, 20, 56, 403
Suffrage, 353–355, 362–363
Sullivan, A. M., 371, 411
Suspensory Act, 400
Sutherland, George, 225, 266–267
Sutherland v. Mayer, 271 U.S. 272 (1926), 265–266
Sweden, 110, 117, 187, 354
Swedish Trading Company, 112
Swinton, Ernest, 166
Switzerland, 7, 187
Sykes, Mark, 403, 445, 477
Syria, 398
Szold, Robert, 225, 276–277

T
Taft, William Howard, 5, 124, 237, 264, 293
   arms embargo to the Americas, 246
   China, 66
   creation of National War Labor Board, 331
   foreign policy, 64–66
   legal profile, 65–66
   Nicaragua, 65
   Second Philippine Commission, 49
Talaat Pasha, 395
Taliban, 272
Tampico Incident, 245–246
Taney, Roger B., 54
Tangier Crisis, 32–33, 62
Tankosić, Vojislav, 80–81
Tanks, 85, 139
Taxation, 341–343
Taylor, Alfred, 29–30
Tear gas, 379
Tehcir Law, 381
Temple, Henry John, Lord Palmerston, 13
Tennessee Valley Authority, 302
Texas annexation, 39
Thiers, Adolphe, 3, 7–8
   Histoire de la Revolution, 7
   Le Consulat et l'Empire, 8
Third French Republic, 7, 10
Third Naval Law, 33
Thirteenth Amendment, U.S. Constitution, 53, 301
Thomas, James Francis, 4, 31

Tibet, 20
Tirpitz, Alfred von, 119
Tisdall, Sara, 175
Tisza, István, 70, 73–74
Trading with the Enemy Act, 238, 259–260, 261, 268, 270, 469
Traité de droit commercial (Renault), 27
Transjordan, 403
Transportation Act of 1920, 340
Treachery Act, 221
Treason
    cases, 202–220
    by newspapers, 214–217
    political, 209–212
    statutes, 96–97, 200–202
    subsequent events, 220–221
Treason Act of 1351, 200, 218, 409, 410, 418
Treaties
    agreements and nation-building, 5–19
    alliance-building agreements, 19–31
    peace, 449–463
    United States, 465–466
Treaty of Berlin, 15, 17, 34, 36, 131, 133, 380, 465, 467–468, 469
Treaty of Brest-Litovsk, 405
Treaty of Bucharest, 38
Treaty of Constantinople, 38
Treaty of Fez, 34
Treaty of Frankfurt, 9–10, 11
Treaty of Lausanne, 395, 462
Treaty of Locarno, 221
Treaty of London, 8, 16, 18, 19, 75, 83

Treaty of Neuilly-sur-Seine, 461
Treaty of Ouchy, 37
Treaty of Paris, 6, 42, 50, 52
Treaty of Saint-Germain-en-Laye, 461–462
Treaty of San Francisco, 474
Treaty of San Stefano, 13–14, 15
Treaty of Sèrves, 462
Treaty of Sèvres, 403
Treaty of Shimonoseki, 48
Treaty of Trianon, 462
Treaty of Versailles, 428, 452–461, 466, 467, 469, 470–471, 472, 491
Treaty of Vienna, 11, 16
Trench dogs, 435, 441
Trench warfare, 95–96
Tribunal at The Hague, 60
Les tribunaux militaires, 96
Triple Alliance, 19
Triple Alliance agreement, 21–22
Triple Entente, 19–20, 68
Turkey, 37, 462
Turko-Italian War, 3, 37
Tweed, William "Boss," 63
Twenty-First Amendment, U.S. Constitution, 365

U

U-boat attacks. *See* Unrestricted submarine warfare
U-boats, 120–123, 125, 135, 192, 193–194, 388–391, 409
Ukraine, 17, 405
UN Charter, 118
UN Security Council, 118, 148, 421
Unemployment, 366

Uniform Code of Military Justice,
   293–294
United Kingdom, 5–6, 13
   Anglo-Russian Entente, 19–20
   blockade of Germany, 69,
      108–111, 116–117
   British mandate for Palestine,
      414–416, 420
   China and, 66
   civilian supply, 176–178
   conscription laws, 86–88
   declarations of war, 74–77
   Eight-Nation Alliance, 47
   emergency powers, 152–164
   Entente Cordiale, 19–20
   execution of soldiers, 95
   Irish uprising, 399–400,
      407–408
   Law and Usages of War on
      Land, 372
   Messenger Dog Service, 436
   military plans, 68
   Naval Agreement of 1912, 19
   pardoning executed soldiers,
      107
   parity in the empire, 421–428
   rationing, 176–178, 185
   reasons for starting war, 82
   relative position of before start
      of war, 67–68
   reparations payments to, 471
   secret agreements with Italy, 22
   significant impact of war on
      women in, 365–366
   Treason Act, 200
   Treaty of London, 83

Triple Entente, 19
uprisings, 399–404
Venezuela blockade, 59, 60
women's suffrage, 353–354, 365
United Nations, 137, 420
United States
   arming of merchant ships, 228
   arms embargo to the Americas,
      246
   Articles of War, 278–294
   biological warfare capabilities
      prepared in, 258
   conflicts involving, 2
   declaring neutrality, 226–230
   declaring war, 231–234
   distance neutrality, 226–243
   Eight-Nation Alliance, 47
   enemy asset and export
      controls, 259–272
   espionage and freedom of
      expression, 298–315
   expansion of continental
      territory, 39–40
   German involvement in
      schemes/attacks on U.S. soil,
      244–258
   influenza pandemic, 475–476
   Insular Cases, 50–54
   Mixed Claims Commission,
      131–133
   mutinies, 105
   Panama Canal, 56–57
   peace treaty with Austria, 466
   peace treaty with Germany, 466
   peace treaty with Hungary, 466
   Philippine-American War, 49

INDEX | 535

problems of empires, 46–49
reparations payments to,
    472–473
role in mediating global
    disputes, 61–62
role in Tangier Crisis, 33
Roosevelt Corollary, 59–60
Rules of Land Warfare, 372
sedition, anarchists and enemy
    aliens, 316–323
Selective Service, 272–277
Spanish-American War, 2,
    41–42
supplying war effort, 323–341
takeover of Dominican
    Republic, 258
treaties, 465–466
war funding, 341–349
women and the war, 350–367
United States ex rel. Milwaukee Social
    Democratic Publ'g Co. v. Burleson,
    Postmaster Gen. of the U.S., 255 F.
    407 (1919), 312–313
United States Steel Products
    Company (United States) v.
    Germany, 241
United States v. Bentley, 107 F.2d 382
    (1939), 484
United States v. Chem. Found., Inc.,
    272 U.S. 1 (1926), 268–269
United States v. L. Cohen Grocery
    Co., 255 U.S. 81 (1921), 337
Unrestricted submarine warfare
    cases, 125–136
    modern applicability, 138–139
    statutes, 119–123

subsequent events, 137–138
use by Germany, 231
Uprisings
    cases, 406–418
    India, 401–402, 412–413
    Ireland, 399–400, 407–408,
        418–419
    Middle East, 402–404, 414–416
    modern applicability, 420–421
    Russia, 404–406, 417–418
    statutes, 398–406
    subsequent events, 418–419
U.S. Congress
    address on severance of
        diplomatic relations with
        Germany, 233–234
    American Relief
        Administration, 340
    arms embargo to the Americas,
        246
    bans on alcohol, 357
    declaration of war, 234
    declaring neutrality, 226–227
    joint resolution terminating
        state of war, 465
    Nolan Act, 467–468
    Panama Canal Purchase Act, 56
    Railroad Control Act, 325
    retired military dogs, 442
    sale authorization of Liberty
        bonds, 344
    Taft message to, 64
    war funding, 341–343
    War Industries Board, 327
    Wartime Prohibition Act, 358
    women's suffrage, 354

U.S. Constitution, 50
    Article I, 275
    Article III, 313
    Eighteenth Amendment, 364, 365
    Eighth Amendment, 313
    Fifth Amendment, 313, 364
    First Amendment, 301, 303, 313, 321
    National Prohibition Act, 358–359
    Nineteenth Amendment, 354, 359, 362, 362–363, 365
    Sixteenth Amendment, 341
    Sixth Amendment, 313
    Thirteenth Amendment, 53, 301
    Twenty-First Amendment, 365
U.S. Department of Defense, 442
U.S. Department of Justice, 319
U.S. Department of the Treasury, 272, 344, 434
U.S. Food Administration, 198
U.S. Navy, 44, 63, 291–292
U.S. Public Health Service, 476
U.S. Senate, 33, 65
U.S. Shipping Board, 334
U.S. Signal Corps, 438
U.S. Sugar Equalization Board, Inc., 329
U.S. Supreme Court, 58, 255
    cases of German involvement in Americas, 249–250
    damages or profits, 486
    encouraging others to avoid the draft cases, 276
    enemy ownership of shares case, 261–263
    excess profits tax case, 347
    Food and Fuel Administrations export v. domestic prices case, 338
    Food and Fuel Administrations reasonable rates case, 337
    Insular Cases, 50–54
    Liberty Bonds redemption case, 348–349
    minimum wage for women cases, 360–362
    National Prohibition Cases, 363–364
    neutrality, 235–240
    NWLB impact of wage decisions case, 338–339
    opinion regarding horses in military, 434
    partnership valuation, 266
    Railroad Administration penalties case, 335
    Railroad Administration rates case, 333–334
    rule on implicit contracts, 485–486
    Sedition Act case, 320–321
    selective draft law cases, 274–275
    Sixteenth Amendment and, 341
    suffrage case, 362–363
    tax on Liberty Bonds case, 348
    veterans' claims, 482
    War Industries Board market rates case, 336

War Industries Board price
changes case, 335–336
USS *Maine* (warship), 41, 44–45
USS *Vincennes* (guided missile cruiser), 138

V

Van de Weyer, Sylvain, 4, 18–19
van Devanter, Willis, 225, 264
van Fleet, William, 225, 253
Vanderbilt, Alfred G., 133
Vandervelde, Emile, 444
Venezuela, 59, 60–61
Vernon, Charles Alfred, 169
Versailles Treaty, 116, 133, 143, 163, 197, 378, 392
Vesnić, Milenko Radomar, 445, 462
Veterans
    bonuses, 484–485
    issues, 478–479
    March on Washington, 484–485
Vichy France, 104
Vietnam War, 105, 118
Villa, Francisco "Pancho," 247, 249–250, 280
Village of Euclid v. Ambler Realty Co., 272 U.S. 365 (1926), 302
Viviani, René, 70, 78, 97
Volstead Act. *See* National Prohibition Act
von Brincken, Wilhelm, 252
von Hindenburg, Paul, 179, 378
von Jagow, Gottlieb, 121, 123
von Rintelen, Franz, 258
von Schack, Hans, 389
Vreeland board of inquiry, 44

W

Wainwright, Jonathan Mayhew, 371, 394
Waldow, Wilhelm von, 151, 181
Walsh, Frank P., 297, 332
War contracts, 485–487
War crimes
    Armenian massacre, 380–382
    atrocities in Belgium, 376–377, 383–387
    cases, 383–396
    on land and sea, 378–379
    Leipzig war crimes trials, 388–391
    modern applicability, 397–398
    personal responsibility, 374
    statutes, 372–382
    subsequent events, 397
    use of poisonous gases, 379–380
War Damages Act of 1965, 162
War effort, supplying
    cases, 333–339
    food and fuel, 328–330
    labor, 331–332
    railroads, 323–325
    statutes, 323–332
    subsequent events, 340
    War Industries Board, 326–327
War Finance Corporation, 345
War funding
    cases, 346–348
    credit to businesses, 345–346
    money supply and, 343–344
    sale of government bonds, 344–345
    statutes, 341–346
    subsequent events, 348–349
    taxation and, 341–343

War Industries Board, 472
War Industries Board (WIB), 326–327, 335–336
War Labor Conference Board (WLCB), 331
War Labor Policies Board (WLPB), 331
War Measures Act, 422
War of 1812, 39
War Precautions Act, 422, 426
War Revenue Act of 1917, 342
War risk insurance
    control, 239–240
    premium claims, 241–242
War Risk Insurance Act, 233, 478, 483
War risk insurance bureau, 233
War, starting
    cases, 79–81
    declarations of, 74–77
    July Crisis, 71–73
    modern applicability, 84–85
    reasons for, 82
    statutes, 71–77
War Trade Board, 267, 326, 466
Warrior (horse), 433
Wartime Prohibition Act, 358, 364
Washington Naval Conference, 64, 78, 392
Waters, Cecilia Streett, 362
Watts, Watts & Co. v. Unione Austriaca di Navigazione, 248 U.S. 9 (1918), 237
WCTU. *See* Women's Christian Temperance Union (WCTU)
Webb, Edwin Y., 296, 300

Weber, Max, 445, 477
    Economy and Society, 477
    (Protestant) *The Protestant Ethic and the Spirit of Capitalism*, 477
Wells, H.G., 173
Western Front, 95
Wheat, Alfred A., 297, 336–337
Wheeler, Wayne, 297, 359
Whiskey Rebellion, 356
White Army, 405
White, Edward Douglass, 4, 54, 55
White v. United States, 270 U.S. 175 (1926), 482
Whitlock, Brand, 152, 207, 208–209
Whittlesey, Charles White, 371, 439
WIB. *See* War Industries Board (WIB)
Wickersham Commission, 302
Wickersham, George, 293
WikiLeaks, 315
Wilde, Oscar, 117–118
Wilhelm I, King of Prussia, 9, 13
Wilhelm II, King of Prussia and German Kaiser, 30, 32, 77, 196–197, 207, 226, 375, 447
William II, King of Scotland, 5
Wilson, Woodrow, 121, 124, 224, 268, 300, 346
    Address to Joint Session of Congress, 449–451
    creation of Committee for Public Information, 314
    declaring neutrality, 227–228
    declaring war, 232–234
    enemy aliens, 317–319
    Exec. Order No. 2012, 226

executive orders, 243
legal profile, 231
proclamation taking control of railroads, 324
Prohibition and, 357
"Strict Accountability" warning, 120
Tampico Incident, 245–246
The Wind and the Lion (movie), 35
Wire of Death, 190
Witton, George, 31
    Morant court-martial, 29–30
    Scapegoats of the Empire, 30
Wobblies, 306–307, 426
Women, war and
    cases, 360–364
    conscription, 93
    employment, 350–352
    minimum wage for, 352–353, 360–362
    pressed into service, 177
    Prohibition, 356–359
    statutes, 350–359
    subsequent events, 365–366
    suffrage, 353–355, 362–363
    unemployment of, 366
Women's Christian Temperance Union (WCTU), 357, 359
Women's Land Army, 177, 350

Woodhull, Victoria, 355
Woolf, Virginia, 93
Woolsey, John M., 224, 238
Work v. United States ex rel. Rives, 267 U.S. 175 (1925), 486–487
World Court, 73
World War Adjusted Compensation Act, 484
Wounded Knee Massacre, 40
Wozniak, Theodore, 256

Y

Yardley, Herbert, 174
Yeats, W. B., 93
Yom Kippur War, 421
Young, Owen D., 445, 473, 474
Young Plan, 473
Yugoslavia, 84, 148, 420

Z

Zelle, Margaretha Geertruida. *See* Mata Hari
Zeppelin airship L-33, 142
Zeppelins, 142, 143
Zimmermann, Arthur, 224, 234
Zimmermann telegram, 174, 244
Zistler, Rudolph, 80
Zohrab, Krikor, 370, 382
Zola, Émile, 23